# APPLICATIONS
# OF BEHAVIOR
# MODIFICATION

# APPLICATIONS OF BEHAVIOR MODIFICATION

*Edited by*

## *TRAVIS THOMPSON*

*Psychiatry Research Unit and
Department of Psychology
University of Minnesota
Minneapolis, Minnesota*

## *WILLIAM S. DOCKENS, III*

*Psykologiska Institutionen
Uppsala Universitet
Uppsala, Sweden*

ACADEMIC PRESS   New York   San Francisco   London

*A Subsidiary of Harcourt Brace Jovanovich, Publishers*

ACADEMIC PRESS, INC.
111 Fifth Avenue, New York, New York 10003

*United Kingdom Edition published by*
ACADEMIC PRESS, INC. (LONDON) LTD.
24/28 Oval Road, London NW1

Library of Congress Cataloging in Publication Data

International Symposium on Behavior Modification, 1st,
    Minneapolis, 1972.
    Applications of behavior modification.

    Includes bibliographies and index.
    1.    Behavior therapy—Congresses.    I.    Thompson,
Travis I., ed.    II.    Dockens, Williams S., (date)    ed.
III.    Title.    [DNLM:    1.    Behavior therapy—Congresses.
W3 IN916AM 1972a / WM420 160Sa 1972]
RC489.B4157 1972        616.8'914        74-17970
ISBN 0-12-689550-3

PRINTED IN THE UNITED STATES OF AMERICA

*To Our Parents*

# CONTENTS

LIST OF CONTRIBUTORS — xi

PREFACE — xv

ACKNOWLEDGMENTS — xvii

## I. Treating Anxiety

1 Flooding: Results and Problems from a New Treatment for Anxiety — 3
   *Michael Gelder*

2 The Impact of Research on the Clinical Application of Behavior Therapy — 11
   *V. Meyer*

3 Laboratory-Derived Clinical Methods of Deconditioning Anxiety — 33
   *Joseph Wolpe*

## II. Modification of Maladaptive Social and Somatic Behaviors

4 Behavioral Treatment of Anorexia Nervosa — 45
   *John Paul Brady and Wolfram Rieger*

5 The Assessment of Sexual Function — 65
   *J. T. Quinn, P. Joan Graham, J. J. Harbison, and H. McAllister*

6 Behavioral Remedies for Marital Ills: A Guide to the Use of Operant–Interpersonal Techniques — 79
   *Richard B. Stuart*

7 Behavior Therapy in the Treatment of Bronchial Asthma — 97
   *N. J. Yorkston*

## III. Modification of Preacademic and Academic Skills in Children

8 Mothers as Educateurs for Their Children — 107
   *Teodoro Ayllon and Michael D. Roberts*

9  Some Effects of Direct Instruction Methods in Teaching
   Disadvantaged Children in Project Follow Through                    139
   *Wesley C. Becker*

10  Behavioral Diagnosis and Assessment in Teaching
    Young Handicapped Children                                         161
    *Sidney B. Bijou and Jeffrey A. Grimm*

11  Reciprocal and Self-Management in Educational Communities         181
    *Wells Hively and Ann Dell Duncan*

12  Behavior Technology in Higher Education                           201
    *Richard W. Malott and Beverly Louisell*

13  Verbal Development in Preschool Children                          221
    *Emilio Ribes-I., Silvia Gomar-Ruiz, and Leticia Rivas*

14  Effects of Peer Tutoring and Homework Assignments
    on Classroom Performance                                          237
    *James A. Sherman and V. William Harris*

## IV. Behavior Modification with Disturbed Children

15  Toward a Community Approach to Behavior Modification with
    Emotionally Disturbed Children                                    265
    *Lawrence E. Dettweiler, Margaret A. Acker,*
    *Barnaby F. Guthrie, and Charles Gregory*

16  Self-Control in Individual and Group Behavior Modification
    Programs for Emotionally Disturbed Children                       285
    *Hans Heiner*

17  Multiple Evaluations of a Parent-Training Program                 299
    *G. R. Patterson*

## V. Modifying Behavior of Retardates and Psychotics

18  Kin Kare: A Community Residence for Graduates of an Operant
    Program for Severe and Profound Retardates in a Large Institution 325
    *Garry L. Martin and Glen H. Lowther*

19  A Back Ward Routine and the Effects of Instructions               345
    *Luis Otávio de Seixas Queiroz*

20  Application of Operant Principles to Mentally Retarded Children    365
    *Kaoru Yamaguchi*

## VI. Modifying Drug-Related Behavior Problems

21  A Behavioral Program for Intravenous Amphetamine Addicts     387
    *K. Gunnar Gotestam, G. Lennart Melin,*
    *and William S. Dockens, III*

22  Use of Behavior Modification in the Reduction of Alcohol
    Related Road Accidents     399
    *S. H. Lovibond*

## VII. Theoretical and Ethical Issues

23  Environmental Design: Realities and Delusions     409
    *Arthur D. Colman*

24  Operant Conditioning: A General Systems Approach     425
    *William S. Dockens, III*

25  Humanism and Applied Behaviorism     443
    *Travis Thompson*

## VIII. Training Behavior Therapists

26  A Comprehensive Training Program for Behavior Therapists     451
    *Sten Rönnberg*

27  Training Nonprofessionals in Behavior Modification     469
    *James M. Gardner*

## IX. Control and Countercontrol: A Panel Discussion

Patrick Bateson     487
Willard F. Day     491
Herbert McClosky     501
Paul E. Meehl     509
Jack Michael     523

AUTHOR INDEX     525
SUBJECT INDEX     535

# VI. Modifying Drug-Related Behavior Problems

# LIST OF CONTRIBUTORS

Numbers in parentheses indicate the pages on which the authors' contributions begin.

MARGARET A. ACKER (265), Liberal and Applied Arts Division, Camosun College, Victoria, British Columbia, Canada

TEODORO AYLLON (107), Department of Psychology, Georgia State University, Atlanta, Georgia

PATRICK BATESON (487), Sub-Department of Animal Behaviour, University of Cambridge, Madingley, Cambridge, England

WESLEY C. BECKER (139), Department of Special Education, University of Oregon, College of Education, Eugene, Oregon

SIDNEY B. BIJOU (161), Department of Psychology, University of Illinois, Champaign, Illinois

JOHN PAUL BRADY (45), Department of Psychiatry, Hospital of the University of Pennsylvania, Philadelphia, Pennsylvania

ARTHUR D. COLMAN (409), Department of Psychiatry, University of California Medical Center, San Francisco, California, and School of Environmental Design, University of California, Berkeley, California

WILLARD F. DAY (491), Department of Psychology, University of Nevada, Reno, Nevada

LUIS OTÁVIO DE SEIXAS QUEIROZ* (345), Instituto de Neuro-Psiquiatria, Itapira, São Paulo, Brazil

LAWRENCE E. DETTWEILER (265), The Pacific Centre for Human Development, University of Victoria, Victoria, British Columbia, Canada

*Present address: Clinica do Comportamento, Rua Padre José Teixeira, 107, Campinas, São Paulo, Brazil.

WILLIAM S. DOCKENS, III (387, 425), Psykologiska Institutionen, Uppsala Universitet, Uppsala, Sweden

ANN DELL DUNCAN (181), Spaulding Youth Center, Tilton, New Hampshire

JAMES M. GARDNER (469), Department of Psychology, University of Queensland, St. Lucia, Australia

MICHAEL GELDER (3), Department of Psychiatry, University of Oxford, The Warneford Hospital, Oxford, England

SILVIA GOMAR-RUIZ (221), Department of Experimental Psychology and Methodology, National Autonomous University of Mexico, Mexico City, Mexico

K. GUNNAR GÖTESTAM (387), Psychiatric Research Center, University of Uppsala, Ulleraker Hospital, Uppsala, Sweden

P. JOAN GRAHAM (65), Departments of Mental Health, Psychology and Social Studies, Queen's University of Belfast, Belfast, Northern Ireland

CHARLES GREGORY (265), Pharmakologisches und Anatomisches Institut (Abt. Embryonal-Pharmakologie), der Freien Universitat Berlin, Berlin, Germany

JEFFREY A. GRIMM (161), Thistledown Regional Center, Rexdale, Ontario, Canada

BARNABY F. GUTHRIE (265), The Pacific Centre for Human Development, Victoria, British Columbia, Canada

J. J. HARBISON (65), Department of Mental Health, University of Belfast, Belfast, Northern Ireland

V. WILLIAM HARRIS* (237), Department of Human Development and Family Life, University of Kansas, Lawrence, Kansas

HANS HEINER (285), Paedologisch Institut, Prins Hendriklaan, Amsterdam, The Netherlands

WELLS HIVELY (181), Spaulding Youth Center, Tilton, New Hampshire

BEVERLY LOUISELL (201), Behaviordelia, Kalamazoo, Michigan

*Present address: Southwest Indian Center, Tucson, Arizona

S. H. LOVIBOND (399), University of New South Wales, Kensington, New South Wales, Australia

GLEN H. LOWTHER (325), The Manitoba School for Retardates, Portage La Prairie, Manitoba, Canada

H. McALLISTER (65), Departments of Mental Health, Psychology, and Social Studies, Queen's University of Belfast, Northern Ireland

HERBERT McCLOSKY (501), Department of Political Science, University of California, Berkeley, Berkeley, California

RICHARD W. MALOTT (201), Department of Psychology, Western Michigan University, Kalamazoo, Michigan

GARRY L. MARTIN (325), Department of Psychology, St. Paul's College, University of Manitoba, Winnipeg, Manitoba, Canada

PAUL E. MEEHL (509), Psychiatry Research Unit, University of Minnesota, Minneapolis, Minnesota

G. LENNART MELIN (387), Psykologiska Institutionen, Uppsala Universitet, Uppsala, Sweden

V. MEYER (11), Academic Department of Psychiatry, Middlesex Hospital Medical School, University of London, London, England

JACK MICHAEL (523), Department of Psychology, Western Michigan University, Kalamazoo, Michigan

G. R. PATTERSON (299), Oregon Research Institute, Eugene, Oregon

J. T. QUINN (65), Belfast City Hospital and the Royal Victoria Hospital, Department of Mental Health, Queen's University of Belfast, Belfast, Northern Ireland

EMILIO RIBES-I. (221), Department of Experimental Analysis of Behavior, National Autonomous University of Mexico, Mexico City, Mexico

WOLFRAM RIEGER (45), Eastern Pennsylvania Psychiatric Institute, Philadelphia, Pennsylvania

LETICIA RIVAS (221), Department of Experimental Psychology and Methodology, National Autonomous University of Mexico, Mexico City, Mexico

MICHAEL D. ROBERTS (107), Community Mental Health Center of Palm Beach County, West Palm Beach, Florida

STEN RÖNNBERG (451), Institute of Education, Stockholm University, Stockholm, Sweden

JAMES A. SHERMAN (237), Department of Human Development and Family Life, University of Kansas, Lawrence, Kansas

RICHARD B. STUART* (79), Center for Human Growth and Development, University of Michigan, Ann Arbor, Michigan

TRAVIS THOMPSON (443), Psychiatry Research Unit and Department of Psychology, University of Minnesota, Minneapolis, Minnesota

JOSEPH WOLPE (33), Department of Psychiatry, Health Sciences Center, Temple University, Philadelphia, Pennsylvania

KAORU YAMAGUCHI (365), Research Institute for the Education of Exceptional Children, Tokyo Gakugei University, Nukui Kita-Machi, Koganei-Shi, Tokyo, Japan

N. J. YORKSTON[†] (97), Departments of Psychiatry and Medicine, University of Minnesota, Minneapolis, Minnesota

*Present address: Department of Psychiatry, University of British Columbia, Vancouver, British Columbia.
[†]Present address: Friern Hospital, New Southgate, London, England.

# PREFACE

It began as a few novel experiments in animal laboratories, with rats and pigeons serving as subjects. Then there were reports on the periphery of clinical practice that retardates and autistic children responded to the same procedures as the animals in the novel experiments. Next, teaching machines and programmed texts began exciting curiosity in education and industry, while small experimental cultures blossomed and wilted in response to the same stimuli from experimental laboratories. Suddenly, wards of psychotic patients, sheltered workshops for the retarded, clinics for alcoholics, industrial departments, university classes, prisons, correction centers, aerospace laboratories, and outpatient clinics were responding to the same principles. A literature quickly developed, and applied behaviorism became not only a major force in psychology, but also an unquestionable reality in an array of disciplines ranging from industrial psychophysics to human pharmacology. And such is the range of topics expounded on in the present volume.

It has become difficult enough to keep abreast of developments in one's own community or region; attempting to maintain even superficial awareness of activities in other nations across linguistic barriers is next to impossible. It was with this problem in mind that an International Symposium on Behavior Modification was held in Minneapolis, Minnesota on October 4–6, 1972, as the first realization of much needed international communication.

We believe this volume demonstrates that investigators in this highly dynamic area can be brought together to exchange their findings and thoughts concerning applications of behavioral principles to significant human problems. In it the reader will find some exciting revelations, with a number of surprises and reports of major impact. Thus we can say, without immodesty, that this volume bears careful reading.

# ACKNOWLEDGMENTS

Any effort at international communication is necessarily complex and requires the cooperation of many people, not the least of whom are the participants themselves. The conference was sponsored by the department of Psychiatry of the University of Minnesota, the Psykologiska Institutionen, Uppsala Universitet, and the Nolte Center for Continuing Education, University of Minnesota. Financial support by the University of Minnesota is most gratefully acknowledged.

Numerous individuals played critical roles in the organization of the conference. In particular, Gordon Amundson and his staff at the Nolte Center performed an amazing job in coordinating and organizing the often mind-boggling complexities of such an international conference. Mary Timmerman Belmonte and Judy Volinkaty served invaluably in administrative matters and in preparation of manuscripts for publication. The administrative support of Leonard Heston and William Hausman was most appreciated. Finally, the editors wish to acknowledge the cooperation and support of Professor David T. Lykken for helping to bring the volume to realization.

# I TREATING ANXIETY

# 1 FLOODING: RESULTS AND PROBLEMS FROM A NEW TREATMENT FOR ANXIETY[1]

## Michael Gelder

Treatment by flooding, or implosion, has attracted attention as a possible alternative therapy for anxiety states and other neurotic disorders. The literature on the results of flooding treatment is full of contradictions, however, and in this respect it is in sharp contrast to the much more consistent reports about desensitization. Some of these differences may have arisen because studies have been uncontrolled or poorly designed. But if attention is restricted to investigations that appeared to be well controlled, differences are still found. Thus, Barrett (1969) found flooding at least as effective as desensitization, while Mealiea and Nawas (1971) report that it is no more effective than control procedures. Such a difference might be due to variations in procedure or to differences in the subjects of the two investigations.

Marks, Boulougouris, and Marset (1971) have drawn attention to the importance of differences between subjects, and suggest that flooding is more effective than desensitization only with subjects who are very anxious (for example, agoraphobic patients). However, this was not confirmed by Hussain (1971), whose results suggested the reverse. On the other hand, Prokaska (1971), studying students with examination anxiety, reports that the subjects who responded best were those who were made most anxious by the flooding procedure.

[1] The original investigations described in this paper were undertaken by a research team, which included Drs. D. H. Gath, D. Johnstone, A. M. Mathews, P. M. Shaw, and Mrs. M. Munby, with the support of the Medical Research Council of Great Britain.

3

Several procedural differences may be important. Some investigators use themes based on psychoanalytic interpretations of symptoms (e.g., Stampfl and Levis, 1967); others link the emotive material more directly with the patients' manifest anxieties (e.g., Marks *et al.,* 1971); in some investigations, tape recordings are used; in others, themes are presented by the therapists; some investigators rely mainly on imaginal treatment; others lay emphasis on exposure to the real situations. However, critical examination of the literature does not indicate that any one of these factors can by itself explain the differences between investigations, although some interaction between them might still be important. Two other important variables are the degree of emotional arousal evoked and the length of exposure, but these also fail to explain all the differences among investigations.

All this indicates that flooding is a complicated precedure and that, correspondingly, proper investigation is likely to be time consuming. In view of the conflicting results from "preclinical" controlled studies and the lack of a comparative controlled investigation of a patient population, we decided to carry out a controlled clinical trial in which flooding treatment was compared with desensitization and with a procedure designed to include the most important nonspecific elements common to the two behavioral procedures.

Thirty-six phobic patients were allocated to a four-level factorial design in which there were three therapists, three treatments, two kinds of phobic disorder (agoraphobic patients and those with other varieties of phobia), and two levels of expectancy. The latter was manipulated by an induction interview designed to increase the expectations of success of half the patients. In fact, the procedure did not lead to measurable differences between the two groups, and this variable need not be considered further. Equally, no differences were found between the results of the three therapists, and this part of the investigation will not be discussed here.

The three procedures—flooding, desensitization, and the control— were standardized carefully, and sessions were of equal length. Therapists were trained thoroughly in all three techniques before the investigation. Desensitization was carried out following the procedure described by Wolpe (1969). Flooding made use of fear-provoking scenes related directly to the phobia or its manifest associations; we did not use material derived from psychoanalytic interpretations. The control procedure was designed to include nonspecific elements common to the behavior treatments: A period of undirected fantasy based on free association was combined with discussion of symptoms and their effects, and with strong encouragement.

All three treatments included a period of practice, but the degree and speed of exposure varied; thus, in flooding sessions exposure was intensive and evoked much anxiety, in desensitization it was gradual and anxiety was avoided, and in the control procedure it was left to the patient to practice as much as he felt able.

A comprehensive series of measures of improvement were used, including clinical ratings, attitude tests, and psychophysiological measurements, but here we shall consider only a few variables. One special feature of the investigation was the inclusion of an objective behavioral test carried out before and after treatment by an assessor who remained unaware of the treatment given. Such behavioral avoidance tests have shown their value in studies with volunteers with mild phobias but do not appear to have been included in any published report of behavior therapy with psychiatric patients, no doubt because they are time consuming and difficult to administer. Results were subjected to analysis of covariance, the covariate being the pretreatment score, in an analysis in which the main effects and most important first-order interactions were examined. This account will deal only with the main effects of the three treatments, as shown by three indices (Figure 1.1).

When rating scores are considered, whether these were made by a psychiatrist (who was not aware of the treatment received) or by the patient,

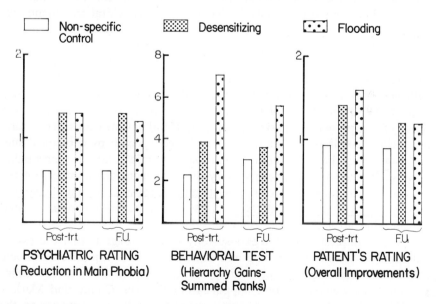

*Figure 1.1.*

there was no significant difference between the effects of flooding and those of desensitization, although both led to significantly more improvement than the control procedure. With the behavioral test, there was a tendency for patients who received flooding to improve more than desensitization patients, but the difference did not reach an acceptable level of statistical significance. This pattern of results had not changed significantly when patients were reexamined 6 months after the end of treatment. The other ratings, attitude scales, and physiological measurements all pointed to the same conclusion: Flooding and desensitization affected phobias equally, and significantly more than the control treatment; and they did not differ in other important ways. There was, in addition, no evidence that agoraphobic patients responded any differently from those with other phobias.

This finding, which might disappoint an enthusiastic advocate of flooding treatment, is in fact of great interest. Two very different treatments produced similar effects on phobic symptoms; and they are unlikely to have done so by virtue of shared nonspecific elements because both differed significantly from the control procedure, which incorporated the main nonspecific elements common to the behavior therapies. Therefore, another explanation must be sought.

First, it is possible that flooding and desensitization have quite different psychological mechanisms and that in our investigation these have led, by chance, to the same amount of improvement in the two groups of patients. The second possibility is that the two behavioral treatments, although apparently very different from one another, nevertheless share the *same* psychological mechanism—and a specific mechanism rather than one of the nonspecific treatment factors that were incorporated in the control treatment. A replication of our experiment is required to distinguish with certainty between these two possibilities, but the first appears less likely because the effects of the treatments were so similar on the whole range of symptomatic, physiological, and attitudinal measures. Therefore, the second possibility—that there is a shared specific psychological mechanism—must be considered even though it might appear improbable because the treatments appear so very different from one another. Of the possible psychological processes, systematic exposure to phobic stimuli must be given special consideration, as Marks *et al.* (1971) have pointed out on other grounds.

In its simplest form, the exposure hypothesis suggests that the essential common feature in flooding and desensitization is exposure to phobic stimuli and that the level of anxiety that is adopted is relatively unimportant. This view gains some support from Watson, Gaind, and Marks's (1971) finding that specific phobias respond rapidly to exposure to the phobic object even when no measures are taken to control anxiety. This simple hypothesis will not account for our results, because although the amount of exposure in the two behavioral treatments was quite different—being much longer in flooding—the final therapeutic effects were equal.

To meet this difficulty, modifications of the exposure hypothesis can be considered: first, that exposure at low levels of anxiety is more effective than exposure at high levels, and second, that intermittent exposure is more effective than continuous exposure; or there might be an interaction between these two variables.

We decided to investigate this question further in the less complex situation of a study using volunteers with simple phobias. Volunteer subjects were selected who presented with fears of spiders and who failed a behavioral avoidance test with a live spider. Each of 40 female students was allocated at random to one of four conditions: continuous presentation of highly arousing themes, discontinuous presentation of highly arousing themes, continuous presentation of less arousing themes, and discontinuous presentation of less arousing themes. The usual rationale of flooding leads to the prediction that continuous presentation of highly arousing material would have greatest therapeutic effect. By contrast, the rationale of desensitization leads to the prediction that intermittent exposure to less arousing themes would be more effective.

Each student was assessed before and after a single treatment session, using a behavioral avoidance test (following Bandura, Blanchard, and Ritter, 1969) and attitude measurements. The behavioral measurements showed most change with the low-arousal–massed-presentation condition, least with the high arousal massed presentation condition (Table 1.1). Thus, neither prediction was confirmed, but the optimal condition was one that might explain some of the results with patients. There were also differences in attitude measures, highly arousing material tending to reinforce subjects' conception of spiders as unpleasant and dangerous, low-arousal themes tending to the opposite effect. These attitude changes were transient, however, and were reversed by the subjects' subsequent experience in the behavioral test.

**TABLE 1.1**

Items Gained on Behavior Test under Four Treatment Conditions

| Treatment condition | Behavioral avoidance test | | Items gained |
|---|---|---|---|
| | 1 | 2 | |
| High anxiety—massed | 11.0 | 11.6 | 0.6 |
| High anxiety—spaced | 12.7 | 14.0 | 1.3 |
| Low anxiety—massed | 11.4 | 13.8 | 2.4 |
| Low anxiety—spaced | 11.9 | 13.0 | 1.1 |

A test was then carried out to test the hypothesis that continuous presentation at low arousal is particularly effective in relieving phobic symptoms. For this investigation, we returned to the study of agoraphobic patients. A small group of patients with very severe agoraphobia was studied. Flooding was performed under two conditions, in the usual way and also while the patient received an anxiety-reducing drug. At the same time, "attribution" effects were examined by introducing two further conditions: In one the patient received the anxiety-reducing drug but was unaware of this, while in the other he received no anxiety-reducing drug but thought that the drug had been given. Every patient received each of the four treatment conditions in balanced order. The means of examining attribution effects was as follows: All patients received a syrup which they were led to believe was to facilitate the physiological monitoring carried out in treatment sessions. On half the occasions this was inert, on the other half it contained the anxiolytic agent (diazepam 20–30 mg). On half the occasions patients also received a capsule which they were led to believe was the anxiolytic agent but which was always inert. Thus, the conditions were as follows: (a) inactive syrup, no capsule—the patient believes correctly that he has not received an anxiolytic; (b) active syrup, no capsule—the patient believes incorrectly that he has not received an anxiolytic; (c) inactive syrup plus capsule—the patient believes incorrectly that he has received the anxiolytic; (d) active syrup plus capsule—the patient believes correctly that he has received the anxiolytic. Assessment was again by behavioral tests, ratings, and attitude measurements (Table 1.2).

The results were clear: Flooding was most effective when carried out with an anxiolytic and with the patient's knowledge of this. It was least effective when the patient was correctly informed that he had received no anxiolytic. Flooding with an anxiolytic given without the patient's knowledge was not significantly more effective than flooding given when

**TABLE 1.2**

EFFECT OF DIAZEPAM AND AN INERT CAPSULE ON THE RESULTS OF FLOODING TREATMENT

| Condition | Behavior test: items gained |
|---|---|
| Diazepam plus capsule | 4.50 |
| Diazepam, no capsule | 2.50 |
| No diazepam, capsule | 2.25 |
| No diazepam, no capsule | −0.25 |

[Overall $\chi^2 = 9.23$; $P < 0.05$]

the patient was wrongly informed that he had received an anxiolytic. These results lend further support to the idea that continuous exposure is most effective when carried out at low levels of arousal. They also indicate that attribution effects have powerful effects, which are comparable to those of the drug. We shall not consider the interpretation of these attribution effects further here, but instead restrict ourselves to the main finding.

Although this result can be explained retrospectively in terms of simple learning processes, it is not one that was predicted from them; nor, as far as I know, has it been suggested, on the basis of laboratory studies of conditioning, that these would be the optimal conditions for alleviating phobias. Although several assumptions are involved in drawing together the results from the three studies with their different patient populations, the attempt does appear to be useful, because it suggests new experiments as well as some modifications to existing therapeutic procedures. In addition, it suggests that cognitive processes which cannot be understood solely in terms of the learning principles that have been discovered with laboratory animals are important in behavior therapy. A synthesis will therefore be attempted.

One of the small pieces of evidence pointing to the importance of cognitive factors comes from the study, which was the second to be described, of subjects with phobias of spiders. Here, high-anxiety themes led to even more unfavorable attitudes to spiders, while low-anxiety themes tended to do the opposite. When subjects were subsequently confronted with a spider in a behavioral avoidance test, these attitude changes were reversed—the unfavorable attitudes of the high-anxiety group became more favorable, and the opposite change took place in the low-anxiety group. These changes, which have been replicated in a further experiment, appear consistent with the idea that the flooding session acted, among other things, as a persuasive message. Thus, even in this simple experimental treatment, cognitive processes are apparently added to simple learning.

With the more intense phobias met in psychiatric patients, the situation is no doubt even more complicated. Watson and Marks (1971) have shown that emotionally arousing material that has nothing to do with the phobia can, under some circumstances at least, be as effective as material related to the fears. Perhaps, therefore, there is also in flooding a component of learning to cope with fear—a suggestion that seems quite probable on clinical grounds because it is known that many phobic patients avoid experiencing even mild degrees of anxiety and therefore do not learn that they can tolerate more, or that anxiety elicited by phobic stimuli eventually declines.

We are beginning to see reasons for the inconsistent results that have been reported from investigations of flooding treatment. The procedure may well have several psychological components, and each may be optimal in rather different conditions. At the same time, the subjects who are roughly grouped as "phobic" differ in the structure of the psychological disorder that they present. In some, avoidance behavior and conditioned anxiety responses predominate; in others, unrealistic attitudes to the feared object; in still others a vicious circle in which the symptoms of anxiety generate more fear.

If we accept that there are psychological components at work in flooding treatment, then we cannot necessarily specify a single set of optimal treatment conditions. Nevertheless, our results indicate that one condition that is likely to be particularly effective is *continuous exposure to phobic situations under conditions that prevent the development of anxiety.* Whether this exposure is best carried out within real situations, in imagination, or with some combination of the two, is a question we are investigating at present. Of course, further experiments will be required to test these ideas more thoroughly, but whatever their outcome it is already clear that the study of flooding treatment is leading to important new questions about anxiety states and their treatment.

## References

Bandura, A., Blanchard, E. B., and Ritter, D. The relative efficiency of desensitization and modeling approaches for inducing behavioral affective and attitudinal changes. *Journal of Personality and Social Psychology*, 1969, **13**, 173–199.

Barrett, C. L. Systematic desensitization versus implosive therapy. *Journal of Abnormal Psychology*, 1969, **74**, 581–592.

Hussain, M. Z. Desensitization and flooding (implosion) in treatment of phobias. *American Journal of Psychiatry*, 1971, **127**, 1509–1514.

Marks, I. M., Boulougouris, J., and Marset, P. Flooding versus desensitization in the treatment of phobic patients: A crossover study. *British Journal of Psychiatry*, 1971, **119**, 353–375.

Mealiea, W. L., and Nawas, M. N. The comparative effectiveness of systematic desensitization and implosive therapy in the treatment of snake phobia. *Journal of Behavior Therapy and Experimental Psychiatry*, 1971, **2**, 85–94.

Prokaska, J. O. Symptom and dynamic cues in the implosive treatment of test anxiety. *Journal of Abnormal Psychology*, 1971, **77**, 133–142.

Stampfl, T. G., and Levis, D. J. Essentials of implosive therapy: A learning theory based on psychodynamic behavioural therapy. *Journal of Abnormal Psychology*, 1967, **72**, 496–503.

Watson, J. P., Gaind, R., and Marks, I. M. Prolonged exposure: A rapid treatment for phobias. *British Medical Journal*, 1971, **1**, 13–15.

Watson, J. B., and Marks, I. M. Relevant and irrelevant fear in flooding. *Behaviour Therapy*, 1971, **2**, 275–293.

Wolpe, J. *The Practice of Behaviour Therapy*. Oxford: Pergamon, 1969.

# 2 THE IMPACT OF RESEARCH ON THE CLINICAL APPLICATION OF BEHAVIOR THERAPY

V. Meyer

The last decade has witnessed a rapid development in the field of behavior therapy. The accelerating rate at which publications accumulate has been well documented (Ernst, 1971). It seems that the peak of novelty and enthusiasm has passed, and that critical evaluations are now being undertaken concerning its efficacy, theoretical basis, definition, and ethical implications (e.g., Franks, 1969).

The emphasis in the literature is on the experimental approach to various problems in the field, and the majority of textbooks on behavior therapy have been written by authors who have little or no experience in the clinical application of the principles of behavior therapy. As a result, the current literature deals mainly with various problems and issues for pure and applied research and prepares the reader only to become a research worker in the field. Clinical practice and training, and the problems involved in these aspects of behavior therapy, are relatively ignored. This is unfortunate, because in many countries behavior therapy has been officially recognized as an established form of therapy, although there are no adequate behavior therapy training centers. Thus, would-be behavior therapists find very little help from the literature concerning the nature of their duties and the problems pertaining to their role as clinicians.

The purpose of this paper is to identify and discuss the various limitations of research in the field of behavior therapy from the point of view of a clinician. I started applying the principles of behavior therapy in 1955 and have keenly followed all the developments in the field. For the last 10 years, I have worked exclusively as a behavior therapist, having easy access

11

to a whole range of psychiatric conditions. Apart from some lecturing to medical students, my time is wholly taken up with training clinical psychologists and psychiatrists in behavior therapy (1-year course) and conducting clinical research.

In the early writings on behavior therapy (e.g., Wolpe, 1958; Eysenck, 1960), one finds statements to the effect that this form of treatment is based on "modern learning theory" supported by sound experimental findings. Its formulations are readily testable, and the clinician will be provided with treatment techniques whose range of applicability, efficacy, the relevance of various components, and the processes underlying them will be tested experimentally. Let us see to what extent these objectives have been attained.

First of all, it is important to point out that despite numerous books and articles concerning the design of investigations and procedural tactics for accumulating knowledge about therapy, one can find hardly a single report that satisfies all the stringent requirements of a good investigation. Is it possible to fulfill these criteria, as expanded by Paul (1969a) in behavior-modification research on clinical material? This question should be considered in the light of Paul's conclusion that ultimately the questions to be answered appear to be: "What treatment, by whom, is most effective for this individual, with that specific problem, under which set of circumstances, and how does it come about?"

As regards the efficacy, all one can conclude is that some techniques of behavior therapy, namely, systematic desensitization for phobics (Gelder, Marks, and Wolff, 1967), bell and pad for enuretics (Forrester, Stein, and Susser, 1964; Werry and Cohrssen, 1965; De Leon and Mandell, 1966), token economies for chronic hospitalized patients (e.g., Henderson and Scales, 1970; Lloyd and Abel, 1970; Marks, Sonoda, and Schalack, 1968; Birky and Chambliss, 1971; Gripp and Magaro, 1971; Shean and Zeidberg, 1971), and aversion therapy for homosexuals (Feldman and McCulloch, 1971) appear to produce better outcome results than no treatment or some other form of therapy, mainly psychotherapy. I am fully aware of the vast literature on therapy-analog research using students with various "excessive fears" (see Paul, 1969c) but, despite superior experimental designs and methodology, the utility of the findings is limited by analog research errors that preclude significant contributions to clinical practice (Bernstein and Paul, 1971).

More recently, a number of studies have attempted to compare the efficacy of certain behavior-therapy techniques. The findings of these are on the whole inconsistent. For instance, in six studies comparing systematic desensitization with implosion, three showed no difference between the two techniques, all producing significantly better improvement than no-treatment controls (Barrett, 1969; Calf and Maclean, 1970; De Moor, 1970). Two research projects (Mealiea and Nawas, 1971; Willis and Edwards, 1969) indicated that desensitization was significantly better than implosion, the latter giving no better results than no-treatment controls. The last published study that used phobic patients and physiological features found a better outcome with implosion (Marks, Boulougouris, and Marset, 1971). An unpublished study in Professor Gelder's department at Oxford, on the other hand, found no difference between the two techniques as applied to phobics.

This lack of consistency can even be found when researchers accurately apply identical treatment procedures. For instance, Hodgson and Rachman (1970), using Kirchner and Hogan's (1966) implosion technique, failed to demonstrate the dramatic effects of implosion reported by the latter authors. Similarly, Kent, Wilson, and Nelson (1972) were unable to replicate Valius and Ray's (1967) findings of "cognitive desensitization."

Another area of lively research purports to assess the relevance of various components in treatment techniques, and efforts have been made to evaluate the role of nonspecific elements that enter into any form of therapy, for example, therapeutic sensitizations and therapist–patient relationship. Systematic desensitization, or rather four identifiable procedural "packages," have been most widely and intensively investigated. Consistency for findings, as regards the role of relaxation and exposure and the combination of these, is much better, but far from being perfect (see Paul, 1969b, 1969c), and all the published work has been in incidents with "excessive fears." Lack of consistency is prominent in studies dealing with "therapeutic instructions." Thus, some studies provide evidence to the effect that therapeutic instructions alone increase the efficacy of experimental desensitization to a lesser or greater degree (e.g., Leitenberg, Agras, Barlow, and Oliveau, 1969; Oliveau, Agras, Leitenberg, Moore, and Wright, 1969; McGlynn, Mealiea, and Nawas, 1969; McGlynn, Reynolds, and Linder, 1971a; Parrino, 1971; Woy and Efran, 1972); also, Borkovec (1972) supports this finding and, in addition, finds an expectancy manipulation effect on implosion. On the other hand, some reports fail to demonstrate this effect with analog imaginal or contact desensitization (e.g., McGlynn and Mapp, 1970; McGlynn and Williams, 1970; Lomont and Brock, 1971; McGlynn, Reynolds, and Linder 1971b). Most recently, Miller (1972) adduced some evidence suggesting that the presentation of therapeutic instructions does not appear to enhance the desensitization effect. It is the presentation of misleading instructions that appears to reduce the effectiveness of analog desensitization. In passing, this study demonstrates the importance of controlling for the subjects' awareness of the therapeutic nature of these experiments. This awareness appears to be related to better outcome. Research of this nature has been extended to patients treated with aversion therapy (see Rachman and Teasdale, 1969), a version-relief therapy (Solyom, McClure, Heseltine, Ledwige, and Solyom, 1972), and operant techniques (see Ayllon and Azrin, 1968; Davison, 1969).

Closely related to this type of research, attempts have been made to explore the underlying processes of treatment methods—the question, "How does it work?" This area abounds in theoretical speculations, with a paucity of experimental findings clearly supporting the postulated theoretical interpretations. Alongside the original model of Wolpian reciprocal inhibition, which has been the subject of severe criticism (Wilson and Davison, 1971), we have now several interpretations, namely: extinction, habituation, operant conditioning, attribution theory, and a combination of processes couched in Guthrian terms. Most of these models indicate moderate to radical modifications of systematic desensitization as derived from the Wolpian theoretical standpoint.

The role of muscular relaxation in desensitization has been questioned (Davison, 1966; Rachman, 1968), and a number of studies have attempted to evaluate the physiological effects of relaxation (e.g., Paul, 1969d; Lader and Mathews, 1970). Also, recently, the psychophysiological aspects of systematic desensitization have received increased attention (e.g., Lang, Melamed, and Hart, 1970; Van Egeren, 1971). At the moment, it is difficult to draw any firm conclusion from this area of research.

While therapeutic effectiveness of aversion therapy appears to be promising, its theoretical basis is still a matter of dispute. Rachman and Teasdale (1969) favor the classical conditioning model in an attempt to account for the effects of the three main procedures used, that is, classical conditioning, anticipatory avoidance (Feldman and McCulloch, 1971), and punishment (Azrin and Holz, 1966). Feldman and McCulloch (1971) report a controlled study comparing the anticipatory avoidance paradigm with the classical model and psychotherapy using homosexual patients. Both conditioning models were equally successful, and both were more successful than psychotherapy in cases of "secondary" homosexuality. All three treatments were largely unsuccessful with "primary" homosexuals and "severe personality disorders" irrespective of prior heterosexual history.

Some very limited physiological evidence in support of a classical conditioning theory on patients with sexual disorders has been adduced (Feldman and McCulloch, 1971; Hallam and Rachman, 1972). These studies showed that there are changes in cardiac responsiveness following aversion therapy, and that successes and failures can be discriminated in terms of cardiac responses. However, a better-controlled study by Hallam, Rachman, and Falkowski (1972) on alcoholics furnishes results that are very embarrassing for a conditioning interpretation of aversion therapy; no conditioning effect was observed after aversion therapy using cardiac and skin-resistance responses.

"Cognitive desensitization" found support for a reinterpretation in terms of an aversion-relief model (Gaupp, Stern, and Galbraith, 1972). Baker (1969) and Turner, Young, and Rachman (1970) failed to demonstrate the evidence for an expected conditioning effect, over a period of 4 weeks, with a bell-and-pad apparatus for the treatment of enuresis, when placebo and arousal factors were controlled.

One could have predicted this state of affairs in this type of research on the basis of the past experience of early experts in the field of learning, working with infrahumans in relatively well-controlled settings. They concluded that crucial experiments to decide between important theoretical issues are very hard to come by, and nowadays researchers concentrate their efforts on parametric studies.

Leaving aside the general problems of research and the difficulties involved when working with clinical material in poorly controlled settings, research endeavors have shown so far that the original assumptions of behavior therapists were oversimplified, and after a decade of research more questions have been raised than answered.

As was pointed out at the outset, most of the writings on behavior therapy by "experts" are experimentally oriented and advocate a technological approach to treatment by giving "scientific respectability" to the techniques that have been derived from learning principles and intensively investigated. This no doubt has an influence on the practice of behavior therapy. It is not surprising, therefore, that many practicing behavior therapists apply certain prescribed techniques to certain psychiatric conditions. Also, psychologists and psychiatrists seeking training in behavior therapy expect to be grilled in techniques and the range of their applicability. Originally, I did subscribe to this approach, but, after gaining wide clinical experience, I was struck by its considerable limitations and its inappropriateness in many cases (Meyer and Chesser, 1970). The problems of technology are twofold. First, not all patients sharing the same complaint respond to the procedural requirements of techniques. For example, in the case of systematic desensitization, some patients find it difficult to relax, some fail to conjure up clear images of phobic scenes in relevant modalities, some do not report anxiety to clearly imagined phobic stimuli, and a proportion fail to generalize adequately to real-life situations. Second, and more important, one seldom finds cases with isolated complaints in psychiatric clinics. It is more likely that one is confronted with a number of complaints and problems that may or may not be directly related to the main complaint presented by the patient; or the main complaint may turn out, according to the therapist's assessment, to be other than what the patient himself believes it to be.

The research-oriented behavior therapist tends to ignore individual differences and to lump together subjects who exhibit something in common. The clinician, on the other hand, tends to consider individual differences carefully and adopts his own approach to them.

It is not very difficult to understand these differences in approach, and learning principles may be of help here. Basically, the objectives and the sources of associated reinforcement are different. The experimentally orientated therapist searches for generalizations and theoretical explanations for techniques that appear to work. To attain these goals, he attempts to conduct rigorous experiments. His reinforcement for this type of work comes mainly from the establishment and from editors of learned journals. The surest way to attain these objectives is to adopt an acceptable methodology using groups of subjects, exerting rigorous controls over relevant variables so that the findings can be meaningfully evaluated and therefore warrant the conclusion drawn from them. Individual differences are a nuisance for the experimentalist, and it is understandable that he would rather ignore them.

The clinician, on the other hand, addresses himself to the immediate practical problems presented by patients, which require solution in fact and not in principle. It is his duty to accept therapeutic responsibility for his patients, and his main sources of reinforcement are his patients.

What are the advantages and disadvantages of each approach? Obviously, in order to improve the theoretical and practical status of behavior therapy, knowledge must be advanced and research into its pure and applied aspects is essential. However, the stringent requirements of a good experiment, because of methodological and practical difficulties when working with clinical material, direct the experimentalist's efforts to nonpatient populations. Clinical research, on the other hand, has serious limitations because experimental rigor demands that all the patients in a group be treated in exactly the same way, and the design does not allow for any modifications to accommodate individual differences in response to the requirements of a particular technique. Also, individual differences in the breadth of complaints and problems are ignored provided all patients have a similar main or most-incapacitating complaint in the opinion of the experimenter.

On the basis of a research project for phobic patients in which we attempted to compare the efficacy of systematic desensitization alone with systematic desensitization plus immediate *in vivo* training, we are surprised that other workers with similar samples have not drawn attention to these problems. In terms of certain responses of some patients, it was obvious that they were not being desensitized. Some patients' treatment was hampered by additional anxiety due to stress at work, marriage, interpersonal relationships, or financial problems; two patients left treatment because the therapist ignored their pleas to help them with additional problems that became acute. In some patients, the basic problem turned out to be strong reinforcement obtained from their phobic behavior. In our role as research workers, we had to follow the research design and ignore these problems; but, as therapists with clinical responsibility, we were very frustrated. Such limited therapeutic programs no doubt reflect limited therapeutic outcomes. Gelder *et al.* (1967), for example, report superiority of desensitization of phobic patients over individual and group psychotherapy, but the average improvement from 4.1 to 2.5 points of a 5-point scale leaves a number of patients in the desensitization group with phobic complaints.

After a pilot study to assess clinically the efficacy of a response-prevention method for compulsive patients with ritualistic acts, we have now embarked on a project comparing the efficacy of 24 hours prevention with 1 hour daily prevention. The project is already bedevilled with the problems of individual differences. Some patients do not gain freedom from rituals within the time allowed for inpatient treatment and demand further treatment. Some, in whom additional complaints are thought by the selecting psychiatrist to be reactions to the compulsive behavior, respond to treatment very well but are left with other complaints and demand additional treatment. Some of the chronic cases obviously require social work before they can be discharged with any hope of making some adjustment to everyday life outside the hospital setting.

It is easy for the purpose of research to form a group of patients with a common complaint and without further consideration treat them with a technique according to the strict prescriptions of a research design. However, is it therapeutically commendable? It is not surprising that following final assessment, research workers frequently continue treatment during the follow-up period (e.g., Rachman, Hodgson, and Marks, 1971; Marks *et al.,* 1971). In the field of token economy projects, apart from group-administered reinforcement programs, individualized treatment programs have been recommended and introduced (e.g., Atthowe and Krasner, 1968; Davison, 1969; Lloyd and Abel, 1970; Birky and Chambliss, 1971; Shean and Zeidberg, 1971; Pomerleau, Bobrove, and Harris, 1972).

The greatest advantage of a clinical approach is that it allows for flexibility to accommodate the individual differences and requirements of patients. The clinician adjusts his approach to the patient and does not force the patient to fit the prescribed treatment. The cost of this approach, however, is great: It precludes the accumulation of scientific knowledge about treatment. The clinician may contribute to theoretical and practical advances by making observations, posing questions, and reporting failures in as much detail as successes. He can test specific hypotheses in individual patients undergoing treatment. The time series and the equivalent time-sample designs for the individual case studies can furnish valuable information, but there are considerable limitations to these designs and, at best, their levels or product provide only hypotheses about cause–effect relationships between variables (Paul, 1969a; Bandura, 1969). One of the problems with research on clinical cases is that accepting therapeutic responsibility is almost antagonistic to following stringent reinforcements of sound research. In my role as both clinician and researcher, I see it as a dilemma for which no easy solution has occurred to me.

It is not surprising that there is a rift between the researcher and the clinician. According to the former, the latter does now know what he is doing and does not bother to find out. The clinician, on the other hand, retaliates by pointing out that the researcher is divorced from reality and that his findings are seldom practical or useful in dealing with clinical problems. Apart from that, he is alarmed by the rapid growth of journals and the rapid accumulation of studies that, more often than not, have no clinical relevance, and the quality of which has gradually declined. He is also disappointed about an alarming inconsistency of findings and the usual repetitive, concluding remark: "Further research is greatly needed." Even when he comes across interesting and valuable results, he is well conditioned to wonder immediately whether anyone else will ever reproduce them.

A very disconcerting aspect of most textbooks is their neglect of the practical application of behavior therapy in a clinical setting. The would-be behavior therapist is told a great deal about treatment techniques—referred to by some as a "box of tricks"—but there is little material on some extremely important aspects of behavior therapy, that is, interviewing patients, the kind of information required for the decisions about the designing of treatment programs and management, discharge from treatment and the social work involved, and competence in dealing with patients and in "know-how" in cooperation with associated disciplines in clinical settings.

Obviously, one's activities as a behavior therapist will be largely determined by one's previous training, theoretical orientation, and the type of cases seen for treatment.

As a Maudsley product, I still lean toward two-factor learning theory and still experience twinges of anxiety when confronted with experimental evidence against it. With the passing of time and with experience in the application of behavior therapy, the intensity of my anxiety has diminished but, at the same time, antipathy about technology, including Lazarus' technical eclecticism (Lazarus, 1971), has increased. This brings us to the question of what behavior therapy is and what behavior therapists do. I will give my own view on this, bearing in mind that what therapists say they do and what they in fact do may be two different things. Apart from that, therapists of different orientations will no doubt interpret their activities according to their theoretical models.

My therapeutic activities from the first interview to the termination of treatment are basically guided by learning principles. By principle, I mean an empirical generalization about a lawful relationship between two variables. For example, the principle of extinction refers to the general curve of a decline and the eventual cessation of responding to the repeated lack of a certain event following the occurrence of the response. Apart from that, there is a considerable amount of information obtained through parametric studies, concerning variables and conditions affecting the rate of the decline.

It is important to bear in mind that principles, defined in this way, refer to observable phenomena and by themselves are not indicative of any specific theoretical explanations for the observed relationships. In fact, there are some five different theoretical explanations for extinction, but none of them accounts satisfactorily for all the known findings.

In the attempt to deal with problems presented by patients, I do not go about thinking in terms of "modern learning theories" but in terms of relatively well-established factual knowledge. Patients cannot afford to wait for crucial experiments designed to decide between competing theoretical explanations.

It is also important to bear in mind the limitations of learning principles, particularly when applied to acquisition, maintenance, and change of disordered behavior (see Buchwald and Young, 1969). First of all, they have been established in laboratory research and only extrapolated to the clinic, without the necessary intervening steps to determine whether they apply in this environment to this kind of behavior. Second, some of these empirical generalizations have been shown not to hold in certain situations. Third, they are very general, lacking the necessary precision concerning rules for application to specific instances of behavior and for explaining the relationship between antecedent events and disordered behaviors. Fourth, there are other determinants of behavior change, that is, organic factors; but even behavior that this has triggered is subject to modification by learning principles. Fifth, the attempts to extend learning principles to cover cognitive events is fraught with dangers because these events are quite different from those on which the principles have been established.

The limitations of etiological formulations become enormous when one considers classical, instrumental conditioning, learning principles, hereditary predisposition, and organismic variables, the vicissitudes of the patient's life, environmental experiences, and reinforcement history. Furthermore, interoceptive conditioning may obscure the genesis of a given pattern of responsiveness. Moreover, vicarious conditioning and learning and mediational processes are additional and complicating variables. This gives the learning approach to etiology of disordered behaviors a wide explanatory power, which is not necessarily indicative of either its validity or pragmatic value in the choice of therapy.

Granted these limitations, the relevance of learning principles to acquisition, maintenance, and change of behavior have been demonstrated on a variety of animal species and on humans. If one adopts very stringent criteria for establishing an empirical generalization, then very little can be salvaged from experimental psychology for practical application. The usefulness of extrapolating the available experimental findings in the field of learning, in the form of paradigms and analogs, to the problems of psychiatric patients has been demonstrated beyond any doubt. Also, fruitful and promising extensions of this knowledge to covert events has been shown recently (e.g., Mahoney, 1970; Cautela, 1971) and to such complex behaviors as modeling (Bandura, 1969) and interpersonal relationships (e.g., Lewinsohn, Weinstein, and Alper, 1970; Liberman, 1970); and attempts have been made to identify and maximize therapeutic learning components in so-called intangible therapeutic events, such as therapist–patient relationships (e.g., Goldstein, Heller, and Sechrest, 1966; Wilson, Hannon, and Evans, 1968).

Thus, as a therapist, I attempt to guide all my activities in terms of learning principles, no matter whether the goal of treatment is to modify motor, autonomic, or cognitive aspects of disordered behavior. For myself, as for Kanfer and Phillips (1970), behavior therapy is an ongoing process during which observations are collected, hypotheses put forward to account for them, tests of hypotheses carried out, adjustments to new observations made, and so on.

Of course, I do not plan every bit of my behavior in advance by specific reference to learning principles. Some of the interactions, such as establishing rapport with patients, flow so swiftly that I work "off the cuff." Also, a great deal of decision making is made on the basis of clinical experience, and sometimes explanations for them in terms of learning principles can only be made *post hoc*. Therapy is a very complex situation, and no empirical generalizations exist that can program every bit of the therapist's behavior.

Obviously, the actual implementation of treatment frequently acquires the aid of general experimental psychology, and the relevant knowledge available in other disciplines such as physiology, anatomy, pharmacology, neurophysiology, sociology, and electronics. Even here I attempt to introduce these aids in accordance with learning principles. Whenever relevant and possible, help is sought from semiprofessionals, that is, nurses, social workers, and relatives of the patient.

Lazarus, introducing technical eclecticism (Lazarus, 1971), implies that a number of useful techniques cannot be encompassed within the framework of learning principles. My contention is that a behavior therapist can structure the introduction of these techniques in terms of this framework. Many behavior therapists, for example, do this when using Masters and Johnson's techniques (1970).

The advantage of the approach advocated here is that the clinician would be able to formulate treatment programs for every patient that would be flexible enough to meet the myriad problems and practical obstacles found when treating patients and would not be obliged to put technical straightjackets on his patients. It is not the technological approach but the application of the principles that has enabled behavior therapy to be extended to virtually every type of psychiatric picture.

In my opinion, learning principles offer a distinct contribution in the attempt to understand etiology and to design treatment for psychiatric disorders. Apart from differences concerning etiological formulations and goals of treatment, the only difference between my activities and those of psychotherapists is that I attempt to structure my approach explicitly and systematically in terms of learning principles.

One of the most difficult aspects of behavior therapy, which has received little attention, is the initial interviewing. The importance of this is obvious, since decisions about the goal and choice of treatment depend on the kind of information elicited from the patient. Kanfer and Saslow

(1969) have proposed a very useful set of guidelines for the behavior analysis of patients' problems in a manner that suggests specific treatment and target behaviors for modification. The analysis covers psychological, biological, economic, and social variables in the patient's history, as well as his current circumstances. It stresses the need for the construction of therapeutic strategies that are adapted to the unique requirements and behavior characteristics of each individual patient. It does not envisage a list of treatment techniques.

The main sources of information are the patient's verbal report, non-verbal behavior during the interview, and response to psychological tests. In addition, the therapist has at his disposal other means of gathering information, such as seeing the relatives of the patient, observing the patient in his own environment, or getting the patient to observe and record his own behavior.

The scheme is Skinnerian in orientation. It does not attempt to determine to what extent the complaint may be due to autonomic disturbances or to faulty knowledge or attitudes; nor does it deal sufficiently with such variables as self-attitudes, self-reinforcement systems, and aspirations. Apart from this, rigid adherence to the scheme can render the interview a very unwieldly and clumsy procedure. An experienced therapist easily formulates one or more hypotheses about the nature of the complaint during the interview, and this shapes the course of the interview and makes it more fluent. The danger here is that the skillful interviewer may elicit the information he expects to find.

Kanfer and Saslow (1969) also seem to neglect another aspect of interviewing. It is extremely important and useful to explore historically the development of the complaint, and to attempt to link one's formulation of the current problem with events in the past, in terms of learning principles. Such information may not only support one's formulation, but it may also help in designing treatment strategy. For instance, a behavioral analysis of an "agoraphobic" may indicate that being outside home (place of security) elicits anxiety but particularly when psychologically or physically restrained. Furthermore, it may turn out that the subject is afraid of failing in any sphere of activities and of an associated criticism by certain people. This formulation would be supported by the findings that the patient's parents put a special premium on achievement and correct behavior, and punished failure, or even second best. In addition, scholastic, occupational, and sexual history may provide evidence to strengthen the formulation.

On the basis of the initial interviews, the therapist should also have some idea which sort of behavior on his part would be reinforcing and which punishing for the patient. This will help the therapist in establishing rapport with the patient. Initial interviewing, before the decision about treatment strategy, may take 4–5 hours on average.

The patient is then given the formulation in simple terms, and the objective of treatment is discussed with him. The subject should give his consent concerning the goal of treatment. Close relatives should also be consulted about it, particularly when the target behavior is social behavior. The therapist should consider the patient's wishes within the context of his own formulation, and it should be his duty to attempt to adjust the patient to the environment to which he wishes to be discharged, if possible.

Following this, the patient is given a simple general outline of possible treatment procedures and the rationale underlying them. The therapist emphasizes the tentative nature of his formulation, but he also indicates that the patient's responses early in treatment may demonstrate any necessary modifications. While motivating the patient to undertake treatment, the therapist at the same time attempts to give him a realistic expectation for the outcome. In addition, the patient is told that he is expected to be an active participant in the treatment, and that as soon as possible he will be required to become his own therapist and to exert self-control. Understanding of every step undertaken in therapy is essential and will enable him to cooperate and participate actively.

These therapeutic instructions are given because there is some evidence to the effect that they add to the therapeutic potency of specific treatment procedures and reduce the patient's general anxiety about his condition in that he feels someone "understands" him and gives him a hopeful outlook.

As regards the treatment itself, the first problem is the setting in which the treatment will be carried out; in particular, one must decide whether or not admission is necessary. The simple rule in our practice is that if no control can be exerted over the repetitive disordered behavior between treatment sessions, admission as an inpatient is at least initially indicated. For instance, it will hinder treatment if an agoraphobic gets frightened traveling to and from therapy sessions, or if a compulsive-ritualistic patient engages in his ritualistic behavior between treatment sessions.

For a relatively isolated complaint, well-established behavior-therapy techniques can be given, for instance, systematic desensitization for phobias. However, if the patient reports anxiety due to any other ongoing stresses, it may be beneficial to deal with it, because anxiety appears to be additive—and apart from that, may interfere with the treatment of a specific complaint. Frequently, the therapist has several treatment techniques at his disposal for the same complaint, for instance, desensitization, *in vivo* training, a combination of these, anxiety-management training and various forms of flooding, or classical conditioning, avoidance training, punishment, covert sensitization, or a combination of these for sexual deviations. Among the many factors determining the choice, the most obvious ones are the facilities available, the patient's resources, and the personal preferences and previous experience of the therapist. Nevertheless, the patient should be consulted about his own preferences.

Complex cases present considerable problems in the choice of target behavior. Let us take as an example an agoraphobic who also complains of bouts of depression, derealization, depersonalization, poor interpersonal relationships, and frigidity. If the original analysis indicated a basic problem under which all the complaints could be subsumed, then an attempt to deal mainly with this problem could be tried. Lack of such a formulation would necessitate a pragmatic approach, selecting the most incapacitating complaint for treatment. In such cases, the initial treatment approach is usually introduced as a further exploration. Lack of progress or fluctuations in the patient's response calls for reappraisal of the case. During this ongoing process, the therapist may use a combination of orthodox behavior-therapy techniques, or design new ones to deal with specific problems that arise.

Let us take the problem of homosexuality and alcoholism to illustrate further the approach advocated here. In the case of homosexuality, the primary goal should be the development of heterosexual behavior, if the patient wants the change for positive reasons. Some sort of aversion therapy would be considered for an exclusively homosexual patient who has no resources to resist temptations. In view of suggestive findings on exhibitionists by Evans (1970), one would also try to eliminate abnormal masturbatory fantasy. At the same time, one should concentrate therapeutic efforts on any difficulties experienced by the patient when relating to the opposite sex, and so any fears or misconceptions he may have about sexual intercourse. If surrogate therapists cannot be found, an indirect approach, through the modification of masturbatory fantasy and desensitization to heterosexual activities, must be tried. Bancroft's comparison study (1970) suggests that both desensitization and aversion therapy (pairing electric shocks with penile erections) produce reduction in homosexual behavior. It is of interest to note that this change appears to be due to the increase in heterosexual erections, irrespective of treatment.

On the other hand, one would not hastily give aversion therapy to a homosexual who lacks social skills and practices homosexuality as his sole means of establishing social contacts, and who with continuous encouragement can refrain from overt homosexuality. In this case the development of social skills, particularly in relation to females, would be more relevant.

Similarly, the indiscriminate administration of aversion therapy to alcoholics without taking into consideration the reasons for their drinking constitutes an excessively simplistic approach. Leaving aside the problems of the nature of aversive stimulation (Rachman and Teasdale, 1969; Wilson and Davison, 1969) and the goal of treatment, that is, total abstinence versus moderate social drinking (Lovibond and Caddy, 1970; Mills, Sobell, and Schaefer, 1971; Sobell, Sobell, and Christelman, 1972), a successful elimination of drinking invites the emergence of new behavior that may be maladjustive (see Cahoon, 1968). Aversion therapy in cases of addicted alcoholism is usually indicated because drinking would hamper the treatment of the basic problems. On the other hand, in many cases alcoholism could be treated by directing therapeutic efforts toward basic problems, such as social anxiety (Kraft, 1968) or existential depression.

Inpatient treatment, particularly when operant procedures are involved, requires the cooperation and participation of the nursing staff, occupational therapists, and sometimes of other patients on the ward. The therapist must prepare the ward by explaining, in detailed but simple terms, the objective of treatment, the therapeutic methods to be used, and the underlying rationale. At the outset, demonstrations and supervision may be essential.

Discharge from treatment, particularly of inpatients, often presents the problem of generalization, and the extension of treatment to the patient's environment may be indicated (Gruber, 1971). During treatment, but particularly when discharging chronic patients or those who have longstanding problems in keeping jobs and earning money, social work is frequently essential, that is, evaluating social circumstances, finding accommodation, a job, helping the patient in establishing social contacts, and so on. Psychiatric social workers trained in the behavioral approach would be an ideal asset to the clinic (Jehu, Hardiker, Yelloly, and Martin, 1972).

In his daily work, the behavior therapist frequently requires help from the referring psychiatrist and from allied disciplines. It would also be difficult to work without a technician who can make various gadgets required for specific treatments. In recent years, interest in the treatment methods of muscular tensions, cramps, and headaches involving biofeedbacks has increased (Macpherson, 1967; Budzynski, Stoyva, and Alder, 1970; Gannon and Sternbach, 1971); such an approach requires the assistance of physiologists and technicians.

In order to facilitate cooperation, the behavior therapist should be able to communicate with others without using technical jargon. The cooperation with psychiatrists can be greatly improved if the behavior therapist understands their language, formulations, and methods. A knowledge of descriptive psychiatry helps the behavior therapist not only to communicate in this way but also in dealing with patients. Having intensively trained 40 psychologists and psychiatrists in the application of behavior-therapy principles, I find it easiest to train psychologists who have a sound knowledge of learning principles and of descriptive psychiatry, and who also have clinical experience. Psychiatrists find it difficult to switch to analyzing and conceptualizing clinical problems in terms of learning principles. Psychologists, even those who are extremely well trained in experimental psychology but who lack clinical experience, tend to feel lost when confronted with patients. But after all, to be able effectively to shape a pigeon's behavior, it is not sufficient to know the principles of shaping; one must also know the habitual behavior of the pigeon.

Thus, in his clinical work the behavior therapist, of necessity, gets involved in a great variety of activities for most of which there are no strict prescriptions. It is only through experience that he acquires know-how, competence, and confidence.

As regards research, I find laboratory parametric studies in the field of learning most helpful in my clinical work. For instance, the review of parametric studies of punishment by Azrin and Holz (1966) provides the most valuable information on how one should set about eliminating behavior by punishment. Obviously, one would like these studies to be extended to humans, including psychiatric patients. I also find the case reports in sections of behavior-therapy journals extremely useful inasmuch as they give ideas about various possible ways of conceptualizing and treating psychiatric conditions.

In addition, two types of studies appear to be promising and should be encouraged. The first aims at a precise description of disordered behavior using behavioristic analysis (e.g., Schaefer, Sobell, and Mills, 1971; Nathan and O'Brien, 1971; and Sobel *et al.,* 1972). The findings of these studies are bound to help in designing treatment strategies. The other type involves the investigations of therapeutic situations, applying the learning framework (e.g., Truax, 1966; Liberman, 1970). Other than this, most of the literature the research worker greatly appreciates is, so far, least helpful in my clinical work. Despite a great number of studies on systematic desensitization, one still does not know the most efficient and effective method of desensitizing the American student "complaining" of examination or snake fear.

Studies purporting to evaluate the relevance of various components of treatment techniques should continue, but it is high time to pool our resources and carry them out using better designs, and not the usual sample $N = 10$, and extending them to psychiatric populations.

I see no good reason to encourage studies that attempt to compare the efficacy of behavior-therapy techniques with other methods, or those that try to conduct "crucial" experiments to decide between theoretical issues.

In this article, I have tried to evaluate the current status of behavior therapy as objectively as possible. However, I do realize that my views on behavior therapy are firmly established, some might say to a degree of being almost fixated, by the high amount and frequency of primary and secondary reinforcement I get from being this sort of behavior therapist. I am also fully aware that I am highly motivated to influence the reader and, applying learning principles to this effect, I may have stretched a point or two. The reason for doing this is simple: Producing proselytes and supporters is very reinforcing.

## References

Atthowe, J. M., and Krasner, L. Preliminary report on the application of contingent reinforcement procedures (token economy) on a "chronic" psychiatric ward. *Journal of Abnormal Psychology,* 1968, **73**, 37–43.

Ayllon, T., and Azrin, N. H. *The Token Economy: A Motivational System for Therapy and Rehabilitation.* New York: Appleton-Century-Crofts, 1968.

Azrin, N. H., and Holz, W. C. Punishment. In W. K. Honig (Ed.), *Operant Behavior: Areas of Research and Application.* New York: Appleton-Century-Crofts, 1966.

Baker, B. L. Symptom treatment and symptom substitution in enuresis. *Journal of Abnormal Psychology,* 1969, **74**, 42–49.

Bancroft, J. H. J. A comparative study of aversion and desensitization in the treatment of homosexuality. In L. E. Burns and J. L. Worsley (Eds.), *Behaviour Therapy in 1970's.* Bristol: Wright, 1970.

Bandura, A. *Principles of Behavior Modification.* New York: Holt, Rinehart & Winston, 1969.

Barrett, C. Systematic desensitization versus implosive therapy. *Journal of Abnormal Psychology,* 1969, **74**, 587–592.

Bernstein, D. A., and Paul, G. L. Some comments on therapy analogue research with small animal "phobias." *Journal of Behavior Therapy and Experimental Psychiatry,* 1971, **2**, 225–237.

Birky, H. J., and Chambliss, J. E. A comparison of residents discharged from a token economy and two traditional psychiatric programs. *Behavior Therapy,* 1971, **2**, 46–51.

Borkovec, T. D. Effects of expectancy on the outcome of systematic desensitization and implosive treatments for analogue anxiety. *Behavior Therapy*, 1972, **3**, 29–40.

Buchwald, A. M., and Young, R. D. Some comments on the foundations of behavior therapy. In C. M. Franks (Ed.), *Behavior Therapy: Appraisal and Status*. New York: McGraw-Hill, 1969.

Budzynski, T., Stoyva, J., and Alder, C. Feedback-induced muscle relaxation: Application to tension headache. *Journal of Behavior Therapy and Experimental Psychiatry*, 1970, **1**, 205–211.

Cahoon, D. D. Symptom substitution and the behavior therapies: A reappraisal. *Psychological Bulletin*, 1968, **69**, 149–156.

Calf, R. A., and Maclean, G. D. A comparison of reciprocal inhibition and reactive inhibition therapies in the treatment of speech anxiety. *Behavior Therapy*, 1970, **1**, 51–58.

Cautela, J. R. Covert conditioning. In A. Jacobs and L. B. Sachs (Eds.), *The Psychology of Private Events: Perspectives on Covert Response Systems*. New York: Academic, 1971.

Davison, G. C. Anxiety under total curarization: Implications for the role of muscular relaxation in the desensitization of neurotic fears. *Journal of Nervous and Mental Disease*, 1966, **143**, 443–448.

Davison, G. C. Appraisal of behavior modification techniques with adults in institutional settings. In C. M. Franks (Ed.), *Behavior Therapy: Appraisal and Status*. New York: McGraw-Hill, 1969.

De Leon, G., and Mandell, W. A comparison of conditioning and psychotherapy in the treatment of functional enuresis. *Journal of Clinical Psychology*, 1966, **22**, 326–333.

De Moor, W. Systematic desensitization versus prolonged high intensity stimulation (flooding). *Journal of Behavior Therapy and Experimental Psychiatry*, 1970, **1**, 45–52.

Ernst, F. A. Behaviour therapy and training in clinical psychology: A students perspective. *Journal of Behavior Therapy and Experimental Psychiatry*, 1971, **2**, 75–79.

Evans, D. R. Subjective variables and treatment effects in aversion therapy. *Behaviour Research and Therapy*, 1970, **8**, 147–152.

Eysenck, H. J. (Ed.) *Behaviour Therapy and the Neurosis*. Oxford: Pergamon, 1960.

Feldman, M. P., and McCulloch, M. *Homosexual Behaviour: Therapy and Assessment*, Oxford: Pergamon, 1971.

Forrester, R. M., Stein, S., and Susser, M. W. A trial of conditioning therapy in nocturnal enuresis. *Developmental Medicine and Child Neurology*, 1964, **6**, 158–166.

Franks, C. M. (Ed.) *Behavior Therapy: Appraisal and Status*. New York: McGraw-Hill, 1969.

Gannon, L., and Sternbach, R. A. Alpha enhancement as a treatment for pain: A case study. *Journal of Behavior Therapy and Experimental Psychiatry*, 1971, **2**, 209–213.

Gaupp, L. A., Stern, R. M., and Galbraith, G. G. False heart-rate feedback and reciprocal inhibition by aversion relief in the treatment of snake avoidance behavior. *Behavior Therapy*, 1972, **3**, 7–20.

Gelder, M. G., Marks, I. M., and Wolff, H. H. Desensitization and psychotherapy in the treatment of phobic states: A controlled inquiry. *British Journal of Psychiatry*, 1967, **113**, 53–73.

Goldstein, A. P., Heller, K., and Sechrest, L. B. *Psychotherapy and the Psychology of Behavior Change.* New York: Wiley, 1966.

Gripp, R. F., and Magaro, P. A. A token economy program evaluation with untreated control ward comparison. *Behaviour Research and Therapy*, 1971, **9**, 137–149.

Gruber, R. P. Behavior therapy: Problems in generalization. *Behavior Therapy*, 1971, **2**, 361–368.

Hallam, R. S., and Rachman, S. Some effects of aversion therapy on patients with sexual disorders. *Behavior Research and Therapy*, 1972, **10**, 171–180.

Hallam, R., Rachman, S., and Falkowski, W. Subjective, attitudinal and physiological effects of electrical aversion therapy. *Behaviour Research and Therapy*, 1972, **10**, 1–13.

Henderson, J. D., and Scales, P. E. Conditioning techniques in a community-based operant environment for psychotic men. *Behavior Therapy*, 1970, **1**, 245–251.

Hodgson, R. J., and Rachman, S. An experimental investigation of the implosive technique. *Behaviour Research and Therapy*, 1970, **8**, 21–27.

Jehu, D., Hardiker, P., Yelloly, M., and Martin, S. *Behaviour Modification in Social Work.* London: Wiley-Interscience, 1972.

Kanfer, F. H., and Phillips, J. S. *Learning Foundations of Behaviour Therapy.* New York: Wiley, 1970.

Kanfer, F. H., and Saslow, G. Behavioral diagnosis. In C. M. Franks (Ed.), *Behavior Therapy: Appraisal and Status.* New York: McGraw-Hill, 1969.

Kent, R. N., Wilson, G. T., and Nelson, R. Effects of false-heartrate feedback on avoidance behaviour: An investigation of cognitive desensitization. *Behavior Therapy*, 1972, **3**, 1–6.

Kirchner, J. H., and Hogan, R. A. The therapist variable in the implosion of phobias. *Psychotherapy: Theory, Research and Practice*, 1966, **3**, 102–104.

Kraft, T. Experience in the treatment of alcoholism. In H. Freeman (Ed.), *Progress in Behaviour Therapy.* Bristol: J. Wright & Sons, 1968.

Lader, M. H., and Mathews, A. M. Comparison of methods of relaxation using physiological measures. *Behaviour Research and Therapy*, 1970, **8**, 331–337.

Lang, P. J., Melamed, B. G., and Hart, J. A psychophysiological analysis of fear modification using an automated desensitization procedure. *Journal of Abnormal Psychology*, 1970, **76**, 220–234.

Lazarus, A. A. *Behavior Therapy and Beyond.* New York: McGraw-Hill, 1971.

Leitenberg, H., Agras, W. S., Barlow, D. H., and Oliveau, D. C. Contribution of selective positive reinforcement and therapeutic instructions to systematic desensitization therapy. *Journal of Abnormal Psychology*, 1969, **74**, 113–118.

Lewinsohn, P. M., Weinstein, M. S., and Alper, T. A behavioral approach to the group treatment of depressed persons: A methodological contribution. *Journal of Clinical Psychology*, 1970, **26**, 525–532.

Liberman, R. A behavioral approach to group dynamics. *Behavior Therapy*, 1970, **1**, 141–145 and 312–327.

Lloyd, K. E., and Abel L. Performance on a token economy psychiatric ward: A two year summary. *Behaviour Research and Therapy*, 1970, **8**, 1–9.

Lomont, J. F., and Brock, L. Cognitive factors on systematic desensitization. *Behaviour Research and Therapy*, 1971, **9**, 187–195.

Lovibond, S. H., and Caddy, G. Discriminated aversive control in the moderation of alcoholic's drinking behavior. *Behavior Therapy,* 1970, **1**, 437–444.

McGlynn, F. D., and Mapp, R. H. Systematic desensitization of smoke-avoidance following three types of suggestion. *Behaviour Research and Therapy,* 1970, **9**, 197–201.

McGlynn, F. D., Mealiea, W. L., and Nawas, M. M. Systematic desensitization of smoke-avoidance under two conditions of suggestion. *Psychological Reports,* 1969, **25**, 220–222.

McGlynn, F. D., Reynolds, E. J., and Linder, L. H. Systematic desensitization with pre-treatment and intra-treatment therapeutic instructions. *Behaviour Research and Therapy,* 1971, **9**, 57–64. (a)

McGlynn, F. D., Reynolds, E. J., and Linder, L. H. Experimental desensitization following therapeutically oriented and physiologically oriented instructions. *Journal of Behavior Therapy and Experimental Psychiatry,* 1971, **2**, 13–18. (b)

McGlynn, F. D., and Williams, C. W. Systematic desensitization of smoke-avoidance under three types of suggestion. *Journal of Behavior Therapy and Experimental Psychiatry,* 1970, **1**, 97–101.

Macpherson, E. L. R. Control of involuntary movement. *Behaviour Therapy and Research,* 1967, **5**, 143–145.

Mahoney, M. J. Toward an experimental analysis of coverant control. *Behavior Therapy,* 1970, **1**, 510–520.

Marks, I., Boulougouris, J., and Marset, P. Flooding versus desensitization in the treatment of phobic patients. A cross over study. *British Journal of Psychiatry,* 1971, **119**, 353–375.

Marks, J., Sonoda, B., and Schalack, R. Reinforcement versus relationship therapy for schizophrenics. *Journal of Abnormal Psychology,* 1968, **73**, 397–402.

Masters, W. H., and Johnson, V. E. *Human Sexual Inadequacy.* Boston: Little, Brown, 1970.

Mealiea, W. L., and Nawas, M. M. The comparative effectiveness of systematic desensitization and implosive therapy on the treatment of snake phobia. *Journal of Behavior Therapy and Experimental Psychiatry,* 1971, **2**, 85–94.

Meyer, V., and Chesser, E. S. *Behaviour Therapy in Clinical Psychiatry.* Harmondsworth: Penguin Education, 1970.

Miller, S. B. The contribution of therapeutic instructions to systematic desensitization. *Behaviour Research and Therapy,* 1972, **10**, 159–169.

Mills, K. C., Sobell, M. B., and Schaefer, H. H. Training social drinking as an alternative to abstinence for alcoholics. *Behavior Therapy,* 1971, **2**, 18–27.

Nathan, P. E., and O'Brien, J. S. An experimental analysis of the behavior of alcoholics and non-alcoholics during prolonged experimental drinking: A necessary precurser of behavior therapy? *Behavior Therapy,* 1971, **2**, 455–476.

Oliveau, D. C., Agras, W. S., Leitenberg, H., Moore, R. D., and Wright, D. E. Systematic desensitization, therapeutically oriented instructions and selective positive reinforcement. *Behaviour Research and Therapy,* 1969, **7**, 27–33.

Parrino, J. J. Effects of pretherapy information on learning in psychotherapy. *Journal of Abnormal Psychology,* 1971, **77**, 17–24.

Paul, G. Behavior modification research: Design and tactics. In C. M. Franks (Ed.), *Behavior Therapy: Appraisal and Status.* New York: McGraw-Hill, 1969. (a)

Paul, G. L. Outcome of systematic desensitization. I: Background procedures, and uncontrolled reports of individual treatment. In C. M. Franks (Ed.), *Behavior Therapy: Appraisal and Status.* New York: McGraw-Hill, 1969. (b)

Paul, G. L. Outcome of systematic desensitization. II: Controlled investigations of individual treatment, techniques variations, and current status. In C. M. Franks (Ed.), *Behavior Therapy: Appraisal and Status.* New York: McGraw-Hill, 1969. (c)

Paul, G. L. Inhibition of physiological response to stressful imagery by relaxation training and hypnotically suggested relaxation. *Behaviour Research and Therapy,* 1969, **7**, 249–256. (d)

Pomerleau, O. F., Bobrove, P. H., and Harris, L. C. Some observations on a controlled social environment for psychiatric patients. *Journal of Behavior Therapy and Experimental Psychiatry,* 1972, **3**, 15–21.

Rachman, S. The role of muscular relaxation in desensitization therapy. *Behaviour Research and Therapy,* 1968, **6**, 159–166.

Rachman, S., Hodgson, R., and Marks, I. M. The treatment of chronic obsessive-compulsive neurosis. *Behaviour Research and Therapy,* 1971, **9**, 237–247.

Rachman, S., and Teasdale, J. *Aversion Therapy and Behaviour Disorders: An Analysis.* London: Routledge & Kegan Paul, 1969.

Schaefer, H. H., Sobell, M. B., and Mills, K. C. Baseline drinking behaviours in alcoholics and social drinkers: Kinds of drinks and sip magnitude. *Behaviour Research and Therapy,* 1971, **9**, 23–27.

Shean, G. D., and Zeidberg, A. Token reinforcement therapy: A comparison of matched groups. *Journal of Behavior Therapy and Experimental Psychiatry,* 1971, **2**, 95–105.

Sobell, I. C., Sobell, M. B., and Christelman, W. C. The myth of "one drink." *Behaviour Research and Therapy,* 1972, **10**, 119–123.

Solyom, L., McClure, D. J., Heseltine, G. F. D., Ledwige, B., and Solyom, C. Variables on the aversive relief therapy in phobics. *Behavior Therapy,* 1972, **3**, 21–28.

Truax, C. B. Reinforcement and nonreinforcement in Rogerian psychotherapy. *Journal of Abnormal Psychology,* 1966, **71**, 1–9.

Turner, R. K., Young, G. C., and Rachman, S. Treatment of nocturnal enuresis by conditioning techniques. *Behaviour Research and Therapy,* 1970, **8**, 367–381.

Valius, S., and Ray, A. Effects of cognitive desensitization on avoidance behavior. *Journal of Personality and Social Psychology,* 1967, **7**, 345–350.

Van Egeren, L. F. Psychophysiological aspects of systematic desensitization: Some outstanding issues. *Behaviour Research and Therapy,* 1971, **9**, 65–77.

Werry, J. S., and Cohrssen, J. Enuresis: An aetiological and therapeutic study. *Journal of Pediatrics,* 1965, **67**, 423–431.

Willis, R. W., and Edwards, J. A. A study of the effectiveness of systematic desensitization and implosive therapy. *Behavior Research and Therapy,* 1969, **7**, 387–395.

Wilson, G. T., and Davison, G. C. Aversion techniques in behaviour therapy: Some theoretical and metatheoretical considerations. *Journal of Consulting and Clinical Psychology,* 1969, **33**, 327–329.

Wilson, G. T., and Davison, G. C. Processes of fear reduction in systematic desensitization: Animal studies. *Psychological Bulletin,* 1971, **76**, 1–14.

Wilson, G. T., Hannon, A. E., and Evans, W. I. M. Behaviour therapy and the therapist–patient relationship. *Journal of Consulting and Clinical Psychology,* 1968, **32**, 103–109.

Wolpe, J. *Psychotherapy by Reciprocal Inhibition.* Stanford, Calif.: Stanford University Press, 1958.

Woy, R., and Efran, J. S. Systematic desensitization and expectancy in the treatment of speaking anxiety. *Behaviour Research and Therapy,* 1972, **10**, 43–49.

# 3 LABORATORY–DERIVED CLINICAL METHODS OF DECONDITIONING ANXIETY

Joseph Wolpe

Fear habits are a function of the autonomic nervous system. I use "anxiety" and "fear" interchangeably because of their indistinguishable physiological manifestations, applying these terms to the individual organism's characteristic pattern of autonomic responses to noxious stimulation. That pattern is relatively easily conditioned to contiguous stimuli. When unadaptive fear habits present themselves in the clinic as anxiety neuroses, they can only be weakened by procedures that have impact on the autonomic responses patterns involved in these habits. The neuronal pathways serving fear belong to a very "primitive" part of the nervous system, in which responses are characterized by immediacy and are not subject to cortical control—except in some instances, by cortical events that have previously been conditioned to countervailing or augmenting autonomic effects. That is why experiments on animals have particularly direct implications for the treatment of human patients.

The most studied process of habit elimination has, of course, been experimental extinction, the progressive decrease in habit strength that follows repeated evocations of a response without reinforcement. When it became evident (Pavlov, 1941; Masserman, 1943; Wolpe, 1948, 1952a, 1952b) that the anxiety responses that characterize experimental neuroses did not become weaker when they were repeatedly evoked without reinforcement, attempts were made at "counterconditioning" (Wolpe, 1952a). This was done by offering the animal food in the presence of stimuli to neurotic anxiety. The anxiety had to be at low intensity; otherwise it would inhibit eating. Each act of eating weakened the anxiety response, so that it was

33

eventually eliminated. Apparently, by inhibiting anxiety, each act of feeding left behind some degree of conditioned inhibition of the anxiety habit (see the following). Besides suggesting several parallel methods for clinical use, this observation indicated that conditioned inhibition might be built on *any* procedure that could inhibit anxiety. Some of these methods are discussed below.


### Conditioned Inhibition Based on Reciprocal Inhibition by an Incompatible Response (Counterconditioning)

A response may be progressively weakened if an incompatible response is repeatedly made to interfere with its execution, a process that has been alluded to as *counterconditioning* (Guthrie, 1935). The potency of counterconditioning in eliminating anxiety-response habits was revealed in the treatment of experimental neuroses. An experimental neurosis is a very intense and persistent laboratory-induced habit of responding with anxiety to stimulus situations that carry no objective threat. It can be induced by placing an animal in a confined place and then subjecting it either to strong ambivalent stimulation (e.g., Pavlov, 1941; Dworkin, 1939) or to strong noxious stimulation (e.g., Masserman, 1943; Wolpe, 1952b; Smart, 1965), either of which evokes a high level of anxiety—marked autonomic arousal characterized by prominent sympathetic effects such as mydriasis, tachycardia, tachypnoea, and pilo-erection. After several repetitions of the stimulation, the high anxiety is found to be conditioned to the experimental environment. Weaker anxiety responses are manifest in other environments to the extent that they resemble the experimental environment, in accordance with the principle of primary stimulus generalization.

Treatment consists of proffering food in a place where anxiety is weak, so that eating takes place. The manifestations of anxiety are reciprocally inhibited, and with repetition diminish—eventually to zero. The animal will then eat in a place more like the experimental environment. The same treatment is repeated through several stages, leading finally to the deconditioning of the anxiety in the original experimental environment.

For human neurotic anxiety, also, feeding was the first response competitive with anxiety to be deliberately put to use (Jones, 1924). In recent years, many other counteranxiety responses have been employed (Wolpe, 1969), assertive and relaxation responses being the most frequent. The most frequently used procedure is systematic desensitization (Wolpe, 1958, 1961, 1969), in which anxiety-arousing stimuli are presented to the imagination of the deeply relaxed patient—deep muscle relaxation having been shown to have autonomic effects that are the precise opposite of those of anxiety (e.g., Jacobson, 1938; Lang, 1969; Paul, 1969). For each class of phobic stimuli, a hierarchy is set up—a list that ranks the stimuli in order of strength of evoked responses. The fully relaxed patient is first asked to imagine a scene embodying the least disturbing member of an anxiety hierarchy. This scene is presented again and again until it ceases to evoke any disturbance whatsoever. The next hierarchically higher scene is then dealt with in the same way. Eventually, even the highest is deprived entirely of its ability to evoke anxiety, and the patient can then accept the corresponding real situation without anxiety.

Other emotional responses can also be systematically employed as the counterconditioning agents in desensitizing operations. Emotional responses to the therapist ("positive transference," in the loose sense), in those patients in whom it is both strong and nonanxious, is probably the main basis for the successes of nonbehavior therapies that act by inhibiting the anxiety responses to verbal stimuli during interviews. This can also be used to inhibit the effects of anxiety-evoking stimuli *systematically* introduced at graded strength. Deliberately induced anger can act as a counterconditioner (Wolpe, 1958; Goldstein, Serber, and Piaget, 1970), and the same applies to other emotions.

Recent experiments that have compared counterconditioning and "pure" extinction (see below) in the elimination of conditioned emotional reactions leave little doubt of the greater potency of the former. The first well-controlled experiment was reported by Gale, Sturmfels, and Gale (1966). Some anxiety-conditioned rats received repeated presentations of anxiety-evoking stimuli alone, and others the same stimuli accompanied by feeding. The latter animals showed significantly faster anxiety-response decrements. A more elaborate experiment by Poppen (1970), which featured stimuli in graduated strength, showed that typical desensitization was more effective than five other procedures involving either extinction or counterconditioning.

## Conditioned Inhibition Based on Intraresponse Reciprocal Inhibition

Competition can occur between the elements *within* a response, so that under one set of circumstances one element is strengthened and becomes dominant while another is weakened, whereas under opposite circumstances the dominance is reversed. Mowrer and Viek (1948) showed that slight and decreasing anxiety was conditioned in animals repeatedly shocked in a rectangular cage if the shock was consistently terminated when the animal jumped into the air, in contrast to the development of greater and more persistent anxiety in "experimental twins" who received exactly the same duration of shock without reference to what they were doing at the time of its termination. Since a different act would coincide with each termination in these "twins," no particular act was reinforced. In the group in which the jumping response was consistently reinforced by shock reduction, that response became progressively stronger. Presumably, on attaining a certain strength, it produced inhibition and consequent weakening of the concurrent autonomic response.

Deliberate therapeutic use of this principle has so far applied only to a very small number of patients. The patient is instructed to close his eyes and imagine a slightly disturbing situation (out of a hierarchy) and to signal to the therapist when the image is clearly formed. The therapist then delivers a rather mild faradic shock to the forearm, continuing it until the patient briskly flexes his forearm. In a successfully treated case of agoraphobia, it was found that about 20 forearm flexions were usually needed to reduce to zero the anxiety response to a particular scene (Wolpe, 1958, pp. 174–180).

## Conditioned Inhibition Based on External Inhibition

Experimenting with mild electrical stimuli on the basis of the published account of the foregoing case of agoraphobia, Philpott (1964) noted that by repeatedly administering weak galvanic stimuli to a patient's forearm he could often progressively decrease pervasive ("free-floating" anxiety. Similarly, if a patient is asked to imagine a scene from a hierarchy (as in systematic desensitization), and if during the scene two or three weak galvanic stimuli are delivered to his forearm, the anxiety-arousing effect of the scene noticeably decreases with repetition. As a general rule, it takes between 10 and 30 presentations of a scene to reduce its anxiety-arousing effect to zero. There are some patients in whom very weak galvanic stimuli are ineffective, but in whom if the stimulation is judiciously increased—sometimes to the extent of inducing local muscular contraction—the desired decrements of anxiety are obtained.

The mechanism by which this procedure produces change is seemingly *conditioned inhibition based on external inhibition.* If this supposition is correct, then stimuli in other sensory modalities should also be sources of external inhibition available for therapeutic purposes. The special virtue of electrical stimulation is the facility with which it can be controlled.

## Conditioned Inhibition Based on Direct Inhibition—
## "Anxiety-Relief" Conditioning

It has been shown in a variety of contexts that the repeated presentation of a stimulus at the time of the cessation of a response may lead to that stimulus becoming conditioned to the negative of the response (e.g., Zbrozyna, 1957). Reasoning that inhibition of anxiety might be similarly conditioned, I investigated the effects of applying a fairly strong, steady faradic shock to the forearm of the patient, and then switching off the shock as soon as the patient said a word—"calm." In some individuals the word became conditioned to an anxiety-inhibiting response, so that uttering, or even thinking that word in any anxiety-arousing situation produced a decrease of anxiety (Wolpe, 1958). This technique is called "anxiety-relief conditioning." In some cases (Wolpe, 1969) the systematic use of a word to which "anxiety relief" has been conditioned has the effect of gradually building a conditioned inhibition of anxiety to the stimulus situations involved. Segundo, Galeano, Sommer-Smith, and Roig (1961), in an electroencepalographic study, have directly demonstrated that schedules of this type produce conditioned inhibition of the responses to noxious stimulation.

## Conditioned Inhibition Based on Transmarginal Inhibition

If a conditioned stimulus is administered to an animal at increasing intensities, it is usually found that the strength of the responses increases until it reaches an asymptote—that is, it remains at its top level no matter how much stronger the stimulus is made. But sometimes, in some animals, after the response has reached a maximum strength, its evocation paradoxically becomes weaker and weaker as the intensity of stimulation is further increased. Pavlov (1927) used to call this kind of inhibition of response *transmarginal inhibition,* but he also referred to it as *supramaximal inhibition* and *protective inhibition.* By analogy with the other response-inhibiting processes described in this paper, it might be expected that habit strength would be decreased by transmarginal inhibition.

In recent years, a number of therapists (e.g., Malleson, 1959; Frankl, 1960; Stampfl and Levis, 1967; Wolpin and Raines, 1966; Wolpe, 1969) have reported the overcoming of neurotic fears by exposing patients either in reality or in imagination for several minutes to strongly anxiety-arousing stimuli. Many of these patients have improved markedly, and in them change has usually been rapid.

A fact that favors a transmarginal inhibition hypothesis for these effects is that the beneficial effects seem to depend on *insistent and prolonged* exposure to the anxiety-evoking stimulation. In a study by Rachman (1966) in which the highest hierarchy item of subjects with phobias for spiders was given repeatedly for 2 minutes at a time, no benefit was recorded. By contrast, Wolpin and Raines (1966) were successful with exposures of 6–10 minutes.

Such heroic methods as flooding should be used with caution until we know more about the factors on which their effects depend. In experimental neuroses, prolonged exposure to the most highly disturbing stimuli has so far not proved ameliorative (Pavlov, 1941; Wolpe, 1952b, 1958; Goldstein, 1971). And in human anxiety states, high-level exposure to anxiety-evoking stimulation can sometimes make the patient very much worse.

## Experimental Extinction

Operationally, experimental extinction is the progressive decline in the strength of a response that is repeatedly presented without reinforcement. While this procedure is enormously potent in diminishing motor habits, there is no clear evidence of its efficacy in overcoming the durable and often intense anxiety habits that are the nucleus of most neuroses. Even in the apparent "extinction" of weak anxiety in laboratory experiments (e.g., Kimble and Kendall, 1953), it is quite likely that the autonomic response declines because of inhibition by an accompanying motor response (*vide supra*). To say this is not to rule out that extinction, as such, may have or could have a *role* in the elimination of autonomic habits. Indeed, the likelihood appears greater now than it ever did before. Previously I believed that autonomic responses were impervious to the presense or absence of contingent reinforcement. But recently there has been an impressive accumulation of evidence that consequences can determine the strengthening or weakening of specific visceral responses (e.g., Kimmel, 1967; Miller and Banuazizi, 1968). The implications of this should not, however, be taken too far. The reinforcing events that have figured in these studies seem feeble by comparison with the reinforcement available from reduction of the strong drive antecedent to neurotic anxiety, which follows removal of the organism from exposure to the anxiety-evoking stimulus.

### Secondary Unadaptive Anxiety Habits

All the foregoing methods are applied to detaching anxiety responses from stimuli to which their attachment is judged unadaptive. It is necessary to be aware of an important class of unadaptive habits that involve anxiety but in which the therapeutic tactic is not to break the bond between a stimulus and an anxiety response but between a stimulus to which anxiety is an adaptive response and an antecedent stimulus. What is involved here is an inappropriate bond at the level of cognition. This is illustrated in Figure 3.1.

Suppose that a particular stimulus configuration ($S_1$), which may be as simple as the sound of a siren or as complex as the sight of a funeral procession, constantly evokes, unadaptively, the response of anxiety ($rs_1$). The first consequence of $S_1$ is the neural complex of excitations ($rs_1$) producing the image (perception) of $S_1$. If this percept is directly conditioned to $r_a$, we have an anxiety habit to break. But sometimes $rs_1$ is conditioned to the evocation of another image ($rs_2$), and it is $rs_2$ that is conditioned to the anxiety ($r_a$). Now, anxiety may be an *appropriate* response to $rs_2$. When that is so, clearly, the correct therapeutic strategy will be to de-

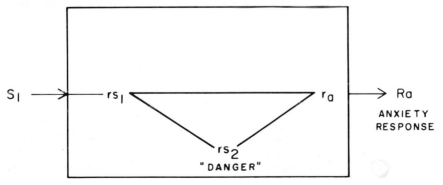

*Figure 3.1.*

condition the cognitive chain $rs_1$–$rs_2$. For example, the awareness of a pain in the chest may evoke the verbal response, "I am going to die," and this may produce an anxiety response. The way to eliminate this anxiety response would be to break the link between the pain and the verbal response, which in many cases would be effected by demonstrating that electrocardiograms and other tests are negative.

# References

Dworkin, S. Conditioning neuroses in dog and cat. *Psychosomatic Medicine*, 1939, **1**, 388.

Frankl, V. Paradoxical intention: A logotherapeutic technique. *American Journal of Psychotherapy*, 1960, **14**, 520.

Gale, D. S., Sturmfels, G., and Gale, E. N. A comparison of reciprocal inhibition and experimental extinction in the psychotherapeutic process. *Behaviour Research and Therapy*, 1966, **4**, 149.

Goldstein, A. Prolonged exposure of neurotic animals to stimuli of different intensities. Unpublished manuscript, 1971.

Goldstein, A., Serber, M., and Piaget, J. Induced anger as a reciprocal inhibition of fear. *Journal Behavior Therapy and Experimental Psychiatry*, 1970, **1**, 67.

Guthrie, E. R. *The Psychology of Human Learning.* New York: Harper & Row, 1935.

Jacobson, E. *Progressive Relaxation.* Chicago: University of Chicago Press, 1938.

Jones, M. C. A laboratory study of fear: The case of Peter. *Pedagogical Seminary* 1924, **31**, 308–315.

Kimble, G. A., and Kendall, J. W. A comparison of two methods of producing experimental extinction. *Journal Experimental Psychology*, 1953, **45**, 87.

Kimmel, H. D. Instrumental conditioning of autonomically mediated behavior. *Psychological Bulletin*, 1967, **67**, 337.

Lang, P. J. The mechanics of desensitization and the laboratory study of human fear. In C. M. Franks (Ed.), *Behavior Therapy: Appraisal and Status.* New York: McGraw-Hill, 1969.

Malleson, N. Panic and phobia. *Lancet*, 1959, **1**, 225.

Masserman, J. H. *Behavior and Neurosis.* Chicago: University of Chicago Press, 1943.

Miller, N. E., and Banuazizi, A. Instrumental learning by curarized rats of a specific visceral response, intestinal or cardiac. *Journal of Comparative Physiology and Psychology*, 1968, **65**, 1.

Mowrer, O. H., and Viek, P. Experimental analogue of fear from a sense of helplessness. *Journal of Abnormal Social Psychology*, 1948, **43**, 193.

Paul, G. L. Physiological effects of relaxation training and hypnotic suggestion. *Journal of Abnormal Psychology*, 1969, **74**, 425.

Pavlov, I. P. *Conditioned Reflexes*, trans. by G. V. Anrap. New York: Liveright, 1927.

Pavlov, I. P. *Conditioned Reflexes and Psychiatry,* trans. by W. H. Gantt. New York: International Publications, 1941.

Philpott, W. M. Personal communication. 1964.

Poppen, R. Counterconditioning of conditioned suppression in rats. *Psychological Reports,* 1970, **27,** 659.

Rachman, S. Studies in desensitization: II. Flooding. *Behaviour Research and Therapy,* 1966, **4,** 1.

Segundo, J. P., Galeano, C., Sommer-Smith, J. A., and Roig, J. A. Behavioral and EEG effects of tones "reinforced" by cessation of painful stimuli. In J. F. Delafresnaye (Ed.), *Brain Mechanisms and Learning.* Oxford: Blackwell, 1961.

Smart, R. G. Conflict and conditioned aversive stimuli in the development of experimental neuroses. *Canadian Journal of Psychology,* 1965, **19,** 208.

Stampfl, T. G., and Levis, D. J. Essentials of implosive therapy: A learning-theory-based psychodynamic behavioral therapy. *Journal of Abnormal Psychology,* 1967, **72,** 496.

Wolpe, J. An approach to the problem of neurosis based on the conditioned response. Unpublished manuscript, M.D. thesis, University of Witwatersrand, South Africa, 1948.

Wolpe, J. Experimental neurosis as learned behavior. *British Journal of Psychology,* 1952, **43,** 243. (a)

Wolpe, J. Formation of negative habits: A neurophysiological view. *Psychological Reviews,* 1952, **59,** 290. (b)

Wolpe, J. *Psychotherapy by Reciprocal Inhibition.* Stanford, Calif.: Stanford University Press, 1958.

Wolpe, J. The systematic desensitization treatment of neuroses, *Journal of Nervous and Mental Disease,* 1961, **112,** 189.

Wolpe, J. *The Practice of Behavior Therapy.* Elmsford, N.Y.: Pergamon, 1969 (second edition, 1973).

Wolpin, M., and Raines, J. Visual imagery, extinction, as possible factors in reducing fear and avoidance behavior. *Behaviour Research and Therapy,* 1966, **4,** 25.

Zbrozyna, A. The conditioned cessation of eating. *Bulletin de L'Academie Polonaise des Sciences,* 1957, **5,** 261.

Last, J. E., *Conditioned Reflexes and Psychiatry*. Trans. by W. H. Gantt. New York: International Publishers, 1941.

Philpott, W. M. Personal communication, 1964.

Razran, G., Stimulus generalization of conditioned responses. *Psychol. Bull.*, 1949, 46, 337-365.

# II MODIFICATION OF MALADAPTIVE SOCIAL AND SOMATIC BEHAVIORS

# 4 BEHAVIORAL TREATMENT OF ANOREXIA NERVOSA[1]

John Paul Brady

Wolfram Rieger

Anorexia nervosa is a rare disorder characterized by profound weight loss due to self-imposed restriction of food intake and often aggravated by excessive exercise, self-induced vomiting, and purgation. This intriguing and baffling disorder presents a difficult treatment problem and has attracted the attention of many writers. It has been subjected to behavioral analysis and treatment only in the last few years. In this paper we shall give a clinical description of the disorder, emphasizing the unusual relationship in these patients between the ingestion of food and reinforcement contingencies. The treatment results in 16 patients with anorexia nervosa at the Hospital of the University of Pennsylvania will be described in detail. Finally, we shall outline some general guidelines for the behavioral treatment of these patients on the basis of our experience in this area.

## The Clinical Syndrome

Marked weight loss has long been recognized as an occasional accompaniment of psychiatric disorder. A thousand years ago, Avicenna reported the case of a Persian prince with delusions, self-imposed starvation, and profound weight loss (Shafir, 1972). However, the first clear description of anorexia nervosa as a distinct clinical entity was provided by Gull

[1] This research was supported in part by a U.S. Public Health Service Research Scientist Award (K3–MH–22, 682) from the National Institute of Mental Health.

45

in 1874. Since then the disorder has been the subject of intensive clinical study and extensive description (Bliss and Branch, 1960; Dally, 1969; Thoma, 1967). The condition occurs chiefly in females (sex ratio about 10:1) and chiefly in the 14–25 age range. The clinical picture is remarkably similar in most cases (Stunkard, 1972). Typically, the early physical and psychological development of these patients is not remarkable. They tend to be model children: obedient, quiet, eager to please, and both conscientious and successful in their school work. Mild obesity or "chubbiness" in adolescence often occasions a self-imposed dieting regime. However, the patient continues to diet and lose weight after excessive fat has been lost, despite reassurances from the parents that she is no longer overweight. Menstruation often stops at this time. These parental reassurances gradually turn to admonitions and then stronger measures to get the patient to eat normally again, as a state of emaciation sets in. The efforts of the family physician and others to get the patient to resume an adequate caloric intake appear to have the same paradoxical effect of intensifying the patient's insistence that she is still fat and her determination to continue to lose weight. At this point, other behavioral disturbances usually emerge, some of which are exaggerations of preexisting personality traits; one may see pronounced social withdrawal, compulsive rituals, and excessive exercise. The patient's manner of eating and choice of foods may take on bizarre qualities. Surreptitious vomiting and the use of laxatives in large dosages often occur as well. Hospitalization is usually resorted to as a state of cachexia is approached. The struggle over eating is now typically carried out between the patient and the hospital nursing and medical staff. The patient tends to be aloof, reticent, and negativistic, warding off the efforts of the hospital staff to help her. Usually the patient will continue to insist that she is eating an adequate amount of food and is not too thin despite the gruesome cachectic state that is developing from starvation and the danger of death from inanition or intercurrent infection.

It should be mentioned that the term "anorexia" used in this condition is a misnomer, since most of these patients do not report loss of appetite. Indeed, in an experiment reported by Silverstone and Russell (1967), anorexia nervosa patients did not differ from normal controls in gastric motility or the occurrence of so-called hunger contractions. Rather, they appear to have what might be termed a food or weight "phobia." Characteristically, they show intense emotional discomfort on ingesting food and have an inappropriate and unrealistic concern with growing fat. The patient may occasionally eat an ample amount of food or even go on an eating "binge," only to induce vomiting minutes later and redouble her efforts to avoid weight gain by intensive exercise.

## DIFFERENTIAL DIAGNOSIS

It is usually not difficult to differentiate anorexia nervosa from medical conditions such as panhypopituitarism (Simmonds' disease) and regional enteritis in which the physiological disturbance is primary. The normo- or hyperactivity of the anorexia nervosa patient in the presence of even marked cachexia is especially striking. When the state of malnutrition is severe, endocrine abnormalities usually develop secondarily, especially decreased gonadal function (Russell, 1969). Other physiological changes commonly observed in these patients include arterial hypotension, bradycardia, hypothermia, edema (Stunkard, 1972) and sometimes pancytopenia (Rieger and Brady, 1972). These and other physiological changes are secondary to the malnutrition and are similar to those observed in externally imposed starvation (Dally, 1969).

Patients with anorexia nervosa may differ considerably from one another in clinical psychological features. Concurrent psychiatric diagnoses often made in these patients include schizoid personality and obsessive–compulsive neurosis. However, the cluster of observable characteristics described above identifies the syndrome. There are, of course, other psychiatric disorders in which weight loss may be present, but these can be differentiated from anorexia nervosa on clinical grounds. Thus, true anorexia (loss of appetite) often occurs in depression, and moderate weight loss may result. A schizophrenic patient with delusions of being poisoned may refuse to eat for a time. However, marked weight loss (more than 20% of body weight) is rare in this condition, and other clinical features of anorexia nervosa are generally absent. So-called hysterical vomiting is sometimes misdiagnosed as anorexia nervosa, but in the former condition marked weight loss is rare, menses are retained, and the problem is mainly one of not retaining food after it is ingested.

## FOOD, WEIGHT GAIN, AND CONTINGENCIES OF REINFORCEMENT

Perhaps the most striking feature of anorexia nervosa is the relationship of eating and weight gain to reinforcement contingencies. Eating when hungry is one of the most prepotent of behaviors. When an experimental organism has been deprived of food, food is one of the most powerful of reinforcers for the shaping and maintenance of other behaviors. Among severely autistic children, access to food when hungry is one of the few powerful reinforcing events available to the therapist. Thus, food has been used by Lovaas (1966) and others in the early shaping of verbal and social behaviors in this difficult patient group.

"Eating problems" sometimes are seen in chronically hospitalized psychiatric patients. Ayllon and Haughton (1962) demonstrated that these problems are often maintained by their unrecognized social consequences. Thus, when nurses and psychiatric aides no longer responded to these patients' refusal to eat with coaxing, spoon feeding, conducting the patient to the dining room, and other forms of special attention, much of the problem was eliminated. In fact, all problem eaters in one of their experimental wards learned to enter the dining room within 5 minutes and to eat adequately without assistance when access to food was contingent on these self-help behaviors. In these patients, food still functions as a positive reinforcer, since it maintains a complex behavioral chain (going to the dining room, putting food on the plate, ingesting the food) once the confounding inability-to-eat behavior is placed on extinction by the withdrawal of social reinforcement.

One of the ways in which these institutionalized "problem eaters" differ from true anorexia nervosa is that the latter will not usually begin to eat with this simple extinction procedure (Leitenberg, Agras, and Thompson, 1968). They behave rather as though they suffer from an eating phobia—eating generates anxiety, and their failure to eat represents avoidance. In other words, their cessation of eating after ingesting a very small portion of a meal (or removing it from the body by self-induced vomiting) is reinforced by anxiety reduction. From such an analysis, two treatment procedures suggest themselves: deconditioning the anxiety associated with eating and/or shaping eating behavior (and hence weight gain) by making access to powerful reinforcers contingent on eating. These are the two categories of behavioral procedures that have been used in the treatment of anorexia nervosa (*vide infra*).

ETIOLOGY

The cause of anorexia nervosa is not known. A genetic factor has not been identified and, as mentioned before, there is no evidence of a primary physiological disturbance. There is some evidence that the condition is more common in middle and higher socioeconomic classes (Stunkard, 1972).

Many authors have speculated on the symbolic meaning of food, eating, and weight gain in these patients. In particular, eating as a sexual or aggressive act has been assigned an etiologic role (e.g., Waller, Kaufman, and Deutsch, 1940). However, these clinical hypotheses have not been adequately tested and verified.

Many clinicians have commented on the tempestuous relationship often observed between the anorexia nervosa patient and her mother. Nemiah (1958) described it as "a peculiar relationship between the patient and her mother . . . a mixture of solicitous overconcern for the daughter's welfare and aggressive domination of every aspect of her life. . . . Mother and daughter form a restless and turbulent symbiotic unit . . . [p. 258]." However, it is difficult to know what features of the mother–child relationship observed by the clinician existed before the onset of the disorder and may therefore have played an etiologic role. The disturbed eating and other behavior of the anorexia nervosa child tend to evoke guilt and frustration in the parent, and it is possible that much of the parent–child interaction is a consequence rather than a cause of the disorder when first seen by the clinician.

Whatever its etiological significance, however, one can usually observe an intense struggle in these patients with their parents, and especially with their mothers. The patient tends to be compliant and dependent in most areas while steadfastly refusing to ingest and retain adequate amounts of food. It is as though the patient's struggle for independence and autonomy were being fought on the inappropriate battlefield of the dinner table. We believe that these observations are relevant to the behavioral treatment of anorexia nervosa. During the early (weight-gain) phase of treatment, it is important that intense, affect-laden interaction with the patient over eating be avoided. Later in treatment, it is essential that the patient acquire (learn) age-appropriate independence and autonomy in important life areas so that eating can again come under the control of the usual and adaptive biological forces and social influences.

## Nonbehavioral Treatment Procedures

A great variety of procedures have been described and recommended for the treatment of anorexia nervosa. These include tube feeding, bed rest, hormones, chlorpromazine and other ataractic drugs, subcoma doses of insulin, electroconvulsant therapy, and prefrontal lobotomy (Dally, 1969), and psychological approaches include hypnosis, dynamically-oriented individual or family psychotherapy, and psychoanalysis (Nemiah, 1958). It is difficult to compare the efficacy of these various procedures, because reports of clinical treatment trials are often based on quite different patient samples. As with most disorders, the patient's accessibility to treatment, the immediate prognosis, and the ultimate outcome vary with the duration and severity of the illness at the time of therapeutic intervention. All authors agree, however, that these patients are difficult to treat and that the relapse rate is high. Estimates of death from inanition vary from 3 to 20% in different outcome studies (Stunkard, 1972).

Perhaps the best results reported for the treatment of a substantial number of anorexia nervosa patients are those of Dally and Sargant (1960, 1966). Their treatment consists of large doses of chlorpromazine (up to 1600 mg daily), modified (subcoma) insulin therapy (usually 40–60 units daily), and "bed rest." They do not emphasize the contribution of "bed rest" to the treatment program, but apparently their patients are put to bed at the start of treatment and are not permitted to get up until a predetermined weight has been gained. In a later publication, Dally (1969) states: "Bed rest is at first total and no visitors are permitted. She is given weight targets and their attainment is rewarded by progressive relaxation of restrictions. If at any time she should lose weight and fall below a target level restrictions are reimposed [p. 51]." They do not conceptualize their treatment as behavioral, but it clearly is. They do present data to the effect that bed rest wihout "specific treatment" is somewhat less effective than bed rest with chlorpromazine and insulin, but their report of this comparison is retrospective and unconvincing. A well-controlled prospective trial comparing their "bed rest" procedure with clear specification of the actual contingencies with and without chlorpormazine and subcoma insulin would be interesting. Our own experience in treating these patients with large dosages of chlorpromazine and carefully planned behavioral contingencies suggests that the latter is the important ingredient.

## Behavioral Treatment Procedures

We know of seven previous reports concerning the treatment of anorexia nervosa by behavior therapy. The first two employed predominantly desensitization procedures and the others operant-reinforcement procedures.

1. Lang (1965) treated a 23-year-old nurse with a 20-pound weight loss by applying desensitization to several heirarchies of anxiety-producing social situations associated with inability to eat. Assertive training was also employed, especially in helping the patient to be more direct and autonomous with her mother and other family members, who tended to con-

trol and criticize her a great deal. Lang reported that the patient regained the lost weight, improved in her social relationships, and sustained these changes at a 12-month follow-up. However, he did not report the patient's actual weight and provided no information on menses.

2. Hallsten (1965) treated a 12-year-old girl who was afraid of gaining weight and becoming fat by pairing Jacobsonian relaxation with graded scenes of eating at home (systematic desensitization). The patient's weight rose from 57 pounds to 78 pounds over a 50-day period (height, 57 inches). At 5-month follow-up, the patient was "eating good" and her general social and school adjustment was satisfactory. No menstrual data are given.

3. Bachrach, Erwin, and Mohr (1965) reported the first explicit operant–reinforcement approach to anorexia nervosa in treating a 37-year-old woman whose weight fell from 118 to 47 pounds over a 7-year period (height, 64 inches). Initially the patient took all her meals in her room with the experimenters, who used social (verbal) reinforcement to shape eating responses. Access to other reinforcers such as watching TV, walks with other patients, and visitors was made contingent on eating progressively larger meals. However, the patient's weight soon stabilized at about 63 pounds, and the experimenters surmised that she was secretly vomiting. At this point, reinforcers were made contingent on weight gain rather than the ingestion of food. After some additional weight gain, the patient was discharged and gained an additional 14 pounds during outpatient care. She was rehospitalized briefly for additional study and gained 7 more pounds with the previous behavioral regimen. However, on follow-up, 18 months after her last hospitalization, the patient reported that she had become more active professionally and socially and that her weight had fallen to 72 pounds. She was amenorrheic during this entire period.

4. Leitenberg, Agras, and Thompson (1968) report two patients whom they treated in a design that included some experimental control procedures. The first patient was a 14-year-old girl with amenorrhea and a 22-pound weight loss whose treatment was divided into three phases. The first was a baseline period of normal nursing care and the second a "nonreinforcement" period during which all references to the patient's symptoms and food were ignored. During both of these periods, the patient could not leave the ward and could engage in no pleasurable ward activities. Her weight remained stable throughout. During the third phase, specific and presumably rewarding consequences such as praise and ward privileges were attached to eating and weight gain. During this 45-day period the patient's weight rose from 76 to 92 pounds. At 9-month follow-up, the patient weighed 98 pounds and was attending school regularly. The

second was a 17-year-old girl with amenorrhea and a 22-pound weight loss. Initially she was instructed to count mouthfuls of food and chart her daily weight, with the suggestion that this would facilitate weight gain. It did not. She did gain weight on a positive-reinforcement regime similar to that given the first patient. After the patient gained 7 pounds, a reversal procedure was tried—praise and tangible reinforcers were withdrawn (extinction) to ascertain whether weight gain would cease, and then reinforcement was again instituted. However, the patient continued to gain weight through the extinction period as well as the reinstituted reinforcement procedure. On discharge the patient weighed 95 pounds. At 4-month follow-up she weighed 92 pounds and was working full time as a waitress. Leitenberg *et al.* argue that these two cases indicate the specificity of the operant-reinforcement paradigm, since the sympathetic attention of the therapists, therpeutic instructions, suggestion, and patient expectancy all failed to bring about weight gain before the positive-reinforcement procedures were instituted. The reason for the second patient's continued weight gain during the reversal period is not known.

5. Azerrad and Stafford (1969) reported the treatment of a 13-year-old girl with "anorexia nervosa" by a token system in which the patient, by eating and weight gain, earned points that were redeemable for material items, special privileges, and home visits. During this regimen her weight rose from 62 to 84 pounds over a 3½-month period. This case is difficult to evaluate, however, because the authors failed to give the patient's height, the number of pounds she lost before hospitalization, or the state of her menses. Thus, it is not clear that the patient suffered from anorexia nervosa.

6. Scrignar (1971) described the outpatient treatment of a 14-year-old girl with "anorexia nervosa," but again the diagnosis is questionable. The history suggests rather "hysterical vomiting" in that the eating disturbance consisted mainly of episodes of hyperphagia followed by self-induced vomiting. She was 62 inches tall and weighed 84 pounds. Since this means that she was only 26% below her "standard weight," she would not have met our criteria for anorexia nervosa (*vide infra*). Menstrual data are not given. Treatment entailed limiting the amount of food the patient was allowed to eat at each meal. Also, she was only allowed to eat the foods she preferred most at the end of meals or as snacks at bedtime. Thus, these preferred foods were used as positive reinforcers. The patient's weight rose to 106 pounds on this program, and she weighed 112 pounds at 6-month follow-up.

7. The final study is that of Blinder and Ringold (1967) and Blinder, Freeman, and Stunkard (1970), who reported a series of six pa-

tients treated at the Hospital of the University of Pennsylvania. Case 1 was a 22-year-old female with a 31% weight loss (from the onset of her illness). Case 2 was a 15-year-old girl with a 29% weight loss, and Case 3 was a 20-year-old college coed with a 63% weight loss. All were unmarried and amenorrheic. The authors noted that hyperactivity was a striking feature in each case despite her state of inanition. During baseline observational periods, the daily physical activity of each was estimated by means of a mechanical pedometer attached to the leg. The authors report that these patients averaged 6.8 miles per day, which contrasts with an average of 4.9 miles per day for women of normal weight living in the community. This documented hyperactivity prompted the authors to make access to activity contingent on a minimal daily weight gain. Specifically, the patient was permitted a 6-hour unrestricted period outside the hospital on any day on which her morning weight was at least ½ pound above her previous morning weight. On this regimen, each patient gained weight promptly during her hospitalization (20.0, 21.5, and 26.0 pounds, respectively). Interestingly, each showed improvement in her interpersonal relationships after a substantial weight gain was effected. Two of the patients (Cases 2 and 3) made good adjustments after discharge (follow-ups of 10 and 8 months, respectively). However, Case 1 did not. Despite a good initial posthospitalization adjustment, this patient committed suicide after an intensely stormy encounter with her mother.

Cases 4, 5, and 6 are described in less detail. Access to activity did not prove to be an adequate reinforcer for these patients, but each gained substantial weight with other contingencies. Three of the patients treated by Blinder *et al.* (Cases 1, 3, and 4) are included in the present series of 16 cases reported in the following.

## The Present Program

Sixteen patients with a diagnosis of anorexia nervosa were treated in the Psychiatric Inpatient Service of the Hospital of the University of Pennsylvania during the last 5 years. We will describe the patient sample, the behavioral treatment procedures, the immediate clinical outcome, and the results of a follow-up survey.

PATIENT SAMPLE

The criteria for anorexia nervosa used in this retrospective survey were as follows: (1) age between 15 and 35 years, (2) a history of progressive weight loss due primarily to self-imposed restrictions of food intake resulting in a body weight at least 30% below the standard for his height, and (3), if female, amenorrheic for at least 6 months. Male patients were included if they met the first two criteria. In these patients, weight loss is aggravated by self-induced vomiting and vigorous exercise, but these were not required for the diagnosis. We used as a weight criterion a minimal percentage below a standard rather than percentage of weight loss because specifying the onset of the "present illness" is often difficult and arbitrary. Also, these patients are often actually overweight when they start to reduce. Some studies have excluded patients if they had a concurrent diagnosis of schizophrenia. In our sample there were two patients with a questionable diagnosis of schizophrenia. However, neither of these patients differed markedly from the rest in their response to the behavioral treatment.

Table 4.1 summarizes the patient sample. Note that all but two were female. On admission their weights ranged from 30 to 51% (mean 38.4%) below the standard weights for their sex and height. Cases 1, 2, and 16 correspond to Cases 1, 3, and 4, respectively, in the reports of Blinder *et al.* (1967, 1970). Case 16 is also described in a recent publication of Stunkard (1972). Case 9 was rehospitalized for a second course of behavioral treatment (9A and 9B).

## TREATMENT

All 16 patients were treated in an operant–reinforcement paradigm in which access to powerful reinforcers was made contingent on a minimum daily weight gain. With minor variations, the general procedure was as follows. The patient was weighed every morning upon arising under standardized conditions (same scales, nurse, clothing, etc.). For the first 4 or 5 days of hospitalization, these weights were simply recorded. During this observational period, note was made of the patient's general activity— her daily habits and how she spent most of her time. A reinforcer or set of reinforcers sufficiently powerful to bring about weight gain can usually be identified through these behavioral observations. The contingent reinforcer we used most often was simply permission to leave the hospital ward during the day. This was especially effective with the typically hyperactive patients, since it allowed them to walk, run, climb stairs, and exercise in other ways. If the patient's morning weight was at least $\frac{1}{2}$ pound more than his weight the previous morning, he would have a 6-hour offward pass for that day. If he failed to gain this weight, he was restricted

## TABLE 4.1

### Resumé of Patient Characteristics and Treatment Results at Discharge and at Follow-up

| Case number | Sex | Age | Height (inches) | Weight on admission | Percent below standard weight [a] | Ataractic medication [b] | Weight at discharge | Pounds gained per week | Months since discharge | Weight | Percent below standard weight [a] | Menstruation returned | Current adjustment [c] |
|---|---|---|---|---|---|---|---|---|---|---|---|---|---|
| | | | | | | | | | | | | | Follow-up |
| 1 | F | 22 | 66 | 90 | 30 | P.T | 110 | 3.8 | — | — | — | | died |
| 2 | F | 20 | 63 | 64 | 45 | P | 90 | 4.1 | 59 | 104 | 10 | + | F |
| 3 | F | 34 | 68 | 75 | 45 | P | 90 | 3.5 | — | — | — | | died |
| 4 | F | 18 | 69 | 93 | 34 | P | 113 | 3.2 | not obtainable | | | | — |
| 5 | M | 18 | 63 | 81 | 36 | P.T | 103 | 6.6 | 23 | 132 | -4 | | G |
| 6 | F | 21 | 70 | 74 | 33 | P.T | 102 | 1.8 | 10 | 117 | 19 | | F |
| 7 | F | 29 | 65 | 77 | 37 | T | 92 | 5.8 | 24 | 120 | 3 | | G |
| 8 | F | 18 | 62 | 67 | 41 | P | 87 | 2.7 | 14 | 110 | 3 | + | F |
| 9A | F | 20 | 62 | 69 | 39 | T | 78 | 1.7 | — | — | — | | — |
| 9B | F | 21 | 62 | 74 | 34 | T | 79 | 1.7 | 8 | 68 | 40 | | P |
| 10 | F | 18 | 60 | 59 | 45 | P | 84 | 1.8 | 37 | 77 | 28 | | P |
| 11 | F | 15 | 62 | 74 | 34 | P | 95 | 9.1 | 15 | 89 | 17 | + | F |
| 12 | F | 16 | 59 | 73 | 30 | — | 84 | 3.3 | 4 | 93 | 11 | | G |
| 13 | M | 20 | 73 | 117 | 30 | P | 126 | 3.3 | 26 | 133 | 21 | | F |
| 14 | F | 20 | 66 | 68 | 47 | P | 78 | 10.3 | 12 | 110 | 14 | | G |
| 15 | F | 16 | 63 | 69 | 41 | — | 78 | 4.0 | 29 | 95 | 18 | + | G |
| 16 | F | 17 | 59 | 51 | 51 | P | 78 | 2.7 | 49 | 47 | 55 | | P |
| Mean | | 20.2 | 64.2 | 75.0 | 38.4 | | 92.2 | 4.07 | 23.8 | 99.6 | 18.1 | | |

[a] From "New Weight Standards for Men and Women," *Metropolitan Life Insurance Company Statistical Bulletin*, **40**, 1 (1959).
[b] P = phenothiazines, T = tricyclic antidepressants.
[c] See text for explanation of G, F, and P.

to the ward (and in some cases to his room) for that day. All other discussion of food, eating, weight, and so on was avoided by the entire hospital staff. If the patient failed to gain weight after 3 or 4 days on this regime, an empirical search was made for a more potent reinforcer, and its effect on weight gain was ascertained in the same manner. This was the principal contingency used in Cases 1–9. Hyperactivity was not a striking feature of Cases 10, 11, and 12, but all had strong social behavior in the evening and spent much time socializing with other adolescents in a common day room. The contingency for these patients was permission to socialize with other patients in this room between the evening meal and bedtime. In contrast, Patient 13 tended to spend long periods of time alone in his room, where he frequently studied his college textbooks. Access to his room and books during the day was contingent on a $\frac{1}{2}$ pound daily weight gain. This proved to be an effective reinforcer for him. Patient 14 was a highly compulsive girl with an exaggerated concern with personal hygiene and cleanliness. Access to her toothbrush, hair comb, and daily clean linen was made contingent on weight gain. Thus, these other psychopathological symptoms (obsessional concerns with bodily cleanliness) were exploited to bring about weight gain. A token system was employed with Patient 15. She earned points by weight gain with bonuses earned by eating snacks during the day and finishing entire meals. She spent points to obtain her mail, use a phone and radio, and for special privileges such as walks outside the hospital. Finally, an unusual arrangement was set up with Patient 16 when only modest success was obtained with the off-ward passes. This patient greatly resisted taking her chlorpromazine medication (400 mg daily) and frequently asked for a reduction in dosage. Accordingly, her daily dosage was made contingent on the amount of weight she gained over the previous day; she was required to take 400 mg if there was no weight gain, 300 mg if she gained $\frac{1}{4}$ pound, 200 mg if she gained $\frac{1}{2}$ pound, 100 mg if she gained $\frac{3}{4}$ pound, and no chlorpormazine if she gained a pound or more. This worked very well.

As can be seen in Table 4.1, the use of ataractic drugs was individualized. Most patients also received phenothiazine during their hospitalization. This was usually chlorpromazine in the 200–500 mg daily dosage range. Others received tricyclic antidepressants, usually imipramine, in the 100–250 mg daily dosage range. Still others received both or neither. There was no clear relationship between the drugs prescribed during hospitalization and weight gain. Phenothiazines were discontinued with two patients who developed an alarming leukopenia (Cases 13 and 14). Both continued to gain weight on the behavioral paradigm, and their blood counts returned to normal after several weeks.

All patients were managed on a day-to-day basis by their individual psychiatric residents. All participated in the milieu therapy program on the unit (group meetings, occupational therapy, etc.). The median length of hospitalization in our acute psychiatric unit for the sample was 6 weeks (range 2–18 weeks).

## RESULTS

The clinical results are given in Table 4.1. All patients gained weight (mean of 17.2 pounds). Note that the mean rate of increase was 4.07 pounds per week (based on the time the patient was actually on a behavioral regimen). Only one patient (Case 1) had regained her menses at discharge—this is probably related to the brief periods of hospitalization. [Dally and Sargant (1966) found that average time for menstruation to return in the patients was 14 months after discharge.] Many patients showed improvement in other areas as well. In particular, many recognized that they had in fact been dangerously underweight and needed to gain more weight. With some exceptions they were less defensive, more open in their feelings, and generally more accessible to psychotherapy. Since most were referred to our unit from outside the Philadelphia area, they were referred back to their local psychiatrists or psychotherapists for further care. Our recommendations for further treatment usually included family therapy.

## FOLLOW-UP ASSESSMENTS

Follow-up data were collected on all but one patient (Table 4.1). These were obtained by letter and telephone interviews with the patient, members of his family, and/or his present therapist. They range from 4 to 59 months after discharge (mean of 23.8 months). Two of the patients died. Case 1 committed suicide 1 month after discharge, and Case 3 died 1 year after discharge from causes that were probably related to another episode of severe weight loss. The adjustment of the remaining patients was categorized as follows: G (good adjustment) if the patient is maintaining his weight and functioning well in most important life areas (family, community, school, work, etc.); F (fair adjustment) if the patient is maintaining his weight but functioning only marginally in one or more central life areas; and P (poor adjustment) if the patient is not maintaining his weight or is functioning inadequately in one or more important life areas (e.g. currently hospitalized for a psychiatric disorder, unable to keep a

job, shows marked social isolation). Note in Table 4.1 that 5 of the surviving patients were judged to have a good adjustment, 5 a fair adjustment, and 3 were regarded as poorly adjusted. At follow-up, 4 of the
surviving 11 female patients (36%) on whom information was obtainable
reported a return of menstruation. Note also that 3 of the patients (23%)
were markedly underweight (25% or more below standard weight). Three
patients required rehospitalization (Cases 10, 13, and 16).

## DISCUSSION

There seems little doubt that an operant–reinforcement procedure is
an efficient way to bring about weight gain in anorexia nervosa patients;
our patients gained an average of 4.07 pounds per week. As noted in the
preceding, other more adaptive behaviors emerged as well. It is not possible to identify in this retrospective study the factors responsible for these
other changes. However, it is our impression that these were as much a
result of the altered eating hehavior and consequent weight gain as the
result of concurrent treatment procedures. It is often noted in behavior
therapy that modification of presenting target behavior is followed by
improvement in other areas (Bandura, 1971; Brady, 1971). In some of our
patients, this included the acquisition of limited "insight," that is, awareness
of some of the discriminative stimuli and contingencies of reinforcement
that were controlling their eating behavior (Brady, 1967).

As noted, many patients did poorly after discharge. There were two
deaths (13%), and four others required rehospitalization (29%), of
which three (21%) were judged to have a poor adjustment at follow-up.
It is clear that almost all of these patients required continued treatment
after weight restoration in the hospital. Ideally, this would be a continuation of their hospital program, with increasing attention to family problems and relationships (see recommendations that follow).

It is difficult to compare our results with those of others because of
differences in patient sample and criteria for improvement. Among the most
favorable results are those of Dally and Sargant (1966) mentioned earlier,
whose regimen entailed a combination of chlorpromazine, subcoma insulin, and bed rest. However, they required only a 10% weight loss (from
the "premorbid" level) for inclusion in the study, so some of their patients
were probably less severely disordered than those in our sample. Their
program brought about an average weekly gain of 4.7 pounds (in contrast
to our 4.07 pounds). Their long-term results were also similar. One of
their 30 patients died (3.3%), 33% required readmission for weight loss
within 2 years of discharge, and 28% failed to reach the criteria for "well-
adjusted socially and satisfactory weight" at 3–5 year follow-up.

## Recommendations for Treatment

Severely malnourished anorexia nervosa patients, such as those in our series, often present a medical emergency. Although none of our patients died in the hospital from inanition, this is not an uncommon development (Bruch, 1971). For this reason priority should be given to the restoration of weight. Also, in our experience, efforts to make therapeutic progress with the patient's various interpersonal difficulties come to naught while he is still succeeding in avoiding weight gain. As mentioned earlier, after appreciable weight has been gained, most patients seem more amenable to psychotherapeutic procedures aimed at improving their interpersonal behaviors. Our experience with weight restoration by operant-reinforcement procedures suggests some general principles or guidelines to be followed:

1. From the start, it is essential to obtain and record reliable daily weights under standardized conditions. These weights are the relevant dependent variable of interest to the behavioral clinician. [Some anorexia nervosa patients enter the hospital with 3 or 4 pounds of edematous fluid, presumably due to restricted protein intake. Such patients should be given a mild diuretic (e.g., chlorothiazide, 50 mg) so that a valid estimate of body weight can be obtained.]

2. The patient should be observed for 3 or 4 days to obtain baseline weight data and knowledge of his daily habits. These observations often suggest an adequate reinforcer for eating and hence weight gain. In general, behaviors that have a high frequency (high-probability behaviors) can be used contingently as reinforcers for less frequent behaviors (Premack, 1965). In our series this often proved to be vigorous physical activity, daily access to which was made contingent on weight gain. Other reinforcers are described above.

3. Once a reinforcer is selected, the contingencies should be spelled out unequivocally to the patient, the nursing staff, and other relevant persons. The usual daily requirement is a minimum weight gain of $\frac{1}{2}$ pound for access to the selected reinforcer. It is essential that the therapist and hospital staff be completely consistent in applying the contingencies.

4. If the patient gains weight consistently (with only occasional, small losses), the contingencies should be continued until weight is in the normal range. If he does not, a more potent reinforcer must be selected and tried in the same manner. In an extreme case, complete bed rest without access to social reinforcement or diversion may be necessary.

5. Confrontation and interaction with the patient over the issue of food, eating, or weight gain should be restricted to carrying out the contingencies described above. Measures such as coaxing, cajoling, or pleading to get the patient to eat—measures that have usually proved ineffective with the patient in the past—are contraindicated. In our experience, they tend to aggravate the patient's determination not to eat. For the same reason, having the patient consult with a dietitian or preparing special meals is also counterproductive. Parents or other visitors are also instructed not to discuss food, weight, or eating with the patient. In instances in which visitors persisted in doing so, we made their continued visiting privileges contingent on their total avoidance of comments in this area.

6. In general, the contingency should not involve the direct reinforcement of eating behavior. With this arrangement, the patient may indeed ingest more food but then surreptitiously remove it by vomiting. Rather, it is better to allow the patient to choose what he eats, when he eats, and how he eats. With the single requirement that he gain weight, this allows the patient maximum choice and freedom and facilitates his working out the issue of autonomy and independence in a more appropriate arena.

7. When the patient gains weight, his attitude is less negativistic and, as his discharge from the hosptital draws near, preparations for outpatient therapy, in most cases behaviorally oriented family therapy, should be arranged. When feasible, we have begun these sessions during the last week or so of the patient's hospitalization.

## LONG-TERM (OUTPATIENT) PHASE

If the patient does not continue to gain weight after discharge, or to maintain a normal weight, a system of weight-contingent reinforcement may be instituted similar to the inpatient program. This can often be designed and monitored by the therapist but executed by the patient's parents or other significant persons. With one of our recently discharged patients (Case 12), attending high school classes in her community was made contingent on a daily weight gain. With further progress, more reliance can usually be made on direct positive reinforcers (rather than the avoidance of the withdrawal of positive reinforcers). Thus, with this patient new clothes and verbal reinforcements in the form of compliments about her appearance were used when the school year ended.

Since much of the psychopathology of these patients entails intrafamilial conflicts, especially over the issues of independence and autonomy, many clinicians recommend family therapy as the principal treatment modality (Barcai, 1971). Behavioral techniques are particularly useful here as well, especially the use of contingency management to facilitate the development of new relationships among the family members and the growth of independence in the patient.

## Research Needs

It is clear from our review of the literature and our own largely retrospective survey that controlled clinical research on the behavioral treatment of anorexia nervosa is very much needed. Two kinds of studies are necessary. One-control, single-organism studies of the "A–B–A–B" design are needed to identify unequivocally the therapeutic environmental contingencies that control eating behavior (Baer, Wolf, and Risely, 1968). As mentioned earlier, after the partial restoration of lost weight, a change occurs in many anorexia nervosa patients in that eating again appears to come under the control of ordinary physiologic and environmental events; that is, therapeutically contrived contingencies are no longer necessary. An important research problem is to identify the physiological and/or behavioral events that signal this change and to determine its implications for the nature of the disorder.

A complementing clinical research strategy would be controlled clinical comparisons of the short- and long-term efficacy of an operant–reinforcement approach to the disorder versus more traditional medical and psychiatric regimens. The longer-term, posthospitalization phase of treatment especially warrants controlled clinical study.

## References

Ayllon, T., and Haughton, E. Control of the behavior of schizophrenics by food. *Journal of Experimental Analysis of Behavior,* 1962, **5**, 343–352.

Azerrad, J., and Stanford, R. L. Restoration of eating behavior in anorexia nervosa through operant conditioning and environmental manipulation. *Behaviour Research and Therapy,* 1969, **7**, 165–171.

Bachrach, A. J., Erwin, W. J., and Mohr, J. P. The control of eating behavior in an anorexic by operant conditioning techniques. In L. P. Ullmann and L. Krasner (Eds.), *Case Studies in Behavior Modification.* New York: Holt, Rinehart & Winston, 1965, pp. 153–163.

Baer, D. M., Wolf, M. M., and Risely, T. R. Some current dimensions of applied behavior analysis. *Journal of Applied Behavior Analysis,* 1968, **1**, 91–97.

Bandura, A. Psychotherapy based upon modeling principles. In A. E. Bergin and
    S. L. Garfield (Eds.), *Handbook of Psychotherapy and Behavior Change.* New
    York: Wiley, 1971, pp. 653–708.
Barcai, A. Family therapy in the treatment of anorexia nervosa. *American Journal
    of Psychiatry,* 1971, **128**, 286–290.
Blinder, B. J., and Ringold, Alan L. Rapid weight gain in anorexia nervosa. *Clinical
    Research,* 1967, **15**, 473 (Abstract).
Blinder, B. J., Freeman, D. M., and Stunkard, A. J. Behavior therapy of anorexia
    nervosa: Effectiveness of activity as a reinforcer of weight gain. *American
    Journal of Psychiatry,* 1970, **126**, 1093–1098.
Bliss, E. L., and Branch, C. H. H. *Anorexia Nervosa: Its History, Psychology and
    Biology.* New York: Hoeber, 1960.
Brady, J. P. Psychotherapy, learning theory, and insight. *Archives of General Psy-
    chiatry,* 1967, **16**, 304–311.
Brady, J. P. Metronome-conditioned speech retraining for stuttering. *Behavior
    Therapy,* 1971, **2**, 129–150.
Bruch, H. Death in anorexia nervosa. *Psychosomatic Medicine,* 1971, **33**, 135–144.
Dally, P. *Anorexia Nervosa.* London: William Heinemann Medical Books, 1969.
Dally, P. J., and Sargant, W. A new treatment of anorexia nervosa. *British Medical
    Journal,* 1960, **1**, 1770–1773.
Dally, P., and Sargant, W. Treatment and outcome of anorexia nervosa. *British Med-
    ical Journal,* 1966, **2**, 793–795.
Gull, W. W. Anorexia nervosa. *Transactions of the Clinical Society (London),* 1874,
    **7**, 22–28.
Hallsten, E. A., Jr. Adolescent anorexia nervosa treated by desensitization. *Behavior
    Research and Therapy,* 1965, **3**, 87–92.
Lang, P. J. Behavior therapy with a case of nervous anorexia. In L. P. Ullmann and
    L. Krasner (Eds.), *Case Studies in Behavior Modification.* New York: Holt,
    Rinehart & Winston, 1965, pp. 217–221.
Leitenberg, H., Agras, W. S., and Thompson, L. E. A sequential analysis of the
    effect of selective positive reinforcement in modifying anorexia nervosa. *Be-
    haviour Research and Therapy,* 1968, **6**, 211–218.
Lovaas, O. I. A program for the establishment of speech in psychotic children. In
    J. K. Wing (Ed.), *Childhood Autism.* Elmsford, N.Y.: Pergamon, 1966.
Nemiah, J. C. Anorexia nervosa, fact and theory. *American Journal of Digestive
    Diseases,* 1958, **3**, 249–274.
Premack, D. Reinforcement theory. In D. Levine (Ed.), *Nebraska Symposium on
    Motivation: 1965.* Lincoln, Neb.: University of Nebraska Press, 1965, pp. 123–
    180.
Rieger, W., and Brady, J. P. Unpublished data, 1972.
Russell, G. F. M. Metabolic, endocrine and psychiatric aspects of anorexia nervosa.
    In *The Scientific Basis of Medicine, Annual Reviews.* London: Athlone Press,
    1969, pp. 236–255.
Scrignar, C. B. Food as the reinforcer in the outpatient treatment of anorexia nervosa.
    *Journal of Behavior Therapy and Experimental Psychiatry,* 1971, **4**, 31–36.
Shafir, M. A precedent for modern psychotherapeutic techniques: One thousand
    years ago. *American Journal of Psychiatry,* 1972, **128**, 1581–1584.
Silverstone, J. T., and Russell, G. F. M. Gastric "hunger" contractions in anorexia
    nervosa. *British Journal of Psychiatry,* 1967, **113**, 257–263.

Stunkard, A. New therapies for eating disorders. *Archives of General Psychiatry,* 1972, **26**, 391–398.

Thoma, H. *Anorexia Nervosa,* t rans. by G. Brydone. New York: International Universities Press, 1967.

Waller, J. V., Kaufman, M. R., and Deutsch, F. Anorexia nervosa. A psychosomatic entity. *Psychosomatic Medicine,* 1940, **2**, 3–21.

# 5 THE ASSESSMENT OF SEXUAL FUNCTION[1]

J. T. Quinn

P. Joan Graham

J. J. Harbison

H. McAllister

The application of traditional methods of psychological assessment to the area of behavior modification has become a relatively unpopular exercise. Valid criticisms have been leveled at the traditional psychometric approach (Mischel, 1968), and although we accept many of these strictures, we feel that we have, in a previous paper (Harbison, Graham, Quinn, and McAllister, 1972), discussed some of the ways in which the traditional psychometrics may be utilized in behavior modification. In this paper we would like to extend this argument with illustrations of some of our more recent research in the area of sexual deviation and dysfunction. We shall use the terms "sexual interest," "sexual orientation," and "sexual evaluation." Conceptually, these form three apparently separate entities, but this distinction may or may not have empirical support. For the purpose of this paper, we suggest provisional definition of these terms as follows: "Sexual orientation" attempts to describe the direction of preference toward male and female sexual objects, "sexual interest" describes the intensity of attraction toward either object, and "sexual evaluation" describes the level of esteem placed upon any sexual behavior or interest.

[1] This research was carried out as part of a M.R.C.-supported project (M.R.C. G970/340/C) under the general direction of Professor J. G. Gibson.

**The Use of Psychological Tests in the Description and
Discrimination of Deviant Behavior**

Homosexuality

In the assessment of homosexuality, it is important to be able to describe both the degree of homosexual–heterosexual orientation and to monitor any changes in this orientation produced by therapeutic intervention. The Sexual Orientation Method (SOM) introduced by Feldman, MacCulloch, Mellor, and Pinschoff (1966) is a 120-item attitude questionnaire that assesses the degree of homoerotic and heteroerotic orientation of either males or females.

Feldman and MacCulloch (1971) summarized the work with the SOM to date. They have shown that there are significant differences between the scores of normals and homosexual patients on this test. We were interested in replicating and extending this work using discriminant-analysis techniques. Discriminant analysis can be used when one has a set of measures of test scores for individuals who are known to belong, on the basis of other evidence, to two or more distinct criterion groups. The aim of the analysis is to establish whether, and to what extent, the individuals can be allocated to the original criterion groups on the basis of their test scores.

Our first study (Woodward, McAllister, Harbison, Quinn, and Graham, in press) employed two groups of subjects, matched for age and intelligence. The first group comprised 43 male patients referred to the Department of Mental Health, Queen's University of Belfast, as homosexuals; the second group was composed of a similar number of non-selected males. Both groups completed SOM, which was computer scored to produce four measures: homosexual orientation, heterosexual orientation, homosexual inconsistency, and heterosexual inconsistency. The final two scores are based on the subject's consistency in responding to the 120 items of the scale. For each of the two sexual-orientation scales, a limited number of consistent response patterns are possible. We are thus able to derive a consistency–inconsistency measure (which appears to be an interesting variable in its own right).

Table 5.1 shows results of this first study. It can be seen that SOM was highly successful in discriminating between the two groups, and 84 of 86 subjects were correctly classified. Only 1 subject was misclassified in each group. This study confirms Feldman and MacCulloch's findings and might suggest that discriminating between cooperative normal and homosexual groups may be a relatively straightforward task.

**TABLE 5.1**

"Hits and Misses" Table Derived from Discriminant Analysis Using Two Criterion Groups (Normals and Homosexuals) and Four SOM Scores

| | Predicted group | |
|---|---|---|
| Actual group | Homosexual | Heterosexual |
| Homosexual | 42 | 1 |
| Heterosexual | 1 | 42 |

In our second study (McAllister, Quinn, Graham, and Harbison, 1973), we added three other diagnostic groups to the previous groups of normals and homosexuals. The three additional groups used were impotent patients, a group of husbands of females who presented with problems of frigidity, and a group of male psychiatric patients with no obvious sexual difficulties. There were 25 subjects in each of the five groups. The first 25 subjects from the normal and homosexual groups described above were used.

Table 5.2 shows the results of this second study. It can be seen that again SOM discriminated successfully between the homosexual group and the four other diagnostic groups. Twenty-one of the 25 homosexual patients were correctly classified, and only 2 of the 100 other subjects were wrongly classified as homosexual. Table 5.2 also indicates that although SOM by itself discriminated successfully between the homosexual and the four other groups, it does not enable members of these four groups to be efficiently allocated to their correct diagnostic category. This in itself may not be surprising, although it is interesting that the impotent subjects do

**TABLE 5.2**

Discriminant Analysis of SOM Scores from Five Groups of Males: "Hits and Misses" Table [a]

| Forecast group | Actual group | | | | |
|---|---|---|---|---|---|
| | F | A | N | I | C |
| F | 3 | 3 | 3 | 2 | 4 |
| A | 1 | 21 | 0 | 1 | 0 |
| N | 11 | 1 | 17 | 9 | 11 |
| I | 0 | 0 | 2 | 3 | 0 |
| C | 10 | 0 | 3 | 10 | 10 |

[a] Key: F (husbands of frigid women); A (homosexual patients); N (normals); I (impotent patients); C (psychiatric controls).

not appear significantly different from any of the other three nonhomosexual groups. In fact, the table indicates that while 21 of 25 homosexual subjects are correctly allocated by use of the SOM, only 33 of 100 of the remaining four groups are correctly placed.

The same five groups also completed the Cattell 16 P.F., which measures 16 personality traits. Table 5.3 presents the results of a discriminant analysis, and this time we find that the 16 P.F. is less successful than SOM in discriminating between the homosexual and the other four diagnostic groups.

Sixteen of 25 homosexuals were correctly classified, while 11 of the 99 nonhomosexual subjects are classified as homosexual. The table also shows, in contrast, that the 16 P.F. is more successful than SOM in correctly classifying subjects within the nonhomosexual groups (57 of 99 correct). One subject of the impotent group had not completed the 16 P.F.

The final stage of this set of analyses is to combine both tests in a further discriminant analysis.

Table 5.4 shows the results of this analysis. With the combined measures, there is a further slight improvement, with 23 of the homosexual group correctly allocated, and only 2 of the remaining 99 subjects misclassified as homosexuals. The combined measures are also the most successful in correctly classifying within the nonhomosexual groups, with 69 of the 99 subjects being correctly allocated to their respective groups.

Obviously, it is possible to extend this work. We are at the moment utilizing discriminant analysis with groups of sexually disordered and other subjects, and investigating as to whether ratings of psychiatric disability,

**TABLE 5.3**

DISCRIMINATE ANALYSIS OF 16 P.F. SCORES FROM FIVE GROUPS OF MALES: "HITS AND MISSES" TABLE [a]

| Forecast group | Actual group | | | | |
|:---:|:---:|:---:|:---:|:---:|:---:|
| | F | A | N | I | C |
| F | 16 | 1 | 4 | 1 | 4 |
| A | 2 | 16 | 3 | 3 | 3 |
| N | 3 | 2 | 13 | 2 | 4 |
| I | 1 | 0 | 1 | 14 | 0 |
| C | 3 | 6 | 4 | 4 | 14 |

[a] Key: F (husbands of frigid women); A (homosexual patients); N (normals); I (impotent patients); C (psychiatric controls).

**TABLE 5.4**

DISCRIMINATE ANALYSIS OF SOM AND 16 P.F. SCORES FROM FIVE GROUPS OF MALES: "HITS AND MISSES" TABLE [a]

| Forecast group | Actual group | | | | |
|---|---|---|---|---|---|
| | F | A | N | I | C |
| F | 17 | 0 | 2 | 1 | 3 |
| A | 1 | 23 | 0 | 1 | 0 |
| N | 2 | 1 | 19 | 2 | 5 |
| I | 1 | 0 | 3 | 16 | 0 |
| C | 3 | 1 | 1 | 3 | 17 |

[a] Key: F (husbands of frigid women); A (homosexual patients); N (normals); I (impotent patients); C (psychiatric controls).

sexual attitudes, and other variables will improve the efficiency of our descriptive process even further.

## THE DESCRIPTION OF MARITAL INTERACTION

The concept of the marriage unit and its importance in sexual dysfunction has increasingly been acknowledged, particularly through the work of Masters and Johnson (1970). To date little attempt has been made to compare the interactions that occur within normal marriages and within those in which a sexual problem is known to exist. We have been attempting to obtain some objective measures of marital interaction, and to relate this interaction both to the type of sexual problem that exists and the prognosis of the sexual problem.

Drewery (1969) has introduced a psychometric technique that he calls the Interpersonal Perception Technique (I.P.T.). This technique is based on the Edwards Personal Preference Schedule, and both the husband and wife complete the questionnaire three times. Table 5.5 shows how the two marriage partners complete the marriage questionnaire: "as I would fill it in for myself," "as my husband/wife would fill it in," and "how my husband/wife thinks I would complete it." It is then possible to derive a number of correlations between the scores derived from these protocols. A comparison can be made between, for example, how the husband sees himself and how the wife sees him, how he thinks his wife sees him and how his wife really sees him, and so on. Drewery and Rae (1969) have used this technique to describe normal and alcoholic marriages, and discriminate

**TABLE 5.5**

INTERPERSONAL PERCEPTION TECHNIQUE: WAYS HUSBAND/WIFE ARE ASKED TO
COMPLETE QUESTIONNAIRE

| Husbands' protocols coded | Respondent asked to describe | Wives' protocols scored |
|---|---|---|
| A | Myself as I am | B |
| A1 | My spouse as I see him/her | B1 |
| A2 | Myself as I think my spouse sees me | B2 |

between good-prognosis (stable) alcoholic marriages and bad-prognosis (unstable) alcoholic marriages.

We have been employing the I.P.T. with all subjects who present with sexual problems within a marital setting. Table 5.6 indicates the results of a study that compares the various interpersonal perceptions derived from the test in four groups of marriages: a group of normal marriages ($N = 17$), a group of marriages in which one patient is suffering from a psychiatric illness although not presenting with a major sexual problem ($N = 20$), a group of marriages in which the man has presented with a diagnosis of impotency ($N = 21$), and a group of marriages in which the female has presented with a diagnosis of frigidity ($N = 21$). The analysis of the results in Table 5.6 is at an early stage, but it can be seen that the two groups of couples in whose marriage a sexual problem has developed appear as successful in their interpersonal perceptions as do couples with no sexual problems (the normal and psychiatric control groups). Table 5.6 also shows the results obtained by Drewery and Rae with normal and alcoholic marriages. These workers suggest that the failure in the disturbed patient marriages lies in the poor match between self-description and spouse description ($A \times B1$) and ($B \times A1$), which are both low, and the failure on the part of these couples to anticipate this poor match, shown by the high correlations between ($A \times A2$) and ($B \times B2$).

We feel that this method of describing couples' perceptions of each other may also be of considerable value in predicting the outcome of therapy, and also in indicating which aspects of deviant perceptions may possibly be concentrated upon in therapy. There are also suggestions (Cooper, 1969) that differing groups of impotent patients exist, with both differing etiologies and response to treatment. We hope at a later stage to study the interperceptions of these different groups of impotent subjects and their wives.

# TABLE 5.6

MEAN PRODUCT MOMENT CORRELATION COEFFICIENT FOR I.P.T. MEASURES, WITH GROUPS OF FRIGID, IMPOTENT, PSYCHIATRIC CONTROL AND NORMAL CONTROL COUPLES [a]

| | Frigid (N = 21) | Impotent (N = 21) | Psychiatric control (N = 20) | Normal control (N = 17) | Drewery and Rae normal control (N = 51) | Alcoholic Good prognosis (N = 16) | Bad prognosis (N = 17) |
|---|---|---|---|---|---|---|---|
| B × A1 | .43 | .49 | .43 | .49 | .53 | .58 | .28 |
| B1 × A2 | .42 | .60 | .50 | .63 | .51 | .52 | .55 |
| A × A2 | .32 | .37 | .38 | .45 | .68 | .69 | .55 |
| A × B1 | .43 | .44 | .41 | .46 | .50 | .36 | .18 |
| A1 × B2 | .54 | .62 | .67 | .58 | .51 | .57 | .42 |
| B × B2 | .18 | .20 | .17 | .30 | .71 | .69 | .55 |

[a] Also included are Drewery and Rae normal couples and two alcoholic groups (good prognosis and bad prognosis).

## The Use of Psychological Tests to Describe Differences in Sexual Behavior and to Assess Changes in Behavior

Our experience with patients suffering from potency disorders and frigidity suggested the need to quantify sexual interest as defined earlier. The literature suggested that no suitable psychological measures existed, so we constructed our own objective measure of sexual interest. We have called this the Sexual Interest measure (SIN), and it is fully described elsewhere (Harbison, Graham, Quinn, and McAllister, 1973). Briefly, SIN is a 140-item questionnaire that assesses interest in five areas of sexual behavior (kissing, being kissed, touching sexually, being touched sexually, and sexual intercourse) and also allows a global measure of sexual interest to be derived. The construction of SIN is similar to that of SOM, already mentioned, and again it is possible to obtain measures of inconsistency of responding. This questionnaire appears to be both reliable and valid, and Table 5.7 indicates the differing levels of sexual interest shown by groups of normal impotent and frigid subjects. It can be seen that not only are impotent and frigid subjects significantly different from normal male and female subjects at all levels of sexual behavior and interest, but that the frigid group is significantly lower on the various aspects of sexual interest than is the impotent group.

This questionnaire has also been used to assess changes in sexual interest that occur over treatment. A recent study by O'Gorman, McAllister, Quinn, Graham, and Harbison (1973) demonstrated the use of a group desensitization procedure with frigid patients. The SIN question-

**TABLE 5.7**

MEAN (AND STANDARD DEVIATION) OF SEXUAL INTEREST SCORES FOR NORMAL, IMPOTENT, AND FRIGID GROUP [a]

| Group | K | BK | T | BT | I | Total sexual interest |
|---|---|---|---|---|---|---|
| Normal | 29.7 | 30.2 | 28.8 | 30.0 | 31.2 | 149.8 |
| (N = 40) | (3.89) | (3.33) | (5.89) | (1.38) | (1.18) | (12.04) |
| Impotent | 23.9 | 24.1 | 26.1 | 25.2 | 26.4 | 125.7 |
| (N = 20) | (6.03) | (5.90) | (5.40) | (5.42) | (5.50) | (26.48) |
| Frigid | 16.0 | 16.3 | 15.5 | 16.1 | 15.1 | 78.2 |
| (N = 15) | (6.34) | (5.56) | (6.33) | (6.74) | (6.57) | (29.8) |

[a] Areas of sexual behavior assessed are "kissing" (K), "being kissed" (BK), "touching sexually" (T), "being touched sexually" (BT), and "sexual intercourse" (I).

naire was administered to all subjects at the beginning and the end of treatment. Of the 12 patients in the treatment regime, 7 patients improved significantly on both clinical and self-report ratings and 5 patients either did not improve or deteriorated. Table 5.8 indicates the mean SIN scores of both groups before and after treatment. It can be seen that the improved patients showed a significant increase in overall SIN scores, and the unimproved group showed virtually no change. These differences are statistically significant ($p < 0.05$). The other point of interest to note is that although the group of patients who improved significantly did indicate an overall significant increase in SIN scores, these final sexual interest scores were still significantly lower than those shown by normal females. This indicates the importance of having a method for quantifying sexual interest; although the patients showed significant improvement after treatment, they still do not reach normal levels of sexual interest.

**TABLE 5.8**

SEXUAL INTEREST SCORES OF "IMPROVED" GROUP, "UNIMPROVED" GROUP OF FRIGID PATIENTS BEFORE AND AFTER TREATMENT [a]

| Group | Before therapy | After therapy |
|---|---|---|
| "Improved" ($N = 7$) | 69.0 | 126.7 |
| "Unimproved" ($N = 5$) | 64.0 | 60.4 |

[a] Normal female mean, 148.5.

## The Analysis of Relationships between Different Components of Sexual Response

The assessment of sexual orientation has obvious practical value for the classification of patients, for the description of the severity of the homosexual problem, and for the prediction or monitoring of treatment change.

In the introduction to this paper, we attempted to suggest three working definitions of separate aspects of human sexual responding. We would not regard this attempt as at all satisfactory, but no worker has to date attempted to draw any serious distinction between such terms as sexual orientation, attitude, and arousal. In the main, two psychological measures of sexual attitude and orientation appear in the literature, the Sexual Orientation Method (Feldman *et al.,* 1966) and measures of attitude derived from the semantic differential, such as Bancroft (1970). Zuckerman (1971), in a review, concludes that the only specific psychophysiological measure of sexual arousal is the phallic response, and a number of workers have used phallic responding as an indicator of the direction of sexual orientation (reviewed by Bancroft, 1971).

The present study attempted to relate these measures of sexual attitude and orientation in a group of 35 homosexual subjects, each of whom completed a standard psychophysiological measure of sexual responding, the Sexual Orientation Method, and a semantic differential.

Each subject was assessed in terms of his penile response to a balanced number of male and female pin-up slides. The procedure was a simplified version of the measure of sexual orientation developed by Lee-Evans (1971) on the basis of a detailed analysis of psychophysiological responding of a number of homosexual subjects. Fuller details of this technique can be obtained elsewhere (Graham, Harbison, McAllister, and Quinn, 1973).

The four measures of sexual orientation described earlier were obtained from SOM as well as a "homosexual preference score" based on the homosexual orientation score minus the heterosexual score. Homosexual and heterosexual attitudes were derived from a semantic differential test; this measure enabled a homosexual, a heterosexual, and a homosexual preference score to be derived in terms of evaluative, activity, and potency factors.

Fifteen variables altogether were derived from these three measures of sexual responding; these variables were intercorrelated, and a varimax rotation analysis was completed on the principal components that emerged. Table 5.9 shows the significant correlations obtained from the crucial variables among the three different measures of sexual response. It can be seen that the psychophysiological measure (penile response) was significantly related to two of the SOM scores (the homosexual preference score and the heterosexual score). There were no significant relationships found between the penile response and any semantic differential score. A considerable number of significant relationships were found, however, between SOM scores and semantic differential scores.

Table 5.10 shows the factor weights emerging from the varimax rotation of the data above. Three factors were obtained. The first factor, which accounted for approximately 30% of the variance, appears to be determined almost entirely by the semantic differential scores. Neither the psychophysiological measure nor the SOM variables have any significant weighting on this factor. Factor II, which accounts for 19.5% of the variance, is determined largely by the psychophysiological measure and the

## TABLE 5.9

Abbreviated Table of Correlations between Psychophysiological Score (1), Three Scores from the SOM (2, 4, 6), and Three Evaluative Factor Scores from the Semantic Differential (7, 10, 13)

| Score | Penile response | SOM | | | Semantic differential | | |
|---|---|---|---|---|---|---|---|
| | | Heterosexual score | Homosexual score | Homosexual preference score | Heterosexual E | Homosexual E | Homosexual preference E |
| 1 | | | | | | | |
| 2 | $+0.34^a$ | | | | | | |
| 4 | $-0.32$ | $-0.37^a$ | | | | | |
| 6 | $-0.40^a$ | $-0.84^b$ | $+0.82^b$ | | | | |
| 7 | $+0.06$ | $+0.68^b$ | $-0.42^a$ | $-0.67^b$ | | | |
| 10 | $+0.21$ | $-0.23$ | $+0.16$ | $+0.24$ | $-0.41^a$ | | |
| 13 | $+0.10$ | $-0.53^b$ | $+0.34^a$ | $+0.53^b$ | $-0.82^b$ | $+0.85^b$ | |

[a] $p < 0.05$.
[b] $p < 0.01$.

**TABLE 5.10**

Abbreviated Table of Weightings of Psychophysiological Variable (1), SOM
Variables (2, 4, 6), and Semantic Differential Variables (7, 10, 13) on Three
Factors Derived from Varimax Rotation Analysis

| Variable | Factor I (30% variance) | Factor II (19.5% variance) | Factor III (20% variance) |
|---|---|---|---|
| 1 | +0.22 | +0.62 | +0.16 |
| 2 | −0.23 | +0.55 | +0.59 |
| 4 | +0.19 | −0.85 | +0.04 |
| 6 | +0.26 | −0.84 | −0.35 |
| 7 | −0.59 | +0.40 | +0.56 |
| 10 | +0.87 | +0.06 | +0.04 |
| 13 | +0.88 | −0.19 | −0.30 |

sexual orientation scores. The semantic differential is not involved in this
factor to any degree. The third factor, which again accounts for about
20% of the variance, is a rather heterogeneous factor and appears to be
comprised of mainly heterosexual scores derived from the semantic differential and SOM.

The results of this study indicate that no one has a satisfactory description of the components of sexual responding. The first and largest
factor is the easiest to equate with our present conceptions in that it is
mainly derived from the evaluative scale of the semantic differential and
offers some support for our concept of sexual evaluation. The second factor suggests at least that questionnaire measures of sexual orientation and
physiological arousal overlap, and are different from evaluation. It can be
seen that this second factor is more difficult to integrate into our previous
postulated system, since it cannot be regarded as a pure interest or preference factor. The third factor is composed mainly of heterosexual scores
comprising the SOM heterosexual rating and the semantic differential
heterosexual evaluative score.

The factor analysis suggests that there are difficulties in defining orientation in terms of preference, since preference scores appear in both
Factor I and Factor II. This analysis does not help to clarify our concept
of sexual interest, since the measures used are not focally concerned with
sexual interest and it is impossible with our present data to relate any intensity measures from the above analysis to the other proposed test of
sexual interest (the SIN) on which preliminary data is presented above.
Clarification of this situation requires further analysis and extension of the
data.

## Summary

This paper indicates ways in which it is possible to employ psychological assessment methods within the area of behavior modification and, particularly, with sexual problems. Among the ways in which psychological techniques can be of assistance is in the description of various clinical groups, in the assessment of change produced by treatment, and in analyzing the relationship between different aspects of sexual response. We make little apology to purists in the behavior modification field who may claim that all the measures described earlier are indirect and not really behavioral.

The quantification of sexual behavior by direct observation is extremely difficult, in contrast to the ease with which such quantification can be carried out in other areas, such as object phobias.

We have indicated elsewhere (Quinn, McAllister, Graham, and Harbison, 1972) that we regard physiological and psychophysiological measures of sexual response as part of a general sexual response class. Perhaps one reason for investigating different assessment procedures is so that we can tap as many components of such response classes as possible, thereby making it more likely that we shall be making meaningful measurements of sexual behavior in real life. In some senses, this argument is an empirical one, and we look forward to extended experience with these and other assessment procedures to answer this question.

## References

Bancroft, J. A comparative study of aversion and desensitization in the treatment of homosexuality. In L. E. Burns and J. L. Worsley (Eds.), *Behavior Therapy in the 1970's.* Bristol: Wright, 1970.

Bancroft, J. The application of psychophysiological measures to the assessment and modification of sexual behavior. *Behavior Research and Therapy,* 1971, **9**, 119–130.

Cooper, A. J. Disorders of sexual potency in the male: A clinical and statistical study of some factors related to short term prognosis. *British Journal of Psychiatry,* 1969, **115**, 709–719.

Drewery, J. An interpersonal perception technique. *British Journal of Medical Psychology,* 1969, **42**, 171–181.

Drewery, J., and Rae, J. B. Interperceptions in alcoholic marriages. *British Journal of Psychiatry,* 1969, **115**, 287–300.

Feldman, M. P., and MacCulloch, M. *Homosexual Behavior: Therapy and Assessment.* Oxford: Pergamon, 1971.

Feldman, M. P., MacCulloch, M. J., Mellor, V., and Pinschoff, J. M. The sexual orientation method. *Behavior Research and Therapy,* 1966, **4**, 289–299.

Graham, P. Joan, Harbison, J. J. M., McAllister, H., and Quinn, J. T. The relationship between psychological and psychophysiological measures of sexual response. *European Issues in Behavior Therapy,* 1973.

Harbison, J. J. M., Graham, P. Joan, Quinn, J. T., and McAllister, H. The psychological assessment of sexual dysfunction. In J. C. Brengelmann and W. Tunner (Eds.), *Behavioral Therapy.* Munich: Urban & Schwarzenberg, 1972.

Harbison, J. J. M., Graham, P. Joan, Quinn, J. T., and McAllister, H. A questionnaire measure of sexual interest, 1973. (*Submitted for publication.*)

Lee-Evans, M. Penile plethysmographic assessment of sexual orientation. Paper presented at Third Conference on Behavior Modification, Wexford, Ireland, 1971.

McAllister, H., Quinn, J. T., Graham, P. Joan, and Harbison, J. J. M. A discriminant analysis of the S.O.M. In *European Issues in Behavior Therapy,* 1973.

Masters, W., and Johnson, V. E. *Human Sexual Inadequacy.* Boston: Little, Brown, 1970.

Mischel, W. *Personality and Assessment.* New York: Wiley, 1968.

O'Gorman, Ethna, McAllister, H., Quinn, J. T., Graham, P. Joan, and Harbison, J. J. M. The treatment of frigidity by group desensitization. In *European Issues in Behavior Modification,* 1973.

Quinn, J. T., McAllister, H., Graham, P. Joan, and Harbison, J. J. M. An approach to the treatment of homosexuality. In J. C. Brengelmann and W. Tunner (Eds.), *Behavioral Therapy.* Munich: Urban & Schwarzenberg, 1972.

Woodward, R., McAllister, H., Harbison, J. J. M., Quinn, J. T., and Graham, P. Joan. A comparison of two scoring methods for the Sexual Orientation Method. *British Journal of Social and Clinical Psychology.* (*In press.*)

Zuckerman, M. Physiological measures of sexual arousal in the human. *Psychological Bulletin,* 1971, **75**, 297–329.

# 6 BEHAVIORAL REMEDIES FOR MARITAL ILLS: A GUIDE TO THE USE OF OPERANT–INTERPERSONAL TECHNIQUES[1]

## Richard B. Stuart

Behavior modifiers have paid surprisingly little attention to the modification of marital discord despite the importance of marital success to physical and mental health (Stuart and Lederer, 1975). Goldiamond (1966) referred to the importance of controlling the concomitants of aggressive exchanges in an early anecdotal report; Stuart (1969a, 1969b) suggested the use of token reinforcement to monitor and facilitate the contractual exchange of behaviors; Goldstein and Francis (1969) trained wives to alter the contingencies of their husbands' behavior; Liberman (1970) suggested the sophisticated use of stimulus-control techniques; Rappaport and Harrell (1972) used a slightly expanded concept of behavioral contracting; and Welch and Goldstein (1972) explored the relative importance of lectures on contingency control and the counting of nonspecified positive and negative behaviors. Of these reports, only the last utilizes an experimental design. In more recent work, however, Hunt and Azrin (1973) have experimentally evaluated the importance of marital behavior change for modification of alcoholics' drinking behavior; Turner (1972) has evaluated the effectiveness of couple, group, and no treatment on changes in marital interaction; and Patterson and Hops (1973) and Weiss, Hops, and Patterson (1973) have laid the groundwork for an extensive experimental evaluation of a complex experimental package. At this time, then, the literature concerning behavioral approaches to marital treatment contains a wealth of descriptions of potentially useful techniques with but scant validation of their effectiveness. Because there is increasing recognition of the importance of marital interaction as a mediator of adaptive or deficit functioning in other areas, because marriage breakdown has rapidly acquired public recognition as a major social problem, and because measurement and intervention techniques have reached a new level of efficiency, a rapid growth in the extent of behavioral research in this area can be anticipated.

This paper offers a description of one approach to marital treatment based on operant–interpersonal theory. It is the approach that is currently being tested in an experimental program at the University of Michigan, and it should be carefully compared to a similar program in operation at the University of Oregon (Weiss *et al.*, 1973). Data reflecting the preliminary evaluation of results will be given in a paper presently being prepared for publication elsewhere (Stuart, in press).

## A Theoretical Basis for Marital Treatment

George Levinger (1965) suggested that the strength of a marital relationship is "a direct function of the attractions within and barriers around the marriage, and an inverse function of such attractions and barriers from other relationships [p. 19]." Therefore, any effort to modify marital behavior must utilize a theoretical approach that permits prediction of spousal interaction in the light of the relationship between spouses, between each partner and social forces outside the marriage, and between the couple as a unit and these outside forces. To be suitable for an operant–interpersonal approach, this theory must also yield refutable hypotheses so that the effectiveness of intervention can be tested in light of its theoretical underpinning.

The functional analysis of behavior provides an ideal means of understanding observational data, particularly when the analysis includes both the antecedents and consequences of social behavior (e.g., Patterson and Cobb, 1972). Exchange theory represented by the work of Thibaut and Kelley (1959), Homans (1961), and Blau (1964) provides an ideal means of predicting and explaining such behavioral observations. Thibaut and Kelley, for example, devised a way of predicting individual choices in social situations through reference to both the absolute standards by which a person evaluates the adequacy of each of his or her alternatives (the Comparison Level) and the relative superiority of one existing alternative over another (Comparison Level for Alternatives). For example, a husband might spend more evening time working than with his family, being nagged by his wife to stay home and seduced by his employers to put in more hours. The exchange theorist would identify the husband's absolute preference to relax at home rather than at work, and would also demonstrate that his actual experience nevertheless presents more powerful inducements for work instead of spending time with his family. The functional analyst can then formulate a hypothesis that a change in the husband's use of his evening hours can occur through an increase in the value of reinforcements mediated by the wife relative to the constant level of work-mediated reinforcements. When the theories of the communications analysts are added to this evaluation (Watzlawick, Beavin, and Jackson, 1967), an extremely effective theoretical basis for therapeutic intervention becomes available. This composite approach, which reflects an ecological perspective on behavior through verifiable constructs, can be characterized as the "operant–interpersonal" approach to marital and family treatment.

## Goals of Intervention

Marriage counselors are typically asked to work toward one of two goals: to help spouses improve their interaction or to help them explore the desirability of dissolving their marriage. To help couples improve their interaction, it is necessary to help them modify the contingencies that each sets for the behavior of the other. To help couples reach a sound decision to dissolve their marriage, it is necessary to facilitate their experiencing their relationship at its best within the limits of existing external pressures. This can be done by asking each to act "as if" the marriage were a success for a period of from 3 to 5 weeks. If this trial does lead to greater satisfaction, then consecutive trial periods can follow. Therefore, no matter which of the two major goals clients request, intervention procedures typically have a single focus, that of improving the quality and quantity of positive experiences within the marriage.

Within the general objective of improving spousal interaction, specific change goals must be set. This is done by identifying the base rate of the occurrence of selected positive behaviors, identifying the target rate of these behaviors, which can be specified on a graph, and singling out stages of progress toward these goals that can be considered successive approximations of the target. Thus, a wife might wish that her husband "respect

her more." This can translate into her wishing that he assume some responsibility for arranging babysitters for the children since they both work,
that he accommodate to the occasional demand that she work into the
early evening by preparing his own and the children's dinner and that he
prepare his own lunches. The husband might wish that his wife "show some
consideration for him" by joining him on skiing trips, by helping to enter-
tain his business associates occasionally, and by sharing use of the family
car. Each can be helped to achieve the goal of selected changes in the behavior of the other. And when these goals are achieved, it is reasonable
to expect that the wife will feel more "respected" and the husband more
"considered" because both of these feelings result from the way in which
each behaves toward the other. The ultimate goal of marital counseling is
thus to change the way each feels about the other, but the means to the
attainment of that goal is a change in the way each behaves toward the
other.

## Assessment of Marital Interaction

In 1969 Olson observed that "considerable research is needed in the
field before adequate methods can be developed for diagnosing marital dynamics in a valid manner which can be useful to a marriage counselor
[p. 1]." Since that time, effort has gone into the development of direct observation techniques for use in natural (e.g., Patterson and Cobb, 1972;
Weiss *et al.,* 1973) and laboratory (e.g., Olson and Straus, 1972; Braver
and Stuart, in press) environments. These techniques are costly, however,
and the question of how reactive they may be has not yet been resolved.
Effort has also been expended on the development of both indirect (e.g.,
Olson and Ryder, 1970) and direct (e.g., Stuart, 1972a) measures of a
variety of areas of marital adequacy. These latter approaches have been
designed to obtain information that overcomes the generality and conven-
tionality (Edmonds, 1967) of the familiar indices of marital satisfaction
(Burgess and Wallin, 1953; Locke and Wallace, 1959), which can be efficiently collected and which yield data needed by clinicians for the planning
and evaluation of intervention. The Stuart Marital Precounseling Inventory
(Stuart, 1972a), for example, collects socially and self-monitored behavioral data, measures evaluative reactions to multiple areas of marital
functioning, assesses commitment to the marriage, provides means of
assessing the extent to which one partner concurs with and understands the
views of the other in many areas, and provides data on the sources for interactional change available to the couple.

## Intervention Structure

There are four issues to be resolved in the structuring of marital treatment. The first is whether the couple should be seen jointly or separately. Joint contact increases the likelihood that descriptions of interactional events occurring outside treatment will be accurate, it creates invaluable emphasis on the role of both partners in generating and changing problematic behaviors, and it permits the therapists efficiently to investigate changes in the behavior of both partners simultaneously rather than having to rely on the more costly process of working through one spouse to reach the other. The one dubious advantage of individual contact is that one spouse or the other might feel more comfortable about self-revelation in the other's absence. But this means that the therapist used as a confidant is in the awkward position of having to violate a confidence or of entering into collusion with one mate against the other. Therefore, in addition to restricting treatment to joint contacts only, it is also prudent to make a formal agreement that any information given to the therapist in person, by phone, or in writing by either spouse will be treated as though it were common knowledge.

The second issue is whether the couple should be seen by one therapist or by a man–woman therapist team, and whether they should be seen as a separate couple or as members of a couples group. While there is good reason to believe that therapist teams are effective in the treatment of sexual problems (LoPiccolo, in press; Masters and Johnson, 1972), there are no available data to support the use of teams in treating marital problems in which sex plays a secondary role. That is, there is no clear justification at this time to assume that the value of cross- and same-sexed models outweighs the cost of doubling therapist time. There is also no evidence currently available that would aid in making the programatic decision about couple or couple group therapy, although work currently in progress (Turner, 1972) will shed light on this question.

A third issue is whether the duration of treatment should be short or long and whether treatment sessions should be frequent or more broadly timed. The psychotherapeutic finding that longer treatment programs tend to be more effective is frought with methodological problems (Luborsky, Chandler, Auerbach, Cohen, and Bachrach, 1971). Recent research with delinquents (Adams, 1967; Stuart, Tripodi, and Jayaratne, in press a) and in social agencies (Reid and Shyne, 1969) has shown short-term treatment to be advantageous and, based on similar findings, Meltzoff and Kornreich (1970) concluded that "there is very little good evidence that time in

therapy past some unidentified point brings commensurate additional benefits [p. 346]." Therefore, it is prudent to limit time in treatment in the
service of economy and effectiveness, with six to eight sessions being a
reasonable allowance. Establishing this time limit prior to the start of
treatment has the advantage of allowing both the therapist and the clients
to organize their use of treatment time to maximum advantage.

On the question of the optimal spacing of therapeutic sessions, Lorr
(1962) concluded a decade ago "therapist time can be spread over more
patients with fewer contacts and at less cost to patients [p. 140]." Since
there has been little contrary evidence adduced since that statement was
made, it can be assumed that the optimal spacing of sessions might be
biweekly, allowing for the gradual fading-in of behavior changes and for
the maintenance of those changes once they have been initiated.

The degree of structure of the content of sessions is the final pretreatment issue. Structure of interview contact has been shown to be highly
beneficial both because it helps bring order to the clients' often chaotic
perceptions of their problems (Frank, 1962) and because it increases the
concreteness of specificity of the therapist's behavior (Lennard, Bernstein,
and Hendin, 1960; Stuart *et al.,* in press a; Truax and Charkhuff, 1964). In
marital treatment, carefully designed and prestructured content of treatment interviews helps to reduce the likelihood that the clients will fruit-
lessly use the time to engage in the negative practice of prolonged fighting,
and it also facilitates the therapist's efforts to mobilize the client's problem-
solving efforts. Treatment content can be prestructured through several
means. Precounseling forms (e.g., Stuart, 1972a) can be used to cue
clients to state their goals positively and to provide the counselor with
organized data, which facilitate the immediate initiation of change efforts.
Explanation of the logic of the intervention (e.g., Stuart, 1969a) gives the
clients an opportunity to organize their own efforts. Further, the case
records and tapes can be used as positive role models of client behavior.
In addition to these client-focused structural aids, therapist recording of all
instigations, and even the prestructuring of instigations (Stuart, Jayartne,
and Tripodi, in press b) facilitate the constructive use of every contact
hour.

In summary, it has been suggested that all marital treatment should
involve conjoint sessions only, that treatment should be limited in duration,
with a planned timing of sessions, and that the content of each interview
should be optimally structured. Use of a precounseling form as a means
of anticipatorily socializing clients into treatment and use of a treatment
contract such as that presented in Table 6.1 are two effective means of
achieving the necessary structure.

**TABLE 6.1**

Marital Treatment Contract

Mr. —————————— and Mrs. —————————— have requested counseling to help with the improvement of their relationship. They agree to participate in ——————— joint counseling sessions which will be held at intervals of ——————— days. It is understood that any written, telephoned, or spoken messages to the counselor by either spouse will be assumed to be common knowledge. This assumption is necessary in order to assure both spouses of the impartial help of the counselor. Finally, both spouses agree to complete every behavioral assignment to which he or she agrees, whether this assignment requires the completion of written forms, the graphing of changes in behavior, or changes in actions toward the other.

The counselor agrees to help both spouses equally toward the attainment of those goals to which all three parties agree. The counselor also agrees to explain to both spouses the logic of all therapeutic procedures, to evaluate the effectiveness of each of these procedures, and to ask spouses to perform only those tasks that are believed essential to the attainment of their goals. Finally, the Counselor agrees to be available by telephone between sessions solely to help with the avoidance of conflict.

Mr. ———————————— Mrs. ———————————— Dr. ————————————
Date ————————————

## Intervention Procedures

The procedures used in this intervention approach can be divided into five hierarchically ordered categories, analogous to the modules set forth by Weiss *et al.* (1973), with the procedures at each higher level subsuming those at earlier levels. The five steps can be summarized as follows:

1. Begin by helping each spouse to identify those positive changes in his or her own behavior as well as that of the other, which would significantly increase both the individual and shared mutual enjoyment of the marriage; then,
2. Help the partners to develop a dependable means of exchanging these desirable behaviors which permits them both to maintain an adequate level of personal and mutual satisfaction while simultaneously rebuilding trust in each other,
3. Help each member of the pair to evolve an effective channel of verbal and nonverbal communication so that each has an unambiguous, readily available means of expressing his or her wishes and of communicating his satisfaction; then,
4. Help the couple to devise a strategy of decision making which accords each partner a consensually agreed-upon measure of control over the form and content of the marital interaction; and
5. Finally, develop with the couple a means of maintaining these changes in a climate of flexibility which allows them to adapt to the evolving internal and external demands upon their marriage [Stuart, 1972b, pp. 2–3].

Each of these steps leads to the development of an important skill of interpersonal competence. The first leads to the shaping of a behaviorally specific interpersonal vocabulary in which experience is described with precision in a manner stressing the individual's influence over his or her experience. The second leads to the acquisition of skill in interpersonal influence based on positive, incremental techniques. The third leads to an increased ability in eliciting and utilizing feedback about one's own behavior and information about the other's desires. The fourth leads to the strengthening of effective norms governing the allocation of power to replace coersion as the basis for decision making. And the fifth leads to the development of efficient techniques for naturally cueing and maintaining all phases of interaction change. Each of these procedures will now be described in more detail, with an expanded discussion available elsewhere (Stuart and Lederer, 1975).

1. *Shaping a new interpersonal vocabulary.* Clients entering marital counseling generally have long histories of faulty labeling of their own behavior and that of their spouses. Hurvitz (1970) has succinctly described the problem in these labeling systems as an overdependence on "terminal hypotheses" that "may or may not be 'true' and . . . may 'fit' the information available but do not offer possible plans of action that can be utilized to change the relationship [p. 66]." That is, no matter how great their chance accuracy might be, reliance on terminal hypotheses such as "psychodynamic interpretations," "pseudoscientific explanations," or "psychological name-calling" reify the problem as unchangeable. If George Kelly's assertion is correct and "a person's processes are psychologically channelized by the ways in which he anticipates events [1955, p. 46]," then maintenance of terminal hypotheses function as negative cues for change efforts and would weaken the likelihood of their occurrence. Therefore the first step in this treatment program is aimed at introducing the use of "instrumental hypotheses . . . [which] explain behavior, meanings or feelings . . . in such a way that something can be done to change the existing situation [Hurvitz, 1970, p. 67]." To do this, past efforts to explain *why* problems developed (e.g., "You always come home late for dinner because you resent your mother's domination so!") are replaced with explanations of *how* desired repertoires can be established (e.g., "I will be home on time if we agree to have dinner at 6:30 each day").

Couples are trained to use this process vocabulary in place of more static terminology, coupled with efforts to particularize general statements and relate all behavioral descriptions to the situations in which the actions take place. Each spouse then learns to express his or her wishes for changes in other's behavior in the form of a behavioral prescription. While Weiss *et al.* (1973) ask their couples to express their "pleases" and "displeases" —that is, acceleration and deceleration change targets—the present approach cues clients to state all goals in terms of positive changes. This is done for three reasons. First, the technology available for acceleration is more compatible with constructive marital interaction than the technology of behavioral suppression. Second, couples facing marital discord typically overstress negative scanning, and a purely positive data-collection process aids in overcoming this bias (Stuart, 1969a). Third, it has been noted that ". . . there seems to be substantial support for the proposition that negative information carries greater weight than positive information [Kanouse, Hanson, and Reid, 1972, p. 15]." Therefore, the collection of both positive and negative information carries with it the risk that the negative data will outweigh the effects of the positive data. For these reasons, it seems that only the collection of positive data offers multiple advantages.

2. *Shaping new techniques of interpersonal influence.* It has been suggested elsewhere (Stuart, 1969b) that couples with marital discord are more likely to use coercion than reciprocity as a norm in their interaction. Coercion and reciprocity have been defined as the use of negative and positive reinforcements, respectively (Patterson and Reid, 1970). While some negative reinforcement in the form of nagging is probably inevitable in marital interaction, if nagging becomes a high-frequency strategy by either or both partners, the marriage loses much of its luster for the victim. To overcome the excessive use of coersion, it is neccessary to convince both partners that the exchanges they enjoy in their marriages are privileges and not rights. A privilege is "a special prerogative which one may enjoy at the will of another person upon having performed some qualifying task [Stuart, 1971, p. 3]," in contrast to a right, which implies inalienable access to a reinforcer. To earn privileges, one must reinforce the other: to enjoy rights, one need only insist on his due. By conceptualizing preferred marital pleasures as privileges, reciprocity becomes the only means of gaining access to them, replacing coersion as the means to securing rights.

Building on the notion of privileges, behavioral contracts provide for the equitable exchange of favors by spouses (Stuart and Lott, 1972). Contracts specify the responsibilities that each must meet in order to enjoy his privileges. Contributing to the technology of contracting, Weiss *et al.* (1973) suggest that it is probably advisable to allow each spouse to choose from among several privileges each time that an obligation has been fulfilled. Early contracts begin with very specific behavioral options (e.g., if the wife takes the garbage out by 7:30 she may either have first access to the evening paper, choose the movie, television program, or other entertainment for the evening, or have her choice of leaving the bedroom windows open or shut. Later contracts are often less specific but nevertheless continue to provide a broad framework for behavioral exchanges with means of monitoring all contract-governed behaviors. Contracts thus help the couple to schedule the exchanges that nondistressed couples make naturally and, as with any behavioral prosthetic, they can be faded when they are no longer needed.

3. *Developing new means of information exchange.* While marriage counselors frequently assess their client's as having "no communication," couples seeking treatment frequently complain that their marriages include too much communication that is aversive (Bienvenu, 1970; Levinger and Senn, 1967). The effort to overcome communicational problems through this program is premised on four axioms, each of which is discussed more fully elsewhere (Stuart and Lederer, 1975). Briefly stated, they are as follows:

1. One cannot not communicate (Watzlawick, 1964). This axiom stems from the findings of numerous studies that demonstrate a continuous flow of nonverbal communication. Thus, a husband who enters and picks up the paper without greeting his wife has very clearly communicated his displeasure with his wife.
2. Measured honesty is required for the enrichment of relationships. This axiom stems from the repeated requests by clients that their spouses use "selective communication" (Bienvenu, 1970, p. 28) or the "selective disclosure of feelings" (Levinger and Senn, 1967, p. 256). Thus, spouses are encouraged to ask each other only for those changes that can reasonably be granted.
3. Positive information can change relationships, while negative information can only stabilize them. This axiom is based on the logic of systems theory (von Bertalanffy, 1950), which suggests that servomechanisms that provide negative feedback can correct errors in functioning while new, positive information is needed for system change. Thus, spouses are encouraged to use the shaping principle in their interaction, making limited and very judicious use of negative feedback.
4. Every interactional description must include the first speaker's cue, the first response of the second person, and the consequence supplied by the first person for the last response of the second period. This axiom stems from the work of Watzlawick *et al.* (1967), who stress the importance of "punctuation" in behavioral chains. For example, a wife might complain that her husband

enters without greeting her: He entered, she waited, and he did something other than express a greeting. Her three-unit description (two of her husband's behavior bracketing one of hers) makes her appear guiltless. But one cannot hear such a description without wondering whether she greeted him. Her husband's next maneuver would be quite different if it was silence following a greeting rather than silence following silence. The way in which the exchange is punctuated—that is, in odd number of units of three or more, which would bias matters to the speaker's advantage, or in even number of units of four or more which would place the behavior of both in an appropriate context—would greatly influence the way in which the speaker planned his or her own next actions. Training in the proper punctuation of communication chain thus greatly increases skill in constructive information exchange.

Taken together, these axioms provide the building blocks for a model of effective marital communication. The first axiom leads to the adoption of a strategy in which positive messages are communicated both verbally and nonverbally while negative messages are expressed primarily in words. The second axiom leads to the expression of requests rather than condemnations, with the requests selected with kindness. The third axiom leads to a strong emphasis on constructive communication, which is itself a reinforcer as well as being a means to the end of increasing the attractiveness of one spouse to the other (Byrne and Rhamey, 1965). The fourth leads to acceptance by each spouse of the responsibility for changing painful communication patterns. A variety of techniques are available for achieving these changes, ranging from the scheduling of a standard half-hour each evening for a quiet review of the happenings of the day, to a rule that requires one to ask at least two questions as an indication of his interest in what the other has to say, the use of poker chips to serve as a means of on-line signals of positive evaluation, and the tape recording of stressful exchanges to identify the problematic punctuation of events. [See Stuart and Lederer (1975) for a full description of these and other communication-change techniques.]

4. *Developing new decision-making norms.* While there is no generally agreed-upon measure of power in a marital relationship (Olson and Rabunsky, 1972; Turk and Bell, 1972) and no common pattern for distributing power (Stuart, 1972b), power can be understood to mean the ability to control decision making. Couples make a myriad of choices ranging from monumentally important decisions such as whether to have children or whether to remain together to far less momentous decisions

such as whether to invite in-laws for a holiday or what color to paint the living room. Successful couples develop dependable norms to allocate the power in each of these areas at varying stages in their lives. Distressed couples fail to develop effective norms and therefore must resort to the frank use of power to cope with recurring conflict. Successful and distressed couples can therefore be differentiated according to the proportion of areas of decision: (1) shared equally; (2) shared unequally by agree-

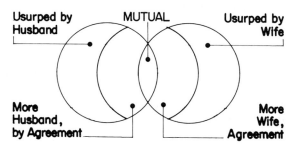

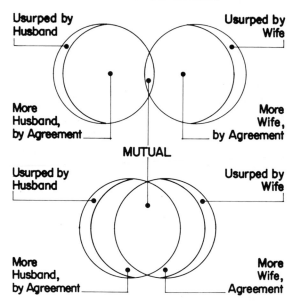

*Figure 6.1* Models of unsuccessful and successful divisions of decision-making authority.

ment; or (3) usurped by one and contested by the other. Various matters of power allocation are shown in Figure 6.1 in which it can be seen that nonfunctioning couples may vary in the extent of mutual aid offered to allocating power, but they differ greatly from distressed couples in the amount of usurped power. In general, the person with the least to lose in the dispute has the most to gain (Waller, 1938), but the balance of power in a relationship is far more complicated than this being sensitive to a matrix of forces both within and beyond the spouses themselves.

Efficiency and comfort in the marriage is certainly related to the degree to which both partners accept the existing balance of power. To improve an unsatisfactory condition, it is necessary to follow three steps. First, identify the areas in which each presently exercises power. Then identify the areas in which each would ideally like to exercise power. This is followed by contracting for agreements governing power distribution. During these contracting sessions, the role of the therapist is that of mediator. Both spouses generally know in advance what concessions they will have to make, but neither has offered to give up his claim to an area for fear of loss of face. (Pruitt and Johnson, 1970). By directing both partners to change, the therapist facilitates accommodation to the inevitable, leading to the development of new norms of interpersonal influence.

5. *Building techniques for maintaining change.* After one person has changed his actions, the new behaviors will fall under the social control of the other. But because marriages are not closed systems but rather are open to a myriad of outside influences over and above the changing demands caused by maturation of the spouses themselves, it is always necessary to protect the new behavioral balance. This can be done efficiently by developing a set of "relationship rules" for each couple that can serve as explications of norms of interaction and cues for behavior change. Stuart and Lederer (1975) offer an extensive collection of such rules. Listed here are but a few.

1. Respect the core symbols of the marriage. Following this rule protects both spouses from attacks on their security in the relationship. It sets the limits within which arguments will occur so that the relationship is not wasted over petty disagreements.
2. Strive to end arguments, not to win them. Following this rule protects the partners from the futility of attempting to "one-up" each other. It stresses efforts to enhance rather than thwart reciprocity as a means of increasing personal satisfaction.
3. Communicate the expectation that your spouse will fulfill your wishes. Following this rule provides continuous cues for constructive behavior, while simultaneously avoiding the trap of cueing negative behaviors.
4. Encourage the behaviors you desire, in order to strengthen the chances of

getting what you wish. For example, when one says, "I love you," saying "thank you" reinforces the thought while saying "no, you don't" weakens it.

Finally, couples can also be helped to maintain changed interactional patterns by undergoing a periodic self-assessment of the strengths and targets for change in their relationship. This can be conveniently undertaken by estimating the extent to which preset goals have been achieved and by matching perceptions of the current interaction against the type of interaction to which the couple aspires. If treatment succeeded, these assessments should cue each spouse in how he or she can develop new strategies to create the conditions for change in the other. On the other hand, treatment will have failed if each uses the assessment experience as an occasion to condemn the other.

## Conclusion

This paper has set forth the rationale and a procedural guide for the operant-interpersonal treatment of marital discord. The overall design of the method is outlined in Figure 6.2, which reveals a series of decisions beginning with the decision of the couple to embark upon treatment and ending with the final stages of fading out intervention techniques. At each stage, the techniques and the criteria for their selection can be precisely stated. This sets the operant–interpersonal approach apart from the other systems of marital treatment (Broderick, 1971; Olson, 1970), since it permits the experimental validation of the importance of each set of procedures through factorial experimental I designs (e.g., Welch and Goldstein, 1972), it permits the techniques to be taught to other practitioners and students, and it provides clients with a cogent system that they can potentially self-apply to improve their marriages. Therefore, while the returns are not yet in, it appears that the operant-interpersonal approach will offer the best hope yet of couples moving from poor to good and from good to better marriages.

## References

Adams, S. Some findings from correctional caseload research. *Federal Probation,* 1967, **31**, 48–57.
Bienvenu, M. J. Measurement of marital communication. *The Family Coordinator,* 1970, **19**, 26–31.

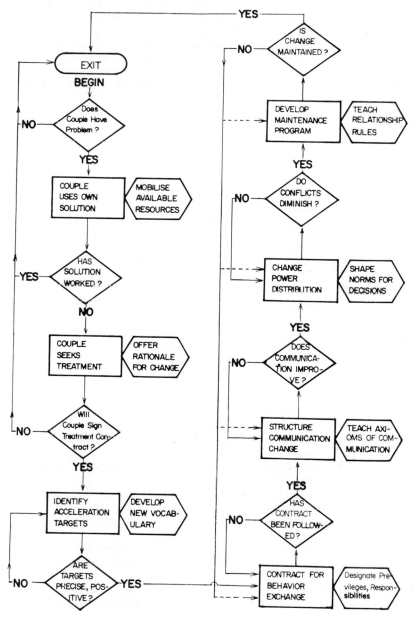

YES

IS CHANGE MAINTAINED ?

NO

EXIT

BEGIN

NO

Does Couple Have Problem ?

YES

DEVELOP MAINTENANCE PROGRAM

TEACH RELATIONSHIP RULES

COUPLE USES OWN SOLUTION

MOBILISE AVAILABLE RESOURCES

YES

DO CONFLICTS DIMINISH ?

NO

YES

HAS SOLUTION WORKED ?

NO

CHANGE POWER DISTRIBUTION

SHAPE NORMS FOR DECISIONS

COUPLE SEEKS TREATMENT

OFFER RATIONALE FOR CHANGE

YES

DOES COMMUNICATION IMPROVE ?

NO

Will Couple Sign Treatment Contract ?

NO

STRUCTURE COMMUNICATION CHANGE

TEACH AXIOMS OF COMMUNICATION

YES

IDENTIFY ACCELERATION TARGETS

DEVELOP NEW VOCABULARY

YES

HAS CONTRACT BEEN FOLLOWED ?

NO

ARE TARGETS PRECISE, POSITIVE ?

NO

YES

CONTRACT FOR BEHAVIOR EXCHANGE

Designate Privileges, Responsibilities

*Figure 6.2.*

93

Blau, P. M. *Exchange and Power in Social Life.* New York: Wiley, 1964.

Braver, J., and Stuart, R. B. "Differential reinforcement of spouses and strangers: An index of marital satisfaction. *Family Process.* (*In press.*)

Broderick, C. B. Beyond the five conceptual frameworks: A decade of development in family theory. In C. B. Broderick (Ed.), *A Decade of Family Research and Action.* Minneapolis, Minn.: National Council on Family Relations, 1971.

Burgess, E. W., and Wallin, P. *Engagement and Marriage.* New York: Lippincott, 1953.

Byrne, D., and Rhamey, R. Magnitude of positive and negative reinforcements as a determinant of attraction. *Journal of Personality and Social Psychology,* 1965, **2**, 884–889.

Edmonds, V. H., Marital conventionalization: Definition and measurement. *Journal of Marriage and the Family,* 1967, **27**, 681–688.

Frank, J. D. The role of cognitions in illness and healing. In H. H. Strupp and L. Luborsky (Eds.), *Research in Psychotherapy.* Washington, D.C.: American Psychological Association, 1962.

Goldiamond, I. Self-control procedures in personal behavior problems. In R. Ulrich, T. Stachnick, and J. Mabry (Eds.), *Control of Human Behavior.* Glenview, Ill.: Scott, Foresman, 1966.

Goldstein, M. K., and Francis, B. Behavior modification of husbands by wives. Paper presented at the annual meeting of the National Council on Family Relations, Washington, D.C., 1969.

Homans, G. C. *Social Behavior: Its Elementary Forms.* New York: Harcourt Brace Jovanovich, 1961.

Hunt, G. M., and Azrin, N. H. A community-reinforcement approach to alcoholism. *Behavior Research and Therapy,* 1973, **11**, 91–104.

Hurvitz, N. Interaction hypotheses in marriage counseling. *The Family Coordinator,* 1970, **19**, 64–75.

Kanouse, D. E., Hanson, L., and Reid, W. J. *Negativity in Evaluations.* Morristown, N.J.: General Learning Press, 1972.

Kelly, G. A. *The Psychology of Personal Constructs, Vol. 1.* New York: Norton, 1955.

Lennard, H., Bernstein, A., and Hendin, E. *Anatomy of Psychotherapy.* New York: Columbia University Press, 1960.

Levinger, G. Marital cohesiveness and dissolution: An integrative review. *Journal of Marriage and the Family,* 1965, **27**, 1, 19–28.

Levinger, G., and Senn, D. J. Disclosure of feelings in marriage. *Merrill-Palmer Quarterly of Behavior and Development,* 1967, **13**, 252–258.

Liberman, R. Behavioral approaches to family and couples therapy. *American Journal of Orthopsychiatry,* 1970, **40**, 106–118.

Locke, H. J., and Wallace, K. M. Short marital-adjustment and prediction tests: Their reliability and validity. *Journal of Marriage and Family Living,* 1959, **21**, 251–255.

LoPiccolo, J. Behavior therapy of sexual dysfunction. In L. A. Hamerlynck, L. C. Handy, and E. J. Mash (Eds.), *Critical Issues in Behavior Modification.* Champaign, Ill.: Research Press. (*In press.*)

Lorr, M. Relation of treatment frequency and duration to psychotherapeutic outcome. In H. H. Strupp and L. Luborsky (Eds.), *Research in Psychotherapy.* Washington, D.C.: American Psychological Association, 1962.

Luborsky, L., Chandler, M., Auerbach, A. H., Cohen, J., and Bachrach, H. M. Factors influencing the outcome of psychotherapy: A review of quantitative research. *Psychological Bulletin,* 1971, **75**, 145–185.

Masters, W. H., and Johnson, V. E. The rapid treatment of human sexual dysfunctions. In C. J. Sager and H. S. Kaplan (Eds.), *Progress in Group and Family Therapy.* New York: Brunner/Mazel, 1972.

Meltzoff, J., and Kornreich, M. *Research in Psychotherapy.* New York: Atherton Press, 1970.

Olson, D. H. Diagnosis in marriage counseling using SIMFAM, MMPI's and therapists. *American Association of Marriage Counselors Newsletter,* Spring 1969, 1.

Olson, D. H. Marital and family therapy: Integrative review and critique. *Journal of Marriage and the Family,* 1970, **32**, 501–538.

Olson, D. H., and Rabunsky, C. Validity of four measures of family power. *Journal of Marriage and the Family,* 1972, **34**, 224–234.

Olson, D. H., and Ryder, R. G. Inventory of marital conflicts (IMC): An experimental interaction procedure. *Journal of Marriage and the Family,* 1970, **31**, 433–448.

Olson, D. H., and Straus, M. A. A diagnostic tool for marital and family therapy: The SIMFAM technique. *The Family Coordinator,* 1972, **21**, 55–62.

Patterson, G. R., and Cobb, J. A. Stimulus control for classes of noxious behaviors. In J. F. Knutson (Ed.), *The Control of Aggression: Implications for Basic Research.* Chicago: Aldine, 1972.

Patterson, G. R., and Hops, H. Coercion, a game for two: Intervention techniques for marital conflict. In R. E. Ulrich and P. Montjoy (Eds.), *The Experimental Analysis of Social Behavior.* New York: Appleton-Century-Crofts, 1973.

Patterson, G. R., and Reid, J. B. Reciprocity and Coercion: Two facets of social systems. In C. Neuringer and J. Michael (Eds.), *Behavior Modification in Clinical Psychology.* New York: Appleton-Century-Crofts, 1970.

Pruitt, D. G., and Johnson, D. F. Mediation as an aid to face saving in negotiation. *Journal of Personality and Social Psychology,* 1970, **14**, 239 246.

Rappaport, A. F., and Harell, J. A. A behavioral-exchange model for marital counseling. *The Family Coordinator,* 1972, **21**, 203–212.

Reid, W. J., and Shyne, A. W. *Brief and Extended Casework.* New York: Columbia University Press, 1969.

Stuart, R. B. Operant-interpersonal treatment for marital discord. *Journal of Consulting and Clinical Psychology,* 1969, **33**, 675–682. (a)

Stuart, R. B. Token reinforcement in marital treatment. In R. Rubin and C. M. Franks (Eds.), *Advances in Behavior Therapy.* New York: Academic Press, 1969. (b)

Stuart, R. B. Behavioral contracting within the families of delinquents. *Journal of Behavior Therapy and Experimental Psychiatry,* 1971, **2**, 1–11.

Stuart, R. B. *Marital Pre-counseling Inventory.* Champaign, Ill.: Research Press, 1972. (a)

Stuart, R. B. *Marital Pre-counseling Inventory: Counselors Guide.* Champaign, Ill.: Research Press, 1972. (b)

Stuart, R. B. Techniques for assessing marital interaction and change. *Journal of Behavior Therapy and Experimental Psychiatry.* (*In press.*)

Stuart, R. B., and Lederer, W. J. *How to Make a Bad Marriage Good and a Good Marriage Better.* New York: Norton, 1975.

Stuart, R. B., and Lott, L. Behavioral contracting: A cautionary note. *Journal of Behavior Therapy and Experimental Psychiatry* 1972, **3**, 161–170.

Stuart, R. B., Tripodi, T., and Jayaratne, S. The family and school treatment model of services for predelinquents. *Journal of Research in Crime and Delinquency.* (*In press.*) (a)

Stuart, R. B., Jayaratne, S., and Tripodi, T. Modifying deviant adolescent behavior through reprogramming the behavior of parents and teachers. *Canadian Journal of Behavioral Science.* (*In press.*) (b)

Thibaut, J. M., and Kelley, H. H. *The Social Psychology of Groups.* New York: John Wiley, 1959.

Truax, C. B., and Carkhuff, R. R. Concreteness: A neglected variable in research in psychotherapy. *Journal of Clinical Psychology,* 1964, **20**, 264–267.

Turk, J. L., and Bell, N. W. Measuring power in families. *Journal of Marriage and the Family,* 1972, **34**, 215–223.

Turner, A. J. Couple and group treatment of marital discord: An experiment. Paper presented at the Fifth Annual Meeting of the Association for the Advancement of Behavior Therapy, New York, 1972.

von Bertalanffy, L. An outline of general system theory. *British Journal of Philosophy,* 1950, **1**, 134–165.

Waller, W. *The Family: A Dynamic Interpretation.* New York: Gordon, 1938.

Watzlawick, P. *An Anthology of Human Communication.* Palo Alto, Calif.: Science and Behavior Books, 1964.

Watzlawick, P., Beavin, J. H., and Jackson, D. D. *Pragmatics of Human Communication.* New York: Norton, 1967.

Weiss, R. L., Hops, H., and Patterson, G. R. A framework for conceptualizing marital conflict, a technology for altering it, some data for evaluating it. In L. A. Hamerlynck, L. C. Handy, and E. J. Mash (Eds.), *Critical Issues in Behavior Modification.* Champaign, Ill.: Research Press, 1973.

Welch, J. C., and Goldstein, M. K. "The differential effects of operant-interpersonal intervention." Paper presented at the Fifth Annual Meeting of the Association for the Advancement of Behavior Therapy, New York, 1972.

# 7 BEHAVIOR THERAPY IN THE TREATMENT OF BRONCHIAL ASTHMA

N. J. Yorkston

## Introduction

This paper discusses some evidence that a behavioral approach can contribute to the treatment of bronchial asthma. This evidence comes from a study of 27 patients, and further data are expected from another 27 who were treated at the University of Minnesota.

Before reviewing this evidence, let us remind ourselves about the disorder called bronchial asthma. "Asthma" is a Greek word that means panting. Breathlessness can arise from many causes, but in clinical medicine two main types of asthma are usually recognized: cardiac asthma and bronchial asthma. In cardiac asthma the person becomes breathless when the left side of the heart fails and the blood congests the lungs. In bronchial asthma the patient becomes breathless when involuntary muscles in the small airways contract. (Occasionally, of course, someone has both cardiac and bronchial asthma.) Because contracting of the airways is a kind of behavior, a study of bronchial asthma might profit from examining the experimental methods for analyzing behavior.

## Analysis of Behavior and Bronchial Asthma

Work in the experimental analysis of behavior prompts us clinicians to look for the answers to three key questions:

1. What is the altered behavior in bronchial asthma?
2. What agents govern this altered behavior?
3. How can we control those agents?

In passing, may I say that this behavioral model fits perfectly with the medical model. They concur, it seems to me, because both are examples of a systematic attempt to apply knowledge to defining a practical problem, looking for its possible causes, and trying to solve the problem, preferably by removing its causes.

## What Is the Altered Behavior in Bronchial Asthma?

The essential disorder is that the involuntary muscles in the small airways contract. This reduces the caliber of the airways, obstructs the flow of air, especially on expiration, and makes the patient breathless. This resistance to the flow of air can be measured objectively. Other changes accompany the muscular contractions and add to the obstruction; for example, the mucous membranes lining the airways become edematous and the glands in the mucous membranes secrete mucus.

Other changes in behavior may be regarded as secondary to the narrowed airways. The person makes respiratory efforts to overcome the obstruction. Any behavior that relieves the obstruction, such as taking an effective medicine, tends to be repeated. Other autonomic and related reactions may accompany these changes in the small airways. A patient may sweat, feel his heart palpitate, and become generally aroused. He may become tense, anxious, or even panicky.

A person with asthma thinks. During an attack his immediate thought is to find relief. If relief does not come, he wonders what will happen next. His thoughts may make him more anxious; he may even wonder if he is going to die. When he has time to reflect, he wonders about the causes of the attack. He may appropriately identify the agents concerned, although sometimes his views about causation seem strange and probably depend on some accidental circumstances. In either case, whether appropriate or not, he begins to avoid the situations that he believes can provoke an attack.

These changes in behavior often disrupt his normal activities. Asthma may hinder a person's work. In children, asthma accounts for one-quarter of the absenteeism from school that arises from chronic illness (Schiffer and Hunt, 1963). Attacks of asthma may impede social life, family life, and sexual behavior. All this might suggest a serious disruption to the personality, but personality tests do not provide evidence of differences between asthmatics and normals (Falliers, 1969; Zealley, Aitken, and Rosenthal, 1971). However, in bronchial asthma there is a great range of altered behavior that may distress the patient, impede his daily activities, and shorten or even take his life.

## What Agents Govern the Altered Behavior?

If the essential behavioral disorder in bronchial asthma is that the airways contract, what agents govern that reaction? If airway contraction is the dependent variable, what are independent variables of which the contraction is a function? If we can identify those independent variables, we may be able to deal with them and thus control the unwanted reaction.

Various agents may play a part in bronchial asthma. Different factors may be important in different individuals, or at different times in the same person. Before dealing with some of the psychological variables, a few of the other factors are mentioned briefly.

*Organisms.* Microorganisms that infect the respiratory passages may provoke asthma. Intervention against the invading organism, such as taking an antibiotic, may help to relieve the asthma.

*Physical or Chemical Irritants.* Occasionally there are obvious irritants, as in the case of the man whose job was demolishing buildings, raising clouds of coarse particles into the air he breathed. Extremes of heat or cold or humidity, or sudden changes in these variables, are often thought to induce asthma, and may be controlled by central heating or air conditioning. Tobacco smoke irritates the airways of some asthmatic patients.

*Allergens.* An allergy is an altered reaction; an allergic person reacts to an agent that is intrinsically neutral for most people, and that perhaps was originally neutral for that person himself. Allergens include, for example, pollens and molds. Steps can be taken to avoid contact with the allergens, for instance by taking a vacation at the time when a perennial pollen disperses, or by repairing a damp basement that fosters the growth of molds. Allergens have also been dealt with by desensitizing the patient with graduated injections of the allergen. Thus, in allergy, as in behavior therapy, practitioners use the concept of desensitization, although the techniques in the two disciplines are quite different.

*Psychological Factors.* Psychological factors are widely thought to play a part in the development of bronchial asthma. Shepherd, Cooper, Brown, and Kalton (1966) found that physicians ranked asthma first among the diseases in which they thought psychological factors were important. Sometimes these factors seem obvious, such as when an attack of asthma follows an argument or occurs when a person becomes excited or anxious. Walton (1960) described a man who developed asthma whenever he had to assert himself with other people, but his attacks improved considerably when he learned to act appropriately in his job as a manager.

Among the less obvious psychological factors that may initiate or exacerbate an attack are the patient's thoughts. There is evidence that an asthmatic's airways may react to his own thinking. An early example is the case report by Mackenzie (1886) of a lady who developed hay fever and asthma when she was shown an artificial rose. "For the purpose of the experiment, I obtained an artificial rose of such exquisite workmanship that it presented a perfect counterfeit of the original. To exclude every possible error, each leaf was carefully wiped, so that not a single particle of foreign matter was secreted within the convolutions of the artificial flower." Within 5 minutes of seeing it, she had developed severe hay fever and "the feeling of oppression in the chest began, with slight embarrassment of respiration. . . . As the discomfort was rapidly increasing, and as I considered the results of the experiment sufficiently satisfactory, I removed the rose and placed it in a distant part of the room."

Luparello, Lyons, Bleecker, and McFadden (1968) misled 40 asthmatic patients into believing that they were inhaling an irritant or allergen that typically precipitated their asthma when in fact they were breathing nebulized saline. In 19 patients the airways resistance increased, and 12 of them developed obvious asthma.

How Can We Control the Agent?

How can we control the agents that govern the altered behavior in bronchial asthma? How can we manipulate the independent variables and thus avoid (or reduce) the contraction of the muscles in the airways? Some examples from general medicine have been given. If the patient develops evidence of the airways narrowing when he thinks about either the agents that provoke an attack or the attack itself, one aim of treatment is to teach the patient to think about these things calmly. This has been done by verbal desensitization (Sergeant and Yorkston, 1969).

**Verbal Desensitization**

The process of verbal desensitization may be sketched in the following steps. First the history is taken with particular reference to the attack of asthma, tracing its apparent precipitants, its early symptoms, and its progress to its worst manifestations. The thoughts that accompany the asthma are carefully noted, particularly the thoughts that raise the patient's anxiety. The following procedure is then carefully explained in sufficient detail to meet the individual patient's interest. The patient is taught to relax himself by a simple and brief method (Yorkston and Sergeant, 1969). While well relaxed, the patient is then taught to discriminate between statements that leave him perfectly calm and those that make him even slightly uncomfortable. Verbal desensitization is then carried out by progressing through a series of carefully graded statements, ensuring that the patient is perfectly calm after listening to one statement before proceeding to the next. These steps are taken very gradually because of the danger of provoking an attack of asthma, which is uncomfortable, difficult to control, and, although rarely, is potentially fatal. Because of the risks involved, techniques like those used in implosion therapy are carefully avoided.

*Internal Stimuli.* Verbal desensitization is begun with symptoms, starting with a benign statement such as, "Everyone gets breathless at some time in his life." The patient is desensitized to such words as "breathless," "wheeze," "tight chest," "palpitations," and "asthma." The process is extended to describe the development of the individual's own attack and the anxious thoughts that occur during it. The description is gradually elaborated, phrase by phrase and sentence by sentence, until the patient can listen to his own description of his worst attack but remain perfectly relaxed.

*External Stimuli.* After the individual is desensitized to these internal stimuli, he is desensitized to the external stimuli—the circumstances in which the attacks occur. It is thus possible to describe the apparent cause and effect, or, more accurately, the circumstances and the nature of the attack. For example, "When the weather is very humid, you often develop a severe attack of asthma in which your chest gets tighter and tighter . . ." and so on.

Finally, all the known stimuli are combined in a vivid description of the circumstances of the attack, the symptoms, and the accompanying thoughts.

Practical desensitization follows verbal desensitization: The patient deliberately enters intrinsically neutral situations that had previously made him uneasy.

The term "verbal desensitization" was proposed (Sergeant and Yorkston, 1969) to distinguish this method of desensitization from the method of desensitization to allergens by graduated injections. The term also distinguishes the verbal method from the practical behavioral method of desensitization through actually facing the situation.

## Results

The first patient treated by this means was a woman who was given 8 hours of verbal desensitization in addition to a full medical treatment for asthma (Sergeant and Yorkston, 1969). Verbal desensitization appeared to be the turning point in her history, and after the improvement she remained well and free of asthma for the 5 years over which her progress was followed.

Norah Moore (1965) made a comparative study of relaxation, relaxation with suggestion, and relaxation with verbal desensitization. She gave two of these treatments (each for eight half-hour sessions) to 12 patients with asthma. By subjective ratings all three treatments had equal success, but on objective measurement of lung function, relaxation with verbal desensitization gave significantly more improvement than the other two treatments. No follow-up study was possible because each patient had received two treatments.

In another controlled study of 14 adults, relaxation was compared with verbal desensitization (Yorkston, McHugh, Brady, Serber, and Sergeant, 1974). Two men and six women were assigned randomly to relaxation, and two men and four women to verbal desensitization. Before treatment the groups were comparable in lung function. Measurements of lung function over six sessions showed no improvement in the relaxation group, but the verbal desensitization group improved significantly. Summarizing estimates of the progress of the two groups were expressed in terms of the percentage of the predicted forced expiratory volume in 1 second ($FEV_1$). Averages of these showed that the relaxation group changed from 68% to 63%, but the verbal desensitization group rose from 56% to 76%. Follow-up ratings 2 years later did not reach the 5% level of significance, but the verbal desensitization group was rated as considerably more improved than the relaxation group.

A similar study of 27 patients in Minnesota is nearing completion.

## Conclusions

The results of these studies suggest that verbal desensitization can supplement the existing treatments for bronchial asthma.

The treatment of asthma is not easy, as a physician who himself "suffered under the Tyranny of the Asthma" observed in 1717: "Since the Cure of the *Asthma* is observed by all physicians, who have attempted the Eradicating of that Chronical Distemper, to be very difficult, and frequently unsuccessful; I may thence infer, That either the true Nature of that Disease is not thoroughly understood by them, or they have not yet found out the Medicines by which the Cure may be effected [Floyer, 1717]." All that remains true, but it seems that the analysis of behavior may contribute something both to understanding the nature of bronchial asthma and to its treatment.

# References

Falliers, C. J. Psychosomatic study and treatment of asthmatic children. *The Pediatric Clinics of North America,* 1969, **16**, No. 1, 271–286.

Floyer, Sir John *A Treatise of the Asthma, Divided into Four Parts,* 2nd ed., corrected. London: Printed for R. Wilkin and W. Innys, 1717.

Luparello, T., Lyons, H. A., Blecker, E. R., Jr., and McFadden, E. R. Influences of suggestion on airway reactivity in asthmatic subjects. *Psychosomatic Medicine,* 1968, **30**, 819–825.

Mackenzie, J. N. The production of the so-called "rose cold" by means of an artificial rose. *American Journal of Medical Sciences,* 1886, **91**, 45–57.

Moore, N. A. Behaviour therapy in bronchial asthma: A controlled study. *Psychosomatic Research,* 1965, **9**, 257–276.

Schiffer, C. B., and Hunt, E. P. Illnesses among children. *Children's Bureau,* U.S. Department of Health, Education, and Welfare, 1963, cited by T. L. Creer, and C. Yoches in The modification of an inappropriate behavioral pattern in asthmatic children. *Journal of Chronic Diseases,* 1971, **24**, 507–513.

Sergeant, H. G. S., and Yorkston, N. J. Verbal desensitisation in the treatment of bronchial asthma. *Lancet,* 1969, **ii**, 1321–1323.

Shepherd, M. Cooper, B., Brown, A. C., and Kalton, G. *Psychiatric Illness in General Practice.* London: Oxford University Press, 1966.

Walton, D. The application of learning theory to the treatment of a case of bronchial asthma. In H. J. Eysenck (Ed.), *Behavior Therapy and the Neuroses.* Oxford, London, New York, Paris: Pergamon, 1960.

Yorkston, N. J., McHugh, R. B., Brady, R., Serber, M., and Sergeant, H. G. S. Verbal desensitization in bronchial asthma. *Psychosomatic Research,* 1974, **18**, 371–376.

Yorkston, N. J., and Sergeant, H. G. S. A simple method of relaxation. *Lancet,* 1969, **ii**, 1319–1321.

Zealley, A. K., Aitken, R. C., and Rosenthal, S. V. Personality and bronchial asthma. *Proceedings of the Royal Society of Medicine,* 1971, **64**, 825–829.

# III MODIFICATION OF PREACADEMIC AND ACADEMIC SKILLS IN CHILDREN

# 8  MOTHERS AS EDUCATEURS FOR THEIR CHILDREN[1]

Teodoro Ayllon

Michael D. Roberts

Three women averaging a third-grade educational background were trained to develop the cognitive skills of disadvantaged preschool children. Four behavioral areas—receptive language, expressive language, prepositional language, and body awareness—were operationally defined. A research design involving multiple baselines was employed to assess experimentally the relative effectiveness of repeated stimulation on culturally deprived children. Irrespective of the race, sex, or educational level of the person presenting the stimulus, the children did not learn when exposed repeatedly to the stimulus material. When reinforcement was introduced in the form of paired praise and consumables, however, the children learned cognitive skills. Using a nonacademic "cookbook" method, three mothers were trained to use reinforcement procedures with one child each. To test for generalization, two of the mothers were each asked to teach an additional child. The learning exhibited by the children demonstrated generalization of the mothers' teaching skills within the experimental setting. This study illustrates an effective and inexpensive method of training people to remediate the developmental deficits of disadvantaged children in their own community.

The behavioral demands made by modern, industrial, urban society on its members are greater than those ever conceived by any previous society. Bloom, Davis, and Hess (1965) pointed out that as society develops more and more rapidly, the skills and abilities necessary for even minimal

[1] This report is based on a project supported in part by Economic Opportunity of Atlanta, Inc. (grant 8100).

107

individual functioning, economic security, social maturity, and independence must increase at the same rate. Toffler, in his widely read *Future Shock* (1970), elegantly reiterates this concept and states that rather than decreasing or at least progressing at the same rate, society's rate of development is increasing and, in fact, the rate of increase itself is accelerating. It is Toffler's premise that, in the near future, even those persons who presently function well in society must be prepared to assimilate new concepts and learn new skills. What will the impact of the future society be on those persons who cannot cope with the present one?

The awareness of present and future problems of so-called socio-cultural-economically "deprived" people has led to increasing scientific research in this area, especially with regard to racial factors. Stimulated by the emerging modern civil rights movement of the late 1950s and the early 1960s, evidence mounted that the effects of "deprivation" on educational potential and progress, intellectual functioning, and children's cognitive development were devastating to blacks and other minority groups. Shuey (1966) found that, across 81 different tests of intellectual ability, blacks averaged one standard deviation (15 IQ points) below the average of the white population. He reported that the longer these children remain in school, the farther behind they fall. This cumulative deficit has been noted on tests of general intelligence (Deutsch and Brown, 1964; Kennedy, Van de Riet, and White, 1963; Pettigrew, 1964) and also on measures of academic achievement (Deutsch, 1960; Kennedy *et al.,* 1963). Frost and Hawkes (1966) reported that children from low-income families (less than $3000 per year) drop out of school at a much higher rate than those from middle-income (greater than $7000 per year) families. And, as might be expected from their test performance, a disproportionate number of disadvantaged children are placed in special classrooms for the mentally retarded, although few suffer any apparent neurological defects (Frost and Hawkes, 1966).

What are the causes for the lower IQs, higher rate of retardation, and poorer rate of academic success among disadvantaged children? There are several views.

Evidence accounting for these deficiencies may be found in the educational setting of the children: the environment of poverty (Riessman, 1962; Deutsch, 1960, 1967), the child-rearing techniques (Deutsch, 1960, 1967; Riessman, 1962; Bronfenbrenner, 1967; Frost and Hawkes, 1966; Miller and Swanson, 1960; Siller, 1957), and the middle-class biases of the public schools (Goldberg, 1967; Hunt, 1967; Keller, 1963; Deutsch, 1960, 1967; Kennedy *et al.,* 1963). Other evidence cites the genetic differences between black and white children (Jensen, 1969; for rebuttals to this position, see also Hebb, 1970; Anastasi, 1971).

Presumably, if these conditions were radically altered, the learning deficits shown by disadvantaged children would be quickly remediated, if not eliminated altogether. While the conceptualizations offered to account for these deficits may be correct, it remains unclear as to how one can remediate or prevent these deficits without the aid of reliable procedures and techniques.

Fortunately, recent findings from behavior research indicate that such procedures and techniques may already be available. Developed in extensive laboratory experimentation (Skinner, 1938; Sidman, 1960; Ferster and Skinner, 1957), these operant principles have been successfully extended to a variety of applied settings (psychiatric hospitals: Ayllon and Michael, 1959; Ayllon and Azrin, 1968; public schools: O'Leary and Becker, 1967; Madsen, Becker, and Thomas, 1968; private homes: Wolf, Risley, and Mees, 1964; nursery schools: Baer and Sherman, 1964). These methods are not dependent on highly sophisticated psychological tests nor trained clinical judgment, but define behavior and its consequences in operational terms (Ayllon and Roberts, 1972). They are therefore well suited to use by paraprofessionals (Ayllon and Wright, 1972).

Previous experimenters have used operant techniques to modify the language of disadvantaged and normal children. These efforts, however, have largely been concentrated in increasing certain parts of speech (descriptive adjectives: Hart and Risley, 1968; Lahey, 1971; comparative and superlative adjectives: Baer and Guess, 1971; quantity of verbalization: Reynolds and Risley, 1968). Some efforts have involved the use of reinforcement to modify the context of verbalizations (Guess, Sailor, Rutherford, and Baer, 1968; Wheeler and Sulzer, 1970). Largely because of the difficulty of definition and observation, the cognitive aspects of verbal behavior have been generally avoided in operant research. The importance, however, of these cognitive aspects of behavior—recognition, understanding, expression, synthesis, and so on—cannot be ignored.

Until recently, operant techniques have mostly been applied by professionals. Currently, however, these techniques are being used by paraprofessionals with middle-class educational backgrounds to remedy the behavioral problems presented by their children (Zeilberger, Sampen, and Sloane, 1968; Gardner, Pearson, Bercovici, and Bricker, 1968) or to increase nonverbal, easily observable, appropriate behaviors (Hall, Cristler, Cranston, and Tucker, 1970). Indeed, several books, designed as guides for parents to use in managing their children's behavior, are available (Becker, 1971; McIntire, 1970; Zifferblatt, 1970). The systematic extension of paraprofessional training in operant methods of teaching children to lower-class, inadequately educated, or even illiterate individuals, has not previously been reported.

The origins of this apparent neglect probably lie in the nature of the problems presented by these children, and in the communication and educational handicaps of their parents. As stated above, the cognitive deficits of disadvantaged children manifest themselves in behaviors that present grave problems of definition and observation. Parents of lower economic class themselves present problems to training through the usual methods. They tend to have few, if any, skills in language or reading. Typically, they have no familiarity with books as a means of acquiring new skills.

Yet it seems obvious that the need for effective educational remediation is so great that any attempts to solve these problems would be a step in the right direction.

The present research represents an attempt to devise: (1) an effective method of training paraprofessional personnel with relatively limited educational backgrounds to implement (2) procedures suitable to develop (and, where needed, to remediate) the cognitive skills of disadvantaged preschool children. (See Roberts, 1972, for a detailed report.)

## Experiment I

The initial problem involved in developing procedures is that of defining target behaviors. With young children, and especially deprived children, there exists a multitude of behaviors that the child either lacks or possesses only minimally. It was determined that the behaviors to be selected should meet two general requirements: (1) They must be cognitive in nature (the research previously presented concludes that it is in cognitive skills, especially in the verbal area, that these children are most deficient), and (2) they must be functional, not only in the child's present environment, but also in the classroom environment he will soon enter. Four behavioral areas were selected, all involving instructions (mands) (Skinner, 1957) or questions involving an implied response. All four make contact with events usually termed "cognitive." All are response modes common to developmental and intelligence tests, and all are functional in home and school environments. They are as follows:

1. *Receptive language.* The child is required to respond to an instruction in a nonvocal manner. In this case, his task was to identify a verbally named object by pointing to a picture of it. This task represents a behavior that contains verbal and preverbal understanding of the child's environment.
2. *Expressive language.* The child is required to respond to instruc-

tions in a vocal–verbal manner. In this case, his task was to identify vocally a pictured object, representing not only an understanding of the instruction and a knowledge of his environment but also the ability to verbalize and communicate this knowledge.

3. *Prepositional language.* The child is required to position an object according to a specified spacial arrangement. In this case, his task was to place a figure relative to a box according to verbally presented instructions. This task represents a high-order receptive response form, requiring not only knowledge of the environment but also knowledge of the interrelations of parts of the environment.

4. *Body awareness.* The child is required to identify parts of his own body. In this case, his task was to respond to combined vocal and nonvocal instructions by identifying vocally a portion of his own anatomy. This task represents a high-order expressive response form requiring cognitive knowledge of himself as a part of the identifiable environment as well as the ability to synthesize mixed-modality stimulation. (See Church, 1961, for an analysis of "active" and "passive" language.)

To develop effective methods of teaching these cognitive skills to children, two approaches were considered: (1) repeated presentation of the cognitive material by an adult (thus maximizing child–adult interaction) to facilitate the learning of the material, and (2) the use of techniques of reinforcement to facilitate the child's learning. Since an obviously critical factor in the child–adult interaction approach is the identity of the adult who is interacting with child, we selected a white male professional, a black female professional, and the child's own mother.

Certain methodological problems are raised when several independent variables are manipulated at one time, the major problem being the determination of the causal factor in a behavioral change. While the traditional pre- and post-test, with control groups, indicates the presence or absence of change, this design *does not* reveal the specific causal factor involved. In order to control for this problem, a multiple-baseline research design was selected (Baer, Wolf, and Risley, 1968; Hall *et al.,* 1970), that requires preexperimental baseline measurements to be taken on several behaviors. The experimental variable is then applied to only one behavior at a time, while baseline measurement of the other behaviors is continued. If a change is noted in the behavior paired with the experimental variable while no changes are observed in the other behaviors, evidence is accumulated that supports the causal nature of the experimental variable. The evidence becomes more compelling as the other behaviors are successively paired with the experimental variable with the same result.

The present study employed the multiple-baseline technique in a like manner, except that periodic (every second or third session) behavioral probes were substituted for continuous measurement at certain times in order to keep each session relatively short. During original baseline measurements, each of the four behaviors was assessed at each session. With the initiation of the experimental conditions, however, only two behaviors were assessed at each session; the behavior under the experimental condition and only one of the remaining three behaviors under baseline conditions. The experimental condition was applied for several continuous sessions to a single behavioral area, and behavioral changes were noted. Sessions during the original baseline at which all four behaviors were measured lasted approximately 30 minutes. Sessions at which one behavior was assessed under experimental conditions and one behavior was probed under baseline conditions lasted approximately 15 minutes.

## METHOD

### SUBJECT AND SETTING

The subject of this study was Johnnie Lee, a 37-month-old black male child whose family members were participants at the Center. The child's mother was present during all sessions and received minimal training in the presentation of stimuli. Sessions were conducted by either of two professionals who were graduate students in psychology, one a white male and the other a black female.

All work was conducted at a Parent and Child Center in urban Atlanta, Georgia. Funded by state and federal governments, the Center offered child day care, monetary incentives, and social services to community residents. Center participants were admitted to the program on the basis of family income (below the current government-determined "poverty level"), the membership of at least one child under 5 years in the family, and a score by the child of less than standardized means on certain developmental and intelligence measures (The Bayley Scales of Infant Maturity and the Stanford-Binet). The families had from one to four participating children. Less than 50% of the families included fathers. The mean age of the participating mothers was 28 years, and their approximate mean educational history was third grade. (Educational data were unreliable, since self-report was the only measure available.)

PROCEDURE

The procedures were similar in all four behavioral areas:

1. *Receptive language.* The adult presented the child with three pictures of different common objects and asked the child to point to the object named verbally, for example, "Point to the cow." Ten pictures of common objects were presented at each session: cow, ball, car, baby, block, key, girl, drum, leaf, and bird. Since the commands given to the children specify their own reinforcement, they are referred to here as *mands* (see Skinner, 1957). The adult's statement, "Point to the cow," for example, would be reinforced by the child's correct response of pointing to the picture of the cow. Pointing to the appropriate picture was recorded as a correct response. After each mand, the adult allowed the child 10 seconds in which to respond. Responses occurring after more than 10 seconds, as well as pointing to an inappropriate picture and not responding, were recorded as incorrect responses. The adult recorded the response and then proceeded to the next mand without differential comment as to the correctness of the child's response.

2. *Expressive language.* The adult presented the child with a picture of a common object and asked him to name the object. Ten pictures of common objects were presented at each session: horse, shoe, bus, dog, turtle, sock, kite, clock, flower, and boy. A clear and audible response by the child was recorded as correct. "Car" was the correct response to the mand given while the adult was showing the child a picture of a car. The adult allowed the child 10 seconds to respond after the presentation of the mand. Responses occurring after more than 10 seconds, as well as inappropriate responses, inaudible responses, and not responding, were recorded as incorrect responses. The adult recorded the response and then proceeded to the next mand without differential comment as to the correctness of the child's response.

3. *Body awareness.* The adult placed her finger on a particular part of the child's anatomy and asked the child, "What is this called?" Ten different body-awareness mands were presented at each session: ear, eye, nose, hair, hand, mouth, teeth, finger, leg, and neck. An appropriate, clear, and audible response by the child was recorded as correct. "Ear," therefore, was the correct response to the mand given while the adult was touching the child's ear. The adult allowed the child 10 seconds after the presentation of the mand in which to respond. Responses occurring after more than 10 seconds, as well as inappropriate responses, inaudible responses, and not responding, were recorded as incorrect responses.

During baseline procedures the adult recorded the response and then proceeded to the next mand without differential comment as to the correctness of the child's response. During reinforcement procedures, however, the adult, following a correct response, praised the child and reinforced him with a piece of sweetened cereal. Following incorrect responses, the adult either verbalized or modeled the correct response while holding the body part.

4. *Prepositional language.* The adult presented the child with a verbal instruction requiring him to place a small wooden figure of a boy in some spatial relationship to a box on the table before him. The child had 10 seconds in which to respond to the mand appropriately. Each of five relationships—on top, in, under, behind, and in front—was presented twice at each session. Placing the figure on top of the box, for example, was the correct response to the mand, "Put the boy on top of the box." Any response occurring after more than 10 seconds was recorded as "incorrect," as was placing the figure incorrectly or not responding. The adult recorded the response and then proceeded to the next mand without differential comment as to the correctness of the child's response.

The adult presented stimuli from all four behavioral areas during the first four sessions. He then presented receptive language stimuli and stimuli from one of the other areas during each of the next three sessions. The child's mother presented expressive language stimuli and stimuli from one of the other three areas during each of the next three sessions. The black female professional presented body-awareness stimuli and stimuli from one of the other three areas during each of the next three sessions. During each of the remaining sessions (sessions 14–26) the adult reinforced responses to body-awareness stimuli while assessing one of the other three areas under baseline conditions.

## RESULTS

Repeated stimulus presentation, without reinforcement, did not improve the child's cognitive skills. However, when reinforcement was used, the child's skills were immediately developed. Figure 8.1 shows Johnnie Lee's low frequency of response in all four areas. Receptive language ranged from 0 to 30% correct, with a mean of 13%; expressive language ranged from 0 to 20%, with a mean of 10%; body awareness ranged from 0 to 20%, with a mean of 10%; and prepositional language ranged from 0 to 20%, with a mean of 13%.

Intensive exposure to each individual area resulted in no behavioral

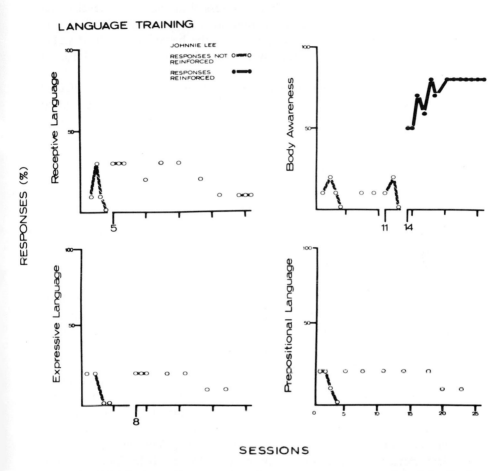

*Figure 8.1* Johnnie Lee—the percentage of correct responses across four behavioral dimensions. Beginning with session 5 and continuing through session 26, two of three dimensions (receptive, expressive, and prepositional language) were selected at random for evaluation. Through session 13, evaluation of body awareness was also random. Reinforcement was introduced at session 14 and was continued through session 26, but was confined to body awareness. Procedural changes that did not prove to be significant are indicated by breaks in the abscissa on days 5, 8, and 11 (see text).

change over baseline observations. Nor was there any change in any of the other three behaviors that were monitored concurrently.

When body awareness, which was assessed at the lowest level of all four behaviors, was then selected for reinforcement, the 80% level of performance was reached in eight sessions, and the behavior remained stable thereafter. No concurrent increases were noted in any of the nonreinforced behaviors.

To determine whether or not the child's performance was affected by the person working with him, three adults were alternately asked to present the material, including the child's mother, a white male professional, and a black female professional. In spite of differences in the educational level, sex, and race of the adults, no systematic effects on the child's performance were noted.

## DISCUSSION

The use of an experimental approach involving multiple baselines, as suggested by Baer *et al.* (1968), appears to be particularly useful in identifying the specific variable responsible for behavioral change. It is apparent that neither long-term repeated stimulus presentation, nor the adult–child interaction according to sex, race, education, and relationship to the child, is critical in the process of cognitive learning. Although not completely demonstrated, it is equally apparent that, as others have suggested (Hart and Risley, 1968; Reynolds and Risley, 1968), reinforcement of the language responses of disadvantaged preschool children is effective in strengthening these behaviors. The effectiveness of the reinforcement procedure is realized in a very short time, and increases in cognitive skill are immediate when food is used as a reinforcer. The increases are specific as well, having an effect only on the behavior that is reinforced. The use of probes rather than continuous measurement seems to be promising as a methodological device for time-saving purposes. Probed behaviors remained stable, and there was no apparent loss of data. Their use, therefore, with young children may be recommended in solving problems associated with long sessions and short attention spans.

The demonstration of the effectiveness of reinforcement in developing behavior in children confirms previous findings (Coleman, 1970; Hopkins, Schutte, and Garton, 1971). The literature in the operant area would suggest that reinforcement is effective when applied by a professional. In this study, no differences were noted in the child's responses irrespective of the sex or race of the adult professional working with him. The pertinent question raised by this demonstration is whether or not persons averaging a third-grade education can be trained to use reinforcement procedures to teach children cognitive skills. Experiment II addresses itself to this issue.


## Experiment II

The outcome of Experiment I indicated that a trained professional can use reinforcement techniques to teach cognitive skills to a deprived child. While it might be desirable to use professionals to achieve similar objectives, the cost to a community-sponsored program is prohibitive. An obvious alternative would be to use trained paraprofessionals to teach the children. Indeed, paraprofessionals are already involved in such programs. Typically they work as aides, caring for the children and exposing them to various experiences such as art, music, personal care, group and interpersonal social behaviors, directed play, and psychomotor activities. This traditional "exposure" method, however, has been found to be largely ineffective in modifying the verbal behavior of children (Hart and Risley, 1968). In addition, each aide must be responsible for the physical needs of 15–20 preschool children (dress, undress, change diapers, take to bathroom, feed, administer first aid, clean up after, etc.), and therefore has little time to do individual, concentrated teaching with the children.

An untapped source for paraprofessional psychology training in deprived communities is the children's mothers. These individuals differ, however, from the educated middle-class mothers who have previously been trained. Their formal education has usually not exceeded the third-grade level. Their reading ability is inadequate. They are not responsive to lecture methods of training or learning. Their history does not lead them to expect that they could be effective teachers of children. They usually communicate in terms of dialects different from those used by professionals. In summary, they seem totally unsuitable for training in imparting cognitive skills to children. There is, however, an urgent need for persons to teach these skills to disadvantaged children, and the children's mothers seem to be the only available group for training. Furthermore, these mothers are the individuals most directly affected by the success or failure of their children. The critical question is whether or not these mothers can be trained to use reinforcement procedures effectively.

In order to avoid some of the more troublesome aspects of training paraprofessionals to teach children (lack of rapport, the child's fear of strangers, the trainee's self-consciousness in teaching someone else's child, racial differences, etc.), it was decided to attempt the training with a person whose relationship with the child avoids these problems: the child's own mother.

The method of training to be attempted with the mother was tailored to her needs and skills. Although she had only a minimal academic background, training was thought to be possible since the reinforcement techniques depend on the specification of (1) the stimulus material as presented by the trainee to the child, (2) the response of the child to the stimulus, and (3) the differential consequences provided by the trainee according to the child's response. The techniques, therefore, involve only observable events and do not require any conceptualizations or analysis of these events.

The differences between academic and topographical behavior training are most clearly evident in the difference in teaching methods used by a teacher and those used by an athletic coach. The teacher deals with abstract conceptual responses that the student can learn and emit only in a verbal form, that is, spoken or written. The coach, on the other hand, deals exclusively with concrete physical responses. His student can learn and emit topographically appropriate responses without any conceptual orientation. The coach demonstrates the behavior, and the student then attempts to match it. He may try a back flip off the high board after watching the coach or another member of the swimming team perform the dive. As he practices matching his behavior to that of the coach, he is given feedback by the coach as to his performance, such as, "Keep your feet together next time." As he observes, practices, and redefines his dive under the coach's guidance, he may be instructed to observe critical environmental contingencies of his behavior. "Do you see how you go higher when you bend your knees more?" The coach may indicate how the student can tell when he has made the appropriate responses. "Remember, the less splash you feel yourself making, the better your dive was." The coach does not expect a perfect dive on the first try, but he does require closer approximations with practice. All along the way, he praises his student's efforts, giving less and less advice, and successively raising his criteria for praise until the target response is made. The student does not need to attain a knowledge of aerodynamics, water surface tension, or coaching methods to perform successfully. All he needs is someone to give him feedback as he attempts to match the observed behavior, and someone to draw his attention to the "natural" environmental consequences of the behavior.

It was this "coaching" method of training, which includes the use of modeling, shaping, social reinforcement, response-contingent behavioral feedback, and fading, which was attempted to train the mother in the reinforcement procedures. Thus, the paraprofessional would gradually assume more and more of the teaching behaviors utilized by the professional.

Since the objective of the training was to bring about an increase in the child's behavior, the trainee's competence in behavioral procedures was evaluated in terms of the child's performance. Based on subjective judgment and the objective behavior of the subject in Experiment I, the child's criteria for success in each behavioral area was defined in terms of his level of competence (80% correct or greater), and variability for at least two consecutive sessions.

## METHOD

### SUBJECT

The subject of this study was Delvin, a 30-month-old black male child whose mother was a participant at the Center. The child's mother was present during all sessions and was trained in the teaching procedures. She had attended school through the fourth grade and was able to read well. Training was conducted by the white male professional.

### PROCEDURE

*Teaching Mothers.* The major objective in developing a training method for individuals in this setting was the emphasis on "cookbook"-type procedures. For this purpose, the concepts of stimulus, response, and reinforcement were translated into specific, tangible, and observable events. Thus, all materials presented to the child, as well as all verbal prompts to be made by the trainee, were explicitly defined and taught as the first step toward determining what the child's reaction to this stimulation would be. The trainer said, for example, "Place one of these ten pictures on the table in front of the child like this." Then he showed the mother where to place the picture. He told her to say, "Delvin, what is this a picture of?" The second step consisted of observing the child's reaction to the stimulus and to the accompanying instruction. The trainer told the mother, "As soon as you finish telling him what to do—remember, say it only once—start your watch. Wait exactly 10 seconds, then mark down 'Yes' or 'No' on this piece of paper. Mark 'Yes' if he said exactly what you told him to say. Mark 'No' if he said anything else or if he did not say anything during the 10 seconds." The third step required that the trainee apply a differential consequence to the child's response. He explained, "If he said exactly what you told him to say and you marked the paper 'Yes,' give him one piece of

cereal and say 'Good boy!' or 'Very good!' If you marked 'No,' either because he said the wrong thing or did not say anything at all, do not praise
him or give him any cereal. Instead, put your finger on the picture you
asked him about and say 'This is a car.' Do this only once, then put the
next picture on the table and start again."

Initially, the trainee simply observed the professional presenting the
stimuli and consequating, timing, and recording responses. She was then
encouraged to record responses, then time and record, then present and
consequate, and finally present, consequate, time, and record. As the professional gradually faded himself out of the teaching role, he shaped the
appropriate behavior of the trainee by praising her attempts, suggesting
improvements, and drawing her attention to those behaviors of the child
that necessitated critical observation. Only the functional aspects of the
reinforcement procedure were taught to the trainee. Abstract generalizations concerning reinforcement principles were excluded. No verbalization
of the methodological or theoretical implications of the procedure were
required of her. To maximize the mother's realization of the relationship
between her behavior and that of her child, certain contingencies were
pointed out in common language, for example, "Did you see how Delvin
tried harder the next time he was asked a question, after you rewarded
him for getting the right answer?" It was made clear to the trainee that she
was not being tested, and that the child's performance or lack of it during
baseline was no reflection on her as a mother, nor on her child's intelligence. The procedure was described as "a good way to teach things to
children" that she might find useful in helping her child to learn many
things he "needs to know." The trainees were specifically asked to avoid
any use of punishment or threat to control the subject's behavior.

*Teaching Children.* The procedures for teaching skills to the child
were similar to those used in Experiment I:

1. *Body awareness.* The trainee placed her finger on a particular
part of the child's anatomy and asked the child, "What is this called?" Ten
different body-awareness mands were presented at each session: ear, nose,
hair, mouth, teeth, finger, leg, neck, and hand. An appropriate, clear, and
audible response by the child was recorded as correct. "Ear," therefore,
was the correct response to the mand given while the trainee was touching
the child's ear. The trainee allowed the child 10 seconds after the presentation of the mand in which to respond. Responses occurring after more than
10 seconds, as well as inappropriate responses, inaudible responses, and
not responding, were recorded as incorrect responses.

During baseline procedures, the trainee recorded the response and
then proceeded to the next mand without differential comment as to the

correctness of the child's response. During teaching procedures, however, she praised the child following a correct response by making a comment such as "Very good," and reinforced him with a piece of sweetened cereal. Following incorrect responses, the trainee verbalized or modeled the correct response while holding the body part (such as saying "ear" while holding the child's ear).

2. *Expressive language.* The trainee presented the child with a picture of a common object and asked him to name the object. Ten pictures of common objects were presented at each session: horse, shoe, bus, dog, turtle, sock, kite, clock, flower, and boy. A clear and audible response by the child was recorded as correct. "Bus," for example, was the correct response to the mand given while the adult was showing the child a picture of a bus. The trainee allowed the child 10 seconds after the presentation of the mand in which to respond. Responses occurring after more than 10 seconds, as well as inappropriate responses, inaudible responses, and not responding were recorded as incorrect responses. During baseline, the trainee recorded the response and then proceeded to the next mand without differential comment as to the correctness of the child's response. During teaching procedures, however, the trainee, following a correct response, praised the child (such as saying "Very good"), and reinforced him with a piece of sweetened cereal. Following incorrect responses, the trainee verbalized or modeled the correct response while showing her child the appropriate picture (such as saying "bus" while showing the picture of a bus).

3. *Prepositional language.* The trainee presented the child with a verbal instruction requiring him to place a small wooden figure of a boy in some spatial relationship to a box on the table before him. The child had 10 seconds in which to respond to the mand appropriately. Each of five relationships—on top, in, under, behind, and in front—was presented twice at each session. Placing the figure on top of the box, for example, was the correct response to the mand, "Put the boy on top of the box." Any response occurring after more than 10 seconds was recorded as incorrect, as was placing the figure incorrectly and not responding. The trainee recorded the response and then proceeded to the next mand without differential comment as to the correctness of the child's response.

4. *Receptive language.* The trainee presented the child with three pictures of different common objects and asked the child to point to the object named verbally, for example, "Point to the cow." Ten pictures of common objects were presented at each session: cow, ball, car, baby, block, key, girl, drum, leaf, and bird. Pointing to the appropriate picture was recorded as a correct response. The child's response of placing his

finger on the picture of the cow, for example, was considered the correct response to the mand, "Point to the cow." The trainee allowed her child 10 seconds after the presentation of the mand in which to respond. Responses occurring after more than 10 seconds, as well as pointing to an inappropriate picture and not responding, were recorded as incorrect responses. The trainee recorded the response and then proceeded to the next mand without differential comment as to the correctness of the child's response.

The professional presented stimuli for all four behavioral areas at each of the first six sessions. The trainee then reinforced body awareness while assessing one of the remaining three areas under baseline conditions. After body awareness had attained the performance and variability criteria of 80% or greater correct for two consecutive sessions, the trainee began teaching expressive language while periodically assessing the other areas, until it reached criteria.

## RESULTS

When Delvin's mother used the reinforcement procedures, the cognitive skills of her child increased significantly over baseline levels. Figure 8.2 shows that Delvin's baseline measurements were characterized by variability. Body awareness ranged from 0 to 80% with a mean of 30%; expressive language ranged from 40 to 60% with a mean of 52%; prepositional language ranged from 0 to 30% with a mean of 15%; and receptive language ranged from 0 to 80% with a mean of 48%.

After receiving training, Delvin's mother began reinforcing her child's body awareness. Within four sessions, body awareness had reached the competency and variability criteria (80% or greater for two consecutive sessions). She then reinforced expressive language and it reached criteria in three sessions, the last two being 100%.

No concurrent increases were noted in any of the nonreinforced behaviors that were also measured by the mother.

## DISCUSSION

It appears that the "cookbook" method of training was effective, since Delvin's cognitive skills, which were reinforced by his mother, clearly improved. The trainee learned to use the procedure quickly (approximately 2 hours of training time), and was able to conduct all phases of the pro-

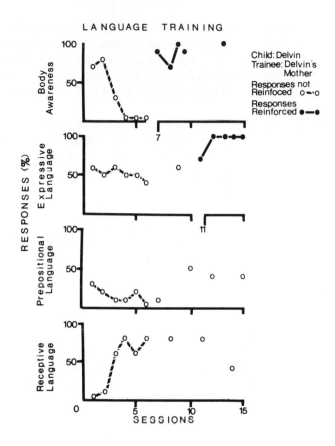

*Figure 8.2* Delvin—the percentage of correct responses across four behavioral dimensions. Delvin's mother conducted sessions 7–15. Reinforcement procedures were initiated on the 7th session for body awareness, and on the 11th session for expressive language. Connected points represent continuous data, and isolated points are probes.

cedure: presenting stimuli, timing, recording, and consequating responses. The consequences used—praise and sweetened cereal—appeared to have been effective in reinforcing cognitive skills, and the criteria used to judge their development (80% or greater for two consecutive sessions) seemed to have been an appropriate and sensitive measure for cognitive responses.

Some problems were encountered, however, in the trainee's subjective reactions to her child's performance. During baseline she seemed to be embarrassed by Delvin's poor performance. Although this embarrassment was replaced by pride as the child's performance improved during reinforcement, it appeared that the mother had felt that her qualifications as "a good mother" were somehow being evaluated. It seemed that more training emphasis should have been placed on the reason baseline was being taken. In other words, she should have been told that the purpose was "to get an idea of what Delvin does not know now so that we will know what to teach him."

The training procedure itself, though effectively demonstrated as appropriate in Experiment II, remained only "promising," since certain questions of its effectiveness were left unanswered by Experiment II: (1) Was training effective only because of certain characteristics of Delvin's mother, such as high intelligence, strong motivation, and so on? (2) Is the training method dependent on the mother–child relationship? (3) Can the mother teach skills successfully to any other child besides the one she was trained to teach? Experiment III was designed to answer these questions.

## Experiment III

Experiment II showed that mothers can be trained to use the reinforcement procedures effectively in teaching cognitive skills to their own children. Wide applicability of such procedures, however, was still open to question. If only the mother can work effectively with her child, the usefulness of the procedure is limited. Some children do not have mothers. Many mothers work outside the home if jobs are available. Even if the mother does not work, the number of children she could help would be limited to her own offspring. If any mother, however, could be trained to work with any child, the usefulness of the procedure to a community center would be greatly increased. Trainees would not be limited to working with their own children, but could work with many children during a single day.

Before endorsing the reinforcement procedure, the paraprofessional training, and the evaluation procedures for each as an effective "teaching package" for community centers, therefore, two central questions must be answered: First, can trainees use the procedure with children who are *not* their own? Second, once trained to work with one child, can the trainee generalize her skills to teaching the material to another child?

To answer the first question, the training of two mothers to teach children who were not their own was attempted. To answer the second question, two trainees, Delvin's mother and one of the new trainees, were instructed to teach a second child once they had finished teaching their own. Once again, the trainees' criteria for achieving competence was defined as improvement in the behavior of the particular child with whom they worked.

## METHOD

### SUBJECTS

The subjects of this study were three black children, two females and one male. Stephy was 33 months old, Maria was 36 months old, and Delvin was 37 months old. Three women were trained to use the reinforcement procedures. They were selected to maximize the possibilty of the effects of trainee reading ability on the outcome of training. $T_1$, who was trained in Experiment II, had attended school through the fourth grade and was able to read well. $T_2$ had attended school through the third grade and was able to read with difficulty. School attendance data on $T_3$ were unavailable, but she could not read. Training was conducted by the white male professional.

### PROCEDURE

*Teaching Mothers.* Training was similar to that conducted in Experiment II.

*Teaching Children.* The procedures for teaching the cognitive skills to the children were similar to those used in Experiment I, with the addition of reinforcement procedures for prepositional language and receptive language.

1. *Prepositional language.* Baseline procedures were similar to those conducted previously. During reinforcement procedures, however, the trainee, following a correct response, praised the child (such as saying "Very good") and reinforced him with a piece of sweetened cereal. Following incorrect responses, the trainees modeled the correct response while giving its verbal description (such as, "The boy is *on top* of the box").

2. *Receptive language.* Baseline procedures were similar to those conducted previously. During reinforcement procedures, however, the trainee, following a correct response, praised the child (such as saying "Very good"), and reinforced him with a piece of sweetened cereal. Following incorrect responses, the trainee modeled the correct response while giving its verbal description, (such as pointing to the car and saying "This is the car").

The professional presented stimuli for two behaviors to each child until sufficient baseline measurements were obtained (four to six sessions per child).

A trainee then reinforced one of the behaviors while assessing the others under baseline conditions for each child. After the first behavior had reached criteria, the trainee began reinforcing the other until it too reached criteria (80% or greater for two consecutive sessions).

$T_1$ and $T_2$ each worked with one child. $T_3$, however, was instructed to work with a second child after she had brought her first child to criteria on two behaviors.

## RESULTS

After receiving training, all three trainees were equally able to increase the cognitive skills of children by using the reinforcement procedure. No increases were observed in the absence of reinforcement.

Delvin's mother, $T_1$, reinforced Stephy's receptive language, which had previously been assessed by the trainer as ranging from 20 to 40% with a mean of 26% under baseline conditions. Figure 8.3 illustrates that while Stephy's receptive language did not reach criteria during six reinforced sessions, all of these sessions exceeded baseline limits, the last two points being 80% and 70%. $T_1$ later probed receptive language under reinforcement conditions, resulting in percentages of 80% and 90%.

Concurrent with her reinforcement of receptive language, $T_1$ conducted two probes of Stephy's prepositional language under baseline conditions, and observed it at 20% and 40%, which was slightly higher than baseline limits of 0 to 20% with a mean of 8%. When she made reinforcement contingent upon Stephy's correct prepositional language responses, the behavior reached criteria within seven sessions, the last two being 90% and 80%.

$T_2$ reinforced Stephy's expressive language, which had previously been assessed by the trainer as ranging from 20 to 50% with a mean of 34% under baseline conditions. As Figure 8.4 shows, Stephy's responses to expressive language appeared to have leveled off at 70% by session 10. Although this level was below prearranged criteria, it was more than twice the mean percentage observed under baseline conditions and was stable. Responses to body awareness, assessed by the trainer as ranging from 0 to 90% with a mean of 38% under baseline, reached criteria in the minimum of two reinforced sessions, both at 90%.

Maria's baseline measurements were nearly nonexistent. During four sessions (80 stimulus presentations), she emitted only one correct response. As Figure 8.5 shows, reinforcement of her receptive language stimuli presentation by $T_3$ resulted in a drastic change in the response rate, as Maria attained criteria in the minimum of two sessions and reached

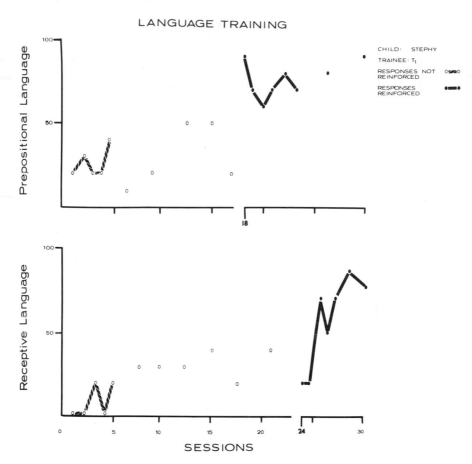

*Figure 8.3* Stephy—the percentage of correct responses across two behavioral dimensions. $T_1$ conducted sessions 17–30. Reinforcement procedures were initiated on the 18th session for prepositional language, and on the 24th session for receptive language. Connected points represent continuous data, and isolated points are probes.

100% during the third reinforced session. Responses to prepositional language stimuli presentations by $T_3$ reached criteria in nine sessions, the last two both being 80%.

A probe of prepositional language taken under baseline conditions by $T_3$, concurrent with the reinforcement of receptive language, resulted in 0% responding. As shown in Figure 8.6, a subsequent probe under reinforcement conditions by $T_3$ indicated that receptive language remained at criteria level.

When $T_3$ applied the reinforcement procedure to Maria's prepositional

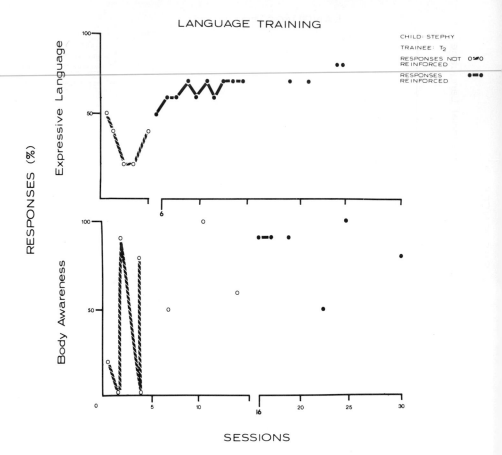

*Figure 8.4* Stephy—the percentage of correct responses across two behavioral dimensions. T$_2$ conducted sessions 5–30. Reinforcement procedures were initiated on the 6th session for expressive language and on the 16th session for body awareness. Connected points represent continuous data, and isolated points are probes.

language, criteria was reached within nine sessions and remained stable at the 80% level for two additional sessions.

At this point, T$_3$ was instructed to discontinue working with Maria and to reinforce Delvin's prepositional language, which had previously been assessed by the trainer as ranging from 0 to 30% with a mean of 15%, and had been observed to increase 10 to 20 percentage points during subsequent probes. T$_3$ brought Delvin's prepositional language to criteria within four sessions.

Concurrent with her reinforcement of Delvin's prepositional language, T$_3$ conducted a probe under baseline conditions of his receptive language and observed it at 10%, which was well within baseline limits.

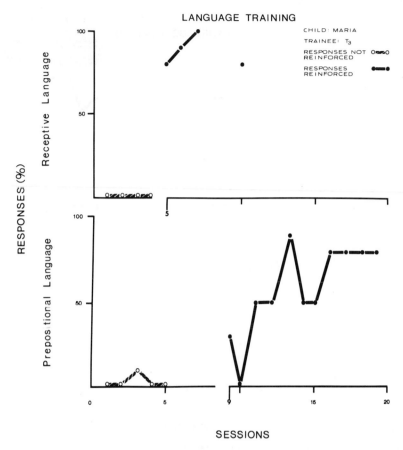

*Figure 8.5* Maria—the percentage of correct responses across two behavioral dimensions. $T_3$ conducted sessions 5–19. Reinforcement procedures were initiated on the 5th session for receptive language, and on the 9th session for prepositional language. Connected points represent continuous data, and isolated points are probes.

When she applied reinforcement to his receptive language, which had previously been assessed by the trainer as ranging from 0 to 80% with a mean of 48%, the behavior reached criteria in the minimum of two sessions, both at 90%.

## DISCUSSION

Experiment III confirmed the effectiveness of the "cookbook" training method demonstrated in Experiment II. Furthermore, the training was extended to persons with only a third-grade ($T_2$) education (or possibly

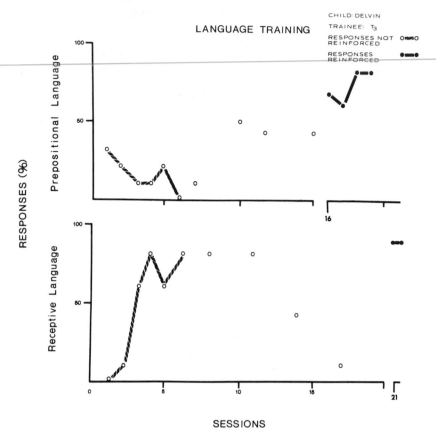

*Figure 8.6* Delvin—the percentage of correct responses across two behavioral dimensions. $T_3$ conducted sessions 16–21. Reinforcement procedures were initiated on the 16th session for prepositional language, and on the 21st session for receptive language. Connected points represent continuous data, and isolated points are probes.

even less in the case of $T_3$, on whom educational data were unavailable). This effectiveness does not appear to be dependent on trainee characteristics such as high intelligence or strong motivation (i.e., based on the desire for one's own child to succeed), nor, more importantly, on the mother–child relationship. It is clearly evident, on the basis of the performance of Delvin's mother and $T_3$, that, once trained, the trainee can generalize her teaching skills to other children, irrespective of whether her training was conducted with her own or another child. The degree of child and task generalization are necessarily empirical questions subject to further study.

## Discussion and Conclusion

This study demonstrates that the training of adults who have had minimal formal education in the application of reinforcement procedures can be accomplished if the training is specifically modified to the needs and abilities of this population. It is obvious that many seemingly complex and technical behaviors, now performed exclusively by professionals, can be learned by paraprofessionals. Although the systematic development and evaluation of such procedures relied on professional expertise, the procedures themselves—presentation of the stimulus material, observation and recording of the child's response, and differential consequation of the response—are topographical behaviors and, as such, can be learned and applied, through imitation, by nonprofessionals. While the analysis of the data requires professionals, the actual implementation of the procedures can, and in the case of the present study, should be accomplished by paraprofessionals. When the needs of any given population far outstrip the physical capabilities of the professionals available, it is the responsibility of those professionals to devise ways of meeting these needs. That is, the professionals must give their skills to those who need skills most (Miller, 1969). This is not to suggest that paraprofessionals will or can replace professionals. It is suggested, rather, that the appropriate use of the paraprofessional will serve to extend the services of the professional, and will also allow him greater opportunities to develop and analyze new procedures and techniques (Ayllon and Wright, 1972).

In the present study, new ways of defining and expanding procedures for the improvement of the cognitive behavior of disadvantaged children were demonstrated. It is clear that these kinds of behavior *are* suited to manipulation by operant procedures. So-called mentalistic concepts, which are of great concern to most people, need not be avoided as the subject of behavioral research. When operationally defined, these concepts become as observable, and therefore measurable, as a bar-press or an "out-of-seat" response. It is appropriate and necessary that the specific needs and intrinsic behaviors of any given population be considered in the application of applied psychology.

Through the course of the present study, several interesting and perhaps population-specific relationships were observed. In the present setting, paraprofessional training was a requirement of the Center's administration rather than an expressed desire of the trainees. Although daily appointment schedules were agreed upon by the trainees a week in advance, they came to the training sessions only about 8% of the time. If, however, the professionals found and reminded them of their appointments at the time they were scheduled, this percentage rose to about 77%. (The remaining 23% of total represented instances in which trainees could not be found or were engaged in some other Center activity that precluded training. No trainee ever refused to come.) This phenomenal nonattendance in the absence of contingent material reinforcement has previously been observed in similar low-income groups (Miller and Miller, 1970). An effort to alleviate this problem was attempted with one trainee in the form of a "verbal contract." The terms of the contract stated that for each day she came to the room used for the training and teaching sessions at or prior to her scheduled time, she would earn $1.00, payable at the end of the week. Furthermore, if she was "on time" each day during the normal 4-day week, she was to receive an additional $1.00 "bonus." It was therefore possible for her to supplement her income by an additional $5.00 a week for an approximate half-hour per day of work. The trainee was "on time" each of the first 3 days of the experiment. On the last day of the week, however, she did not come to the training–teaching session because she attended a special event involving all of the mothers at the center. The attendance procedure and this trainee's participation in the study abruptly ended the following week, when she entered the hospital for minor surgery and was unable to attend the Center during the rest of the study. Although this unfortunate event precluded the identification of any definite effect of the attendance procedure, it was noted that the record of three consecutive days of "on time" behavior attained by this trainee was not matched by any other trainee.

Although the use of punishment to promote the children's cognitive skills was strictly disallowed in experimental sessions, all mothers at the Center were commonly observed to rely on aversive control to affect the behavior of their children outside the experimental setting. This method was never attempted by trainees who were not working with their own children, but on two or three occasions, threats were used by trainees working with their own children in the experimental session. When used to gain the child's attention or to induce him to respond, aversive control always took the form of threats of physical punishment, which were never carried out in experimental sessions. When punishment was used, it appeared to be severe and excessive for children of this age. The fact that mere threats seldom resulted in any observable change in the children's behavior may well have been an effect of the inconsistency between threat and actual punishment. Supportive data for the use of "cookbook" training methods may be found relative to the Center administration's efforts to reduce this use of physical punishment. In the role of "staff member," the professional was required to conduct periodic lectures and discussions with the participants. If, for example, the required lecture concerned the alternatives to using punishment as a means of controlling their children's behavior, few questions would typically be raised during discussion. The mothers would all agree as to the effectiveness of these methods, and verbalize that they might use them. If, however, an example was given, such as, "Suppose you found your child writing on the living room wall with crayons, what would you do?," the mother's typical response indicated a definite lack of understanding of the content previously discussed, such as: "I'd bash him in the head."

Not only does this kind of response demonstrate the futility of lectures and discussions as a method of changing the behavior of this population, it also confirms the social approach taken by the authors. It is held that no professional should attempt to change the behavior of any population, either against their will or without their knowledge. Nor should this be done merely to conform to the norms of some other group. The effort here, in regard to the use of aversive control with children, was not intended to preempt the mothers' style of child rearing nor to change it to fit middle-class norms. Alternative methods of influencing children's behavior were presented because they are considered to be more effective and potentially less harmful (physically and psychologically) to the welfare of the child. In any case, the final decision to use or abandon punishment remained the mother's, once she had been exposed to alternative means. The observation that trainees working with their own children tended to rely on threat and punishment, while trainees working with other people's children never did so suggests that, for maximum effectiveness, training and subsequent paraprofessional activities should *not* pair a mother with her *own* child.

Some evidence of generalization of procedures and influence of principles was observed. One trainee excitedly reported that she had taught her child (who had not been involved in the study) to say "banana" at breakfast that morning by making availability of the fruit contingent upon his verbalizing the name of the fruit, "banana." On another occasion, one of the subjects was having a tantrum during a training session. This behavior was routinely placed on an extinction schedule (Zimmerman and Zimmerman, 1962). The child's own mother, who was not a trainee, came into the room and removed the child. (This and similar behavior by the child's mother resulted in the child's being dropped from the study.) Without prompting, both of the trainees present at the time expressed the opinion that the mother's behavior would only strengthen her child's tantrum response, since she was reinforcing it. (This was not expressed in technical jargon, of course.)

This evidence of generalization is most encouraging. Although the present study did not include an attempt to produce generalization of the trainee's learned abilities to other settings, the desirability of such generalization is clearly great and should be the object of future research.

Although this study avoided the traditional use of large numbers of subjects, control groups, and statistical analysis, the results and conclusions derived from the study are held to be general, reliable, and scientifically important. The experimental methodology used to arrive at these conclusions has been demonstrated both empirically (Hall *et al.*, 1970) and theoretically (Sidman, 1960). This method of research does not force the researcher to disregard the differences among individuals, or to summate the performance of all of the individuals in order to make some general statement. Rather, through repeated measures and systematic application of the independent variable, critical relationships and empirical methods of influencing behavior are identified. The individuality of each research subject is accounted for and, while the basic procedure remains constant, changes in detail, such as the type of reinforcer used, the number of sessions conducted, and so on, are altered to meet individual needs and requirements.

In summary, then, what has been presented here is a means of training paraprofessionals with low academic qualifications (third grade or less), to teach cognitive skills to disadvantaged preschool children. This is seen as fulfilling a critical social need, in that this type of training enables many children to receive early help and perhaps prevents them from being social failures for the rest of their lives. This training is not limited to the mothers of these children. It is suggested that any community organization—a church, a club, a school, a political group, an economic group, or a social action group—could help its community in this way. By consolidating community interest and finances, and by providing a setting for people who desire this type of training, be they mothers, Neighborhood Youth Corps, or just interested neighbors, the group could help the community's children. If rapid social change is to occur, it will be accomplished by people helping each other to build a better community.

## ACKNOWLEDGMENTS
Grateful acknowledgment is due to Evelyn D. Brown, Director of the Edgewood Parent and Child Development Center, for her constant support and encouragement, and to her staff for their assistance and cooperation.

## References

Anastasi, A. More on heritability: Addendum to the Hebb and Jensen interchange. *American Psychologist*, 1971, **26**, 1036–1037.

Ayllon, T., and Azrin, N. H. *The Token Economy: A Motivational System for Therapy and Rehabilitation.* New York: Appleton-Century-Crofts, 1968.

Ayllon, T., and Michael, J. The psychiatric nurse as a behavioral engineer. *Journal of the Experimental Analysis of Behavior,* 1959, **2**, 323–334.

Ayllon, T., and Roberts, M. D. The token economy: Now! In W. S. Agras (Ed.), *Behavior Modification: Principles and Clinical Application.* Boston: Little, Brown, 1972.

Ayllon, T., and Wright, P. New roles for the paraprofessional. In S. Bijou and E. Ribes-Inesta (Eds.), *Behavior Modification: Issues and Extensions.* New York: Academic Press, 1972.

Baer, D. M., and Guess, D. Receptive training of adjectival inflections in mental retardates. *Journal of Applied Behavior Analysis,* 1971, **4**, 129–139.

Baer, D. M., and Sherman, J. A. Reinforcement control of generalized imitation in young children. *Journal of Experimental Child Psychology,* 1964, **1**, 37–49.

Baer, D. M., Wolf, M. M., and Risley, T. R. Some current dimensions of applied behavior analysis. *Journal of Applied Behavior Analysis,* 1968, **1**, 91–97.

Becker, W. C. *Parents Are Teachers: A Child Management Program.* Champaign, Ill.: Research Press, 1971.

Bloom, B. S., Davis, A., and Hess, R. *Compensatory Education for Cultural Deprivation.* New York: Holt, Rinehart & Winston, 1965.

Bronfenbrenner, U. The psychological costs of quality and equality in education. *Child Development,* 1967, **38**, 909–925.

Church, J. *Language and the Discovery of Reality.* New York: Vintage Books, 1961.

Coleman, R. A conditioning technique applicable to elementary school classrooms. *Journal of Applied Behavior Analysis,* 1970, **3**, 293–297.

Deutsch, M. Minority group and class status as related to social and personality factors in scholastic achievement. *Monograph of the Society for Applied Anthropology,* 1960, **2**, 1–32.

Deutsch, M. (Ed.) *The Disadvantaged Child: Selected Papers of Martin Deutsch and Associates.* New York: Basic Books, 1967.

Deutsch, M., and Brown, B. Social influences in Negro–white intelligence differences. *Journal of Social Issues,* 1964, **20**, no. 2, 24–35.

Ferster, C. B., and Skinner, B. F. *Schedules of Reinforcement.* New York: Appleton-Century-Crofts, 1957.

Frost, J. L., and Hawkes, G. R. (Eds.) *The Disadvantaged Child.* Boston: Houghton Mifflin, 1966.

Gardner, J. E., Pearson, D. T., Bercovici, A. N., and Bricker, D. E. Measurement, evaluation, and modification of selected social interactions between a schizophrenic child, his parents, and his therapist. *Journal of Consulting and Clinical Psychology,* 1968, **32**, 543–549; 537–542.

Goldberg, M. L. Factors affecting educational attainment in depressed urban areas. In A. H. Passow, M. Goldberg, and A. J. Tannenbaum (Eds.), *Education of the Disadvantaged.* New York: Holt, Rinehart & Winston, 1967.

Guess, D., Sailor, W., Rutherford, G., and Baer, D. M. An experimental analysis of linguistic development: The productive use of the plural morpheme. *Journal of Applied Behavior Analysis,* 1968, **1**, 297–306.

Hall, R. V., Cristler, C., Cranston, S. S., and Tucker, B. Teachers and parents as researchers using multiple baseline designs. *Journal of Applied Behavior Analysis,* 1970, **3**, 247–255.

Hart, B. M., and Risley, T. R. Establishing use of descriptive adjectives in the spontaneous speech of disadvantaged preschool children. *Journal of Applied Behavior Analysis,* 1968, **1**, 109–120.

Hebb, D. O. A return of Jensen and his social science critics. *American Psychologist,* 1970, **25**, 568.

Hopkins, B. L., Schutte, R. C., and Garton, K. L. The effects of access to a playroom on the rate and quality of printing and writing of first- and second-grade students. *Journal of Applied Behavior Analysis,* 1971, **4**, 77–87.

Hunt, J. M. The psychological basis for using preschool enrichment as an antidote for cultural deprivation. In A. H. Passow, M. Goldberg, and A. J. Tannenbaum (Eds.), *Education of the Disadvantaged.* New York: Holt, Rinehart & Winston, 1967.

Jensen, A. R. How much can we boost I.Q. and scholastic achievement? *Harvard Educational Review,* 1969, **39**, 1–123.

Keller, S. The social world of the urban slum child: Some early findings. *American Journal of Orthopsychiatry,* 1963, **33**, 823–831.

Kennedy, W. A., Van de Riet, V., and White, J. C., Jr. A normative sample of intelligence and achievement of Negro elementary school children in the Southeastern United States. *Monograph of Social Research in Child Development,* 1963, **28**, 6–13.

Lahey, B. B. Modification of the frequency of descriptive adjectives in the speech of Head Start children through modeling without reinforcement. *Journal of Applied Behavior Analysis,* 1971, **4**, 19–22.

McIntire, R. W. *For Love of Children: Behavioral Psychology for Parents.* Del Mar, Calif.: C.R.M. Books, 1970.

Madsen, C. H., Jr., Becker, W. C., and Thomas, D. R. Rules, praise, and ignoring: Elements of elementary classroom control. *Journal of Applied Behavior Analysis,* 1968, **1**, 139–150.

Miller, D. R., and Swanson, G. E. *Inner Conflict and Defense.* New York: Holt, Rinehart & Winston, 1960.

Miller, G. A. Psychology as a means of promoting human welfare. *American Psychologist,* 1969, **24**, 1063–1075.

Miller, L. K., and Miller, O. L. Reinforcing self-help group activities of welfare recipients. *Journal of Applied Behavior Analysis,* 1970, **3**, 57–64.

O'Leary, K. D., and Becker, W. C. Behavior modification of an adjustment class: A token reinforcement program. *Exceptional Children,* 1967, **33**, 642–673.

Pettigrew, T. F., *A Profile of the Negro American.* New York: Van Nostrand Reinhold, 1964.

Reynolds, N. J., and Risley, T. R. The role of social and material reinforcers in increasing talking of a disadvantaged preschool child. *Journal of Applied Behavior Analysis,* 1968, **1**, 253–262.

Riessman, F. *The Culturally Deprived Child.* New York: Harper & Row, 1962.

Roberts, M. D. *Training Third-Grade Educated Women to Teach Cognitive Skills to Disadvantaged Children* (M.A. thesis, Western Michigan University). Ann Arbor, Mich.: University Microfilms, 1972.

Shuey, A. M. *The Testing of Negro Intelligence,* 2nd ed. New York: Social Science Press, 1966.

Sidman, M. *Tactics of Scientific Research.* New York: Basic Books, 1960.

Siller, J. Socioeconomic status and conceptual thinking. *Journal of Abnormal and Social Psychology,* 1957, **55**, 365–371.

Skinner, B. F. *The Behavior of Organisms: An Experimental Analysis.* New York: Appleton-Century-Crofts, 1938.

Skinner, B. F. *Verbal Behavior.* New York: Appleton-Century-Crofts, 1957.

Toffler, A. *Future Shock.* New York: Random House, 1970.

Wheeler, A. J., and Sulzer, B. Operant training and generalization of a verbal response form in a speech deficient child. *Journal of Applied Behavior Analysis,* 1970, **3**, 139–147.

Wolf, M. M., Risley, T., and Mees, H. Application of operant conditioning procedures to the behavior problems of an autistic child. *Behavior Research and Therapy,* 1964, **1**, 305–312.

Zeilberger, J., Sampen, S. E., and Sloane, H. N. Modification of a child's problem behaviors in the home with the mother as therapist. *Journal of Applied Behavior Analysis,* 1968, **1**, 47–53.

Zifferblatt, S. M. *You Can Help Your Child Improve Study and Homework Behaviors.* Champaign, Ill.: Research Press, 1970.

Zimmerman, E. H., and Zimmerman, J. The alteration of behavior of a special classroom situation. *Journal of the Experimental Analysis of Behavior,* 1962, **5**, 59–60.

# 9 SOME EFFECTS OF DIRECT INSTRUCTION METHODS IN TEACHING DISADVANTAGED CHILDREN IN PROJECT FOLLOW THROUGH[1]

**Wesley C. Becker**

In 1967, the U.S. Office of Education undertook an experimental compensatory education program to evaluate possible strategies for overcoming problems in teaching children of the poor. Siegfried Engelmann and the author were given the opportunity to design a program for children in kindergarten through third grade. Officially, we were called a program sponsor—one of 12 selected to begin work in school districts in the fall of 1968. The program we developed was based on Engelmann's earlier work with Bereiter in using direct instruction methods with disadvantaged children and our own work in applied behavioral analysis of classroom problems. During the first year, 13 communities, involving 2000 children in kindergarten and first grade, elected to work with our model. The next year a new grade level was added along with six new communities, raising our total population to 5000 children. In 1970–1971, one more community was added and a new grade level at continuing sites, bringing the number of children in the program to 8000. This year the program is continuing in 20 communities, involving nearly 10,000 children.

Undertaking a field operation of this magnitude has necessitated the development of training, monitoring, and management techniques for

[1] Parts of this paper are taken with permission from W. C. Becker, A teaching-management system to make learning happen, *Florida State University First Annual Conference on School Psychology*, 1972. These studies were supported by grant OEG–0–70–4257 (286) from the U.S. Office of Education.

which we had little experience. This report describes some of the procedures that were developed and preliminary outcome data. The basic
problem was to devise a system to get more teaching going in the classroom. Only if disadvantaged children were taught more could they learn
more.

## Getting More Teaching Going—The University of Oregon
## Follow Through Model (Engelmann–Becker)

There are six basic components to the system:

1. Manpower in the classroom was increased by adding two aides.
2. The daily program was structured so that the teaching personnel
   had a clear plan of action.
3. Daily programmed lessons were provided to insure that the teaching personnel knew what was to be taught in what sequence.
4. A teaching method was instituted that utilized basic operant behavioral principles to insure efficiency in teaching.
5. Continuing training was provided for in the use of the programs.
6. Progress of the children and the skills of the teachers and aides
   were monitored to ensure that the system was functioning.

### INCREASED MANPOWER IN THE CLASSROOM

When children cannot read, the primary means available for instruct-
ing them is by talking to them. It is true that some highly sophisticated
computers could be used to do the job at some point in the future, but
such systems are not now economically feasible. If every child is to be
involved and the school day is fully utilized for instruction at a faster than
average rate, more than one teacher is required for 25–30 children. Because of cost considerations, teacher aides were used rather than more
teachers. For the most part, the aides were parents of the children. This
decision was made for two reasons. First, in providing the legislation that
led to Follow Through, Congress specified that there should be maximum
involvement of the communities to be served in selecting, operating, and
evaluating the programs. Second, it was our belief that parents who learned
good teaching skills would be in a better position to facilitate their children's learning, particularly the learning of their preschool children.

## STRUCTURING THE DAILY PROGRAM

Manpower by itself does not ensure that more teaching goes on in the classroom. The organization of the school day, a good program, and training are needed to use the added manpower effectively. The classrooms are set up so that the three "teachers" are each working in booths (for sound control) with groups of 4–7 children. The teachers and aides become specialists in one of the three basic programs (reading, language, and arithmetic), and a schedule is devised to fit each school's timetable to rotate the children through teaching groups and other activities when the children work on their own. Approximately 30 minutes are used for small-group instruction in each subject area at levels I and II. At level III, 15 minutes of instruction is followed by 30 minutes of self-directed practice in workbooks.

## PROGRAMMED LESSONS

From a behavioral view, the act of teaching involves maximizing the likelihood that children will make the right responses in the presence of the right stimulus. When the teacher presents a letter *m* and asks, "What sound is this?" the children are to learn to respond "Mmmmmmmmmmmm" and not to emit some other response. To achieve the theoretically simple goal of getting children to make the right response in the presence of the right stimulus, however, the teacher must have tools and skill. The primary tool the teacher needs is an effective instructional program, whether the teacher designs it or uses one that is commercially available. If used properly, this tool should help the teacher in the following ways:

It should provide the teacher with examples of concepts that are clear. It should indicate in detail how the teacher can phrase tasks, questions, and directions so that they are clear and unambiguous.
It should sequence the various skills that are to be taught so the children proceed a step at a time.
It should further sequence skills so that the teacher uses teaching time efficiently, by dealing with more than one skill during a lesson.
It should teach "the general case" so that the children master generalized concepts and operations that can be applied to many situations (rather than learning facts and idioms that apply only to limited situations).

An effective instructional program is a potentially powerful tool. As noted later, however, the teacher must have presentational skills in order to take advantage of it. The concepts will not jump from the instructional program into the children's heads and be manifested in their behavior. They must be transmitted through the teacher. If the teacher does a poor job of transmitting, the child cannot be blamed for not receiving. In other words, the problem of "teaching" is not totally solved when an effective instructional program has been introduced; however, the introduction of the program provides a focus for solving the other teaching problems.

The instructional programs used in our Follow Through classrooms are the DISTAR ™ programs (reading, arithmetic, and language). These programs are potentially powerful—particularly with respect to teaching the general case. Consider the following examples.

ARITHMETIC

Let us consider the discrimination approach to teaching arithmetic. It is possible to teach addition as a series of specific problems of this form:

| Stimulus | | Response |
|----------|---|----------|
| 9 + 1 | = | 10 |
| 4 + 5 | = | 9 |
| 7 + 2 | = | 9 |
| 2 + 5 | = | 7 |

The children practice their addition facts (with sums up to 10) until they have learned all problems of this form. Then they can be presented with higher numbers and practice some more. Simple discriminative responses are being taught. In the presence of a particular stimulus, a particular response is very probable.

Alternatively, the task can be broken down into a series of concepts and operations, as Engelmann does in DISTAR, and teach the general case so that the child can solve any of the 40 problems (with sums up to 10) of the form $2 + 7 = \square$.

1. The child is taught to count to any specified number. This is a rote chain.
2. The child is taught to use this chain as a basis for teaching him to count objects. Counting objects is an operation for determining how many are in a group.
3. Symbol identification is taught using concept-teaching rules.
4. Given a numeral, the child is taught to make as many lines as the numeral stands for. This is also an operation.
5. The concepts of plus and equality are taught. "Plussing" is getting some more. Equality is a rule: "As many as we have on this side

of the equal sign we have to have on this side of the equal sign."
The operation of counting is used to verify the equality rule, or to
produce equality. Now when a child is presented with a problem
like

$$4 + 5 = \square$$

he can solve it by putting five lines under the five, touching the 4
and saying "four," and counting "5, 6, 7, 8, 9" as he touches successive lines.

6. A little later, the lines are dropped and fingers are used in the
   operation. "We have four and we plus five." (The children put out
   five fingers on the cue, "and we plus five.") Then they say "Fouu-
   urrr," and count "5, 6, 7, 8, 9," touching each of the five fingers.
7. Still later the children are taught to count from a number to a
   number. They can now handle 40 new problems like this:

$$4 + \square = 9$$

they just need to draw a line or stick out a finger each time they
count "5, 6, 7, 8, 9," and they can produce the answer. With a
slight variation on counting from a number to a number, they can
also do 40 problems of this form:

$$9 = 4 + \square$$

While this approach may take a little more time in building up
basic operations, the dividends are great since the children can
solve whole sets of new problems after completing just a few of
them with their teacher. The basis is also laid for solving algebraic
equations. Note too that each example gives the child practice on
the rote facts. At the end of each example he is trained to say
the whole statement, "four plus five equals nine."

## READING

It is instructive to compare a hypothetical sight-reading program
with the DISTAR reading-by-sounds program. There is no doubt that a
child could be taught to give responses to ten words faster than he could
be taught responses to ten symbols for sounds. It is easier to find words
and word sounds that are markedly different from each other than it is to
find ten letters and sounds that differ in many ways. However, by the time
sounds and blending skills have been taught, the potential basis has been
laid for reading-by-sounds some 720 three-sound words, 4320 four-sound
words, and 21,600 five-sound words. Not all these "words" would have

meaning, but all could be decoded using the basic skills. By the time 40 sounds have been taught, a basis has been established for reading a large percentage of the English language. Irregularities still need to be taught, but the child now has skills that permit an attack on any new words. He has the basic 224 operations for reading.

The strategy of teaching concepts and operations is a powerful one. The child is taught component operations, *which can be recombined* in any number of ways. In the DISTAR reading program, some of the operations taught are *holding* continuous sounds, *switching* to a new sound with no pause (sssssssssssaaaaammmmmm), speeding up the sounds to "say it fast," (sam), and *blending* a stop sound (t, p, b) with the next continuous sound (taaaaannnnn). Also, the child is taught to produce the sounds for any order of letters, even nonsense words. The combination of these operations is reading.

Engelmann's view of concepts and operations leads to considerable power in programming, since it leads one to look for sets of concepts and operations that can be taught using a common format; thus it generates the great savings in teaching associated with so-called learning-set phenomena. For an overview of the DISTAR program, the reader is referred to the DISTAR teacher manuals or to Becker (1972).

## AN EFFICIENT TEACHING METHOD

The DISTAR programs are just words on paper. To teach these skills, which is the objective of the program, the teachers and aides must understand the concepts and operations they are teaching and must have a number of basic teaching skills. These skills involve management of the children and organization of the teaching materials so that both the children and the teacher are ready to work when they sit down in an instructional group. Beyond that, the teacher needs to know how to teach a task—any task. Programs can be broken down into tasks. Tasks also have components:

| Pre-Task | Task | | Post-Task |
|----------|------|--|-----------|
| Get everyone's attention | Present a task signal(s) and teach the children how they are to respond | Signal the children to respond | Reinforce or correct |
| "Listen" | Show the letter *m*: "This is mmmmmm" | "What sound is this?" | "Good" |

Figure 9.1 provides an example from a DISTAR teaching manual (Engelmann, Osborn, and Engelmann, 1970) illustrating the nature of the teacher materials. Each lesson day is broken down into a number of tasks. The visual materials the teacher needs for that task are provided, or she is instructed what to draw on a chalk board. The teacher is given further instructions on what he or she should do (in black) and what should be said (in color). The required child responses are given in italics.

Efficient teaching aims at attaining a high rate of correct child responses within the teaching time available. To accomplish this, the teacher needs to know the formats (tasks) in the program well. The teacher needs to know how to use attention signals most appropriate for each task, and must learn to use a variety of signals to induce the children to respond together (or individually) on cue. These latter signals are called "do it" signals, since they tell the children that it is their turn to "do it." In small-group instruction, "do it" signals are critical to ensuring that each child learns what the teacher is teaching, rather than just imitating what another child is saying. The teacher also needs to learn how to pace each task

**100**                                                                                                      MULTIPLE ATTRIBUTES

Praise the children for correct responses. Correct mistakes immediately.

**Task 2**
Group Activity
**a.** Point to the dogs. What are these? *These are dogs.* Call on one child.
Find the dogs that are little. Everybody, tell me about these dogs.
Repeat, using the dogs that are wearing a hat, are big, and are not wearing a hat.

**b.** Point. Is this dog little? *Yes.*
Is this dog wearing a hat? *Yes.*
Is this dog little and wearing
a hat? *Yes.*
Say the whole thing.
*This dog is little and wearing
a hat.*

**c.** Point. Is this dog little? *Yes.*
Is this dog wearing a hat? *No.*
Is this dog little and wearing
a hat? *No.*
Say the whole thing.
*This dog is not little and
wearing a hat.* Why not?
*This dog is not wearing a hat.*

**d.** Point. Is this dog little? *No.*
Is this dog wearing a hat? *Yes.*
Is this dog little and wearing
a hat? *No.*
Say the whole thing.
*This dog is not little and
wearing a hat.* Why not?
*This dog is not little.*

**e.** Point. Is this dog little? *No.*
Is this dog wearing a hat? *No.*
Is this dog little and wearing
a hat? *No.*
Say the whole thing.
*This dog is not little and
wearing a hat.* Why not?
*This dog is not little and not
wearing a hat.*

Individual Activity
**f.** Call on individual children. Point to a picture. Is this dog little and
wearing a hat? If the dog is not little and wearing a hat, ask: Why not?
Correction Procedure: If children answer "Is he little?" by saying "No, he is
big," say: Yes, but is he little?
If children have trouble, point to a dog. Is he little? Is he wearing a hat?
When a child says "No," say: Well, that's why he's not little and wearing a
hat. He is not little **(or)** wearing a hat.

*Figure 9.1* An example of tasks from a DISTAR lesson.

appropriately, quickly enough to hold attention, yet going slowly when required to give the children "time to think."

The teacher must learn to use reinforcers effectively to strengthen correct responding, and how to correct mistakes in a way that permits all children to learn each task (criterion teaching). Often, teacher praise or confirmation for correct responses may be sufficient reinforcement when the teacher's signals and pacing are sharp. Occasionally, tokens or edible rewards are needed to get the process going. Efficient correction procedures are based on an analysis of the kinds of errors children make. For elementary tasks, there are just three. If the child cannot make the motor response, the teacher leads him through it several times or breaks it into a simpler response and then synthesizes it. If the child has responded to the "do it" signal with a response in the appropriate class, but has made the wrong response (the child says "sss" to $m$), he is given the answer and the task is repeated. If the child fails to respond in the right class (he says "yes" to $m$), the task is modeled (and often several related tasks are given) to teach him to respond to the signal that calls for a sound rather than "yes" or "no." The teacher must never pass over a mistake, and must repeat the entire task after a correction is made to ensure that correction has been effective. With advanced tasks involving more complex formats, the teacher needs to learn how to pinpoint the error and present a pair of tasks selected to teach a critical discrimination. Throughout, what counts is the outcome—whether the children can perform the tasks being taught.

TRAINING AND SUPERVISION

The goal of teacher training is to provide the teacher with the skills outlined in the preceding. This is accomplished in a 2-week preservice workshop, continuing inservice sessions of about 2 hours a week, and through classroom supervision. A number of detailed procedural manuals have been prepared for trainers and participants in training. The key is to specify what the teachers should be able to do, and to devise procedures to teach the required skills. It should be recognized that precision in specifying and training essential teaching skills is possible only within a structured teaching system.

The preservice workshop focuses on teaching the general requirements for teaching any task. This is accomplished through a variety of exercises that involve analyzing a task into its components and through demonstration and practice with a variety of key tasks from each of the programs. The use of signals, precise presentation of tasks, reinforcement, and corrections are emphasized. The procedure is not unlike an actor learning a new role in a play. The participants work mostly in small groups, with a supervisor serving as a coach. Checkouts for proficiency are required periodically throughout the workshop. Time is also devoted to planning classroom schedules and the use of continuous testing for monitoring of progress and regrouping of the children.

A videotape library illustrating administration of key tasks in the program is provided for inservice training. While the preservice training focuses on general requirements for teaching and the key formats for the first 30–60 days of given program, inservice training sessions focus mainly on preparing teachers for new formats arising in their programs. The procedure is still basically the same: practice, critique, practice, checkout. The videotape library allows teachers to practice new formats on their own. Videotapes of classroom teaching are also used in training. Some of these tapes are sent to the sponsor for review and critique.

Another phase of inservice training involves a programmed course in behavior modification and the teaching principles underlying the model (Becker, Englemann, and Thomas, 1971). This is conducted on site, and course credit is provided for this training through the University of Oregon.

Classroom supervision is provided by consultants trained by the sponsor. Many of these are former teachers from the local site. There is approximately one local supervisor for every 200 children in the program. In working with teachers (and aides, of course), the supervisor observes the performance and provides a critique. The supervisor may actually stop a teacher presentation and give a demonstration to the teacher, using her group. Assignments may be given on a specific skill to be checked out on the supervisor's next visit.

Teacher supervisors are also required to make periodic videotapes of their supervision procedures, which are reviewed by our project managers.

## Monitoring

The management of the progress of more than 10,000 children in 20 locations around the country requires a carefully designed monitoring system.

### BIWEEKLY REPORTS AND CONTINUOUS PROGRESS TESTS

Built into the DISTAR programs are teacher-given tests to check each new skill as it is taught. To monitor child progress independently of the teacher, continuous progress tests are given in each area every 6 weeks by paraprofessionals at the Follow Through sites. Every 2 weeks, test results in one area are summarized by child on four-copy IBM forms (with names and numbers preprinted by group). These biweekly reports also show absences for the 2-week period and show where each group is in each program. Copies of the reports go to the teacher, the supervisor, the Follow-Through director, and our data-analysis center. The reports can be used locally to regroup the children directly or to provide special remediation or acceleration. They also provide a basis for summary analyses of progress for management by the sponsor. Trouble spots can be determined and worked on.

The Arithmetic I Continuous Test will be used as an example for all of the tests. The test consists of several tracks covering the major skills in the program. Examine the child record form in Figure 9.2. The abbreviations across the top of the form stand for the skills. OC stands for object counting; CTN stands for counting to a number. Lesson ranges are listed along the left side. The first range is from 1 to 43; the others progress in 10-day intervals. A child fits within one of the lesson ranges according to his lesson day in program when he is tested. The lesson range determines which skills will be tested and the expected scores (baseline) for each child. A child on day 100 in the program should pass test items 7, 15, 25, and 30. He should fail items of a higher number in the given tracks and should pass those of a lower number. Since each item is selected to reflect 10 days of progress in the track, the scores may be interpreted directly. For example, a child at program day 100 who passes only item 23 in track CFNTN (counting from a number to a number) is 20 days behind where he should be in that track. He should pass item 25, but he falls two items below. Each item is worth 10 days. Similarly, a child who passes item 27 in the same track would be 20 days ahead of where he is placed in his group. To make the continuous tests maximally useful to the teachers, keys are provided. The Continuous Test Keys look like Figure 9.2 but give the teacher precise information about where to find examples in DISTAR lessons of the skills that need remediation. For example, if a child fails item 25, the Key tells the teacher to go to Lesson 100, Task 1. For each test item there is an item specified in the program to show the teacher what skills need to be taught. With these procedures, diagnosis is immediate and directly informative to the teacher.

Management reports are produced by computer from the biweekly reports. These reports keep track of group gains in lesson days and on the Continuous Progress Tests. Projections are made and compared with target goals for each group for the year. When projections fall behind goals, adjustments in the program can be made at the site to attempt to reach goals before it is too late to do anything about it. Management reports also

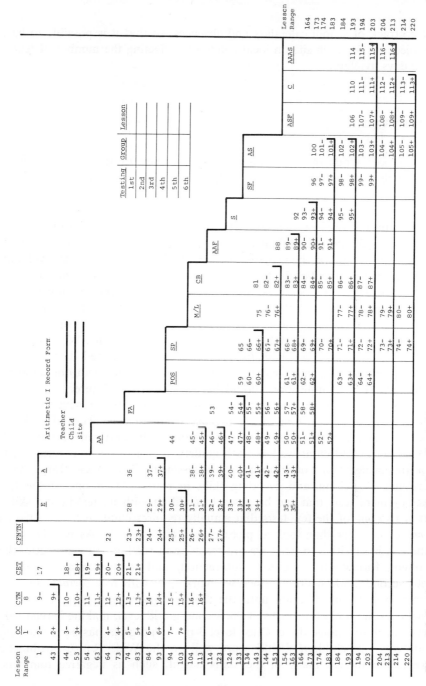

*Figure 9.2* Continuous test recording form for Arithmetic I.

149

keep track of school calendars and absences, so that it is possible to base projections for each site on local conditions affecting the number of teaching days available.

## Outcomes

Three kinds of evaluations are being made of the various Follow Through projects. Stanford Research Institute is largely responsible for a national evaluation with sponsor program comparisons and control group data. Many local school districts are making their own comparisons on tests typically used in their district. After the first year of the program, a sponsor evaluation was initiated to provide the teachers and ourselves with comparative data on the progress of each child, classroom, grade level, and district. The national evaluation is not yet available in a form that identifies sponsors. Data are being withheld in order to protect the longer-term experimental aspects of the project. Many local school district comparisons are available for our projects from the local districts—for example, E. Las Vegas, New Mexico; Grand Rapids, Michigan; and Racine, Wisconsin.

In this report, we shall discuss only sponsor-collected data, and we cannot release data that compare identified communities with one another, although such identification should be possible in the future.

The decision was made in the spring of 1969 to test with the Wide Range Achievement Test and the Slosson Intelligence Test. The Wide Range was selected because it is given individually and can be used with Head Start children as well as sixth graders, and it fit the long-term needs of the project for some normative assessment. The Wide Range tests arithmetic, spelling, and decoding skills in reading. It is one of the few achievement tests that can be given to children with no test-taking skills. It is also one of the few tests that actually requires children to read words out loud, rather than look at pictures and circle words. As will be seen, the test is sensitive to what we are teaching in reading. In arithmetic, the column formats for addition, subtraction, and multiplication handicap our second-grade children, since we work only with row formats in subtraction and multiplication until the third program year. Also, the arithmetic test has only four items at the second-grade level, making it relatively insensitive to change there. Once level 3 of the program has been reached, however, our children should score well on the Wide Range Arithmetic Test even though many of the skills taught, such as negative numbers, factoring, and revaluing, and most of the fractions taught are not covered by the test. Spelling data are not included in this report, but are available and generally parallel those for arithmetic.

The Slosson Intelligence Test is a short IQ test modeled after the Stanford-Binet. It can be given and scored in 20 minutes. It was included in an attempt to measure progress in conceptual skills taught by all three of our programs, but especially the language program. The lack of first-year pre-test data has hindered our evaluation of findings with this test, but some preliminary analyses of interest can be presented. Basically, we still lack a good evaluation of our language program beyond our Continuous Progress Test.

TEACHING AND TEST PROGRESS

The first data presented here demonstrate that teaching can make a difference. There are, surprisingly, very little data of this nature in educational research today. Figure 9.3 plots classroom means for scores on WRAT reading against classroom means for final day in program for DISTAR reading. The figure is based on data from 3700 children. This graphic display indicates a very close relationship between the number of lessons taught to children and their test scores in reading. This function implies that efforts to ensure that more lessons are taught to each child are likely to lead to improved rates of skill development.

A similar relation between teaching and test progress is given in Figure 9.4 for arithmetic. Note that during level 2, classroom progress is not as closely mirrored by the WRAT as during levels 1 and 3. As suggested earlier, this is very likely due to the fact that most work with column functions is delayed until level 3, and the WRAT focuses on column addition, subtraction, and multiplication. By the end of level 3, however, the children in our program should score at least at the fourth grade level on the WRAT.

GAINS

Figures 9.5 and 9.6 present 2-year gains by grade groups, separated for sites with and without kindergarten in our program. The children for whom there were no data in 1972 were not eliminated from the previously calculated gains between 1970 and 1971. Thus, there is some small distortion in viewing these data as pure gain scores. The reader should note

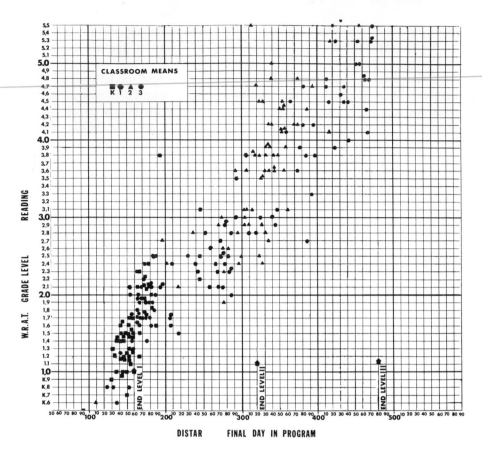

*Figure 9.3* Relationship of average final day in program, DISTAR reading, to Wide Range reading performance. Based on 3700 children. Each dot is a classroom mean.

that the data presented in Figures 9.5 and 9.6 are based only on OEO-defined children of the poor. Nonpoor children in our programs have been eliminated from these analyses. It should also be noted that the WRAT measures decoding skills in reading, not comprehension. However, our continuous tests show that comprehension skills are also being mastered.

    With a little extrapolation, it can be seen from Figure 9.5 that the gain in reading from pre-kindergarten to post-third grade is 4.8 grade levels. The gain from pre-first to post-third grade is 4.1 grade levels. It is worth noting that the expected gain for economically disadvantaged children has typically been reported at about 0.6 grade levels per year. Also note that the gains of children starting in kindergarten are nearly the same as those of children starting in first grade. This evidence strongly contra-

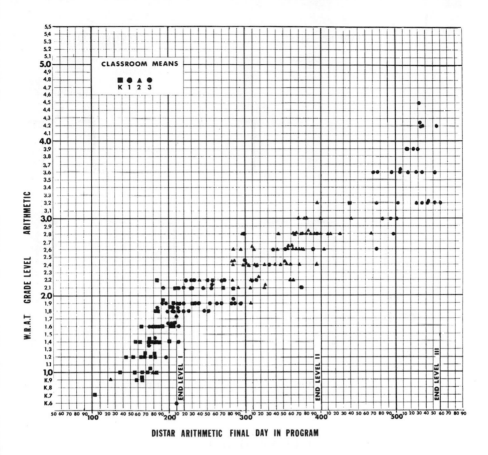

*Figure 9.4* Relationship of average final day in program, DISTAR arithmetic to Wide Range arithmetic performance.

dicts opinions that kindergarten children are not ready to learn to read, and these data are on *disadvantaged kindergarten* children.

The gain data in arithmetic presented in Figure 9.6 are not as dramatic as those in reading, but they show that generally a year of test gain for a year of instruction is being obtained with disadvantaged children. With children starting in kindergarten, we are matching or beating national norms. With those starting in first grade, we are still falling short of this objective. Part of the difficulty is that we have no means of ensuring that all our poor children complete 3 years of the program in 3 years of time. Because priority has been given to reading, arithmetic has sometimes been slighted.

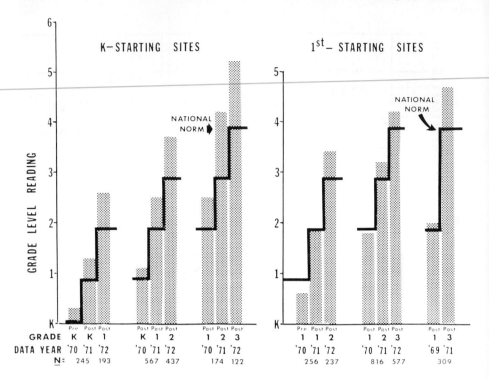

*Figure 9.5* Wide Range reading gains for poor children in program for at least 130 days per year. See text for qualification of gain scores.

GAINS AS A FUNCTION OF LESSON DAYS TAUGHT

Figures 9.7 and 9.8 present each gain analysis from Figures 9.5 and 9.6 respectively, and plot WRAT gains as a function of lesson days taught in the program each year. Both figures show that for various groups of children, the gains in lessons taught are closely related to gains in test performance. Whether children start in first grade or kindergarten has little effect on gain scores (parallel slopes), but children starting in first grade tend to start with more skills.

The important benefits of starting reading earlier is further supported by the analysis of Figure 9.9. Comparisons are made at the end of first grade and at the end of second grade between groups of children who had our kindergarten program (E-B kg) and those who had a traditional kindergarten or no kindergarten. At the end of the first grade, those children in the Follow Through kindergarten program were 0.7 grade levels

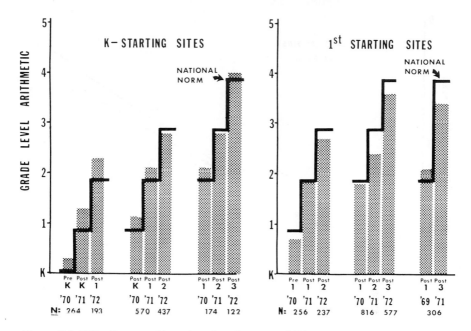

*Figure 9.6* Wide Range arithmetic gains for poor children in program at least 130 days per year.

ahead of the other two groups. At the end of second grade, these same children were 1 year ahead of the other two groups and more than 1 year above grade norms. This kind of evidence shows that just any kind of kindergarten experience will not necessarily contribute to the development of reading skills. It also shows that one way to give disadvantaged children a running start in skills they will need to be successful in school is to start teaching them earlier.

## EVIDENCE OF PROGRAM IMPROVEMENT

With good monitoring of field studies, it should be possible to demonstrate continual improvement in implementation. Figures 9.10 and 9.11 compare overall performance of our children (poor and nonpoor) from the same classrooms over 2 consecutive data years. These averages include late-entering children (e.g., third-grade children starting at level 1). With one exception, the performances for the various grade groupings show improvement for 1972 over that for 1971. The gain in performance averages about 0.3 grade levels for the 8000 children tested. While it is not

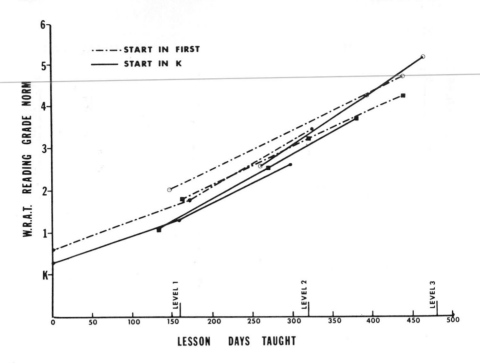

*Figure 9.7* Reading gains on the Wide Range as a function of lessons taught.

possible to isolate the program changes responsible for their gains, our guess is that improved training methods are largely responsible.

Studies are currently being initiated to examine the contributions of teacher performance and management variables to program effectiveness.

## Summary

We have described a teaching–management system for basic instruction for disadvantaged children. The program is based on the assumption that children can learn if they are taught more in a given period of time. The basic components of the Engelmann–Becker Follow Through model involve increasing manpower in the classroom, providing a structured plan of action, providing programmed materials for small-group direct instruction, utilizing operant behavioral principles to ensure efficient teaching at the level of single tasks, providing continuous training, and monitoring the progress of teachers and children to be sure the system is working.

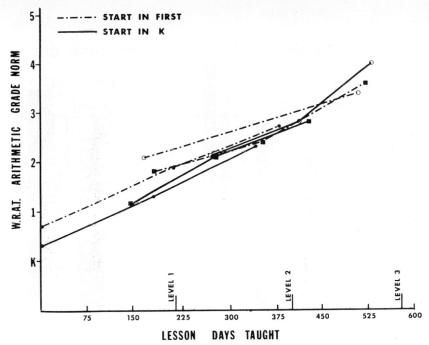

*Figure 9.8* Arithmetic gains on the Wide Range as a function of lessons taught.

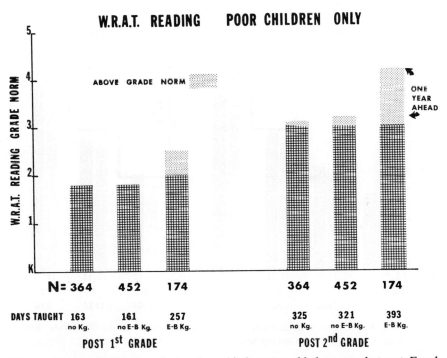

*Figure 9.9* Analysis of the effects of no kindergarten, kindergarten but not Engelmann–Becker kindergarten, and Engelmann–Becker kindergarten on reading levels at the end of first and second grades.

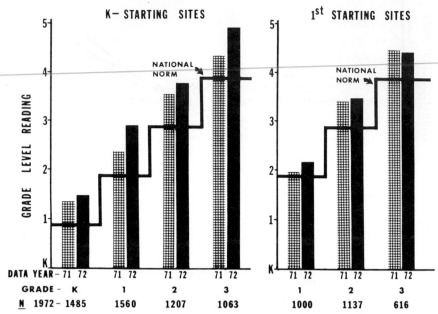

*Figure 9.10* Improvement in average reading performance on the Wide Range from spring testing, 1971, to spring testing, 1972.

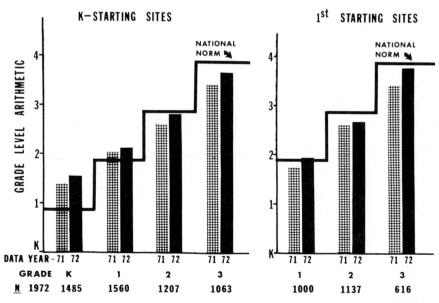

*Figure 9.11* Improvement in average arithmetic performance on the Wide Range from spring testing, 1971, to spring testing, 1972.

The results after 4 years are extremely encouraging in reading and promising in arithmetic. The results to date show that it is valuable to start instruction in kindergarten, if the idea is to give the children a strong start.

These findings with disadvantaged children support the idea that better applications of what we know about the learning process could do much to alleviate many school problems now attributed to the children and their backgrounds rather than the system of instruction.

## References

Becker, W. C. A teaching-management system to make learning happen. *Florida State University First Annual Conference on School Psychology,* Tallahassee, Florida, February, 1972.

Becker, W. C., Engelmann, S., and Thomas, D. R. *Teaching: A Course in Applied Psychology.* Chicago: SRA, 1971.

Engelmann, S., Osborn, J., and Engelmann, T. *DISTAR Language 1.* Chicago: SRA, 1970.

# 10 BEHAVIORAL DIAGNOSIS AND ASSESSMENT IN TEACHING YOUNG HANDICAPPED CHILDREN[1]

Sidney W. Bijou
Jeffrey A. Grimm

This paper discusses behavioral diagnosis and assessment as it applies to teaching, particularly to teaching young retarded and emotionally disturbed children. Teaching is viewed as the arrangement of conditions to expedite learning by a child (Skinner, 1968). The conditions refer to the curriculum materials, the pedagogical practices of the teacher, and the social and physical setting, which is the class and classroom. The target behaviors of teaching in this instance are academic tool subject behaviors and personal–social behaviors that facilitate learning (e.g., good attending behavior). In this paper we shall be dealing with children between the ages of 5 and 8 who have demonstrated serious behavior problems in kindergarten or the first grade in the public schools.

## Diagnosis

The diagnostic practices in the special education of retarded and emotionally disturbed children cannot be adequately discussed without a consideration of the concept of etiology. Etiology, a term borrowed from medical practice, generally refers to the cause of a school problem. For

[1] The research described here was supported by the U.S. Office of Education, Division of Research, Bureau of Education for the Handicapped, project 23–2030, grant OEG–0–9–232030–076.

example, reading disability is said by some to be caused by a single factor such as organic impairment or dysfunction (e.g., primary dyslexia). Others view reading disability as being caused by many factors, some empirically defined (e.g., visual defects and social maladjustment) and some hypothetical constructs (e.g., poor auditory association and limited short-term memory).

The search for or creation of single or multiple causal factors, empirically or hypothetically defined, is based on the assumption that a school problem is a symptom of some pathology. This is a tenable assumption if one accepts the illness model for analyzing school problems. However, the adequacy of this model for conceptualizing behavior problems in and out of school has in recent years been seriously questioned on the basis of empirical findings (e.g., Bringmann, Mueller, Balance, and Matijiw, 1970b, 1971).

It has also been seriously questioned on theoretical grounds (e.g., Bringmann, Mueller, Balance, and Matijiw, 1970a). From the point of view of an experimental analysis of behavior (Skinner, 1953, 1968), for example, a school problem is important in its own right and not as an indication of some underlying condition. The behavior is of concern because it is aversive to someone (in many instances the child himself) and because it is the phenomenon that must be analyzed and altered in arranging a treatment program, educational or otherwise. Problem behavior, like *any* class of behavior, is caused by, or is a function of, the genetic and personal history of the individual and his current situation. We take his genetic history as given and try to understand the child's personal history.

To know the personal history of a child with a school behavior problem requires knowledge of the actual interactions that have constituted his development (Bijou and Baer, 1961, 1965). Information of this sort is not ordinarily available to the teacher or school psychologist, and attempts to obtain even faint hints from secondary sources (e.g., retrospective accounts, questionnaires, and psychological tests) have proven wholly inadequate (Yarrow, Campbell, and Burton, 1968). The difficulty of identifying the historical determinants of a class of behavior does not degrade the diagnostic endeavor, because knowledge of a child's past interactions with the environment is *not* necessary. Remedial education cannot undo or redo the history of a child. It can, instead, arrange an environment that encourages a child to learn the behavior repertoires he lacks and to modify those behaviors that have proven disadvantageous from the point of view of cultural demands. Knowledge and application of behavior principles, not knowledge of the child's history, can serve to accomplish these ends.

To contend that it is unnecessary to know the actual interactional events in the history of a child does not mean that background material about him should be ignored. Information that is ordinarily considered a "history" throws light on a child's current home and neighborhood conditions, and such data must be taken into account in planning ways to augment and generalize school learning.

Let us consider the usual diagnostic practices in special education. Diagnosis generally refers to the use of psychometric, medical, educational, and clinical techniques to obtain data used to place a child in one or more classification categories, such as psychiatric (autistic), intelligence (borderline), or educational potential (trainable). It may also involve a prediction of the child's performance. This concept of diagnosis is based on three highly questionable assumptions: (1) that there is currently available a specific treatment program for children included in each of the diagnostic categories, (2) that these treatment techniques are well known to the teacher, and (3) that the teacher has the facilities, equipment, and personnel to put them into operation as needed. Although there is considerable discussion about the need for differential treatment of the autistic, the brain injured, and the deprived, the remedial program proposed for one category is *not* contraindicated for children in other categories. For example, a program developed on a population of clinically inferred, brain-damaged children could be used without detrimental effects on a group of hyperactive children not diagnosed as brain damaged. In regard to the second and third points, the programs described in the literature or on the market for presumably specific categories of children are not necessarily known to special teachers, and those that may be known cannot be readily actualized under most existing school conditions.

A variation of the classification and treatment format is the diagnostic hypothesis-testing model articulated by Bateman (1967). For her, diagnosis consists of the following:

1. Determination that a problem exists.
2. Behavior analysis of the problem area.
3. Diagnostic testing of possible correlates or underlying disability areas in receptive language (tactile–kinesthetic, visual, and auditory), internal processes (assimilation, storage, and retrieval), and expressive language (motor and social).
4. Formation of a diagnostic hypothesis that leads directly to the remediation of the primary disability area and then to broadening the scope of remediation to include (a) related disability areas and (b) general application to problem area as indicated in (1) above.

Although these procedures focus on an analysis of an individual child, they are unnecessarily circuitous. This roundabout course is necessitated by the assumption of underlying hypothetical variables or conditions. It includes (1) determination and analysis of the problem, (2) a search for the presumed underlying primary disability areas, (3) the preparation of a program designed to remedy the primary disability areas, (4) the preparation of a program designed to remedy related disability areas, and (5) the preparation of a program designed to remedy the problem behavior. An alternative direct procedure would involve only the first and last steps: determination and analysis of the problem, and preparation of a program to remedy the problem behavior.

Diagnosis, from the point of view of behavioral analysis, consists neither of placing a child in a diagnostic category, nor of making a prediction, nor of speculations about previous historical interactions, nor of a search for hypothetical underlying areas, neurological or otherwise. Diagnosis is, instead, *oriented toward determining the conditions that would probably develop new behavior and modify the problem behavior.* It consists of ascertaining the relevant repertories in objective behavioral terms and of specifying in concrete ways the kinds of educational programs that would probably remediate the problem. Since impressions or hypotheses of the required conditions change with the availability of new information, the diagnostic procedure starts with the initial evaluation and continues throughout the treatment process.

### Assessment for Diagnosis

The behavioral approach to diagnosis involves three sets of interrelated assessment procedures arranged chronologically with respect to the entire treatment procedure. The first set provides information about the child's repertoires in the areas that are the instructional target (baseline). These findings are the basis for decisions concerning the appropriate starting places in a child's educational program. Starting a child at the level of his strengths gives him an opportunity to make progress in school work at the outset and to be reinforced for his efforts. This is a well-known remedial practice, as Bateman (1967) points out: "A basic premise of remediation in cases of learning disability is that one must determine exactly where the child is functioning and begin instruction at or slightly below that point. Diagnostic testing is a valuable aid in this determination [p. 22]." In a behavioral approach, however, the teacher does not seek to determine "where the child is functioning" but rather what the child can *actually do* in the task that is presenting the problem. Furthermore, diagnostic testing, if it means assessing behavior inventories, is not only "a valuable aid" but an *indispensible* tool, as we shall see.

The second set of assessments yields running accounts of the adequacy of the program, including teaching materials, response contingencies, response requirements, and contextual factors. These measures provide essential information on which to base decisions about changing the programs. The third set of assessments indicates the child's competencies at the end of training. The differences between the baseline and terminal measures indicate, in objective terms, the child's progress over the treatment period.

All assessments can and should be made by the teacher. In most school systems the school psychologist assesses the abilities and achievements of the child. Using psychometric tests and a modified form of psychoanalytic theory, he attempts to categorize the child, predict his performance in class, and analyze his personality in "dynamic" terms. Little of the information in the psychologist's report is helpful to the teacher in planning an instructional program, because generally it does not refer to the *specific things* the child can do. Even if the school psychologist were trained to provide the kind of information that is relevant to individual program planning, it would still be preferable for the teacher to evaluate her own pupils. The assessment process gives the teacher first-hand acquaintance with what the child can do, his style of performing, and his responsiveness to social contingencies. This kind of direct knowledge is far more helpful to him or her than a verbal account by someone whose responsibility to the child is already finished.

## ASSESSMENT PRIOR TO INSTRUCTION (BASELINE)

As we indicated earlier, assessment prior to remedial instruction provides information for preparing tailor-made instructional programs for the child. Data for this purpose are derived from (1) direct observation, (2) reports and interviews, (3) psychometric tests, and (4) inventories and behavioral surveys.

### DIRECT OBSERVATION

Direct observation of a child's social and academic behaviors, both in the classroom from which he was referred and in the special class during the first few weeks after enrollment, can be recorded by verbal descriptions, rating scales, and checklists. However, the most serviceable technique found to date is counting the frequency of occurrence of selected classes of behavior. Since this technique of recording has been discussed in detail elsewhere (Bijou, Peterson, and Ault, 1968; Bijou, Peterson, Harris, Allen, and Johnston, 1969), and since the literature on its use in the school has been comprehensively reviewed recently (Bersoff, in press), only examples will be given here.

One such example pertains to observations of a 6-year-old boy in the first-grade classroom from which he was referred. The data, collected during the reading period, are presented in Table 10.1 under "A." Each box represents a continuous 10-second period. There are 30 boxes representing 6 minutes. On-task behavior (working appropriately with the reading materials) and off-task behavior (anything other than on-task behavior) are coded as N and F, respectively. Each 10-second box was scored for the occurrence of either or both of these behaviors. Of the entries, 50% were Ns and 44% were Fs, with an overall observer reliability of 97%. Hence, the child was on-task for only a bit more than half of the total 6-minute observation periods and had a high rate of switching from reading to nonreading behavior (five times).

A second example is the behavior of another 6-year-old boy during a reading period in a public school first-grade classroom. The method of collecting data, shown under "B" of Table 10.1, gives more information about the child's off-task behavior as well as some indication of its social consequences. The child was on-task 33% and off-task 67% of the observation period. Off-task behaviors, which included physical aggression, teasing, destroying materials, disrupting other children's study, and sitting quietly doing nothing were recorded in the third row of the data sheet. The only off-task behaviors observed in the sample data shown in Table 10.1 were "disrupting other children's study," shown as 3, and "sitting quietly doing nothing," designated as 6. When the child was off-task, he disrupted other children 27% of the time and sat quietly 73% of the time. The consequences of his behavior (e.g., peer attention, teacher attention, approval, and teacher admonishment), shown as "I" entries in the second row of the "B" section of Table 10.1, indicate the intervals in which the teacher paid attention (talked) to the child. (See boxes 13, 20, and 21 in the first row.) Although the child was on-task 33% of the time, the teacher paid attention to him primarily when he was off-task. It is quite possible that the teacher's differential attention at least partially controlled this child's high rate of off-task behaviors.

Data from direct observation of a child in the classroom from which he had been referred should be interpreted with caution. First, the presence

**TABLE 10.1**
EXAMPLES OF DATA ON TWO CHILDREN (A AND B) TAKEN IN A PUBLIC SCHOOL CLASSROOM

**A**

| 1 | 2 | 3 | 4 | 5 | 6 | 7 | 8 | 9 | 10 | 11 | 12 | 13 | 14 | 15 | 16 | 17 | 18 | 19 | 20 | 21 | 22 | 23 | 24 |
|---|---|---|---|---|---|---|---|---|----|----|----|----|----|----|----|----|----|----|----|----|----|----|----|
| N | N | N | N | N | N | F | F | F | F | F | F | F | F | F | F | F | N | N | N | N | F | F | N |

| | | | | | | 25 | 26 | 27 | 28 | 29 | 30 | 31 | 32 | 33 | 34 | 35 | 36 |
|---|---|---|---|---|---|----|----|----|----|----|----|----|----|----|----|----|----|
| | | | | | | N | F | N | N | F | N | F | N | N | N | N | N |

**B**

| 1 | 2 | 3 | 4 | 5 | 6 | 7 | 8 | 9 | 10 | 11 | 12 | 13 | 14 | 15 | 16 | 17 | 18 | 19 | 20 | 21 | 22 | 23 | 24 |
|---|---|---|---|---|---|---|---|---|----|----|----|----|----|----|----|----|----|----|----|----|----|----|----|
| N | N | N | N | N | N | N | F | F | F | N | N | F | N | N | N | N | N | F | F | F | F | N | N |
| | | | | | | | | | | | | I | | | | | | | I | I | | | |
| | | | | | | | 6 | | 6 | | | 6 | | | | | | 6 | 3 | 3 | 3 | | |

| 25 | 26 | 27 | 28 | 29 | 30 | 31 | 32 | 33 | 34 | 35 | 36 | 37 | 38 | 39 | 40 | 41 | 42 | 43 | 44 | 45 | 46 | 47 | 48 |
|----|----|----|----|----|----|----|----|----|----|----|----|----|----|----|----|----|----|----|----|----|----|----|----|
| F | N | F | F | F | F | F | F | F | F | F | F | F | F | F | F | F | F | F | F | F | F | F | F |
| I | | | | | | | | | | | | | | | | | | | | | | | |
| 6 | | 3 | 3 | 3 | 3 | 3 | 3 | 3 | 6 | 6 | 6 | 6 | 6 | 3 | 6 | 6 | 6 | 6 | 6 | 6 | 6 | 6 | 6 |

| 49 | 50 | 51 | 52 | 53 | 54 | 55 | 56 | 57 | 58 | 59 | 60 | 61 | 62 | 63 | 64 | 65 | 66 |
|----|----|----|----|----|----|----|----|----|----|----|----|----|----|----|----|----|----|
| F | F | F | F | F | F | F | F | F | F | F | F | F | F | N | N | N | N |
| | | | | | | | | | | I | I | I | I | I | | | |
| 6 | 6 | 6 | 6 | 6 | 6 | 6 | 6 | 6 | 3 | 6 | 6 | 6 | 6 | | | | |

167

of an observer in the room may suppress or facilitate the behavior output of the child. The observer can minimize these effects by entering the classroom unobtrusively, by immediately breaking eye contact with the child, should it occur, and by making observations at different times of the day (Bijou *et al.*, 1968). Second, the presence of an observer in the room may cause the teacher to alter her usual classroom behavior, with resulting changes in the child's behavior. Third, some problem behaviors (e.g., physical aggression toward other children) have wide daily variability. Fourth, the data collected usually constitute only a small sample of the child's usual behavior in the classroom.

Another example of using direct observation for baseline information pertains to a child's on-task behavior when he is with a tutor or a teacher and when he is assigned to work alone (e.g., coloring with crayons or copying letters from a model). Figure 10.1 shows the behavior of a 6-year-old girl, R. B., in 21 tutored and 15 untutored academic sessions in the remedial classroom. Each successive 10-second period during an observation session was scored if she was on-task for more than half of the interval. It can readily be seen that R. B. was consistently on-task when being tutored, and generally off-task when the teacher gave her attention only intermittently. The arrows indicate the sessions in which reliability measures were taken. Reliabilities for tutored sessions ranged from 0.94 to 1.00 and for untutored sessions from 0.97 to 1.00. The information obtained suggested that R. B.'s daily program should include tutoring, and that the tutoring sessions should be designed not only to help her make rapid progress in the academic subjects but to teach her how to work alone productively. The latter would be accomplished by the proper use of percentage and intermittent schedules of reinforcement (Bijou, 1972).

REPORTS AND INTERVIEWS

The second source of baseline information is medical reports and interviews with parents, teachers, and school psychologists. It goes without saying that any mention in the medical reports of poor health, physical disability, or ongoing treatment regimes is taken into account in preparing a program for a child, and any indication of sensory or motor disability or problem is referred for specialized medical evaluation and treatment.

As we indicated earlier, information from interviews with parents, teachers, and school psychologists is not viewed as providing clues for the reconstruction of a child's history but rather as indicators of the conditions prevailing in his current situation. Leads on the kind of support and cooperation the teacher may expect from the parents are of special interest.

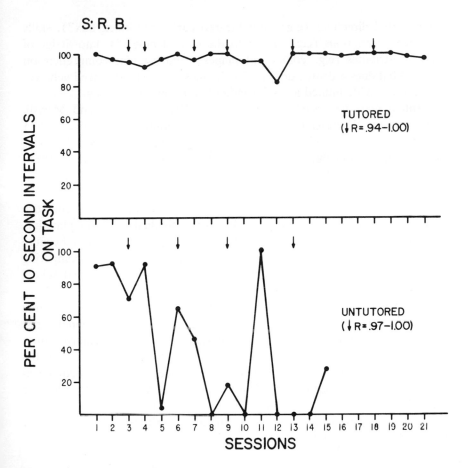

*Figure 10.1.*

STANDARDIZED TESTS

The third source of information is the child's performance on standardized tests. Standardized tests of intelligence and school achievement both yield information about the child's performance as compared with other children of the same chronological age. Standardized school achievement tests yield measures of the child's academic behavior based on selected samples and are expressed in terms of average grade level or age norms. Because of their low "floors," the Wide Range Achievement Test (Jastak, Bijou, and Jastak, 1965) and the Caldwell Preschool Test (Caldwell, 1967) are often used. The Wide Range Achievement measures oral word reading and writing, spelling, and arithmetic; the Caldwell measures personal information (e.g., name, address, and body parts), ability to follow verbal directions (e.g., "put the red car in the black box"), skills in numerical relations (e.g., "point to the second object"), knowledge of physical attributes (e.g., colors and shapes), and listening comprehension (e.g., "What does a dentist do?"). For the most part, standardized achievement tests provide limited leads for individual program planning.

Intelligence tests such as the Stanford-Binet (Terman and Merrill, 1960) and the Wechsler Intelligence Scale for Children (Wechsler, 1967) indicate a child's aptitude for work in the regular public school classes as they are now constituted, organized, and conducted (Anastasi, 1968; Humphreys, 1971). Because each can be administered in 10–20 minutes, the Peabody Picture Vocabulary Test (Dunn, 1959) and the Slosson Intelligence Test (Slosson, 1963) are often used for this purpose. Intelligence tests provide practically no information for individual program planning. They are often given in a behaviorally oriented special class only because they provide data for school personnel who are interested in comparing a child's school aptitude with children of similar age in a typical school grade placement.

Recently, the use of psychometric tests to evaluate school children has come in for considerable criticism by parents and professionals. The position usually taken is that almost all such tests are particularly unfair to children who are disadvantaged in one way or another, and are, because of their emphasis on school-type experiences, less than adequate as measures of intelligence even for so-called normal children. Demands have been heard that such tests should be abandoned by the schools or used only with the consent of the parents. In further criticism of psychometric tests, Cronbach (1970) writes:

> I am more convinced than ever that the solution to the ills is to develop sound knowledge of aptitude-treatment interactions. Then we can shift from a selection model or a prediction model to an allocation model, and use test procedures to pick the educational, therapeutic, or other approach that promises best results for the individual. This is both socially and logically right. . . . When we have cross-validated evidence as to what *person* variables and *treatment* variables interact, we will be in a position to generate a new kind of practical testing [p. xxix].

Two things need to be said about current testing practices. First, one may support the continued use of intelligence and school achievement tests as long as school personnel continue the practice of selecting and grouping children on the basis of school achievement. However, the purpose of such tests should be merely to ascertain academic achievement as revealed by a particular test and to measure aptitude in the public schools *as they are now constituted.* Second, it is not at all certain that the ills of testing will be eliminated when test constructors can relate personal variables and treatment variables. Such a prediction assumes that the needed transition to a treatment model can be made within the framework of current psychometric theory and practice. This is a questionable assumption. One may argue that the change requires a shift from group analysis to individual analysis. It is quite probable that the tests of the future will not be based on normative concepts, comparative measures, and group research methodology, but rather on functional concepts, behavioral repertory measures, and individual research designs. Those tests or assessment procedures will reveal in detail what a child can do in relation to an explicit program of instruction or training (Ribes-Inesta, 1972; Risley, Reynolds, and Hart, 1970). Our next topic, assessment by means of behavior inventories, deals with this approach in detail.

BEHAVIOR INVENTORIES AND SURVEYS

Three basic behavior inventories are necessary: (1) a child's abilities in preacademic and academic tool subjects, (2) his social behaviors, and (3) his likes (functional reinforcers). Academic skills may be assessed by pre-tests from the reading, writing, spelling, arithmetic, and language programs used in the class. Below is an example of assessing a child for program placement in a laboratory class. N. B., a $5\frac{1}{2}$-year-old boy, was referred to the Laboratory School because "he does not relate with adults, has emotional problems, and does not follow or join in group activities." On the reading pre-test, N. B. was successful on picture, letter, and word discrimination tasks, so it was not necessary to place him in the prereading program, which is designed to improve attending behavior. However, he could not identify or sound out phonetically any of the words on the general reading pre-tests and could not identify any of the ten words in the first subset pre-test of the reading program, although he was able to imitate verbally all ten words when they were presented orally. Since the latter performance was the prerequisite for the first subset of the reading program, N. B.'s first assignment in reading involved unit one in set one.

In writing, N. B. held the pencil correctly and copied all the printed letters of the alphabet on unlined paper without major errors. However, his writing showed marked hand tremors. Lined paper (no. 1) was used in the training program, in order to reduce gradually the unevenness of his strokes.

In arithmetic, he named the numbers from 1 to 10 and counted sequentially from 1 to the 30s. He was given the pre-test for the arithmetic program, which showed that he could imitate the numbers 1–20 presented orally in random sequence; could count from any number (1–19) to any other number (2–20); could identify (name and point to) any written number from 1 to 20; could make equal sets; and could match sets and numerals. N. B. was started on the finger-counting unit, a set arranged to help him learn elementary addition and subtraction.

N. B. was able to recite the alphabet and name the primary colors. He could name all of the uppercase letters (printed models) and all of the lowercase letters except d, b, l, i, g, and p. He was assigned to work on these six lowercase letters during the language and writing periods. Since N. B. had been unable to identify any words in the reading program he was not given a spelling test, because spelling is not introduced until a child has a sight vocabulary of at least ten words.

Social behavior inventories center on a child's ability to participate as a member of a group. Observations in group situations produce data on which to make decisions about preparing informal programs aimed at shaping peer interactions and participation in academic groups (e.g., does the child "volunteer" or does he have to be "called upon?").

Finally, behavior inventories are taken of the child's likes (reinforcers). Because most handicapped children have had an unpleasant experience with school work, close attention must be paid to the assessment of response consequences that support the acquisition and maintenance of academic and social learning. These include teacher attention, school-related activities, and marks (tokens) exchangeable for objects and activities.

An assessment of the reinforcing value of the teacher's attention can be accomplished rather quickly. If the teacher's attention is not reinforcing to a child, he will probably go off-task in tutored situations, including the administration of tests. If the teacher is uncertain about the value of her attention for a child, she can quickly evaluate it by making her attention contingent on some simple low-frequency behavior. Hand raising is an example. If her attention is a reinforcer for a child, his hand-raising behavior will increase when she gives him her attention as soon as she sees the raised hand; hand raising will decrease when the teacher ignores the raised hand and reserves her attention for other behaviors.

Activities such as recess, play time, or art may also function as reinforcers. They should be evaluated, especially if teacher attention is a weak reinforcer.

Nonexchangeable marks, such as gummed stars, rubber stamps, seals, and numerical and letter grades may function as weak reinforcers for academic learning for some children. The reinforcing value of this class of marks is probably related directly to the strength of contingent teacher attention and comments of approval. If the teacher's attention and statements of support are not reinforcing to the child, it is likely that nonexchangeable marks will not be reinforcing for him. If, on the other hand, the teacher's contingent responses are reinforcing, these symbols will very likely increase the range of reinforcers and minimize decreases in performance correlated with satiation.

When teacher attention and comments of approval are not reinforcing for a child, other stimuli that are likely to be reinforcing to the child should be used. These include small toys, candies, school objects, such as pencils, erasers, crayons, chalk, and colored paper, participation in preferred activities, and so on. Instead of giving them contingent correct responses, it is best to use them as "backups" for marks or tokens. Such a mark or token system has several advantages over dispensing "backup" reinforcers directly: (1) A large number of marks can be dispensed over short intervals; (2) each mark can be given immediately after a response; and (3) the satiation–performance-decrement effect that comes with giving a large number of "backups" can be avoided.

There are several instruments available that may be used as an aid in evaluating the reinforcing function of stimuli for a child. One is the Children's Reinforcement Survey (Clement and Richard, 1971). This two-page set of rating scales requests the informant to rank in order the people, places, and things that a child spends most of his time with or on during each week. Others are discussed by Ackerman (1972), Ayllon and Azrin (1968), and Birnbrauer, Burchard, and Burchard (1970).

## ASSESSMENT DURING INSTRUCTION

It is generally agreed that diagnosis is, or should be, continuous throughout treatment, but progress evaluation is often carried out in ways that are not functional for this purpose, such as oral or written subjective impressions, periodic notes, test grades, or scores on standardized tests at the beginning and end of treatment. To convert this dictum into a workable reality, a systematic approach is needed that yields objective measures consistent and compatible with those obtained during the initial assessment period described above.

Three types of monitoring techniques fit this requirement. The first utilizes the actual products of the child's behavior, his work output. Completed writing assignments, sheets of arithmetic problems, written spelling pages, and tape recordings are scrutinized, scored, and entered on progress charts each day. The second technique involves the use of pre- and post-tests from the instructional materials. If the academic pre- and post-tests are constructed so that they accurately measure the behaviors the programs are designed to teach, they are the best criteria for evaluating the effectiveness of the programs.

The third technique is direct observation of behavior, which was referred to in assessing baseline behaviors. This technique as a monitoring measure can take many forms, ranging from simple frequency, counts (e.g., number of prompts, or number of correct responses) accumulated in daily or weekly units to automated recording along a continuous-time line (e.g., electronic teaching machines). The equipment required under ordinary circumstances is a mechanical hand counter or a tally sheet. The reliability of observations, however, is sometimes a problem. A more dependable procedure is one in which data are collected by an observer (teacher, aide, parent, or student) who records instances of antecedent and consequent stimulus events and the child's responses on a sheet with successive time units (Bijou *et al.,* 1968; Bijou *et al.,* 1969). If the stimulus and response events are defined in clearly discernible, observable terms, so that two or more observers can agree on their occurrences, this method can be used to record the behavior of a child in relation to the academic tasks, the instructional procedures of the teacher, the behavior of peers, and response contingencies from all of these sources.

Monitoring the frequency of occurence of behaviors has two other advantages. First, it provides an effective technique for training teachers, teacher's aides and assistants, and parents. Systematic observation of behavior is the cornerstone of effective teaching skills. Second, it yields objective information on small changes in behavior. Trends indicating increases in a child's desirable behavior can be a powerful reinforcer for both teacher and pupil. Trends indicating decreases in desirable behavior can serve as indicators that one or more of the following interacting aspects of the learning environment requires attention: (a) conditions supporting interfering precurrent behavior (e.g., academic material is too easy), (b) ineffective response contingencies (e.g., intrinsic reinforcement from the task), (c) conditions preventing the occurrence of appropriate responses (e.g., academic material is too hard), and (d) setting or contextual factor (e.g., illness or chaotic conditions in classroom). All four of these factors interact with one another all the time. Hence, information from the monitoring procedures must be such that the teacher can discern which one or ones are probably responsible for a specific instance of deceleration. Some examples are given in the next two pages.

EXAMPLE 1: MONITORING INTERFERING PRECURRENT BEHAVIORS

Most decreases in the strength of interfering behaviors occur as the result of strengthening appropriate behaviors. One source of interfering emotional behavior generates from a child's enrollment in a new class. Although such behavior generally decreases over the course of 1 or 2 weeks, more interactions over a longer period are occasionally necessary. The resulting decrease in emotional behavior often allows the child to display knowledge and academic skills not observed in the initial assessment. For example, R. B., a child in the Laboratory School, initially behaved in many ways best described as fearful. He tended to remain in unoccupied rooms or close to walls, crossed open spaces very quickly, and often hid his face in his hands when approached by an adult or another child. These behaviors made it difficult for the teacher to administer the academic pretests and her impression, from the lack of responses, was that R. B. possessed only minimal academic skills. Two months later, after observational data showed that the interfering behaviors had decreased, she again presented him with the general pre-test for the reading program. Exerpts from the teacher's report follow:

> Of the 40 words on the first page, R. B. read 22 quite clearly. Others were read so that the initial sounds were correct, but he didn't pronounce the last syllables or sound. On the second page of the test, R. B. read 4 out of 13 phrases perfectly. I was not able to tell whether R. B. could understand what he read or not; he did not answer questions about the words he read orally.

Clearly this child did have some academic skills, skills that would not have been discovered so promptly had the teacher not monitored the child's precurrent behavior. Several weeks later, R. B. also demonstrated reading comprehension defined as following simple written instructions.

EXAMPLE 2: MONITORING ADEQUACY OF ACADEMIC MATERIALS

If a child's normally satisfactory performance in academic work suddenly deteriorates, or if he does not acquire a new academic task as readily as he had in the past, the difficulty may lie in the way the academic materials were programmed for him. An example is provided by the performance of a $6\frac{1}{2}$-year-old girl, K. D., in the Laboratory's beginning reading program. After some initial difficulties with discriminated responses to letters, K. D. was placed in the reading program and was doing well. Her performance on Units 35–41 is shown in the graph at the top of Figure 10.2. The "A" portion of the overall-percent-correct curve shows that

K. D.'s performance on oral reading and comprehension (solid line) was generally accurate and stable. She was reinforced with tokens about 25% of the time, as shown by the broken line. Unit 42 introduced and concentrated on the word "day." Units 43–47 each introduced a new word, but also included systematic reviews of the word "day." The "B" portion of the overall-percent-correct curve shows that no major difficulties occurred in Units 42, 43, and 44. However, the curve representing accuracy for the word "day," shown in the "B" panel of the middle graph, indicates that K. D.'s performance on the reviews of the word "day" declined to 50% in Unit 44. Previously, during the administration of Units 37–44, an attempt had been made to decrease the frequency of contingent marks. This decrease is shown by the dashed curve in the "B" panel of the upper graph in Figure 10.2. (The frequency of teacher approval for correct responses, rather than marks, varied between 96% and 100% for all the reading units shown, and thus has not been plotted.) On the assumption that this decrease in the frequency of marks might be the condition responsible for the decrease in K. D.'s accuracy, the rate was increased at the beginning of Unit 45 (the first data point in the dashed curve shown in the "C" portion of the upper graph of Figure 10.2). However, accuracy for the review of "day" declined even further, as shown in the "C" portion of the middle graph, and K. D. failed to acquire the new word "a," as shown in the "C" portion of the lower graph. She was given Unit 45 again on the following 2 days and, as shown in the middle and lower graphs, again failed to meet the criterion. It was noted that K. D. usually responded with the word "day" to the written word "a" and vice versa. Accordingly, a short remedial unit was constructed that (1) emphasized discrimination between the written "a" and "day" and (2) utilized a much condensed version of the normal transition from the reading-discrimination task. This remedial unit proved to be effective, and K. D. moved on to the next units of the program—46 and 47. The "D" portion of the upper graph of Figure 10.2 shows K. D.'s overall accuracy; the "D" portion of the middle graph shows her accuracy for the review of the word "day"; and the "D" portion of the lower graph shows her accuracy for the review of the word "a." All were at 100%.

## Assessment at the End of Instruction (Terminal)

Assessment at the end of the school year or at the end of the treatment period consists of (1) administering the standardized intelligence and achievement tests given at the beginning of treatment, (2) describing the

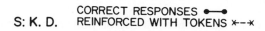

S: K. D.

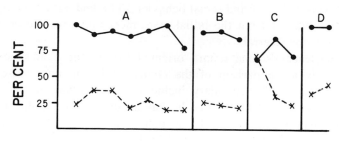

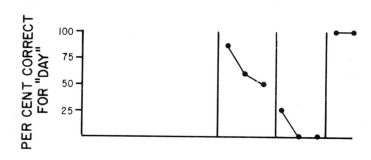

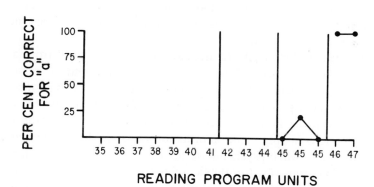

*Figure 10.2.*

child's performance on his last set of post-tests, and (3) describing his school-work behavior and social behaviors. The findings are compared with the data obtained from the initial assessment and with the description of the reason for referral.

The teacher's final report, oriented toward the child's next teacher, is generally a comparison of the child's beginning and end-of-year behavioral status. The summary includes a description of the social and academic skills and knowledge he has acquired. To aid the new teacher in planning for the child, the response contingencies used successfully during the last month are described in detail. Recommendations are based on extensions of the academic materials and teaching procedures that have been effective and on the specific techniques that were successful in strengthening desirable behaviors and weakening undesirable behaviors. Summary comments on the work with parents are also included.

## Summary

Diagnosis is an integral part of the remedial teaching of the retarded and emotionally disturbed young child. However, diagnosis from the point of view of behavior analysis is not concerned with placing a child in one or several diagnostic categories, or predicting his performance in a regular or special class, or making statements about the presumed etiology of his problem. Instead, it involves arriving at a set of decisions, in concrete and specific behavioral terms, for designing an academic program that will meet a child's specific academic and social needs. The initial set of decisions is considered tentative, changing throughout the period of instruction as new findings are revealed.

Information for diagnostic decision making is derived from assessing the child's performance before, during, and at the end of remedial instruction. Assessment before instruction (baseline) involves medical reports, interviews, psychometric tests, direct observation, and behavior inventories, with the latter two techniques supplying most of the essential data. Interviews supply some information on a child's current home and family situation, while psychometric tests provide information on selection and grouping primarily for public school personnel. Assessment during instruction (monitoring data) consists of direct observation, pre- and post-tests from the classroom instructional programs, systematic evaluation of the child's productions, and "counts" of indicators of progress. Assessment at the end of instruction (terminal measures) consists of performances on the last post-tests, scores form the readministration of psychometric tests, and descriptions of the child's precurrent and social behavior from objective measures and accounts.

Designating a child, or a group of children, as retarded or emotionally disturbed may serve a useful purpose in mustering support for special educational programs, in fabricating legislation, and in establishing administrative policies. But such labeling does not help a teacher to devise an effective remedial plan for the child so designated. Only knowledge and systematic application of behavioral principles can serve that purpose.

# References

Ackerman, J. M. *Operant Conditioning Techniques for the Classroom Teacher.* Glenview, Ill.: Scott, Foresman, 1972.

Anastasi, A. *Psychological Testing,* 3rd ed. New York: Macmillan, 1968.

Ayllon, T., and Azrin, N. *The Token Economy: A Motivational System for Therapy and Rehabilitation.* New York: Appleton-Century-Crofts, 1968.

Bateman, B. Learning disabilities—yesterday, today, and tomorrow. In E. C. Frierson and W. B. Barbe (Eds.), *Educating Children with Learning Disabilities.* New York: Appleton-Century-Crofts, 1967, pp. 10–25.

Bersoff, D. N. Behavioral approaches to assessment and observation in the school. In J. Magary (Ed.), *Handbook of School Psychology Services.* St. Louis: C. V. Mosby. (*In press.*)

Bijou, S. W. Technology of teaching young handicapped children. In S. W. Bijou and E. Ribes-Inesta (Eds.), *Behavior Modification: Issues and Extensions.* New York: Academic Press, 1972.

Bijou, S. W., and Baer, D. M. *Child Development: A Systematic and Empirical Theory,* Vol. 1. New York: Appleton-Century-Crofts, 1961.

Bijou, S. W., and Baer, D. M. *Child Development: The Universal Stage of Infancy,* Vol. 2. New York: Appleton-Century-Crofts, 1965.

Bijou, S. W., Peterson, R. F., and Ault, M. H. A method to integrate descriptive and experimental field studies at the level of data and empirical concepts. *Journal of Applied Behavior Analysis,* 1968, **1,** 175–191.

Bijou, S. W., Peterson, R. F., Harris, F. R., Allen, K. E., and Johnston, M. S. Methodology for experimental studies of young children in natural settings. *Psychological Record,* 1969, **19,** 177–210.

Birnbrauer, J. S., Burchard, J. D., and Burchard, S. N. Wanted: Behavior analysts. In R. H. Bradfield (Ed.), *Behavior Modification: The Human Effort.* San Rafael, Calif.: Dimensions, 1970.

Bringmann, W. G., Mueller, R. H., Balance, W. D. G., and Matijiw, S. L. Medical model bibliography I: Logical and conceptual analysis. *Psychological Center Research Bulletin No. 7,* University of Windsor, Department of Psychology, 1970. (a)

Bringmann, W. G., Mueller, R. H., Balance, W. D. G., and Matijiw, S. L. Medical model bibliography II: Applications and implications. *Psychological Center Research Bulletin No. 8,* University of Windsor, Department of Psychology, 1970. (b)

Bringmann, W. C., Mueller, R. H., Balance, W. D. G., and Matijiw, S. L. *Psychological Center Research Bulletin No. 9,* University of Windsor, Department of Psychology, 1971.

Caldwell, B. M. *The Preschool Inventory.* Princeton, N.J.: Educational Testing Service, 1967.

Clement, P. W., and Richard, R. C. *Children's Reinforcement Survey.* Graduate School of Psychology, Fuller Theological Seminary, Pasadena, Calif., 1971.

Cronbach, L. J. *Essentials of Psychological Testing.* New York: Harper & Row, 1970.

Dunn, L. M. *Peabody Picture Vocabulary Test.* Minneapolis, Minn.: American Guidance Service, 1959.

Humphreys, L. G. Theory of intelligence. In R. Cancro (Ed.), *Contributions to Intelligence.* New York: Grune & Stratton, 1971.

Jastak, J. F., Bijou, S. W., and Jastak, S. R. *Wide Range Achievement Test,* rev. ed. Wilmington, Del.: Guidance Associates, 1965.

Ribes-Inesta, E. Discussion: Methodological remarks on a delinquency prevention and rehabilitation program. In S. W. Bijou and E. Ribes-Inesta (Eds.), *Behavior Modification: Issues and Extensions.* New York: Academic Press, 1972, pp. 86–87.

Risley, T., Reynolds, N., and Hart, B. The disadvantaged: Behavior modification with disadvantaged preschool children. In R. H. Bradfield (Ed.), *Behavior Modification: The Human Effort.* San Rafael, Calif.: Dimensions, 1970.

Skinner, B. F. *Sciences and Human Behavior.* New York: MacMillan, 1953.

Skinner, B. F. *The Technology of Teaching.* New York: Appleton-Century-Crofts, 1968.

Slosson, R. L. *Slosson Intelligence Test for Children and Adults,* 1968 ed. East Aurora, N.Y.: Slosson Educational Publications, 1963.

Terman, L. M., and Merrill, M. *Stanford-Binet Intelligence Scale. Manual for the Third Revision: Form L-M.* Boston: Houghton Mifflin, 1960.

Wechsler, D. *Wechsler Preschool and Primary Scale of Intelligence Manual.* New York: Psychological Corp., 1967.

Yarrow, M. R., Campbell, J. D., and Burton, R. V. *Child Rearing: An Inquiry into Research and Methods.* San Francisco: Jossey-Bass, 1968.

# 11 RECIPROCAL AND SELF-MANAGEMENT IN EDUCATIONAL COMMUNITIES

**Wells Hively**

**Ann Dell Duncan**

Today, few people would deny that behavior analysis has become a powerful technology. This International Conference on Behavior Modification marks an important point in the history of our professional community. Our community is becoming a technocracy, and it may help to get some perspective on ourselves. To what uses are we putting our skills? To whom are we passing them on? What variables influence our professional behavior?

As behavior technologists, we are at the center of what Victor Ferkiss (*Technological Man,* 1970) describes as an "existential revolution":

> Power over himself and his environment puts man in a radically new moral position. Throughout his history he has lived with certain concepts of freedom and identity. Freedom was doing what you wanted to do. You were restricted by other men or an intractable physical environment. But the degree to which other men could control you or restrict your freedom was limited by the fact that the environment limited their powers also. You lived in a society, an economy, a physical environment that was difficult to alter. If worst came to worst you could run away. You could hide. Or you could remain true to yourself at the stake. Identity, by the same token, was a limited problem. You were the result of a combination of circumstances—your childhood, your surroundings, your own desires. These might be determined by fate, but not by anyone else, certainly not by yourself.
>
> In an era of absolute technology, freedom and identity must take on new meanings. . . . Other men can change your society, your economy, and your

181

physical environment. Eventually, they will be able to force you to live in a
world with neither trees nor oceans if they choose. Running and hiding become
increasingly difficult. They can make you love them so you need not go to the
stake. They can alter your identity by controlling how you are brought up and
what your experiences are; they can even program your children genetically in
advance of birth. But perhaps more disturbing is the fact that you can do all
these things yourself: you can change your appearance . . . your moods and
your memories, you can even decide what you want your children to look like.
But if you can be whatever you want to be, how will you distinguish the "real"
you from the chosen? Who is it that is doing the choosing [p. 31]?

The problems generated by this existential revolution are now becoming serious, and the time for solving them is growing short (Meadows, Meadows, Randers, and Behrens, 1972). Behavior technologists must face them very directly. For example, although we are fairly successful at analyzing the behavior of individuals, we are not yet skilled at analyzing the behavior of groups. Few of us are even seriously concerned with analyzing our own behavior. Therefore, we are in considerable danger of being seduced by some prevailing contingencies of reinforcement, which may generate behavior we shall later regret.

We are, like many other professions, becoming a priesthood. We tend to speak an unnecessarily opaque private language, to form closed professional societies, and to emphasize theory more than exploratory method. We tend to fall into methodological orthodoxies and to forget our imaginative empiricism.

Our tendency to drift into the stream of institutional professionalization may have low long-range survival value. Those who swim with this stream believe that therapy (behavioral or otherwise) should be done only by trained and certified therapists, teaching by certified teachers, health care by certified medical personnel, and so on. But some thoughtful people are saying that this trend may be unfortunate. They point out that more people need help than ever before, more are being helped in ways that prevent them from learning how to help themselves, more professional helpers seem to be needed, and the costs tend to become unsupportable (Goodman, 1969; Illich, 1970).

Alternative behavior is possible, and conditions could be arranged so to make it a lot more probable. We can learn to talk a technical language much closer to basic English, and we can work out much more effective ways of sharing tools and techniques with others (Lindsley, 1972). By emphasizing data and functional analysis rather than jargon and theory, we can build bridges with other professionals. Above all, we can examine our own behavior with our own techniques. We can study the conditions that generate trust, reciprocity, and mutual growth as well as those that generate institutional obedience. We can take precise personal management seriously. And in the analysis of reciprocity and personal management, we might find some answers to the problems generated by Ferkiss' existential revolution.

For a start, a simple way to study our own behavior is to examine the frequencies with which we engage in projects involving (1) *other* management, (2) *self*-management, and (3) *reciprocal* management. Consider the following example.

Ruth was a bright 10-year-old who knew a counselor in her school. The counselor asked if she would help her with some school work at the university. Ruth eagerly asked what it involved. After some mutual exploration, Ruth decided that the project would be to help her teacher praise the class members more. The children had been talking about it during recess, and it seemed an important thing to do. Ruth started by counting every time the teacher praised anybody in the class. A praise could be as mild as "That's good" or as extreme as "I really liked what you just did." The topography was not important, so long as it could be considered praise. She jotted down the things the teacher said that she thought were praise and kept the list nearby while counting. As Figure 11.1 shows, the first 2 weeks were not so good—only one, or mostly two praises for an entire school day. The teacher did not know that Ruth was counting.

At the end of the 2-week period, the children decided to put up a large sign that said "We Like Praise." The teacher was greeted one Monday morning with this banner in the back of her class. She asked what it was all about, and Ruth then told her about the project, but did not show the teacher her counts or her chart.

What a dramatic change with just one large banner! The teacher found all sorts of things about which to express her pleasure, and Ruth and the class enjoyed it so much they kept the banner up for 4½ weeks. Then there was a PTA meeting scheduled for Wednesday night, and the teacher asked if she could take the sign down on Tuesday. They all took it down together, and Ruth kept her counts going to see whether the teacher had been helped permanently. She slipped a bit, but she was not nearly as bad as she had been in the beginning.

That was an example of straight *other* management. Each step in the experimental sequence—pinpoint, record, chart, and change,—was carried out by 10-year-old Ruth. Her "'subject," the teacher, took no part in choosing the behavior to be examined, recording its frequency, choosing the change procedure, or delivering it. And during the time the study went on, we have no record that the teacher was permitted formally to pinpoint, chart, or change any of Ruth's behavior. By these standards, neither *self*-management nor *reciprocal* management were involved. Ruth managed the behavior of her teacher in an authoritarian and arbitrary way. (Teachers have sometimes been known to do the same thing to children.)

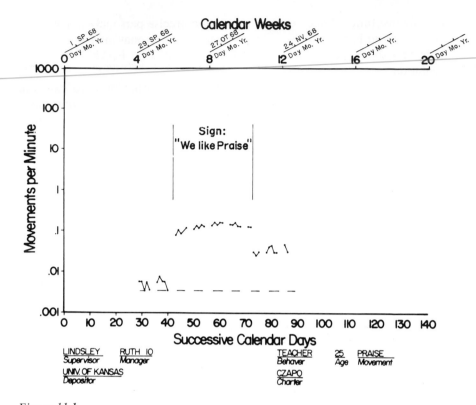

*Figure 11.1.*

What happens when there is some reciprocity?

Before moving to Israel, Judi Hirsch taught in a Junior Guidance class in New York City (the New York label for children with emotional/behavioral problems). One of the boys in her class was Frankie, a slight, frail child. Judi thought that one problem with Frankie's academic progress was that it was difficult to tell how well or poorly he was doing. His papers were always a shambles: full of erasures, torn, covered with atrocious handwriting, so that it was hard to give him the benefit of the doubt for what he knew.

Judi decided to help Frankie produce neater papers by counting, charting, and changing. Five weeks of counting showed an average of only one neat paper a day. That did not do Frankie much good, and it certainly did not help Judi.

Judi decided that one of the problems might be the delay in giving Frankie feedback on his performance. So the change she instituted was to correct each paper immediately and praise him for every small improvement. She also asked him to become involved in the project by tallying the number of neat papers he completed each day. (See Figure 11.2). The results were encouraging to both of them (a leap up to an average of nine neat papers a day for 3 weeks).

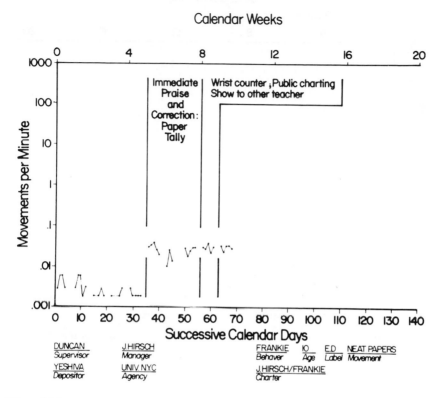

*Figure 11.2.*

They then tried giving Frankie a wrist counter (like the one Miss Hirsch wore), putting his chart up on the bulletin board, and showing his work to another teacher for judgment of neatness. This stabilized his neat papers at ten a day. After the formal change procedures were withdrawn, he continued to be neat about his work. Quite a change from the shambles he had been producing 10 weeks before!

Judi is the kind of teacher who believes that children should be worked *with, not at.* She offered to share what she was learning about precision teaching with any of the children who were interested. Frankie said he wanted to help too, but what could he do? Judi suggested there might be something about her behavior that he might want to count, chart, and change. Frankie picked Judi's yelling at the class. The first day he counted over 20 yells and showed her the results at the end of the day. Judi had known it was a problem, but not a 20-a-day problem! As can be seen on the chart (Figure 11.3), the frequency of yells dropped dramatically after that first high day and continued to go down to one or two a day, with the last 5 weeks at zero . . . no yells at all. . . . There was no need to put in a formal change procedure for this

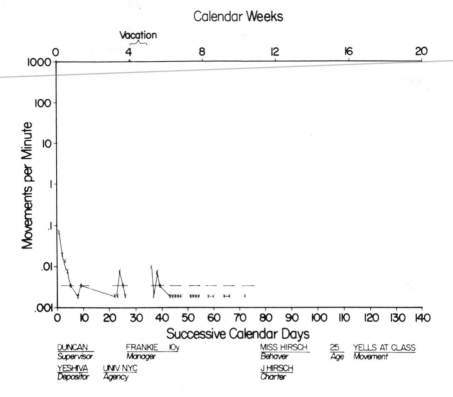

*Figure 11.3.*

project. The act of a child's recording and sharing the information with her was sufficient to bring Judi's yells down to zero. Judi reported that every time she felt like yelling, she would look at Frankie with his pencil poised and take a deep breath and try an alternative way to communicate with the children.

Interactions such as these between Judi and Frankie are so compli- cated that detailed count sheets are needed to keep track of them. On our count sheets (see Tables 11.1–11.4) the basic activities that occur in precise-behavior management are listed down the left, while across the top are listed column headings for *self-* and *other* management. (Each of those columns is subdivided into four phases so that a single count sheet can be used for a project that includes a before phase and up to three tries at making changes.) We write the names of the people who performed the activities in each phase in the cells in the table under the appropriate column headings.

Table 11.1 shows the count sheet for the project devoted to acceler-

**TABLE 11.1**

COUNT SHEET FOR RECIPROCITY IN STUDIES OF PRECISE BEHAVIOR MANAGEMENT [a]

| Phases | Other management (someone else does it for the behaver) | | | | Self-management (the behaver does it himself) | | | |
|---|---|---|---|---|---|---|---|---|
| | 1 | 2 | 3 | 4 | 1 | 2 | 3 | 4 |
| 1. Choose movement cycle (Behavior to be recorded) | Judi | — | — | — | X | — | — | — |
| 2. Record | Judi | X | X | Judi | X | Frank | Frank | X |
| 3. Choose program (General antecedent conditions) | Judi | Judi | Judi | Judi | X | X | X | X |
| 4. Set up program | Judi | Judi | Judi | Judi | X | X | X | X |
| 5. Choose programmed event (Specific antecedent stimuli) | Judi | Judi | Judi | Judi | X | X | X | X |
| 6. Deliver programmed event | Judi | Judi | Judi | Judi | X | X | X | X |
| 7. Choose arranged event (possible consequence) | — | Judi | — | — | — | X | — | — |
| 8. Set arrangement (schedule) | — | Judi | — | Judi | — | X | — | X |
| 9. Deliver arranged event | — | Judi | *other teacher* — | — | — | X | X | — |

Source of Study

| Frankie | 10½ | E.D. | Neat papers |
|---|---|---|---|
| Behaver | Age | Label | Movement |
| Judi Hirsch | 8-Nov.-68 | 2-Sept.-68 | 46 |
| Charter | Last data day | First data day | Total data days |
| Ann Dell Duncan | Yeshiva University, N.Y.C. | | |
| Depositor | Agency | | |

[a] This count sheet prepared by Wells Hively, Psycho-Educational Center, Pattee Hall, University of Minnesota, Minneapolis, Minnesota 55455.

ating Frankie's neat papers. (We put X's in cells that have been preempted by other activities and dashes to indicate when activities did not take place at all.) From the count sheet you can see that Frankie kept his own records, and Judi did everything else.

Table 11.2 shows the count sheet for the project devoted to decelerating Judi's yells. Frankie carried out two activities to manage Judi: He chose the movement cycle, and he counted it. Three activities were done cooperatively: Frankie and Judi agreed that he would show her the record every day (she had to look and he had to be willing to show her). So together they (1) chose the arranged event and (2) set the arrangement. Sometimes Judi remembered to go to Frankie's desk at the end of the day for a look at the record, and sometimes Frankie took it to her. So both of them occasionally (3) delivered the arranged event.

The count sheets provide a convenient bird's-eye view of the patterns of reciprocity shown in Judi and Frankie's cooperative projects. For example, one can see that Judi took a sizable part in the project to decelerate

**TABLE 11.2**

COUNT SHEET FOR RECIPROCITY IN STUDIES OF PRECISE BEHAVIOR MANAGEMENT [a]

| Phases | Other management (someone else does it for the behaver) | | | | Self-management (the behaver does it himself) | | | |
|---|---|---|---|---|---|---|---|---|
| | 1 | 2 | 3 | 4 | 1 | 2 | 3 | 4 |
| 1. Choose movement cycle (behavior to be recorded) | Frank | | | | X | | | |
| 2. Record | Frank | | | | X | | | |
| 3. Choose program (general antecedent conditions) | X | | | | Judi | | | |
| 4. Set up program | X | | | | Judi | | | |
| 5. Choose programmed event (specific antecedent stimuli) | — | | | | — | | | |
| 6. Deliver programmed event | — | | | | — | | | |
| 7. Choose arranged event (possible consequence) | Frank and Judi | | | | Frank and Judi | | | |
| 8. Set arrangement (schedule) | Frank and Judi | | | | Frank and Judi | | | |
| 9. Deliver arranged event | Frank and Judi | | | | Frank and Judi | | | |

Source of Study

| Judi | 25 | Teacher | Yells at class |
|---|---|---|---|
| Behaver | Age | Label | Movement |
| Judi Hirsch | 8-Nov.-68 | 2-Sept.-68 | 30 |
| Charter | Last data day | First data day | Total data days |
| Ann Dell Duncan | Yeshiva University, N.Y.C. | | |
| Depositor | Agency | | |

[a] This count sheet prepared by Wells Hively, Psycho-Educational Center, Pattee Hall, University of Minnesota, Minneapolis, Minnesota 55455.

her own yelling. Of seven activities, she helped to carry out five. In contrast, Frankie took little part in the project to accelerate his own neat papers. Of 26 activities, he helped to carry out 2.

From these count sheets, we can get a score for reciprocity: the number of pairs of cells that can be found by taking an activity in which Frankie managed Judi and matching it with an activity in which Judi managed Frankie. There were five such pairs, if we include the activities in which Frankie and Judi cooperated to manage Judi's yells.

Formal accounts do not reflect the warmth and trust between Judi and Frankie, and operationally speaking, it may look as if their relationship was pretty authoritarian. But on the other hand, how does their relationship compare to the relationships among teachers and students in other special-education classrooms in which behavior modification occurs? Warmth and trust may be rather closely related to countable frequencies of *self-*, *other,* and *reciprocal* management.

The significance of the following example is not in changes exhibited in the data, but rather in that it shows a $3\frac{1}{2}$-year-old child learning to manage her own life.

Christine volunteered to help Ray in his assignment from his university class, which was to teach a child to manage his own inner and outer behaviors. She thought about what she wanted to change, and since it had been part of a recent discussion with her mother, she selected being selfish. This was translated into selfish thoughts and selfish acts to form an "impulse pair." Christine wanted to count these behaviors only while she was in nursery school (about 300 minutes a day). She wore two wrist counters, one for the thoughts and one for the acts. Every day, when she returned home from school, she would tell her mother how that day had gone, and they would put the counts onto the charts (see Figures 11.4 and 11.5). After 2 weeks of counting, Ray noticed that the trend for selfish thoughts was accelerating at about $\times 1.3$ (or 30% per week). They talked about making a change, and with a little help from her mother, Christine decided to tell each selfish thought out loud whenever it happened. Her mother decided to contract with money for decreases in selfish acts. For fewer than 15 acts she earned 10 cents; if she kept under 10 acts she would have 20 cents a day. After 2 weeks Christine had earned $1.90, and they stopped the contract. Her selfish thoughts dropped in frequency too, but started to trend back up. It could be that revealing the thought was rewarded by someone in her nursery school. Count sheets for Christine's impulse pair are shown in Tables 11.3 and 11.4.

Christine did her inner-behavior project, selfish thoughts, almost completely by herself. She chose the pinpoint, did the counting, decided where and when to do it, worked out a change with her mother (saying the thought aloud) and delivered it. Christine also picked the outer pinpoint and recorded it, but her mother put in the change procedure.

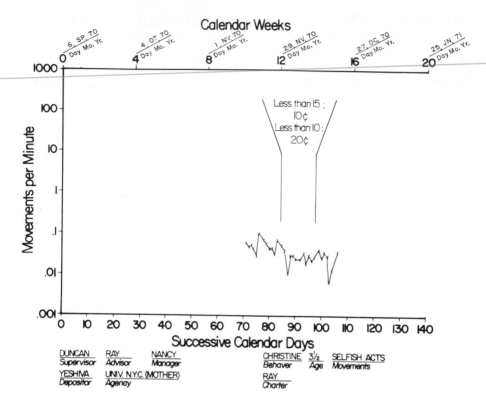

*Figure 11.4.*

We could get an idea of the frequency with which all the members of an educational community—an institution, classroom, family, or therapy group—engage (precisely) in *other, self-*, or *reciprocal* management by collecting their records of precise-behavior-management projects and diagramming each of them on the count sheet for reciprocity. Then we could add up the total numbers of filled cells under each of the main column headings, across all the projects, to get the total numbers of *other* management and *self*-management activities. We could also count the total number of reciprocal pairs, as we did with Judi and Frankie, across all projects, to get an index of reciprocity.

These numbers could be turned into meaningful frequencies by dividing them by the total number of data days from all the projects. The resulting measures might be very useful in the evaluation and comparison of behavior-modification programs.

A similar approach may be taken to the analysis of written reports

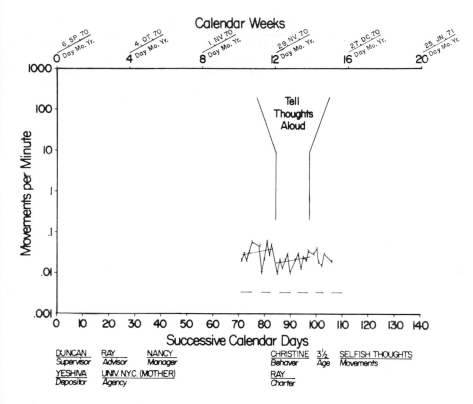

*Figure 11.5.*

or spoken presentations at conferences such as this. A count sheet for that purpose is shown in Table 11.5. [Down the left is the familiar list of activities making up precise-behavior-management projects (with two additional activities added at the beginning of the list).] Across the top are column headings referring to *other, self-* and *reciprocal* management. Using the count sheet, an observer can work his way through an article looking for descriptions of, or references to, each of the activities and tallying each reference under its appropriate column. Here are some examples.

> All 15 students in a fifth-grade class for low-track readers were included in the study: Score 1 in row 1, column 1; and 1 in row 2, column 1.
> Robert was told he would receive a token every 10 minutes if he did not crack his knuckles: Score 1 in each of rows 9 and 10 under column 1.
> Joan did her work in a class where assignments were made on an individual basis. The teacher instructed those who raised their hands. . . . : Score 1 each in each of rows 5, 6, 7, and 8 under column 1.

**TABLE 11.3**

COUNT SHEET FOR RECIPROCITY IN STUDIES OF PRECISE BEHAVIOR MANAGEMENT [a]

| Phases | Other management (someone else does it for the behaver) | | | | Self-management (the behaver does it himself) | | | |
|---|---|---|---|---|---|---|---|---|
| | 1 | 2 | 3 | 4 | 1 | 2 | 3 | 4 |
| 1. Choose movement cycle (behavior to be recorded) | X | — | — | | Chris | — | — | |
| 2. Record | X | — | — | | Chris | — | — | |
| 3. Choose program (general antecedent conditions) | X | — | — | | Chris | — | — | |
| 4. Set up program | Teacher | — | — | | X | — | — | |
| 5. Choose programmed event (specific antecedent stimuli) | — | — | — | | — | — | — | |
| 6. Deliver programmed event | — | — | — | | — | — | — | |
| 7. Choose arranged event (possible consequence) | — | mother | — | | — | X | — | |
| 8. Set arrangement (schedule) | — | mother | mother | | — | X | X | |
| 9. Deliver arranged event | — | mother | — | | — | X | — | |

Source of Study

| Christine Vane | 3½ | | Selfish acts | |
|---|---|---|---|---|
| Behaver | Age | Label | Movement | |
| Ray Vane | 24-Dec.-70 | 15-Nov.-70 | 31 | |
| Charter | Last data day | First data day | Total data days | |
| Ann Dell Duncan | | Yeshiva University, N.Y.C. | | |
| Depositor | | Agency | | |

[a] This count sheet prepared by Wells Hively, Psycho-Educational Center, Pattee Hall, University of Minnesota, Minneapolis, Minnesota 55455.

Note that when there is ambiguity, references tend to be tallied as *other* management. In the last example, the children might have chosen, or helped to choose, their own assignments, in which case the activities should not have been scored in column 1. But it is a good bet that they did not choose for themselves. In any case, habitual use of the passive voice in report writing perpetuates such ambiguity. We could do a lot to improve our communication with people outside the "profession" by writing in the active voice and being clear about who did what to (or for) whom:

We posted a notice advertising a precise tutoring program for people who feel they read too slowly. Eight people volunteered: Score 1 in each of rows 1 and 2 under column 2.

Students exchanged papers, checked each other's work, and helped each other plot the number of words correct on their daily charts: Score 1 in row 4 column 3, and 1 in row 11, column 3.

## TABLE 11.4

COUNT SHEET FOR RECIPROCITY IN STUDIES OF PRECISE BEHAVIOR MANAGEMENT [a]

| Phases | Other management (someone else does it for the behaver) | | | | Self-management (the behaver does it himself) | | | |
|---|---|---|---|---|---|---|---|---|
| | 1 | 2 | 3 | 4 | 1 | 2 | 3 | 4 |
| 1. Choose movement cycle (behavior to be recorded) | X | — | — | | Chris | — | — | |
| 2. Record | X | — | — | | Chris | — | — | |
| 3. Choose program (general antecedent conditions) | X | — | — | | Chris | — | — | |
| 4. Set up program | Teacher | — | — | | X | — | — | |
| 5. Choose programmed event (specific antecedent stimuli) | — | — | — | | — | — | — | |
| 6. Deliver programmed event | — | — | — | | — | — | — | |
| 7. Choose arranged event (possible consequence) | — | Chris and mother | — | | — | Chris and mother | — | |
| 8. Set arrangement (schedule) | — | Chris and mother | father | | — | Chris and mother | X | |
| 9. Deliver arranged event | — | X | — | | — | Chris | — | |

Source of Study

| Christine Vane | 3½ | | Selfish thoughts | |
|---|---|---|---|---|
| Behaver | Age | Label | Movement | |
| Ray Vane | 24-Dec.-70 | 15-Nov.-70 | 31 | |
| Charter | Last data day | First data day | Total data days | |
| Ann Dell Duncan | Yeshiva University, N.Y.C. | | | |
| Depositor | Agency | | | |

[a] This count sheet prepared by Wells Hively, Psycho-Educational Center, Pattee Hall, University of Minnesota, Minneapolis, Minnesota 55455.

A practiced auditor can also use this count sheet to record spoken presentations as well as written ones. To bring spoken and written presen-

**TABLE 11.5**

Count Sheet for Reciprocity in Reports of Precise Behavior Management [a]

| | References to other management (someone else does it for the behaver) | | References to self management (the behaver does it himself) | | References to reciprocal management (two or more people do it for each other) | |
|---|---|---|---|---|---|---|
| | Number | F | Number | F | Number | F |
| 1. Choose who is to be the Behaver | | | | | | |
| 2. Assign label to the behaver | | | | | | |
| 3. Choose movement cycle | | | | | | |
| 4. Record | | | | | | |
| 5. Choose program | | | | | | |
| 6. Set up program | | | | | | |
| 7. Choose programmed event | | | | | | |
| 8. Deliver programmed event | | | | | | |
| 9. Choose arranged event | | | | | | |
| 10. Set arrangement | | | | | | |
| 11. Deliver arranged event | | | | | | |

Presenter:_____ Observer:_____ Date:_____
Title of presentation: _____
Place (or publication): _____
Time stop:_____    Note: For written material assume
Time start:_____    reading rate of 200 words/min.
Duration: _____

[a] This count sheet prepared by Wells Hively, Psycho-Educational Center, Pattee Hall, University of Minnesota, Minneapolis, Minnesota 55455.

tations into a common metric, we may summarize the data in a special way. The auditor simply records the frequency of occurance of each type of reference and constructs charts that show the frequencies with which the presenter refers to various kinds of *other, self-,* and *reciprocal* management.

The reader imagines that he is reading at about 200 words per minute (the more or less standard lecture rate) and calculates the frequency of references on that basis.

Table 11.6 shows the results of performing this kind of analysis on Elery Phillips' article, "Achievement Place: Token Reinforcement Procedures in a Home-Style Rehabilitation Setting for Pre-delinquent Boys"

**TABLE 11.6**

FREQUENCIES OF REFERENCE TO MANAGEMENT ACTIVITIES

| Activities | Other | | Self | | Reciprocal | |
|---|---|---|---|---|---|---|
| | Phillips | Sheil | Phillips | Sheil | Phillips | Sheil |
| Assign label | 0.24 | 0.50 | 0.00 | 0.00 | 0.00 | 0.00 |
| Choose movement | 1.80 | 0.10 | 0.00 | 0.29 | 0.04 | 0.50 |
| Record | 0.80 | 0.00 | 0.00 | 0.00 | 0.00 | 0.00 |
| Choose program | 0.24 | 0.10 | 0.00 | 0.04 | 0.00 | 0.00 |
| Set up program | 0.20 | 0.00 | 0.00 | 0.09 | 0.00 | 0.20 |
| Choose programmed event | 0.24 | 0.60 | 0.00 | 0.20 | 0.00 | 0.28 |
| Deliver programmed event | 0.24 | 0.60 | 0.00 | 0.24 | 0.00 | 0.28 |
| Choose arranged event | 1.00 | 0.50 | 0.00 | 0.25 | 0.00 | 0.40 |
| Set contingency | 1.80 | 0.20 | 0.08 | 0.15 | 0.04 | 0.25 |
| Deliver arranged event | 0.56 | 0.30 | 0.08 | 0.15 | 0.08 | 0.40 |
| Overall frequency | 6.97 | 3.30 | 0.16 | 1.50 | 0.16 | 2.50 |

| | Phillips | Sheil |
|---|---|---|
| All management activities | 8.00 | 8.00 |
| Charts or tables | 0.70 | 0.00 |

(Phillips, 1968), one of a famous series of studies, being carried out at the University of Kansas under the leadership of Montrose Wolf—studies that have laid the groundwork for a whole new orientation toward the rehabilitation of juvenile offenders.

If we imagine Elery Phillips reading his article at the rate of 200 words per minute, we find him referring to management activities, *other, self-,* or *reciprocal,* about eight times a minute. Of these, nearly all are references to *other* management. He mentions *self*-management four times and *reciprocal* management four times in the 25 minutes it would take to read the article.

The highest frequencies of references to *other* management are concerned with choosing the behaviors to be modified (about two a minute), choosing the arranged events (one a minute), setting arrangements (about two a minute), and delivering the arranged events (about one every 2 minutes). Frequencies of reference to programmed events and antecedant conditions are low, as they tend to be in most behavior-modification projects. Seven of the eight total references to *self*- and *reciprocal* management also concern setting arrangements and delivering arranged events. One is concerned with pinpointing a movement cycle.

Overall, the pattern is clearly an authoritarian one. The boys occasionally delivered rewards to themselves and to one another, but they never took part in recording, choosing behavior to accomplish, or programming their environment. Operationally speaking, Achievement Place, based on the data from Phillips' report, was a dictatorship.

It is revealing to compare the report of Achievement Place with the report of a self-actualizing classroom conducted by teacher Barbara Sheil and quoted in Carl Roger's *Freedom to Learn* (Rogers, 1969). It is not easy to see explicit management references in Barbara Sheil's prose, but the process is roughly the same as that described by Charlie Ferster for analyzing the behavior of a skilled therapist in operant terms (Ferster, 1971). To get an idea of the auditor variability, try putting Sheil's article on the count sheet yourself.

Table 11.6 shows the results of our analysis of Sheil's report. Her references to management activities in general were just as frequent as Phillips'. Although she was devoted to self-actualization, Sheil talked more often about *other* management (three times a minute) than about either *self*-management (between one and two times a minute) or *reciprocal* management (between two and three times a minute). But she talked a lot about all three. And, as one might expect from a group-process enthusiast, she talked more frequently about *reciprocal* management than about *self*-management.

Sheil's emphasis on each different type of management activity was strikingly different from Phillips'. In her references to *other* management, Sheil talked most often about (1) assigning labels (she categorized the children frequently), (2) choosing, and (3) delivering programmed events, and less often about arranged events.

The picture that emerges from Sheil's description is one in which the teacher set up the main programmed and arranged events, then gave the children a major say in choosing specific behavioral targets within the preestablished overall program, and allowed them to set up the details of their programs for themselves. Operationally speaking, her program appears as a kind of benevolent monarchy.

The most striking thing about Sheil's project is, of course, that she does not mention *recording* by anybody. Phillips' presents a graph or table showing changes in the boys' behavior about once every minute and a half. Sheil's does not present any. The data from a series of precise-behavior-management studies, in an educational community whose practices are evolving experimentally, make the interrelationships among the members especially transparent. What went on in Achievement Place is much clearer than what went on in Sheil's classroom. This makes Achievement Place both more vulnerable to criticism and more capable of evolution.

As B. F. Skinner so clearly argued (Skinner, 1948), keeping your eye on the data, as Phillips does, ought to ensure progress. Taken all together, empiricism, reinforcement theory, and a concern for the long haul should yield continuously improving education and government.

One may argue that when faced with tough problems, like those taken on by Elery Phillips, Montrose Wolf, and their coworkers in Achievement Place, it is necessary to start with *other* management. Then, after some of the minimal behavioral criteria set by others are met, the boys may be given more control over their own lives. Phillips says at the end of his report that the boys were beginning to take over more and more in the management of their community. If this is the strategy, over time the data from Achievement Place ought to show a move to higher frequencies of *self-* and *reciprocal* management. But of two subsequent reports, one (Phillips, Phillips, Fixen, and Wolf, 1971) contains essentially the same pattern of frequencies, and the other (Fixen, Phillips, and Wolf, 1972) describes the failure of an attempt to introduce self-recording.

An alternative strategy would be to search from the start for areas in which each boy can manage his own behavior and arrange circumstances to support him in doing so. If the long-range goal is competent self-management together with effective citizenship, the data ought to lead us to the most effective mixture of approaches.

The long-range goal may not always be reciprocity or self-management. Some projects, like Achievement Place, may be designed simply to produce a specific change in behavior, after which the citizens are released to the larger community with, hopefully, a better chance to survive.

So how one feels about high frequencies of *other* management may depend on several things—the constitution of the community, in both the demographic and governmental senses; the stage of evolution of the experiment; the political philosophy of the viewer; and whatever scientifically grounded beliefs the viewer may have about how individuals and groups survive.

The projects by Elery Phillips and Barbara Sheil are classic representations of a profound split in our current culture. Tough-minded, careful researchers working within a framework of *other* management, guided by data and scientific method, and serving the goals of institutions, are squaring off against tender-minded humanitarians, serving individual goals and working within a framework of reciprocity, but with little reliance on data or scientific method.

That is not how it has to be. Data and method can serve individual as well as institutional goals. Everything we know can be used just as well by individuals to guide themselves and help each other (Duncan, Hively, and Spence, in press). This is what O. R. Lindsley calls "humane science."

Charles Madsen, Carl Thoresen, Roger Ulrich, Joseph and Elaine Zimmerman, and others have started the work, but a general survey of the field will show the reciprocity frequencies to be very low.

The count sheets for reciprocity may be used not only to evaluate ongoing projects but also to help guide more strategic project planning. Most of us have had the experience of working with "subjects" who responded beautifully to a program designed with great care by us, directed by us, and implemented by us with a little help from teachers or parents. But go back and visit the people who took part in the projects you alone mainly controlled. What are the children and their helpers doing now? How lasting were the effects? What happened to the institutions after you left? Much of the work in which *other* management had predominated seems to have had little lasting effect. The more reciprocity and self-management are built into a community, the more lasting the effects may be.

At another session in this conference, there was a panel discussion on "Control and Countercontrol," in which the discussion was devoted exclusively to the philosophical status of radical behaviorism. But it really does not matter whether the theoretical foundations of behaviorism are complete, whether they take into account all human activity, or whether they are rationalized with currently prevailing philosophies. The point is that the technology produces results, and the consequent sense of power tends to trap us into theoretical and provisional orthodoxies and leads us to lose sight of the overall social context in which we work.

The technology produces its results mainly because of its method—pinpoint, record, chart, and change. In that method is the power, and from it must come the counterbalance. If we allow ourselves to lose sight of the experimental method that concentrates on data and its search for function, we cease to grow and to make contact with others. If we stay with it, traditional behavior modifiers, far-out precision teachers, group-process advocates, and humanists can all continue to make science together. If we do not stay with it, we deserve to become extinct.

So stay with the data, delicately, continuously, and with an open mind. If you are a governor who loves his citizens, you can study and help them that way. If you are a citizen who values his freedom, in that way you can study yourself, protect yourself, and help the ones you love. Do unto yourself as you would do unto others. Care enough to chart and the data may help to keep us free.

### ACKNOWLEDGMENTS
Many people whose names do not appear in this paper have helped us learn about reciprocity, especially A.D.D.'s colleagues and students at Yeshiva University,

too numerous to name, and our current coworkers in the Psycho-Eduactional Center: Judi Curtis, Bob Graham, and Chris O'Brien.

Special thanks go to Carole Bland for careful counting, Eric Haughton for careful reading, and Roger Wilk for encouragement. And special gratitude to the behavers—Ruth, Judi, Frankie, and Christine—for sharing a portion of their lives with all of us through their charts.

# References

Duncan, A. D., Hively, W., and Spence, I. *Precision Teaching and Precise Personal Management.* New York: David McKay, Inc. (*In press.*)

Ferkiss, Victor. *Technological Man.* New York: New American Library (Mentor), 1970.

Ferster, C. B. The use of learning principles in clinical practice and training. *Psychological Record,* 1971, **21**, 353–361.

Fixen, D., Phillips, E., and Wolf, M. Achievement Place: The reliability of self-reporting and peer-reporting and their effects on behavior. *Journal of Applied Analysis Behavior,* 1972, **5**, 19–33.

Goodman, Paul *New Reformation,* New York: Random House (Vintage), 1969.

Illich, I. *Deschooling Society,* New York: Harper & Row, 1970.

Lindsley, O. R. From Skinner to precision teaching: The child knows best. In J. Jordan, and L. S. Robbins (Eds.), *Behavioral Principles and the Exceptional Child.* Arlington, Va.: Council for Exceptional Children, 1972.

Meadows, D. H., Meadows, D. L., Randers, J., and Behrens, W. *The Limits of Growth.* Washington, D.C.: Potomac Associates, 1972.

Phillips, E. L. Achievement Place: Token reinforcement procedures in a home-style rehabilitation setting for pre-delinquent boys, *Journal of Experimental Analysis Behavior,* 1968, **1**, 213–223.

Phillips, E., Phillips, E., Fixen, D., and Wolf, M. Achievement Place: Modification of behaviors of pre-delinquent boys with a token economy. *Journal of Applied Analysis Behavior,* 1971, **4**, 45–61.

Rogers, C. R. *Freedom to Learn.* Columbus, Ohio: Charles Merrill, 1969.

Skinner, B. F. *Walden Two.* New York: Macmillan, 1948.

# 12 BEHAVIOR TECHNOLOGY IN HIGHER EDUCATION

**Richard W. Malott**

**Beverly Louisell**

We are trying to design an optimum learning system for higher education. Learning systems include two major components: the teacher and the student.

The student wants to learn—he would love to have all "A" grades—but there are many competing variables that prevent such a performance. He has difficulty determining the important aspects of the material and

*Figure 12.1.*

*Figure 12.2.*

therefore often spends precious time studying the wrong things. At a typical university, 25% of the freshmen are on academic probation. (Malott, 1972). Instructors deplore poor student performance, grades continue to fall into the bell-shaped curve, students often miss the important points in the material presented, and each new group of students has difficulty with the same concepts semester after semester. "In spite of this state of affairs, it may be that all students meeting the normal college entrance requirements are capable of doing 'A' level work [Malott and Svinicki, 1969]."

The development of the present learning system was initiated because traditional college education is not adequately accomplishing its goal. What is the purpose of education? It is not simply to provide the student with a chance to learn but rather, *the purpose of education is to teach.* A good teacher does not expect students to "get it on their own"—he maximizes the chances of learning. He sets up the learning environment so that it is virtually impossible for the student *not* to achieve.

Bearing in mind the shortcomings of traditional college education, our courses were designed using the principles of systems analysis: The behaviors desired from the students were clearly *specified,* whether or not those behaviors occurred was *observed,* and *consequences* for those behaviors were provided in the form of appropriate rewards and punishments.

## Specification

Since the instructor knows the important concepts that are presented in his material, it makes sense for him to specify exactly what it is he wants the students to learn. The student does not learn less because he is told what is important—as a matter of fact, he probably learns more because he does not inadvertently spend valuable time on unimportant aspects of the material; if there is something he finds particularly interesting but not essential in the course, he is free to study it at his leisure. Therefore, at the beginning of each semester, each of our students receives written objectives for the course material. These objectives are in the form of multiple-choice questions covering the important ideas to be learned. Clarification of especially difficult areas is included.

Along with the objectives, a written course syllabus describing the grading system, and course policy on attendance and tardiness, is given to

*Figure 12.3.*

*Figure 12.4.*

each student. The class meets for 1 hour 4 days a week. Each day the student is quizzed over a 1-hour reading assignment. The daily quizzing is to help the student study in the most effective way possible—short, daily study sessions. Students will almost always study just before a test, but tests are not given often enough to control daily study behavior; instead, the student "crams" before the test, which means that he spends less time on each individual aspect of the material, retains less, and gets a lower grade than he is actually capable of achieving.

## Observation and Consequation

Daily study behavior is observed through daily quizzes. The answers are read in class right after the quiz, so the student gets immediate feedback as to how well he performed. The grades are then posted the following day, before class, by student number, so he can always tell exactly what his grade is in class at any given time.

*Figure 12.5.*

The grading scale is absolute, so each student has an equal chance to get an "A"—he is competing with an absolute standard, not other students. The criteria for an "A" in the course are (1) 90% mastery of daily activities and (2) 90% mastery of the concepts presented on a final exam. The final exam includes questions on all the material covered during the semester. The final exam is used only to raise grades; it can never subtract from a student's in-class performance. Students are also required to demonstrate a functional comprehension of the principles of behavior by completing four laboratory experiments. Two rewrites are allowed for each report, so points are seldom, if ever, lost for lab work.

All students do not learn at the same speed. Some require teacher-guided remediation, whereas others do not. One of the long-standing problems of education has been how to handle remedial activities— what do you do with those who do not need them? We solved the problem by presenting all the material in the first 10 weeks of a 15-week semester. This has proved to be a reasonable pace for the average student. At the end of 10 weeks, those students with "A" in the course are no longer required to attend class. The other students are given 5 weeks of remedial

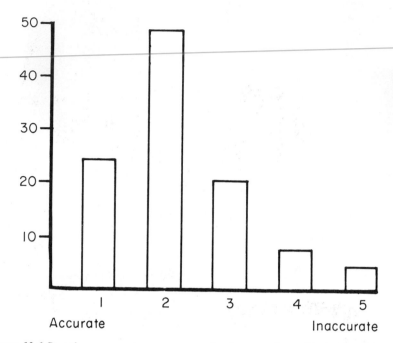

*Figure 12.6* Sample response to a course-evaluation question asking, "Are the grades you are receiving in this course an accurate measure of how much you are learning?"

quizzes, followed by another final. Most raise their course grades by at least one letter grade during these last weeks. Thus, we accomplish several goals: Students with 90% mastery at the end of 10 weeks are reinforced by not having to attend class for 5 weeks, by the social prestige of finishing class early, and by avoidance of remedial activities they do not need; students who need a little extra help get it in an efficient, systematic way and receive a grade in no way affected by the performance of the "fast learners" in their class.

Obviously, in such a system absences can seriously affect a student's grade. The material is cumulative, and days missed lower the probability of 90% mastery on subsequent days. So a rather strict absence policy is observed, consisting of excused and unexcused absences issued through a "central excuse system." Excused absences are those for which a student has verifiable proof that his absence was unavoidable. Each student is allowed 4 unexcused absences—the 5th drops his grade one letter; or

*Figure 12.7.*

he can have 14 excused absences, but with the 15th his grade is lowered one letter. Any combination of excused and unexcused absences totaling 15 also lowers the course grade one letter.

Class time is extremely valuable. There are 5 minutes for questions before the quiz, the quiz is given, answer sheets are collected, the answers are read, quizzes are collected, and generally the rest of the time is spent working with the rats. It would be disruptive and inefficient for students to enter after quizzes are handed out, so tardiness has been defined as any time following 1 minute after class is scheduled to begin. The consequence for tardiness is that the student is not allowed to take that day's quiz and receives an unexcused absence for the day.

Make-up quizzes are given Saturday mornings; *any* missed quiz may be taken, whether the absence was excused or unexcused.

*Figure 12.8.*

## Recycling

This is our learning system as it exists today. Since its inception in the fall of 1966, it has undergone many changes. One of the primary rules of systems analysis is that after (1) the behavioral objectives have been specified, (2) the behavioral systems has been designed, and (3) implemented, (4) the system must be evaluated if necessary, and (5) recycled through the above-mentioned phases of systems analysis. Most of our course changes resulted from student suggestions or complaints, performances not up to par with our expectations, expectations that proved to be unreasonable, and data gathered from master's theses.

Initially, the daily quizzes consisted of two short essay questions. It was impossible to make up enough different questions for the 58 sections

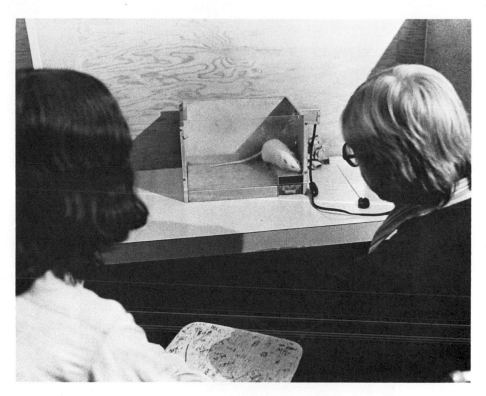

*Figure 12.9.*

handling the 1000 students typically enrolled in the course; by the afternoon, students knew the questions they were going to be asked. The solution to this problem was a system utilizing multiple-choice questions. There are ten questions on a quiz and four different forms of each quiz. Every week a schedule is made up so that, in a random manner, two of the four forms are given in a section.

When the two short-answer questions were being used, there was a 100% mastery requirement in effect. Six make-up quizzes were offered for each reading assignment, the first preceded by a 40-minute remedial lecture on the evening of the regular quiz. A student had to demonstrate 100% mastery on one of the quizzes for a particular reading assignment or drop the course, or get an "E" if it was too late to drop. We have since altered our policy due to the manpower required in administering so many remedial quizzes and because students and those running the course found this system unduly aversive. At present, the mastery requirement is 90%.

*Figure 12.10.*

On Friday, a remedial lecture is given over the material with which students had difficulty that week, following which a two-question multiple-choice quiz is given covering the lecture. The points a student earns on the lecture quiz are "extra"; they are bonus points that are added to his in-class grade. We feel this to be a much more efficient and reinforcing way to handle remediation, but we must admit that academic achievement is lower than with our previous mastery requirement.

Hubbard (1971), Hesse (1971), and Janczarek (1970) conducted

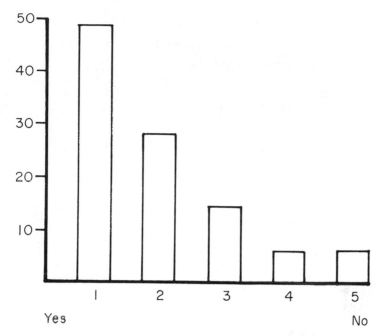

*Figure 12.11* Sample response to a course evaluation question asking, "Is this course designed and managed so that you could achieve a high level of mastery?"

research on the effect of daily quizzes on hour-examination performance. Their data indicated that students who took daily quizzes performed significantly higher on the midterm and final examinations than those who took the examinations without daily quizzes. These results gave credence to our earlier supposition that if a student learns material in short, daily study sessions, he will not only perform better, but he will also retain a higher percentage of the concepts presented.

Included in our educational goals has been a desire to help the students demonstrate a conceptual mastery of the principles of behavior. This has proven to be an extremely difficult task. In the early development of our course, students were required to participate in discussions emphasizing the proper use of four attitudes of science as they applied to various articles. Extensive research revealed that final examination scores were not positively affected by the discussion procedures, so this aspect of the course was eliminated (Malott and Rollofson, 1972).

Being able to apply a knowledge of the principles of behavior still seemed a worthwhile skill, so our effort to teach conceptualization was pursued. Hubbard (1971), after analyzing the final-examination perfor-

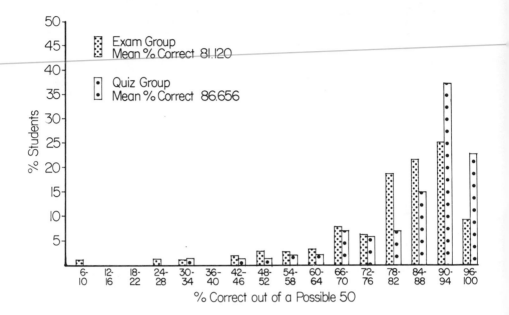

*Figure 12.12* A comparison of scores on a final examination in introductory psychology for students who took only a midterm and final exam (Exam Group) and students who also took daily quizzes (Quiz Group).

mance of students, suggested that the texts and class procedures were adequate for students to learn at the recognition level (Espich and Williams, 1967). Further study indicated that the materials were also adequate for learning at a conceptual level. What was needed to ensure that such conceptual learning occurred was supplementary materials geared toward the multiple-choice format. Reese and Woolfenden (1973) and Woolfenden (1972) obtained results with programs using the multiple-choice format that demonstrated conceptual learning by both the identification and writing of examples. Several of these programs have been incorporated into our present course materials. Another area in which the students failed to meet our expectations was data graphing. Graphs were usually incorrect because the axes were not labeled, there was no legend, or the scales were not assigned numerical values of equal intervals. Katzenberg (1974) developed a programmed text on graph construction. The standard for the graph was that it should meet the publication requirements of the American Psychological Association. The program was successful in teaching the concept of graphing laboratory data.

**TABLE 12.1**
DECILE DISTRIBUTION OF EXAMINATION SCORES SHOWN IN FIGURE 12.12

| | Midterm exam | | Final exam | |
| --- | --- | --- | --- | --- |
| Scores | Exam Group | Quiz Group | Exam Group | Quiz Group |
| 90–100 | 44% | 60% | 35% | 61% |
| 80–89 | 23% | 24% | 34% | 19% |
| 70–79 | 13% | 11% | 14% | 12% |
| 60–69 | 3% | 2% | 9% | 4% |
| Below 60 | 17% | 3% | 8% | 4% |

*Figure 12.13.*

Thus, we are constantly revising our source materials in an effort to reach our educational goal of "teaching as much as possible to as many as possible."

## Student-Centered Education Project

The technology with which we were successful in individual courses has been applied to an entire curriculum at Western Michigan University. It is the Student-Centered Education Project, begun in the fall semester of 1969 and comprising 35 students who volunteered to take all or most of their courses in the project. Two apartment buildings serve as university-approved dormitories for 21 of the SCEP students. These dorms are an important part of the project—students share common interests and goals and are all committed to spending a greater than average amount of time on their academic work.

Each course offered in SCEP has applied the principles of systems

*Figure 12.14.*

*Figure 12.15.*

analysis. The desired behavior is specified, observed, and consequated. At the beginning of the class meeting, the student goes to a study carrel, where he reads for 30 minutes while referring to study objectives he has been given. He then goes over the study objectives again, making sure he can answer them. The quiz is given and, when answered and collected, the "teaching apprentice" reads the correct answers—this provides the student with immediate feedback. The grading scale is set up to encourage maximum learning.

Courses offered in SCEP include General Social Studies; Philosophy: Introduction to Logic; Management: Fundamentals of Management (management as it applies to social or behavioral systems such as mental hospitals, classrooms, and families); Social Basis of Human Behavior; and Introductory Mathematics. In comparison to the traditional courses they have had, students rated the contents of their SCEP courses as vastly superior. They strongly prefer studying in the SCEP system, they work much harder, and they prefer daily quizzes to hour exams. They are under slightly more pressure than traditional students, but most feel that the

*Figure 12.16.*

pressure is not too intense. There is considerable academic interaction among students in the SCEP dorms, where they can use the technical vocabulary they are learning. Everyone involved in the program is more than satisfied.

## Teaching Apprentices

One of the most important factors in the implementation of our educational system has been the use of teaching apprentices. These are students who took the course previously and showed an "A" mastery of its

*Figure 12.17.*

contents. The T.A. is in charge of a class of 24 students, for which he answers questions about the day's assignment, administers and grades the quizzes, supervises laboratory work, and helps monitor the weekly lecture sections, make-up labs, or make-up quizzes. For performance of these duties, the T.A. receives 3 hours of academic credit, teaching experience early in his college career, and increased knowledge in the subject area.

After serving as teaching apprentices, 13 students are picked to serve as advanced teaching apprentices during the following term. The advanced teaching apprentice monitors the performance of the teaching apprentices in the discussion/laboratory sections. He has a rating form that he uses to grade the teaching apprentices on the basis of classroom performance, reliability of performing clerical work, accuracy of seminar monitoring, quiz grading, and laboratory report grading. In addition, the advanced teaching apprentice helps with more advanced administrative aspects of the course. Grades are posted daily and cumulated weekly.

### Assistants

Four paid undergraduate assistants each work 20 hours a week on the course. Their duties are arranged so that one assistant is primarily responsi-

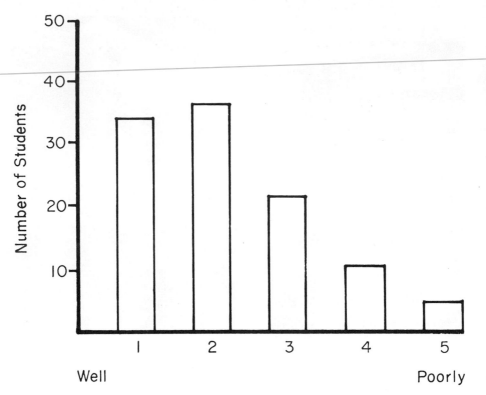

*Figure 12.18* A course-evaluation question asking, "How well do the faculty, assist-ants, and apprentices for this course seem to have mastered the information and skills the course is attempting to teach?"

ble for supervising the laboratory sections, another the lectures, and a third the reading quizzes; the fourth acts as a general administrative assist-ant. They are also responsible for evaluating the performance of the ad-vanced teaching apprentices. Paid graduate assistants develop new course materials based on an analysis of quiz results. Through this system of teaching apprentices, advanced teaching apprentices, undergraduate assist-ants, and graduate assistants (T.A.s, A.T.A.s, U.G.A.s, and G.A.s), a large number of students (about 1000) can be taught each semester with no loss of individual attention for the student. Students are involved in every aspect of the course—in fact, it is their course. Changes are made as a result of their suggestions on student evaluations. They take this re-sponsibility seriously and are doing everything they can to help us accom-plish our goal of designing an educational system that provides the best education possible for as many as possible.

ACKNOWLEDGMENTS

We wish to thank Jim Smith for the photography and Pat Hartlep for the artwork that appears in this article.

## References

Espich, J. E., and Williams, B. *Developing Programmed Instructional Materials.* Palo Alto, Calif.: Fearon Publishers, 1967.

Hesse, R. M. The effects of daily quizzes on hour examination performance in a junior level psychology course. Unpublished master's thesis, Western Michigan University, Kalamazoo, Michigan, 1971.

Hubbard, M. C. Daily quizzes with review and remedial quizzes and examination performance. Unpublished master's thesis, Western Michigan University, Kalamazoo, Michigan, 1971.

Janczarek, K. M. The effects of daily quizzes on hour examination performance. Unpublished master's thesis, Western Michigan University, Kalamazoo, Michigan, 1970.

Katzenberg, A. C. *How to Draw Graphs.* Kalamazoo, Mich.: Behaviordelia, 1974.

Malott, R. W. *Contingency Management in Education,* 2nd ed. Kalamazoo, Mich.: Behaviordelia, 1972.

Malott, R. W., and Palm, J. M. Contingency management revisited. *Journal of the Scientific Laboratories,* 1971, **52**, 9–13.

Malott, R. W., and Rollofson, R. L. An empirical evaluation of student-led discussions. *Psychological Reports,* 1972, **30**, 531–535.

Malott, R. W., and Svinicki, J. G. Contingency management in an introductory psychology course produces better learning. *Psychological Record,* 1969, **2**, 79–83.

Reese, D. G., and Woolfenden, R. M. *Behavioral Analysis of Everyday Life: A Program for the Generalization of Behavioral Concepts.* Kalamazoo, Mich.: Behaviordelia, 1973.

Woolfenden, R. M. The development and empirical validation of programmed instructional materials to improve conceptual mastery, the development and empirical validation. Unpublished master's thesis, Western Michigan University, Kalamazoo, Michigan, 1972.

# 13 VERBAL DEVELOPMENT IN PRESCHOOL CHILDREN

Emilio Ribes-I.

Silvia Gomar-Ruiz

Leticia Rivas

With the exception of a few cases (Risley, Reynolds, and Hart, 1970), most studies on verbal behavior in normal children deal with individual training situations. Nevertheless, it is important to stress the social nature of verbal development and the necessity of designing and evaluating experimental programs in social situations that better describe natural conditions affecting language acquisition and maintenance in preschool children. In this chapter we shall report some data referred to individual children in a group situation. The study is part of an experimental project for developing verbal behavior in nursery school children.

The program to be described has been applied to children attending a public nursery school in Mexico City. Most of the children come from low or middle-low income social classes and range from 3 to 5 years old. The program covers three basic objectives: (1) to increase the frequency of talking (verbal rate), (2) to extend the range (amplitude) of the verbal repertoire or vocabulary, and (3) to establish differential environmental control of verbal behavior.

In the following sections, we shall describe each of the particular projects and its outcome. Since each of the program objectives was developed simultaneously but in separate form, we shall discuss first the project related to the development behaviors differentially controlled by the environment.

221

**Differential Environmental Control of Verbal Behavior**

Although most programs in verbal behavior try to establish a varied vocal topography, it is necessary to discriminate between different functional repertoires in terms of the environmental control exerted on verbal behavior. Some programs acknowledge this fact (Lovaas, 1968). In our study we have tried to develop differential verbal repertoires according to Skinner's (1957) classification of environmentally determined response classes.

Three types of verbal classes are considered in this program, in reference to the discriminative stimuli and reinforcers related to them.

The first are *mands*. These responses lack antecedent stimulus control and are defined by the consequences following the behavior, which are specified by the behavior itself—commands, questions, petitions, and so on. Although lacking observable discriminative stimuli, mands may increase in probability through the manipulation of previous deprivation or aversive conditions (setting events). Mands are generally reinforced through the threat of potentially aversive consequences represented by the speaker, although many other contingency interactions might be described (Skinner, 1957, p. 40). In this program children are taught to use *softened* mands, that is, verbal responses whose reinforcement is not mediated by the removal of potential aversive consequences on the listener.

The second type of verbal responses are *tacts*. Tacts are responses controlled and defined by an antecedent nonverbal stimulus and maintained by generalized and educational reinforcers. These verbal responses generally involve labeling or identification responses, and are closely related to the "meaning" of language. Although *extended* tacts are an essential component of concept formation, we shall restrict ourselves to the development of nonextended tacts or at most of *generic* extensions.

The third type of verbal responses included in this program are *intraverbal* responses controlled by antecedent verbal stimuli lacking formal correspondence to the behavior and maintained by generalized reinforcers. Intraverbal behavior is related to conventional talking and conversation. Most verbal behavior is intraverbal, at least in terms of partial determinants comprising its multiple causation.

The objectives of this program were to increase the number of complex intraverbal responses (to three or more words), to increase the number of cases, and to increase the number of softened mands. The design of the program involved four periods: (1) baseline period, (2) reinforcement of tacts, complex intraverbal with mixed tact components, and softened mands, (3) reversal to baseline conditions, and (4) reinstatement of period 2.

The experimental situation involved an arrangement that allowed simultaneous reinforcement of three types of terminal behaviors. The experimental setting was a small room where the teacher and five children were seated around a table, watched by two observers located in the corner of the room, who recorded the children's behavior. The materials on the table consisted of cards, pictures, and objects. Each session lasted 15 minutes and the recording was made through an instantaneous *flash* sampling technique. Every 5 seconds, the observers recorded whether one of the five children emitted one or another type of verbal response. The recording was sequential, so each sample corresponded to a different child: Each child was included in a total of 36 samplings per session. Reliability estimates were obtained by dividing the number of agreements by the number of agreements plus nonagreements and then discarding those agreements indicating nonoccurrence of behavior.

During the baseline period, the situation was arranged as a free-operant situation, in which the teacher sat with the children, made materials on the table available without explaining what the materials were about or their use, while at the same time trying not to prompt any response through questions or verbal indications. The teacher encouraged the children to remain in the experimental setting for a 15-minute period covering the experimental session. This total experiment involved a minimum of 20 sessions.

In the first experimental period, the teacher presented the materials to the children, giving them general instructions and prompting the response to be reinforced. Afterwards, she asked each of the children, in sequential order, the object's name or its use, reinforcing the child first for emitting the correct tact, and then for emitting a tact mixed with an intraverbal response. She also reinforced responses each time they were more complex in terms of the number of words. The objects or pictures were available to the children if they emitted softened mands. Tacts and mixed tacts-intraverbals were reinforced through a point system, where points could be redeemed for access to the play yard and toys, candies, or sodas. Social reinforcement, such as praise and attention, were provided for each correct response. It is important to note that observation samplings did not coincide with the questions the teacher addressed to each child. On the contrary, samplings were made independent of whether or not the teacher was asking a particular child being observed. This was done to avoid a procedural artifact that might contaminate the recordings by an artificial increase in the number of correct responses. This experimental period lasted a minimum of 20 sessions.

The reversal period involved two phases. In the first, lasting five sessions, conditions were the same as during baseline. In the second phase, lasting a minimum of five sessions, the teacher presented new materials to the children as in the experimental period without reinforcing or prompting verbal responses to these materials.

In the fourth period, new materials were presented, with probes in the last day of each week (every fifth session), during which no reinforcers or minimal prompts were provided. This period involved a minimum of ten sessions. Reliability in the recordings was of 88%, with a range of 80% to 96%.

Since the data obtained in the four groups of five children each are very similar, we shall show the data of only one of these groups. Figure 13.1 depicts the outcome of the various periods described earlier.

The baseline section shows a very low percentage of tacting behavior. The peak reached only 30%, while the score during the lowest session was 4%, with a mean of 17.1% in the 22 sessions. Intraverbal behavior was somewhat higher, with a peak at 80% and the lowest session at 31%. The mean was 52.3%. Mands were intermediate in frequency, with a peak at 60% and the lowest session at 10%. The mean score was 29.6%.

During the first experimental period, when social reinforcement and the point system were introduced, marked changes in the foregoing behaviors were observed. In general, the graph shows a separation of the three behaviors, tacts increasing, intraverbal behavior showing a moderate decrease, and mands practically disappearing. The peak for tacts was at 83%, with the lowest session at 40%, and a mean score of 60.3% in 20 sessions. Intraverbal behavior had its peak at 55% and the lowest session at 18%, with a mean of 31.9%. Mands had its peak at 27%, the lowest session at zero, with a mean of 6.2%.

In the reversal period, the distribution of the verbal response classes returned toward the conditions prevailing during baseline. Tacts decreased, mands increased to an intermediate frequency, and intraverbal behavior became the highest. Tacts had its peak at 52%, the lowest session being at 9%, with a mean score of 25.6% in nine sessions. Intraverbal behavior had its peak at 63%, with the lowest score at 23% and a mean of 42.6%. Mands had its peak at 33% and the lowest score at 23%, with a mean of 27.5%. It should be observed, nevertheless, that tacts showed a higher level than during the baseline period.

In the second experimental period, including probe sessions, conditions seemed to replicate the data obtained in the first experimental period. Tacts increased again, with a peak at 84%, the lowest session at 53%, and a mean of 70% in 11 sessions. Tacts increased in frequency compared with the previous experimental period. Intraverbal behavior decreased again, with its peak at 40%, the lowest session at 8%, and a mean score

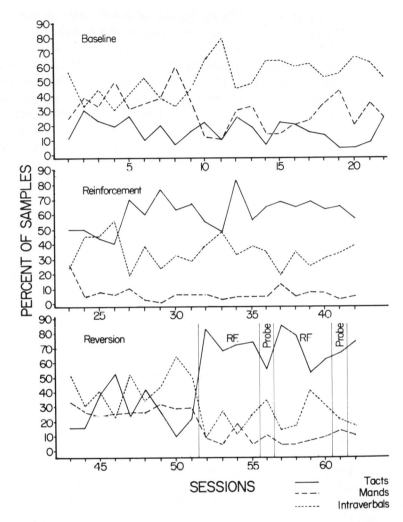

*Figure 13.1.*

of 21.5%. Mands also decreased dramatically, with a peak at 18%, the lowest session at 3%, and a mean score of 8%.

Several interesting facts appear in these data. First, the reinforcement procedure in a group situation seemed to be effective only in relation to tacts. Intraverbal responses always tended to decrease when tacts were reinforced as the main experimental target. This might be accounted for in two ways. It could be that in the particular situation described, with presentation of visual material, both classes of verbal behavior were incompatible. The effect could also be determined by the verbal behavior of the teacher which, through reinforcing correct tacts, fostered the emission of short responses controlled exclusively by the visual material presented.

Another interesting feature of the data is the relation between tacts and mands. Mands tended to increase when no reinforcement was provided in the situation. When tacts were reinforced in the experimental periods, mands decreased dramatically. This is a clear demonstration of the differential environmental control on verbal response classes, since mands did increase in probability through a deprivation procedure, as the baseline and reversal periods indicate.

## Verbal Repertoire Range or Amplitude

Another important aspect in the development of verbal behavior is related to the relative amplitude of members of the *verbal repertoire* of a particular subject. This diversity in verbal responses involves two different situations: the difference *per se* in the verbal responses emitted in a given situation and the different responses controlled by the same or a similar nonverbal stimulus (synonyms).

In this program both objectives were pursued, and the general design involved three periods: (1) baseline period, (2) increase of verbal diversity, and (3) increase of verbal diversity under the control of a nonverbal stimulus.

In order to avoid resorting to reversal periods, DRO probes were included in periods (2) and (3).

The experimental situation consisted of a room with various tables and chairs. Thirty children were divided into three groups of ten each, distributed in three different sections of the room for observation and reinforcement.

During baseline, which involved a minimum of 20 sessions of 45 minutes each, a temporal sampling system was used. Each 30 seconds a different child was observed for 5 seconds, and the number of different words emitted was transcribed on the recording sheet. Each child was sampled nine times per session. During this time, the observers were in the room and did not interact in any way with the children. Materials were absent.

In the first experimental period, reinforcement was introduced to increase the diversity of the children's verbal repertoire. Materials were also

introduced for the first time. Reinforcement consisted of points to be redeemed (marks on a sheet), social approval, and praise. Reinforcement
was dispensed by an adult, who interacted with each child in sequential
order every 20 seconds, attending 135 times to the group of children and
13–14 times to each child. If the child did not speak during the first 10
seconds of the 20-second sample, the adult prompted the response. The
criterion was increased progressively by two words every session. Every
2 weeks, a DRO probe was introduced to verify the procedure's effectiveness.

The second experimental period was initiated when children were
capable of emitting a sufficient number of different verbal responses per
session (14 different words per sample). During this period, the adult
questioned a child every 20 seconds (according to a previously arranged
sequential order) as to which other way he could designate an action, object, or stimulus property. If the child did not respond within 5 seconds
after the question was addressed, the response was prompted through imitation and the child was reinforced. The following two samples consisted
of tests involving synonym acquisition, so that every child could learn
four synonyms per session. These synonyms were repeated during four
sessions. In the fifth session a general test was provided to determine
whether the child was able to emit the complete list of synonyms acquired
during the previous weeks. In this period the recording system was
changed. The responses recorded were those asked by one observer who
did not prompt or reinforce. The observer sampled a different child every
30 seconds according to a sequential order different from the one followed
by the experimenter. A test was also performed by the experimenter, who
did not reinforce the children.

In this program, recordings were checked for reliability by an observer
who intermittently recorded the responses of every group of children working under a different observer. Responses by each group of ten children
were recorded separately. Agreement between observers yielded a percentage of 90.2, with a range of 80.5 to 100%.

The outcome of this program is presented in Figures 13.2, 13.3, and
13.4. Figure 13.2 shows the number of different words emitted in a session
by a group of ten children during a 45-minute period. The other three
groups showed similar results. Each point represents the number of words
in the corresponding session. The dotted line shows the mean frequency
per treatment. During the baseline period, the average was 25 different
words, with a range of 0 to 52. In the first experimental treatment, the
mean increased to 50 words, with a range of 65 to 34 words. In the first
DRO probe, the mean increased to 56 words. In the second experimental

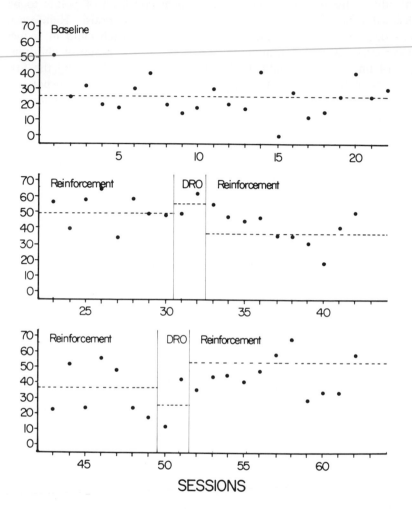

*Figure 13.2.*

treatment, there was a decline in the mean to 37 words with a range of 55 to 18 words. In the second DRO probe, the mean decreased even more, to 26 words, and then finally increased in the third experimental period to a mean of 52 words, with a range of 68 to 29. It should be stressed that these data were recorded in those time samples in which the experimenter was not interacting with the particular child.

Figure 13.3 shows how the various response criteria were achieved

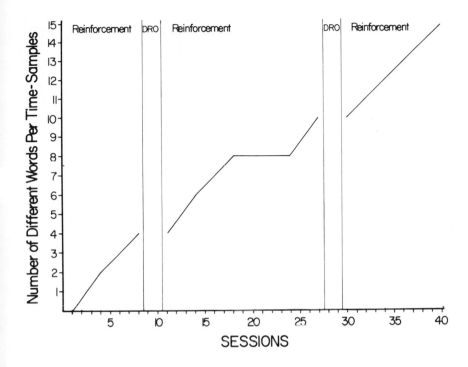

*Figure 13.3.*

by the group as a whole. No data are provided for the DRO probes, but on the average, the children obtained a larger number of reinforcers in these periods than during the experimental periods. This means that the number of different responses emitted in each sample was under that session's criterion. In session 4, children were capable of emitting two different words per sample; in session 8, four different words; in session 14, six different words; in session 18, eight different words; in session 27, 10 different words; in session 34, 12 different words; and in session 40, 14 different words per sample. This was the terminal repertoire specified by the program. This repertoire of 14 different words per sample was maintained during the rest of the sessions.

Figure 13.4 presents the acquisition of synonyms. The graph shows the percentage of correct responses during the reinforcement periods and test sessions. This program is still under way, so we shall present only partial data involving 14 sessions. Since the program is a continuation of the verbal amplitude program, no baseline was measured. In the first experimental treatment, the percentage of correct responses increased from 25

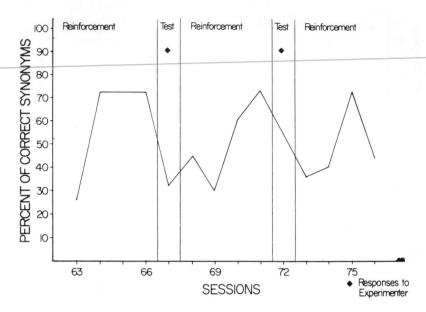

*Figure 13.4.*

in the first session to 73 in the other three sessions. In the first test session the percentage decreased to 32 when an observer asked for the synonyms from the children, but when the experimenter was the questioner, the percentage was about 63%, in spite of the fact that no reinforcement was provided. In the second experimental treatment, with different synonyms, correct responding increased from 45% in the first session to 74% in the fourth session. In the second test session, the same effect was replicated. The percentage of correct responses decreased to 55% according to the observer, but increased to 84% according to the experimenter. In the third experimental period, with new synonyms, correct responding increased from 36% in the first session to 73% in the third session. For unknown reasons, correct responding in the fourth session decreased to 44%.

## Discussion

The relevant findings in this program are as follows. First, the size of vocabulary can be increased in a group situation by using reinforcement procedures. Children learned 14 different words in a brief time sample in only 40 sessions, and in 62 sessions they learned to emit an average of 50 different words without prompting. This is a remarkable vocabulary for children of preschool age from low-income classes in Mexico. Also, it has been shown that synonyms may be acquired under the same conditions at a rate of four per week, and that these changes are maintained in the absence of arbitrary reinforcers.

It should be mentioned that the data reflect the influence of natural generalized reinforcers in the situation and the discriminative control gained by the experimenter. In the amplitude section of the program, the data were taken during "no-reinforcement" samples. This means that the children were emitting a great deal of different verbalizations in a momentarily unstructured situation, probably controlled only by their peers. In the synonyms section of the program, the test sessions showed quite clearly the degree of stimulus control achieved by the experimenter on the verbal behavior of children. This is relevant to Skinner's (1957) discussion of the audience and to some experimental results concerned with the audience effects on verbal behavior in natural settings (de Souza e Silva, 1971).

One point remains to be explained, concerning the increment observed in the first DRO probe in the amplitude section of the program. The effect was not consistent, since amplitude increased in the second DRO probe. Two reasons could be advanced. The first concerns the probe length. The probe period might be too short to produce generalized effects outside of the experimental samples. The second concerns the partial irreversibility of natural reinforcers established in the experimental setting and the prompting properties acquired by people even in a DRO situation.

It should also be noted that the introduction of reinforcement for increased vocabulary size reduced the variability between sessions in the group scores compared with those obtained in the baseline and DRO probe sessions. This effect is observed when no reinforcement was provided, which means that in one or another way reinforcement restricts the elements of the verbal class of the group defined as a behaving unit.

The last aspect of verbal development that we shall discuss is response rate. In this program, we tried to increase the frequency of verbal behavior independently of the topography or functional characteristics of the behavior. This has been one of the areas in which operant conditioning procedures have proven to be most successful.

In this case, conserving the group setting, the program involved five periods: (1) baseline period, (2) reinforcement for talking, (3) reversal period, (4) reintroduction of reinforcement, and (5) stretching out reinforcement ratio.

The experimental setting was the same as the one used for the program to increase vocabulary size. Thirty children divided into three ten-children subgroups were introduced into a room with material for 30 minutes a day. Reinforcement in this situation consisted, as in the rest of the programs, of a point system redeemable for back-up reinforcers and social reinforcement (praise, etc.).

During baseline, observations were made every 5 seconds using an instantaneous time sampling procedure. This system was changed for another consisting of continuous 5-second observation intervals, in sequential order for every child in the room. In both sampling procedures, each sample was always scored as a single count, independent of the number of words emitted during the sample. The number of observation samples was the same in both systems: 360 samples for the group as a whole and 36 for every child. The difference consisted of the time duration of the observation sample: instantaneous or 5 seconds long. This was done in order to obtain a more sensitive measure of the experimental treatment effects. No experimenter interacted with the children at all during the baseline period.

The instantaneous sampling procedure was used until session 43, when the second sampling system was in use simultaneously with one subgroup in order to compare the differences produced in measurement with both time-recording procedures. In this period, an experimenter was introduced into the situation for each subgroup. The talking child was reinforced according to a time sampling procedure of 20 seconds arranged in sequential order. The criterion for reinforcement was simply that the child talk. Content or any other feature of speech was ignored. The observation time for the experimenter did not coincide with those of the observers. This was done in order to avoid contamination of the recordings by observing only the samples when children were reinforced. From the second week on, the experimenter provided prompts to those children whose rate of verbalization was low as shown by the recordings taken in the first week of the reinforcement procedure. The criterion for changing to the reversal period was specified in terms of the visually judged stability of the recordings. Each child was reinforced nine times per session. This means that children were under a FI schedule of reinforcement (200 seconds). This period lasted 40 sessions.

In the reversal period, the conditions were the same as during baseline. The experimenter was absent, and no reinforcement was provided. This period lasted 10 days.

In the second experimental treatment, which lasted 13 days, conditions were the same as during the first experimental period.

Finally, in the fifth period, reinforcement was faded out by the experimenter. In the first week the number of reinforcement samples would be half of those in the experimental periods, that is, four or five. In the second week, only one reinforcement sample would be provided for every child, and in the third week, reinforcement would be completely discontinued in order to assess the permanence of the changes in verbal rate. This part of the study is still in progress.

Reliability in the recordings reached 88%, with a range of 80 and 96 during the whole program.

Figure 13.5 presents the course of this program in one group. All groups showed the same effects. During the baseline period, frequency of verbalization never exceeded 27%, with a mean score of 13.1%. In the first experimental treatment, when reinforcement was introduced, no significant changes were observed. Although the peak showed a higher score than in the baseline period (54%), mean frequency per sample was only 15.3% until session 43. At this point an additional recording system was introduced in order to make the observation system more sensitive to the changes that had been observed informally. From session 43 to session 62 (when the period terminated), some differences were observed among the data yielded by the two recording systems. The initial recording system through *flash* samples every 5 seconds, yielded an average frequency of 19.1%. The second observation procedure, involving single counts taken in a continuous sample of 5-seconds duration, showed 30%.

In the reversal period, both observation systems were used. With the instantaneous sampling procedure, the average score was 16.6%. With the continuous sampling procedure, the average score was 26.6%. The same effect was obtained as in the other programs, where verbal changes seem to be partially irreversible. This was possibly due to the natural contingencies emerging during the experimental treatment. Here, for instance, it was observed that children did not stop talking among themselves in this period.

Finally, in the second experimental treatment, only the continuous sampling procedure was used, since it had proved to be more sensitive to changes in the situation being observed. In this period a very significant increase was observed. We do not know if this increase was due to the maintenance of the particular experimental treatment or to induction effects from the vocabulary program. The average percentage score was 48.7%, with the last six sessions having scores of 68, 70, 80, 75, 50, and 60%, respectively.

As a final comment, it should be mentioned that the data in this program seem to stress the importance of audience control and natural consequences playing an important role in the emission of verbal behavior. The difficulty of decreasing response rates during the reversal periods, and the

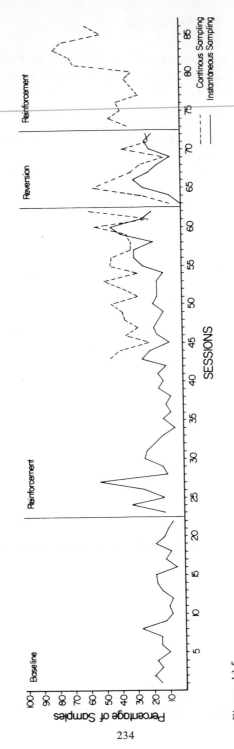

*Figure 13.5.*

increasing trend over sessions shown in the last section of Figure 13.5, relate to these factors.

## Concluding Comments

These data illustrate the possibility of arranging a social situation for developing verbal behavior in preschool children. Some factors, essential to the development and maintenance of verbal behavior, seem to be intrinsic to social arrangements where natural reinforcers gradually become the main sources of control (Ferster, 1967). A common outcome in the three programs described was the increased verbal interaction among children resulting from somewhat artificial experimental procedures employed in this study. These interactions were observed during DRO and reversal periods, and neutralized the expected effects of these manipulations in some instances. Additional research should be designed in order to evaluate the relative influence of different social variables acting in complex verbal episodes.

This study suggests the independence of functionally defined verbal repertoires, either in terms of environmental control or of response quantitative criteria. The three programs described here were carried on independently of each other, with apparently little interference. This means that it is possible to analyze and develop separate, different, functional verbal repertoires. In the future, research should be addressed to the experimental study of how these repertoires interact in the development of language in children.

### ACKNOWLEDGMENTS

The authors are most indebted to the group of students at the National University of Mexico who participated in the development of this project, but very specially to Enriqueta Galván, Vicente García, Ignacio Castro, and Lamberto Villaneuva.

The facilities provided by Dr. Lino Carbajal and Dr. David Fragoso, whose assistance is acknowledged, enabled us to carry out this project.

## References

de Souza e Silva, Sebastiao Vocalización Espontánea y Provocada en un sujeto retardado en tres—"Medios-Audiencia" naturales. Unpublished master's thesis, Department of Psychology, University of Veracruz, 1971.

Ferster, C. B. Arbitrary and natural reinforcement. *Psychological Record,* 1967, **17,** 341–347.

Lovaas, O. I. A program for the establishment of speech in psychotic children. In H. N. Sloane and B. D. Mac Aulay (Eds.), *Operant Procedures in Remedial Speech and Language Training.* Boston: Houghton Mifflin, 1968.

Risley, T., Reynolds, N., and Hart, B. The disadvantaged: Behavior modification with disadvantaged preschool children. In R. H. Bradfield (Ed.), *Behavior Modification, the Human Effort.* San Rafael, Calif.: Dimensions, 1970.

Skinner, B. F. *Verbal Behavior.* New York: Appleton-Century-Crofts, 1957.

# 14 EFFECTS OF PEER TUTORING AND HOMEWORK ASSIGNMENTS ON CLASSROOM PERFORMANCE

James A. Sherman

V. William Harris

The past 5 years have seen the ever-increasing application of behavior modification procedures with normal students in a variety of classroom situations. Some of the most extensive work has involved the use of behavioral consequences to reduce students' inappropriate social and disruptive behavior (e.g., Becker, Madsen, Arnold, and Thomas, 1967; Thomas, Becker, and Armstrong, 1968; Barrish, Saunders, and Wolf, 1969; McAllister, Stachowiak, Baer, and Conderman, 1969; Schmidt and Ulrich, 1969) and to increase attending or study behaviors (e.g., Bushell, Wrobel, and Michaelis, 1968; Hall, Lund, and Jackson, 1968; Broden, Bruce, Mitchell, Carter, and Hall, 1970; Packard, 1970). Although the definitions of inappropriate social and disruptive behavior and of attending and study behavior have varied from study to study, inappropriate social and disruptive behavior generally includes behaviors such as talking to classmates during individual study times, throwing objects, striking other students, and wandering around the room. Attending or study behavior generally includes orientation toward classmates when they are reciting, looking at books or study materials, writing, and working cooperatively with other children.

One reason for attempting to reduce disruptive behaviors and to increase attending and study behaviors in the classroom is based on the assumption that these changes will have beneficial effects on the students' performance with curriculum materials. It is assumed that reducing disruptive behavior or increasing study behavior will improve the rate and/or accuracy at which the students in the class complete academic assignments. Although the results of several studies suggest that improved academic performance was apparently related to increases in study behavior and reductions in disruptive behaviors (e.g., Hall *et al.,* 1968; O'Leary, Becker, Evans, and Saudargas, 1969; Surrat, Ulrich, and Hawkins, 1969), this relationship has not been found consistently in those studies that have attempted to investigate it systematically. In a study by Ferritor, Buckholdt, Hamblin, and Smith (1972), tokens, exchangeable for candy, ice cream, toys, and activities, were delivered when students were attending to academic tasks, including looking at or writing on paper and looking at the teacher when she was talking. They found that tokens for attending behavior did increase attending behavior somewhat, but had little effect on the rate of math problems completed correctly or overall accuracy. Similar results were found by Sulzer, Hunt, Ashby, Koniarski, and Krams (1971). However, a study by Harris and Sherman (1973a) showed that reductions in disruptive behavior produced by a group game procedure, in which children received permission to leave school early for nondisruptive behaviors, were consistently associated with small increases in accuracy of math performance of elementary school children. These small increases in accuracy appeared to be a function of decreasing the rate at which children completed math problems incorrectly rather than increasing the rate at which they completed math problems correctly.

At the present time, then, the precise relation between study behavior, disruptive behavior, and academic performance is not clear. It seems likely that any such relation would depend on at least three factors: the initial levels of attending and disruptive behavior of the students, the magnitude of effect that the experimental procedures had on increasing attending behavior and decreasing disruptive behavior, and the initial level of academic performance of the students. The results obtained in research up to this time, however, indicate that the use of consequences to increase attending behavior or to decrease disruptive behaviors may not automatically produce improved academic performance.

There has also been considerable research concerned with the direct use of behavioral consequences to improve the rate and/or accuracy of academic performance of students. Although many of these studies have examined the effects of behavioral consequences using special academic materials or particularly constructed pools of problems or tasks (e.g., Kirby and Shields, 1972; Ferritor *et al.,* 1972), or have employed students with special academic difficulties (e.g., Lovitt and Esveldt, 1970; Chadwick and Day, 1971; Birnbrauer, Wolf, Kidder, and Tague, 1965; Wolf,

Giles, and Hall, 1968; Lovitt and Curtiss, 1969; Tyler, 1967), a number of studies have examined the effects of behavioral consequences on the performance of normal students working on standard academic materials (e.g., Hamblin, Hathaway, and Wodarski, 1971; Sulzer *et al.,* 1971; Evans and Oswalt, 1968; Hanley and Perelman, 1971). Taken together, the results of these studies indicate that rate and/or accuracy of performance in several academic areas such as reading, spelling, and math can be improved by the contingent use of consequences. The consequences that have been used effectively include praise and immediate grading (e.g., Kirby and Shields, 1972), points or tokens that may be used to purchase "back-up" events or items such as candy, inexpensive toys, school supplies, and special activities (e.g., Birnbrauer *et al.,* 1965; Tyler and Brown, 1968; Wolf *et al.,* 1968; Miller and Schneider, 1970; Chadwick and Day, 1971; Ferritor *et al.,* 1972), and contingent availability of free time, whereby students may be allowed access to a play area (e.g., Hopkins, Schutte, and Garton, 1971), leave early for recess (e.g., Evans and Oswalt, 1968; Harris and Sherman, 1973b), leave school early (Harris and Sherman, 1974), or read library books or engage in any school-related activity of their choice (Lovitt, Guppy, and Blattner, 1969).

Although providing consequences directly for academic performance can be effective in producing improved performance in various academic areas, two qualifications should be noted. First, of the published studies, relatively few (e.g., Chadwick and Day, 1971) have reported simultaneous increases in overall accuracy of performance as well as rate of correct performance. Second, in a number of studies the magnitude of effect on either rate correct or accuracy was not extremely large. In view of this, we decided to explore the use of two alternative methods for possibly improving the classroom performance of normal students. One alternative involved the use of peer students to tutor each other. The second alternative involved the assignment of homework to the students. In the evaluation of the effects of tutoring and homework, we also used behavioral consequences both for performance on the homework and performance in the classroom. The consequences employed involved allowing students access to recess and permission to leave school early. These consequences were employed because similar ones seemed to be effective in other studies. They were relatively simple to arrange and involved no additional cost to the school.

The effects of both tutoring and homework assignments have received considerable attention in the education literature. Tutoring of some students by others has been strongly advocated in several articles (e.g., Lippitt, 1969; Fleming, 1969; Rossi, 1969; Archibeque, 1970), and a number of student-tutoring procedures have been reviewed by Thelen

(1969). The relatively few studies that have presented numerical data on the effects of student tutoring procedures indicate that tutoring by other students may have positive effects on academic performance as measured by school grades (e.g., Horst, 1931; Caditz, 1963; Taylor, 1969) and performance on standardized achievement tests (Hassinger and Via, 1969; Landrum and Martin, 1970). However, there is little published information about the possible day-to-day effects of student tutoring. Further, in only one of the studies that provided numerical information about the performance of students (Taylor, 1969) is there direct evidence that the tutoring procedures seemed to be responsible for the academic gains achieved. In this study it was found that students who were tutored received better grades at the end of an academic quarter than did students in a matched control group who received no tutoring. Although no control-group information or other comparison conditions were included in the studies by Hassinger and Via (1969) and Landrum and Martin (1970), the achievement test gains reported were larger than might be expected simply on the basis of the passage of 6 weeks of time, the length of time during which the tutoring program was in effect.

Thus, student tutoring seems to be a widely advocated procedure, and the available data suggest that it may also be academically beneficial to the students involved. Further, the use of some students to tutor others in the classroom seems to have several practical advantages. First, students in a particular classroom may have widely differing academic skills. Using some students to tutor other students may capitalize on these skills and allow the development of more individualized instruction, usually prevented by the high student-to-teacher ratios in most classrooms. Second, using students to tutor other students involves little or no extra cost to the school and does not necessarily increase the total amount of time students are required to spend in the classroom.

The educational literature available on the effects of the assignment of homework on academic performance of students is more difficult to evaluate. A number of articles have been published describing the supposed advantages or disadvantages of assigning homework, or describing the attitudes of students, teachers, and parents about the value of assigning homework (e.g., Schiller, 1954; Strang, 1955; Evans, 1957; Langdon and Stout, 1957; Baker, 1960; Punke, 1961; Check, 1966; and Maertens, 1968). On the basis of several reviews of the experimental literature on the effects of assigning homework (e.g., Otto, 1950; Swenson, Cost, and Taylor, 1955; and Goldstein, 1960), there seems to be little agreement as to whether or not assigning homework produces desirable effects on academic performance. Some studies indicate that the assignment of homework is associated with improved academic performance, and other studies indicate that assignment of homework produces little or no effect on academic performance. The problem of clearly evaluating the effects of homework on the basis of the available literature is further complicated by the diverse measures employed in the homework studies. The measures of performance in the studies range from scores on standardized achievement and intelligence tests to scores on achievement tests constructed by individual teachers to course grades. Further, most studies lack a clear specification of what was assigned as homework. Most important, the available literature is hard to evaluate because measures are not presented as to whether or not the assigned homework was actually completed by the students and, if completed, at what level of accuracy. If homework assignments are to have any effect on academic performance, presumably they would need to be completed by the students at a reasonable accuracy level.

Thus, the published literature does not seem to allow any clear conclusions to be made about whether or not homework assignments have beneficial effects on subsequent academic performance. First, it seems important to provide additional information on this topic because many teachers assign homework to students in their classes under the assumption that homework does benefit the students' academic performance in those areas in which it is assigned. Second, whether or not homework improves academic performance is important because of the additional time required by the teacher to grade homework assignments. Third, homework also requires that students work outside normal classroom periods and, hence, may be aversive to the students.

The studies to be described below involve four experiments conducted with students in the second through sixth grades in an elementary school located in a poor economic area in a small city. In general, the academic skills of the students, as evaluated by standardized achievement tests, were below average in most academic areas.

The basic questions asked in the two studies on peer tutoring were (1) whether a simple, unstructured tutoring situation involving the students in the class produced improved academic performance as compared to no tutoring; and (2) if the tutoring procedures seemed more effective than no tutoring, whether the improvements in academic performance produced by tutoring were greater than those improvements that might be produced if students worked alone on the material for an equivalent amount of time.

The first experiment (Harris, Sherman, Henderson, and Harris, 1972) examined the effects of peer tutoring on spelling performance. Twenty students in a fifth-grade classroom served as subjects in the majority of the experimental conditions. As a pre-test, students were asked to spell words from two 20-word lists on the first school day of each week. As a post-test, students were again asked to spell words from the same two 20-word lists on the last school day of each week. On the days between the pre- and post-tests, students worked on assignments related to both word lists. All words on the spelling tests, as well as intervening assignments, were taken from the regular classroom text, Book D of the Botel spelling series.

Initially, the effects of an unstructured peer tutoring procedure on spelling performance were observed for 3 weeks. Ten minutes prior to administering the post-tests, the teacher gave each student a list of words comprising one of the 20-word tests (the list selected was determined by a coin flip) and simply told the students to arrange themselves in small groups of from two to four students in order to help each other learn the words. The students were not told how to help each other.

The way students helped each other during tutoring sessions took several forms. Occasionally, only one student in a tutoring group would serve as spelling examiner for the entire 10-minute tutoring period. Generally, however, each student in a tutoring group would participate as spelling examiner sometime during the tutoring session. As the spelling examiner called out words from the spelling list, students would write the words on a sheet of paper. Then, within each group, students would compare answers and make appropriate corrections. When a tutorial group was composed of only two students, one student (tutee) frequently would respond vocally to words presented by the other student (tutor) rather than writing the words on a sheet of paper.

Next, an independent study condition was arranged for 3 weeks. This procedure was implemented in order to determine whether the effects of tutoring were a result of interactions between students during tutoring sessions or simply a function of allowing students a 10-minute study period prior to the post-test. All procedures in the independent study procedure were identical to the tutoring procedure except that students had to study by themselves. Thus, under the independent study conditions, students were given one of the 20-word lists (again, selected by a coin flip) and were told to study it by themselves for 10 minutes prior to the post-test.

Three weeks of the independent study condition were followed by additional tutoring and independent study conditions that alternated each week. Mean percent correct on pre-tests and post-tests were calculated over all students who took both the pre-test and post-test during any given week. These scores for the pre-tests and the post-tests for each list of 20 words are displayed in the top set of axes of Figure 14.1. The solid lines connect pre- and post-test scores for the tutored or individually studied word lists, and the dotted lines connect pre- and post-test scores for the comparison word lists. The bottom set of axes in Figure 14.1 shows the percentage point gains of the tutored or independently studied word list over the comparison word list each week.

The gains from pre-test to post-test were consistently higher for

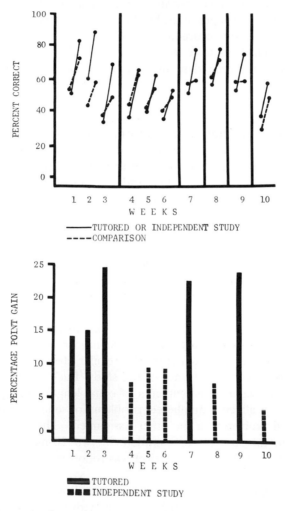

*Figure 14.1* Upper set of axes: mean percent correct for all students on each weekly pre-test and post-test for tutored, independently studied, and comparison word lists. Lower set of axes: mean percentage point gain for tutored or independently studied word list over the comparison word list during each week. (From Harris, Sherman, Henderson, and Harris, 1972.)

tutored word lists than for comparison word lists. The pre- to post-test gains on tutored words ranged from 14 to 25% higher than for comparison words over the 5 weeks during which the tutoring procedure was used. The gains from pre-test to post-test were also higher for individually studied word lists than for comparison word lists. However, the pre- to post-test gains for individually studied words over comparison words (3–9%) were smaller than those gains produced by the tutoring procedure. These results indicate that the tutoring procedure was effective in increasing accuracy on spelling tests. Further, since tutoring produced higher accuracy gains versus comparison words than did the individual study procedure, the results suggest that some aspect of the interactions between children during the 10-minute tutoring periods was functional in improving accuracy on the spelling tests.

Systematic replications of the tutoring procedures were performed in four additional classrooms: a combination second/third-grade classroom (24 students); a combination fourth/fifth-grade classroom (25 students); and two sixth-grade classrooms (22 and 21 students). Figure 14.2 shows the results in these four classrooms. Solid lines connect the mean pre-test and post-test scores for tutored words, and dotted lines connect the mean pre-test and post-test scores for comparison words. The bars show the mean percentage point pre- to post-test gain of tutored words over the comparison words. The results obtained with students in these four additional classrooms were very similar to those obtained with the students in the first classroom: The tutored words gained more (16–23%) from pre-test to post-test than did the comparison words.

A second tutoring experiment (Harris and Sherman, 1973b) was conducted in math in a fourth-grade classroom composed of 24 students. Daily math assignments, taken from the regular classroom textbook, were selected by the teacher in advance of the study. Each daily assignment was divided into two separate assignments of equal length and equivalent difficulty by placing all even-numbered problems on one assignment and all odd-numbered problems on the other assignment. These two assignments were given to the students to complete in two 20-minute math periods (math$_1$ and math$_2$). Each math period was followed by a 20-minute recess period.

Prior to math$_1$ the teacher told the students how to solve the upcoming math problems and demonstrated solutions with sample problems similar to those assigned in the next two math sessions (math$_1$ and math$_2$). After the lecture, a math work period or a tutorial period followed by a math work period began. After completing an assignment in a math work period, a student gave his paper to a grader, who recorded the time taken to com-

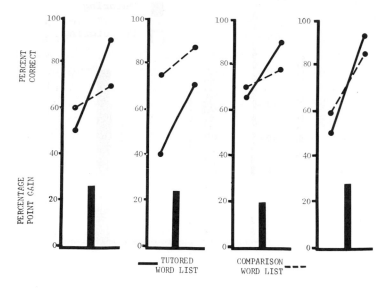

*Figure 14.2* Mean percent correct for all students in each of four classrooms on the pre-test and post test for tutored and comparison word lists. The bar at the base of each set of axes represents the mean percentage point gain for the tutored word list over the comparison word list. (From Harris, Sherman, Henderson, and Harris, 1972.)

plete the assignment as well as the student's score. Then the grader returned the paper to the student, who could rework problems that he missed on the first grading check and give his paper to the grader for a second check. Each student was allowed three grading checks during a math session. Throughout the study, students could receive assistance on solving the problems from the teacher.

First, the effects of peer tutoring alone on arithmetic behavior were investigated. Fifteen minutes prior to one of the two math periods, students were given a copy of the math problems to be assigned in the next math session. The teacher then told the students to arrange themselves in small groups of two or three and to help each other solve the problems. The teacher passed from group to group, praising students who helped each other work the problems, and was available to answer students' questions during the tutorial period. When the tutorial period terminated, tutoring assignment sheets and any work sheets used by the students were collected. The tutoring procedure was first used prior to math$_1$ for several days, then prior to math$_2$ for several days.

Figure 14.3 shows the effects of the peer tutoring procedure. Math sessions preceded by the tutorial period averaged 51% correct, while base-

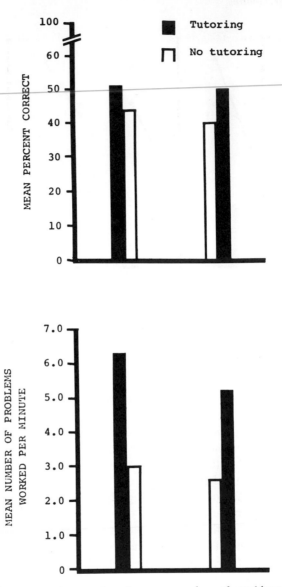

*Figure 14.3* Mean percent correct and mean number of problems worked per minute on the first grading check in math₁ and math₂ within each of the experimental conditions in which the tutoring procedure was evaluated. The first bar in each pair represents math₁; the second bar represents math₂. (After V. William Harris and James A. Sherman, Effects of peer tutoring and consequences on the math performance of elementary classroom students. *Journal of Applied Behavior Analysis,* 1973, **6**, 587–597. Copyright 1973 by the Society for the Experimental Analysis of Behavior, Inc.)

line math sessions averaged 42% correct. Students completed an average of 5.7 problems per minute after peer tutoring, as compared to 2.8 problems per minute without peer tutoring. Thus, the results indicate that students completed problems at more than double the rate after peer tutoring, with an improved accuracy of 9%.

The tutorial procedure was next evaluated in the presence of a consequence procedure for classroom math performance. A student was allowed to leave class immediately for recess after scoring 90% or better on his math assignment in math$_1$ or math$_2$. Peer tutoring was first used prior to math$_1$ for several days, then prior to math$_2$ for several days. This sequence of manipulations was repeated. Figure 14.4 shows the effects of the peer tutoring procedure in the presence of the classroom consequence procedure. Tutored math sessions averaged 60% correct, while baseline math sessions averaged 47% correct. Students completed an average of 2.4 problems per minute in tutored math sessions and only 1.2 problems per minute in baseline math sessions. Thus, the results indicate that students completed problems at double the rate, with an improved accuracy of 13%, after peer tutoring.

The peer tutoring procedure was compared to an independent study procedure in order to assess whether the effects of tutoring were due to the interaction between students during the tutorial period or were simply a function of presenting material to be assigned in the next math session 15 minutes before. In the independent study procedure, students were given the math assignment 15 minutes prior to the next math session and were told to solve the problems individually. Independent study differed from peer tutoring only in that students were not allowed to interact with each other during the independent study period. Initially, independent study occurred prior to math$_2$. Following several days, peer tutoring replaced independent study. These two conditions were repeated. The consequence procedure for 90% or better classroom performance was in effect in both math periods during these manipulations.

Figure 14.5 compares the effects of the tutoring and independent study procedures. The average response rate during math sessions preceded by peer tutoring was 1.08 problems per minute greater than comparison math sessions, while the average response rate during math sessions preceded by independent study averaged only .46 problems per minute greater than comparison math sessions. Tutored math sessions averaged 14% greater accuracy than comparison math sessions, while independent study math sessions averaged only 8% greater accuracy than baseline math sessions. These data suggest that interactions between students during tutoring sessions, not just the opportunity students had to study the math

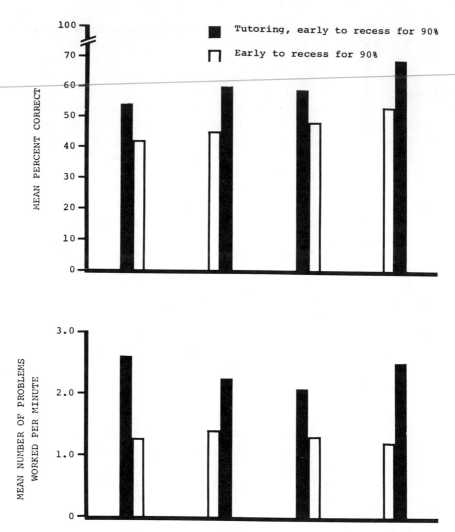

*Figure 14.4* Mean percent correct and mean number of problems worked per minute on the first grading check in math$_1$ and math$_2$ during the experimental conditions in which the tutoring procedure was evaluated in the presence of the consequence procedure for 90% correct or better math performance. The first bar in each pair represents math$_1$; the second bar represents math$_2$. (After V. William Harris and James A. Sherman, Effects of peer tutoring and consequences on the math performance of elementary classroom students. *Journal of Applied Behavior Analysis,* 1973, **6**, 587–597. Copyright 1973 by the Society for the Experimental Analysis of Behavior, Inc.)

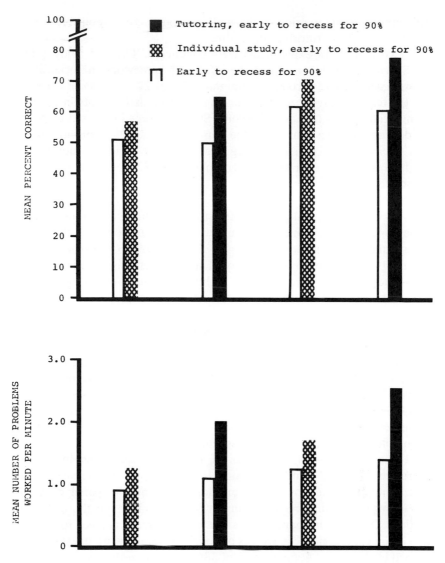

*Figure 14.5* Mean percent correct and mean number of problems worked per minute on the first grading check in math$_1$ and math$_2$ during the experimental conditions in which the effects of the tutoring and independent study procedures were compared. The first bar in each pair represents math$_1$; the second bar represents math$_2$. (After V. William Harris and James A. Sherman, Effects of peer tutoring and consequences on the math performance of elementary classroom students. *Journal of Applied Behavior Analysis,* 1973, **6**, 587–597. Copyright 1973 by the Society for the Experimental Analysis of Behavior, Inc.)

problems 15 minutes prior to the math period, were responsible for part of the effects of the tutoring procedure.

Two homework experiments were conducted. The first study (Harris and Sherman, 1974) examined the effects of homework in social studies in two sixth-grade classrooms containing 25 and 27 students. Each school day, the teachers gave three- or four-page reading assignments in the classroom social studies text as homework. Students were instructed to be prepared to answer questions about the homework assignment during the next day's social studies period. During social studies periods, students were asked 15 questions of a sentence-completion type. These questions were constructed by drawing sentences from the reading assignment with one or two key words missing. The same questions were assigned as part of the homework during several phases of the study. When the questions were part of the homework assignment, students were asked to complete the 15 sentences (questions) in writing and give their papers to the teacher at the beginning of class the following day. The 15 questions asked during the social studies period were answered within the context of a game.

First, the effects of the homework on students' performance in social studies period were investigated. Homework questions (15 incomplete-sentence type questions identical to questions asked in class the next day) were given to each student in the two classrooms for several days. Homework questions were collected at the beginning of class, graded, and returned to the students 30 minutes later. Thus, students were provided feedback regarding homework performance prior to the social studies period. However, students were not allowed to use homework papers during social studies sessions. There were no programmed contingencies for completion of the homework assignment.

Figure 14.6 shows the effects of homework questions in the two classrooms. The top panel of Figure 14.6 shows the percentage of students completing the homework questions. The middle panel of Figure 14.6 shows the mean percentage correct for all students on the homework questions. The bottom panel shows the mean percent correct for all students in the classroom social studies period. When homework questions were assigned in classroom A, an average of 38% of the questions were answered correctly in the classroom social studies periods, while only 14% of the questions were answered correctly when homework questions were not assigned. Similarly, in classroom B the assignment of homework questions was correlated with 31% correct classroom performance, while no assignment of homework questions was correlated with only 13% correct classroom performance. The results indicate that homework questions may improve classroom performance slightly even though an average of only

38% of the students completed the homework assignment in the two classrooms.

Various consequence procedures for homework completion at an 80% accuracy criterion were then employed. The most effective procedure provided students scoring 80% correct or better on the homework questions the opportunity to leave school 15 minutes early at the end of the school day and required students not completing the homework questions at an 80% accuracy to remain in class during the morning recess until the homework assignment was completed at an 80% accuracy. The effects of

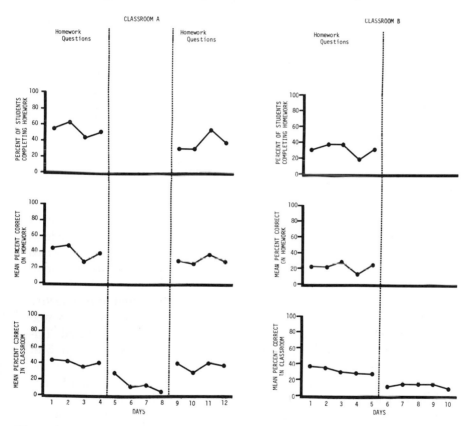

*Figure 14.6* Mean percent of students completing the homework assignment, mean percent correct on the homework assignment, and mean percent correct in classroom A and classroom B when homework questions were assigned and when they were not assigned. (From V. William Harris and James A. Sherman, Homework assignments, consequences, and classroom performance in social studies and mathematics. *Journal of Applied Behavior Analysis,* 1974, **7**, 505–519. Copyright 1974 by the Society for the Experimental Analysis of Behavior, Inc.)

homework questions and this consequence procedure for homework completion were evaluated in classroom A. Figure 14.7 shows the results of this evaluation. When the homework questions were assigned and the early-to-leave-school and recess consequences were employed, a mean of 67% of the students completed the homework assignment at the beginning of class at a mean accuracy level of 70%. Classroom performance averaged 74% correct when the homework questions were assigned and the consequences were employed and averaged only 12% correct in the absence of homework questions.

Figure 14.8 shows an evaluation of providing consequences for accurate completion of homework questions in classroom B. First, the effects of providing students the opportunity to leave school 15 minutes early at the end of the school day contingent on 80% correct homework performance were investigated. Then, the effects of requiring students to remain in the morning recess until reaching an 80% accuracy on the homework questions in combination with the leave-school-15-minutes-early consequence were examined. When either consequence procedure was used, a mean of 73% of the students completed the homework questions at the beginning of class at a mean accuracy level of 67%. Homework questions with consequences for 80% completion were associated with markedly higher classroom performance (mean of 66%) than when no homework questions were assigned (mean of 13%).

In this study, homework performance was observed to be highly correlated with classroom performance. Over the entire study, students who completed the homework at or above an 80% accuracy level answered 87% of the questions correctly in class, while students who did not complete the homework at an 80% or better accuracy level answered only 31% of the questions correctly in class. Consequences were found to be effective in improving the percentage of students completing the homework as well as the accuracy at which the homework assignment was completed. Improvements in homework performance were consistently correlated with improved class-room performance.

Twenty-five sixth-grade students served as subjects in a second homework investigation conducted in math (Harris and Sherman, 1974). Two 30-minute math periods occurred daily. One math session (math$_1$) occurred in the morning and the second math session (math$_2$) occurred in the afternoon. Both math sessions were followed by recess periods. Daily math assignments were taken from the regular classroom math text and were divided into two separate assignments of equal length and equivalent difficulty by placing all even-numbered problems on one assignment and all odd-numbered problems on another assignment. The effects of various

CLASSROOM A

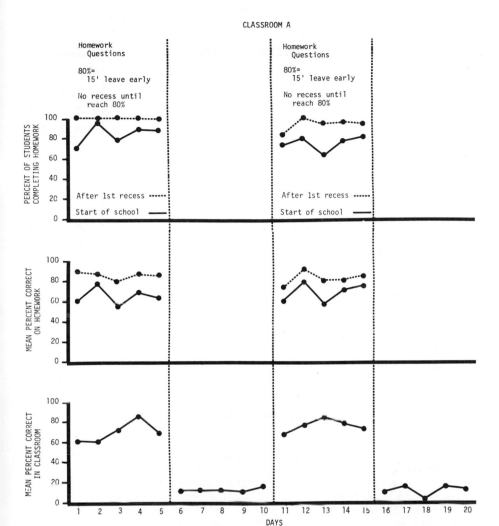

*Figure 14.7* Mean percent of students completing the homework assignment, mean percent correct on the homework assignment, and mean percent correct in classroom A when no homework questions were assigned and when homework questions were assigned and the early-out-of-school and recess consequences were employed. (From V. William Harris and James A. Sherman, Homework assignments, consequences, and classroom performance in social studies and mathematics. *Journal of Applied Behavior Analysis,* 1974, **7**, 505–519. Copyright 1974 by the Society for the Experimental Analysis of Behavior, Inc.)

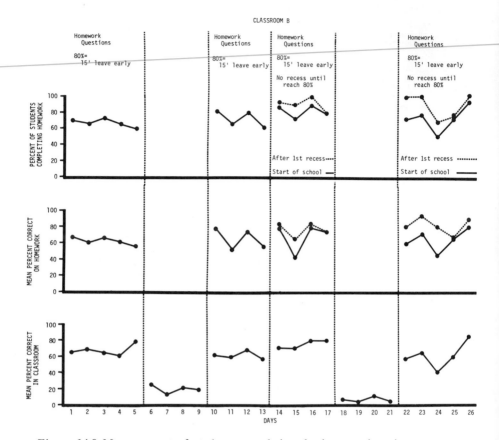

*Figure 14.8* Mean percent of students completing the homework assignment, mean percent correct on the homework assignment, and mean percent correct in classroom B when no homework questions were assigned and when homework questions were assigned and the early-out-of-school and recess consequences were employed. (From V. William Harris and James A. Sherman, Homework assignments, consequences, and classroom performance in social studies and mathematics. *Journal of Applied Behavior Analysis,* 1974, **7**, 505–519. Copyright 1974 by the Society for the Experimental Analysis of Behavior, Inc.)

experimental conditions were evaluated by comparing performances in $math_1$ and $math_2$.

Before the morning math session ($math_1$), the teacher discussed the solution of sample problems similar to the problems assigned in both of the day's math sessions. Following this discussion, the first math period began. After completing an assignment, a student took his paper to a grader, who recorded the time taken to complete the assignment, graded the answers, and returned the paper to the student. Thus, a student received immediate feedback regarding his math performance. Each student could receive up to three grading checks during a math session.

Homework assignments composed of the same problems to be assigned in one of the next day's math sessions were given to the students to be completed at home. Homework assignments were collected at the start of class, graded, and returned to the students at the end of class. Thus, students did not receive feedback regarding homework performance prior to the daily math sessions. Initially, students were allowed to depart for lunch 10 minutes early contingent on completing the homework assignment (i.e., having a written answer to each of the problems). After several days the early-to-lunch consequence was removed, although the students were still encouraged to complete and hand in the homework. Then the early-to-lunch consequence was reinstated. Next, an additional consequence was provided for homework completion in order to increase the percentage of students completing the homework assignment. A student who completed his homework was allowed to leave school 10 minutes early in addition to departing for lunch early. After several days, both consequences for homework completion were removed and, finally, both consequences were reinstated. Figure 14.9 shows the effects of the various consequences on homework completion and accuracy. The percentage of students completing the homework assignment averaged 84% when both consequences were provided for homework completion, 62% when only the early-to-lunch consequence was provided, and only 15% when neither consequence was provided. The mean accuracy on the homework assignment was generally highest when one or both consequences were used. Students averaged 33% correct on the homework assignment in the presence of one or both consequences for homework completion. They averaged only 12% correct when no consequences were provided for homework completion.

The classroom performance of students did not show any marked effects of the various homework conditions, although the average accuracy of classroom performance was slightly higher (2%) for homework math sessions than for comparison math sessions.

The effects of consequences for accurate homework on classroom math performance were investigated in the next set of manipulations. The two consequences employed earlier (i.e., early to lunch and early to leave school) for homework completion were made contingent on *accurate* homework completion. Students completing the homework assignment (all problems answered) at a 60% accuracy level were provided both

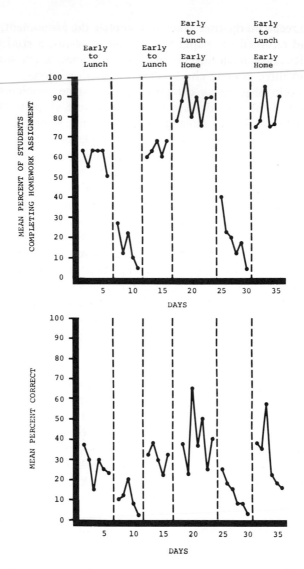

*Figure 14.9* Mean percent of all students completing and handing in the homework assignment and mean percent correct on the homework assignment when there were and were not consequences for completing homework assignments. (From V. William Harris and James A. Sherman, Homework assignments, consequences, and classroom performance in social studies and mathematics. *Journal of Applied Behavior Analysis,* 1974, **7,** 505–519. Copyright 1974 by the Society for the Experimental Analysis of Behavior, Inc.)

consequences. The homework procedures were the same as those employed earlier except for the addition of the accuracy criterion. At first the homework assignment was the same as the problems scheduled for $math_1$. After several days the homework was changed to be the same as the problems scheduled for $math_2$ and then, once again, the homework was made the same as the problems for $math_1$.

Accuracy on the homework increased from an average of 33% scored by students in the previous homework condition with no accuracy criterion to 57% during the homework conditions with a 60% accuracy criterion. About half the class completed their homework assignments under these conditions. Figure 14.10 shows the effects of the homework procedure on classroom math performance. Students averaged 48% correct in homework math sessions and 36% correct in comparison math sessions. They worked problems at an average of 2.05 problems per minute in homework sessions and 1.70 problems per minute in homework math sessions. Thus, students worked problems somewhat faster and with greater accuracy when these problems had been assigned as homework and when there were consequences for completion of the homework assignment at a 60% accuracy level.

The results of these four experiments suggest that peer tutoring and homework can be useful procedures for improving students' academic performance in the classroom. The addition of the tutoring and homework procedures to the classroom required little time and few additional materials. Teachers who used the procedures found them to be practical and convenient and advocated their continued use in other academic areas.

The peer tutoring procedures seemed to be the simplest to use, since they required only that the teacher assign a period of time for tutoring and that she instruct the students to help each other on a specified academic assignment. Use of homework procedures was more complex, since the teacher had to provide homework assignments for students to take home, and homework had to be graded. Further, simple assignment of homework did not have a marked effect on classroom performance. Instead, students' classroom performance was markedly improved only when there were consequences for *accurate* completion of homework assignments. Although the use of these consequences adds to the complexity of the homework procedures, the consequences used (such as permission to leave school early and to go to lunch early) were relatively easy to arrange and involved no additional expense to the school.

It should be noted that in the tutoring studies and the homework studies, the problems or tasks tutored or given as homework were the same

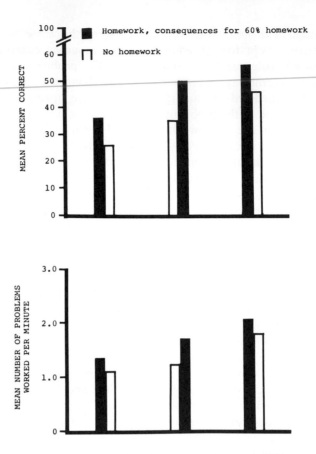

*Figure 14.10* Mean percent correct and mean number of problems worked per minute in the two daily math sessions with homework problems and consequences for 60% performance on the homework problems used in one of the math sessions. The first bar in each pair represents math$_1$; the second bar represents math$_2$. (From V. William and James A. Sherman, Homework assignments, consequences, and classroom performance in social studies and mathematics. *Journal of Applied Behavior Analysis* 1974, **7**, 505–519. Copyright 1974 by the Society for the Experimental Analysis of Behavior, Inc. )

ones as the students worked during subsequent class periods: Students tutored each other over the same words and math problems as they were subsequently asked to spell or solve; the homework assignments consisted of the same questions and problems as the students were subsequently asked to answer. Whether results like those obtained in the present series of studies would be obtained if comparable tutoring or homework procedures were used but students were subsequently asked to answer similar but different questions and problems is unknown. Nevertheless, the success of the procedures used in this series of studies suggests that peer tutoring and assignment of homework with consequences for accurate completion may be useful techniques for the improvement of students' academic performance in the classroom.

# References

Archibeque, J. D. Utilizing the advanced Spanish student as a classroom tutor. *Hispania*, 1970, **53**, 70–72.

Baker, J. B. College students and their assignments. *Journal of Educational Research*, 1960, **54**, 49–53.

Barrish, H. H., Saunders, M., and Wolf, M. M. Good behavior game: Effects of individual contingencies for group consequences on disruptive behavior in a classroom. *Journal of Applied Behavior Analysis*, 1969, **2**, 119–124.

Becker, W. C., Madsen, C. H., Arnold, C. R., and Thomas, D. R. The contingent use of teacher attention and praise in reducing classroom behavior problems. *Journal of Special Education*, 1967, **1**, 287–307.

Birnbrauer, J. S., Wolf, M. M., Kidder, J. D., and Tague, C. E. Classroom behavior of retarded pupils with token reinforcement. *Journal of Experimental Child Psychology*, 1965, **2**, 219–235.

Broden, M., Bruce, C., Mitchell, M. A., Carter, V., and Hall, R. V. Effects of teacher attention on attending behavior of two boys at adjacent desks. *Journal of Applied Behavior Analysis*, 1970, **3**, 199–203.

Bushell, D., Wrobel, P. A., and Michaelis, M. L. Applying "group" contingencies to the classroom study behavior of preschool children. *Journal of Applied Behavior Analysis*, 1968, **1**, 55–61.

Caditz, R. Using student tutors in high school mathematics. *Chicago School Journal*, 1963, **44**, 323–325.

Chadwick, B. A., and Day, R. C. Systematic reinforcement: Academic performance of underachieving students. *Journal of Applied Behavior Analysis*, 1971, **4**, 311–319.

Check, J. F. Homework—Is it needed? *The Clearing House*, 1966, **41**, 143–147.

Evans, G. W., and Oswalt, G. L. Acceleration of academic progress through the manipulation of peer influence. *Behaviour Research and Therapy*, 1968, **6**, 189–195.

Evans, N. D. Homework. *Childhood Education*, 1957, **33**, 218–220.

Ferritor, D. E., Buckholdt, D., Hamblin, R. L., and Smith, L. The noneffects of contingent reinforcement for attending behavior on work accomplished. *Journal of Applied Behavior Analysis*, 1972, **5**, 7–17.

Fleming, J. C. Pupil tutors and tutees learn. *Today's Education*, 1969, **58**, 22–24.

Goldstein, A. Does homework help? A review of research. *Elementary School Journal*, 1960, **60**, 212–224.

Hall, R. V., Lund, D., and Jackson, D. Effects of teacher attention on study behavior. *Journal of Applied Behavior Analysis*, 1968, **1**, 1–12.

Hamblin, R. L., Hathaway, C., and Wodarski, J. Group contingencies, peer tutoring and accelerating academic achievement. In E. A. Ramp and B. L. Hopkins (Eds.), *A New Direction for Education: Behavior Analysis.* Lawrence, Kan.: The University of Kansas Support and Development Center for Follow Through, 1971, pp. 41–53.

Hanley, E. M., and Perelman, P. F. Research resulting from a model cities program designed to train paraprofessionals to aid teachers in elementary school classrooms. In E. A. Ramp and B. L. Hopkins (Eds.), *A New Direction for Education: Behavior Analysis.* Lawrence, Kan.: The University of Kansas Support and Development Center for Follow Through, 1971, pp. 54–71.

Harris, V. W., and Sherman, J. A. Use and analysis of the "good behavior game" to reduce disruptive classroom behavior. *Journal of Applied Behavior Analysis,* 1973, **6**, 405–417. (a)

Harris, V. W., and Sherman, J. A. Effects of peer tutoring and consequences on the math performance of elementary classroom students. *Journal of Applied Behavior Analysis,* 1973, **6**, 587–597. (b)

Harris, V. W., and Sherman, J. A. Homework assignments, consequences, and classroom performance in social studies and mathematics. *Journal of Applied Behavior Analysis,* 1974, **7**, 505–519.

Harris, V. W., Sherman, J. A., Henderson, D. G., and Harris, M. S. Effects of peer tutoring on the spelling performance of elementary classroom students. In *A New Direction for Education: Behavior Analysis.* Lawrence, Kan.: The University of Kansas Support and Development Center for Follow Through, 1972.

Hassinger, J., and Via, M. How much does a tutor learn through teaching reading? *Journal of Secondary Education,* 1969, **44**, 42–44.

Hopkins, B. L., Schutte, R. C., and Garton, K. L. The effects of access to a playroom on the rate and quality of printing and writing of first and second-grade students. *Journal of Applied Behavior Analysis,* 1971, **4**, 77–87.

Horst, H. M. History of student tutoring at West High School, Akron, Ohio. *Junior-Senior High School Clearing House,* 1931, **24**, 69–81.

Kirby, F. D., and Shields, F. Modification of arithmetic response rate and attending behavior in a seventh-grade student. *Journal of Applied Behavior Analysis,* 1972, **5**, 79–84.

Landrum, J. W., and Martin, M. D. When students teach others. One-to-one project, Los Angeles Co. Schools. *Educational Leadership,* 1970, **27**, 446–448.

Langdon, G., and Stout, I. W. What parents think about homework. *National Education Association Journal,* 1957, 370–372.

Lippitt, P. Children can teach other children. *The Instructor,* 1969, **78**, 41–99.

Lovitt, T. C., and Curtiss, K. A. Academic response rate as a function of teacher and self-imposed contingencies. *Journal of Applied Behavior Analysis,* 1969, **2**, 49–53.

Lovitt, T. C., and Esveldt, K. A. The relative effects on math performance of a single-versus multiple-ratio schedules: A case study. *Journal of Applied Behavior Analysis,* 1970, **3**, 261–270.

Lovitt, T. C., Guppy, T. E., and Blattner, J. E. The use of a free-time contingency with fourth graders to increase spelling accuracy. *Behaviour Research and Therapy,* 1969, **7**, 151–156.

McAllister, L. W., Stachowiak, J. G., Baer, D. M., and Conderman, L. The application of operant conditioning techniques in a secondary classroom. *Journal of Applied Behavior Analysis,* 1969, **2**, 277–285.

Maertens, N. Effects of arithmetic homework upon the attitudes of third grade pupils toward certain school related structures. *School Science and Mathematics,* 1968, **68**, 657–662.

Miller, L. K., and Schneider, R. The use of a token system in Project Head Start. *Journal of Applied Behavior Analysis,* 1970, **3**, 191–197.

O'Leary, K. D., Becker, W. C., Evans, M. B., and Saudargas, R. A. A token reinforcement program in a public school: A replication and systematic analysis. *Journal of Applied Behavior Analysis,* 1969, **2**, 3–13.

Otto, H. J. Elementary education—III. Organization and administration. In W. S. Monroe (Ed.), *Encyclopedia of Educational Research,* rev. ed. New York: Macmillan, 1950.

Packard, R. G. The control of "classroom attention": A group contingency for complex behavior. *Journal of Applied Behavior Analysis,* 1970, **3**, 13–28.

Punke, H. H. Pupil–teacher relationships—of high school seniors. *National Association of Secondary-School Principles,* 1961, **45**, 64–71.

Rossi, T. P. Help: Students teach students. *Reading Improvements,* 1969, **6**, 47–79.

Schiller, B. A questionnaire study of junior high school students; reactions to homework. *High Points,* 1954, **36**, 23–27.

Schmidt, G. W., and Ulrich, R. E. Effects of group contingent events upon classroom noise. *Journal of Applied Behavior Analysis,* 1969, **2**, 171–179.

Strang, R. Guided study and homework. *National Education Association Journal,* 1955, **44**, 399–400.

Sulzer, B., Hunt, S., Ashby, E., Koniarski, C., and Krams, M. Increasing the rate and percentage correct in reading and spelling in a fifth grade public school class of slow readers by means of a token system. In E. A. Ramp and B. L. Hopkins (Eds.), *A New Direction for Education: Behavior Analysis.* Lawrence, Kan.: The University of Kansas Support and Development Center for Follow Through, 1971, pp. 5–28.

Surrat, P. R., Ulrich, R. E., and Hawkins, R. O. An elementary student as a behavioral engineer. *Journal of Applied Behavior Analysis,* 1969, **2**, 85–92.

Swenson, E. J., Cost, J. C., and Taylor, G. Y. Research on homework. *Journal of Education,* 1955, **137**, 20–22.

Taylor, R. G. Tutorial services and academic success. *Journal of Educational Research,* 1969, **62**, 195–197.

Thelen, H. A. Tutoring by students. *The School Review,* 1969, **77**, 229–244.

Thomas, D. R., Becker, W. C., and Armstrong, M. Production and elimination of disruptive classroom behavior by systematically varying teacher's behavior. *Journal of Applied Behavior Analysis,* 1968, **1**, 35–45.

Tyler, V. O. Application of operant token reinforcement to academic performance of an institutionalized delinquent. *Psychological Reports,* 1967, **21**, 249–260.

Tyler, V. O., and Brown, G. D. Token reinforcement of academic performance with institutionalized delinquent boys. *Journal of Educational Psychology,* 1963, **59**, 164–168.

Wolf, M. M., Giles, D. K., and Hall, R. V. Experiments with token reinforcement in a remedial classroom. *Behaviour Research and Therapy,* 1968, **6**, 51–64.

# IV BEHAVIOR MODIFICATION WITH DISTURBED CHILDREN

# 15 TOWARD A COMMUNITY APPROACH TO BEHAVIOR MODIFICATION WITH EMOTIONALLY DISTURBED CHILDREN

Lawrence E. Dettweiler

Margaret A. Acker

Barnaby F. Guthrie

Charles Gregory

The use of token economies in residential treatment settings is an established procedure in behavior modification. The comprehensive study by Ayllon and Azrin (1968) described the use of a token economy with institutionalized psychotics. More recently, Phillips (1968) and Phillips, Phillips, Fixsen, and Wolf (1971) have described the exciting residential program at Achievement Place, a home for delinquent boys. The Pacific Centre for Human Development is a residential treatment center in a semirural, rapidly developing area outside Victoria, British Columbia. Originally, a token economy resembling the above programs was designed to alter the inappropriate disruptive and violent behavior occurring among children at the Centre. Although the program still aids in achieving these goals, it now serves to facilitate the child's return to public school and reeducate his family in the methods of child management. Indeed, institution of a token economy not only changed the behavior of the children at the Centre, but led to the retrospectively obvious conclusion that successful treatment involved altering the behavior of staff members, parents, and members of the community to which the child was returning. This, then, is a record not only of the evolution and success of the program, but also of the events that resulted in our dissatisfaction with the residential model and that led to the subsequent founding of what hopefully will be a truly effective community mental health program.

This chapter will present a description of the general residential program instituted at the Centre and the results of this program. A discussion of the effects of the program on the behavior of the staff members and parents will follow. A rationale for expanding the program from the residential treatment center to the public schools and the community at large will be discussed.

## Method

### SUBJECTS

Referrals to the Centre are made by municipal or provincial agencies for various reasons. Although the children in residence are from 6 to 14 years of age and show many different symptoms, the child most likely to be admitted is 6 or 7 years old and has been diagnosed as hyperactive, aggressive, possibly minimally brain damaged, or has received some other psychiatric label indicating a high rate of deviant, unacceptable behavior. All children have been removed from school before referral and are out of control at home if they reside at home. At some time before entering the Centre, drugs have been prescribed for all of the children. For example, a 7-year-old boy was recently admitted who had been receiving 350 mg of chloropromazine daily. All drugs not designed to reduce seizures are terminated upon admission. Many of the children have lived in a series of foster homes, group homes, or other child-care facilities. In most cases the Centre was the last resource available to these children other than juvenile detention centers or institutions providing long-term hospitalization.

Although the population at the Centre was not constant during this study due to the demands of discharge and intake, between 28 and 30 children were involved in the program at all times. Six of these children have been chosen as typical, and the results of our program with these children will be presented.

*Janet.* Janet was 10 when the program began, and had been at the Centre for $2\frac{1}{2}$ years. She had a history of hyperactivity, uncontrollability, and violent physical and verbal attacks on staff and children. Janet has definite brain damage resulting from meningitis and has a history of *petit mal* seizures for which she received heavy sedation before admission.

*Hank.* Hank, an adopted boy who was 10 years old when he entered the study, had been at the Centre for 2 years. Anoxic at birth, he had very strong signs of brain damage. A history of hyperactivity and total irresponsibility for his own well-being were the main reasons for admission.

*Toby.* Toby had been at the Centre for 2 years and was 10 years old when the program began. A product of gross neglect and assault during infancy, he had a history of lying, stealing, torturing animals, temper tantrums, and epilepsy; he also had a history of heavy sedation. Not only had he been dismissed from school and ejected from two foster homes, but he was the target of considerable outrage in the community.

*Peter.* Another 10-year–old, Peter was admitted 9 months before inception of the program. His mother, a divorcee, describes him as a child who cried or fought 90% of the time. He was diagnosed as a hyperactive, dull-normal child with severe dysphasia and perceptual problems. Also, he was sedated heavily at home.

*Arty.* Arty is typical of the children now entering the Centre. He had been admitted at the age of 7, only four months prior to the inception of the program. He was extremely hyperactive, had no bowel or bladder control, showed no social skills, and was uncontrollable. His parents were divorced.

*Stanley.* This epileptic boy was 9 years old and had been at the Centre for a year when the program began. His teachers reported head banging, a short attention span, tantrums, perceptual problems, and hyperactivity. At one time he was receiving Dexadrine, Mellaril, and Dilantin simultaneously.

Janet, Toby, and Stanley received medication for epileptic seizures during the study.

## SETTING

The children lived in a large house on about 80 acres of country property. The school was attached to the house and was organized so that teachers were responsible for the children from the moment they were awakened until 3:00 P.M., when school terminated. The morning began for the five teachers when they coerced and begged the children out of bed and into their morning routine. Clothes were unkempt, dental hygiene was nonexistent, ten children were suffering from gum infections, bedwetting was rampant, the children ate what they pleased, and as many as 14 fights might break out between 7:30 and 9:00, when school began. Although the children were supposed to be in the breakfast room by 8:00, none were, and on the average only 20 of the 28 children ate breakfast. Meals were often interrupted with food fights, and little nourishing food was consumed. The teachers, who were exhausted before their actual teaching began, had five or six children in their rooms from 9:00–10:30, 11:00–12:00, and 1:00–3:00. Needless to say, very little teaching was done, and the teachers lived in constant fear of runaways and violence to the room, property, and other children. Windows were broken, tires were slashed, one teacher was sent to the hospital twice as a result of kicks to the back of the head, and sexual assaults by children upon children and upon members of the staff were common. These overt actions of violence were sometimes met by aversive responses such as hitting, isolation, or threats of violence. At the same time, this behavior was reinforced by trips out to "cool off" and bribes of better treatment for future benefits.

## PROCEDURE

### RECORDING

It was planned originally to record very specific behaviors such as teasing, swearing, hitting, and correct academic responses per minute during the study. The chaotic situation, the lack of personnel, and the failure to obtain reliability resulted in a very simple system, which collapsed the behaviors into the following six easily observed categories:

/    Attending to or participating in an academic activity scheduled for the period.

T+    Positive social interaction from the child toward the teacher or from the teacher toward the child.

T−    Negative social interaction from the child toward the teacher or from the teacher toward the child.

P+    Positive social interaction from the child toward a peer or from a peer.

P−    Negative social interaction from the child toward a peer or from a peer.

X    None of the above.

### BASELINE

Although collecting data was a rather harrowing experience, 10-minute samples on each child were collected in his class on six occasions evenly distributed over a baseline period from December 1, 1970, to January 15, 1971. Observations had been taking place for 2 months prior, so the children were quite accustomed to observers. Data was collected by the second and third authors and occasionally by the senior author on each child. Each observer carried a stopwatch, and at the end of each 10-second interval the observer would look up from his stopwatch and code the child's behavior according to one of the six categories listed above.

## POINT SYSTEM (PS 1)

Although several variations of a token economy were tried between January 15, 1971, and September 1, 1971, the final product was simple but quite effective.[1] Every staff member carried a point sheet on which each child's name was printed next to a space where positive and negative points were recorded. In general, positive points were administered for positive interactions with peers and adults, working on an appropriate activity, politeness, punctuality, compliance, and generally acceptable behavior. Negative points were subtracted from the child's total and were given for physical assaults, verbal assaults, noncompliance, and other deviant behavior. Three negative points resulted in the child missing his next meal. Disruptive behavior resulted in "time out." There were two types of points, academic and behavioral. Academic points were assigned to academic tasks and were spent in the school store, while behavioral points were spent on a level system incorporating those privileges normally earned by the children. A child beginning in level 1 was under constant supervision and spent his points on meals and other necessities. As the child progressed through five levels, he was allowed more freedom but was required to be more responsible for his own behavior and the behavior of his peers. For example, a child in level 4 had to earn at least 200 academic points each week to maintain his position in that level. He spent these points on such articles as phonograph records, hobby materials, and special outings. The child was gradually phased off the point system toward the end of level 4. In level 5 he would attend public school and might work part-time in the community. The value of negative points increased from $-1$ in level 1 to $-50$ in level 5. Time out cost the child in level 1 ten points, but it cost the child in level 5 an entire level.

A yellow token was given to each child after he arose, washed, made his

[1] The conception and implementation of this program is primarily a result of the hard work and dedication of Mr. Roy Bobby, school director (1971–1972), Mr. La Mar Culley, director, Metchosin facility of the Pacific Centre for Human Development, and their respective staff.

bed, and dressed. This token allowed him into the dining room where, upon completion of breakfast, a green token allowed the child to go to brush his teeth. After brushing his teeth, each child was given a red token, which allowed admission to school. School began with physical exercises, an activity in which many points could be obtained. After exercises, each child proceeded to the open area of the school, where he picked up a clipboard containing his daily schedule and sheets of programmed assignments. The day was divided into 20-minute "modules." Children spent 20, 40, or 60 minutes in the open area for work on their programmed assignments or went to one of the classrooms for woodwork, arts and crafts, cooking, social studies, mathematics, science, sewing, or reading and spelling. Twenty-minute breaks in the morning and afternoon were also scheduled. This system was completely operational by September 1, 1971. At this time, data were collected in the same manner as during baseline on eight occasions distributed evenly over a period from September 1 to December 31. As the system was designed, it is impossible to separate the effects of academic points from positive or negative behavior points.

Data from an independent study on one child (Batstone and McMurchy, 1972) has shown that rate of responding (correct arithmetic responses or syllables written per minute) does not correlate with the amount of time spent attending ($/$) or total appropriate behavior ($/$ and T+ and P+). Therefore, a level of academic functioning in mathematics and reading was established by administering a Jastak Wide Range Achievement Test in August 1971.

While the feedback to the children was considered crucial, it was also felt that staff members should be consistent in their point distribution. Graphs of the total points awarded each day, the net points awarded to each child, and the daily positive and negative points given to the child were posted. Also, graphs of the points given out by each teacher were posted, since consistency in the density of reinforcement was quite important. Each child's record of time out was posted.

After the program began, it became obvious that control of destructive and deviant aggressive acts was no longer a primary problem. Simple treatment programs for each child were written and kept in a treatment book to be read and initialed by each member of the staff. Each program tried to pinpoint one or two target behaviors and described which behaviors were to be ignored, positively reinforced, punished, or lead to time out. All six of the children discussed here were given positive points for compliance, negative points for noncompliance, and placed in time out for disruptive behavior.

## POINTS REMOVED (PS OFF)

To determine the importance of the points as a currency system, all points and distinctions between levels were removed on February 1, 1972, for 1 month. Data were collected during five sessions for each child. This was not a true reversal, since the staff had radically altered its conception of the determinants of human behavior and could not resort to previous aversive and ineffectual means of control.

## RATING SYSTEM (RS)

On March 1, 1972, a system of evaluation that did not use behavioral points was instituted in the school. Children received a rating of excellent, very good, good, fair, or poor at the end of each module. These ratings in social studies, mathematics, reading, and the open area determined the child's access to reinforcing events such as woodshop and cooking. No levels were involved. Reinforcers were determined empirically by asking the children in which events they wished to participate. External reinforcers were avoided, but some outings and material reinforcers were available to children who would not perform for the reinforcers in the school. During March and April, data were collected over six evenly distributed sessions. The Jastak Wide Range Achievement Test was readministered in June 1972. This system was in effect until July 1, 1972, when the children left for camp.

## POINT SYSTEM 2 (PS 2)

In August 1972, a positive point system covering both academic and behavioral contingencies was instituted. Although time out was used, negative points were not part of the program. Smaller and immediately obtainable reinforcers were purchased from our store, which was open daily, while some reinforcers took as long as a week or a month to obtain. Modeling procedures were introduced with the help of the older, more advanced children, who had previously been segregated by the levels. Data for each child were collected on three occasions between August 14 and August 28, 1972.

## STAFF

Since the behavior of the staff seemed subjectively more dependent on the presence of points than on the behavior of the children, we began taking data on staff members' interactions with the children after the points were reinstated. We observed 10-minute samples of individual interactions of one staff member and one child in random orders. It was thus possible to inform the staff members not only of their point administraton with respect to other staff members, but also of their behavior in relation to the other staff members. We not only recorded the outcome of interactions, but discriminated between negative or positive behavior toward the children from the staff and negative or positive behavior from the children toward the staff.

## PARENTS

From a behaviorist point of view, it is unwise to alter a child's behavior and return him to the environment that produced the poor behavior. For this reason we began a training program for parents that now involves six families. The training began by obtaining an agreement from the parents that they would work in the program if they wished to have their children returned to them. The parents were observed with their child alone in a playroom while baseline measures were collected. Then they were given a copy of *Living with Children* (Patterson and Gullion, 1968) and told that they would be working in a setting using behavior modification. After reading and discussing the book, the parents' use of a token economy was taught in a closed setting with their child. Later they were immersed in the program at the Centre and were helped to model the counselor's use of contingent social and nonsocial reinforcement and time out.

## Results

### RELIABILITY

After training, reliability was established by requiring the observers to observe one or two 10-minute periods together at least twice each month. Reliability in each category was computed by dividing the number of agreements by the total number of observations. Reliability was always above .85 and in most cases above .95. Two other staff members have participated in tests of reliability on six occasions during the study, and coefficients of reliability greater than .85 were found. On several occasions, naive untrained university students and the observers have viewed videotape of the children, and reliability has been greater than .80. For simplicity of presentation, negative interactions between children (P−) and negative interactions between adults and children (T−) have been combined into a score representing inappropriate behavior. Appropriate participation (/), positive interactions with adults (T+), and positive interactions with peers (P+) have been combined into a score representing appropriate behavior.

## Morning Routine

Although no behavioral data were recorded, introduction of the token economy during the morning routine resulted in increased consumption of food and improved hygiene; breakfast became a pleasant experience, and the staff required to administer the program in the morning was decreased from eight to three.

## Experimental Conditions

The results of the different programs are shown in Figure 15.1.

*Janet.* Janet's low rate and high variability of appropriate behavior during baseline was usually a representation of sulking or withdrawal after a high rate of kicking, hitting, or swearing. The frequency of inappropriate behavior was not surprising in the light of the functional relationship that had existed between children and staff. Data indicated that attention was almost totally contingent on inappropriate behavior and indeed, the most poorly behaved child at the Centre received an average of more than 50% of the attention meted out by his teacher. Janet's response to the point system was phenomenal. Disruptive acts dropped virtually to zero, while her appropriate performance increased greatly. Removal of the points led to a decrease in appropriate behavior, but disruptive behavior did not recur. A high percentage of appropriate behavior was seen when the rating system was introduced. Point system 2 had been in effect for only 2 weeks when the last data were collected. The data indicate that Janet is ready for discharge and is now in the process of returning home.

*Hank.* Although Hank seemed to be attending and engaging in more appropriate behavior when point systems were in effect, his actual academic output was poor and has remained so in spite of repeated individual efforts by members of the staff. Hank has been discharged to a center specializing in the education of children with severe brain damage.

*Toby.* Although Toby's behavior was very similar to Janet's, he would

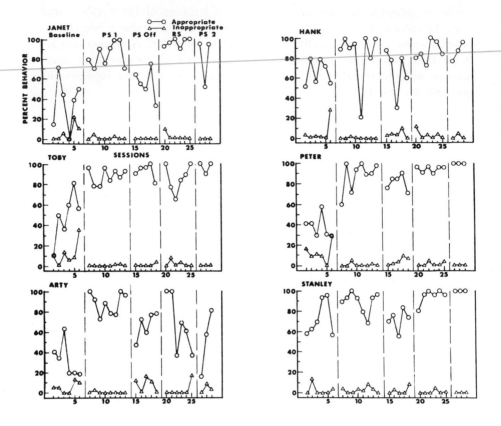

*Figure 15.1* Percentage of appropriate and inappropriate behavior observed in five conditions for six typical children.

stop at nothing to force a teacher to attend to him. He would go so far as faking an epileptic seizure on the roof of the second story or attempting to commit suicide by plunging a knife into electrical outlets. Placing Toby in time out after the program began was very effective in decreasing his inappropriate behavior. As can be seen, removing the points had little effect on Toby, since staff members continued to use withdrawal of attention and time out during this period. Although some backsliding occurred during the use of the rating system, his appropriate behavior was increasing and inappropriate behavior was decreasing when the ratings were terminated. Toby's greatest need now is a good foster home that can provide considerable structure and positive reinforcement.

*Peter.* Peter's performance is representative of the growth of the program at the Centre. A high rate of inappropriate behavior and a low rate of appropriate behavior was altered by the introduction of the point system. Removal of the points resulted in a degeneration in behavior. Performance on the rating system was excellent, but it improved even more with the introduction of the final token economy. Peter is now in public school and should be discharged soon.

*Arty.* Arty's performance on the various programs is also typical of the younger, hyperactive children now entering the program. This child needed constant feedback and did well when points were contingent on behavior, but performed poorly when the points were removed. The rating system also was ineffectual in controlling his behavior. This is not surprising, since data show the correlation between the children's appropriate behavior and the teacher's ratings in the classroom to be .60. As Arty's treatment program becomes more specific and demanding, his progress on point system 2 should continue to improve.

*Stanley.* Although Stanley's behavior did not change drastically during the study, we found him to be more productive and less inappropriate when no points were being awarded for his behavior during the rating period. For this reason, the final condition presented in Figure 15.1 involved points for academic output only. Stanley should be discharged soon.

ACADEMIC PERFORMANCE

As stated earlier, academic performance is not necessarily correlated with overt appropriate behavior. Figure 15.2 shows the increase of performance in mathematics and reading for each child between the first testing, in August 1971, and the second testing, in June 1972, on the Jastak Wide Range Achievement Test. The performance of six additional children is included in order to show the interesting relationship between age and performance on the first and second testing. The diagonal represents a hypothetical normal relationship between age and grade level. In general, the younger child was closer to normal performance, and the slope of his progress was greater than the slope of the line representing normal progress. Progress in mathematics was greater than progress in reading. It is interesting to note the difference between Gene, the youngest child, and Janet, the oldest. Both children suffered from meningitis as young children, experience *petit mal* attacks now, and were diagnosed as hyperactive children. Gene's medical and psychological history is worse than Janet's, but his relative progress is better. This graph covers 10 months, but a comprehensive token economy was in effect during only 5 of these months.

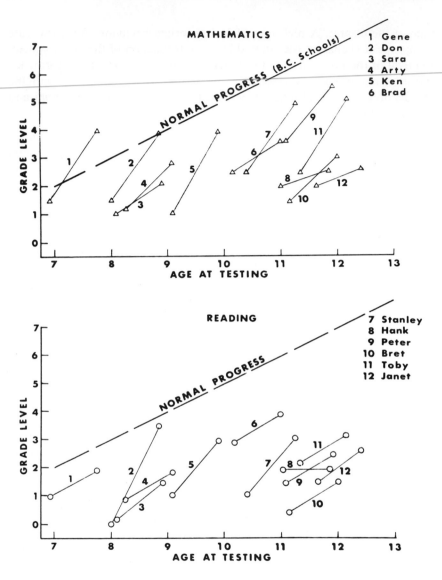

*Figure 15.2* Academic progress of 12 typical children over 10 months.

STAFF

    One of the most important aspects of the program is feedback to the staff. While we have not reported the concurrent program after school, the most deleterious effect of removing the point system in the house was not on the children but on the staff, since they then had no standard by which to measure their own performance. As a result, a positive point system was reinstituted in the house. There were 12 child-care workers in the house, and data taken on each worker indicated that positive behavior toward an individual child took place on 8% of the observations. Since this seemed low, data were posted in graphical form and a program directed at increasing the output of favorable comments to the children by verbally reinforcing such behavior was instituted. The average percentage of positive interactions increased to 14% during the next month. We are now in the process of not posting graphs for 2 months to see if any reversal effects will be seen. Also, we are beginning to record total interactions and continuous data in order to study closer the relationship between the behavior of children and that of adults.

The preceding data and subjective impressions have led the authors to the conclusion that for most children a positive token economy incorporating time out for inappropriate behavior is more effective than the rating system or no points. It has also been found more effective to design tight programs in which necessities must be earned rather than subject the children and staff to the unpleasant effects of a punitive program involving negative points. As programs have become more individualized and staff more experienced, such negative contingencies have become unnecessary.

## A Specific Program

This is the case history of a child referred to the Centre whose progress illustrates the positive aspects of our program but indicates the shortcomings of residential treatment.

## METHOD

### SUBJECT

Gene is a 6-year-old boy who at 18 months of age suffered from a severe case of pneumococcal meningitis complicated by repeated convulsions and the presence of a "huge communicating hydrocephalus." The attending physician described Gene as a "very tragic case" and predicted certain neurological dysfunction in later life. In spite of this poor prognosis, Gene seemed to progress well physically after the operation, although several physicians noted his short attention span and high level of activity, which led to the well-known diagnosis of "organic brain dysfunction." Gene's intellectual progress seemed slow, and the persistent emergence of tantrums and aggressive behavior caused the parents considerable worry. The arrival of a baby sister at 3 years of age seemed to precipitate Gene's worst behavior. Soon after the baby was born, his mother reported that Gene displayed numerous tantrums, required continuous attention, and showed considerable aggressive behavior toward the baby. This behavior, combined with a tantrum during a visit to a physician's office, led to the prescription of 10 mg of Mellaril three times daily. In spite of this treatment, there was a continued increase in the frequency of aggressive acts toward his sister. On several occasions he threw her to the sidewalk, attempted to "bash her head in," and "very deliberately tried to squash her" between doors. He was also beginning to wander from home. After nearly destroying a physician's office on one occasion, he was recommended for psychiatric treatment and eventually was placed in Vancouver General Hospital. He was shortly dismissed with the diagnosis of "hyperkinetic impulse disorder and mental retardation, with secondary behavioral problems characterized by aggressiveness, liability, and manipulative behavior." He was sent on his way with 50 mg of Largactil three times daily, which had the effect of photosensitizing him, but little other benefit was seen. Following this, an inability or refusal to sleep caused his physician to prescribe 150 mg of chlorpromazine before bedtime, which was subsequently reduced to 50 mg. Further destruction of person and property, such as his father's stereo, bay windows, and furniture, caused Gene to be referred for residential treatment with the following statement from his physician: "It is my opinion that Gene is suffering from the results of the meningitis at $1\frac{1}{2}$ years. I do not know of any treatment that could be more effective than what is now being done for the boy at home. . . ." The professionals agreed that Gene would be severely retarded and belonged in a hospital for children who could not function in society, but his mother refused to believe this prognosis. Only her dogged insistence on treatment and refusal to accept such a conclusion kept Gene from such placement.

When Gene arrived at the Centre, he refused to follow any directions, wandered aimlessly, and threw tantrums whenever required to do anything he did not wish to do. His entry into a classroom with four other children was chaotic. He refused to sit in a chair, talked constantly, walked out of class, threw tantrums, whined, and spat. In order to assess his academic ability and introduce him into the highly structured educational system, the frequency of his inappropriate verbal and physical behavior had to be reduced. Secondly, it was necessary to teach the parents to deal with this inappropriate behavior.

## PROCEDURE AND RESULTS

Data recorded as previously described in the school over 1 month are shown in Figure 15.3 and indicate that Gene was behaving inappropriately on an average of 32% of the observations. This rate was fairly steady from day 1 to day 7, and seemed to be increasing toward the end of baseline. No data were recorded on appropriate behavior. Although we did not differentiate between different forms of attention at this stage of the study, the teacher spent 38% of her time attending to Gene.

During the experimental period, Gene received stars for a certain number of consecutive observations on which he was sitting in his chair without misbehaving. These stars purchased various reinforcers, and the

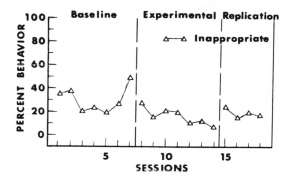

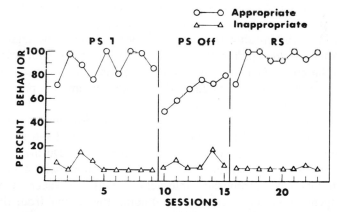

*Figure 15.3* Percentage of Gene's appropriate and inappropriate behavior observed in school.

number of consecutive trials necessary to receive a star was gradually increased when two stars had been awarded without any interruption by Gene. This contingency was increased from 3 to 12 by day 14. Initially in the experimental period, Gene behaved inappropriately on 27% of the observations. By increasing the contingencies for reinforcement, we were able to lower this figure to 9% by day 14. The teacher was attending to Gene on 17% of the observations during this phase, and this figure remained fairly constant during the experimental period of six weeks.

Gene was then sent home for a short visit with his parents. Since much, if not all of Gene's disruptive inappropriate behavior had been shaped by his parents, his behavior should have degenerated during the visit. An increase in the frequency of his disruptive behavior is seen on day 15, the day he returned to school. Although the contingency on day 15 was the same as on day 14, his behavior had degenerated somewhat. Day 16 was begun with a contingency of five uninterrupted observations for reinforcement; we increased the number of consecutive noiseless trials from 5 to 15 over the 1 month represented by days 15–17.

At this time, point system 1 was introduced into the academic program. As can be seen in the lower graph in Figure 15.3, Gene's performance on point system 1 was quite good, but removal of points affected him rather dramatically. Institution of the rating system resulted in an increase in appropriate behavior. Also, as can be seen in Figure 15.2, Gene's progress in mathematics was quite remarkable. Academically and behaviorally, Gene was ready for a remedial reading class in public school.

Gene's parents were brought to the Centre in June 1970 for their first training session. During baseline we introduced Gene, his mother, his sister, and his father into the experimental room in different orders. We shall discuss Gene's sessions with his mother and sister, since they are the most interesting. The functional relationship between Gene and his mother was established after the sister was born. After Gene attacked his sister, mother would separate them and spend all of her time with him. During the baseline, data not represented here indicated his inappropriate behavior to be inversely correlated to the amount of time his parents were in proximity or were talking to him.

During two 1-hour baseline sessions, three 5-minute observations of inappropriate (T− and P−) and appropriate (T+ and P+ and /) behavior were recorded. Data are shown in Figure 15.4. During the training phase, his mother was introduced to a token economy with which Gene could earn lunch by appropriate interactions with his sister. Time out was contingent upon negative behavior. Fading the trainer from the situation between observations four and seven over two training sessions 2 hours in length resulted in an increase in inappropriate behavior and a drop in appropriate behavior. Mother, Gene, and sister alone during another session are represented in observations eight and nine. Day 10 represents the same situation several months later. Obviously, training has not been totally effective. Since the parents understood the method well enough, however, they were introduced into the program at the Centre, where they were responsible for four or five children with severe behavior problems and could model the behavior of staff members. Data are being recorded presently and are most encouraging. We are working with social workers and local teachers to help them implement a program of behavior modification for Gene in his own community.

## The Future

Although our program with Gene and his parents is proving successful, the basic flaw inherent in the very concept of the treatment center should be evident. Gene has spent 2 years away from the environment to to which he will have to return, where he must deal with a hostile community that remembers only his antisocial behavior and knows that he was sent to a school for children who are different. It is highly likely that if Gene is expected to return to his old patterns of behaving, and if members of the community are not ready to reinforce behavior incompatible with his aggressive and inappropriate behavior, he will fulfill their expectations. We are now in the midst of a custody battle for another child, Dwight, who was admitted to the Centre 9 months before the program began and was 11 years old when the program was instituted. This child had been ejected from public school because of truancy, vandalism, lying, stealing, and disturbances in the classroom. At age 10 he was arraigned in juvenile court on 17 counts of theft, shoplifting, breaking and entry, truancy, and arson. His father is an alcoholic who set fire to the furniture and beat the children and their mother. Dwight's older brother is in a penal institution as a result of child molesting, and his sister has been convicted of prostitution. In the words of his former teacher in public school, "Dwight is a deceitful, disobedient, uncooperative child. He is a compulsive liar." His last offense before being admitted to the Centre was to burn down an elderly couple's house while they were in it. Fortunately, they escaped. Dwight has progressed well at the Centre, and entered public school during the period when points were removed. He is presently being considered for foster placement, but if the battle for custody is lost, Dwight

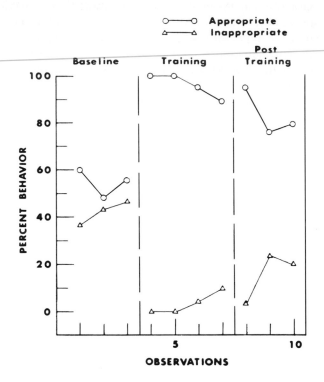

*Figure 15.4* Percentage of Gene's appropriate and inappropriate behavior observed in the presence of his mother and sister before, during, and after training.

will terminate all contact with the Centre. It is unlikely that the environment at home will maintain his present behavior.

The basic justification for treatment centers has been the medical model. A child's deviant behavior results in a diagnosis of unmanageability or emotional disturbance. He is removed from his social environment by an official of society and placed in a center for "treatment." The immediate reinforcing effects on these members of society as a result of removing the child from the community and labeling him as "disturbed" are obvious. An unpleasant, unmanageable child has been removed from the responsibility. The job of the center consists of supposedly flushing the emotions clean and restructuring the psyche of the child. Assuming the operant model, however, places the "pathology" not solely on the child's shoulders but rather on the environment. This places the burden of "cure" on parents, teachers, courts, social agencies, and law enforcement agencies. Our data show an immediate improvement in even the most severely "disturbed" children when they enter a highly structured reinforcing environment. Assuming that it is important and better for the child to remain in society and to learn to deal with society, our institutions must be made more reinforcing for members of the community to restructure the normal environment of the child.

One method of teaching members of the community to manage these disturbed children is to teach them how to manage their own children. This is a most powerful method of involving people in programs, since there is no reinforcer more potent nor punishment more effective than in the behavior of one's own child. Since deviant children often are sent to treatment centers as a result of their effect on the behavior of other children, members of the community must see all children in their community as their responsibility and an area in which they can exercise some authority. One reads much of alienation, anomie, and other terms describing the lack of social responsibility in North American culture. It is our feeling that socially responsible behavior has been placed on extinction in the face of unresponsive institutionalization of society's duties such as education, self-policing and social work.

A dialogue with the community surrounding our Centre has begun as a result of the performance of children from the Centre in the local schools and the progress of local children at the Centre. Volunteers from the community are involved in programs similar to the previously mentioned parent-training program, and will serve with the staff of the Centre as consultants and involved members of the community. Our staff has been allowed to enter a local first grade, with the aim of bringing the parents into the school program. Hopefully, this sort of involvement will reveal problems and solve them in the natural environment before residential care is necessary. A program designed to combat the use of alcohol and other drugs by children in the community is planned with the basic premise that one cannot avoid children's use of drugs without teaching a competing response and removing the social reinforcement contingent upon drug use. Groups of adolescents will contract with local businessmen and residents for jobs, which will supply monetary reinforcement and approval from peer groups while teaching them that their own behavior can affect their environment and well-being.

We began our program as a reaction to unacceptable behavior in a residential treatment center. We then realized that we could not treat children without changing the behavior of staff members and parents. We are now finding that the community at large behaves in a way toward children who require or who have been in residential treatment that is not conducive to adaptive child behavior. It is our contention that the solutions to children's behavioral problems in the community rests on the members of that community. Our job is to teach them and offer positive alternatives to removing children from their natural environment.

## References

Ayllon, T., and Azrin, N. H. *Token Economy: A Motivational System for Therapy and Rehabilitation*. New York: Appleton-Century-Crofts, 1968.

Batstone, D., and McMurchy, M. A token economy for children with learning disabilities. Unpublished honors thesis, University of Victoria, 1972.

Patterson, G. R., and Gullion, M. E. *Living with Children*. Champaign, Ill.: Research Press, 1968.

Phillips, E. L. Achievement Place: Token reinforcement procedures in a home-style rehabilitation setting for pre-delinquent boys. *Journal of Applied Behavior Analysis,* 1968, **1**, 213–223.

Phillips, E. L., Phillips, E. A., Fixsen, D. L., and Wolf, M. M. Achievement Place: Modification of the behaviors of pre-delinquent boys within a token economy. *Journal of Applied Behavior Analysis,* 1971, **4**, 45–59.

# 16 SELF-CONTROL IN INDIVIDUAL AND GROUP BEHAVIOR MODIFICATION PROGRAMS FOR EMOTIONALLY DISTURBED CHILDREN

Hans Heiner

Treatment procedures for emotionally disturbed children that are based on learning principles are confined almost solely to ambulant practices. To date, there are only a few studies that have been conducted in residential settings.

The introduction of behavior modification programs in the Pedological Institute (P.I.) has raised questions concerning both the fields of clinical practice and developmental psychology. The P.I. has a twofold aim: to offer assistance to children, adolescents, and their parents, and to function as an institution for study and research. Both these aims are incorporated in the training of university students. Since the director of the P.I. is also professor of developmental psychology and clinical child and adolescent psychology at the Free University, close cooperation between the P.I. foundation and the university are guaranteed.

The P.I. has three departments: a center for ambulant treatment of children and adolescents; a research center; and a center for residential treatment. It is experience in the last-mentioned that will be discussed in this chapter.

## The Center for Residential Treatment and Observation

### POPULATION

A total of 70 children varying in age between 3 and 13 years are divided into eight resident groups of six to ten children each, depending on the nature of their problem and the duration of their stay.

The school connected with the center has eight classes of eight to ten children each. The duration of stay is 3 months for observation and 1.5–2.5 years for treatment. The children are of normal intelligence, most of them handicapped by somewhat complicated learning and/or behavior difficulties (emotionally disturbed). Intake is by professional referral only.

### THE NATURE OF THE POPULATION

The children admitted for treatment or observation may be categorized roughly into three groups. The first group consists of children who developed disorders primarily as a result of conflict with their environment. In these children, one may observe disturbances for which ambulant treatment offers insufficient help, because the situation at home or in school has become untenable. A light cerebral–organic disturbance predominates among the children of the second group. The third group consists of mostly younger children with severe emotional disturbances or with a developmental retardation. The possibility of favorable influence should be present in such cases.

### WORKING PROCEDURE

A multidisciplinary approach is attempted in the P.I.:

1. Psychological approach. Psychodiagnosis and psychotherapy (e.g., play therapy and behavior therapy). Psychological consultation with coworkers belonging to other disciplines.
2. Special educational training within the living groups. Groups for special activities (creative work, music, etc.).
3. Special education in the school, with possibilities for individual approaches outside the classroom setting by speech therapists, specialized remedial teachers, or physiotherapists.
4. Treatment by social work. Intensive contact with the parents. Family diagnosis and treatment. Contacts with the Mental Health Service.

5. Service for medical treatment and examination by specialists. Special attention is given to neurological diagnosis and psychopharmacological treatment.

Because of the complex nature of the children's problems, it is necessary in nearly all cases that each of the five disciplines contribute to the treatment plan. On the basis of an empirically founded differentiated analysis (among others, a functional analysis), a treatment plan is evolved. Within this plan, either the various psychotherapeutic approaches are used to supplement each other, or a specific approach functions alone as the sole form of therapy in any given phase of the treatment. In the present report, an attempt will be made to present the effects of behavior modification in the total treatment program of the residential setting under discussion. This involves specifically the use of learning principles such as generalization and self-control. The principle of generalization offers dimensions that can help to stimulate the clinician in his consideration of treatment policy in a residential setting.

Although participation of parents is strongly desirable, to date this question has received somewhat one-sided emphasis. In order to make certain aspects of the treatment operational, an attempt is also made to specify the child's role in his own treatment process. To this end, the principle of self-control can be elaborated.

## Mental Health Services to Children

The nature and content of the questions posed, as well as the extent to which those seeking help will themselves be able to contribute to the finding of a solution, determines the form in which assistance is offered and the extent to which cooperation with a professional helper is desired. A range of situations in which assistance can be given is thus essential in order to match the variety of different requests for help from parents, educators, and children. This range of situations can be seen as extending from forms of ambulant help that do not serve to make fundamental changes in the natural milieu, to round-the-clock treatment in a residential setting, which acts as a temporary substitute for the natural milieu (family and school, public schools for normal children). This chapter is concerned primarily with the last mentioned, namely, the residential setting as temporary substitute.

Gelfand and Hartmann (1968) and Bandura (1970) regard this

residential setting as being advantageous to the execution of behavior modification programs, their main argument being that it is easier to gain, and thereafter to maintain, control over such a situation, for example, over the family and normal school. The control over the life situation of the child in the living group and classroom within the residential setting is exercised by the group leaders, that is, by professional educators. In this way, the treatment can be carried out systematically according to a general plan.

We have added another component to the three already included in the triadic model of Tharp and Wetzel (1969), of consultant, mediator, and target. The fourth component, viz. the parents, has been added to adapt the model to embrace the treatment situation in a residential setting, where the group leaders act as mediators instead of the parents. The principal difference between group leaders and parents can be explained very briefly by the concept of professional, as opposed to nonprofessional, educator. In this chapter the term "group leader" is used to imply all persons acting as professional educators in the residential setting; the term "consultant" refers to that member of the team whose task it is to contribute to the treatment by drawing upon his theoretical knowledge of learning principles.

## External Generalization

### COOPERATION BETWEEN MEDIATOR AND PARENTS

Browning and Stover (1971) give an extensive report on the setting up and execution of behavior modification programs in a residential setting. The aim of these programs is to shift the mediating task gradually from the professional educators back to the parents. In this way, residential treatment can become ambulant practice, so to speak. This can succeed only if the residential setting is constructed in such a way as to make generalization to life situations (family, regular school) maximally possible (whaler, 1969). For example, one of the criteria for admission to the institution where Browning and Stover (1971) work is that the parents be intensively involved in the residential treatment. To this end they must live within a 50-mile radius of the institution and must enter a gentleman's agreement to cooperate maximally. Wagner and Mabry (1970) set as a prerequisite to admission to their institution that the client's accomodation be regulated after discharge, and although the details of this requirement may alter during the course of treatment, the principle remains unchanged. These preconditions to admission flow directly from the concept that residential treatment fulfills a role of temporary substitution. This requires that generalization to various situations beyond and within the institution must be attempted (external and internal generalization). Accordingly, a group leader is expected to carry out his task of assisting the child in a temporary replacement capacity, bearing in mind that the parents (as nonprofessional educators) will eventually have to resume the education and guidance of their child.

In clinical practice we find this to be a source of tension. Closer analysis reveals this as tension in the relationship of the group leader to the child (target). The target's behavior evokes many emotions in the group leader. Since such behavior is perhaps partially the result of an unsuitable approach on the part of the parents, the group leader will want to "compensate" in an emotional sense. The setting up and carrying out of a behavior modification program, however, demands activities from a group leader that could sometimes appear "unnatural."

A second field of tension can also emerge between a consultant and a group leader. The consultant must not presume to present a ready-made program, but must arrive at a program via cooperative consultation. The determination of the aim and nature of a treatment can succeed only if consultant and group leader together—that is, all adults involved in the institution—have reached maximal agreement as members of one team. The various tasks must thereafter be allocated according to available knowledge and information concerning the target behavior in question. The fields of tension mentioned above must be reduced to a minimum if it is to be made clear to the parents that none of the group leaders aims to rival the parents in his approach to their child. Success gained by professional educators with the treatment of problem children can evoke feelings of guilt in parents, although such success is meant to give them the confidence and skill they will need to be able to guide their child once he returns home. Generalization can make a great contribution in this respect. The implication of the above for the professional educator is that from the first contact with the client system, a relationship of mutual cooperation must be established, on the basis of which treatment can be begun.

## PARENTS/COMPLAINT RELATIONSHIP

Generally it can be said that case histories deal with the treatment of one clearly circumscribed complaint. Treatment is initially carried out in a traditional therapist–child/client situation. Parents, teachers, and group leaders are named collectively as mediators. The adults from the child's environment receive introduction/training to enable them to carry out a behavior modification program together with the therapist (Tharp and Wetzel, 1969). The actual difference between parents and natural educators as opposed to teachers as professional educators still lacks sufficient explication (Fournier, 1972), but the time has now come to reflect more, especially on the specific implications of the inclusion of parents as mediators. The mediatorship of the parents can be called a subsidiary aim within the total treatment plan of the client system in that the parents should be lead to ever-increasing awareness of their own contribution to their child's problem. Without such insight, the mediatorship of the parents will be reduced to a mere technicality. The treatment of the child will thus be carried out on the authority of the professional therapist. This, in its turn, wrongly equates the complaint of the parents with the target behavior.

## PARENTS/CHILD/COMPLAINT RELATIONSHIP

The feelings of the child (in addition to those of the parents) about the complaint are too often ignored. Complaints are expressed in ways that arise from the parents/clients norms and value patterns, including such concepts as abnormal–normal, well adjusted–maladjusted, and so on. The coding of the complaint by the parents includes, among other factors, a number of cognitive variables. The treatment of the parents begins with the exploration of the parents' own subjective discrimination observation of the target behavior. Agreement between parent and therapist on the fact that a child is to receive treatment is insufficient for the formulation of a treatment goal.

Adults are able to communicate from a position of authority and, in Western cultures, the child is to a large extent dependent on the adult. The feelings of the child about his own so-called deviant behavior must equally be considered and incorporated into the treatment goals. It is the task of the professional therapist to help both parents and child to arrive at maximal clarity concerning the target behavior in order to be able to formulate a treatment goal. The therapist's knowledge of developmental psychology should enable him to contribute to the decision of whether or not treatment is necessary, since he will be able to judge whether there are factors present in the client system that will stand in the way of healthy development.

## Internal Generalization

Ayllon and Azrin (1968) designed a total residential setting (for adult treatment) based on a token economy. One gets the impression that such wards are a last-resort measure, because in the total treatment policy of the institution there is as yet insufficient place awarded to the carrying out of individualized treatment programs based on learning principles. It appears to be difficult to introduce new treatments based on a specific theory. The tendency of the representatives of established current theories is to evaluate anything new in terms of results achieved in a ward or even from a totally isolated individual treatment. Integration into treatment philosophy is thus, alas, often difficult. A theory with its practical clinical possibilities is insufficiently evaluated against scientific criteria. This makes for a certain rigidity in treatment. One regards treatment on the basis of learning principles desirable for the modification of clearly describable target behavior of an individual or group.

Wagner and Mabry (1970) indicate that treatment based on learning principles in a total treatment process—and not merely at the beginning thereof—should be discussed in continual revisions. We regard it as being of the utmost importance that on one hand, the decision for a choice of treatment plan be determined by the degree to which a scientifically responsible treatment experiment can be set up, based on a specific theory. On the other hand, clinical practice demands that one should be able to make a well-motivated choice of a treatment in the best interest of a client, based on a theoretical hypothesis that can seldom, if ever, be tested. The responsibility for such a choice should preferably be borne by a team. This team should have knowledge of, and give due consideration to, other possible alternatives. In this consideration, internal generalization should play a role; that is, the eventual results of the various parts of the treatment should complement each other. Behavior therapists still allow themselves to be persuaded into carrying out treatments that are insufficiently functional within a total treatment plan.

## CHILD–GROUP LEADER RELATIONSHIP

The place of the parent as client and future mediator in the child's treatment in a residential setting specifies the relationship of the child to the group leaders, especially with a view to generalization into normal educational situations. In the formulation of goals, it seems that the child and parent must be given equal consideration. The position of the child within the client system is, however, established only upon his actual admittance to the residential setting. The child is strongly dependent on the group's leaders, and has many confusing feelings about his placement in the institution. We can state that the emotionally disturbed child is not sufficiently able to shape his emotions suitably to his environment. Impressions from the environment and accompanying emotions cannot be integrated. The information-assimilating processes are too underdeveloped, for whatever reason, and do not function optimally. The resulting behavior pattern appears confused and impulsive, while the child's selection of alternative behaviors frequently leads to clashes with the expectations of his environment. The environment reacts negatively and thereby serves to strengthen and maintain the problem behavior. A residential setting provides these children with a measure of external control, which is of great assistance when this aspect is lacking or poorly developed in the child, and when control in a normal family/school situation appears insufficient. The temporary substitution character of the residential treatment will also lead to greater internal control, thereby developing an increasing amount of independence in the child. In this way the child can develop optimally, independent of his environment.

The treatment process should begin from the first contact between the client system and therapist. It is our opinion that insufficient attention has been paid to the development of a theory and method concerning the participation of the child as part of the client system both in the formulation of aims, their execution, and the final evaluation. Clinical findings concerning external and internal generalization according to the nature of the situation, as sketched above, will have to influence the operationalization of this child participation. In addition, developmental psychology must make its influence felt by indicating the level of intellectual and emotional development. In the next part of this chapter, an attempt will be made to elaborate this by examining more closely some ideas and results of self-control programs.

## Participation of the Child

Among the reports on clinical practice with behavior modification, there is occasional mention of the active participation of the child in the setting up of a program. Wahler and Cormier (1970) allow parents and children to make the same observations with the aim of exploring the experience value of a specific problem behavior by means of coding. Similarly, the development of "contingency or behavioral contracts" deserves attention. In the treatment of ambulant cases, one attempts to bring about the exchange of positive reinforcement between two or more persons. A contract presupposes a common basis of cooperation for both parties (compare, for instance, parents and child). The problem with this is that young children are at a stage of development that can lead to a discrepancy in the pattern of cooperation. This intervention model appears, however, to be applicable to cases concerning adolescents and their parents/teachers. Tharp and Wetzel (1969) indicate that a child, by means of an interview, can contribute to the search for feasible reinforcers. This brings us to token-economy programs. The following can serve as an illustration of the problem mentioned.

Token-economy programs will find increasing application in a residential treatment setting for children in imitation of their application in school situations. Bearing in mind the advantages and disadvantages as set out by Sherman and Bear (1969), this technique can be used as an instrument for bringing about new behavior. It can serve as an "initial tool to establish new behavior, which later can be transferred to social control." The dominant role in designing these programs is usually that of the adult. Clinical experience has taught, however, that a group leader is at a disadvantage as a dispenser of social reinforcers (or vicarious reinforcers) in the situation of the living group with its rich variety of behavior. Naturalistic descriptive research in the P.I. has indicated that a mere 30% of the contact between group leader and child was initiated by the group leader. The supposition is justified that this can be ascribed to insufficient training, together with the functional complexity of the events that take place in the living group (de Ruyter, 1971).

To allow this task to be carried out by nongroup leaders carries with it the danger of violating important aspects of the group setting. The use of technical apparatus can only partially overcome this disadvantage.

Both the dominant position and the task of the group leader make the establishing of self-control by the child, to promote independence from a specific environment, essential. Browning and Stover (1971) note the necessity of investigating the reliability of the measures they themselves used for assessing the effects of treatment. In our opinion, the child's experience of his own target behavior must be systematically handled in the development of such measures. The operationalization of concepts such as self-control in treatment experiments can be of very great importance in achieving this end.

## Participation and Self-Control: A Theoretical Viewpoint

For a theoretical explanation, we take our point of departure in the work of Kanfer and Phillips (1970):

> In dealing with human behavior the engineering of fully controlled environments for individuals encounters many obstacles. Not only are there strong social injunctions against rigorous control of individual behavior but there are also characteristic limitations to any such attempts due to man's unique capacity to create his own subjective environment. The result of this special property of human behavior is man's greater independence from his physical environment than is true of any other species and his capacity for regulating his behavior on the basis of these private processes [p. 371].

After an extensive consideration of the use of verbal methods of behavior control, the authors conclude: "The interview at present continues to be used for collection of data about the patient's history, for observation of his behavior under varying interviewing conditions, and for behavior modification." Still, the interview is used for more "specific purposes than as a vehicle for all psychological treatment," although the client can as yet make very little active use of the interview therapy for gaining more information and insight for his guidance in daily life outside the therapy sessions. The authors use techniques that are very similar to these, which they call "instigation therapies"—a form of therapy in which therapists and client work closely together in the treatment.

> These attitudes of participation and self-regulation are especially important in maximizing cooperation among patients who are opposed to external manipulations. The patient's role is also indispensable for execution of programs in his natural environment, particularly applicable when the symptoms do not warrant institutionalization or interference by the therapist in the patient's private life.

The authors note the contribution of self-regulation but do not elaborate upon its limitations.

Clients in a residential setting are as much exposed to external manipulations as are those receiving ambulant treatment. The nature and seriousness of the problem that leads to the admission of clients to such an institution should in no way be allowed to hinder the search for a form of treatment that furthers self-regulation. In fact, it should stimulate effort to find a solution. This is most certainly so when it concerns children who are admitted to an institution almost solely at the request of adults/parents.

A residential treatment home for emotionally disturbed children can be only a temporary substitute for the family. The professional educator at an institution must therefore not only promote generalization toward the parents but also activate the child's potential (among other things, forms of self-regulation) so that he may once again take his place in the family. Kanfer and Phillips all too seldom examine the fundamental importance of self-regulation for treatment in residential settings. Self-regulation in its diverse theoretical and technical developments is still insufficiently proven in clinical practice. Research findings have indicated the great importance of a closer analysis via these theoretical avenues of the cognitive variables (which play a role in each form of therapy and therefore also in behavior modification) and their manipulation in the treatment as experimental variables. Concepts such as self-control, self-monitoring, self-description, and self-administration are attempts at the operationalization of self-regulation.

If Kanfer and Phillips' review of studies concerning the clinical use of self-control procedures in children is examined, mainly laboratory-oriented studies are discussed. The theoretical consideration about these processes in children are scarcely, or not at all, supported by findings from developmental psychology. Without further reference to research, it is stated that a child learns to label his emotions under the influence of external factors. The development described by Gagne and Bijou from a learning psychological point of view are not mentioned. Baldwin (1967), in his discussion of social learning theories, refers equally seldom to Bijou, although he does refer to Gagne. The contact between theorists in the fields of learning psychology and development psychology has apparently advanced very little. In our opinion, the result is that Baldwin regards behavior modification programs as being limited to the treatment of children with monosymptomatic, clearly defined problems, while professing other and "deeper" therapy forms for more complex problems. Kanfer and Phillips wish to break through this barrier by extensive study of the treatment based on learning psychological principles, of the so-called private events that are so difficult to operationalize. Meichenbaum and Goodman (1971) clearly attempt to include cognitive factors in their behavior modification programs.

To summarize: The theoretical contribution of self-control procedures is stimulating for behavior modification in children. These theories are, however, still too seldom borne out in relation to developmental psychological facts. The implications for the clinical use of self-control procedures are still more or less nonexistent, and where they do exist, should be queried as regards their theoretical background.

## Execution of a Behavior Modification Program and Self-Control

Some examples of the child's participation in the setting up of treatment were mentioned, taking Kanfer and Phillips' description of self-regulation as a collective concept for forms of active client contribution to the execution of a treatment. An important contribution to the development of this idea was found in the following studies. Wahler and Pollio (1968) attempted to find an experimental connection between changes in a child's deviant behavior and his verbal description of that behavior. This was done with the help of rating the words that semantically related to his deviant behavior. The findings of Krop, Calhoon, and Verrier (1971) indicate that changes in self-concept by means of covert reinforcement can be brought about in emotionally disturbed children. In this study, the therapeutic application of concepts such as "coverant"—after Cautela (1970)—are employed. Homme, Csanyl, Gonzalez, and Rechs (1969) gave much attention to "self-contracting" or "self-control." Their idea is to give the pupils increasingly more responsibility in the setting up and carrying out of their contracts. They state: "The ultimate goal of contingency contracting can now be redefined as getting the student ready to both establish and fulfill his own contracts and to reinforce himself . . . for doing so." The aim is to decrease external control while increasing internal control. Lovitt and Curtiss (1969) conclude that a pupil will achieve at a higher level when he can determine the contingencies himself and note the results than when the teacher acts as contingency manager. This holds true even when the actual rewards received are fewer. Glynn (1970) makes an important contribution to the discussion concerning the application of self-determined reinforcement. Inconsistency, unpredictability of the teacher's reinforcement strategies—with strong reinforcement at one time and very little reinforcement at another—hinders effective application of self-reinforcement procedures. Research into the factors that bring about self-control in children and serve to maintain it should be considerably increased. The role of mediating processes, that is, discrimination-learning and labelling behavior, are recognized but are still too little operationalized in therapeutic practice. In 1971, Geus and Heiner carried out a token-economy program with a school group in order to modify the work behavior of 11 emotionally disturbed children (mean age 10.5, IQ: normal average). Self-recording ensured active participation of the boys in the program. Rules and activities within a living group cannot be as clearly specified as those for the same group within the structured school situation. In our opinion, it is therefore more difficult to set up a behavior modification program for such a group—whether for the group as a whole or for individual members of the group—than it is for a school group. In accordance with the findings of Geus and Heiner, Fullard, Heiner, Hoekstra, and de Kruijff (1972) carried out a token-economy program in the eating situation of a living group in which the development of self-control over the behavior in this situation was an important aspect. The results of both the above-mentioned treatment programs have, in our opinion, provided enough evidence in favor of continuing the application of self-control in behavior modification programs in school and living groups.

To summarize: Literary evidence and experience in a residential setting leads one to conclude that self-control should be given a more prominent place in behavior modification programs. This becomes even more essential if generalization from the residential setting to situations in normal life is to be promoted.

## References

Ayllon, T., and Azrin, N. *The Token Economy.* New York: Appleton-Century-Crofts, 1968.

Baldwin, A. L. *Theories of Child Development.* New York: Wiley, 1967.

Bandura, A. *Principles of Behavior Modification.* London: Holt, Rinehart & Winston, 1970.

Browning, R. M., and Stover, D. O. *Behavior Modification in Child Treatment.* Chicago: Aldine, Atherton, 1971.

Cautela, J. R. Covert reinforcement. *Behavior Therapy,* 1970, **1**, 33–50.

Fournier, E. P. *Ouders en kinderen in de Gedragstherapie.* Assen: Van Gorcum and Comp. N. V., 1972.

Fullard, J. P. P., Heiner, J. Hoekstra, F., and de Kruijff, G. *Self-Control: Application and Implications Within a Residential Treatment Program.* Amsterdam: Pedological Institute, 1972.

Gelfand, D. M., and Hartmann, D. P. Behavior therapy with children: A review and evaluation of research methodology. *Psychological Bulletin,* 1968, **69**, 204–215.

Geus, R. F. B., and Heiner, J. *Token-Reinforcement Programma's bij kinderen en jeugdigen.* Amsterdam: Pedological Institute, 1971.

Glynn, E. L. Classroom applications of self-determined reinforcement. *Journal of Applied Behavior Analysis,* 1970, **3**, 123–132.

Heiner, J. Gedragstherapie in internaten. In M. J. A. van Spange (Ed.), *Contour en Perspectief in de Kinderbescherming.* Rotterdam: Lemniscaat, 1971, p. 91–127.

Homme, L., Csanyl, A. Gonzalez, M., and Rechs, J. *How to Use Contingency Contracting in the Classroom.* Champaign, Ill.: Research Press, 1969.

Kanfer, F. H., and Phillips, J. S. *Learning Foundations of Behavior Therapy.* New York: Wiley, 1970.

Krop, H., Calhoon, B., and Verrier, R. Modification of the "self-concept" of emotionally disturbed children by covert reinforcement. *Behavior Therapy*, 1971, **2**, 201–204.

Lovitt, T. C., and Curtiss, K. Academic response rate as a function of teacher, and self-imposed contingencies. *Journal of Applied Behavior Analysis*, 1969, **2**, 49–53.

Meichenbaum, D. H., and Goodman, J. Training impulsive children to talk to themselves: A means of developing self-control. *Journal of Abnormal Psychology*, 1971, **77**, 115–126.

de Ruyter, P. A. *De "volgende" groepsleidster: Interacties van Groepsleidsters en kinderen in een centrum voor Residentiele Behandeling* (with English summary). Dissertation, Free University of Amsterdam. Groningen: Wolters-Noordhoff, 1971.

Sherman, J. A., and Baer, D. M. Appraisal of operant therapy technique with children and adults. In C. M. Franks (Ed.), *Behavior Therapy: Appraisal and Status*. New York: McGraw-Hill, 1969, pp. 192–220.

Tharp, R. G., and Wetzel, R. J. *Behavior Modification in the Natural Environment*. New York: Academic Press, 1969.

Wagner, B. R., and Mabry, T. R. PACE: A residentially based behavior modification program for adolescents. Adolf Meyer Zone Center, Decatur, Ill., 1970. Decatur, Ill., 1970.

Wahler, R. G. Setting generality: Some specific and general effects of child behavior therapy. *Journal of Applied Behavior Analysis*, 1969, **2**, 239–246.

Wahler, R. G., and Cormier, W. H. The ecological interview: A first step in outpatient child behavior therapy. *Journal of Behavior Therapy and Experimental Psychiatry*, 1970, **1**, 279–289.

Wahler, R. G., and Pollio, H. R. Behavior and insight: A case study in behavior therapy. *Journal of Experimental Research in Personality*, 1968, **3**, 45–56.

# 17 MULTIPLE EVALUATIONS OF A PARENT-TRAINING PROGRAM[1]

**G. R. Patterson**

This report investigates the efficiency of parent-training procedures designed to alter the behavior of aggressive children. Two sets of criteria were collected during baseline and during treatment to evaluate the outcome.

Boys' aggressive behavior is one of the problems that frequently leads both teachers (Rogers, Lilienfeld, and Pasamanick, 1954; Woody, 1969) and parents (Patterson, 1964; Roach, 1958) to refer children for professional assistance. About a third of the total referrals from either source concern problems of aggression. The empirical findings from longitudinal studies in the classroom showed that these more extreme cases of aggression do not "outgrow" the behaviors. In that setting, the behaviors persisted over the 5- to 10-year periods studied (Beach and Laird, 1968; Benning, Feldhusen, and Thurston, 1968; Westman, Rice, and Bermann, 1967). The follow-up studies by Morris (1956) and Robins (1966) of children diagnosed as aggressive showed that as adults less than one in four were "well adjusted." In the later study, compared to a matched control group, aggressive children contributed disproportionately as adults to major crimes, psychosis, and marginal employment records.

[1] This study was supported by grants MH 10822 and RO1 MH 15985 from NIMH Section in Crime and Delinquency, and Career Development Award 4-K1-MH 40518. Computing assistance was obtained from the Health Sciences Computing Facility, UCLA, sponsored by NIH grant FR-3. A version of this paper was also presented at the Sixth Annual Convention of the Association for the Advancement of Behavior Therapy, New York, October 1972.

When aggressive children are referred to clinics, they are typically diagnosed as "conduct disorders." In one study, only a fourth to a third of cases so diagnosed were offered treatment (Bahm, Chandler, and Eisenberg, 1961). The review by Levitt (1971) showed that of those cases treated, few responded to traditional therapies. Rausch, Dittman, and Taylor (1959) reported modest changes in a small group of severely aggressive boys treated for an extended period in a residential center. Later, clinical follow-up studies of these boys showed that even these modest changes did not persist when the boys were returned to their homes.

It would seem, then, that effective treatment procedures are badly needed for aggressive children. There are, however, two major difficulties. First, techniques for changing the behavior must be developed. Simultaneously, means for increasing relevant behavioral changes must be constructed.

## A Means for Changing Aggressive Behaviors

FORMULATION

In his review of the research literature, Frank (1965) found no variables significantly differentiating families of disturbed and nondisturbed children. However, Hendricks (1972a) compared observed rates of deviant behaviors for matched samples of aggressive and nonaggressive boys. He found that boys referred as conduct disorders displayed significantly higher rates of aggressive behaviors as they interacted with members of their own families.

It is hypothesized that there are certain family interactions that relate to these differences in observed rates. First, the "schedule differences" hypothesis stipulates that deviant families have higher rates of reinforcement (positive and negative) and lower rates of aversive consequences provided for deviant child behaviors. Second, the "responsiveness deficit" hypothesis states that these are differences in the responsiveness of the deviant child to those consequences that are provided. Third, the "density of controlling stimuli" hypothesis describes families of problem children as presenting higher densities of noxious stimuli, which in turn control the rates of occurrence of the aggressive behaviors.

Observation data collected in the homes of five aggressive boys showed that positive consequences occurred for 26% of the deviant responses, aversive consequences also occurred 26% of the time for these behaviors (Patterson, Ray, and Shaw, 1968).[2] Shaw (1971) analyzed the data from 15 matched pairs of aggressive and normal boys. For the combined sample, his data showed deviant child behavior to be positively consequated 33.7% of the time and aversively consequated 24.4%. Wahl (1971) found comparable values for a sample of normal boys. Sallows (1972) analyzed the data from 15 matched pairs of aggressive and normal boys. His data showed that the families of aggressive boys tended to provide more positive consequences for deviant responses, but both sets of families provided about the same rates of aversive consequences. Assuming that Sallows' "positive consequences" were in fact positive reinforcers, his data offer support for one aspect of the "schedule differences" hypothesis.

A review of laboratory analog studies showed aggressive boys to be less responsive to adult-dispensed social reinforcers than were nonaggressive boys (Patterson, 1969). Wahler (1967) not only demonstrated this effect, but altered responsiveness by manipulating several contingencies employed by the parents. Walker and Buckley (1973) demonstrated in the classroom that aggressive boys were less responsive to teacher-dispensed reinforcers than were normal boys. Sequential analyses of observation data by Sallows (1972) showed problem children to be less responsive to aversive consequences than nonproblem children. Responsiveness was measured in terms of its effect on the immediately following response in the time series.[3]

It was assumed by Patterson and Cobb (1971) that much aggressive behavior was controlled by negative reinforcement. Families of aggressive boys would be expected to present higher rates of aversive stimuli to each other than would families of nonaggressive children. A recent comparison

---

[2] All studies carried out thus far have been forced to use a priori groupings for positive and aversive consequences. While the investigators may wish to assume that such a priori groupings correspond to "reinforcers," there is no evidence that such correspondence exists. Therefore, the findings must remain tentative pending empirical identification of "reinforcers" occurring in situ.

[3] It should be noted that testing for the impact of consequences on the probability of a response's immediate recurrence does *not* provide a test of reinforcer effectiveness. The discussion by Patterson and Cobb (1971) outlines the reasons for this. Sallows' findings do suggest that the responsiveness hypothesis should be expanded to include hypotheses about differential responsiveness to stimuli in general, including discriminative as well as reinforcing stimuli. For example, the available data suggest that aggressive boys may be slightly more responsive to stimuli that trigger deviant responses (Patterson and Cobb, 1971). Sallows' data suggest further that they are less responsive to decelerating consequences. They may be, in addition, less responsive to positive and aversive reinforcers.

of matched samples of families of aggressive and nonaggressive children showed the hypothesis to be supported (Patterson, in press). It would also be assumed that these families are more likely to reinforce the aggressive response by removing the aversive stimulus following the occurrence of the aggressive response; that is, aggression "pays off." As yet, there are no studies that have tested this hypothesis.

These preliminary findings offer support for the hypotheses that families of aggressive boys provide richer schedules of positive reinforcement for deviant behaviors, and that the boys are probably less responsive to aversive consequences than are nonaggressive boys. The families also provide higher rates of aversive stimuli, which facilitate the occurrence of aggressive behaviors. Presumably, successful intervention would have to deal with each of these facets of interaction in order to produce long-term effects.

## INTERVENTION

Earlier reports describing applications of social learning procedures to family intervention (e.g., Hawkins, Peterson, Schweid, and Bijou, 1966; Wahler, Winkle, Peterson, and Morrison, 1965; Wolf, Mees, and Risley, 1964) were single-case studies. In some of these, the parents were trained to apply positive and aversive consequences to bring the child's behavior under control. Many of these, and the other studies that followed, relied on observation data collected within the home as criteria for evaluating outcome. Such case studies demonstrated the promise of parent-training procedures. However, the general utility of such procedures as clinical techniques requires investigation of the generalizability of the training, its efficiency for treating consecutive families, its cost in professional time, and the persistence of the effects.

Several large-scale studies fulfill some of these requirements, but each leaves something to be desired. For example, in the major study by Tharp and Wetzel (1969), an attempt was made to have the parents collect systematic observation data for 77 families. However, for many cases the data were not collected, systematic follow-up data were not obtained, nor were data reported for the amount of time expended on each case. Another study by Wahler and Erikson (1969) also involved a large sample of cases. However, the observation data were collected by the therapists themselves, and no follow-up or cost-efficiency data were presented. These two studies constitute major contributions to the development of family-intervention procedures. Both reiterate the promise of a social learning base for such a venture. Both leave unanswered questions concerning general efficiency.

The procedures for intervention and for data collection to be reported here have evolved gradually as a function of experiences obtained with a series of half a dozen unpublished and published studies (Patterson and Brodsky, 1966; Patterson, McNeal, Hawkins, and Phelps, 1967; Patterson and Reidfi 1970). The treatment strategy was (1) to work with consecutive referals; (2) to observe the families in their homes to establish the base rates of deviant and prosocial child behaviors and the parent-mediated consequences; (3) to require the parents to study a programmed text on social-learning-based child-management techniques (Patterson, 1972a); (Patterson and Gullion, 1968); (4) to teach the parents to define, pinpoint, track, and record carefully rates of target deviant and prosocial child behaviors; (5) to help the parents construct and execute modification programs in their homes; and (6) to conduct follow-up investigations designed to determine the stability of treatment effects. Sometimes these required actually going into the homes and modeling the techniques for the parents.

In the first such study (Patterson *et al.*, 1968), parents of five aggressive boys (consecutive referrals) were trained. The observation system used in the previous studies was further developed (Patterson, Ray, Shaw, and Cobb, 1969), and served to evaluate treatment outcome. The data were collected by observers in the homes during baseline, intervention, and a 12-month follow-up. Comparisons of baseline and termination data in the home showed a range of 62–75% reduction in observed rates of total deviant child behavior, comparing baseline with terminal observations.

The follow-up data showed persistence of training effects for three of the four families for whom data were available. An average of 22.8 hours of professional time per family was required to produce the effects.

The training and measurement procedures were further standardized and altered somewhat to fit the requirements of group training. The details are presented in the report by Patterson, Cobb, and Ray (1973). The present report describes the outcome of application of these revised procedures to 28 consecutive referrals. The sample consisted of extremely aggresive boys. Two sets of criterion data were collected in the homes prior to and during treatment. The criteria consisted of (1) observations of family interaction made within the home and (2) parents' daily reports on the occurrence or nonoccurrence of the specified child's referral problem behaviors. Careful records were also kept of the amount of professional time invested in each case. It was assumed that comparisons of baseline and termination data would show significant reductions in both criteria.

## Procedures

### SAMPLE

Twenty-seven families were consecutive referrals by community agencies such as the juvenile court, schools, and mental hygiene clinic during the period from January 1968 through June 1972. They were referred because at least one boy in each family had displayed high rates of aggressive behavior. During the intake interview, the parents were asked whether each of 63 problems, commonly stated by parents seeking treatment at child-guidance clinics (Patterson, 1964), were of immediate concern to them. The problems reported to be of greatest concern to the parents included noncompliance, continued difficulties with siblings, temper tantrums, hyperactivity, aggression, lying, loudness, stealing, and inability to relate to peers. Table 17.1 summarizes the demographic data for the sample.

An intake evaluation, plus diagnostic records from other community agencies, indicated that none of these families included severely retarded, acute psychotic, or severely brain-damaged members. Parents' descriptions of the rate and type of their boys' aggressive behaviors given in the interview, plus reports from community agencies, indicated that all the referred boys had a history of conduct problems. Many of them showed high rates of social aggression.[4] The sample contained more families from lower socioeconomic levels than would be predicted by knowledge of the social structure of the community.

There were also a greater number of father absences than would be expected in the general population. The analysis of family-interaction data by Patterson (in press) showed the father-absent families to be associated with significantly higher rates of aggressive behavior than other families in the sample.

---

[4] A substantial number of boys referred because of "aggressive" behavior showed little or no observable aggressive behaviors in the home. Some of these acted out only in the school. Others displayed few socially aggressive behaviors, but did steal, set fires, and run away. A recent analysis by Reid and Hendriks (1972) showed the current parent-training procedure to be only half as effective for this latter group of boys. The most reasonable means for aggressive children for whom present technology would be appropriate would require home observations *prior* to the decision to accept a case. Setting the acceptance requirement at total rates of observed deviant child behavior at $\geq .4$ responses per minute would have resulted in the rejection of ten cases in the present sample as inappropriate. When applied to a matched sample of 27 normal boys, this decision rule resulted in "misclassifying" 18% of them as deviant (Hendriks, 1972a).

**TABLE 17.1**
DEMOGRAPHIC INFORMATION

| Variable | Sample |
|---|---|
| Number of families | 27 |
| Sex of referred child | All male |
| Age of referred child | Mean 8.7 years |
| | Range 5–13 |
| Race of referred child | 26 Caucasian |
| | 1 Oriental |
| Number of siblings | Mean 2.44 |
| | Range 1–5 |
| Number families with father absent | 8 |
| Socioeconomic level [a] | Mean 4.3 |
| | Range 1–7 |
| Birth order of referred child | Mean 2.11 |
| | Range 1–5 |

[a] Based on system provided by Hollingshead and Redlich (1958) with class 1 denoting higher executive or professional; class 4, clerical; and class 7, unskilled laborer.

Approximately one child in four was receiving medication for "hyperactivity" when the baseline was initiated; all medication was discontinued by termination of the intervention.

THERAPISTS

Five staff members, each spending 2 or more years on the project, carried the bulk of the treatment load. During that time, approximately a dozen trainees supervised by the staff worked with one or more families.

TREATMENT

The treatment procedures used for these families have been presented in detail in Patterson *et al.* (1973). The concomitant classroom procedures, including nine of the children from this sample worked with earlier, was described in Patterson, Cobb, and Ray (1972).

OBSERVATION PROCEDURES

Six to ten baseline observations were made in each home prior to intervention. The version of the observation procedures described in

Patterson *et al.* (1969) was initiated in January 1968 and used throughout the study.

For each session, the observer went to the home at about dinner time and made two 5-minute observations on each family member in a pre-arranged random order. This produced a sequential account of each target subject's behavior and the reaction of other family members to him, in terms of 29 behavior categories. The code was specifically designed to describe family social interaction, emphasizing aversive behaviors and reactions to those behaviors.

During intervention, observational probes were carried out. Each probe consisted of two consecutive observation sessions, during each of which the referred child was observed for 20 minutes and the other family members for 5 minutes. Probes were introduced immediately following the parents' reading of the programmed text, after every 4 and 8 weeks of intervention, at termination, and during follow-up (which is still in progress).

Five professional observers collected the data for this study. To guard against decay in reliability as a function of sessions after initial observer training (Reid, 1970), biweekly observer training sessions and biweekly reliability checks in the homes were conducted.

During 1968, two uninformed "calibrating" observers were employed at regular intervals. However, the analysis of these data by Skindrud (1972a) showed that giving experienced observers information about treatment states did not produce a significant biasing effect. Laboratory (Skindrud, 1972b) and nonlaboratory (Kent, 1972) studies showed that observers using such a code produced unbiased records even when given information likely to bias their recording. For these reasons, no effort was made later in the series to keep observers uninformed.

Presumably, the observers' presence has some impact on the family interaction. However, the nature and magnitude of such an effect has proved difficult to determine (Harris, 1969). Johnson and Lobitz (1972) showed that interaction patterns for normal families could be altered by instructions given to parents to make the child "look good" or "look bad." The data for child behavior showed marked shifts as a function of such instructional sets. However, a study by Walter and Gilmore (1973) showed that parents of deviant children had more difficulty in altering their children's behavior to correspond to sets that they had. In their study, data for parents' expectancies showed that the members of the placebo group believed their children to be improving. Observations in the home showed no changes in deviant child behavior for these families. It is hypothesized that parental expectancies may differentially affect children of normal and deviant families.

A laboratory investigation of mother–child interaction has shown that observer presence was associated with reduced rates of deviant child behavior (White, 1972). An ABAB reversal design controlling for observer presence showed older children to be most effected. The observers' presence was associated with significantly lower rates of deviant behavior and decreased activity rates for these children.

Taken together, the foregoing studies suggest that the effect of the observer may be generally to increase the "noise" in the data (Harris, 1969) and also to produce a certain amount of false negative error *vis à vis* deviant behavior. The magnitude of such distortion remains to be identified.

### VALIDATION OF CODE SYSTEM

The code system was designed to describe the aggressive responses displayed by boys interacting with family members. However, the construct "observed aggressive behavior" is itself a complex term requiring a series of operational tests for adequate definition. In the present report, it is assumed that an aversive stimulus presented to another person constitutes an aggressive act. A priori, 14 different code categories were classified as noxious. This class was labeled Total Deviant behavior.

In a study reported by Johnson and Bolstad (1973), mothers rated descriptions of the code categories for "deviancy." The ratings for the 14 behaviors in the class Total Deviant were consistently rated in the predicted direction. In another study, 20 mothers of preschool children were also asked to rate descriptions of each of the 29 coded behaviors (Patterson, 1972b) on a nine-point scale ranging from (1) "very annoying" to (9) "very pleasing." The mean ratings for all of the aggressive responses were viewed as aversive.

Hendriks (1972c) investigated the relation between the mother's self-description on the MMPI and observers' data describing her actual behavior in the home. The data showed a modest number of significant correlations for some of the MMPI scales. For example, high scores on the Lie scale were correlated positively with the mother's rates of observed Command Negative (.43), Disapproval (.46), Yelling (.33), and her Total Deviant Behavior (.48). In the same report, Hendriks showed that the mother's scores on the Lie scale also correlated positively with five different aggressive responses observed for the problem *child*. A number of the other self-report scales correlated with the child's frequency of Hitting.

The most powerful validational evidence for the code system was supplied by a study in which Hendriks (1972b) investigated the relation between mothers' descriptions of the problem and the observed deviant behaviors. His analysis showed that when the mothers were asked general questions about symptoms, such as "Is he aggressive?", such data produced few correlations with observed deviant child behaviors. However, when asked to describe the child on 47 specific bipolar adjectives (Becker, 1960), the findings were clear cut. Five factor scores summarized the mothers' ratings; of these, the factor Aggression seemed most relevant to validational concerns. The scores on Aggression correlated with the following code variables which were members of Total Deviant: Destructive (.46), Humiliate (.51), Noncomply (.54), Negativism (.49), Physical Negative (.43), Tease (.50), Whine (.46), and Yell (.50).

Taken together, these various studies provide support for the assumption that the code system is indeed measuring something related to child aggressive behaviors.

## STABILITY OF EVENT SAMPLING

Estimates of the "stability" of data require two types of analyses. First, it is necessary to demonstrate that samples of subjects retain their ordinal ranks for any given behavior when that variable is sampled at two different points in time. This would, of course, be analogous to the traditional test–retest correlation. Second, it should be established that there are no changes in *mean level* for rates of that behavior when that variable is sampled over repeated intervals.

Patterson *et al.* (1973) carried out a correlational analysis of the test–retest stability for the first and last half of baseline measures separately for small samples of problem children, mothers, and oldest siblings. The analyses of separate code categories for which sufficient data were available showed a median correlation of .71 for response categories and .60 for consequence categories. (Spearman Brown corrections were not applied to these data.) These preliminary findings were encouraging in showing that individuals' rankings were stable for most code categories.

The *mean levels* for the codes could, of course, vary even though the rankings for individuals were stable. The means for 17 problem children and 14 boys matched for age from nonproblem families were analyzed (Patterson and Cobb, 1971). Each of the code categories was subjected to an ANOVA for repeated measures for sessions 1, 2, 3, 5, 7, 9, and 10. None of the changes in mean level for the categories was significant. It must be concluded that the observation data were moderately stable for most code categories in terms of rankings among individual subjects and for mean rates across time.

As pointed out by Jones (1972a), one might consider both inter- and intrasubject frames of reference in evaluating questions of stability. In another report (Jones, 1972b), mean frequencies were computed for the first and second half of baseline for each of the code categories used in the present study for each of 26 problem children and their mothers, as well as for 20 normal boys and their mothers. A test-retest type of correlation was computed for each subject between the distributions of scores for the code categories. The distribution of scores for each code category were standardized (z-scores), thereby providing a common scale of measurement for the categories. The mean correlations were .42 and .37 for the problem and nonproblem boys, and .57 and .41 for mothers from those samples. From the total sample of 92 stability correlations (subjects), 28% were *non*significant. This suggests that ten observation sessions may not be sufficient for some subjects, and the question of what constitutes stability should probably be estimated individually for each subject.

## CRITERION VARIABLES

*Targeted deviant child behaviors.* Targeted deviant behaviors consisted of any of the 14 deviant behaviors pinpointed by the parents during training and consequently involved in management programs. While most of the parents worked on noncompliance, each family also worked with several other problems. The summed frequency for these responses divided by the number of minutes of observation provided an estimate of the rate of targeted behaviors. The specific behaviors targeted by each family are listed in Table 17.2.

*Parent report data.* Beginning with case 24, parents collected data on the occurrence of symptom behaviors during 1 week of baseline and at the end of treatment. As part of the intake interview, the parents had been asked whether each of the list of 63 "symptoms" was of sufficient concern to warrant changing (Patterson, 1964). Beginning with case 32, these data were collected. On each occasion that the observers came to the home during the baseline and treatment periods, the parents were given a list containing the most easily observed and defined problems from

those previously identified during the interview. They were asked to indicate the occurrence, or nonoccurrence, of each of those events during *that*
day for the time up to, and including, the observation session.

It was assumed that asking parents to make binary decisions (occur–
nonoccur), covering only the preceding 8–10 hours, would minimize dis-
tortions in memory and judgment. The actual symptoms of concern to
each family are listed in Table 17.3.


## Results


### OBSERVED TARGETED BEHAVIOR

The mean rates for targeted behaviors were observed during baseline, after the parents had completed reading the programmed text, after
4 and 8 weeks of training, and at termination. The means for each child
for these periods are listed in Table 17.2.

The mean values graphed in Figure 17.1 reflect a modest reduction in
observed targeted deviant behavior immediately following the parents'
reading of the programmed textbook and further reduction at the fourth-
and eighth-week probe.

By termination there was, on the average, a 60% reduction from the
baseline levels in observed targeted behaviors.[5] This represents substantial
control over the behaviors for which the parents had received specific
training. The ANOVA for repeated measures was carried out for the
data included in baselines 1 and 2, the probes after the book, the fourth
week, eighth week, and termination. The resulting $F$ value of 4.31 ($df =$
5.130) was significant at $p < .01$.

Examination of the data for individual subects showed that 74% of
them showed reductions equal to or greater than 30% from total baseline
levels. In six cases, there were increases in observed rates of targeted behavior.

---

[5] The observation data also suggested that to a limited extent the parents had
generalized the training procedures to include nontargeted deviant child behaviors. To
test this possibility, the targeted behaviors were subtracted from the Total Deviant
score for each subject. The mean of the resulting difference scores was .36 during
baseline and .24 at termination. The ANOVA for repeated measures produced an
$F$ of 2.50, which was not significant at the .05 level.

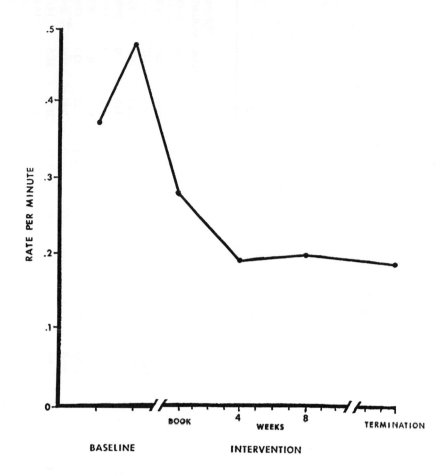

*Figure 17.1* Changes in targeted deviant behavior.

## Parents' Data on Occurrence of Referral Symptoms

The means for each subject during baseline and intervention together with the symptom behaviors of most concern to the parents are listed in Table 17.3, along with the data for each of the 17 cases.

The changes in mean values for the 12 families for whom completed data were available are summarized in Figure 17.2.

During baseline, about two of three referral behaviors occurred each day. While there were modest reductions in occurrences of parent-reported problems following reading of the textbook, there were substantial de-

**TABLE 17.2**
TARGETED BEHAVIORS DURING BASELINE AND INTERVENTION

| Case No. | Behaviors targeted [a] | Mean rate per minute | | | | | | Termination | Minutes of professional time |
|---|---|---|---|---|---|---|---|---|---|
| | | Baseline | | | Intervention | | | | |
| | | BL$_1$ | BL$_2$ | Total | Book | 4 weeks | 8 weeks | | |
| 11 | NC, PN, YE | .025 | .100 | .062 | .100 | .100 | .100 | .200 | 1740 |
| 12 | CN, DI, HU, NC, NE, TE, WH, YE | .950 | 1.000 | .973 | .200 | .200 | .350 | .442 | — |
| 14 | NC, PN | .091 | .117 | .104 | .000 | .020 | .036 | .017 | 834 |
| 15 | CN, DI, HU, NC, NE, WH | .400 | 1.080 | .740 | .100 | .300 | .175 | .400 | 7989 |
| 16 | DI, NC, PN, TE, YE | .260 | .380 | .320 | .400 | .222 | .400 | .400 | 1089 |
| 17 | DS, NC | .000 | .000 | .000 | .000 | .000 | .000 | .000 | 858 |
| 18 | CN, NC, PN | .500 | .340 | .420 | .125 | .075 | .075 | .150 | 1770 |
| 21 | HU, NC | .060 | .020 | .040 | .025 | .050 | .000 | .000 | 906 |
| 22 | HU, NC, NE, PN, TE, WH, YE | .180 | .160 | .170 | .000 | .075 | .000 | .025 | 1412 |
| 24 | DI, DS, NC | .240 | .280 | .260 | .260 | .225 | .100 | .075 | 1479 |
| 25 | NC, NE, PN, TE, YE | 1.440 | .700 | 1.070 | .800 | .200 | .350 | .657 | 1429 |
| 26 | HU, NC, NE, YE | .140 | .660 | .400 | .578 | .050 | .125 | .100 | — |
| 27 | DI, NE, TE | .300 | .920 | .610 | .100 | .075 | .150 | .200 | 558 |
| 28 | NC | .000 | .040 | .020 | .200 | .050 | .050 | .125 | 671 |

| | | | | | | | | |
|---|---|---|---|---|---|---|---|---|
| 29 | NC | .000 | .000 | .000 | .000 | .050 | .050 | .050 | 1180 |
| 31 | HU, NC, TE | .267 | .467 | .367 | .200 | .075 | .075 | .075 | 1040 |
| 32 | DI, NC | .067 | 1.670 | .868 | .200 | .125 | .200 | .050 | 4386 |
| 33 | NC | .067 | .033 | .050 | .000 | .000 | .025 | .025 | 1590 |
| 35 | CN, DI, NC, NE | .167 | .167 | .167 | .225 | .125 | .125 | .000 | 1288 |
| 36 | DS, HR, HU, NC, PN, YE | .367 | .300 | .333 | .325 | .075 | .525 | .200 | 3560 |
| 38 | DI, DS, NC, PN, TE | .300 | .033 | .167 | .050 | .075 | .275 | .275 | 2786 |
| 39 | NC, PN | .167 | .167 | .167 | .150 | .050 | .050 | .025 | 561 |
| 40 | DS, NC, PN | .033 | .200 | .117 | .350 | .050 | .300 | .075 | 1009 |
| 42 | NC | .000 | .067 | .033 | .050 | .000 | .050 | .050 | 998 |
| 43 | CN, DI, HR, HU, NC, PN, TE, YE | .367 | 1.900 | 1.133 | 1.275 | 1.725 | .550 | .750 | 1717 |
| 44 | DS, HR, NC, PN, TE, WH, YE | 2.600 | .867 | 1.732 | .675 | .225 | .100 | .075 | 1967 |
| 45 | DS, NC, PN, TE, YE | 1.017 | 1.233 | 1.125 | 1.246 | .975 | 1.450 | .650 | 5201 |
| Mean | | .371 | .478 | .424 | .283 | .192 | .211 | .190 | 1889 |

[a] CN, Command (negative)    HU, Humiliate    TE, Tease
DI, Disapproval    NC, Noncomply    WH, Whine
DS, Destructiveness    NE, Negativism
HR, High rate    PN, Negative physical contact    YE, Yell

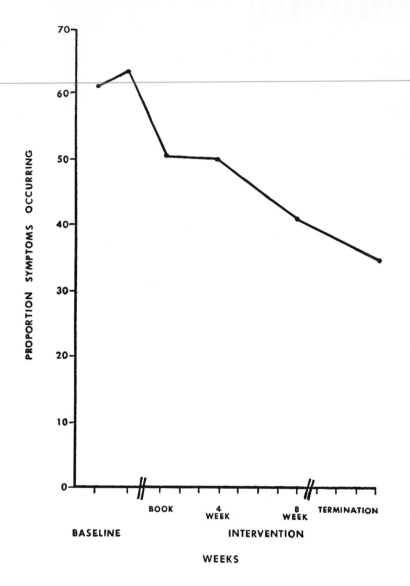

*Figure 17.2* Changes in parents' reports of symptom occurrence (*N* = 12).

creases by the eighth week of training. By termination, the mean daily occurrence dropped to 32.6%. An ANOVA for repeated measures was
carried out for the data available from total baseline and termination. The
analysis produced an *F* value of 15.85, ($df = 1.16$; $p < 0.01$).

**TABLE 17.3**

PARENTS' REPORTS ON SYMPTOMS DURING BASELINE AND INTERVENTION

| Case No. | Behaviors targeted | Proportion of symptoms occurring | | | | | | |
|---|---|---|---|---|---|---|---|---|
| | | Baseline | | | Book | Intervention | | Termination |
| | | $BL_1$ | $BL_2$ | Total | | 4 weeks | 8 weeks | |
| 24[a] | Lies, fights with sibs, steals, tantrums, argues | | | 90 | | | | 26 |
| 25 | Lies, fights, hits, cries, temper tantrums, noncomply, steals | | | 54 | | | | 24 |
| 27 | Fights, cries, temper tantrums, noncomply | | | 50 | | | | 33 |
| 28 | Lies, fights, cries, fears | | | 67 | | | | 33 |
| 29 | Fights, cries, steals, temper tantrums, noncomply, wets bed | | | 38 | | | | 16 |
| 31 | Yelling, tease, noncomply, running around | | 75 | 75 | | | 50 | 50 |
| 32 | Steals, lies, noncomply | 00 | 00 | 00 | 17 | 00 | 00 | 00 |
| 33 | Lies, fights, noncomply | 11 | 56 | 33 | 50 | 100 | 67 | 59 |
| 35 | Lies, steals, noncomply | 100 | 44 | 58 | 17 | 17 | 17 | 00 |
| 36 | Fights, teases, noncomply | 100 | 77 | 83 | 66 | 33 | 66 | 100 |
| 38 | Lies, hits, temper tantrums | 89 | 83 | 87 | 67 | 100 | 67 | 17 |
| 39 | Fights with sibs, steals, sets fires, noncomply, wets bed | 80 | 67 | 73 | 50 | 44 | 40 | 40 |
| 40 | Temper tantrums, not minding, wets bed, soils | 58 | 91 | 75 | 00 | 50 | 25 | 00 |
| 42 | Fights, noncomply, hyperactive, argues, nausea, insomnia, giddiness | 38 | 43 | 40 | 57 | 64 | 36 | 36 |
| 43 | Fights, noncomply, hyperactive, noisy | 75 | 83 | 81 | 88 | 25 | 38 | 21 |
| 44 | Lies, fights with sibs, temper tantrums, noncomply, noisy | 73 | 73 | 73 | 70 | 40 | 30 | 50 |
| 45 | Fights, hits, steals, temper tantrums, noncomply, destructive, screams, wets bed, wets pants, not eat meals | 54 | 72 | 63 | 72 | 78 | 50 | 50 |
| Mean | | 61.6 | 63.7 | 61.2 | 50.4 | 50.1 | 40.5 | 32.7 |

[a] For cases 24–31, data were collected at only two points during the study.

Seventy percent of the families demonstrated reductions $\geq 30\%$. Two families reported their child to be worse.

The correlation of .25 (n. s.) between mean baseline levels would suggest that the two criteria were measuring different aspects of child behavior. The two criteria did, however, assign roughly the same improvement rates. In examining the 17 cases for which both sets of data were available, there were 11 cases identified as "improved" by both criteria. There was, however, no agreement in the identification of cases that were nonimproved. These findings suggest that the two criteria sample different features of the child's behavior and also disagree about "failures."

The amount of professional time required for these families ranged from 561 minutes to 7989 minutes, with an average of 31.5 hours. It should be noted that this did not include the time required for the intake telephone calls, intake interviews, or intake staff conferences. Nine of the boys in this sample also required classroom intervention. Some of these required extensive remedial work for academic as well as social skills. The procedures and outcome data are summarized in a report by Patterson *et al.* (1972). The classroom programs required an average of 27.5 hours of professional time.

## A REPLICATION STUDY

Steven Johnson, Department of Psychology, University of Oregon, has organized a separate laboratory employing adaptations of the measurement and intervention procedures described in the present report. They were used with a group of 15 younger aggressive boys. The families received 12 treatment sessions; pairs of graduate students served as the parent trainers.

The data for targeted deviant child behaviors showed a mean reduction of 40% from baseline levels (Eyberg, 1972). The analysis of the difference scores produced a "t" of 2.6 significant at $p < .02$. These results constitute a modest replication of the findings from the current study, suggesting that it may be possible to train other groups to apply the techniques.

An equally important contribution of the Eyberg report lies in its emphasis on multiple criteria for evaluating outcome. The data showed significant changes in parents' descriptions of the child in a set of bipolar adjectives. These findings replicate the earlier study by Patterson *et al.* (1972), which employed the same instrument for a subset of nine families from the present sample. The parents in the Eyberg study also showed significant changes in their attitudes toward the child.

## SOME PRELIMINARY COMPARATIVE STUDIES

Two studies have been carried out comparing the experimental procedures first to nontreated control families (Wiltz, 1969) and then to families enrolled in a placebo procedure (Walter and Gilmore, 1973). Both studies used families drawn from the sample described in the current report and used a 5-week interval as the basis for comparison. Pre- and post-home observation served as criteria in both studies. In each study, six families were assigned to either a nontreated group or to the "standard" training group. The general assumption was that the experimental procedures would produce reliable decreases in observed rates of targeted deviant child behaviors, while nontreated control groups would show no changes. Following the studies, families in nonexperimental groups were offered the treatment. In the Wahler (1967) study, the first six referrals were placed in the experimental group and the second six families were placed on a no-treatment waiting list for 5 weeks. A comparison of the pre- and post-observations of targeted deviant child behaviors showed no changes in the rates for the control group. The decreases from the baseline measures for members of the experimental group produced an $F$ of 4.33, $p < 0.10$. These trends are reflected in Figure 17.3. When the parents of the control group later received training, they were able to bring the behavior of their problem children under control.

The Walter and Gilmore (1973) study involved 12 new referrals randomly assigned to either a placebo or an experimental group. Families in the experimental group received 4 weeks of the standard training procedures. Families in the placebo group met for an equal number of weekly meetings and discussed tapes they had made concerning problems with their children. There was a nonsignificant *increase* in rates of targeted deviant child behavior for the placebo group. A comparable analysis for the experimental group showed a significant *decrease* in these rates. Similar changes in both groups were obtained when parents' data on referral problem behaviors were analyzed as criterion. Parents in both groups rated their confidence in the treatment procedures being used before and after each session. There were no differences between groups in these expectancies, nor did they change over time.

These two studies attest to the fact that there seems to be *something* (unspecified as yet) in the treatment procedures that produces reliable effects. The effect seems to be unrelated to the mere passage of time, or to that placebo effect attributable to being "involved" in a parent group. The sample size, obvious differences in baseline levels, and short time spans involved in the studies suggest the need for further replication.

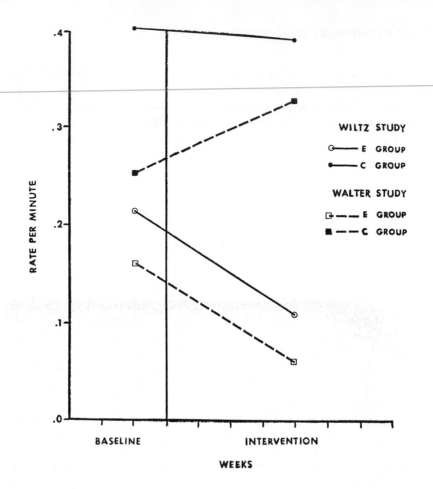

*Figure 17.3* Changes in targeted behavior for two comparison studies.

## Discussion

The findings from the earlier pilot study and the present report concur in suggesting that the procedures are moderately successful in producing changes in the behaviors they were designed to alter. The data from the parents' records of occurrence of symptoms suggest that there is some generalization of training effects to include problems for which the family originally sought professional asistance.

These first 8 years of effort serve to provide the data and experience necessary to design and carry out more definitive studies. Such studies should employ larger numbers of subjects with provisions made for random assignment to treatment and waiting-list control groups. Preferably, the treatment will be carried out by well-trained and supervised paraprofessionals who apply "standardized" treatment packages that are detailed and clearly spelled out. Such studies are currently being planned and will constitute the second stage of the investigation of treatment of social aggression within the group at the Oregon Research Institute.

There are several sets of studies that are now clearly needed before such a treatment technology can be well developed. First, it is necessary to encourage more investigators to carry out replications of the effects within their own laboratories, for instance, the investigations of Steven Johnson's group. The efforts of R. Ray (in press) within our own group has shown the feasibility of training nonpsychologist professionals in community agencies to apply the procedures. Second, it is imperative that an analysis be made of the contribution of various aspects of the treatment procedures. It is not at all clear which of the treatment components are essential, if indeed any of them are. Analyses of this kind would probably underline the fact that some of the components require a good deal of professional time but contribute very little to the overall treatment effectiveness.

As the research proceeds, the rough outline of parenting skills relating to aggressive behaviors has begun to emerge. More intensive analyses of these relations should set the basis for developing research on the prevention of aggressive child behaviors. This is, of course, the focal point of much clinical speculation, but it seems possible that data of the type being collected for these intervention procedures will also serve as a solid empirical base for pursuing such ventures.

### ACKNOWLEDGMENTS

This study represents the cumulative efforts of colleagues including R. Ray, J. Reid, J. Cobb, D. Shaw, K. Skindrud, V. Devine, N. Wiltz, H. Walter, and R. Jones. Each contributed in some unique fashion to the clinical techniques or to the development of measurement procedures. The writer also wishes to thank Allan Levine for his coherent response to repeated demands for yet more data analyses.

## References

Bahm, A. K., Chandler, C., and Eisenberg, L. Diagnostic characteristics related to service on psychiatric clinics for children. Paper presented at the 38th Annual Convention of Orthopsychiatry, Munich, 1961.

Beach, D. R., and Laird, J. D. Follow-up study of children identified early as emotionally disturbed. *Journal of Consulting Clinical Psychology,* 1968, **32**, 369–374.

Becker, W. C. The relationship of factors in parental ratings of self and each other to the behavior of kindergarten children as rated by mothers, fathers, and teachers. *Journal of Consulting Psychology,* 1960, **24**, 507–527.

Benning, J. J., Feldhusen, J. F., and Thurston, J. R. Delinquency prone youth: A longitudinal and preventive research. The Eau Claire County Youth Study. Madison, Wis., Wisconsin State Department, 1968.

Eyberg, S. M. An outcome study of child family intervention: Effects of contingency contracting and order of treated problems. Unpublished doctoral dissertation, University of Oregon, 1972.

Frank, G. H. The role of the family in the development of psychopathology. *Psychological Bulletin,* 1965, **64**, 191–205.

Harris, A. Observer effect on family interaction. Unpublished doctoral dissertation, University of Oregon, 1969.

Hawkins, R. P., Peterson. R. F., Schweid, E., and Bijou, S. W. Behavior therapy in the home: Amelioration of problem parent-child relations with the parent in a therapeutic role. *Journal of Experimental Child Psychology,* 1966, **4**, 99–107.

Hendriks, A. F. C. J. Observed deviancy and age difference in deviant and normal boys. Unpublished doctoral dissertation, Nymegen University, the Netherlands, 1972.(a)

Hendriks, A. F. C. J. Reported versus observed deviancy. Unpublished paper, Nymegen University, the Netherlands, 1972.(b)

Hendriks, A. F. C. J. The MMPI as a predictor of behavior. Unpublished paper, Nymegen University, the Netherlands, 1972. (c)

Hollingshead, A. B., and Redlich, F. C. *Social Class and Mental Illness: A Community Study.* New York: Wiley, 1958.

Johnson, S. M., and Bolstad, O. D. Methodological issues in naturalistic observation. Some problems and solutions for field research. In L. A. Hamerlynck, L. C. Handy, and E. J. Mash (Eds.), *Behavior Change: Methodological Concepts and Practice.* Champaign, Ill.: Research Press, 1973, pp. 7–68.

Johnson, S. M., and Lobitz, G. Demand characteristics in naturalistic observations. Unpublished manuscript, University of Oregon, 1972.

Jones, R. R. Behavioral observation frequency data: Problems in scoring, analysis, and interpretation. *Oregon Research Institute Bulletin,* 1972, **12**, No. 3. (a)

Jones, R. R. Intra-individual stability of behavioral observations: Implications for evaluating behavior modification treatment programs. Paper presented at the Psychological Association Convention, Portland. Oregon, 1972. (b)

Kent, R. N. Unpublished doctoral dissertation, SUNY, Stony Brook, 1972.

Levitt, E. E. Research on psychotherapy with children. In A. E. Bergin and S. L. Garfield (Eds.), *Handbook of Psychotherapy and Behavior Change.* New York: Wiley, 1971, pp. 474–494.

Morris, H. H. Aggressive behavior disorders in children: A follow-up study. *American Journal of Psychiatry,* 1956, **112**, 991–997.

Patterson, G. R. An empirical approach to the classification of disturbed children. *Journal of Clinical Psychology,* 1964, **20**, 326–337.

Patterson, G. R. Behavioral techniques based upon social learning: An additional base for developing behavior modification technologies. In C. M. Franks (Ed.), *Behavior Therapy: Appraisal and Status.* New York: McGraw-Hill, 1969, pp. 341–374.

Patterson, G. R. *Families.* Champaign, Ill.: Research Press, 1972.(a)

Patterson, G. R. Stimulus control: A basis for predicting behavioral events in a natural setting. Invited address presented at the First Texas Conference on Behavior Modification, Houston, Texas, 1972.(b)

Patterson, G. The coercive child: Architect or victim of a coercive system? In L. Hamerlynck, E. J. Mash, and L. C. Handy (Eds.), *Behavior Modification and Families. I. Theory and Research. II. Applications and Developments.* N.Y.: Brunner and Mazell. (*In press.*)

Patterson, G. R., Brodsky, G. A behaviour modification programme for a child with multiple problem behaviours. *Journal of Child Psychology and Psychiatry,* 1966, **7**, 277–295.

Patterson, G. R., and Cobb, J. A. A dyadic analysis of "aggressive" behaviors. In J. P. Hill (Ed.), *Minnesota Symposia on Child Psychology,* Vol. **5**. Minneapolis, Minn.: University of Minnesota Press, 1971, pp. 72–129.

Patterson, G. R., Cobb, J. A., and Ray, R. S. Direct intervention in the classroom: A set of procedures for the aggressive child. In F. W. Clark, D. R. Evans, and L. A. Hamerlynck (Eds.), *Implementing Behavioral Programs for Schools and Clinics.* Champaign, Ill.: Research Press, 1972, pp. 151–201.

Patterson, G. R., Cobb, J. A., and Ray, R. S. A social engineering technology for retraining the families of aggressive boys. In H. F. Adams and I. P. Unikel (Eds.), *Issues and Trends in Behavior Therapy.* Springfield, Ill.: C. C. Thomas, 1973, pp. 139–224.

Patterson, G. R., and Gullion, M. E. *Living with Children: New Methods for Parents and Teachers.* Champaign, Ill.: Research Press, 1968.

Patterson, G. R., McNeal, S., Hawkins, N., and Phelps, R. Reprogramming the social environment. *Journal of Child Psychology and Psychiatry,* 1967, **8**, 181–195.

Patterson, G. R., Ray, R. S., and Shaw, D. A. Direct intervention in families of deviant children. *Oregon Research Institute Bulletin,* 1968, **8**, No. 9.

Patterson, G. R., Ray, R. S., Shaw, D. A., and Cobb, J. A. Manual for coding of family interactions, 1969. Available from ASIS National Auxiliary Publications Service, c/o CMM Information Services, Inc., 909 Third Avenue, New York, N.Y. 10022. Document #01234.

Patterson, G. R., and Reid, J. B. Reciprocity and coercion: Two facets of social systems. In C. Neuringer and J. Michael (Eds.), *Behavior Modification in Clinical Psychology.* New York: Appleton-Century-Crofts, 1970, pp. 133–177.

Rausch, H. L., Dittman, D. T., and Taylor, T. J. The inter-personal behavior of children in residential treatment. *Journal of Abnormal and Social Psychology,* 1959, **58**, 9–26.

Ray, R. S. A program for training in direct-service community agencies. In M. E. Bernal (Ed.), *Training in Behavior Modification.* Belmont, California: Brooks/Cole. (*In press.*)

Reid, J. B. Reliability assessment of observation data: A possible methodological problem. *Child Development,* 1970, **41**, 1143–1150.

Reid, J. B., and Hendriks, A. F. C. J. A preliminary analysis of the effectiveness of direct home intervention for treatment of pre-delinquent boys who steal. Paper presented at the Fourth Banff International Conference on Behavior Modification, Banff, Alberta, Canada, 1972.

Roach, J. L. Some social-psychological characteristics of child guidance clinic caseloads. *Journal of Consulting Psychology,* 1958, **22**, 183–186.

Robins, L. N. *Deviant Children Grown Up: A Sociological and Psychiatric Study of Sociopathic Personality.* Baltimore, Md.: Williams & Wilkins, 1966.

Rogers, M., Lilienfeld, A. M., and Pasamanick, B. *Prenatal and Parental Factors in the Development of Childhood Behavior Disorders.* Baltimore: Johns Hopkins University Press, 1954.

Sallows, G. Comparative responsiveness of normal and deviant children to naturally occurring consequences. Unpublished doctoral dissertation, University of Oregon, 1972.

Shaw, D. A. Family maintenance schedules for deviant behavior. Unpublished doctoral dissertation, University of Oregon, 1971.

Skindrud, K. D. A preliminary evaluation of observer bias in multivariate field studies of social interaction. Paper presented at the Fourth Banff International Conference on Behavior Modification, Banff, Alberta, Canada, 1972. (a)

Skindrud, K. D. An evaluation of observer bias in experimental-field studies of social interaction. Unpublished doctoral dissertation, University of Oregon, 1972.(b)

Tharp, R., and Wetzel, R. *Behavior Modification in the Natural Environment.* New York: Academic Press, 1969.

Wahl, Gail. Operant analysis of family interaction. Unpublished doctoral dissertation, University of Oregon, 1971.

Wahler, R. G. Behavior therapy with oppositional children: Attempts to increase their parents' reinforcement value. Paper presented at the meeting of the Southeastern Psychological Association, Atlanta, Georgia, 1967.

Wahler, R. G., and Erickson, M. Child behavior therapy: A community program in Appalachia. *Behaviour Research and Therapy,* 1969, **7**, 71–78.

Wahler, R. G., Winkle, G. H., Peterson, R. F., and Morrison, D. C. Mothers as behavior therapists for their own children. *Behaviour Research and Therapy,* 1965, **3**, 113–124.

Walker, H., and Buckley, N. K. Teacher attention to appropriate and inappropriate classroom behavior: An individual case study. *Exceptional Children,* 1973, **5**, 5–11.

Walter, H., and Gilmore, S. K. Placebo versus social learning effects in parent training procedures designed to alter the behaviors of aggressive boys. *Behavior Therapy* 1973, **4**, 361–377.

Westman, J. C., Rice, D. L., and Bermann, E. Relationship between nursery school behaviors and later school adjustment. *American Journal of Orthopsychiatry,* 1967, **37**, 725–731.

White, G. The effect of observer presence on mother and child behavior. Unpublished doctoral dissertation, University of Oregon, 1972.

Wiltz, N. A., Jr. Modification of behaviors of deviant boys through parent participation in a group technique. Unpublished doctoral dissertation, University of Oregon, 1969.

Wolf, M., Mees, H., and Risley, T. Applications of operant conditioning procedures to the behavior problems of an autistic child. *Behavior Research and Therapy,* 1964, **1**, 305–312.

Woody, R. H. Behavioral problem children in the schools. New York: Appleton-Century-Crofts, 1969.

# V MODIFYING BEHAVIOR OF RETARDATES AND PSYCHOTICS

# 18 KIN KARE: A COMMUNITY RESIDENCE FOR GRADUATES OF AN OPERANT PROGRAM FOR SEVERE AND PROFOUND RETARDATES IN A LARGE INSTITUTION[1]

Garry L. Martin

Glen H. Lowther

The history of society's concern for the mentally retarded is beset with examples of misinformation and misconception. For many decades, retardation was viewed as a poor cousin of mental disease, and the care of the retarded who could not be maintained by society fell on the established mental hospitals. Then, about the latter part of the nineteenth century, institutions for the retarded began to be built, although the decor generally was largely that of a collection of army medical barracks and penitentiary buildings located somewhere out in the country, where land was cheap and communications were poor. Unfortunately, progress in treatment did not accompany the construction of the institutions. In addition to its early association with mental illness, there are at least four more general influences that contributed to the myths and confusion surrounding the treatment of the retarded.

The first influence relates to the theory, current around the turn of the century, that the "submerged tenth" of the population would ultimately outnumber the rest of society and threaten the middle-class way of life. The solution to the growth of this lowest socioeconomic group of

[1] The preparation of this paper was supported in part by National Health grant 606-7-255.

"borderline intelligence" in society was to place the mildly retarded in large, barracks-like institutions where the aim was not rehabilitation, but rather, the prevention of reproduction.

A second factor contributing to the developing of these institutions was the specific impact of the income taxes primarily on the upper and middle classes, which meant, in effect, that the tolerably wealthy had to foot the bill for assuming the role of their brother's keeper. They were only slightly less willing to do this than they were of the consequences for failing to do so, with the result that they acquitted themselves of the responsibility with a degree of parsimony that was monumental, namely, committing the retarded to large institutions away from large cities.

The third influence was that of the church, which somehow managed to equate original sin with reproduction. To this guilt and fear was added the Calvinist doctrine of Vicarious Atonement, which said, essentially, that all men were sinful, but that Providence had picked a few at random to pay for the guilt of all. From there it was but a short step to relate the sin of carnality with the birth of an abnormal child. The result of the shame of such unmentionable events was that the retarded were confined to the large, distant, custodial barracks, growing up at a safe and respectable distance from the large population centers.

A final influence was that the direction of many of the early facilities for retardates fell to the lot of medical administrators who had frequently spent many years as army medical officers and who continued the "lord of the manor" status of the regular army officers of those days. The story is on record of one medical superintendent, a retired colonel of the British medical corps, who had himself a golf course built between the buildings of his institution, which occupied a delightful area of parkland in a southern English county. He came out of his mansion each morning, bade goodbye to his numerous retainers, and teed off to the administration building. There, after a few minutes of perusing the scanty incoming mail, he continued to the second tee en route to the next green, which was located strategically just outside the male colony building. He continued his rounds from greens to buildings, dispensing medical and military prescriptions along the way. The good colonel may not have achieved very many improvements in the lot of the mentally ill or the retarded, but he was known to run a tight administrative organization, while his golfing handicap was the envy of his admiring colleagues.

Throughout these developments, treatment and training programs for all levels of retardation were minimal, to say the least, and they were the most limited for the severe and profound levels. With the increasing acceptance of the classification of mentally retarded into idiots, imbeciles, and morons in the early twentieth century, the tendency developed for all levels of retardation to be committed to the same institution, with the inevitable result that the bulk of the nursing care for the more severe levels of retardation was provided by the mildly retarded group.

The earliest form of control of undesirable behavioral patterns in these crowded, mass-living institutions was primarily physical restraint. Abnormal behavior, much of which was regarded as sinful since it frequently involved stripping of clothing, smearing of feces, and masturbation, consisted primarily of the application of canvas straitjackets to residents for prolonged periods of time. About the middle of the twentieth century, with the arrival of the "chemical revolution" in the management of behavior problems, it became much more effective and aesthetically acceptable to dose patients who engaged in antisocial behavior with any one of the succession of tranquilizers that made their appearance in a steady stream in the 1950s and 1960s. Institutional budgets for canvas, metal eyelets, and restraint rope plumetted, but there was a corresponding astronomical increase in their pharmacy budgets. The atmosphere in these institutions is difficult for us to imagine in these more enlightened days, consisting as it did of a fine blend of urine, paraldahyde, feces, body odor, and halitosis.

With the development in recent years of training programs and training centers in the community for moderately and mildly retarded individuals, the large outlying institutions found themselves with an increasing proportion of those individuals labeled as severely and profoundly retarded, and these latter groups received primarily custodial care.[2] However, during the past 6 or 7 years, several workers using the principles of behavior modification have brought about changes in the behavior of the severely and profoundly retarded that experts in the field would have said were impossible just a few short years ago. A review of these procedures and developments can be found in Gardner (1971), and a detailed description of the development of behavior modification programs at one institution (Faribault State Hospital, Minnesota) was recently described by Thompson and Grabowski (1972). It is a pleasure to report today that to a large extent at least, as a consequence of some of these recent developments, the use of paraldahyde has been discontinued, body odor has been Banned, halitosis has been Scoped (either menthol or regular), while urine and feces find their way more frequently into institutional white porcelain

---

[2] According to the American Association for Mental Deficiency classification system for mental retardation, individuals who show an IQ of 20–35 are labeled "severely retarded" and those who show an IQ score of below 20 are labeled "profoundly retarded."

toilets (many, alas, still without seats), to a chorus of "Good boy" and a diet of M&M's.

Our program of behavior modification for severely and profoundly retarded residents at the Manitoba School for Retardates began in 1968. The Manitoba School is the main residential institute for retardates in the Province of Manitoba. It houses approximately 1200 retardates, with about 700 of those falling in the severe and profound ranges. Our behavior modification program began with the opening of Cedar Cottage. This was a new cottage facility for 30 residents, consisting of three levels. Bedrooms for three were provided, with individual clothing storage for each resident. There were ample play and sitting areas and a cafeteria-style dining room. Construction was cement block, which lent an institutional atmosphere to the surroundings, but it was distinctly superior to the previous decor.

Thirty severely and profoundly retarded girls were transferred into the new cottage from another unit that had housed 86 children and adults. Prior to the move, the amount of abnormal behavior exhibited was enormous. Some residents stripped off their clothes every few minutes, some played with and smeared feces, some tore their clothes and the curtains, some picked at plaster work, some looked for discarded cigarette butts and other kinds of refuse and placed it in their bodily orifices. Many wandered around aimlessly emitting shrieks or moans, masturbating, spitting, voiding, and defecating. The 30 girls who were transferred to Cedar Cottage were selected primarily because they exhibited the worst behavior problems.

The conditions under which the project was initiated was favorable in many respects. First, nursing staff who were to come into Cedar chose that building rather than transferring to another residence. Those who came were an extremely keen and enthusiastic group. They had been familiarized with the nature of the program and were told that they would be required to learn about behavior modification, write examinations, and develop new training techniques. Second, four undergraduate psychology students from the University of Manitoba, who had previous experience in applying behavior modification techniques with autistic children (Martin, England, Kaprowy, Kilgour, and Pilek, 1968; Martin and Pear, 1970), were hired to supplement the cottage staff during the initial 2 months. These students worked closely with the cottage staff in the gradual development of the behavior modification program to teach self-care skills to the 30 residents. Third, the program initiated in a completely new environment for the residents. The program was initiated as soon as the residents moved into Cedar. This meant that, to some extent, some of the behavior problems did not present themselves, since the new environment did not provide the discriminative stimuli that controlled many of the undesirable behaviors in the previous residence.

The Cedar project was dramatically successful in a variety of respects, and it led the second author, in his role as medical superintendent of a large institution, to endorse strongly behavior modification as the appropriate methodology for training the profoundly and severely retarded (Lowther, 1970, 1971), and to begin programming the institution so that the (approximately) 700 severe and profound retardates in residence would be trained in operant programs. As for the Cedar Cottage girls, they showed excellent improvement in self-care skills, work skills, social skills, and academic skills over the first 2 years of the project. However, they were still institutionalized. The second author had previously described a retarded family community residence unit for the moderate retarded (Lowther, 1968), and has been instrumental in initiating several such units in the Province of Manitoba. Based on the experience with those units, it was felt that it would be desirable to examine similar units for placement of our severely and profoundly retarded girls from Cedar Cottage. Despite the improved condition at Cedar, it was clear that the community could provide opportunities and reinforcers that simply were not available at the institution, including such things as the opportunity to play with normal neighborhood children; greater accessibility of corner stores to visit and to develop purchasing behaviors; the opportunity to operate and participate in a variety of household tasks that are difficult to arrange in an institutional setting, such as vacuuming, preparing meals and baking, and performing different household chores. Accordingly, arrangements were made to find a suitable house in the city of Portage la Prairie (a rural community of approximately 12,000 population), to which a small group of graduates from our Cedar program could be transferred and studied in an experimental project. The Kinsmen Club of Portage la Prairie actively assisted the program by offering to purchase the home for six young graduates, and the whole project became known as "Kin Kare." In the months since their admission to Kin Kare in October 1971, the six former residents of the Manitoba School made further startling gains in their behavior, and it it the purpose of the remainder of this report to describe the Kin Kare project as it evolved from the program at Cedar Cottage.

## Subjects

The characteristics of the subjects are summarized in Table 18.1. Their behavioral scores on a variety of tasks and measures are described in the tables in the remainder of this report. These subjects were selected for the Kin Kare project from among the 30 girls in the Cedar Cottage program primarily on the basis of two criteria: (1) They were among ten of the most advanced girls of the Cedar program, and (2) they were 15 years of age or younger at the start of the Kin Kare project (several of the Cedar girls were as advanced as these subjects, although several years older).

### The Initial Program at Cedar Cottage

The details of the training programs for the residents and the staff in the Cedar project have been described elsewhere (Lowther, Martin, and McDonald, 1971; Martin, 1972; Martin, England, and England, 1971; Martin, Kehoe, Bird, Jensen, and Darbyshire, 1971; Martin, McDonald, and Omichinski, 1971; Martin and Treffry, 1970; Treffry, Martin, Samels, and Watson, 1970). In general, the children were token trained, their attention spans were increased, and undesirable behaviors were eliminated. The subjects were then taught a variety of self-care and work skills in which each task was broken down into small steps and taught using primarily techniques of shaping, chaining, and fading. Some additional features of the Cedar project were the following:

1. A great deal of time was expended initially in the residence teaching the staff to train the children and managing the residence environment to maintain staff behaviors as well as resident behaviors (discussed in detail in Martin, 1972).

2. The institutional staff/resident ratio was improved so that there were always from three to six nursing staff working during the waking hours of the residents, with four and five staff being most common. Thus, the staff/resident ratio during waking hours, excluding a clothing room person and a cleaning person, varied from one/ten to one/five, and this was better than in most other residences.

3. All the staff in the cottage learned behavior modification and participated in the program with the exception of a night staff, a clothing room person, and a cleaning person.

4. Through the cooperation of the medical staff, medication was discontinued with the exception of anticonvulsant drugs.

5. Daily individual and group training sessions were scheduled for an hour in the morning and 3 hours in the afternoon.

6. In addition to the training sessions, daily routines such as dressing, grooming, mealtime, playtime, bathing, and so forth were structured to allow for reinforcement of improvement and independent behaviors of residents to as great a degree as possible.

**TABLE 18.1**

CHARACTERISTICS OF THE SUBJECT

| Subject | Diagnosis | Current age (Sept. 1/72) Years | Months | IQ when entered Cedar | I Q when last tested at Cedar | IQ now | IQ points increased |
|---|---|---|---|---|---|---|---|
| Agnes | Encephalopathy due to unknown or uncertain cause, with the structural reaction alone manifest; epilepsy | 15 | 8 | IQ 25 [Peabody Picture Vocabulary Test (PPVT). Mental age: 2 yrs. 8 mo.] | IQ 33 [July 11, 1969. Stanford-Binet Intelligence Scale (S-B). Mental age: 3 yrs. 5 mo.] | IQ 22 (May 16, 1972. S-B. Mental age: 3 yrs. 6 mo.) | —3 |
| Gail | Cerebal palsy | 13 | 9 | IQ 24 (PPVT. Mental age: 2 yrs. 5 mo.) | IQ 37 (March 17, 1969. Mental age: 3 yrs. 13 mo.) | IQ 41 (May 16, 1972. S-B. Mental age: 4 yrs. 8 mo.) | 17 |
| Ginette | Hyperkinetic syndrome (possible expresive aphasia) | 9 | 11 | IQ below 20 [Wechsler Intelligence Scale (WISC.)] | IQ 28 (October 26, 1970. S-B. Mental age: 2 yrs. 2 mo.) | IQ 35 (February 3, 1972. S-B. Mental age: 3 yrs. 4 mo.) | > 15 |
| Giselle | Down's syndrome (mongolism) | 15 | 7 | IQ 19 (PPVT. Mental age: 2 yrs. 3 mo.) | IQ 25 (July 10, 1969. S-B. Mental age: 3 yrs. 1 mo.) | IQ 31 (February 3, 1972. S-B. Mental age: 3 yrs. 10 mo.) | 12 |
| Lori | Encephalopathy associated with primary cranial anomaly; microephaly | 13 | 2 | IQ 33 (PPVT. Mental age: 2 yrs. 7 mo.) | IQ 39 (November 3, 1970. S-B. Mental age: 3 yrs. 10 mo.) | IQ 46 (May 16, 1972. S-B. Mental age: 5 yrs. 0 mo.) | 13 |
| Louise | Craniostenosis scaphocephaly | 10 | 2 | IQ below 20 (WISC.) | IQ 40 (November 17, 1970. S-B. Mental age: 3 yrs. 7 mo.) | IQ 42 (May 16, 1972. S-B. Mental age: 4 yrs. 2 mo.) | > 22 |

331

**TABLE 18.2**

Self-Care and Work Behaviors Acquired at Cedar Cottage [a]

| | Agnes | | Gail | | Ginette | | Giselle | | Lori | | Louise | |
|---|---|---|---|---|---|---|---|---|---|---|---|---|
| | Baseline (B) | Final performance (FP) | B | FP | B | FP | B | FP | B | FP | B | FP |
| Dressing | | | | | | | | | | | | |
| Undershirt | 3 | 1 | 4 | 1 | 4 | 1 | 2 | 1 | 3 | 1 | 3 | 1 |
| Underpants | 2 | 1 | 2 | 1 | 2 | 1 | 1 | 1 | 2 | 1 | 2 | 1 |
| Bra | 4 | 1 | 4 | 3 | 4 | 4 | 4 | 1 | 4 | 3 | 4 | 4 |
| Dress | 4 | 1 | 4 | 3 | 4 | 2 | 3 | 1 | 3 | 1 | 4 | 1 |
| Buttons | 2 | 1 | 3 | 1 | 2 | 1 | 2 | 1 | 2 | 1 | 3 | 1 |
| Zippers | 3 | 1 | 2 | 1 | 3 | 2 | 3 | 1 | 3 | 1 | 4 | 1 |
| Slacks | 2 | 1 | 3 | 1 | 3 | 1 | 2 | 1 | 3 | 1 | 3 | 1 |
| Blouse | 3 | 1 | 3 | 1 | 4 | 1 | 2 | 1 | 2 | 1 | 3 | 1 |
| Socks | 2 | 1 | 3 | 1 | 2 | 1 | 1 | 1 | 2 | 1 | 2 | 1 |
| Shoes | 2 | 1 | 3 | 1 | 2 | 1 | 1 | 1 | 2 | 1 | 2 | 1 |
| Lace shoes | 3 | 1 | 3 | 1 | 3 | 2 | 2 | 1 | 4 | 1 | 3 | 1 |
| Tie knot and bow | 4 | 1 | 4 | 1 | 4 | 3 | 4 | 1 | 4 | 1 | 4 | 1 |
| Average | 2.8 | 1 | 3.2 | 1.3 | 3.0 | 1.6 | 2.3 | 1 | 2.6 | 1.1 | 3.1 | 1.2 |

| | | | | | | | | | | | | |
|---|---|---|---|---|---|---|---|---|---|---|---|---|
| Washing and drying hands and face | 4 | 1 | 4 | 1 | 3 | 1 | 3 | 1 | 3 | 1 | 4 | 1 |
| Combing hair | 3 | 1 | 3 | 1 | 3 | 1 | 3 | 1 | 3 | 1 | 3 | 1 |
| Brushing teeth | 4 | 1 | 3 | 1 | 4 | 1 | 3 | 1 | 3 | 1 | 4 | 1 |
| Table setting | 3 | 1 | 3 | 1 | 3 | 2 | 2 | 1 | 2 | 1 | 3 | 2 |
| Serving in dining room | 3 | 1 | 3 | 1 | 3 | 2 | 2 | 1 | 2 | 1 | 3 | 2 |
| Bedmaking | 4 | 3 | 4 | 3 | 4 | 3 | 4 | 2 | 4 | 3 | 4 | 3 |
| Store time | 3 | 1 | 2 | 1 | 3 | 1 | 2 | 1 | 2 | 1 | 3 | 1 |
| Overall average | 3.1 | 1.1 | 3.1 | 1.3 | 3.1 | 1.6 | 2.4 | 1.0 | 2.7 | 1.1 | 3.2 | 1.3 |

[a] Each of the behavioral items were scored on a 1–4 rating scale. In each case the test items or set of instructions was presented to the subject. The subject's behavior was then scored as follows:

1. The behavior was performed appropriately in all respects without prompting or guidance of any kind.

2. The behavior was performed appropriately after several (up to five) additional verbal commands or prompts were provided by the tester.

3. The behavior was performed appropriately after additional verbal commands *and/or* physical prompts *and/or* a "little physical guidance" were provided by the tester. Physical prompts include pointing, gesturing, etc., where there is no physical contact between the tester and subject. "A little physical guidance" refers to the amount of guidance a tester can provide by touching the subject appropriately for a maximum of 30 seconds.

4. More than the physical guidance necessary for a score of 3 was required for the behavior to be performed appropriately.

**TABLE 18.3**

UNDESIRABLE BEHAVIORS DEALT WITH SUCCESSFULLY AT CEDAR

| Agnes | Gail | Ginette | Giselle | Lori | Louise |
|---|---|---|---|---|---|
| Vomiting for attention | Washing too slowly | Stealing at mealtime | Disobedience | Extreme temper tantrums | Self-abuse |
| Eating dessert with fingers | Throwing away clothes | Pushing other children | Slapping other residents | Swearing | Playing with food |
| Licking food tray | | | Bossing other residents | Clothes tearing | Refusing to enter dining room |
| Stealing food | | | | Babbling | Leaving bedroom at night |
| | | | | | Mumbling nonsense |

7. Undesirable behaviors were dealt with primarily through the use of brief periods of "time out," administered by placing a child in a specially designed time-out room.

8. The girls in the cottage participated in a token program. In general, tokens were earned in grooming, individual, and group-training sessions of various sorts and were exchanged for back-up reinforcers at one of the two regular store times from 15 minutes to 3 hours after they were earned. At the store, a variety of edibles and trinkets could be purchased with the tokens. In exceptional cases, tokens were required to obtain meals.

9. Six months prior to the beginning of the Kin Kare project, the six girls at the cottage who had been chosen for Kin Kare were placed in a special program designed to prepare them for their new home. From the time the girls arose in the morning until they went to bed at night, they spent most of their time interacting with each other and specially chosen staff rather than with the rest of the girls in the cottage. They ate together at mealtimes, were trained together in one of the training rooms, and received tokens on a separate system. The token system was a check system in which the children received checks and points on 3 × 5 cards which they carried in their purses at all times. The girls could earn checks for dressing, grooming, table manners, classroom performance, and work behaviors. They could lose checks for disobedience, fighting, stealing, swearing, and

temper tantrums. With their checks they purchased their meals and a variety of edibles, privileges, and trinkets.

As a function of the training at Cedar, the six girls acquired a variety of self-care and work behaviors (see Table 18.2), and numerous undesirable behaviors were eliminated (see Table 18.3). In addition, they learned a variety of responses to verbal instructions. Training began with imitation training. Twenty items were chosen for instruction training. The specific items used for imitation training and later for instruction following were

1. Touch your nose.
2. Raise your hand.
3. Touch your ear.
4. Stand up and sit down.
5. Touch your hair.
6. Clap your hands.
7. Touch your arm.
8. Open your mouth wide.
9. Tap the table.
10. Say "mmm."
11. Walk around the room.
12. Look in the mirror.
13. Open the door.
14. Shut the door.
15. Throw the object in the garbage can.
16. Put the object on the table.
17. Take the object off the table.
18. Show me your tongue.
19. Jump.
20. Put the object under the table.

No additional items were taught in structured sessions. However, instructions were given in all kinds of tasks—dressing, grooming, bed making, and so on—and after participating in the imitation and instruction-following sessions, the subjects generally learned to follow instructions in a variety of other situations. The elementary academic skills acquired at Cedar are summarized in Table 18.4.

In addition to the behaviors developed at Cedar and described in Tables 18.2 and 18.4, several behaviors were developed for which only casual observational and anecdotal data were recorded. For example, a four-phase program was developed to teach the girls to behave appropriately when taken to stores in downtown Portage la Prairie by a staff member. The first phase involved teaching the girls to go to the store at Cedar Cottage. The store was simply a big box with a variety of goods on display, and in front of each set of goods was a slot into which tokens could be placed. At store time, the girls were called from their chairs one at a time, and their task was to walk up to the store, deposit their tokens, and take the items of their choice appropriate to the number of tokens that they had earned. The second phase consisted of taking groups of three or four residents to the school canteen, located on the institutional grounds. Arrangements had been made for the girls to exchange their tokens with the

**TABLE 18.4**

ACADEMIC BEHAVIORS TAUGHT AT CEDAR[a]

| Subject | | Behaviors | | | |
|---|---|---|---|---|---|
| | | Imitating | Instruction following | Picture and object naming | Tracing and printing |
| Agnes: | Baseline | 3/20 | 5/20 | 5/100 | None |
| | Final | 20/20 | 20/20 | 20/100 | Can print her own name and numbers 1–5 |
| Gail: | Baseline | 6/20 | 4/20 | 15/100 | None |
| | Final | 20/20 | 20/20 | 70/100 | Can print her own name |
| Ginette: | Baseline | 2/20 | 3/20 | 2/100 | None |
| | Final | 18/20 | 20/20 | 4/100 | Not worked on |
| Giselle: | Baseline | 9/20 | 4/20 | 20/100 | None |
| | Final | 20/20 | 19/20 | 70/100 | Can print her own name and numbers 1–10 |
| Lori: | Baseline | 7/20 | 7/20 | 30/100 | None |
| | Final | 20/20 | 20/20 | 75/100 | Can print her name and numbers 1–5. |
| Louise: | Baseline | 6/20 | 5/20 | 11/100 | None |
| | Final | 18/20 | 20/20 | 69/100 | Can print her name |

[a] The scores given for imitating and instruction following are the number correct out of 20, where the test items were those listed in the body of the paper. The scores for picture and object naming are the number correct out of a pool of 100 items.

clerk who worked in the canteen so that canteen interactions were, to a large extent, simply an extension of store time. Following successful canteen performance on several occasions, the girls were taken in small groups to the city park, where they were allowed to play collectively on the swings and engage in various activities. Undesirable behaviors were punished by a sharp slap on the fingers, and desirable behaviors were further reinforced with more tokens. Since the park was rather sparsely populated, the staff was able to apply strict contingencies to develop appropriate play behaviors and observing behaviors of the children, and to eliminate various undesirable disruptive activities. The fourth and final phase consisted of taking the children downtown to a small restaurant, then to small stores, and finally to a larger department store. By this time they had been taught to stay with the staff member and to refrain from grabbing various items and generally engaging in disruptive activities. On numerous occasions, comments were received from the storekeepers that our children were much better behaved than many normal children. The Cedar children clearly enjoyed the downtown trips, as did the staff from Cedar.

To train appropriate social interaction, staff at Cedar Cottage arranged for the girls to have parties for approximately an hour at a time with some of the male severely retarded residents from another cottage that was also involved in a behavior modification program. The children were taught to sit in an alternating boy/girl sequence, to dance with each other, and to engage in various party activities, all of which were reinforced with tokens. At the end of the dance, tokens could be exchanged for juice and cookies, ice cream, soft drinks, and a variety of activities. Undesirable behavior was punished by placing the children in a time-out room that was nearby.

When the time came for six of the Cedar girls to graduate to Kin Kare, those chosen were well prepared in many respects.

## The Kin Kare Program

### Setting

The house is an older, two-story structure such as is commonly found in any Mid-West town. There are four bedrooms and a bathroom upstairs, and a living room, kitchen, dining room, and a larger room used as a classroom on the main floor. It has front and back porches and a stone basement.

### Staff

Initially, staff who had previously worked at Cedar Cottage with the children, and who were well trained in behavior modification procedures, were provided such that one staff member was available for an overlapping 6-hour shift. Thus, the staff-resident ratio was either one/three or one/six depending on the time of day and the situation. One of the staff members served as housemother and stayed with the children at night.

## PROCEDURES AND RESULTS

Our initial program at Kin Kare involved close staff supervision and monitoring of the subjects' behaviors in most situations. The girls rose each morning and dressed and groomed themselves under supervision. After breakfast the girls worked in teams of two, with one team cleaning the kitchen, one team making beds, and the third team dusting. They then attended class, where a variety of verbal skills were taught. Following lunch were more cleaning and more classroom training, and then the girls returned to Cedar for the evening meal. After supper the subjects helped the Cedar staff groom some of the less advanced residents there, and returned home at about 7:00 P.M. Following the evening bath there was time for object naming, TV watching, and game playing before the 9:30 bedtime. In general, weekends followed the same routine, although there was greater flexibility. The girls would sometimes go downtown and visit some of the stores in Portage la Prairie, or they might go to the town park, or they might spend a good portion of the day playing outside, sometimes supervised and sometimes unsupervised, sometimes with neighborhood children and sometimes by themselves.

Within this general routine the program was characterized by the following features:

1. A token economy was not used during the daily activities with the exception of the classroom training. Rather, social and existing reinforcers were made directly response contingent in most situations. For example, girls were not allowed to go for breakfast unless they passed the dressing and grooming inspection. As another example, coffee and cookies available at the usual morning coffee break were contingent on the work behaviors emitted after breakfast.

2. The classroom utilized a pegboard token economy in which tokens were dispensed contingent on verbal behaviors and attending behaviors and were exchanged for candies at the end of the class period.

3. Objective data were taken regularly on some tasks, while other behaviors were checked regularly but no records were kept. Behaviors recorded regularly included dusting, washing and drying dishes, washing floors, preparing meals, mimicking and picture naming, vacuuming the rug, bedmaking, and social interaction. The data invariably combined a frequency count with a quality assessment. For example, floor washing

was assessed by counting the number of clean 8-inch by 8-inch tiles before and after washing, where a "clean" tile was defined precisely.

Other behaviors were inspected regularly and placed on reinforcement contingencies for a variety of natural reinforcers, but no data were consistently taken. Such activities included grooming, dressing, playing, watching TV quietly, and going downtown with the staff. For the most part, these behaviors had reached acceptable levels and our primary concern was to maintain them. Undesirable behaviors were primarily dealt with by extinction in the situation or time out.

In general, the results have been extremely encouraging. Some of the objective behavioral changes are summarized in Table 18.5. Much more dramatic, however, are the instances of "normal" behaviors that the girls are emitting more and more often. These include such behaviors as

playing Twister and other games with each other during unsupervised quiet periods rather than emitting typical institutional rocking behavior;

hiding dirty dishes in the kitchen so they will not have to be washed;

seeking out their "boyfriends" when they return to the institution for their evening meal;

hiding clothes that they do not like so that they can wear preferred items;

initiating hand shaking and "introductions" to visitors at Kin Kare.

During the past 3 months, the program has been altered in several respects, all of them leading to more individual freedom and less immediate supervision of the girls. This was necessitated in part by staff changes that allowed only one staff member to be with the children through most of the day, and in part was instituted because of the progress made. The girls now make the beds and do the dusting with only random spot checks (one check approximately every third day). They groom themselves and dress themselves without immediate supervision. Two of the girls make sandwiches for lunch with only occasional quality-control inspections. In short, their repertoires are expanding rapidly, and it is impossible at this time to guess what the outer limits of their progress might be.

## Discussion

The material contained in the present report is primarily programmatic. Specific procedures and detailed results related to our Cedar Cottage

**TABLE 18.5**

Some Behaviors Acquired at Kin Kare[a]

| Behaviors | Agnes | | Gail | | Ginette | | Giselle | | Lori | | Louise | |
|---|---|---|---|---|---|---|---|---|---|---|---|---|
| | Baseline (B) | Final performance (FP) | B | FP | B | FP | B | FP | B | FP | B | FP |
| Clearing kitchen table | 4 | 2 | 3 | 3 | 3 | 1 | 2 | 1 | 3 | 1 | 4 | 3 |
| Washing and drying dishes | 3 | 2 | 3 | 2 | 3 | 2 | 3 | 1 | 3 | 2 | 4 | 3 |
| Dusting | 3 | 2 | 3 | 2 | 3 | 2 | 3 | 2 | 3 | 1 | 4 | 3 |
| Washing floor | | | | | | | 3 | 1 | 3 | 2 | | |
| Vacuuming rug | 3 | 2 | 3 | 2 | 3 | 2 | 3 | 1 | 3 | 1 | 4 | 3 |
| Store excursions | 2 | 1 | 2 | 1 | 3 | 2 | 2 | 1 | 2 | 1 | 2 | 1 |

[a] Each of the behavioral items were scored on a 1–4 rating scale. In each case the test items or set of instructions was presented to the subject. The subject's behavior was then scored as follows:

1. The behavior was performed appropriately in all respects without prompting or guidance of any kind.
2. The behavior was performed appropriately after several (up to five) additional verbal commands or prompts were provided by the tester.
3. The behavior was performed appropriately after additional verbal commands *and/or* physical prompts *and/or* a "little physical guidance" were provided by the tester. Physical prompts include pointing, gesturing, etc., where there is no physical contact between the tester and subject. "A little physical guidance" refers to the amount of guidance a tester can provide by touching the subject appropriately for a maximum of 30 seconds.
4. More than the physical guidance necessary for a score of 3 was required for the behavior to be performed appropriately.

training project have been described in other publications. It is clear that our behavior modification programs at the Manitoba School have produced significant behavioral changes in large numbers of severely and profoundly retarded residents. The program at Kin Kare for six of our graduates from the Manitoba School, and the corresponding implication of returning the severely and profoundly retarded to the community and housing them in small-group living units, located on an ordinary street in an ordinary city, is a dividend of behavioral training techniques that we had not envisaged a few short years ago.

The relative costs for caring for the severely and profoundly retarded in cottages such as Cedar Cottage at the Manitoba School and in the Kin Kare home in the community represents an interesting comparison. The last cottage unit built at the Manitoba School cost in the neighborhood of $230,000, an expenditure of approximately $7600 per bed. The comparative cost of a bed in the Kin Kare community residence is $1500, or approximately 20% of the institutional cost. The per diem cost of maintenance at the community residence and the institution are about equal, so that the remaining variable to be considered is the quality of care provided. There is little doubt that the quality of care in the smaller unit in the community is vastly superior in terms of the responses of the residents, their social progress, their choice of experiences, and their general enjoyment of life.

Although we have not yet conducted research to evaluate which of a variety of conditions are essential to the success of a project such as Kin Kare, we do feel that we are in a position to comment on some major contributing factors, the most important of which would seem to be the following:

1. Many of the specific behavioral prerequisites for subjects to participate succesfully in a project such as Kin Kare were previously developed at Cedar Cottage. This included token training, training at various self-care skills, instruction-following skills, and some social skills (for example, the girls were taught not to run up to other people in the streets and hug and kiss and maul them, a behavior not infrequently observed in severely and profoundly retarded children in institutions).

2. Three of the four staff members had had extensive experience in the behavior modification program at Cedar prior to managing the Kin Kare program. The other staff member, the housemother, had some experience in our Cedar project, and was given a good deal of feedback during the first few days at Kin Kare.

3. The community home was established in such a way that daily contact was maintained with the Cedar Cottage program in particular, and the Manitoba School in general. The return of the girls and the staff to

Cedar each day for the evening meal contributed to the encouragement and support for the obvious behavioral changes that were brought about at Kin Kare. In addition, the unit supervisor responsible for management at Cedar and other cottages was also responsible for staff management and supervision at the Kin Kare home.

4. One of our behavior modification psychologists at the Manitoba School was assigned to Kin Kare (approximately a half day per week) to provide advice, reinforcement, and general encouragement for the staff and residents there.

5. A good deal of effort went into preparing the community in the immediately surrounding vicinity of Kin Kare for the initiation of the program. Each family living in the immediate vicinity was contacted and the program was discussed. The members of the community were encouraged to visit Kin Kare at any time, talk with the staff, interact with the residents, and to report any undesirable activities of the residents.

A major implication of Kin Kare is that the role of the large institution for the care of the severely and profoundly retarded must be reconsidered. Some outspoken individuals have been sounding the death knell of large institutions for the retarded located in small communities outside major population centers (Kugel and Wolfensberger, 1969). Community programs for the retarded in the state of Nebraska, for example, are clearly influencing future planning for large institutions, although not all in that state are in agreement with some of Wolfensberger's notions that the large institutions be planned out of existence (compare Wolfensberger, 1972, to LaMontia, 1972). In our view, we should not strive to tear down immediately the large residential institutions located in small outlying communities. Rather, we envisage the role of these institutions as providing a source of trained staff and trained retardates for community residences. It is further necessary to provide maintenance programs of reinforcement for both staff and residents and to provide behavioral training centers and retraining centers for behavioral problems that simply cannot be managed feasibly in a community setting. Finally, it is necessary to have back-up service available to deal with emergency situations in community residences, which may occur at any time of the day or night. The large residential-care facilities would seem to be ideally suited for the role of providing acute emergency intervention for all facilities and services serving the mentally retarded in the community. If the large residential-care facility can adapt itself in this way, it may survive and succeed in living down the unenviable image it was forced to develop in its earlier years.

In summary, the success of our Kin Kare project has had a profound impact on our future social planning for the severely and profoundly retarded, at least in the province of Manitoba. We see the Manitoba School (which many would have seen formerly as a typical, army-barracks institution) as becoming a training center for both residents and staff who will be transferred together to community residences of one sort or another, and as the backbone of maintenance contingencies that are necessary for those community residences that are successfully initiated.

### ACKNOWLEDGMENTS
Numerous people deserve a great deal of credit for the development and continuation of the Kin Kare program. We gratefully acknowledge the staff of Cedar Cottage for their contributions toward the development of the residents of Kin Kare, the Kinsmen of Portage la Prairie for their purchase of the Kin Kare home, and Mr. Gordon England for his contribution to the development and maintenance of the Kin Kare behavior modification program. Finally, we want to mention the contributions of the devoted staff of Kin Kare, and particularly Mrs. Vicki Jensen and Mrs. Dorothy Frie.

## References

Gardner, S. I. *Behavior Modification in Mental Retardation.* Chicago: Aldine-Atherton, 1971.

Kugel, R., and Wolfensberger, S. (Eds.) *Changing Patterns in Residential Services for the Mentally Retarded.* Washington, D.C.: U.S. Government Printing Office, 1969.

LaMontia, M. Statement published in quarterly Newsletter of North Central Region of American Association on Mental Deficiency, 1972.

Lowther, G. H. The retardate family as a social unit in the management of moderate mental retardation. In B. W. Richards (Ed.), *Proceedings of the First Congress of the International Association for the Scientific Study of Mental Deficiency.* Reigate, Surrey, England: Michael Jackson Publishing Company, 1968.

Lowther, G. H. Science and sentimentality. *The Manitoba School (M.S.) Journal,* 1970, **2**, 4–5.

Lowther, G. H. Behavior modification procedures in the management of severe and profound mental retardation. Paper presented at the 2nd Western Regional Meeting of the Canadian Psychiatric Association, Vancouver, B.C., 1971.

Lowther, R., Martin, G. L., and McDonald, L. A Behavioral checklist for assessing behavior modification skills in an operant training program with severely and profoundly retarded. Paper presented at the Canadian Psychological Association Meeting, St. John's, Newfoundland, 1971.

Martin, G. L. Teaching operant technology to psychiatric nurses, aides and attendants. In F. Clark, D. R. Evans, and L. O. Hamerlynck (Eds.), *Implementing Behavioral Programs for Schools and Clinics.* Champaign, Ill.: Research Press, 1972.

Martin, G. L., England, G., and England, K. Use of backward chaining to teach bed-making to severely retarded girls. *Psychological Aspects of Disability,* 1971, **18**, 35–40.

Martin, G. L., England, G., Kaprowy, E., Kilgour, K., and Pilek, V. Operant conditioning of kindergarten class behavior of autistic children. *Behavior Research and Therapy,* 1968, **6**, 281–294.

Martin, G. L., Kehoe, B., Bird, E., Jensen, V., and Darbyshire, M. Operant conditioning of dressing behavior of severely retarded girls. *Mental Retardation,* 1971, **9**, 27–31.

Martin, G. L., McDonald, S., and Omichinski, M. On operant analysis of response interaction during meals with severely retarded girls. *American Journal of Mental Deficiency,* 1971, **76**, 68–75.

Martin, G. L., and Pear, J. J. Short-term participation by 130 undergraduates as operant conditioners in an ongoing project with autistic children. *Psychological Record,* 1970, **20**, 327–336.

Martin, G. L., and Treffry, D. Elimination of self-destructive behavior and development of self-care skills of a severely retarded girl. *Psychological Aspects of Disability,* 1970, **17**, 125–131.

Thompson, T., and Grabowski, J. *Behavior Modification of the Mentally Retarded.* New York: Oxford University Press, 1972.

Treffry, D., Martin, G. L., Samels, J., and Watson, C. Operant conditioning of grooming behavior of severely retarded girls. *Mental Retardation,* 1970, **8**, 29–33.

Wolfensberger, W. Ideology power. *Quarterly Newsletter* of North Central Region of American Association on Mental Deficiency, 1972.

# 19 A BACK WARD ROUTINE AND THE EFFECTS OF INSTRUCTIONS

Luis Otávio de Seixas Queiroz

Itapira is a small town, with 45,000 inhabitants, in the interior of Sao Paulo, in the south of Brazil. It is here that Fundação Espirita Americo Bairral, a religious organization, maintains the Instituto Bairral de Psiquiatria, a hospital housing 1000 mental patients. Several forms of therapy, such as occupational therapy, recreational therapy, therapeutic community and, more recently, a program of behavior modification, have been developed in a ward for chronic patients. This presentation will deal with the behavior modification program.

This report is divided in two sections: (1) back ward routine, where a general view of the whole procedure is presented; and (2) a study of the effects of instructions on some behaviors as a part of the whole procedure.

## Back Ward Routine

My primary job at the hospital was to take care of a few patients, selected by physicians, and to test the effects of some environmental changes on the patients' behavior. The results of such experience were so stimulating that the hospital board of directors accepted the idea of organizing a chronic patient ward where operant-conditioning principles developed by Skinner (1938, 1953) could be applied to a psychiatric population (see Ayllon and Azrin, 1965, 1968; Atthowe and Krasner, 1968; Schaefer and Martin, 1966, 1969).

345

The ward studies included 51 chronic male patients with a mean of 5 years hospitalization, diagnosed as schizophrenic or mental defective with psychotic reactions. They received a maintenance dose of phenothiazine derivatives or butyrophenone derivatives.

The ward was an open ward situated on a hill and surrounded by large gardens where patients could move freely. The ward setting contained four dormitories (13 patients each) with bathroom, hall, nurse's station, meeting room, clothing room, kitchen, barber shop, individual interview room, and lean-to, as shown in Figure 19.1. The "action area" of the program included all the ward's rooms and the surrounding grounds up to a maximum limit of 10 meters radius.

The ward staff included one psychiatrist (4 hours a day), one general practitioner physician (1 hour a day), three psychologists (two working 2 hours a day and one working 1 hour a day), two attendants (in each daily shift), and one attendant (night shift).

We started by teaching all five attendants operant-conditioning principles, how to observe and record a patient's behavior, and the manipulation of environmental conditions to promote behavior changes. We then established a token economy (Ayllon and Azrin, 1968) with the purpose of changing the patients' selected daily routine behaviors. All the contingencies and records were performed by the attendants on duty (one attendant for 25 patients).

Table 19.1 shows the behaviors selected to be included in the new routine, the place, the time, and the number of tokens. The behaviors chosen to be reinforced were those our facilities permitted, and they represented an opportunity for the patient to engage in socially approved activities, to take care of personal hygiene, and to achieve greater social interaction.

The behavioral contingencies were introduced in sequence, over a period of 2 months, according to the following program:

1. Working and watching TV.
2. Physical education.
3. Response cost for lying in bed.
4. Morning hygiene, bathing, getting shaved, and having a haircut at the barber's.
5. Cleaning food tray.

Table 19.2 shows the back-up reinforcers, the number of tokens required for each, and the time schedules that were available to the patients.

The methods by which behaviors were recorded changed according to the specific behavior and the attendant time available.

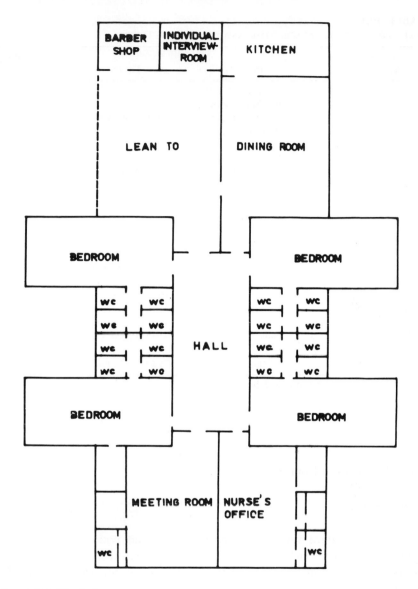

*Figure 19.1* Ward plan.

Data to be presented in this report were collected by time sampling technique, similar to Ayllon (1963) and Schaefer and Martin (1966). These records include (1) lying in bed, recorded hourly, (2) working, recorded each 15 minutes during the working periods, and (3) watching

**TABLE 19.1**
SELECTED BEHAVIORS, PLACE, TIME, AND NUMBER OF TOKENS

| Behavior | Place | Time | Number of tokens |
|---|---|---|---|
| Morning hygiene | | | |
| tooth brushing | Washing room | | 1 |
| face washing | Washing room | 7:00–7:30 A.M. | 1 |
| hair combing | Washing room | | 1 |
| Physical education | | | |
| to be present | Football field | | 1 |
| to participate | Football field | 8:00–8:40 A.M. | 2 |
| Working | | | |
| sanding wood | Lean-to | | 12[a] |
| weaving carpet | Lean-to | 9:00–11:00 A.M. | 18[a] |
| gardening | Garden | | 18[a] |
| attending class | Dining room | and | 18[a] |
| office work | Hall | | 18[a] |
| translating | Hall | 2:00–4:00 P.M. | 18[a] |
| Cleaning food tray | Kitchen | after lunch and | 1 |
| | | after dinner | 1 |
| Bathing | Wash room | 4:00–5:00 P.M | 1 |
| Asking to be shaved | Barber shop | 4 days a week | |
| Asking to have hair cut | Barber shop | 8:00–12:00 A.M. | 1 |
| Watching TV | Dining room | 7:00–9:00 P.M. | 8[a] |

[a] For an entire period of 2 hours.

TV, recorded each 15 minutes during the established period (from 7 to 9 P.M.).

## Some Results and Comments

### LYING IN BED

The procedure used at the hospital to avoid patients lying in bed from 8 to 11 A.M. and from 2 to 4 P.M. involved keeping the bedroom doors closed. Before introducing the contingencies for working and TV watching behaviors, the four bedroom doors were kept open during the day for a 15-day period.

Figure 19.2 shows the mean number of patients lying in bed during the four phases of the procedures. These four phases refer to data collected (1) with the bedroom doors closed; (2) with the bedroom doors open, with no contingency; (3) with the bedroom doors open and rein-

**TABLE 19.2**

<small>Dispensible Reinforcer, Unities, Number of Tokens Required, and Time They Were Available</small>

| Reinforcer | Unity | Number of tokens | Time |
|---|---|---|---|
| 1. Cigarette | | | |
| First class | 1 cigarette | 3 | 7:00–7:30 A.M. |
| Second class | 1 cigarette | 2 | 11;00–12:00 A.M. |
| Third class | 1 cigarette | 1 | |
| 2. Candy | 1 candy | 10 | |
| 3. Coffee | 1 demitasse | 5 | 3:00–4:00 P.M. |
| 4. Artificial drink | 1 glass | 6 | 5:00–6:00 P.M. |
| 5. Soft drink | 1 bottle | 15 | 9:00–9:30 P.M. |
| 6. Watch movie | session | 10 | 6:00 P.M. |
| 7. Walk to town (unescorted) | 2 hr | 40 (20/20)[a] | 6:00–8:00 P.M. |
| 8. Private audience with ward physician, psychologist, social worker | 15 minutes | 20 | with appointment |
| 9. Breakfast | at lib. | 1 | 7:30–8:00 A.M. |
| 10. Lunch | at lib. | 0/4[b] | 11:00–11:30 A.M. |
| 11. Dinner | at lib. | 0/4[b] | 5:00–5:30 P.M. |

[a] In order to obtain the pass to go to town, the patient had to ask for a private audience with the social worker and pay 20 tokens. If he was well groomed and had a doctor's authorization, then the patient had to pay an additional 20 tokens in order to get his pass.

[b] The number of tokens necessary to enter the dining room for lunch and dinner (main meals) was variable (from none to four). If the patient paid one token for lunch, he paid three for dinner. Thus, he had to pay a total of four tokens for the two meals.

forcement of working behavior; (4) with the bedroom doors open, reinforcement of working behavior, and response cost for patients lying in bed.

When the bedroom doors were open, the mean number of patients lying in bed increased rapidly. During the phase of reinforcement of working behavior, a decrease in the mean number resulted that remained steady for a 9-week period.

After this period a new procedure was introduced: the response cost for lying in bed. The patient had to pay two tokens if he was observed lying in bed at 8, 9, 10, and 11 A.M. or at 2, 3, 4, 5, 6, and 7 P.M., when the attendant was recording. Sometimes patients had no tokens or refused

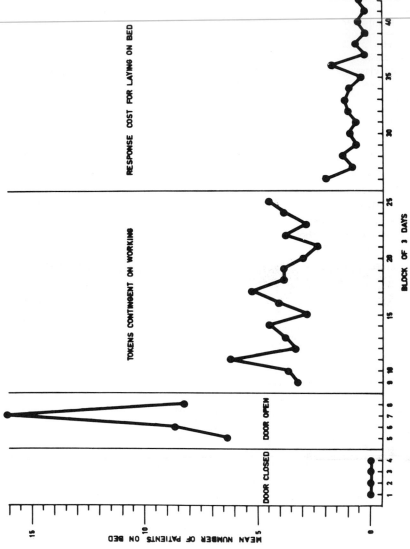

*Figure 19.2* Mean frequency of patients lying in bed from 8:00 to 11:00 A.M. and from 2:00 to 4:00 P.M. under four conditions.

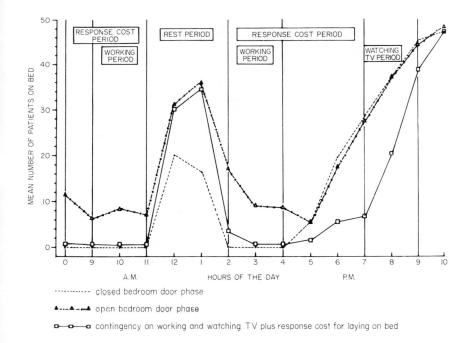

*Figure 19.3* Mean frequency of patients lying in bed during all day hours under three conditions: (1) closed bedroom doors; (2) open bedroom doors; and (3) contingency (see text).

to pay. On such occasions they were not compelled to pay immediately, but had to settle accounts before they could get another reinforcer, including meals. This procedure led to a further decrease in the mean number of patients lying in bed, to near zero, as shown in Figure 19.2. Thus, using response cost and reinforcement for working, we reproduced about the same mean number of patients lying in bed as when the bedroom doors were closed.

Figure 19.3 shows the difference in the general mean number of patients lying in bed, during the whole day (from 8 A.M. to 10 P.M.), under three conditions: (1) with the bedroom doors closed; (2) with the bedroom doors open, with no contingency; and (3) with the bedroom doors open and the contingencies (reinforcement of working and TV watching behaviors and response cost for lying in bed). Data refer to a period of 5 months.

Figure 19.3 shows that using these procedures we (1) reached a mean frequency for lying in bed that approaches the original (with bedroom doors closed) with the advantage of having now an additional condition of reinforcement and deprivation, since the beds were available to the patients all day long; (2) encouraged patients to make more adequate use of bed [the increase of the mean number of patients observed in bed from approximately 12 P.M. to 2 P.M. (rest period) was recorded twice with a mean percentage increase of 27% in each hour]; (3) reduced the number of patients in bed to a mean of about 13% in each hour (7, 8, and 9 P.M.) with a mean total reduction of 40% for the three observations, using the reinforcement of watching TV.

We could verify, otherwise, that the response-cost procedure contributed to the reduction of the number of patients in bed, extending its effects beyond 7 P.M. when it was no longer in force. During the TV-watching period, we got an additional reduction to a mean of 15% in each hour. The total reduction achieved by the two procedures (reinforcement of watching TV and response cost for lying in bed) for this period in relation to the first condition was 84%, with a mean of 28% in each hour.

Although it is hard to conclude a relationship, it seems worth mentioning that while the introduction of response-cost contingency produced a 6% reduction of lying-in-bed behavior during the working period, a 4% mean increase has been observed in the working behavior of patients.

## WORKING BEHAVIOR

The observed frequency of working behavior, as recorded by time sampling, increased from a mean of 45% in the first month to a mean of 75% in the tenth month. There was no special contingency associated with this increment. This effect may be due to adaption to the program. Although some patients were transferred during the tenth month, such transfers occurred at a low rate. The presence of new patients with a more frequent working behavior was not sufficient to justify this increase.

## TV-WATCHING BEHAVIOR

Our program included TV-watching behavior as one to be reinforced, a different goal from the majority of published articles on the same sub-

ject, which make use of such behavior as a reinforcer for other weak behaviors. This was because the frequency for watching TV was low (7%),
and we intended to create an opportunity to expose patients to social situations. The chosen TV-watching period was from 7 to 9 P.M. because
that was the period of prime-time programming. In addition, this time
period would not compete with other routine activities.

The frequency of watching TV increased from 7% in the baseline
week to 34% in the 16th week. Afterwards the frequency decreased to a
level of 15% in the 35th week. When the reinforcement was discontinued,
the frequency returned to the baseline level. This decrement in the frequency of watching TV may be due to the combination of two factors:
(1) lying in bed was more reinforcing than the tokens earned; and (2) the
development of other routine behaviors (working, for instance) provided
patients with a number of tokens sufficient to ensure the reinforcers. This
being true, the patients preferred to go to bed, neglecting the tokens that
could be earned by watching TV.

At the end of the first year after the introduction of this token-economy program, 80% of the patients were ready for discharge, according to
the ward psychiatrist.

## The Effects of Instructions

The procedures described above required all patients to participate
in all programmed activities. This situation could encourage patients to
emit only a few behaviors, which could guarantee highly desirable reinforcers. In such conditions those behaviors that occurred at a very low
frequency tended to remain unchanged. This problem showed up very
clearly with a group of patients who did not present the behaviors of
morning hygiene with a desirable frequency, although the procedure we
used was efficient for other patients. To avoid this problem we chose a
smaller number of patients and organized individual programs for each of
them. This was also the solution arrived at by Schaefer and Martin (1969)
for the Patton State Hospital.

The work reported in this section was an effort to use combined oral
instructions and reinforcement (tokens), applied to the morning hygiene
behaviors of the previously mentioned group of patients, as Ayllon and
Azrin (1964) described more clearly as the "prompting-shaping rule"
(Ayllon and Azrin, 1968).

While most behavior modification programs in psychiatric wards have used the reversal (ABAB) design, we chose to use the multiple-baseline technique as a practical alternative. The procedures suggested by Baer *et al.* (1968) and applied by Hall, Cristler, Cranston, and Tucker (1970) to a classroom situation was the one selected for our study. It consisted in selecting two or more behaviors of the same subjects, collecting a baseline for each one, and making the experimental condition contingent on each one of them on different occasions. An identifiable change in the performance of each behavior is evidence of a relationship between the experimental condition and the performance change.

## Method

SUBJECTS

Eight patients with low frequency in morning hygiene responses were chosen as subjects. We initially had 12 subjects, but 4 were dropped because they were removed from the ward during the procedure.

Table 19.3 shows age, duration of hospitalization, diagnosis, and medication of the patients. The patients' mean age was 35 years, with a range of 21 to 45 years; the mean time of hospitalization was $8\frac{1}{2}$ years, with a range of 4 to 20 years. All patients received a maintenance dosage of tranquilizing drugs, five receiving phenothiazine derivatives and three butyrophenone derivatives.

Morning hygiene behaviors were selected as a result of several considerations: (1) the objectivity of the behavioral description; (2) the specification of time and place of behavior occurrence; (3) availability of a back-up reinforcer in close temporal connection with the behavior-example entering dining room for breakfast; (4) the personal hygiene carelessness characteristic of the chronic patients.

The morning hygiene routine included three responses, as follows:

1. Tooth Brushing (TB): Pick up the toothbrush. Place the toothpaste on the brush. Move the brush up and down all over the teeth. Rinse the mouth. Rinse the toothbrush.

2. Face Washing (FW): Soap the hands. Rub soaped hands all over the face. Rinse the face and hands. Dry the face.

3. Hair Combing (HC): Pick up the comb. Comb the hair in the usual style.

**TABLE 19.3**
Patients, Age, Duration of Hospitalization, Psychiatric Diagnosis, and Tranquilizing Drugs

| Patient | Age | Years of hospital-ization | Diagnosis (psychiatric) | Tranquilizing drugs |
|---|---|---|---|---|
| M. B. | 35 | 5 | Schizophrenic reaction, chronic undifferentiate | Butyrophenone derivative |
| J. C. R. | 34 | 8 | Schizophrenic reaction, chronic undifferentiate | Phenothiazine derivative |
| A. M. | 44 | 20 | Schizophrenic reaction, chronic undifferentiate | Phenothiazine derivative |
| W. S. | 27 | 5 | Schizophrenic reaction, hebephrenic type | Phenothiazine derivative |
| J. B. | 45 | 10 | Schizophrenic reaction, catatonic type | Butyrophenone derivative |
| J. I. | 31 | 10 | Schizophrenic reaction, hebephrenic type | Butyrophenone derivative |
| R. D. S. | 29 | 6 | Schizophrenic reaction, hebephrenic type | Phenothiazine derivative |
| N. L. | 21 | 4 | Schizophrenic reaction, hebephrenic type | Phenothiazine derivative |

## Observations

From 6:30 to 7:00 A.M. the patients assembled in a line in front of the only lavoratory in the dormitory bathroom. Morning hygiene behaviors emitted at another time and place were not recorded as having occurred and did not earn tokens. The attendant of the night shift assumed a place beside the lavoratory and filled in a special observation form, using a behavior code for each one of the responses emitted by the subjects in this setting. The attendant was instructed to leave his place at the end of the time period scheduled for morning hygiene routine or after all patients had performed the behaviors.

## Procedure

*Phase 1: Baseline.* Under baseline conditions, subjects did not receive instructions related to morning hygiene behaviors. The occurrence of every response was reinforced with one token. Six months before starting this procedure, the patients had received the following instructions: "Tooth brushing, face washing, and hair combing are good hygiene habits and help to keep you in good health. For brushing the teeth, washing the face, and combing the hair, you will receive three tokens, with which you may enter the dining room and have breakfast." These instructions were delivered to the group of patients on the evening before, and repeated to each one on the morning of the first procedure day as they approached the bathroom.

During this phase, patients had to pay one token at the dining room door in order to enter the dining room and have breakfast. Phase length was 60 days.

*Phase 2: Correction of face-washing recording.* Since it was noted during the baseline phase that the attendants were not recording FW responses correctly, they were instructed to register and reinforce FW response only if patients used soap in washing their faces. No additional instructions were given to the patients. This phase lasted 24 days.

*Phase 3: Free breakfast.* During phase 3 the patients were not required to pay a token at the dining room entrance. This change of the procedure did not include any special instruction to the patients. This phase lasted 15 days.

*Phase 4: Former instructions repeated.* In phase 4 the instructions mentioned in phase 1 were presented again to all patients. These instructions were delivered to the group of patients on the evening before and repeated to each one as they approached the bathroom on the morning of the first experimental day. These instructions were not repeated during this phase. One token was required from each patient to enter the dining room for breakfast, with no further instructions. Phase 4 lasted 15 days.

*Phase 5: Increasing token requirements.* Again without additional instructions to the patients, three tokens were required to enter the dining room during phase 5. This requirement corresponded to the maximum number of tokens the subjects could earn in morning hygiene. This phase lasted 21 days.

*Phase 6: Prompting–shaping tooth brushing. First day.* When the patient came into the bathroom, the following instructions were delivered: "If you bring your toothbrush, with toothpaste on it, and move the toothbrush up and down all over the teeth, they will become clean. Then rinse your mouth and rinse the toothbrush, and you will receive the three tokens for breakfast."

*Second day.* From the second day the patients who went to the bathroom with their toothbrushes and toothpaste were told "Good guy! Now brush your teeth." At the end of the response, the attendant said: "Very well! You got three tokens for breakfast." If some TB item were omitted, instructions were repeated. This procedure was followed to the end of the phase.

*Twenty-fourth day.* At this point, in order to check the reliability of attendant observations, a second observer, a staff psychologist, was introduced during morning hygiene scheduled time. Hidden in the shower box, he was able to record patient behavior in the dormitory bathroom. The percentage agreement between the two observers was 96%. The simultaneous observation was continued for 15 days; thereafter it followed an intermittent schedule with a mean of twice a week (ranging from one to three simultaneous observations).

During this phase the former contingencies on face washing and hair combing were removed. Phase length: 39 days.

*Phase 7: Prompting–shaping tooth brushing and face washing.*

*A.* In order to encourage patients to bring the necessary items (e.g., toothbrush) to the bathroom, a new prompt was introduced in relation to TB and FW responses. Upon entering the dormitory to wake up the patients, the attendant would say: "Let's get up! Pick up the toothbrush and toothpaste. Pick up a towel and soap too!"

*B.* The attendant moved to the bathroom and said to the patients arriving with all tools: "Very good! Now brush your teeth!" When TB was completed, attendant would say to the patient: "Very well! Now soap your hands, rub your hands all over your face, including your eyes. Rinse your face and dry it. If you do all that you will get the three tokens you need for breakfast."

In this phase the three tokens were contingent upon TB and FW occurrence.

However, if the patient came into the bathroom without all the required tools, the attendant would say: "Very well! You brought (mentioning tools brought) but you forgot (mentioning tools missed). Go and get them!" When the patient brought everything, attendants performed as described in B. This phase lasted 15 days.

*Phase 8: Prompting–shaping tooth brushing, face washing, and hair combing.* The only changes in the procedure at phase 8 (42 days) were the introduction of special instructions for hair combing, similar to those for tooth brushing and face washing (phase 7), and reinforcement contingent upon the emission of all three responses.

*Phase 9: Decreasing token requirements.* Without any further instructions, during phase 9 only one token was again required for access to the dining room. This phase lasted 18 days.

*Phase 10: Increasing reinforcement.* Without any further instructions during phase 10 (36 days), ten token reinforcements were given contingent on the emission of all three responses.

*Phase 11: Delayed reinforcement.* Without further instruction during phase 11 (21 days), tokens were provided at the end of the scheduled time (7:00 A.M.). On achieving the three responses, the patient received the following instruction: "When everybody completes morning hygiene you will get your ten tokens in the lean-to. Wait for me there."

## Results

Figure 19.4 shows the varying mean percentage, in blocks of 3 days of morning hygiene behaviors in relation to the mean percentage of patient entrance into dining room, for all experimental phases.

The upper half of the figure shows the mean frequency of TB, FW, and HC behaviors emitted by the subjects. In the lower half are the mean frequency of patients who satisfied the required number of tokens for entering the dining room and the mean frequencies of those who came to the dining room door without the required number of tokens.

The baseline data show that, from the three morning hygiene responses, only FW (with or without the use of soap) was being emitted by about 73% (phase mean frequency) of the subjects. TB and HC occurred at very low frequencies (TB 3% and HC 0.2%).

During the baseline period the mean frequency of patients entering the dining room (lower half, first column) is somewhat higher than the frequencies of emitted morning hygiene responses, suggesting that some patients were using tokens earned in activities other than the morning hygiene routine to enter the dining room.

With the correction introduced (phase 2), the FW frequency decreased to a mean of 16%; HC mean frequency increased to 22% (phase mean), whereas TB mean frequency remained unchanged. As far as entering the dining room is concerned, of the 85% of the patients who entered in this phase, a mean of 46% received the token only after emitting the morning hygiene behavior.

When tokens were not required for breakfast, morning hygiene be-

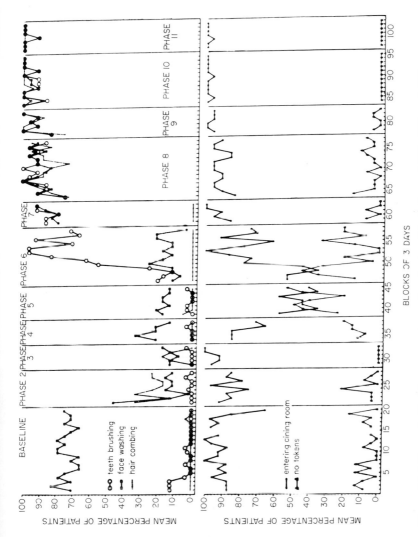

*Figure 19.4* Upper half: Mean percentage of patients who performed TB, FW, and HC responses, in blocks of 3 days, during all experimental phases (see text). Lower half: Mean percentage of patients who entered dining room door and did not have the required number of tokens (see text).

haviors decreased slightly, while the mean frequency of entering the dining room reached 100% during the last 6 days of this phase.

With the reintroduction of oral instruction (fourth column, Figure 19.4), only FW behavior showed an increase in frequency, from a mean of 13% in phase 3 to a mean of 22% in this phase. Entering the dining room decreased to a mean of 78%.

The mean frequency of morning hygiene behavior did not change with the increased token requirement, but the frequency of entering the dining room decreased sharply (phase 5), to a mean of 46% (ranging from 37 to 75%).

With the introduction of the prompting–shaping procedure for TB and three tokens, a minor increase in mean frequency initially occurred. By the 11th day of this phase, TB behavior showed a progressive increase in the mean frequency, reaching almost 100%. But this frequency was not maintained to the end of the phase.

In this phase the TB mean frequency increased up to 59%; FW and HC behaviors were not affected.

In introducing the prompting–shaping procedure in phases 7 and 8, a marked increment in the mean frequencies of FW and HC behaviors resulted. An increase in the TB frequency could be noticed as well (mean frequencies: phase 7, TB 87%, FW 84%, HC 0%; phase 8, TB 92%, FW 90%, and HC 87%).

After decreasing token requirements and increasing reinforcement without any further instruction (phases 9 and 10), the patients showed, during the last 15 days of this procedure, a mean percentage of 98% of TB and 98% of FW (both ranging from 87 to 100%) and 100% of HC behavior. The delay of reinforcement contingency did not affect frequency of these responses. During phases 6–11, the changes in (entering dining room) frequency corresponded to changes in the frequency of morning hygiene behavior.

**Discussion**

As a consequence of the token-economy system used in our chronic patient ward, it was observed that morning hygiene (MH) responses of the selected group of patients showed a stable low frequency. The baseline data indicate that about 75% of the subjects tended to perform only one of the three MH responses. Since only one token was necessary for access to breakfast and each MH response earned one token, it was unnecessary to emit more than one MH response. On the other hand, a number of these patients ordinarily retained tokens earned through other activities. This meant that they had the token required for access to the dining room and did not need to emit the MH responses.

The manipulations introduced (free breakfast, former instructions repeated, and increasing token requirement) had no significant effects on the MH response frequencies, except for a small increase in face washing (FW) frequency when oral instructions were repeated. The only effect observed was the reduction of the number of patients entering the dining room in phase 5 (the mean percentage was 46%, ranging from 37 to 75%).

These data also show that the response cost alone did not produce improvements in the MH response frequencies. But the last manipulation (increasing token requirement) did establish a deprivation condition favorable for the introduction of prompting–shaping procedures.

A dramatic change in the response frequency was observed as a consequence of the introduction of prompting–shaping procedures. As the instructions were applied to individual responses, an immediate increase in the frequency was observed. There was, however, an oscillation of tooth brushing (TB) behavior in the first 10-day period. The new prompt (introduced at phase 7), asking patients to pick up their morning hygiene items before leaving the bedroom, probably contributed to a further improvement of overall response frequency.

The instructions of phases 6, 7, and 8 were different from those in phase 4 in the following ways: (1) They were repeated daily; (2) they refer to only one response in each phase; (3) they more accurately described what the patient was supposed to do; and (4) the instructions for another response were introduced only when the previous response was being performed by the majority of patients.

Another important change was in the way tokens were provided. During the first five phases of the study, each response could be reinforced by one token. In phase 6, the emission of TB responses alone produced three tokens, but in phase 7 it required both TB and FW to produce the same reinforcement. To these two responses, hair combing (HC) was added in phase 8. All three responses of MH routine had to be performed in order for the patient to earn the three tokens. We are thus dealing with response chaining, where the lack of one response has as a consequence the total loss of reinforcement.

These two differences in the procedure and the achieved results suggests that the prompting–shaping procedures were responsible for the improvement in response frequencies, while the chaining of the three responses was responsible for maintaining the frequences.

Additional improvement in response frequencies was achieved when the token reinforcement value was increased. In phase 9, when the required number of tokens to get into the dining room was reduced, patients could save two tokens. In phase 10, with the increase of the number of tokens contingent to the emission of MH responses, patients could save nine tokens. The reduction of the mean frequency shows the improvement.

The reinforcement delay introduced to permit a further analysis (not referred to in this report) on the effect of fading out of the instructions, did not affect the high frequency, which remained during the last 15 days of phase 10.

This study used the multiple-baseline design described by Baer, Wolf, and Risley (1968) and by Risley and Baer (1974). The procedure involved collecting baselines of two or more behaviors and applying consecutively, on different occasions, the experimental condition to each one of the recorded behaviors. An immediate change in the performance in each behavior is evidence of the relation between the experimental condition and the change in the behaviors performed.

Originally, this multiple-baseline design was proposed for single-subject studies. Hall *et al.* (1970) applied the procedure to a group of students to solve classroom behavior problems, showing that it is adequate for a group of subjects if the group is treated as single organism.

The prompting–shaping procedure successively applied to individual responses of MH routine used this multiple-baseline design. If phase 5 is taken as a baseline for the three responses, as shown in Figure 19.5, an immediate change in the frequency of TB can be observed in phase 6. It can also be observed that FW and HC frequency remained unchanged, until the prompting–shaping was applied to them. When this occurred, a marked increase in the frequency was observed. This high frequency remained stable up to the end of the study.

This being the case, it was not necessary to use the common reversal test in order to conclude that the oral instructions were responsible for the patient's behavioral modification.

A last comment should be presented on the changes observed in TB frequency as a consequence of the introduction of a second observer. The general agreement between the two observers was 96% for all the simultaneous observations, which is a high index of reliability. Nevertheless, a marked decrease in TB frequency was observed on the fourth day after the introduction of the second observer (phase 6). He was able to record that some patients were entering the dining room without paying for it. When the attendant's vigilance was corrected, those patients could not get into the dining room without paying the token. Interestingly enough, al-

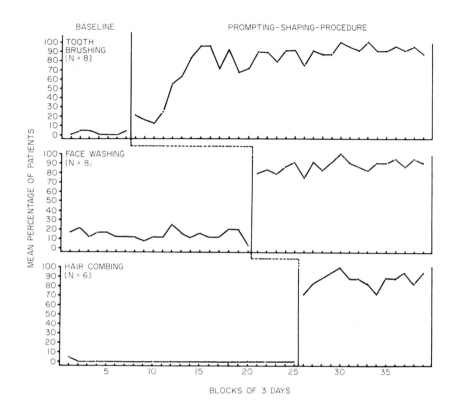

*Figure 19.5* Same data as Figure 19.4, phases 5–8 redrawn in order to show more clearly the multiple-baseline design. Baseline: before prompting–shaping; Prompting–shaping: when instructions were delivered.

though he performed the TB response, the patient usually stated that he had no tokens. On the third day it was observed that three of those patients did not actually perform the TB response. This was observed twice before instructions for FW were introduced. This fact could be analyzed as a function of the tokens' reduced reinforcing value, imposed by increased vigilance.

Entering the dining room set the occasion for obtaining breakfast and getting other reinforcers at the canteen. If the patient could enter without paying, he would save three tokens. This way he might purchase three cigarettes at the canteen, and receive free breakfast. When the increased vigilance impeded patients' entrance without paying, they chose to save their tokens and change them for cigarettes at the canteen at the next opportunity (11:00 P.M.). In this way, the reinforcing value of these tokens decreased for three patients, and may be an explanation for the decline of TB mean frequency in this period. As the vigilant procedure was not discontinued, patients performed the behavior as expected, adapting their behavior to the lower reinforcing effect of tokens.

ACKNOWLEDGMENTS
    The author wishes to thank the Board of Directors of Fundacao Espirita Americo Bairral, whose support made this work possible, and Dr. Francisco B. Calil, Clinic Director, for his encouragement. The author is indebted to Jose M. Munhoz, Oswaldo J. Germano, Eli Mendes, Nelson Topan, Jose B. Santos, and Augusto C. Baldino, ward attendants who made all records and applied contingencies. Grateful acknowledgment is given to Jose A. Batista and Marilena K.O.S. Leite, ward psychologists, who helped in performing the work in many ways. Suggestions received from Dr. Carolina M. Bori were appreciated.

# References

Atthowe, J. M., and Krasner, L. Preliminary report on the application of contingent reinforcement procedures (token economy) on a "chronic psychiatric ward." *Journal of Abnormal Psychology,* 1968, **73**, 37–43.

Ayllon, T. Intensive treatment of psychotic behavior by stimulus satiation and food reinforcement. *Behavior Research and Therapy,* 1963, **1**, 53–61.

Ayllon, T., and Azrin, N. H. Reinforcement and instructions with mental patients. *Journal of Experimental Analysis of Behavior,* 1964, **7**, 327–331.

Ayllon, T., and Azrin, N. H. The measurement and reinforcement of behavior of psychotics. *Journal of Experimental Analysis of Behavior,* 1965, **8**, 357–383.

Ayllon, T., and Azrin, N. H. *The Token Economy: A motivational System for Therapy and Rehabilitation.* New York: Appleton-Century-Crofts, 1968.

Baer, D. M., Wolf, M. M., and Risley, T. R. Some current dimensions of applied behavior analysis. *Journal of Applied Behavior Analysis,* 1968, **1**, 91–97.

Hall, R. V., Cristler, C., Cranston, S. S., and Tucker, B. Teachers and parents as researchers using multiple baseline designs. *Journal of Applied Behavior Analysis,* 1970, **3**, 247–255.

Risley, T. R., and Baer, D. M. Operant conditioning: "Develop" is a transitive active verb. In B. Caldwell and H. Ricciuti (Eds.), *Review of Child Development Research, Vol. III: Social Influence and Social Action.* Chicago: University of Chicago Press, 1974.

Schaefer, H. H., and Martin, P. L. Behavioral therapy for "apathy" of hospitalized schizophrenics. *Psychological Reports,* 1966, **19**, 1147–1158.

Schaefer, H. H., and Martin, P. L. *Behavioral Therapy.* New York: McGraw-Hill, 1969.

Skinner, B. F. *The Behavior of Organisms: An Experimental Analysis.* New York: Appleton-Century-Crofts, 1938.

Skinner, B. F. Ciência e Comportamento Humano. Brasilia: Editora da Universidade de Brasilia, 1967. (original 1953)

# 20 APPLICATION OF OPERANT PRINCIPLES TO MENTALLY RETARDED CHILDREN

**Kaoru Yamaguchi**

It was just 5 years ago that operant principles were first applied to behavior control of mentally retarded children in Japan. Since then, however, the number of researchers who are concerned with an operant approach to retardation has been increasing rapidly each year (Yamaguchi, 1970, 1971). These projects are an outgrowth of and related to recent research in the United States (Bijou and Baer, 1961; Thompson and Grabowski, 1972). We have been applying operant principles to retarded children in reference to the establishment of abilities and the modification of deviant behavior. This chapter will briefly describe some of our studies on a case-by-case basis.

## Case 1.  Application of Operant Principles in Toilet Training

SUBJECT

The subject was a moderately retarded 12-year-old girl whose retardation was attributed to brain damage. Her problem was diurnal enuresis. She was incontinent four times a day on an average. Her parents consulted physicans who prescribed medication. The parents either forced her to go to sit on the toilet periodically or punished her, but these methods were ineffective.

## HISTORY

The mother's pregnancy was normal and the girl weighed 3600 grams (7.9 pounds) at birth, but she was in a condition of syncope. One hour after birth she had convulsions. She began to walk at the age of 2 years and 2 months and began to speak at the age of 4.

## MEDICAL TREATMENT

The frequency of her convulsions increased to 7–8 per day at 1 week after birth. She had an EEG examination and was diagnosed as epileptic. She received anticonvulsant medicine until she was 3 years old, after which the medication was stopped because she had had no convulsions. When she was 8 years old, minor epilepsy began and she was hospitalized for 40 days. At that time both diurnal enuresis and lack of bowel control were significant problems.

Physical examination revealed no physical deficiency, and medication proved to be ineffective.

When she was 4 years old, an intelligence test was administered and it was discovered that her IQ was 20–25. She was sent to a day-care center for a week, but the center refused to permit her to continue attending due to her toilet problems.

## BASELINE PERIOD

The baseline period was 3 days, but, from information supplied by her mother, it was clear that her frequency of enuresis was about four per day. Her frequency of wetting and correct toilet usage (both self- and other-initiated) were recorded. The results are shown in Figure 20.1.

## REINFORCEMENT PERIOD I

At the first interview with her mother we learned that she was very fond of cakes, so we decided to use cake as a reinforcer. We gave her two pieces of cake for both self- and other-initiated toilet usage immediately after her toilet usage.

## REINFORCEMENT PERIOD II

As can be seen in Figure 20.1 the reinforcement procedure was ineffective. We observed her usual daily consumption of cake and con-

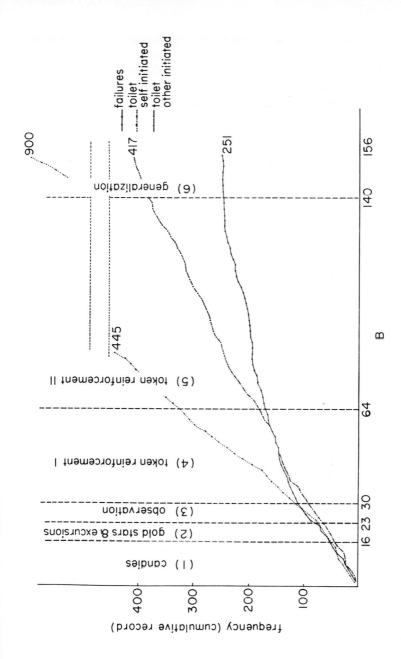

*Figure 20.1* Toilet training (enuresis diurna).

367

cluded that cake was a completely ineffective reinforcer since her mother frequently provided her with cake, fruit, and so forth, not contingent on correct toileting. Consequently, we changed the reinforcer. Now she was given gold stars as a reinforcer and taken on excursions when she accumulated 20 stars. This procedure was still ineffective.

## REINFORCEMENT PERIOD III

In period III we introduced a token-reinforcement system. She was given two tokens for each self-initiated use of the toilet and one token for each other-initiated use of this facility. The tokens were presented to her by her mother after each successful usage. Failures were ignored during this period.

She accumulated the tokens in a small purse which she hung around her neck and removed at bedtime. She was able to exchange the tokens as follows:

1 token: Receive nothing.
2 tokens: Receive cake or fruit.
3 tokens: Receive Coca Cola, orange drink, or other beverage.

In addition to this, she was *not* able to obtain cake, fruit, or soft drinks unless she presented the tokens. If she requested any of these items and did not present the tokens, the mother consistently refused to give her any. This occasionally brought about crying and a general display of frustration, but this behavior was ignored.

When the results in Table 20.1 for reinforcement period III are compared with the results for reinforcement periods I and II, it can be readily observed that the frequency of incontinence decreased from 3.1 in period

**TABLE 20.1**
FREQUENCY OF FAILURES AND TOILET USAGES (PER DAY)

| Period | Failure | Toilet self-initiated | Toilet other-initiated | Other |
|---|---|---|---|---|
| Baseline period | 3.0 | 4.0 | — | 7.0 |
| Reinforcement I | 3.1 | 2.9 | 2.6 | 8.6 |
| Reinforcement II | 3.5 | 3.8 | 3.0 | 10.3 |
| Observation period | 5.3 | 5.4 | 3.6 | 14.3 |
| Reinforcement III | 1.8 | 6.4 | 2.8 | 11.0 |
| Reinforcement IV | 1.0 | 5.8 | 2.7 | 9.5 |
| Generalization | 0.2 | 6.5 | 2.0 | 8.7 |

I and 3.5 in period II to 1.8 per day (on the average) in period III. In addition to this, the frequency of self-initiated toilet usage increased from 2.9 in period I and 3.8 in period II to 6.4 per day (on the average) in period III.

### REINFORCEMENT PERIOD IV

In addition to the above procedures in period III, in period IV one token was taken away from her for each failure. In this period the problem of controlling the number of tokens she possessed arose. The tokens were small, plastic flowers of various colors. Although she spent the tokens regularly, she liked to keep them in her small purse and look at them frequently. Since it was possible for her to save all the tokens she felt she wanted and then abandon her developing toilet habits, we believed it was necessary to control the number of tokens she had. Since she removed her purse before retiring each night, we had the mother remove all tokens in excess of four. Thus, she began each day with the remainder of the previous day's tokens up to a maximum of four.

The results of this period were even more striking. The number of failures dropped to 1.0 per day, the number of self-initiated toilet usages increased to 5.8 per day, and the number of other-initiated toilet usages was 2.7 per day on the average. In this period the number of failures was much less than in periods I and II and less than in period III.

During this period she had a physical examination including an EEG. Medication was discontinued at this time. Later, in the period of generalization, medication was administered for 4 days and finally stopped entirely. This medical treatment changed her behavior to some extent but had no influence on her bladder control and toilet behavior.

### PERIOD OF GENERALIZATION

After 140 days of training, reinforcement was discontinued. For the first 2 days she was incontinent twice, but she had no failures after this. At this point we considered her training to be complete.

### SUMMARY AND CONCLUSIONS

The cumulative record of her bladder control and toilet behavior (failure, self-initiated, and other-initiated) is shown in Figure 20.1. This shows that in the token-reinforcement period the number of failures began to decrease *and* the number of self-initiated usages began to increase. After we added punishment to the positive reinforcement, this tendency was accelerated. After we stopped the reinforcement, the tendency toward self-control of the bladder was maintained. Thus, we can conclude that her toilet training was successful.

This was the first case in which we applied operant principles to a mentally retarded child. There are some deficiencies in the procedures. For example, the baseline period was actually insufficient, and observation of the patient was not sufficiently precise. Also, since the observer was the mother, there was a lack of objectivity. The results of our study were sufficiently gratifying, however, to encourage us to pursue further research in applying operant principles to the mentally retarded.

In parallel to the above study, we applied operant principles to her bowel-control problem using a token-reinforcement system. In the baseline period she sometimes went to the toilet by herself, but usually soiled herself almost every day. After the 36 days of the baseline period, she was given three tokens for self-initiated bowel control. After 8 days, in addition, two tokens were taken from her for failure. The cumulative record of soiling and self-initiated toilet usage is shown in Figure 20.2. This shows that, 1 month after the beginning of the reinforcement, the number of soiling incidents decreased significantly and was approaching zero. Later, the number of failures increased for a short period but soon decreased to almost zero. Even after the token reinforcement stopped, there were almost no failures. It is safe to conclude that her bowel-control habits were finally established.

## Case 2.   Application of Operant Principles to Training in Changing Clothes

### SUBJECT

The subject was a moderately retarded 15-year-old girl. She had Down's syndrome and cerebral palsy contracted when she was 2 years old. The daily tasks of life, such as walking, dressing, and undressing, consumed an inordinate amount of time, making it very difficult for her to participate in group activity. However, we found that she could react faster

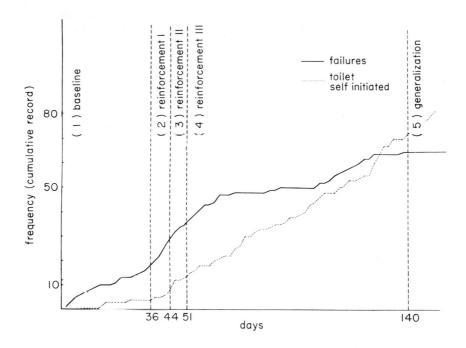

*Figure 20.2* Toilet training (feces).

than usual when she was engaging in those activities that she most enjoyed. Therefore, we tried to apply operant principles with the objectives of decreasing the amount of time required for changing her clothes.

## HISTORY

The mother's pregnancy and delivery were normal. However, the child's early development (both physically and mentally) was extremely slow. For instance, her first tooth erupted when she was 1 year and 3 months old, babbling began at 1 year and 2 months, crawling at 10 months, and standing at 1 year and 6 months. She began walking at the age of 2.

PSYCHOLOGICAL EXAMINATION

Her social age (SA) was 11 years and 3 months, and her social quotient (SQ) was 84. Her WISC VQ was 40, her PQ was 53, and her total IQ was 39. On the Binet scale, her MA was 6 years and 3 months and her IQ was 41.

BASELINE PERIOD

To establish the baseline, we observed the following three behaviors. The first was going to school. She was late almost every day. Second, there was the problem of changing her clothing. She wore a uniform to school, where she changed into play clothes. This procedure was repeated in reverse in the afternoon when she returned home to her dormitory. Changing her clothing each morning took from 30 to 50 minutes, because she would stop changing and wander around before she had completed this task. Third, changing her clothing took less time in the afternoon, but it still took from 20 to 40 minutes. Also, she always asked to be helped in changing her clothing.

The following objectives were set:

1. Arrive at school at 8:15 from the dormitory.
2. Change clothing in the morning in at most 20 minutes, decreasing this duration if possible by successive approximations.
3. Change clothing in the evening in at most 25 minutes, decreasing this duration by successive approximations.

In this process we used a timer which she usually operated herself. If she was successful in performing the task within a certain period of time, she received a star; for example, if she arrived at school on time, she received a star from the teacher. Also, if she performed her morning and afternoon clothing changes within a certain duration, as set on the timer, she received a star each time.

Each Saturday she returned home, and, if she had accumulated 12 stars during the week, she could listen to her favorite phonograph record as much as she liked.

The time that she was allowed to change her clothing was shortened by 1 minute each week.

RESULTS

The results of 9 weeks of training shows that the time needed to change clothes in the morning decreased from 20 minutes to 13 minutes

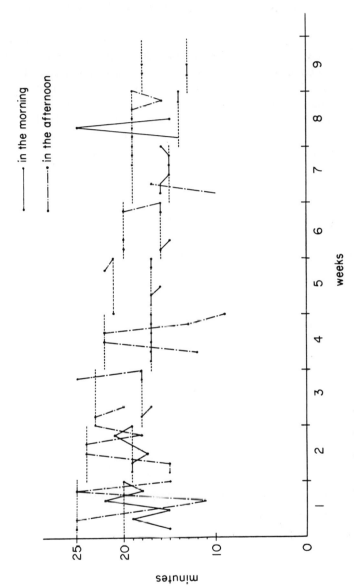

*Figure 20.3* Dressing and undressing.

(Figure 20.3). The time needed in the afternoon decreased from 25 to 18 minutes.

After our participation in the experiment ended, the teacher continued to train her using the timer. After 10 months of training, the time that it took for her to change in the morning was less than 10 minutes. The afternoon change took less than 15 minutes. This is almost the same amount of time that it takes for the other students at this school. At this point, the teacher stopped using the timer. According to the post-check, the time required to change clothes varied from 4 to 30 minutes, averaging 13.9 minutes in the morning and 12.5 minutes in the afternoon. This is a significant improvement over the time consumed prior to the training.

### Case 3.   Application of Operant Principles to Tricycling Behavior

#### SUBJECT

The subject was a severely retarded 14-year-old girl. Her behavior problem was taking tricycles from preschool children and riding them while going to and from school.

#### HISTORY

Her mother had a normal pregnancy and delivery. The subject weighed 3000 grams (6 pounds, 4 ounces) at birth and began to walk when she was 1 year and 10 months old. She has anamnesis of epilepsy.

#### PSYCHOLOGICAL EXAMINATION

The results of her psychological tests are as follows:

Social age (SA): 4.11
Social quotient (SQ): 36
Picture-drawing test: MA, 2.6
Binet test: MA, 3.0; IQ, 28.

#### BASELINE AND REINFORCEMENT PERIOD

The frequency of riding tricycles was 1.8 per day on the average. During this period we investigated the things that she was fond of and found that she liked Coca Cola and Calpis (a milk beverage). Therefore, we used these as reinforcers. When she did not ride a tricycle she was given Coke or Calpis immediately after returning home, as a means of decelerating taking tricycles from preschool children.

## RESULTS

The results of this training show that the frequency of riding tricycles decreased to .2 per day on the average during the reinforcement period (Figure 20.4). After 4 months of training, the reinforcement was stopped. After this, no significant change was found in her behavior.

We attempted to define a new baseline period, but it cannot be fruitfully discussed at this time because of a lack of precise records. In field experience in schools or institutions, it is of crucial importance to train teachers or mothers to observe properly and to record the behavior of the subject.

## Case 4. Application of Operant Principles to Toilet Training

### SUBJECT

The subject was a moderately retarded 14-year-old boy who had never excreted without an enema since he was 9 months old. At the age of 9 he suffered from meningitis, and has since then had epileptic attacks for which he received medication.

### PRELIMINARY OBSERVATIONS

He received an enema every 2 days, administered by his mother, father, or brother. We investigated to see if there was any difference in the subject's reaction depending on who administered the enema, but no difference was discovered.

### PSYCHOLOGICAL EXAMINATION

His Binet test scores are MA 5.10 and IQ 43.

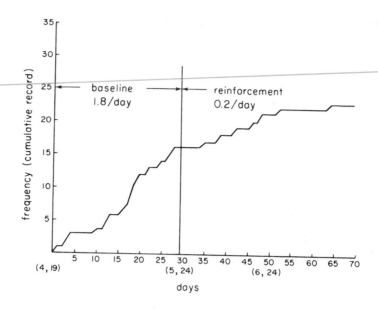

*Figure 20.4* Riding a tricycle.

## PROCESS OF TRAINING

We applied fading procedures; that is, he had an enema every 2 days as before, but the quantity of glycerin was gradually decreased while the total quantity of the enema remained the same. The date and time of the enema, the quantity of glycerin and water, the duration of the excretion, and the condition of the feces were recorded. As a reinforcer we used black tea, of which he was very fond. Immediately after finishing his bowel movement he was given black tea and the verbal reinforcement of saying "good boy."

As is shown in Figure 20.5, after nearly 90 days the quantity of glycerin was decreased from 5 cc of water to 2 cc per 18 cc of water. Subsequently, we kept the amount of glycerin the same while gradually decreasing the quantity of water.

After nearly 120 days from the commencement of the training, the total quantity of liquid decreased to 8 cc, composed of 2 cc of glycerin and 6 cc of water.

We repeated this process of alternately decreasing the amount of glycerin and water.

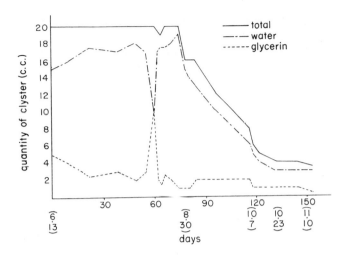

*Figure 20.5* Toilet training.

After 180 days of training he had a bowel movement immediately after having the empty container touched to his buttocks. Finally, normal excretory behavior was established.

## CONCLUSIONS

We can consider this case to be the one in which fading procedures worked most effectively, although the reinforcing function of the black tea is not precisely ascertainable.

## Case 5. Application of Operant Principles to Training in Walking

### SUBJECT

The subject was a profoundly retarded 5-year-old girl who could stand and walk to some extent by holding a railing but could never walk by herself.

### HISTORY

The mother's pregnancy and delivery were normal. The subject weighed 3500 grams (7 pounds, 8 ounces) at birth. Her development was quite normal until 2 months after birth, when she had a combined small-pox, diphtheria, and whooping cough inoculation. At this time she had a convulsion. When she was 4 or 5 months old she had another convulsion. Hereafter, the convulsions increased regularly. When she was 8 months old she was diagnosed as an epileptic.

Her first tooth erupted at the age of 10 months, and she first stood at the age of 1 year and 3 months. This is not too slow, but because of the frequency of her convulsions, she spent most of her time in bed until she was 3 years old. Her convulsions were so severe that the doctor repeatedly told her parents that there was no hope for the subject and that she would soon die.

When she was 4 years old she was allowed to attend a private day-care center for severely retarded children. At that time her condition was as follows. She turned to the caller and smiled when her name was called. When she was frustrated she cried or got angry. She could recognize those people of whom she was fond. She said "oh, oh" and "ah, ah." She crawled and could walk for short distances while holding a rail.

## Psychological and Medical Examinations

Her development quotient (DQ) was 12. Before training she had a physical examination to determine if she was sufficiently strong to walk. It was determined that the development of her leg muscles, though not good, was sufficient to enable her to walk. It was also thought that training in walking would not have an untoward effect on her convulsions.

## Procedures

A similar procedure to that of Meyerson, Kerr, and Michael (1967) was used. That is, two chairs and one organ were arranged as shown in Figure 20.6.

She was put on the floor between the two chairs. A trainer who sat on one chair encouraged her to hold on to the back of the chair and stand up by herself. Another trainer urged her to move to the other chair by calling her name. Immediately after she succeeded in moving from one chair to another she was given a reinforcer.

Several kinds of reinforcers were tried in the following sequence:

1. Ice cream
2. Toys

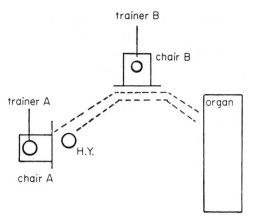

*Figure 20.6* Training in walking.

3. Lid of an ice cream container
4. Chocolate
5. Crackers
6. Mirror
7. Lunch
8. Throwing down the lid of an aluminum lunch box

The last was found to be the only effective reinforcer.

The distance between the chairs, which began at 86 cm, was gradually increased.

### PROGRESS OF THE TRAINING

The result of the training (48 sessions in total) is that we could see very slow progress as the distance between the chairs reached 118 cm by the 33rd session. During this period convulsions continued, but after 36 sessions the frequency of the convulsions increased rapidly until they occurred almost once each day. This made it impossible for us to continue training after 48 sessions.

### DISCUSSION

The distance of 118 cm is equivalent to only one or two steps from one chair to the other. We cannot state that this was successful training. Her failure to walk might be due to her physical condition, since perhaps her legs were not sufficiently developed, but it was more probably due to her severe epileptic seizures. During the last half of the training period her medication was changed 12 times, and all medicines were found to be ineffective. If her convulsions had stopped, she probably could have succeeded in learning to walk. One year after the training was stopped she had frequent convulsions and showed a regression in her ability to walk.

The positive finding of this experiment is that we found the throwing down of the lid of the aluminum lunch box to be an effective reinforcer for her after trying many other reinforcers, all of which were ineffective. Even food was ineffective, since she soon spit out any food that she was given. At that time, the lid of an aluminum lunch box accidentally fell on the floor. She laughed at this incident. In this way we fortuitously discovered that this was an effective reinforcer. I have read a report from the United States where it was found that tearing an old shirt was an effective reinforcer for a severely retarded subject. I think that these two incidents show that we must be highly resourceful in attempting to find successful, effective reinforcers.

## Case 6.  Application of Operant Principles to the Behavior Modification of an Autistic Mentally Retarded Girl

### SUBJECT

The subject was an autistic, retarded 13-year-old girl who had behavior patterns such as holding particular students (mainly men), smelling their heads, and inserting her finger into their ears.

### HISTORY AND AUTISTIC BEHAVIOR PATTERNS

Her mother had a normal pregnancy and delivery. The subject weighed 3500 grams (7 pounds, 8 ounces) at birth. At the age of 6 months her father died in an accident, and her care was given over to foster parents. She was a very quiet baby, but her physical development was quite good and she was able to walk at the age of 14 months. She had a poor appetite, however. When she was taken for a walk in a stroller, she remembered the path immediately and pointed out the way to go the next time.

Before the age of 2 she was humming popular songs, recalling the exact melody, rhythm, and tone of the original. From the time she was 7 months old she enjoyed making noises by scratching rough surfaces. She also liked to smell and feel velvet cloth. This behavior continued until she was 10 years old.

When she was 4 years old, her mother scolded her with very rapid speech. The girl immediately repeated this, with the same accent, although she could hardly speak except to ask for water and to go to the toilet, for which she used baby talk. She also said "mama." Furthermore, at this time she actively disliked having doors partly open. At the age of 6 she entered a special class for mentally retarded children. She became interested in colors, and could give the names of 35 different colors. At the age of 7 she began to collect beads, tiddlywinks, and crayons. She also began to talk to herself and to walk around the room speaking some words that had no meaning. At this time she began to show an interest in origami. At the age of 8 she began to manifest the behavior of holding boys who had short hair and smelling their heads. At the age of 10, she was very skillful at rolling paper into long ropes to make a very strong twine. At 11, she talked to herself more often and began to laugh inappropriately.

## PSYCHOLOGICAL EXAMINATION

The results of her psychological tests are as follows:

Social age (SA), 4.9
Social quotient (SQ), 38
Picture-drawing test, MA 3.7
Binnet test, MA 4.7, IQ 34
MoA, 4.8
MoQ, 38

She was given a physical examination by a psychiatrist when she was 3 years and 6 months of age. She continued under his care on a weekly basis until she was diagnosed as autistic when she was 4 years and 2 months old.

## BASELINE

We observed her behavior patterns, specifically holding male students, smelling their heads, and putting her fingers into their ears, for 10 days.

REINFORCEMENT PROCEDURE

Tiddlywinks were used as reinforcers. She was excessively fond of them and in fact valued them as treasures. When she came to school, she brought five tiddlywinks along with her in a small purse every day. Whenever she showed any of the baseline behavior patterns, one of her tiddlywinks was immediately taken away from her. Whenever one tiddlywink was left at the end of the school day, she was given a badge (similar to Boy Scout merit badges). She could exchange 10 badges for a crayon. The results of this procedure are shown in Figure 20.7. In this figure, the records for 1 week are missing because the teacher was absent.

The problem behavior patterns decreased rapidly from one per day in the baseline period to .3 per day in the reinforcement period.

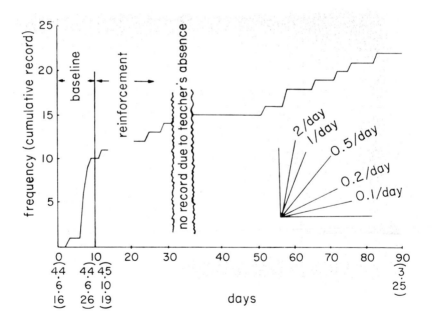

*Figure 20.7* Autistic behavior.

## DISCUSSION

This study is concerned with the modification of maladaptive behavior patterns of an autistic mentally retarded girl by using tiddlywinks as a reinforcer. From a psychotherapeutic point of view, it is not advisable to weaken autistic symptoms themselves. Some psychotherapists would say that the patient would exhibit a symptom substitution for a symptom that is weakened. As far as this subject is concerned, no symptom substitution was found.

The weak points of this study are the lack of records for one week because of the teacher's absence, our inability to establish a second baseline, and the fact that our instructions were not necessarily strictly obeyed. We asked for the cooperation of all members of the school but did not receive this cooperation.

## CURRENT RESEARCH

Recently we began to apply operant principles to teach academic skills to retarded children. We made a special machine (with two projectors) to teach reading to young retarded children. From one a picture (for instance, "hand") is projected on the screen in a frame. From the other projector a letter (which means "hand" in Japanese) is superimposed on the picture. At the beginning, the letter is projected and the subject watches it but cannot read it. Then the picture corresponding to the letter appears superimposed in the letter. While repeating this procedure, the picture, which is the cue to read the letter, is being faded out and the subject begins to read the letter without the cue. Each time the subject read the letter correctly, he was reinforced by the light and a buzzer. Letters were randomly divided into groups. One group was taught with this teaching machine and the other with conventional teaching methods.

The subjects were a severely retarded 14-year-old girl, for whom learning to read was considered impossible, and two mildly retarded 7-year-old boys. Principal findings were that all subjects learned to read the letters better and afterwards showed a higher ratio of retention with the machine than with the conventional procedure.

## Summary and a Look Toward the Future

The applications of operant principles to retarded children that we have conducted so far have been concerned with personal hygiene, deviant behavior, and academic skills. Among them the most effective results were gained in training in personal hygiene and the modification of deviant behavior. Although better results in teaching academic skills were also gained in comparison with conventional teaching, our emphasis was on rote learning of simple discriminations rather than more complex intellectual actions.

## References

Bijou, S. W., and Baer, D. M. *Child Development: A Systematic and Empirical Theory,* Vol. 1. New York: Appleton-Century-Crofts, 1961.

Meyerson, L., Kerr, N., and Michael, J. L. Behavior modification in rehabilitation. In S. W. Bijou and D. M. Baer (Eds.), *Child Development: Readings in Experimental Analysis.* New York: Appleton-Century-Crofts, 1967.

Thompson, T., and Grabowski, J. *Behavior Modification of the Mentally Retarded.* New York: Oxford University Press, 1972.

Yamaguchi, K. Application of operant principles to the training of mentally retarded children. *Bulletin of the Research Institute for Education of Exceptional Children,* 1970, **3**.

Yamaguchi, K. Application of operant principles to the training of mentally retarded children. *Bulletin of the Research Institute for Education of Exceptional Children,* 1971, **4**.

# VI MODIFYING DRUG-RELATED BEHAVIOR PROBLEMS

# 21 A BEHAVIORAL PROGRAM FOR INTRAVENOUS AMPHETAMINE ADDICTS[1]

K. Gunnar Gotestam

G. Lennart Melin

William S. Dockens, III

## Formulation of the Problem

In general, treatment results with amphetamine addicts have been rather poor and in the same range as the results of medical treatment of heroin addicts, with about 15% of patients being drug free 1 year after treatment (Andersson and Gunne, 1969). This was true for the very heavy drug addicts who frequented our clinic, most of whom were intravenous amphetamine users. Although efforts had been made to establish a treatment ward for such people, the management of the ward had become more and more difficult, and the regulations that were necessary for the medical treatment, and for the staff, were poorly accepted by the patients. Sometimes dangerous threats were vocalized and executed. The poor prognosis and the immediate problem of difficulty with ward management had two implications: (1) the need for a management program on the ward, with modification of the ward behavior, and (2) the need to develop a specific treatment program to reduce drug self-administration outside the ward.

[1] This study was supported by research grants from Anton and Dorotea Bexelius' Foundation and the Foundation for Psychiatric and Neurologic Research at the Medical Faculty University of Uppsala.

## Contingency Management on the Ward

Ayllon and Azrin (1968) have set forth rules for ward organization and behavior modification on a ward. The most important principle of a token-economy system (a system built on operant principles) is a principle described by Premack (1959), which states that any behavior that occurs at a low frequency can be increased in frequency if its occurrence is followed by the availability of high-frequency behavior. This general principle has been verified in many operant–conditioning studies. In accordance with this, behaviors of high natural frequency should be arranged as reinforcers by allowing patients to engage in them according to certain prearranged contingencies.

Since this study deals with a semiopen ward with a high turnover both for patients and staff, it would have been very difficult to establish a token economy; that is, our control over the patients' behavior would have been less than necessary to make such an economy effective. Thus, our method of choice was a more direct application of Premack's principle (Homme, 1966). In short, we attempted to link directly low-frequency behaviors to high-frequency behaviors according to certain principles.

As we see behavior modification as a means to an end, it remains to be answered as to what kind of terminal behaviors should be sought. Our choice was to attempt to strengthen behaviors that could be of use in society. Ayllon and Azrin called this the "rule of relevance" (1968). Target behaviors were selected and a management program was designed to increase the frequency of these relevant behaviors.

### Earlier Management of the Ward

#### Subjects

The ward was somewhat small, but quite new. It was relatively well equipped and with a staff-to-patient ratio of 1:2. Figure 21.1 shows the ward. As can be seen, there was one room with three beds, two rooms with two beds, and five rooms with one bed. There was no systematic distribution of beds to patients other than availability.

#### Medical Criteria

The patients had two kinds of medical status: intoxicated and detoxified. These criteria were confirmed by a daily urinalysis. If remains of drugs (i.e., amphetamine or morphine) were found in the urine the patients were considered intoxicated, and if urines contained no remains the patients were considered detoxified. The urine analysis had very profound consequences. The patients in the intoxicated state were not allowed any privileges such as leave, outdoor walks with staff, and visitors, but as soon as there were no drugs found in the urine analysis, they were immediately entitled to outdoor walks with personnel and after a week they were also entitled to other privileges.

When the patient with privileges became intoxicated again, he had to return to detoxification and lost the privileges. It was, however, very diffi-cult to maintain these regulations, especially if the patient came to one of

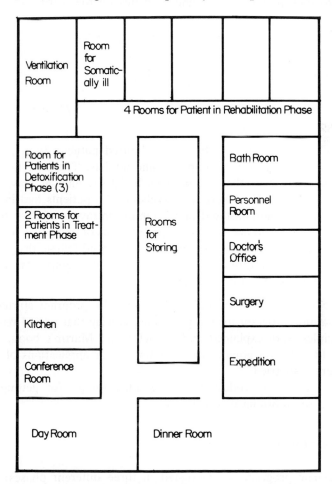

*Figure 21.1.*

the staff and said that she had taken drugs. It was difficult to punish this honesty, and many patients kept some of their privileges even if they were intoxicated during their stay on the ward.

SOCIAL CRITERIA

Every detoxified patient was to take part in the daily activities offered to her; these were occupational therapy, physical therapy, classes, and excursions. There was also a rule that every detoxified patient was to get up and dress before 8 A.M. There was some prompting in an attempt to get patients to take part in the routine activities on the ward. An important thing to note here is that there were no consequences, positive or aversive, tied to the patient's activities, other than drug taking.

BEHAVIORAL PROGRAM I

The behavioral program started August 31, 1971, and ended April 23, 1972.

*Patients.* In all, 18 of about 50 admitted patients took part in the study, and all of them were amphetamine addicts. The criteria for inclusion in the study were that the patients had to remain at least 1 day in each phase and that they were not psychotic. All patients had in common that they had self-administered amphetamine intravenously for from 1 to 15 years, but they also had several other problems of neurotic and psychotic character. The ward was to take the most advanced female drug addicts in the country, and therefore one could expect that the sample was not representative of Swedish addicts in general.

*Introduction of the behavior program.* The program started with a 14-day training program for the personnel. During that period basic learning principles were explained and Schaefer and Martin's book, *Behavior Therapy* (1969) was gone through. A few minor applications of the principles were also tried.

Base rates were collected, among other things, for getting up and dressing in the morning before 8 A.M.

THE MANAGEMENT PROGRAM

The new program was designed in three different phases: (1) detoxification, (2) treatment, and (3) rehabilitation. These three phases were physically separated on the ward; that is, the room with three beds was for detoxification, the two rooms with two beds each were used for the treatment phase, and the single rooms were used for the rehabilitation phase (see Figure 21.1). This change was made because the personnel were convinced from experience that privacy was a reinforcing privilege. Private rooms could be decorated as chosen by patients, but the detoxification room was to be considered a sickroom and looked very sterile. The two treatment rooms were somewhat less sterile than the detoxification rooms, but were not as flexible and colorful as the private rooms.

DETOXIFICATION PHASE

Every patient was allocated to this phase on admission. She had to stay in this phase as long as drugs were found in her urine. When she no longer had any drugs in her urine, she was given the opportunity to join the program. If the patient was not interested in the program she was, after having been offered social assistance, discharged from the ward. In this phase the patient was considered ill and was not allowed to take part in any activities on the ward whatsoever.

TREATMENT PHASE

In the treatment phase the patient was not allowed to take sleeping pills, except in exceptional cases. She stayed in one of the nicer rooms with two beds. In this phase, low-frequency behaviors were tied to high-frequency behaviors to a certain extent. High- and low-frequency behaviors were selected based on patient ratings of preferred activities and also on personnel ratings (Table 21.1).

REHABILITATION PHASE

When the patient had functioned well in the treatment phase for a week, she was moved to the rehabilitation phase. However, if she had not met the requirements of phase 2, she had to stay longer in that phase. The rehabilitation phase contained more high-frequency behaviors, reinforcers, than the treatment phase. The low-frequency behaviors on the ward could also be exchanged for work off the ward. If the patient did not get on very well in this phase, she was moved back to the treatment phase, and if she relapsed to taking drugs she was moved back to the detoxification phase.

**TABLE 21.1**

Relations between High-Frequency Behaviors and Low-Frequency Behaviors in the Rehabilitation Phase

| Low-frequency behaviors | High-frequency behaviors |
| --- | --- |
| 1. Up in the morning by 8 A.M. (dressing, making bed, cleaning room) | 1. Staying in private room |
| 2. Attending morning conference | 2. Leaving ward for a few hours |
| 3. Routine work on ward (with contact man) (scouring, sweeping, dusting) | 3. Leave for a whole day or more |
| 4. Physical therapy | 4. Taking visitors in own room during the afternoon |
| 5. Covert conditioning | |
| 6. Activities 2–4 could be exchanged for off-ward activities, i.e., work in hospital area or in town | |

## Behavioral Program II

When the program had been running for about 4 months, all personnel working on the ward came together to discuss the program. All personnel who had also worked on the ward before the program was started were convinced that it had meant an improvement. By improvement they meant better contact with patients because of the more explicit rule system, fewer tantrums for the same reason, and more productive activity on the ward.

The biggest disadvantage was found to be the distribution of sanctions for not getting along well in the program. Both the personnel and the patients felt that the conditions for moving a patient back to a lower phase were too arbitrary and often led to conflicts between the patients and the personnel. Because of this disadvantage, a point system was developed. This was done by assigning weights (points) to low-frequency behaviors according to a principle that the lower frequency of a specific behavior, the higher its weight (Table 21.2).

The modified program was thus quite similar to a token-economy program (Ayllon and Azrin, 1968). There were, however, some differences. The scores could not be used to gain access to specific privileges. Instead, the patient had to meet certain requirements to earn access to *all* the privileges in the phase. Those requirements were that the patient had to earn 5 points to leave the detoxification phase, 25 points to leave the treatment phase, and 25 points per week to remain in the rehabilitation phase.

**TABLE 21.2**
ACTIVITY SCHEDULE[a]

| Phase | Activity | Points | Times per week | Maximum per week |
|---|---|---|---|---|
| I + II + III | Dressed before 8 A.M. | 1 | 6 | 6 |
| | Made bed and room by 9 A.M. | 2 | 6 | 12 |
| II + III | Work 1 | 1 | 2 | |
| | Work 2 | 1 | 2 | 6 |
| | Work 3 | 1 | 2 | |
| | Working therapy | 2 | 3 | 6 |
| | Gymnastics | 3 | 2 | 6 |
| | Bath excursion | 2 | 2 | 4 |
| | Cooking course | 1 | 1 | 1 |
| | Wednesday conference | 1 | 1 | 1 |
| | Searching for work | 4 | 1 | 4 |
| III | Working | 5 | 5 | 25 |

[a] Five points needed to move from detoxification phase (I), 25 points to move from treatment phase (II), and 25 points a week to stay in rehabilitation (III).

RESULTS AND DISCUSSION

Getting up and dressing before 8 A.M.: To avoid placebo effects, all baselines were collected during the month before the beginning of the program. During this preceding month there was no standardized recording of base rate for these particular behaviors. Instead, records of these behaviors were obtained from the "day reports" that were kept on every patient.

As the program began, these behaviors were systematically collected for all patients in all phases. As can be seen in Figure 21.2, there was a systematic increase in these behaviors in Program I and still more in Program II compared to the base rates. This increase in target behaviors goes for all three phases. A Kruskal–Wallis analysis (Siegel, 1956) of the difference between the three periods was statistically significant (.001 level H 28.9; $df = 2$).

Figure 21.3 presents the data from Figure 21.2 as a cumulative record. In these cumulative data on each individual patient in Program I and II, an increase can be seen rather more consistent in Program II than in Program I.

The data from these two programs (I and II) show that it is possible to improve behavior on a ward of this kind. The kinds of behaviors that we have chosen in this study may not be the most relevant behaviors in

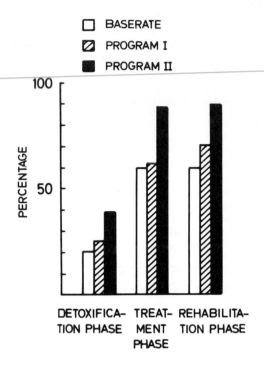

Figure 21.2.

addicts to alter. But, for instance, the behavior of getting up was considered very important, because reliable habits of arising are a prerequisite for holding a job or engaging in any morning activity.

Another gain with the program was that when the rule system was explicitly stated, the discussions, both frequent and without merit, between the personnel and the patient about rules and access to privileges were not as common as before the program.

In behavioral terms, rehabilitation from drug addiction is concerned with increasing effectiveness of vocational and social behavior in terms of rate, precision, and reliability of whatever behaviors are essential to those activities. A ward should provide opportunity to learn relevant behaviors for functioning in society. We therefore think that patients' activities when they are treated for drug addiction should be analyzed according to the "rule of relevance"; that is, behavior sanctioned positively on the ward must have relevance for the patients to engage in (Ayllon and Azrin, 1968). Our general view is that if wards in general mental hospitals and psychiatric clinics cannot provide those relevant activities, perhaps the best

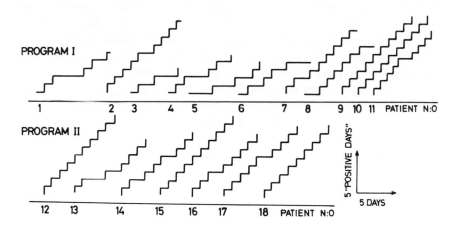

*Figure 21.3.*

way to treat drug addicts would be out in society, apart from a rather short period of detoxification when they require medical treatment.

## "Covert Extinction" of Amphetamine Taking

The traditional treatment for drug addiction has mainly involved depriving the addict of the drug. Rats addicted to morphine and then withdrawn for periods up to 1 year, when given the opportunity to self-administer morphine, take the drug again, indicating that withdrawal from the drug does not affect later drug-taking behavior (Wikler and Pescor, 1967, 1970). Clinical data also show that relapse in amphetamine taking, as well as morphine or heroin, occurs in about 85% of treated addicts during a 6-month follow-up (Andersson and Gunne, 1969).

The common methods for eliminating operant responses are punishing the unwanted response, discontinuing reinforcement, or satiation with the reinforcer (Thompson and Pickens, 1969). Wikler (1971) has proposed the use of an extinction procedure in treating drug addiction. In the present investigation, the extinction procedure was studied as a model for reducing drug taking by amphetamine abusers.

The use of cognitive techniques enables us to use more vivid situations as compared to the restricted environment that would otherwise be used in the hospital ward. Cautela has described a class of therapeutic procedures that were used in the treatment of alcoholism, homosexuality, smoking, and overeating (Cautela, 1970, 1971a, 1971b). He introduces his techniques as the procedures used to modify behavior by presenting imaginary aversive and reinforcing stimuli, and terms them "covert sensitization," "covert reinforcement," and "covert extinction."

The subjective response complex occurring following an intravenous amphetamine injection (the "flash") is thought to be the controlling consequence that acts as a reinforcer for the chain of behaviors terminating in amphetamine injection. Extinction of the chain should therefore occur if the modification program eliminates the occurrence of the flash (Cautela, 1971a).

Four consecutively admitted female amphetamine addicts were interviewed about their injection habits, and two or more of the most common injection situations were recorded. During each treatment session one of these situations was described to the patient, making certain that she could follow and imagine the situation as vividly as possible (see Cautela, 1971a). Finally, the patient was told to imagine that she experienced no flash, and that she feels no effect whatsoever.

Before treatment and during the sixth day of treatment, respiration, pulse rate, pulse volume, and galvanic skin responses were recorded on a Grass recorder on one of the cases.

## RESULTS AND DISCUSSION

In our four cases we have seen that after about 1 week of treatment with the covert extinction procedures, corresponding to about 100 extinction trials, the patient did not react with the autonomic syndrome to verbal descriptions of amphetamine-related situations. At various times all four cases also went AWOL and injected amphetamine, but they reported that they did not experience the flash.

Figure 21.4 shows the physiological measurement of one case, where she was first told to imagine two neutral stimuli, then three highly emotive stimuli dealing with the addiction situation. Note the very marked response in GSR, pulse, and respiration on the emotive stimuli, but no reactions to the neutral ones. Six days later, after the patient had 100 extinction trials, she imagined the "shot situation" but did not respond at all. This reaction is also compared with two other emotive situations, none of which includes addiction situations or behavior. She responded clearly to the two control situations, although to a lesser degree in GSR than in the first recording.

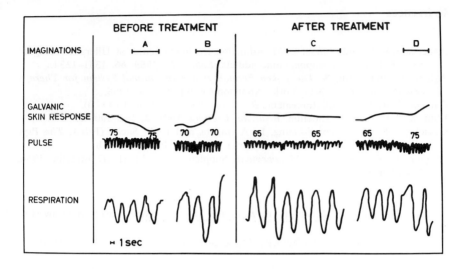

*Figure 21.4.*

This decrease could be explained by a general habituation to the recording situation.

Furthermore, following the treatment, three of the cases (including the "control relapse") have not used central stimulant drugs during a 9-month control period. One has started using stimulants, one has enrolled in classes, and one has gone back to periodic work.

"Covert extinction" is considered to be an extinction procedure. The whole situation (including many discriminative stimuli) is presented, but the drug reinforcer is not. This weakens the relation between the situation and the response—the flash—and the flash becomes weakened. As another later consequence, the craving and drug-seeking behavior will also be extinguished as the terminating consequence—the flash—is extinguished.

Our preliminary data from case studies indicate that it is possible to modify certain aspects of addictive behavior through covert conditioning techniques. We therefore feel justified in applying a learning model to the problem of addiction. We have used a technique that, according to Cautela (1971a), should be named "covert extinction." Our interpretation is that an addict who comes in contact with the drug or with other addicts when he is drug free is rather apt to relapse, because of his autonomic reactions to these stimuli. As these are extinguished, this very small change could be enough to help the addict resist the sight of these items.

# References

Andersson, S. J., and Gunne, L. M. Addiction treatment center at Ulleraker Hospital (3): Follow-up of amphetamine addicts. *Lakartidn,* 1969, **66,** 1331–1334.

Ayllon, T., and Azrin, N. *The Token Economy: A Motivational System for Therapy and Rehabilitation.* New York: Appleton-Century-Crofts, 1968.

Cautela, J. R. Covert reinforcement. *Behavior Therapy,* 1970, **1,** 33–50.

Cautela, J. R. Covert extinction. *Behavior Therapy,* 1971, **2,** 192–200.(a)

Cautela, J. R. Covert conditioning. In A. Jacobs and L. B. Sachs (Eds.), *The Psychology of Private Events.* New York: Academic Press, 1971.(b)

Homme, L. E. *Contingency Management,* Supplement to the IRCD Bulletin, 1966, **2(4A),** 1–3.

Premack, D. Toward empirical behavior laws: I. Positive reinforcement. *Psychological Review,* 1959, **66,** 219–233.

Schaefer, H. H., and Martin, P. L. *Behavior Therapy.* New York: McGraw-Hill, 1969.

Siegel, S. *Nonparametric Statistics for the Behavioral Sciences.* New York: McGraw-Hill, 1956.

Thompson, T., and Pickens, R. Drug self-administration and conditioning. In H. Steinberg (Ed.), *The Scientific Basis of Drug Dependence.* London: J .& A. Churchill, 1969.

Wikler, A. Some implications of conditioning theory for problems of drug abuse. *Behavioral Science,* 1971, **16,** 92–97.

Wikler, A., and Pescor, F. T. Classical conditioning of a morphine-abstinence phenomenon, reinforcement of opoid-drinking behavior and "relapse" in morphine-addicted rats. *Psychopharmacolgia (Berlin),* 1967, **10,** 255–284.

Wikler, A., and Pescor, F. T. Persistence of "relapse-tendencies" of rats previously made physically dependent on morphine. *Psychopharmacologia (Berlin),* 1970, **16,** 375–384.

# 22 USE OF BEHAVIOR MODIFICATION IN THE REDUCTION OF ALCOHOL-RELATED ROAD ACCIDENTS

S. H. Lovibond

It is a truism that road accidents result from a multiplicity of influences that impinge at the point of interaction between the driver, his vehicle, and the road environment. It is also a truism that the influences that may be specified separately vary greatly in importance, and in the extent to which they are available for practical modification. Thus, a factor or influence may be important in the sense that its elimination or modification would change the system to the point of a dramatic reduction in the road toll, and yet it may, for all practical purposes, be essentially unmodifiable. Again, the unmodifiability of a factor may result from un-availability of the technological means of modification; the prohibitive cost of the required program of modification; or the lack of acceptance by the majority of drivers of the required changes.

It is clear that the highest priority should be allocated to programs directed toward modification of the effects of factors in the high/high quadrant, that is, those factors that are of crucial significance in deter-mining the road toll, and that can be modified with the technological means of finance at our disposal in a manner acceptable to the public. It will be argued that the excessive ingestion of alcohol by drivers prior to driving is one factor in road accidents that clearly belongs in the high/high quadrant.

### The Problem of the Drinking Driver

In most motorized communities, recognition that alcohol is involved in at least 50% of serious road crashes has resulted in legislation making it an offense to operate a motor vehicle with a blood alcohol concentration (BAC) above a specified value (most commonly .08% or 80 mg/ 100 ml). Typically a detection system based on the use of breath or blood analysis is supported by a system of penalities including license suspension, fines, and jail sentences. It is now widely recognized that Breathalyzer and blood-analysis legislation has failed to reduce significantly the incidence of alcohol-related crashes. Nevertheless, such legislation has permitted a much more adequate definition of the problem. It is now apparent that the BACs of many drinking drivers who come under police notice are extraordinarily high. In New South Wales, some 12,000 drivers are prosecuted annually under the Breathalyzer legislation. The average BAC of these drivers is of the order of .15%. Australian experience generally suggests that two major groups of drinking drivers may be distinguished: (1) males, aged 35–50 years, very many of whom are alcoholics, and who frequently drive after consuming sufficient alcohol to give Breathalyzer readings in the range of .25–.35%; and (2) young males, aged 18–25 years, who drink excessively and habitually, and who frequently drive after ingesting alcohol sufficient to give Breathalyzer readings in the range .10–.20%.

The ineffectiveness of statutory penalties for drinking–driving has led to suggestions that convicted drivers should be deprived of their driving licenses until they can produce evidence that they do not have a drinking problem or that they have successfully undergone treatment. The attractiveness of such a program is diminished by the complete absence of a method of medical treatment appropriate to the task. The conventional medical approach to the problem of excessive drinking is based on two major assumptions: (1) that excessive drinking is a symptom of a disease called alcoholism; and (2) that the only conceivable goal of treatment is total abstinence.

The concept of alcoholism as a disease has had a number of unfortunate effects, which become particularly apparent when one is faced with the problem of the young drinking driver. In particular, abnormal drinking has become associated in the public mind with the presence of identifiable medical symptoms and skid-row forms of social disarticulation. As a consequence, grossly excessive drinking in the absence of specific symptoms of alcoholism has been accepted as "normal" by the drinker himself and by the general community. The second assumption, that the only conceivable goal of treatment is total abstinence is justifiable in the case of persons whose health is immediately threatened by further ingestion of alcohol. On the other hand, total abstinence is likely to prove an unacceptable and unnecessary treatment goal in the case of the young drinking driver.

What is the alternative? A viable alternative to conventional methods of dealing with excessive consumption of alcohol can be derived from the principles of modern experimental psychology, particularly that branch which is concerned with behavior modification. The essentials of such an alternative approach are as follows:

1. Although excessive consumption of alcohol eventually produces medical symptoms, it is, in essence, a behavioral problem.
2. Excessive drinking, like any other behavior, can be modified.
3. As in the case of any other behavior, criteria of acceptable and unacceptable drinking behavior may be defined in terms of frequency and/or degree.
4. The goal of modification programs should be to reduce drinking to levels that are not ordinarily associated with high risks to health and social competence.

## Modification of Drinking Behavior

The principles outlined have been put into practice in the Behavior Modification Center, School of Applied Psychology, University of New South Wales. Over the past 3 years the Center has developed a program designed to modify rather than totally eliminate the drinking behavior of drinking drivers referred by the courts (Lovibond and Caddy, 1970; Lovibond, Caddy, and Cross, in press). From the outset the disease or illness concept of alcoholism is implicitly rejected, and at all times the subject is treated as an essentially normal person who has a particular behavior problem to overcome. In keeping with this attitude, the responsibility of the patient as an active participant in the program of behavioral change is stressed at all times.

The relationship with the subject is a training relationship in which the subject is helped to learn new skills. He is told the precise nature of the training procedures to be used, the precise goals of training, and the objective probability of achieving the required outcome.

The subject is encouraged to recognize that when he comes to the Center, he is unable to make decisions about his alcohol intake, but that the ultimate goal of training is to bring his drinking behavior under his own control.

The training program includes three major components: discriminated aversive conditioning, training in self-regulation, and education relating to the effects of alcohol (including its effects on driving behavior). Incidental counseling relating to general psychological and social problems is also provided. Discriminated aversive conditioning involves training the subject to discriminate his own BAC, and then rendering drinking aversive only if the BAC is over .05%. In order to assist the subject's efforts at self-control, he is first trained to assess his drinking behavior and its consequences in a more objective manner. As part of this process the subject is required to keep detailed records of his drinking, including estimates of the BAC reached. In addition the subject is taught the elements of behavioral principles, and is required to participate in his own program of behavior modification by manipulating the variables controlling his behavior, that is, the discriminative stimuli and reinforcing events. For example, he is taught to change his drinking environment so that excessive drinking is not as easily stimulated and maintained, and he is taught to interrupt a drinking sequence by substituting another behavior with positively reinforcing consequences.

The total program usually requires 8–10 weekly visits of 2–2½ hours duration. At present all training is given individually, but many components of the program lend themselves to group administration.

## Method

### SUBJECTS

To date, 29 male drinking drivers have completed a behavioral modification program following court referral. Subjects were told that the Center had no legal connection with the courts, but a report of training undertaken would be furnished to the magistrate dealing with the case. Matched control subjects who had not undergone training were available for comparison. Matching criteria were age, marital status, occupation, BAC at time of arrest, and number of drinking–driving convictions. The age range of the subjects was 19–66 years. Almost all subjects were in unskilled, skilled, or clerical occupations. The median BAC revealed by breath analysis following arrest was .18% (range .11–.35%). Median weekly alcohol intake in ounces of beer equivalent was 380 for the controls and 400 for the treatment group. Twenty-two of the training subjects had had previous drinking/driving convictions. Sixteen had had one previous conviction; five had had two convictions; and one had had three convictions.

By comparison with the total population of drivers convicted under the Breathalyzer legislation in New South Wales between 1968 and 1971, the sample undergoing training had a similar age range, a slightly higher BAC on arrest (median .18 cf. .16), a somewhat less favorable socioeconomic background (more unskilled workers), and a much higher frequency of prior convictions (81% cf. 25%).

## Assessment

The drinking behavior of training-group subjects prior to arrest was assessed by means of a comprehensive questionnaire completed in the presence of an associate, usually a family member. Follow-up assessments were made 1 to 9 months after the completion of training. Each individual was interviewed twice in his own home at intervals of approximately 6 weeks. In all cases interviews were conducted in the presence of one or more family members. Control subjects were interviewed in a similar fashion, with the addition that prearrest drinking history was obtained in the interview. Particular emphasis was placed on establishing current drinking patterns with the collaboration of family members. Nine matched control subjects refused to cooperate and were replaced.

Training was conducted by two graduate research assistants who had had prior experience of the treatment of alcoholics by similar methods. Follow-up was carried out by two graduate assistants who had not participated in the training program. The assistants were each assigned a number of cases and worked individually to complete the follow-up interviews.

## Treatment of Results

The current drinking patterns of all subjects were assessed at follow-up in terms of the following three categories:

Complete success: drinking in controlled fashion, exceeding .05% only rarely.

Considerably improved: drinking less, but exceeding .05% once or twice per week.

Slight or no improvement: drinking as much as pretreatment or only slightly less.

## RESULTS

Table 22.1 presents a comparison of the drinking patterns of all subjects at follow-up expressed in frequency of category allocation.

The outcome of training in the case of the young subjects is highly satisfactory, only two subjects failing to meet the criteria of complete success. On the other hand, six of the eight young controls had not changed their drinking patterns following their court appearance. The difference between the drinking behavior of training subjects and controls at follow-up is clearly significant (Exact Test $p < .01$).

The response of the older members of the training group is relatively poor, and compares unfavorably with the response obtained from alcoholics who voluntarily underwent a related program in the earlier studies of Lovibond and Caddy (1970) and Lovibond *et al., in press).

The control subjects in the older age group were quite unresponsive to the pressure exerted by arrest and court proceedings, none of the eight subjects having reduced his alcohol intake significantly as a consequence. Despite their relatively poor response, the 33–66-year-old subjects were significantly improved by comparison with the controls (Exact Test $p < .01$).

It is apparent that the method produces very favorable results in young drinking drivers and, although long-term follow-up is obviously required, it is significant that to date there is less evidence of loss of training gains than in the alcoholics who have undergone similar procedures

**TABLE 22.1**

TRAINING RESPONSE OF DRINKING DRIVERS AND CONTROLS IN IMPROVEMENT CATEGORIES

| Group | | Category | | |
|-------|--|-------------------|-------------------------|--------------------------|
| | | Complete success | Considerably improved | Slight/no improvement |
| 19–32 years | Training | 11 | 2 | 0 |
| | Control | 1 | 1 | 6 |
| 33–66 years | Training | 5 | 5 | 4 |
| | Control | 0 | 0 | 8 |

(Lovibond *et al.,* in press). It would appear that attempts to modify the drinking behavior of older drinking drivers are likely to prove much less rewarding. Given that young men up to 25 years of age are disproportionately represented in the population of apprehended drinking drivers, it seems reasonable to concentrate behavior modification on these young persons.

It should be noted that although aversive conditioning formed part of the training procedure described in the preceding, evidence from another study (Lovibond *et al.,* in press) indicates that considerable success can be achieved in the absence of aversive conditioning.

## Conclusions and Recommendations

The experience of the New South Wales University Behavior Modification Center to date suggests the following conclusions and recommendations:

1. The present statutory penalties for drinking–driving have virtually no effect on the drinking behavior of offenders in the 35–50 age group, and cause only a small number of young offenders to resist their alcohol intake.

2. Although the suspension of an offender's driving license produces little change in drinking behavior, the threat of license suspension is a very effective motivating force in a program of behavioral change.

3. It is possible to modify the drinking behavior of most young drinking drivers, using the methods of modern experimental psychology, if they are referred for training by the courts. Older drinking drivers offer less favorable prospects for behavior modification.

4. Because of the critical role of alcohol in our present high road toll, legislative action should be taken to provide a system of court referral of drinking drivers to behavior assessment and modification centers.

5. Behavior assessment and modification centers should be established under the control of psychologists trained in the principles and techniques of modern behavior modification.

6. The centers should be physically and administratively separate from hospital and psychiatric services. (Administration by departments of motor transport is suggested.)

7. The goal of behavior modification programs, other than in special cases, should be moderation of drinking rather than total abstinence.

8. Males aged 18–25 years with BACs of .15% or higher should be

selected as the initial target group. License suspension and referral of target subjects to the behavior assessment and modification centers should be automatic, unless the subject chooses to be dealt with by the court. Restoration of the offender's driving license should be effected by the appropriate authorities on receipt of evidence that an offender (a) is not an excessive drinker, or (b) has successfully undergone a program of behavior modification designed to moderate his drinking.

9. The total cost of the behavior modification program should be borne by the offender himself. The desire to continue driving is so powerful in the target group (18–25-year-old males) that the majority would opt for training and meet the cost (est. $200) rather than suffer license suspension.

10. The general public is now sufficiently aware of the seriousness of the drinking–driving problem to support the legislative action envisaged.

11. To the extent that programs designed to moderate the drinking behavior of young drinking drivers are successful, they should contribute not only to a reduction of the road toll, but to a reduction of the future population of chronic alcoholics.

## References

Lovibond, S. H., and Caddy, G. Discriminated aversive control in the moderation of alcoholics' drinking behavior. *Behavior Therapy,* 1970, **1,** 437–444.

Lovibond, S. H., Caddy, G., and Cross, M. Self-regulation and discriminated aversive conditioning in the modification of alcoholics' drinking behavior. *Behavior Therapy. (In press.)*

# VII THEORETICAL AND ETHICAL ISSUES

# 23 ENVIRONMENTAL DESIGN: REALITIES AND DELUSIONS[1]

**Arthur D. Colman**

The field of environmental design, particularly the study of the environment–behavior interface, has recently gained some prominence in the academic arena, spurred notably by the mass media. As usual, more questions are asked than answered. Can the designer of our environment become more conscious and self-determining? If so, to what goals should the design point without creating an overplanned society? When and if goals can be agreed upon by the user population, what kinds of models exist for translating these goals into physical and social realities that will support them?

The purpose of this chapter is to explore the usefulness of operant–conditioning concepts in the field of environmental design. To do this, I will attempt to (1) redefine the field of environmental design so that its behavioral effects and implications are clarified, (2) review the uses of operant conditioning as a design model for a variety of sociophysical systems, (3) explore the inadequacies of this model at its current stage of development, particularly in relationship to the problems of scale and intergroup processes, and (4) suggest some future directions for research by operant conditioners and others in the fields of behavioral sciences relating to the problem of environmental design.

[1] First published in Arthur D. Colman and W. Harold Bexton, Eds., *Group Relations Reader*. Berkeley, Calif.: GREX, 1975.

## The Field of Environmental Design

The concept of environmental design—in fact, the word "design" itself—is most often associated with the rearrangement of physical elements in ways that serve an aesthetic or functional purpose. Yet the concept of design is considerably broader. Webster defines it as "the deliberate and purposeful planning of a settled and coherent program for selection of a means and contriving the elements, steps and procedures which will adequately satisfy some need" (*Webster's,* 1965). Obviously such a definition applies to a broad range of situations, including the design of a sophisticated treatment environment for psychotic, retarded, or autistic individuals, the structuring of superior learning environments for graduate students, the design of a playroom in a suburban cottage, and the design of highrise apartment living complex.

The word "environment" is equally restrictive in its current usage. Environment tends to be thought of as land, ocean, water—the external nonliving envelope that encloses our lives and our behavior. In this view, man is seen as external to his environment, except insofar as his tools and waste products add to its dimensions. Such a dichotomy is perceptively false. Recent work has introduced into the vocabulary of the behavioral sciences the term *social space,* a concept that suggests the possibility of a useful comparison between the physical and social dimensions of our perceptual reality. The work of Hall (1966) and Sommer (1969) in the use of space in everyday behavior, and Calhoun (1966) and DeLauwe (1965) on the psychopathology of crowding, to mention some of the more prominent workers in this area, have begun to define a new field. Moreover, human forms are a palapable part of our living space, possibily the most critical "environment" in citified living. Architects are belatedly discovering, for example, that aesthetically pleasing sketches of buildings devoid of human figures bear little relationship to the way that same building looks and functions when it is filled with the people for whom it was built. Once people occupy those empty courtyards, offices, and hallways, the entire environment changes. The interactional chain between the physical and social elements of our environment is extremely complex. The physical shell constrains the type of social structures that may evolve, just as the social structure will in turn affect the social interactions within this space, which will in turn affect further informal and formal modifications of the physical space. A consideration of these complexities is making architects and designers more and more aware that in order to succeed in structuring aesthetically pleasing and operatively useful environments, they must consider both the human and nonhuman elements.

The thin line between the human and nonhuman elements in an environment and their interactive effects on human behavior is exaggerated by some of the autistic children described by Bettleheim (1950), who think of themselves as machines and often relate more comfortably with machines than with people. Colby's (1968) reports of successful use of a "computer therapist" with these children is a logical extension of this aspect of their psychology. Actually, the differentiation between our reaction to "thing" and "person" is becoming increasingly blurred as a function of recent innovations in communication technology. It is only necessary to compare the relevant efficiency of emergency television repair services with medical emergency services to appreciate the intensity that television images have for all of us, especially our children. The more interactive mode that cable TV will soon introduce into our homes will surely increase this relationship. As Sidney Jourard (1971) points out in his book, *The Transparent Self,* the exploration of outer space has been our greatest stimulus to the exploration of inner space. Those of us who have recently lived through the great oil spills in Santa Barbara and San Francisco Bay, or other ecological tragedies, will have personal knowledge of the vast emotional impact of nonhuman environmental catastrophies on our personal selves. In fact, the ecology movement and its apparent interest in the preservation of the nonhuman environment seems to have become a vehicle for the expression of humanistic concern for the individual's psychological survival.

A functional definition of "environmental design" is necessarily changed by the broader reinterpretation of both design and environment sketched above. A more useful definition of environmental design would relate the planning of a coherent program and set of procedures to effect the total human and nonhuman environment in ways that increase the probability that certain goals or "needs" will be achieved. The goal of environmental design would relate to social behavior, such as planning an educational or therapeutic system, as much as to aesthetics such as constructing an awe-inspiring church. Input into environmental design problems must then include knowledge related to modifying human behavior and social systems as well as structural information from engineering or perceptual psychology. The field would expand toward a new view of man, always powerfully effected by his physical and social environment, now actively developing an environmental design model and methodology that would place the effect of the total environment on his behavior more in his own control, and the responsibility for the design and control of the environment of his behavior, in himself.

Such a new definition was predicted and placed in evolutionary perspective by Julian Huxley (1958) in the Arden House Conference on Behavior and Evolution. He said there:

> We are now beginning to see the whole development of man as a unitary process of evolution, and man is the agency by which that process is becoming self-conscious and could become *consciously purposeful*. Evolutionary progress, both in the biological and the human sector, is now seen as a fact that is occurring only rarely and by no means inevitably. We may say that cultural evolution, i.e., evolution in a psycho-social phase, can now be seen as an extension of biological evolution with its own peculiarities of methods and results.

In Huxley's view, evolution seems to have moved toward creating more self-conscious beings—man being the latest product. The inevitable result is that man, with knowledge of his purposes, will now begin to think of how to change his own behavioral development by *designing his environment,* including his own processes and himself. The entire field of organ transplantation, genetic manipulation, and even behavior modification is directly anchored into this evolutionary drama.

## Operant Conditioning as an Environmental Design Model

Certainly these ideas are hardly new to those of us who, as behavioral scientists, have worked in analyzing, planning, and structuring the physical and social space in an effort to control contingencies that modify behavior in predictable directions. The writings of B. F. Skinner (1948, 1971), from *Walden Two* to *Beyond Freedom and Dignity,* particularly the chapter in the latter entitled "The Design of a Culture," have clearly reflected this broader definition of environmental design. The development of the operant test environment, popularly known as "the Skinner box," is an excellent illustration of a purposefully designed environment whose goal is to affect behavior. Using the technology of operant conditioning, the experimenter can design an enclosure that contains specific functional design elements, such as levers operating food, water, and electric shock dispensers, an assortment of lights with superimposed geometrical patterns, patterned and unpatterned sounds, and so on. These elements can then be preprogrammed to provide precise feedback to the responses of animal subjects. It is even possible to include other behaving animals as part of the design. For example, Colman, Liebold, and Boren (1969) and Colman and Boren (1969) showed that in certain monkey pairs, feeding a familiar hungry monkey could be used as a reinforcer. Rice and Gainer (1962) and Masserman, Wechkin, and Terris (1964) have shown that certain monkeys will work harder to prevent another monkey from being punished. In a sense the operant conditioner began to learn how to design simple environments, including both the physical and social elements, that would support specific predictable behavior in the animal experimental situation.

In the last decade, operant principles have been systematically applied to a wide variety of human situations in an effort to both modify behavioral pathology and enhance adaptive learning. At first the designs were adapted directly from the laboratory to single individuals with specific problems of behavior, such as stuttering, self-mutilatory behavior in autistic children, poor toilet control in retardates, and psychotic and chronic schizophrenic individuals (1965). Interpersonal reinforcements such as praise, attention, and affection were added to the armamentarian of reinforcing stimuli to design environments appropriate to extinguishing maladaptive patterns and supporting the behavioral goals. In general, these systems were extremely successful and have challenged more traditional therapeutic modalities to include the operant approaches in standard treatment programs around the country. However, this direct translation of laboratory procedures was limited to single subjects in specialized, quasilaboratory settings and did not affect the larger social networks that, if unchanged, continue to reinforce the maladaptive behaviors and fail to support the new learning.

Ayllon and Azrin (1965) introduced the token-economy concept that has played a critical role in translating operant design principles to technical procedures for redesign of the indigenous environments of hospital wards, nurseries, schools, colleges, and communities, in a manner capable of supporting a variety of behavioral goals for specific individual and group needs. Their idea was to pay the patient or student in artificial currency for specified behaviors. The tokens were then exchangeable for goods and privileges within a specifiable environment. Tokens, like money, became a generalized reinforcer linked to the individual's own preference in his environment. This system allowed the professional with authority in a social system (psychiatrist or psychologist on a treatment ward, teacher in a school room, etc.) to decide, in conjunction with his staff, which behaviors were appropriate for each individual, and link them to reinforcers available within the environment. Specific behavioral plans could be linked to general reinforcement systems as easily as more general group-behavioral goals. The economic structure of the ward could be modified to reflect the changing value system. In addition, the token economy provided an easily available direct measure of behavior in the environment—both of goal-directed behaviors supported by the reinforcement system and the informal behaviors shown through choices of reinforcers. In other words, the token economy provided a technology that allowed comprehensive design of an environment geared to modification of behavior for groups of individuals, according to preset therapeutic goals, together with the feedback of information from that environment so that it could be continuously redesigned to better approximate the behavioral goals.

The token economies sought to expand the actual design potential of the model beyond the limited experimental situations for either animals or humans. It included the complexities of a hospital ward, school room, or even a hospital or school. By fading the stimulus systems and shifting to more variable or long-term reinforcement schedules from one environment to another (for example, from a chronic hospital ward of a state hospital to a half-way house in the community), techniques could be developed for extending its effects beyond these boundaries into more complex interenvironment and intergroup relationships.

As large-scale and more complex environments were utilized by the behavior modification programs, environmental design in both a physical and a social sense became more of a practical reality. For example, Harold Cohen, a designer by profession, developed the CASE project at a juvenile federal prison in Washington, D.C., which brilliantly synthesized a token economy and physical design principles for a rehabilitation program aimed at improving the social adjustment of the prisoners when released (Cohen, Tilepczak, and Bis, 1966). Academic behaviors were reinforced by a judicious combination of tokens, social reinforcements, and constantly changing colors and forms in the living and study environments. Cohen's response to disciplinary problems varied from increasing prices to differential praise of the inmates with better behavior to redesigning the shape and hue of the study cubicles.

It seems clear that operant-conditioning concepts and their technical derivatives such as the token economy are an extremely relevant area to apply to environmental design, particularly those design problems in which the modification of social behavior is of major concern. That is one of the realities in the field of environmental design today. Having said this, it is time to turn to the limitations of the model and tempting illusions, even delusions, that its current vogue may present to its burgeoning practitioners.

## Limitations of Operant Conditions as an Environmental Design Model

I shall use my own work as a basis for discussing some of the problems and limitations of operant conditioning as an environmental design model. In 1966 I developed a point-economy program designed to change the behavior of severely limited delinquent soldiers for whom the traditional therapeutic milieu mode had failed miserably (Colman and Baker, 1969). The program, described briefly in the following, was an overall success as far as our stated goals were concerned. More than two-thirds of the experimental group received an honorable discharge at least 9 months after return to duty. Less than one-third were in a stockade, AWOL, or dishonorably or administratively discharged after 9 months. In the comparison group that had received conventional hospital treatment, the figures were reversed. Less than one-third of the men were in the success category and more than two-thirds were in the failure category. In addition, behavioral measures within the ward—such as absences, suicide attempts, and psychotic episodes—positive performance in educational tests, and so on, were all dramatically improved over the previous ward. However, despite the utility of the point system and other operant techniques in this program, many of the design problems faced in setting up and operating the ward were of the type for which the operant model provided little understanding or practical help.

The work was done at Walter Reed General Hospital. The subjects were soldiers who entered the hospital diagnosed as "character disorders"; that is, they were not psychotic but were felt to need some kind of treatment or rehabilitation. As a group they were little different from the Army stockade population between 1966 and 1969. These men were not Vietnam dissenters; on the contrary, they were eager to fight "the enemy" but had difficulty handling even the most routine Army assignments, were unpopular with peers, had recurrent fights, and made manipulative suicide gestures and other upsetting behaviors in order to avoid or escape from the more unpleasant aspects of Army and stockade life. Typically these men had enlisted in the Army following difficulty with a court, school, or their family.

Our basic assumptions were that these men had failed in both civilian and military life because of behavioral repertoires that provided inadequate reinforcement when operating legally in social situations. Our curriculum offered opportunities for training in education, occupational, and "group skills" that we felt would be applicable to their usual social and work situations. Details of the treatment program have been given elsewhere (Colman, 1971). Pertinent to this paper is the way in which operant principles were used as a design model for a treatment environment to serve these men's needs. One evening, Doctors Israel Goldiamond and John Boren, the ward's sergeant, David Collins, psychiatric resident James Rumbaugh, who was trained in operant–conditioning principles, and I sat down and designed the framework of a ward that has continued for more than 6 years. We identified the *treatment goals,* the *behavioral requirements* necessary to achieve these goals, and the *social and institutional reinforcement system,* and designed a *measurement system* capable of providing internal and external feedback on the ward's success rate. Educational opportunities and events such as classes, behavioral contracts, tutoring, and so on were linked by a point economy to the ward institutional reinforcers such as TV passes and special classes. We planned the room arrangement, the dress, the posting of signs, the activity schedules; in essence we attempted to design the total environment based on the operant technology.

Designing a point economy based on the institutional reinforcers and the relevant educational program was an important step in changing the environment of the men and modifying their behavior in constructive directions in relation to the goals of the ward. However, designing the *social* reinforcement system to achieve similar ends was considerably more difficult, particularly since analysis of this group of men suggested that the preeminent social reinforcer was approval from their own peer group. This meant that within their value system, the discriminative stimuli for reinforcement within this group had somehow to be changed in order for the program to run at all. One approach to this problem was the development of a *phase two* program, which offered certain men who had functioned well on the ward for 10 weeks access to most of the ward's reinforcers without the use of points in return for their performing general leadership duties such as teaching courses, running the unit at night, and supervising the work program. In other words, leadership within the peer group was offered as a reinforcer to those men who learned behavior appropriate to the ward's goals. By this means, potential "antileaders" within the group were converted to leaders supporting the ward's goals, and their informal social behaviors were thereby placed in the service of the treatment program. Since leadership skills and improved methods for handling authority were among the key required behaviors of the program, becoming a *phase two* member also had learning value aside from this critical restructuring of peer reinforcements.

It is possible now in retrospect to describe the restructuring of peer-group values in operant language. What I want to emphasize here is that except for the most general formulation of the problem we faced, operant concepts and technology were of little use in developing this part of the treatment program. What is at issue is the difference between operant conditioning as an analytic and descriptive system versus operant conditioning as a design model. The analytic system requires only the most general application of operant concepts to an ongoing series of interactions. However, the design model requires a much higher degree of specificity, resting as it does on the availability of a carefully worked-out technology based on experimentation. There was simply no applicable technology that we could apply to the complex issues involved in reshaping the value system of this group of men. It required the sergeant's grasp of the military culture together with an understanding of a complex operation of a late-adolescent group to provide the framework necessary to develop a workable *phase two* program. Clearly, further study of leadership of group functioning from an operant point of view would be of value in the future program of this kind. Our own work on the ward was a contribution in this direction. However, at the time the ward was designed, the research in the field was too general and simplified to be of much practical value, and the same information deficit exists today.

Let me provide what I hope is an even more telling example of the present limitations of the operant model. As difficult as it was to gain control of the authority hierarchy of the delinquent peer group, staff did have control of contingencies important to the patient group. However, even as a leader of the ward in an authoritarian Army hospital structure, I had considerably less control over my own staff. The realities of the Army personnel structure did not allow manipulation of the staff's institutional rewards (pay, time off, discipline, etc.) as a function of how well they performed in their task, except in the case of the most blatant wrongdoing or superb positive effort. Furthermore, the staff represented several different professional and nonprofessional disciplines within the hospital, each with their own values and preferred behavior and each with their own sentient group. In other words, although the ward staff made up a group of which I was the leader, all the staff except the psychiatric residents also belonged to other groups with a different chain of command. This meant that my control of the staff—and the crux of the success of the program rested on that control—could not be based on an institutional reinforcement structure using pay, time off, or promotion. Rather I had to rely on "softer" consequences such as educational opportunities, commitment to the treatment staff, *esprit,* or rapport, in order to develop appropriate behavior and discriminations in staff interactions with patients. It was also necessary to become involved in the politics of the hospital and even at times in the politics of the other parts of the Army system to make sure that my goals with the staff were not actively opposed by reinforcement systems outside my immediate control.

It would be fair criticism at this point to suggest that without stronger control over staff, behavior modification programs should not have been begun. Unfortunately, except for those lucky individuals who can staff their programs with graduate students whose reward structure is singularly well tied to graduate department politics, the luxury of a committed and controllable staff is very rare indeed. For example, in hospitals it is almost always true that the nursing administration controls more of the rewards of the nurses and aides working on the treatment ward than does the head of that ward. The same rewards on which we base our token-economy program with such success are exactly those rewards that are particularly subject to organizational influences such as bargaining, pressure groups, and unions. This means that the head of the treatment program must almost always work through a large social system, beyond the boundaries of the ward, and therefore beyond his immediate authority and control, if the program is to succeed.

In 1968 I spent 3 weeks observing some 20 of the best-known behavior modification programs across the country. I was particularly interested in what factors led to (1) successful outcome for patients or students and (2) survival of the project itself. In almost all cases the internal design, that is, the operant techniques used to control patient behavior, was well thought out and workable. The design of individual behavior plans or token economies was rarely the critical factor in either outcome or survival. We seem to have considerable design competence in that area. What distinguished successful and long-lived programs from less successful and short-lived ones was the extent to which the program leader had taken into account the social and physical boundary relationships between the treatment ward and the surrounding environment, to what extent the program leader had been effective in dealing with factors such as the ward's relationship with other wards in that particular institution, the relationship between critical personnel on the ward and their professional peers in nearby environments, the program leader's relationship with other program leaders and with his administrative superior. For example, I visited a ward that had functioned effectively according to sophisticated operant principles but that was soon to close because no patients were being referred to it. This was blamed on the threat that the ward's success with difficult patients presented to the other, more conventional treatment programs in the hospital. Another excellent program was closing because of some well-meaning but uninformed protest about the use of punishment. Not unexpectedly, the protest was inspired by local treating professionals in the community. A nursery school program was on the rocks because the school board was holding up its accreditation on the advice of "prominent" mental health consultants. In yet another program the staff refused to carry out an operant design for which they had been trained for 3 months previously because their supervisor refused to count their training towards a status pay raise and because the education team had given special status to those who worked with the operant principles best irrespective of previous hierarchical differences based on experience and time on the job. On the other hand, many programs were working because effective relationships had been forged with administrators, peer professionals, staff, and the community. What was most dramatic to me was the extent to which these factors were almost treated as "design" issues, that is, variables capable of analysis and control. Rather they were thought of as serendipitous happenings subsumed under demeaning terms such as "politics" or "administrative crap." I began to wonder whether these larger system boundary issues were not in fact critically important program design issues. If they were, then their exclusion in design schema was probably not simply an oversight but more likely a tacit admission that the operant principles were not yet a relevant technology to utilize in their analysis or manipulation. Alternatively, as Thompson and Grabowski (1972) have suggested, hospital systems designers rarely have sufficient control over contingencies or consequences to carry out an operant analysis of a social system as complex as an entire hospital or portion of such an institution.

It is clear to me now that insofar as these administrative and political factors in part determine success or failure of the program's outcome, they are relevant independent variables and must be included in the design model. Yet there are almost no studies of how to work with these variables from the operant perspective. Descriptions of utopias in which goals, behavior, and reinforcement are logically related to one another will not help to bring this about and, until our studies can demonstrate otherwise, there is always the possibility that interrelating human groups do not operate according to our rules.

If we were to conceptualize our operant concepts and behavior modification techniques as important but limited input into complex environmental design situations, I believe we would have better perspective into the relevant variables affecting the success and failure of our program. In the laboratory, this perspective is not as necessary because that is one institution designed precisely to allow small and carefully delimited design projects or experiments to proceed under a high degree of control. Even this utopian vision of the experimental situation is breaking down in the face of an omnivorous and intrusive media and the increasing politicalization of the scientific enterprise. Once we remove ourselves from the laboratory, our technical skill will become a relatively small factor in our effectiveness compared to covert and overt intergroup variables.

For the past 2 years I have been working in the School of Environmental Design at the University of California in Berkeley. My initial reason for this association was that in many areas of my work, particularly in the ward design project, I was in fact acting as an architect and designer of social systems. Yet I had little expertise in the design process except for my intuition and my knowledge of operant conditioning and of other relevant behavioral sciences. Working with a concentration of professional architects, city and regional planners, public health and public policy planners has made me painfully aware that the behavioral sciences as a group have almost no expertise and even less real experience in the field of design. Except for the design of experiments in the laboratory, most of us will be lucky indeed to take part in the design of a few programs of limited scope. This must be contrasted with the above professionals, who spend their lifetimes designing and planning physical and social systems, spanning microscopic to macroscopic scales. There is much to be learned from them about the effects and interactions and physical factors with social forces and group and individual behaviors. What has been most striking to me is that despite their fund of expertise in working with large-scale, complex social and physical systems, their critical problem is similar to ours, that is, the disparity between technological capability and know-how and their limited knowledge in preventing this technology from being blunted and subverted by the very systems they serve. The parallel of this group with the operant conditioners is very striking. Designers have skills that now enable them to translate the most fanciful designs into realities of steel, plastic, and glass. They are becoming more aware of the importance of ascertaining these requirements in programs and the need for building in behavioral as well as aesthetic goals in the final design. Yet they find themselves frustrated by the political and social institutions with which they must work in order to implement their ideas. Because the physical environment—buildings, space, and territory—is so often equated with personal and political power by human groups, their problems in this regard are considerably more serious than our own. They often end up designing structures that fit the irrational or impractical needs of boards of directors or community power groups rather than the needs of the people who will use and be most affected by the buildings. Behavior modifiers need be less involved by such influences, since hospitals for the chronically ill and schools for the socially deprived are hardly symbols of power compared to a new 50-story high rise in the financial district of New York, San Francisco, or Dallas. When faced with the eroding effects of these intergroup forces on our program, most of us can simply retreat to the laboratory and search for more controlled, smaller-scaled settings in which to work.

It is at this point of retreat that the construction of macroscopic design models for entire cultures is most satisfying. Even in these utopian delusions, we have much in common with other designers. For example, Solari, a disciple of Frank Lloyd Wright, is working on new physical models for cities of incredibly high densities, which he feels will not only solve our population and space problem but will also somehow create a unique interactional system that will support and create a truly different type of man, a breed free of the anger, competition, and strife that current groups of men seem compulsively to reenact.

When I began working at the School of Environmental Design, I was more optimistic about the applications of the operant model into larger areas of environmental design. I soon found that although the model had some use in situations where contingencies could be reliably controlled, most design problems began in contexts in which indeterminant variables are the rule. Recently, I have begun studying the process by which complex sociophysical structures are designed, for example, a college campus and a medical care system, in the hope of isolating some of the control factors. In each case I have tried to examine the extent to which the acknowledged design model affected the outcome. Thus far I have been impressed by how unimportant the overt design model is in shaping what happened. For example, in the case of the college campus, although the architect firmly believed in the importance of student and faculty participation in the designing processes so that their needs could be adequately represented, the outcome most clearly reflected the prejudices of the planners and the administrators toward youth, intellectuals, and the educational process. Similarly, although the designers of the abortion care systems that I studied had planned their program to serve the physical and psychological needs of the women users, the final dehumanized and fragmented system that developed mirrored the providers' unspoken, but active, prejudices about the secret and shady role of the abortionist in their own past history. The process by which objective, clear design guidelines are undercut by less reasoned individual and group motives is obscure. As the scale and complexity of the environmental design situation increases, it apparently becomes more and more difficult for the primary design task to be implemented and for the other contingencies to take over.

What are the implications of these remarks for behavior modification? Some in the field may use them as a further rationale for designing only those environments where control is possible. However, as I have tried to suggest earlier in this chapter, no behavior modification is really immune from the same forces that maladaptively modify the design of a building or a medical care delivery system. We need to study and investigate in larger-scale and more complex systems, if only to develop strategies and techniques for controlling some of the covert factors that may undermine our best-designed programs. More important, if we view our discipline, as I do, as a theoretical and methodological resource for the field of environmental design, I believe we might play an important part in explicating these complexities through our own analytical model.

One approach might be to analyze methodically existing social systems using the operant model in the way that Ferster (personal communication) and Goldiamond and Dyrud (1968) have recently analyzed complex therapeutic systems. Marshall and Colman (1974) have recently begun to look at the encounter group from an operant model, not only to understand its intragroup processes, but also to study the development of satellite groups in reaction to the discontinuous stimuli and reinforcement systems at the boundary between the encounter-group culture and everyday social interactions. These kinds of analyses tend to be more difficult than studying more enclosed, controllable situations. Yet they are necessary if we are fully to test and implement the operant model in more complex environmental design issues.

## References

Ayllon, T., and Azrin, N. H. The measurement and reinforcement of behaviors of psychotics. *Journal of Experimental Analysis of Behavior,* 1965, **8**, 357–383.

Bettleheim, B. *Love Is Not Enough.* Glencoe, Ill.: The Free Press. 1950.

Calhoun, J. B. The role of space in animal sociology. *Journal of Social Issues,* 1966, **22**, 46–58.

Cohen, H. L., Tilepczak, J. A., and Bis, J. S. *Contingencies Applicable to Special Education of Delinquents.* Silver Spring, Md.: Institute of Behavioral Research Press, 1966.

Colby, K. M. Computer-ordered language development in non-speaking children. *Archives of General Psychiatry,* 1968, **19**, 641–651.

Colman, A. D. *The Planned Environment in Psychiatric Treatment. A Manual for Ward Design.* Springfield, Ill.: Thomas, 1971.

Colman, A. D., and Baker, S. L. Utilization of an operant conditioning model for the treatment of character and behavior disorders in military setting. *American Journal of Psychiatry,* 1969, **125**, 1395–1403.

Colman, A. D., and Boren, J. J. An information system for measuring patient behavior and its use by staff. *Journal of Applied Behavior Analysis,* 1969, **2**, 207–214.

Colman, A. D., Liebold, K. E., and Boren, J. A method for studying altruism in monkeys, *Psychological Record,* 1969, **19**, 401–405.

DeLauwe, C. *Des Hommes et des Villes.* Paris: Payot, 1965.

Ferster, C. B. An experimental analysis of clinical phenomena. Unpublished manuscript.

Goldiamond, I., and Dyrud, J. E. Some applications and implications of behavioral analysis for psychotherapy. *Research in Psychotherapy,* 1968, **3**, 54–89.

Hall, E. T. *The Hidden Dimension. New York.* New York: Doubleday, 1966.

Jourard, S. *The Transparent Self.* New York: Van Nostrand Reinhold, 1971.

Marshall, K. E., and Colman, A. D. Operant analysis of encounter groups. *International Journal of Group Psychotherapy,* 1974, **24,** 42–54.

Masserman, J. H., Wechkin, S., and Terris, W. Altruism in monkeys. *American Journal of Psychiatry,* 1964, **121,** 584–585.

Rice, G. E., and Gainer, P. Altruism in the albino rat. *Journal of Comparative and Physical Psychology,* 1962, **55,** 123–125.

Skinner, B. F. *Walden Two,* New York: Macmillan, 1948.

Skinner, B. F. *Beyond Freedom and Dignity.* New York: Knopf, 1971.

Sommer, R. *Personal Space,* Englewood Cliffs, N. J.: Prentice-Hall, 1969.

Thompson, T., and Grabowski, J., Eds. *Behavior Modification of the Mentally Retarded.* New York: Oxford University Press, 1972.

*Webster's Third New Dictionary,* Springfield, Ill.: Merriam, 1965.

# 24 OPERANT CONDITIONING: A GENERAL SYSTEMS APPROACH

**William S. Dockens, III**

The essential difference between *Walden Two* (Skinner, 1948) and other books dealing with utopias is that most of the philosophers, authors, and science fiction writers were dreaming, speculating, warning, or threatening, while the author of *Walden Two* made a statement, a statement he has repeated several times in different contexts. According to Skinner, it is possible for a science of human behavior to design and execute a culture that will lead to consequences far less grim than those offered to us by even the most optimistic of today's social science extrapolations. But the question now is, how do we translate statements and promises into experimental behavior? How do we translate laboratory findings into cultural forces that are constructive rather than oppressive? In short, how should a science of behavior tool itself for the delivery of better cultural alternatives?

The problems seem to center around interactions between the organisms and their environments, with survival as a first prerequisite, human behavior as the primary obstacle, and relationships between responses and events seeming to be the basic data. These relationships fall within a discipline called ecology, which is defined by its originator as "the influence of the physical and biological environment on the behavior of organisms [Ernst Haeckel, 1867]."

Man's search for knowledge in these areas had, by the late 1950s, culminated in a conglomeration of systems, theories, and operations scattered throughout a spectrum of seemingly heterogeneous, overlapping disciplines. When Leonard Duhl (Dockens, 1957–1962) conducted a series of conferences to determine if this knowledge could be assembled into a coherent form and applied to some of the major problems of large cities, the results were almost depressing enough to extinguish any social scientist who had dreams of the grand "field theory." The lack of communication, sloppy language, duplication of effort, arrogance, professional chauvanism, and overall chaos in the scientific conception of society seemed to be exceeded only by the state of the world's political situation. Indeed, social science resembled much more a model for conceptual entropy than it did a coherent discipline. This was especially true of psychiatry and psychology, and the effects were carried over to the social sciences that used either of these disciplines as a base.

Fortunately, the splintering process that was so prevalent in the social sciences was not as rampant in other disciplines. In fact, ordering systems were evolving in several areas of automation and systems engineering, mathematics, biology, communications and computer science, and cybernetics. Under the leadership of Ludwig von Bertalanffy, a theory of systems was conceived and introduced into the field of psychiatry and social science in general. This "general systems theory" is a logicomathematical discipline devoted to the unification and integration of the various systems in science.

While laying the basis for the integration of scientific approaches, von Bertalanffy has also launched a rather bitter attack against "S-R theories" (see von Bertalanffy 1967, 1969a, b). Some behavioral theories have, however, penetrated the defenses of the founding father and are considered to be part of the "general systems" approach (see Gray, Duhl, and Rizzo, 1969). By applying the principles of one of these theories (Auerswald, 1969) to behavioral analysis and several related systems, I shall attempt to show (1) that a general system can evolve from the analysis of behavior, (2) that the resulting system can be integrated with other systems so as to cover the area traditionally conceded to ecology, (3) that the resultant system, or a comparable one, is a necessary extension for the application of operant principles to the design of cultures, and (4) that such a system has been tested on a small scale and has initially been proven successful.

## Three Alternative Approaches

The mass of multidisciplinary data available in today's psychiatric clinics, along with the increasing pressures for its optimal application within the limits of existing facilities, presents both the experimenter and the clinician with four equally difficult problems: (1) collection of data, (2) interpretation of data, (3) communication between cooperating disciplines, and (4) administration of the operations necessary for application of the techniques. The approaches most often applied to these problems are the eclectic, interdisciplinary, and ecological.

Since few individual investigators are competent to collect, judge, and utilize relevant data from more than one or two related disciplines, modern information explosions have often buried would-be eclectics under a pile of data from competing and overlapping systems. As institutions become larger, populations more transient, and the demands—both linguistically and conceptually—more acute, the lack of a suitable frame of reference becomes critical. Under these conditions, the limitations of the eclectic approach become quite apparent.

The choice between interdisciplinary and ecological approaches is, however, a little more difficult than choosing between either of these and the now obsolescent eclecticism. Unlike the eclectic approach, both the interdisciplinary and the ecological approaches are capable of encompassing the full range of knowledge and data in any and all areas. The superiority of the ecological approach lies in its ability to integrate the various disciplines within a single frame of reference. Since this integration is performed through a structural analysis of the field, problems of communication so common in interdisciplinary research, as well as biases within disciplines, are more easily overcome with ecological methods.

According to Auerswald, the accumulation of data within an ecological framework is a sequential process involving the collection of information or data, the ordering of that data within a selected framework, analysis of the data, synthesis of the results into hypotheses, and the construction of a delivery plan for use of these strategies and techniques, the implementation to test its impact, which, of course, leads to the repetition of the first step and the continuation of the process. This is essentially a reformulation of our initial four problems listed earlier. Since the Auerswald formulation introduces a methodology that will prove quite beneficial, I shall now abandon my original formulation and accept both his methodology and formulation. The only modifications that I will make concern treatment of hypotheses, which I will treat according to the philosophy outlined by Sidman (1960).

## Ecology and Mental Health

An ecological approach to "mental health" immediately puts to rest many of the arguments and pseudoarguments that have wasted so many pages of book and journal space. With the risk of eliciting attack responses from some of my behavioral chauvanist friends, I accept here the formulations and definitions of a systems-oriented psychiatrist who states (Duhl, 1960):

> The results of research and observations have made it clear that man is the product of a continual learning process in which he biologically and psychologically learns to adapt to experience. In the continual process of adaptation, the basic constitution is modified by the external environment. Increasingly, the external environment is being created by man and is affecting man in innumerable ways. Clearly the etiology of disease cannot be considered to be due to single factors, but rather to the combinations and permutations of multiple factors ranging from individual biological differences, to environmental differences, and to the processes of interaction between individuals.

The organized complexity implicit in this definition is, according to Duhl, much more than the physical and social environment of the individual—it is the total internal and external series of relationships, which includes man as part of an ecological network that modifies and is modified by human behavior. Duhl (1960) goes on to offer an "operational" definition of disease:

> The normal biological, psychological, or social means of coping with the stresses of the internal and external environment becomes defined (by persons given the authority, consciously or not) as disease only when the individual or group's biological, psychological, or social survival is jeopardized and some permanent or semi-permanent damage to the psychosocial or biological functions of man occurs.

What is most impressive about Duhl's definition is that it comes as no shock to medical doctors, who recognize it as an extension of medical models that had evolved years before the 1960 date of the publication. Since few behaviorists would disagree with either Duhl's definition or the formulation, one of the immediate implications of the above is that much of the argument around so-called medical models is perpetrated by psychologists who know little about medicine or psychiatrists who have forgotten fundamentals learned during their biological studies.

In addition to giving us a common basis with psychiatrists who advocate an acceptable model for society, the Duhl formulation acknowledges the central position of learning while at the same time linking adaption, learning, the biological processes, and general ecology. An important implication that can be drawn from the ecological formulation is that learning, although central and important, must be considered within the context of a much larger, more complex, ecological field. And if the design of cultures is the goal of a science of behavior, it is important, indeed critical, that this science function in conjunction with other disciplines in this field.

The absolute distance between the rat lever or pigeon key in a Skinner box and the human ecological net is but a few inches in time and space, but the conceptual range necessary to accommodate the ecological data space with its almost limitless dimension within the same frame of reference as operant models has presented problems that at first seemed insurmountable to all but the most maniacal behavioral analyst. This is part of the reason that von Bertalanffy cited Skinner's *Verbal Behavior* as one of his references when he attacked "S–R theories" as being both conceptually and ethically inadequate to deal with human behavior within a "general systems" context (see von Bertalanffy, 1967, 1969a, b). He suggested instead the use of Gestalt methods, or even traditional analytical methods, as being better complements for his systems of differential and partial differential equations. These equations, according to von Bertalanffy and others, are a much more "humanistic" way of viewing the human being within the ecological space than the "mechanistic" S–R formulations borrowed from physiology.

Robin Gregson (Gregson, 1971) is more specific in his comparisons. He uses a dog chasing a rabbit along a wall to show the eloquence of mathematical equations and feedback systems in describing behavior. While I agree with both Gregson and von Bertalanffy as far as the superiority of mathematics as a descriptive language is concerned, I feel that both have overlooked the power of an operational, functional system. This can best be demonstrated by taking Gregson's rabbit and dog to a sophomore behaviorist, who with the aid of a tranquilizer and a shock apparatus could easily make the rabbit chase the dog. This event would, no doubt, have a low probability of occurrence in Gregson's mathematical formulations, but a skilled behaviorist could make the probability approach unity in a surprisingly short time.

Unfortunately, the problems facing mankind are not so simple, but it appears that the mechanisms governing behavior within the ecological net seem to be amenable to an extension of the analysis of behavior. In fact, the formulation of behavior in terms of learning theory leads to a convergence of concepts within the ecological net. This convergence becomes quite apparent if a structural analysis of the type advocated by Auerswald is applied to relevant portions of the field. To illustrate this point, let us begin with Bergman's (1960) formulation of a general theory of psychotherapy and show how an analysis-of-behavior approach can extend the range of Bergman's formulation into the ecological field, where it converges with the formulations in the biological and physical sciences.

## Traditional Therapies and Behavioral Formulations

Motivated by his concern with the huge gap between experimental and clinical psychologies, Bergman combined Freud's final anxiety theory, Rober's hypothesis about therapists' empathy, and Jacobson, Schultz *et al.*'s concept of physiological mechanism into a general theory of psychotherapy. He formulated his theory within the framework of learning models, with Shoben and Wolpe serving as primary sources.

According to Bergman, two conditions had to be fulfilled by a general theory of psychotherapy: (1) It should discriminate between the effective, neutral, and harmful effects of any psychotherapy, and (2) it should put psychotherapy into a comprehensive framework of general psychology. He then presents three propositions about psychopathology and three additional propositions concerning psychotherapy.

Bergman postulates two types of primary anxiety stimuli: a species-specific stimulus and an anxiety stimulus that is specific for individual organisms. In this formulation, neutral stimuli can be associated with these primary stimuli whether the latter are exteroceptive or interoceptive. Organisms are said to have behavior that can be called "avoidance," "inhibition," "symptom or anxiety" responses presenting a characteristic pattern termed the "pathological defense" of the organism. Physiological patterns that become attached to interactions between the anxiety-defense behavior and their stimuli are said to give rise to interoceptive stimuli, which in turn become attached to the behavior and achieve various degrees of autonomy. Still other physiological patterns come to function as defenses against these interoceptive stimuli. This may result in the muscular tension of flaccidity, dysfunctional breathing, and lead to the type of a behavior that affects the relationship between the organism and the environment.

Desensitization procedures (Wolpe, 1968), physiological techniques for altering physiological patterns that accompany the provoking stimuli, and removal of any and all behavior that prevents the organism from encountering the anxiety stimuli to be "counterconditioned" form the crux of the therapeutic procedures in the Bergman system.

To behavior modifiers these procedures have become common practice, but a comparison between Bergman's reformulation of more centrally oriented traditional therapies and Ullman and Krasner's (1969) recommendations for replacing and abandoning the nonlearning-theory-oriented therapies is worthy of note. If one first considers the range of variables introduced into the formulations, Ullman and Krasner's take on a much broader range that includes social intercourse, laws, schools, families, and environments, while the Bergman formulation is capable of including only a relatively limited portion of the ecological net. The number of techniques for intervention made possible by Ullman and Krasner's formulation is also considerably greater.

Of course, the traditional Freudian formulation normally includes a conceptual range that is quite comparable to the behavioral approach of Ullman and Krasner, but the operational space, like Bergman's, is severely limited and remains so despite the latter's use of both a behavioral formulation and operations space. The reason for this difference in range is due to the incorporation of the experimental analysis of behavior into the Ullman and Krasner system. The expansion of the operations and data space to include more of the ecological net can be seen by applying an ecological approach to the ecological field generated by the analysis of behavior and noting the points of convergence and area of the field covered.

## Analysis of Behavior and the Ecological Field

The experimental analysis of behavior (Skinner, 1938) employs two distinct types of conditioned reflexes (Skinner, 1935): the Pavlovian reflex (classical) and the operant. Skinner's distinction between the two was challenged by Konorski and Miller (1937), and a controversy ensued concerning the operations involved and whether one paradigm was capable of being reduced to the other. An interesting note in the controversy developed when the combined studies of Miller and Carmona (1967), Konorski (Wyrwicka, 1967), and Brown and Jenkins (1968) indicated that autonomic responses can be controlled by operant procedures and that somatic responses can be controlled by respondent procedures. Catania (1971) resolves the conflict by imposing a procedural space upon four different pairings of stimulus (S) response and (R) relationships.

Catania's procedural space is concerned with two types of events: (1) environmental events called stimuli and (2) organismic (behavioral) events called responses. He defines these events in terms of experimental operations and measurements performed on a stream of transitional states. Catania concerns himself with the specification of probabilities of transitions among events in the stream.

Given the concepts stimulus (S) and response (R), four different pairings exhaust the logical possibilities: R–R, S–R, R–S, and S–S. The procedural analysis is carried out in terms of these paired relationships, so that R–R is used to classify response units and determine their hierarchial properties, S–R units are means by which stimuli can be manipulated and behavior can therefore be controlled by the environment, R–S units are used to show how behavior can be controlled by its consequences, and S–S units represent experimental operations and properties of the environment.

A reference frame is constructed for these units assuming three dimensions:

1. The elicitation dimension, a stimulus dimension divided into aversive, neutral, and appetitive sections.
2. An R–S dimension showing the effects of responses on the environment. This dimension is divided into three sections according to whether a response increases the probability or reduces the probability of stimulus occurrence.
3. An S:R (discriminative control) dimension that shows the relationship between a discriminative stimulus, S:D, and an R:S relationship.

By superimposing the second two dimensions on the first, Catania creates a three-dimensional operational space that can serve as a classification system emphasizing continuities, similarities, and interrelationships among the procedures (see Donahoe, 1971).

In addition to serving as a rather exhaustive data and operational space, Catania's system has a dimensional property that gives it several advantages over typological classification systems, especially when scaling and measurement are desirable (see Ekman, 1951). The result is a set of continua that reduce such controversies as the Konorski–Miller (1937), Skinner (1935, 1969) argument on the distinction between Pavlovian and operant reflexes and the Skinner (1957) Chomsky (1959) debate over verbal behavior to mild misunderstandings about points on an operational continua. Important minisystems such as those of Schoenfeld, Cumming, and Hearst (1956), Sidman (1953), and Premack (1971) are also easily accommodated. And most germane to our discussion here is the fact that many ethological relations can be included as well.

The true power of Catania's formulation comes from the support it gives to the proposition that a peripheralistic, probabilistic approach can be used to analyze stimulus-response relationships without resorting to postulated entities (see Donahoe, 1971). Within this frame of reference, behavior is described and defined according to procedures that control it. This implies that given a description of a procedure and the control over the necessary variables, we have control over the behavior. The procedural space is therefore the modification space.

The consequences of modification, of course, can only be determined empirically. What we need, therefore, is a consequence space, which for the sake of modification should correspond as closely as possible to the operational space. Perhaps some modification of the Catania space can be used, since it is possible to accommodate the majority of our most important minisystems within this space. But, as of now, no such space exists. This means that until one evolves (and it appears that it will evolve within this decade), we shall have to content ourselves with judicious use of the empirically obtained minisystems that have led to the extension of the boundaries of behaviorism into the ecological net.

## Organizational and Systematizing Frameworks

Two minisystems, the "t-system" of Schoenfeld *et al.* (1956) and the "motivational system" of Premack (1971) are of special significance in the construction of a consequence space. Both of these can be accommodated within the Catania procedural space, but since Premack's system can be considered a subset of the Schoenfeld (Schoenfeld and Farmer, 1970) formulation, the former will be discussed within the framework of the latter.

Schoenfeld and Farmer (1970) divided the behavioral stream into two classes, "response" and "nonresponse," then placed both classes on a time continuum. A response within this framework is defined as "a change at some instant in the special arrangement of the organism." The context of a response is specified in terms of the duration of the period in which nonresponses occur. And contingency of a response upon reinforcement is defined as a state where the distribution in time of the response class determines the distribution in time of reinforcements. The utility of this formulation is demonstrated by the experiments of Schoenfeld and Cumming (1956, 1957), which show that by controlling the distributions and density of reinforcers in time, an experimenter can generate all of the known classes of schedules of reinforcement, plus several that have not as yet been investigated. Farmer and Schoenfeld (1966) have explored the effect of an intruded stimulus on fixed-interval schedules, and Snapper *et al.* have extended the paradigm to aversive stimuli.

Of course, the whole Schoenfeld system is dependent on the distribution of "reinforcements," which are not specifically defined. The references, however, to Ferster and Skinner (1957) lead one to assume that a reinforcer is "any event which when used in the temporal relations specified in reinforcement is found to produce the process of conditioning."

This definition is made more precise and free of paradoxes if it is qualified and quantified by making four assumptions advocated by David Premack:

1. Organisms order the discriminable events of their world on a scale of value.
2. The value that an organism assigns to a stimulus can be measured by the probability that the organism will respond to the stimuli. The probability can be estimated from the duration for which the organism responds. Durations can be compared over all stimulus and respond dimensions under constraints that reduce to the requirement that either the rate–time functions for the several responses be comparable, or the probabilities compared be momentary rather than average.
3. Value is a unitary dimension.
4. Motivational phenomena—reinforcement, punishment, contrast, arousal—all result from a common state of affairs: a difference in value.

The empirical evidence supporting these assumptions implies a relationship in which a more probable event is made contingent (see earlier definition) on a less probable event. If probability and duration do in fact have the relationship indicated by Premack's studies, then Premack's formulation performs several functions. (1) It accounts for the relativity of the reinforcement relationship (see Catania, 1971). (2) It converges with Schoenfeld's "t-system." (3) It supports Morse and Kelleher's postulates that schedule-controlled responding is a fundamental property of behavior, and that reinforcement depends not only on favorable temporal relations between behavior and effective consequences, but also on quantitative properties of the preceding behavior.

It appears that a considerable amount of work is necessary in the area of *concurrent operants* (see Catania, 1966) before the full power of behavioral relationships can be felt throughout the ecological net, but a great deal of interesting interdisciplinary convergence has occurred, much of it of structural origin.

## Convergence and Systems

Convergence among the disciplines dealing with the ecological net supplies a great deal of support for S–R relationships as central functional units of psychology. In addition to expansion of these systems throughout the field of experimental psychology (see Honig, 1966) a number of syntheses are taking place with concomitant creation of disciplines that border traditional classes; behavioral pharmacology, animal psychophysics, and behavioral genetics are just a few examples. Even von Bertalanffy's own field, zoology, has begun to contradict his attacks by converging with comparative psychology to form a new field of animal behavior (Hinde, 1970).

The convergence of S–R systems with systems of other disciplines is not, however, limited to joint adventures in the field and laboratory. It is accompanied by a change in language that is barely hinted at by the introduction of hyphenated "behavior-nouns" into areas that border ours in the ecological field. Our field has even at this point advanced to the stage where our truth values are statistically determined (Reichenbach, 1938), measurements and empirical relations have replaced concepts, and our systems have melted into the ecological field. Divisions between disciplines become arbitrary; interphase differences become a matter of structure; relationships and mathematics definitely replace prose, even in areas as basic as schedules of reinforcement (see Snapper, Knapp, and Kushner, 1970). But while our technology and language have matured rapidly, Freudians could still accuse us of extreme egotism with respect to our use of the data and information accumulated in other disciplines. This is especially true in language and small-group ecology, where anthropologist Ray L. Birdwhistle and psychologist R. Sommer have made contributions that should have a powerful influence on the development of a science of behavior.

Drawing heavily from structural and descriptive language techniques and multidisciplinary data, Birdwhistle (1971) has produced a science and notational system for the study of "kinesics." This science of "body motion–communications" is descriptive, structural, and behavioristic to a point that *no* essential differences exist between the Birdwhistle tennets and those of the experimental analysis of behavior. Even the concept of the behavioral stream is literally observed, since the analysis of film is an integral part of Birdwhistle's sampling techniques.

It appears that the behavior described by Birdwhistle's "kinegraphs" are an important class of concurrent operants (see Ferster and Skinner, 1957) which occur in conjunction with a wide variety of social behaviors, including language. Indeed, a cogent argument could be advanced to support the hypothesis that the kinesic units "kine," "kineme," and "kinemorph" may prove to be of greater fundamental value to behaviorists than the more controlled and stylized forms such as speech and writing. Techniques that utilize kinesics as analytical tools are already being applied successfully in some fields of therapy (see Scheflen, 1969). And the cross-cultural comparisons that are possible with this system can be used to give valuable information about the past history, both behavioral and genetic, of men and animals.

Another necessary extension of the behavioral paradigm concerns Sommer's (1969) studies of relations between group behavior and physical space. When these concepts of small-group ecology are combined with those of kinesics, the resulting synthesis extends the science of behavior into the region normally occupied by social psychology. Intrusions into the social areas have begun (McGinnies and Ferster, 1971), but the best efforts of S–R formulations have not as yet advanced to the point where kinesics and small-group ecology can be included within our procedural–consequential space.

## Evolution and Behavioral Ecology

It has been obvious from the beginning that the use of behavior modification without some knowledge of the ecological context in which the modified behaviors are to be maintained is flirting with disaster, Ayllon and Michael's (1959) use of psychiatric nurses as behavioral engineers was the beginning of a new era. The token economies (Ayllon and Azrin, 1968) that followed made it necessary for behaviorists to observe, classify, and reinforce behaviors within restricted environments, where relations between space and behavior as well as communication between people and systems, become important.

Extension of the procedures of observation and modification into the natural environment soon followed, and with it the primordial flow diagrams of systems and operations research (see Tharp and Wetzel, 1969). The resistance by individuals and institutions that normally accompanies any deviance from traditional patterns soon followed, as did the necessity for understanding and modifying a much broader portion of the ecological net. The size of programs has increased exponentially with the success of programs until what was originally behavioral modification on a small scale has become institutional modification on a modest scale and we are now faced with problems of administration for which systems technology (see Throne's, 1970) offers the most promising methods.

## Application of Behavioral Ecology

The jump from behavior modification on an individual basis in a restricted environment to institutional modification programs in extended environments is far from modest. We are suddenly plagued with fallacies of inference that can be disastrous if we assume that data from individual populations can be utilized unaltered for decisions involving aggregates (see Alker, 1969). Physical space is no longer simply an independent variable influencing behavior, but may become a hindrance to effective observation. Observations similar to those made by social anthropologists and ecologists become necessities rather than curiosities and baselines can turn into enigmas, the solutions to which are dependent on quantification of behavior that we heretofore have had difficulty even classifying. All of these problems can be reduced to the answer to a simple question: What is the relationship between the behavior of the organism and the environment? But the answer to this question cannot be found within the boundaries of one discipline.

## An Application of Behavioral Ecology

Amphetamine addiction became a problem for behavioral ecology when addicts and personnel began to come into sharp conflict on a semilocked ward at Ulleraker Hospital in Sweden (Gotestam, Melin, and Dockens, 1975). Since there are almost as many reasons for becoming a drug addict as there are addicts, each case had to be handled as an individual, and within the context of a budget that would allow *no* funds to be spent for expanding the modest facilities already available on the ward.

In place of traditional therapies, a modification of Cautela's "covert-conditioning" procedures (Cautela, 1971) was applied. However, physiological measurements were used to supplement patients' reports, and no mediating constructs were employed to interpret results.

Since money was not available for an Ayllon and Azrin type of token economy, a point system was instituted that utilized Premack's principle by offering freedom from the ward, private rooms, ward privileges, and so on as reinforcers for using available hospital and social rehabilitation facilities. The greatest number of points were given for undergoing "covert conditioning," attending classes on and off the ward, and any activity that (1) had a high probability of being reinforced outside of the hospital setting, and (2) had a high probability of coming into conflict with patterns of behavior associated with drug abuses.

As the patterns of mediation emerged, the administration and organization of the ward went through three stages of development, which culminated in a modification of the formal structure so that both biological and behavioral mediators could be used—without disrupting social patterns that could lead to labor crises, territorial struggles, and so on. Such techniques as using the head nurse as chief instructor for ward personnel, assigning each patient a "contact man" as a mediator, and employing a technician to monitor physiological reactions and coordinate collection of baseline data came from interactions between systems technology and behavioral procedures. Social workers also became an integral part of the ecological approach, as the major stress was placed on *teaching* the patients to utilize institutional facilities *outside* the ward and hospital environments.

Success with the above program lead to a type of security, a tendency to generalize in such a way as to assume that with "only minor modifications" the program might be applied to just about any drug problem. Our optimism was short-lived. As if some ironical program writer had added the next frame to a beginner's text, methadone patients were suddenly substituted for our amphetamine addicts, our behavior modification program was discontinued, and the staff that we had worked so painstakingly to train was left with the chaotic result. But not for long. The ward very quickly became unmanageable, and we were recalled to reinstate our modification program, a task that presented problems we could not readily have forseen.

The stimulus properties of methadone were of such a nature as to set up strikingly different behavioral patterns, which required special attention. Add to this a host of biological, ethical, social, political, and administrative problems that were only partially thought out, and you have a problem of the conceptual magnitude of the Duhl formulation mentioned above.

The specific methods and solutions to the ward problems that arose are beyond the scope of this chapter, but it can be stated without exaggeration that they required the complete range of our ecological field, plus a host of extensions that took us into sensitive areas that our operational space does not adequately equip us to handle (See Dockens, 1973). Partial and temporary solutions were achieved by expanding our net with other disciplines. However, our weaknesses in the areas of group phenomena, communications, and languages, as well as faulty relationships with other disciplines, became more than apparent!

## Conclusions

If we compare the approach used with amphetamine and morphine addicts with the approaches advocated by Bergman and Duhl, it becomes apparent that Bergman's formulation is easily subsumed and replaced by procedures from our procedural-consequence spaces. The use of the environment both as criterion and reinforcement comes quite close to Duhl's formulation of the ecological approach. And the use of physiological techniques, medical personnel, and social workers to expand our use of the ecological field is quite consistent with modern multidisciplinary approaches. Reorganization of the ward form, taking care *not* to create conflicts by unnecessarily disrupting existing social systems or brashly crossing territorial lines, leads us into interesting aspects of operational research in which systems concepts such as those of J. G. Miller (1965, 1971) aid both in interpretation and organization when the strain on communication systems is heightened by fast turnover of patients and personnel as well as boundary disputes.

The methadone program has demonstrated that more research is necessary before our procedural and consequence spaces can be combined and ordered to the point where we can enlarge our area of the ecological field at will by calling in other disciplines such as social anthropology and linguistics. But it seems rather apparent now that learning systems must occupy the core of the ecological field that will be applied to the design of cultures, and that S–R theories are extremely compatible with general systems.

## References

Alker, H., Jr. A typology of ecological fallacies. In M. Dogan and S. Rokkan (Eds.), *Quantitative Ecological Analysis in the Social Sciences.* Cambridge, Mass. M.I.T. Press, 1969.

Ayllon T., and Azrin, N. H. The measurement and reinforcement of behavior of psychotics. *Journal of Experimental Analysis of Behavior,* 1965, **8**, 357–383.

Ayllon T., and Michael, J. L. The psychiatric nurse as a behavioral engineer. *Journal of the Experimental Analysis of Behavior,* 1959, **2**, 323–334.

Auerswald, E. H. Interdisciplinary versus ecological approach. In W. Gray, F. J. Duhl, and N. D. Rizzo (Eds.), *General Systems Theory and Psychiatry.* London: J. & A. Churchill, 1969.

Bergman, P. General theory of psychotherapy. Unpublished manuscript, Bethesda, Md.: NIMH, 1960, and personal communication.

Birdwhistle, R. L. *Kinesics and Context: Essays on Body-Motion Communication.* London: Allen Lane The Penguin Press, 1971.

Brown, P. L., and Jenkins, H. M. Auto-shaping of the pigeon's key peck. *Journal of the Experimental Analysis of Behavior,* 1968, **11**, 1–8.

Catania, A. C. Concurrent operants. In W. K. Honig (Ed.), *Operant Behavior: Areas of Research and Application.* New York: Appleton-Century-Crofts, 1966, pp. 213–270.

Catania, A. C. Elicitation, reinforcement and stimulus control. In R. Glaser (Ed.), *The Nature of Reinforcement.* New York: Academic Press, 1971.

Cautela, J. R. Covert conditioning. In A. Jacobs, and L. B. Sachs (Eds.), *The Psychology of Private Events.* New York: Academic Press, 1971.

Chomsky, N. Review of Skinner's *Verbal Behavior. Language.* 1959, **35**, 26–58.

Dockens, W. S., III (Ed.), *Conference of Social and Physical Environmental Variables as Determinants of Mental Health.* Washington, D.C.: U.S. Department of Health, Education and Welfare, Vols. 1 and 2 (1957); Vols. 3 and 4 (1958); Vols. 5 and 6 (1959); Vols. 7 and 8 (1960); Vols. 9 and 10 (1961); Vols. 11 and 12 (1962).

Dockens, W. S., III. Toward a behavioral ecology: A psychological systems approach to social problems, 1973 (unpublished manuscript).

Dogan, M., and Rokkan, S. *Quantitative Ecological Analysis in the Social Sciences.* Cambridge, Mass.: The M.I.T. Press, 1969.

Donahoe, J. W. Some observations on descriptive analysis. In R. Glaser (Ed.), *The Nature of Reinforcement.* New York. Academic Press, 1971, pp. 221–226.

Duhl, L. J. *The Changing Face of Mental Health.* Washington, D.C.: U.S. Department of Health, Education and Welfare, 1960.

Ekman, G. On typological and dimensional systems of reference in describing personality. *Acta Psychologica,* 1951, **7.**

Farmer, J., and Schoenfeld, W. N. Varying temporal placement of an added stimulus in a fixed-interval schedule. *Journal of the Experimental Analysis of Behavior,* 1966, **9**, 369–375.

Ferster, C. B., and Skinner, B. F. *Schedules of Reinforcement.* New York: Appleton-Century-Crofts, 1957.

Glaser, R. *The Nature of Reinforcement.* New York: Academic Press, 1971.

Gotestam, K. G., Melin, G. M., and Dockens, W. S., III. *A Behavioral program for intravenous amphetamine addicts.* Chapter 21, this volume.

Gray, W., Duhl, F., and Rizzo, N. *General Systems Theory and Psychiatry.* Boston: Little, Brown, 1969.

Gregson, R. A. M. *The Control of Behavior.* Unpublished manuscript presented March, 1971, Canterbury University, New Zealand, and personal communication.

Hinde, R. A. *Animal Behavior: A Synthesis of Ethology and Comparative Psychology.* New York: McGraw-Hill, 1970.

Honig, W. K. (Ed.) *Operant Behavior: Research and Application.* New York: Appleton-Century-Crofts, 1966.

Jacobson, E. *Progressive Relaxation.* Chicago: University of Chicago Press, 1938.

Konorski, J., and Miller, S. On two types of conditioned reflex. *Journal of General Psychology,* 1937, **16**, 264–272.

McGinnies, E., and Ferster, C. B. *The Reinforcement of Social Behavior.* Boston: Houghton Mifflin, 1971.

Miller, J. G. Living systems: Basic concepts: *Behavioral Science,* 1965, **10**, No. 3.

Miller, J. G. The nature of living systems: The group. *Behavioral Science,* 1971, **16**, No. 4.

Miller, N. E., and Carmona, A. Modification of a visceral response, salivation in thirsty dogs, by instrumental training with water reward. *Journal of Comparative and Physiological Psychology,* 1967, **63**, 1–6.

Morse, W. H., and Kelleher, R. T. Schedules as fundamental determinants of behavior. In W. N. Schoenfeld (Ed.), *The Theory of Reinforcement Schedules.* New York: Appleton-Century-Crofts, 1970, pp. 139–183.

Premack, D. Catching up with common sense or two sides of a generalization: Reinforcement and punishment. In R. Glaser (Ed.), *The Nature of Reinforcement*. New York: Academic Press, 1971.

Reichenbach, H. *Experience and Prediction*. Chicago: University of Chicago Press, 1938.

Scheflen, A. E. Behavioral programs in human communication. In W. Gray, F. J. Duhl, and N. D. Rizo (Eds.), *General Systems Theory and Psychiatry*. London: J. & A. Churchill, 1969.

Schoenfeld, W. N., Cumming, W. W., and Hearst, E. On the classification of reinforcement schedules. *Proceedings of the National Academy of Sciences*, 1956, **42**, 563–570.

Schoenfeld, W. N., and Cumming, W. W. Some effects of alternation rate in a time-correlated reinforcement contingency. *Proceedings of the National Academy of Sciences*, 1957, **43**, 349–354.

Schoenfeld, W. N., and Farmer, J. Reinforcement schedules and the "behavior stream." In W. N. Schoenfeld (Ed.), *The Theory of Reinforcement Schedules*. New York: Appleton-Century-Crofts, 1970.

Schultz, J. H., and Luthe, W. *Autogenic Training, a Psycho-physiological Approach in Psychotherapy*. New York: Grune and Straton, 1959.

Sidman, M. Two temporal parameters in the maintenance of avoidance behavior by the white rat. *Journal of Comparative and Physiological Psychology*, 1953, **46**, 253–256.

Sidman, M. Time discrimination and behavioral interaction: A free operant situation. *Journal of Comparative and Physiological Psychology*, 1956, **49**, 469–473.

Sidman, M. *Tactics of Scientific Research*. New York: Basic Books, 1960.

Skinner, B. F. Two types of conditioned reflex and a pseudotype. *Journal of General Psychology*, 1935, **12**, 66–77.

Skinner, B. F. *The Behavior of Organisms*. New York: Appleton-Century-Crofts, 1938.

Skinner, B. F. *Walden Two*. New York: Macmillan, 1948.

Skinner, B. F. *Verbal Behavior*. New York: Appleton-Century-Crofts, 1957.

Skinner, B. F. *Cumulative Record*, revised ed. New York: Appleton-Century-Crofts, 1961.

Skinner, B. F. *Contingencies of Reinforcement: A Theoretical Analysis*. New York: Appleton-Century-Crofts, 1969.

Snapper, A. G., Knapp, J., and Kushner, H. Mathematical description of schedules of reinforcement. In W. N. Schoenfeld (Ed.), *The Theory of Reinforcement Schedules*. New York: Appleton-Century-Crofts, 1970.

Sommer, R. *Personal Space*. Englewood Cliffs, N.J.: Prentice-Hall, 1969.

Tharp, R. G., and Wetzel, R. J., *Behavior Modification in the Natural Environment*. New York: Academic Press, 1969.

Throne, J. M. Organization and administration of the university affiliated facility for mental retardation: Role of systems technology and operant conditioning. *American Association on Mental Deficiency*, Washington, D.C., May 1970.

Ullman, L. P., and Krasner, L. *A Psychological Approach to Abnormal Behavior*. Englewood Cliffs, N.J.: Prentice-Hall, 1969.

von Bertalanffy, L. *Robots, Men and Minds*. New York: George Braziller, 1967.

von Bertalanffy, L. *General System Theory: Foundations, Development, Applications*. New York: George Braziller, 1969.(a) von Bertalanffy, L. General systems theory and psychiatry—An overview. In W. Gray, F. J. Duhl, and N. D. Rizzo, (Eds.), *General Systems and Psychiatry,* London: J. & A. Churchill, 1969.(b)

Wolpe, J. *Psychotherapy by Reciprocal Inhibition.* Stanford, Calif.: Stanford University Press, 1958.

Wyrwicka, W. An experimental approach to the problem of mechanism of alimentary conditioned reflex type II. In G. A. Kimble (Ed.), *Foundations of Conditioning and Learning.* New York: Appleton-Century-Crofts, 1967, pp. 260–268.

# 25 HUMANISM AND APPLIED BEHAVIORISM

## Travis Thompson

The behavioral sciences have reached an important juncture in their development. For the last half-century, applied behavioral scientists have been concerned largely with predictive and descriptive problems, which, with a few exceptions, have failed to deal effectively with any of the major difficulties facing mankind. Over the past decade, politicians, government officials, and scholars have exhorted behavioral scientists to face up to the challenge of society's pressing problems. It is time, we have been told, to stop fussing with our Skinner boxes and get on with the serious business of dealing with mankind's ills. But things are different today, with the blossoming of applied behaviorism. Behaviorism has grown from Watson's (1924, p. 82) grandiose "Give me a dozen healthy infants . . . and I'll guarantee to take any one at random and train him to become . . . doctor, lawyer, artist, merchant-chief, and yes, even beggar man and thief," through Skinner's *Walden Two* (1948), to the diverse range of applications of behaviorist principles mushrooming around us in education, mental health, correction, and rehabilitation. What a different tune we hear sung today when behavior science has something of proven practical value to offer for changing behavior—the principles and techniques of applied behaviorism. With each effective extension of behaviorist principles into new areas, the outcry among professional and public sectors becomes more strident. It is as though the exhortations to action were empty calls based on the assumption that a truly effective behavioral science was beyond the realm of possibility. One of behaviorism's critics got to the heart of the matter when he wrote, "I sin-

443

cerely believe this is such a conflict as may well be termed a battle for man's soul. It is not so much because behaviorism is following a blind alley but *because it is clearly effective.* . . [Bugental, 1967, p. 9]."

There is a lesson to be learned here, but many of us have not been paying attention to the teacher. Behavioral science is safe as long as it remains innocuously impotent; but when it bears practical fruit, it becomes to many a frightening menace. It is a paradoxical corrollary that the public and scientific communities have seen content to support basic behavioral research—while their hair turns gray at the thought of supporting effective applied behavioral research. Don't misunderstand me. Having been trained as an experimental psychologist and continuing to wear two hats, one of the basic laboratory scientist and the other of the applied investigator, I am firmly committed to supporting basic research. Indeed, I do not believe that applied behaviorism would be where it is today without its laboratory beginnings. My point here is to indicate the incongruity of many critics' verbal behavior on one occasion ("By all means we must support basic research . . .") and their verbal behavior on another ("These behaviorists are a menace. . . . If they had their way they'd put all of us in Skinner boxes.").

Behavioral science has reached a turning point. It can either continue as a harmless discipline, making limited practical contributions, or develop into a set of powerful tools useful for solving important human problems. Nothing less is at stake. The fact is that applied behaviorism has already proven to be effective in dealing with behavioral problems with which other approaches in psychology, psychiatry, and education have had limited success. There is a world of pressing problems in mental health, education, correction, retardation, rehabilitation, and related fields that need every bit of assistance that applied behaviorism has to offer. One might naively think that a new and effective approach to dealing with these knotty problems would be welcomed with open arms. But there are some who are so frightened by an effective objective approach to human behavior that they would rather see men suffer than change their way of dealing with his ills. Sometimes such views are couched in compassionate language, lending apparent credence to the good intentions of the critics. Unfortunately, good intentions ar not enough. It is not enough to be concerned, sensitive, and love one's fellow man. One must be able to apply procedures of proven efficacy to deal with his problems.

The controversy will not be settled soon, nor by argumentation. But in the meantime, behaviorists can expect to find themselves in the situation aptly described by Bertrand Russell (1953):

The sentimentalist will say that you are coldly intellectual, and that if you really minded the sufferings of others, you could not be so scientific about them. The sentimentalist will claim to have a tenderer heart than yours, and will show it by letting the suffering continue . . . [p. 90].

## Behaviorism's Communication Failures

But let us be honest: Not all of applied behaviorism's problems have arisen because of irrational, hysterical reactions. Many thoughtful, scientifically trained people, including this writer, shudder at the thought of an effective Machiavellian behavioral science, devoid of humanistic values. Our difficulties here are twofold.

1. In this day and age, antiscientific and antitechnological feelings run deep, and often for good reason. To some nonbehaviorists, an effective behavioral science is viewed as an extension of such technological disasters as the threat of thermonuclear war and environmental pollution. Further, for some, an effective behaviorism conjures up images of *1984,* "brain washing," and political exploitation. Most behaviorists, on the other hand, have taken for granted their deep-felt commitment to humanistic values, but have not rushed out to buy a "I am a humanist" sweatshirt. While I am not advocating that behaviorists resort to sloganism, I *am* suggesteing that behaviorists have done a poor job of visibly incorporating humanistic values into their writing, lecturing, and other communications. This is not a matter of cosmetics. We have failed to promulgate clearly our fundamental humanistic values. If applied behaviorism is to have a lasting impact on the social problems with which many of us are so deeply concerned, we must communicate more about our science than its effectiveness. We must also communicate its integral humanism.

2. There will be those who will say "I'm a scientist. . . I discover truth, and it's up to others to apply it as they see fit." Such a view of applied behavioral science cannot be afforded. Values are an inseparable part of applied science. The problems we attack, the precedures we use, and the people with whom we attempt to work are all determined by our values. Further, scientists are not free from responsibility in the use of their discoveries. The principles underlying applied behaviorism are powerful, and their implications are far reaching. There may be some who would make the techniques of applied behaviorism into the twentieth century's gunpowder—a tool to suppress the dissident and maintain power contrary to democratic principles. We must address ourselves to the task of developing procedures to ensure that these principles find their way

into applications consistent with humanistic values. Applied behaviorists must be the watchdogs over the tools and principles they have developed.

As a group, applied behaviorists have been characterized as abrasive, aggressively critical, and pushy by professional peers. Unfortunately, such descriptions are not entirely without foundation. In the history of many new movements emerging against strong professional opposition, there has been a tendency for the adolescent discipline to devote a disproportionate amount of effort in attacking its professional elders. While such behavior is predictable enough, it is important to remember that not only are such attacks counterproductive, but they are, as well, contrary to the principles that applied behaviorists espouse. If we hope to change the future behavior of our colleagues and students, we shall no doubt be far more effective in using positive reinforcement, fading, and shaping in dealing with their behavior than excessive and indiscriminate punishment.

A related mistake made by applied behaviorists is to appear to thrust themselves into situations where their professional wares are not wanted. Once again, this tactic is destined to generate resistance from many who would otherwise be willing to attend to our data. It is far wiser to wait until one's professional skills can provide meaningful reinforcers for colleagues, clients, and peers. Assisting them in maximizing their own personal and professional reinforcement by serving in a mediating role can only help our cause, while threatening to withdraw such important sources of reinforcement will predictably produce aggression and rejection of applied behaviorism.

## Humanist Values and Applied Behaviorism

What are some of the values of applied behaviorism? Let us recognize from the outset that "humanist" values vary widely. Further, we are not claiming humanism as our exclusive domain, as have some in psychology. Rather, we hope that behaviorism can serve the values and goals of humanism broadly conceived. Julian Huxley (1961) expressed such values as follows: The humanist framework

> must be focused on man as an organism, though one with unique properties . . . [is] necessarily unitary instead of dualistic. . . . Universal instead of particularist, affirming the continuity of man with the rest of life . . . naturalistic instead of supernaturalist . . . and global instead of divisional. . . . As the overriding aim of evolving man, it [humanism] is driven to reject power, or mere numbers of people, or efficiency, or material exploitation, and to envisage greater fulfillment and fuller achievement as his true goal [p. 14].

Applied behaviorists find themselves at home with these values, which are so often reflected in their professional activities. Perhaps the most common goal of applied behaviorist efforts is to enable each individual to function effectively to the limits of his biological ability. Implied in this statement is the concept that man need not be a slave to his environment, but by proper arrangement of environmental contingencies, can determine his own destiny—that is, to be what he wants to be.

In the best pragmatist tradition, behaviorism is highly optimistic. Behaviorists generally hold the view that each person's life can be made more meaningful and enriching by honestly assessing the factors affecting his own behavior, and by rearranging environmental contingencies so as to channel his behavioral growth in the directions he chooses. Thus, human behavior is viewed as a continually changing, open-ended stream, always subject to modification. By periodic reappraisals of one's own individual values and goals, and by applying principles of behavioral change, each person can actively strive to fulfill his own potential.

In his role as a therapist, contingency manager, teacher, or consultant, the behaviorist constantly keeps in mind the principle that each person is unique—an individual behaviorally unlike any other. This emphasis on individual difference makes it second nature to react to subtle differences in history, behavioral predispositions, reinforcer preferences, and objectives.

In many fields, there is the tendency to explain complex phenomena by oversimplifying. Hence, in applied behaviorism we have the "nothing but" problem. This is a pitfall that must be avoided, and that, as more experience is gained, will no doubt grow less common. An applied behaviorist may say, "That's *nothing but* a cause of poor stimulus control" after superficially examining a client's behavior problem. Such a claim may be no more helpful than for a psychoanalyst to say, "That's *nothing but* a case of unresolved transference." Whenever one finds himself saying "That's nothing but," he should always ask himself if things are really *that* simple. Perhaps they are, but one suspects that, more often than not, multiple factors must be considered.

Applied behaviorists are committed to reducing the overall amount of aversive stimulation brought to bear on their fellow man. Thus, there are better ways to deal with behavior problems in the classroom than yelling at children, sending them to the principal, or threatening expulsion from school. Husbands and wives can find greater interpersonal happiness by responding to each other's behaviors positively than by nagging and arguing. In dealing with clients, behaviorists use aversive procedures as a last resort, when all other possibilities have been exhausted. A good policy for anyone working in applied behaviorism is to place himself in the client's position, and ask himself, "How would I like to have my behavior changed in *that* way?" If the answer is, "I wouldn't like it at all," then maybe it is time to go back to the drawing board. This is not to say that client discomfort can always be avoided, but merely to emphasize the goal of reducing the use of aversive procedures.

As applied behaviorism grows, it becomes essential that those whose behaviors are being changed be actively involved in selecting their own behavioral objectives and the procedures to be used to reach those goals. Whether one is dealing with private patients, incarcerated criminals, chronic psychotics, or children in the general classroom, self-regulation and self-determination must be a key part of any humanistic behavioral system. The emphasis must be on the client, not as an object, but as a free person, determining the way his life will be lived.

Finally, it must be emphasized that applied behaviorism is a science of *human* behavior having little to do with Pavlov's dogs or Skinner's pigeons. This is no more rejecting our heritage than it is for a specialist in internal medicine to distinguish his activities from those of a physiologist doing cardiovascular research wth dogs. Applied behaviorism is a science that respects the dignity of man. Indeed, applied behaviorism may offer the only tenable solution to some of our more difficult behavioral problems, and the most effective pathway by which man can realize his potential.

## ACKNOWLEDGMENTS
An edited version of this paper was presented as the Presidential Address at the meeting of the Minnesota Association for the Advancement of Behavior Therapy, April 15, 1972. The author wishes to acknowledge the thoughtful comments of Kenneth MacCorquodale, Paul Meehl, Richard Meisch, and Roy Pickens on earlier drafts of this manuscript.

# References

Bugental, J. F. T. *Challenges of Humanistic Psychology*. New York: McGraw-Hill, 1967.

Huxley, J. The humanist frame. In J. Huxley (Ed.), *The Humanist Frame*. New York: Harper & Row, 1961.

Russell, B. *The Impact of Science on Society*. New York: Simon & Schuster, 1953.

Skinner, B. F. *Walden Two*. New York: Macmillan, 1948.

Watson, J. B. *Behaviorism*. New York: The People's Institute Publishing Co., Inc., 1924.

# VIII TRAINING BEHAVIOR THERAPISTS

# 26 A COMPREHENSIVE TRAINING PROGRAM FOR BEHAVIOR THERAPISTS

**Sten Rönnberg**

The purpose of this paper is to describe a major attempt to train behavior modifiers [1] in Sweden, to point out some of the most important elements needed in behavior modification training programs, and finally, to give a rough outline of a more ideal training program in behavior modification.

## An Attempt to Train Behavior Modifiers in Sweden

In the fall of 1969, a training program in behavior modification was initiated at the Institute of Education at Stockholm University.[2] The program consisted of three courses to be taken in sequence: Behavior Therapy I, II, and III. This program has since been extended and applied at other places in Sweden (Table 26.1) in the form of complementary university courses given by the Center for Behavior Therapy in Stockholm and local ABF organizations, with approximately 75% of the costs of these courses subsidized by the state. It has now become the most substantial behavior modification program in Sweden with regard to enrollment and

---

[1] The terms *behavior therapy* and *behavior modification* are here used interchangeably, with the same broad meaning.

[2] The development of the program and the edition for the academic year 1971/1972 have been described elsewhere (Rönnberg, 1971a).

**TABLE 26.1**

Enrollment,[a] Location, and Teachers: Behavior Modification Program
1969–1972

| Year | Course: Behavior Therapy | | | Held at | Teachers |
|------|------|------|------|---------|----------|
|      | I | II | III | | |
| 1969–1970 | 80 | 40 |    | Stockholm | Sten Rönnberg |
| 1970–1971 | 80 | 60 | 16 | Stockholm–Uppsala | Sten Rönnberg |
|           |    |    |    |                   | Lars-Goran Ost |
|           |    |    |    |                   | Suzanne Oxhammer |
| 1971–1972 | 80 | 80 |    | Stockholm | Sten Rönnberg |
|           |    |    |    | Uppsala   | Lars-Goran Ost |
|           |    |    |    | Linkoping | Susanne Gaunitz |
|           |    |    |    | Lulea     | Suzanne Oxhammer |

[a] Generally, each group started with about 24 students. After a few weeks some students dropped out, leaving approximately 20 in each group for the remainer of the course.

number of locations (Table 26.1), comprehensiveness, and lengths. A description of the program for the academic year 1972/1973 may serve as a basis for the discussion of the education of future behavior modifiers.

BEHAVIOR THERAPY I

Behavior Therapy I is an introductory course stressing the theoretical foundations of behavior therapy. The goals of the course are defined as follows:

1. Knowledge of the most important paradigms of learning in behavior therapy.
2. Knowledge of the theoretical and empirical foundations of behavior therapy.
3. Knowledge of the essentials of discussions concerning ethical problems and goals in behavior therapy.

The literature chosen to meet these ends is Bandura's (1969) *Principles of Behavior Modification* and Skinner's (1971) *Beyond Freedom and Dignity*.

Instruction is in the form of seminars, normally with 20 participants per group.

The course comprises 24 hours, divided into six meetings of 4 hours each. The meetings are held every other week, the whole course covering approximately 3 months.

The course ends with a 4-hour essay examination.

## BEHAVIOR THERAPY II

Behavior Therapy II is more practical, with the following goals:

1. Knowledge of behavior analysis.
2. Knowledge of the behavior therapy techniques most often applied.
3. Ability to plan specific treatment programs and to treat simple problems with guidance.

About 2000 pages of literature are covered in this course. A little less than half of the literature is read by all participants and is supposed to provide fundamental knowledge of behavioral analysis (Rönnberg, 1972), systematic desensitization (Öst, 1971a, 1971b), assertive training (Alberti and Emmons, 1970), and the experimental investigation of the single case (Yates, 1970). After this introduction to the practical applications of behavior therapy, the students are provided with the opportunity to choose one of six different lines of literature:

1. Clinical applications to adults (Lazarus, 1971; Rachman and Teasdale, 1969; Schaefer and Martin, 1969).
2. Clinical applications to children (Blackham and Silberman, 1971; Browning and Stover, 1971).
3. School applications (Eriksson and Österling, 1971; Haring and Phillips, 1972; Sulzer and Mayer, 1972).
4. Counseling (Jehu, Hardiker, Yelloly, and Shaw, 1972; Krumboltz and Thoresen, 1969).
5. Mental retardation (Gardner, 1971; Hamerlynck and Clark, 1971; Thompson and Grabowski, 1972).
6. Families (Becker, 1971; Patterson, 1971; Welander, 1972).

There are 69 hours of instruction in this course, divided into 9 hours of seminars, 12 hours of lectures, 48 hours of group work, and a 4-hour examination meeting. Seminars and lectures are held with the whole group of approximately 20. For group work and examinations, the group is divided into two smaller sections of approximately ten each. A 2-day meeting is held every other week, the whole course covering approximately 6 months. Table 26.2 shows the schedule for every meeting.

In addition to the study of literature, every student is required to treat one case and report on it in writing according to the procedures for presentation of case reports prepared by Rönnberg (1971b). The student is also required to write a report of approximately ten pages on some pertinent problem in behavior therapy.

**TABLE 26.2**
Study Plan for Behavior Therapy II

| Meeting number | Study forms [a] | Hours | Topic |
|---|---|---|---|
| 1 | L | 2 | Behavior analysis |
| 2 | G | 3 | Behavior analysis 1 |
| 3 | G | 3 | Behavior analysis 2 |
| 4 | G | 3 | Behavior analysis 3 |
| 5 | L | 2 | Systematic desensitization |
| 6 | G | 4 | Systematic desensitization 1 |
| 7 | S | 3 | Systematic desensitization |
| 8 | G | 4 | Systematic desensitization 2 |
| 9 | G | 4 | Systematic desensitization 3 |
| 10 | L | 2 | Assertive training |
| 11 | G | 4 | Assertive training |
| 12 | S | 3 | Assertive training |
| 13 | L | 2 | Aversion therapy |
| 14 | S | 3 | Various behavior therapy techniques |
| 15 | L | 2 | Operant techniques |
| 16 | G | 4 | Operant techniques |
| 17 | L | 2 | Social modeling |
| 18 | G | 3 | Social modeling |
| 19 | G | 3 | Discussions of cases and reports |
| 20 | G | 3 | Discussions of cases and reports |
| 21 | G | 3 | Discussions of cases and reports |
| 22 | G | 3 | Discussions of cases and reports |
| 23 | G | 4 | Examination |

[a] L = lectures, S = seminars, G = group exercises.

## Behavior Therapy III

Behavior Therapy III focuses on research. The goals of the course are the following:

1. Good knowledge of research in behavior therapy.
2. Encouragement of participants to do research in behavior therapy and related areas.
3. Good knowledge of how one's own responses influence therapist–patient relationships.
4. Ability to plan and execute treatment programs in behavior therapy.

The literature is chosen individually for each of the five or eight students in every group. Approximately 2000 pages of literature are to be covered by each student. Among the books often preferred are Aronfreed

(1968), Barber *et al.* (1971), Bergin and Garfield (1971), Franks (1969), Jacobs and Sachs (1971), Kaminski (1970), McGinnies and Ferster (1971), Rubin and Franks (1969), Rubin, Fensterheim, Lazarus, and Franks (1971). Suggestions concerning relevant articles are available from computer searches, the ERIC and Medlars system, from current behavior therapy journals, and so on.

In addition to reading, some of the aids used to train therapist–patient relationships include role playing, live demonstrations, ITV, and bug-in-the-ear, a written report on the student's own strengths and weaknesses as a therapist, as well as a program for self-education.

Every participant has to treat three cases and to present a written case report on each. He also has to submit a report on a research problem.

Three-hour meetings are held every other week for a period of approximately 7 months.

## Issues in the Education of Behavior Modifiers

According to the rather informal evaluations made each year, the program described teaches effectively, is liked by most students, and seems to be valuable to them in their work, but it by no means fully answers pertinent questions as to how best to train behavior modifiers. This is an appropriate place to raise a few of the important issues that should concern behavior modification educators. A few of the most important factors needed in behavior modification training programs and other issues will be discussed.

### COMPREHENSIVENESS

There are currently *five important lines of development* within the behavior modification movement: the operant (e.g., Schaefer and Martin, 1969), the Wolpean (e.g., Wolpe, 1969), experimental investigation of the single case (e.g., Yates, 1970), social learning (e.g., Bandura, 1969), the personalistic (e.g., Lazarus, 1971) —the last two being less strictly behavioristic and more on the cognitive side than the others. The question of comprehensiveness deals first with the extent to which each of these approaches should be represented in a behavior modification training program.

In the training program described above, all five lines of development have been included. From a detached Swedish point of view, this seems to be what every behavior modification training program should comprise, except perhaps those that would have to provide training for very special purposes, such as special functions in a token-economy program.

The extent to which the different movements within behavior modification should be stressed may be briefly defined by saying that it is essential that the students be well versed in as large a number as possible of the behavioral *techniques,* as well as other techniques for behavior change that have proved to be useful. It is also important that they be well  acquainted with behavioral diagnostic skills, or the art of *behavior analysis,* including the pinpointing of the problem, choosing priorities and problem targets, establishing the controlling factors, and deciding on the goals. They should also know *how to observe and to evaluate,* and should have a thorough knowledge of *theory and research* in the field.

Comprehensiveness, however, not only involves having a good representative sample of different lines of development; it also deals with the question of what knowledge, outside strict behavior modification, would be required in the education of behavior modifiers. This seems to be a question that is seldom raised or answered in literature on behavior modification.

There are some issues not often mentioned in literature on behavior modification. Let me briefly point out and give some views in favor of the most important of these questions.

There is a need for discussion of and opinions on comprehensive *goals* in all training programs in behavior modification, not only the more limited technological aspects of goal analysis, including the selection of goals, their definition in explicit terms, and breaking them down to behavioral terms, which is already part of most training programs in behavior analysis. What kind of goals are we to favor in behavior modification? What are we to add to Skinner's (1953, 1971), Rogers and Skinner's (1956), and Bandura's (1969) opinions on the subject? Who should decide which goals are to be applied for what patient and for which problems? What about patients who cannot fully decide for themselves, such as children, the mentally retarded, and so on? How should decisions be made about targets of treatment, techniques for change, time, schedule, place, fees, and so on of the behavior modification procedure? How do social background and limited social experience influence decisions made by the therapist? What about change of the individual and/or the environment in which he lives? Are not too many of the effects of deficient social systems so obvious in the field of mental health as to dismiss the question altogether—for instance, the effects of certain legislation, lack of social welfare resources, housing, jobs, schooling, discrimination, and so on (Graziano, 1972; Stuart, 1969, 1972)? What about prevention? Which goals maximize prevention? Prevention of what? Correction or prevention, correction or revolution, freedom or control, and so on? There is a strong need for guidelines for behavior modifiers in these areas, not least because these questions are often raised by students.

A large number of diverse, far-reaching questions requiring answers are often brought up by students and others as soon as behavior modification is mentioned. I do not think that we can omit this topic simply because most of the textbooks on behavior modification tend to avoid it or treat it very superficially. Books or articles devoted entirely to the subject often have very limited views and repeat already well-known arguments (e.g., Karlins and Andrews, 1972; London, 1969, 1971; Skinner, 1971; Szasz, 1970). It would be disastrous for behavior modification to adopt an extreme technological position, leaving all the important decisions on goals to politicians and others and following whatever is expedient.

There are many reasons to support training in *self-knowledge* as an essential part of any training program in behavior modification. Not only are the therapist's own responses an important tool in his interplay with the patient, in dispensing reinforcements and modeling cues, but they also affect each other: The therapist should know how his own actions in the therapist–patient relationship are influenced by his acts and thoughts. A lack of this personnal knowledge may cause total disruption of the behavior change process.

There are not easy steps to train self-knowledge. A few of the ways of meeting the most obvious requirements are participation in long-term marathon groups, traditional individual therapy, long psychotherapeutic experience, precision teaching, programs similar to the one mentioned in the Behavior Therapy III course mentioned earlier, including role playing, self-confrontation on ITV, descriptive accounts of one's own strengths and weaknesses in a psychotherapeutic setting, added to a thorough training program on how to be a better therapist.

That one undoubtedly needs experience from many spheres of life to be a good behavior modifier should also be pointed out. One would need *practice* in other social strata than one's own, especially in those from which most of the patients are likely to come. In addition, practice in meeting different types of patients, problems, and treatment settings would be required. These are things that cannot be fully grasped by reading and from experience in a traditional educational environment.

It follows from the position adopted by behavior modification that many factors, other than the psychological ones, can influence an act (e.g., Bandura, 1969; Stuart, 1969; Wolpe, 1969). Comprehensive education of behavior changers, including such important factors as certain aspects of genetics, medicine, and ecology (Mowrer, 1969) still lags far behind the educations of counselors, psychologists, and psychiatrists. While waiting for better training programs for behavior modification, training should include at least some basic information about nonpsychological matters that often arise in the course of therapy. Some information on relevant aspects of *legislation, literature, physiology, and pharmacology* seems to me to be quite indispensable for behavior modifiers elite (cf. Frederick, 1969).

At the moment it is hard to believe that the new behavior modification trainee does not already have characteristics, traits, a disposition to act in certain ways—or whatever one may wish to call them—that easily make one behavior modifier better than another. They are *facilitative conditions* exemplified by traits such as genuineness, empathy, warmth, concreteness, and so on. How to develop these characteristics in students of behavior modification is still an unanswered question. Perhaps the training schemes of Truax and Carkhuff (1967) and Lazarus (1971) give a partial answer. Selecting trainees who already have some of these characteristics and ignoring the effects of educational training should not be an answer. We cannot shelve the problem, however, considering the increasing number of students who wish to work as behavior modifiers after short courses in behavior modification and no previous experience in psychodynamic therapy.

## LEVELS

There are at least four levels of education for behavior modifiers to consider:

1. An *introductory level,* in which one learns that there is something called behavior modification and what it is about. This is intended for high school students, administrators, politicians, and so on. It consists of rather short courses, of about 2 weeks of full-time work.
2. A *restricted application* level, where one learns to apply some of the techniques for certain purposes. Teachers, families, nurses, medical practitioners, and so on would be the target group. The program for level 2 should be longer than that of level 1. A course of 1 or 2 months would perhaps be ideal.

3. A *professional* level, where one acquires both understanding and application and can act as behavior modifier on his own. At this level psychotherapists, psychologists, psychiatrists, counselors, and so on, may be trained.
4. An *advanced trainer* level, after which one is able to train others to do qualified research in the area, write books, and undertake other leading activities in the field. This level would be for advanced, trained psychotherapists, professors, and so on.

Different programs would be required for each of the levels of competence. Table 26.3 gives an idea about what may be essential at each level.

## THE WAY TO TEACH

Bad teaching methods can destroy the best of training programs. In addition to the general guidelines for promoting learning in students, all teachers should be familiar with such concepts as concreteness, vividness, individualization, student initiative, creativeness, group work, and so on. A few ideas should be kept in mind when considering the most appropriate design for each of the just mentioned training levels.

The introductory-level course can be rather conventional. It would have to fit in with other broad educational schemes and should be taught as part of a subject such as psychology, or as a series of concentrated courses of a few days' duration, combining qualified lectures with home-

**TABLE 26.3**
IMPORTANT ISSUES AT DIFFERENT TRAINING LEVELS [a]

| Issues | Level I | Level II | Level III | Level IV |
|---|---|---|---|---|
| Techniques | | x | x | x |
| Behavior analysis | | x | x | x |
| Observation and evaluation techniques | | x | x | x |
| Theory | x | x | x | x |
| Research | | | x | x |
| Goals and behavior control | x | x | x | x |
| Self-knowledge | | | x | x |
| Practice | | x | x | |
| Facilitative conditions | | | x | x |
| Other subjects | | | | x |

[a] An x means that the topic is particularly essential in courses at this level.

work. Films, ITV material, tapes, demonstrations of equipment, standard assignments, workbooks, and other educational aids would help to enliven the learning process.

The course at level 2 aims at teaching specific skills in certain areas, such as management of schools and homes. It is a technological course, intended mainly for nonprofessionals. It is based on the knowledge acquired in the course at level 1.

There are many ways of learning these specific skills, although there is much to say in favor of the Personalized Instructional System (PSI, also known as the Keller system) in a course of this type. An increasing amount of data is in favor of PSI, showing a great deal of success in many courses (Born, 1971; Corey and McMichael, 1970; Gallup, 1970; McMichael, 1971; PSI Newsletter, 1971–1972). PSI is, moreover, theoretically palatable for a behavioral modifier (Keller, 1968), being based on maximum use of reinforcement, shaping, and so on. The student may also learn something from the design of the course itself.

The third level is the most critical one. It trains the independent field worker. The requirements at this level are what we in Sweden have tried to fulfill in the courses described above. Judging from experience, such an education would have to consist of at least 1 year of full-time work, provided that the courses are not integrated into other wider courses and that the students have a background equivalent to at least a master's degree in psychology. However, there are also possibilities of integrating this course into special postdoctoral training programs for psychotherapists and, in that case, of shortening the course slightly.

Students going into professional training at this level most likely already have some background information through their reading, which corresponds to level 1. Considering that participants work in the fields of psychology, counseling, education, social work, psychiatry, and so on, the course can start at an advanced level.

The application of PSI at this level in more than small sections of the course may not be such a good idea. In this course participants are adults with a great deal of experience. The course at this level would have to be designed so that full advantage is derived from every member's participation in the group. The best way of achieving this would probably be the use of a flexible system, where the heaviest training takes place in small groups of five or ten participants, combined with individual discussions with the instructor, proctor, or mediator, discussions in larger meetings of 20 or 30 participants in seminars, and, finally, lectures for larger audiences where new ideas can be presented. Most of the teaching should be handled by the students so that the whole course becomes in practice more student-centered than teacher-centered.

The system approach in training counselors used by Thoresen and his colleagues at Stanford University (Thoresen, 1972) would be suitable for parts of the program at the third level. Dividing the contents of the course into subsystem areas consisting of sequenced behavioral tasks would be helpful for instruction at this level.

The whole repertory of educational aids should be used in the instruction, in particular, live demonstrations, participation in psychotherapeutic sessions, film and ITV demonstrations.

Education at this level should be combined with practice. What is learned must be put into practice and feedback given to the instructors and other students. It is to be hoped that most of those applying for this level already work in the field of mental health. Taking the course and working at the same time would probably be the best solution for most students. If students are not working, possibilities of internships should be arranged or patients supplied on a private, low-cost practice basis.

Admission to level-4 education should be restricted to highly qualified workers in the field. A short course stressing mircotherapeutic work, workshop assignments, internship, sit-ins, role playing, exchange of materials, and so on may be advisable. A few weeks's training may be sufficient, considering the wide experience already acquired by this group.

## An Outline of a Comprehensive Program

This rough outline is only a first step toward a program of education in line with our earlier discussion. The program must be tested with students, and many revisions incorporated as a result. Some new ideas may also be introduced into the program, and many of these included would have to be worked out in more detail. The literature proposed is very tentative, representing what is available in *English* in Sweden in August 1972. The program can be changed in many places. Bearing in mind all these reservations, the outline may still suggest some new ideas, stimulate discussion, and perhaps even prompt others to try it out.

### AN INTRODUCTORY COURSE

Goals:

1. Knowledge of the fundamentals of the theory of behavior theory.
2. Discussion of the ethics of behavior control.

Literature: Mehrabian (1970), Meyer and Chesser (1970), Schaefer and Martin (1969).

Study forms: Seminars with 20–35 participants, the fewer the better, of course. The literature included in the course should be studied and discussed by students and teachers together. The teacher should raise questions concerning the ethics of behavior control.

Requirements:

1. Attendance of 75% of the meetings.
2. A passing grade on the literature examination.

## A COURSE FOR CHANGE AGENTS

Goals:

1. Knowledge equal to the introductory course.
2. Ability to apply behavior modification techniques for certain purposes.
3. Knowledge of the most important discussion topics of goals and behavior control.

Literature: There will be approximately 1000 pages of required reading for the course. These books should be read by all participants: Neuringer and Michael (1970), Karlins and Andrews (1972); suggested extra reading: Guerney (1969) and relevant articles.

After the introduction to behavior modification, the course is divided into different lines of applications: clinical adults, clinical children, school, counseling, mental retardation, families, token economies, community designs, and so on. Each student may choose one of the following books according to his interest: Patterson and Gullion (1968), Sulzer and Mayer (1972), Krumboltz and Thoresen (1969), Gardner (1971), Graziano (1971), Ayllon and Azrin (1968), Lazarus (1971), McGinnies (1970).

Study forms: Small group discussions, PSI, seminars, lectures. Practical applications.

Requirements:

1. Previous experience, preferably the introductory course and some practice in the field chosen.
2. Attendance of 75% of the meetings.
3. A passing grade on the literature examination.
4. A passing grade on practical applications.

## A COURSE FOR BEHAVIOR MODIFIERS

Goals:

1. Knowledge of behavior analysis.

2. Ability to use behavior modification as a help for treatment and prevention of most human problems.
3. Acquiring some information about other models for treating behavior problems.
4. Knowledge of the effect of one's own responses on the therapist–patient relationship.
5. Knowledge and development of justifiable personal opinion on the ethical issues that are part of behavior therapeutic work.

Literature: About 4000 pages of literature must be read during the course. The following books should be read by all participants: Bandura (1969), Bergin and Garfield (1971), Ferster and Perrott (1968), Yates (1970), Skinner (1971), Kanfer and Phillips (1970), Lazarus (1972), Liberman (1972), Wolpe (1969). Following an overall view, giving a solid background, possibilities are open for specializing in areas such as the ones mentioned in the level-2 course and Behavior Therapy II course described earlier. The introductory literature in these courses may be the same as the literature for this course. Here, however, at least 200 pages of relevant articles should be read in addition and are to be selected by the student himself.

Study forms: Mostly discussions in small groups. A few lectures. Case report seminars, paper report seminars. Microtherapeutic work. Student's own therapy in a group and training of facilitative conditions.

Requirements:

1. Two years of previous experience in the field of mental health, or either a Ph.D. or an M.D.
2. Attendance of 75% of the meetings.
3. Passing examinations on the literature.
4. A written research report of a relevant problem in behavior therapy.
5. Treatment of three cases and written case reports.
6. At least 1 year of participation in group therapy and training of facilitative conditions.

## A COURSE FOR BEHAVIOR MODIFICATION TRAINERS

Goals:

1. Thorough knowledge of the contents of the courses at levels 1, 2, and 3.
2. Ability to train others satisfactorily in behavior modification.
3. Demonstrated ability as a good behavior modifier.

4. Thorough knowledge of research in behavior modification.

Previous experience: Postdoctoral research work. At least 5 years' experience as a psychotherapist.

Study forms: International workshops with highly qualified leaders, including exchange of material, case discussions, live therapeutic performances, and so on. Short courses introducing adjacent areas, such as pharmacology, neurophysiology, medicine, sociology, and literature.

## Discussion

The courses outlined in the last section may seem to be laborius, requiring much work both from students and teachers. One may be tempted to lower one's ambitions. This is, of course, possible, but it should be done only when there are very strong reasons for it. The rule to be followed should be to provide solid education for all behavior modification students at all levels. In the long run this will prove to be the most profitable.

A special problem is the integration of behavior modification training into other forms of education, such as the education of high school pupils, nurses, teachers, social workers, counselors, psychologists, psychiatrists, and psychotherapists. Some changes would then have to be made in the proposed courses. The important thing to remember is that most of the elements mentioned in the second section of this paper should be covered.

Another problem is that of practical applications. Practical training is not required at level 1, but most of the students in the courses at level 2, 3, and 4 probably already work in the field, and have a sufficient supply of patients. For those who do not it is important that teaching institutions and teachers have contacts with other institutions and individuals who can supply patients. Contacts with mental health institutions are also important for the internship period at level 3. There is much to be gained by having the university and the clinic work together.

The integration of practical and theoretical training should be one of the most important tasks of the teachers. A great deal can be gained by arranging live demonstrations, sit-ins, ITV, continual case discussions, and so on.

Individuals trained in courses at level 4 should act as teachers for those in the courses at level 3, while those trained in courses at level 3 can act as teachers in courses at level 1 and 2.

This outline of the different courses cannot but be a sketchy one. Nevertheless, even in its present sketchy form, the outline embodies much

of our experience from courses in Sweden and points out a few directions
to follow in future behavior modification training.

# References

Alberti, R. E., and Emmons, M. L. L. *Your Perfect Right. A Guide to Assertive Behavior.* San Luis Obispo, Calif.: Impact, 1970.

Aronfreed, J. *Conduct and Conscience. The Socialization of Internalized Control over Behavior.* New York: Academic Press, 1968.

Ayllon, T., and Azrin, N. *The Token Economy. A Motivational System for Therapy and Rehabilitation.* New York: Appleton-Century-Crofts, 1968.

Bandura, A. *Principles of behavior modification.* New York: Holt, Rinehart & Winston, 1969.

Barber, T., Kamiya, T. *et al.* Eds. *Biofeedback and Self-control. An Aldine Annual on the Regulation of Bodily Processes and Consciousness.* Chicago: Aldine-Atherton, 1971.

Becker, W. C. *Parents Are Teachers. A Child Management Program.* Champaign, Ill.: Research Press, 1971.

Bergin, A. E., and Garfield, S. L. Eds. *Handbook of Psychotherapy and Behavior Change. An Empirical Analysis.* New York: Wiley, 1971.

Blackham, G. J., and Silberman, A. *Modification of Child Behavior.* Belmont, Calif.: Wadsworth, 1971.

Born, D. G. Effects of the Keller plan on students. Paper presented at the M.I.T. Conference on the Keller Plan, Cambridge, Mass., October 1971.

Browning, R. M., and Stover, D. O. *Behavior Modification in Child Treatment. An Experimental and Clinical Approach.* Chicago: Aldine-Atherton, 1971.

Corey, J. R., and McMichael, J. S.: Using personalized instruction in college courses. Unpublished manuscript, C. W. Post College of Long Island University, 1970.

Eriksson, B., and Österling, L. *Elevvard Goteborg, En Modell for Skolans Elevvardsarbete.* Stockholm: Skandinaviska Testforlaget, 1971.

Ferster, C. B., and Perrott, M. C. *Behavior Principles.* New York: New Century, 1968.

Franks, C. M., Ed. *Behavior Therapy: Appraisal and Status.* New York: McGraw-Hill, 1969.

Frederick, C. J. Future training in psychotherapy. In C. J. Frederick (Ed.), *The Future of Psychotherapy. International Psychiatry Clinics,* 6:3. Boston: Little, Brown, 1969.

Gallup, H. F. Individualized instruction in an introductory psychology course. Paper presented at the Eastern Psychological Association Meetings, Atlantic City, New Jersey, 1970

Gardner, W. I. *Behavior Modification in Mental Retardation.* Chicago: Aldine-Atherton, 1971.

Graziano, A. M., Ed. *Behavior Therapy with Children.* Chicago: Aldine-Atherton, 1971.

Graziano, A. M. In the mental-health industry, illness is our most important product. *Psychology Today,* 1972, **5**, 8.

Gurney, B. G., Jr., Ed. *Psychotheraputic Agents: New Roles for Non-professionals, Parents and Teachers.* New York: Holt, Rinehart, & Winston, 1969.

Hamerlynck, L. A., and Clark, F. W., Eds. *Behavior Modification for Exceptional Children and Youth. The Proceedings of the Second Banff International Conference on Behavior Modification.* Calgary, Alberta: The University of Calgary, 1971.

Haring, N. G., and Phillips, E. L. *Analysis and Modification of Classroom Behavior.* Englewood Cliffs, N.J.: Prentice-Hall, 1972.

Jacobs, A., and Sachs, L. B., Eds. *The Psychology of Private Events. Perspectives on Covert Response Systems.* New York: Academic Press, 1971.

Jehu, D., Hardiker, P., Yelloly, M., and Shaw, M. *Behaviour Modification in Social Work.* London: Wiley-Interscience, 1972.

Kaminski, G. *Verhaltenstheorie und Verhaltensmodifikation.* Stuttgart: Ernst Klett Verlag, 1970.

Kanfer, F. H., and Phillips, J. S. *Learning Foundations of Behavior Therapy.* New York: Wiley, 1970.

Karlins, M., and Andrews, L. M., Eds. *Man Controlled. Readings in the Psychology of Behavior Control.* New York: The Free Press, 1972.

Keller, F. S. Good-bye teacher. *Journal of Applied Behavior Analysis,* 1968, **1,** 79–89.

Krumboltz, J. D., and Thoresen, C. E., Eds. *Behavioral Counseling. Cases and Techniques.* New York: Holt, Rinehart & Winston, 1969.

Lazarus, A. A. *Behavior Therapy and Beyond.* New York: McGraw-Hill, 1971.

Lazarus, A. A., Ed. *Clinical Behavior Therapy.* New York: Brunner/Mazel, 1972.

Liberman, R. P. *A Guide to Behavioral Analysis and Therapy.* Elmsford, N.Y.: Pergamon, 1972.

London, P. *Behavior Control.* New York: Harper & Row, 1969.

London, P. The end of ideology in behavior modification. Paper presented at the Third Annual Southern California Conference on Behavior Modification, Los Angeles, 1971.

McGinnies, E. *Social Behavior: A Functional Analysis.* Boston: Houghton-Mifflin, 1970.

McGinnies, E., and Ferster, C. B., Eds. *The Reinforcement of Social Behavior.* Boston: Houghton-Mifflin, 1971.

McMichael, J. S. Personalized instruction: A symposium in honor of Fred Keller. Paper presented at the American Psychological Association Meeting, Washington, D.C., 1971.

Mehrabian, A. *Tactics of Social Influence.* Englewood Cliffs, N.J.: Prentice-Hall, 1970.

Meyer, V., and Chesser, E. S. *Behaviour Therapy in Clinical Psychiatry.* London: Penguin, 1970.

Mowrer, O. H. Group therapy and therapeutic communities examined in the light of behavior modification principles. Paper presented at the First Annual Southern California Conference on Behavior Modification, Los Angeles, 1969.

Neuringer, C., and Michael, J. L., Eds. *Behavior Modification in Clinical Psychology.* New York: Appleton-Century-Crofts, 1970.

Öst, L.-G. Systematisk desensibilisering. Historisk ututveckling, forskning och teoretiska forklaringar. Psykologuppsats. Pedagogiska Institutionen, Stockholm Universitet, 1971. (a)

Öst, L.-G. Systematisk desensibilisering. Praktisk till-lampning av en beteendeterapeutisk metod. Forskningsrapport. Pedagogiska Institutionen, Stockholm Universitet, 1971. (b)

Patterson, G. R. *Families. Applications of Social Learning to Family Life.* Champaign, Ill.: Research Press, 1971.

Patterson, G. R., and Gullion, M. E. *Living with Children. New Methods for Parents and Teachers.* Champaign, Ill.: Research Press, 1968.

Personalized System of Instruction. *Newsletter* 1971–1972. Washington, D.C.: PSI Newsletter, Psychology Department, Georgetown University.

Rachman, S., and Teasdale, J. *Aversion Therapy and Behaviour Disorders. An Analysis.* London: Routledge and Kegan Paul, 1969.

Rogers, C. R., and Skinner, B. F. Some issues concerning the control of human behavior: A symposium. *Science,* 1956, **124,** 1057–1066.

Rönnberg, S. A training program for behavior therapy in Sweden. Paper presented at the First Meeting of the European Association for Behavior Therapy, July 19–23, 1971. (a)

Rönnberg, S. Anvisningar for utformning av fallredogorelser. Opublisherat manuskript, Pedagogiska Institutionen, Stockholm Universitet, 1971. (b)

Rönnberg, S. Beteendeanalys—ett arbete i vardande. APPU-rapport. Pedagogiska Institutionen, Stockholm Universitet, 1972.

Rubin, R. D., Fensterheim, H., Lazarus, A. A., and Franks, C. M., Eds. *Advances in Behavior Therapy. Proceedings of the Third Conference of the Association for Advancement of Behavior Therapy.* New York: Academic Press, 1971.

Rubin, R. D., and Franks, C. M., Eds. *Advances in Behavior Therapy, 1968.* New York: Academic Press, 1969.

Schaefer, H. H., and Martin, P. L. *Behavioral Therapy.* New York: McGraw-Hill, 1969.

Skinner, B. F. *Science and Human Behavior.* New York: The Free Press, 1953.

Skinner, B. F. *Beyond Freedom and Dignity.* New York: Knopf, 1971.

Stuart, R. B. A critical reappraisal and reformulation of selected mental health problems. In L. A. Hamerlynck, P .O. Davidson, and L. E. Acker (Eds.), *Behavior Modification and Ideal Mental Health Services.* Calgary, Alberta: The University of Calgary, 1969.

Stuart, R. B. The role of social work education in innovative human services. In F. W. Clark, D. R. Evans, and L. A. Hamerlynck (Eds.), *Implementing Behavioral Programs for Schools and Clinics.* Champaign, Ill.: Research Press, 1972.

Sulzer, B., and Mayer, G. R. *Behavior Modification Procedures for School Personnel.* Hinsdale, Ill.: The Dryden Press, 1972.

Szasz, T. S. *The Manufacture of Madness.* New York: Harper & Row, 1970.

Thompson, T., and Grabowski, J. *Behavior Modification of the Mentally Retarded.* New York: Oxford University Press, 1972.

Thoresen, C. E. Training behavioral counselors. In F. W. Clark, D. R. Evans, and L. A. Hamerlynck (Eds.), *Implementing Behavioral Programs for Schools and Clinics.* Champaign, Ill.: Research Press, 1972.

Truax, C. B., and Carkhuff, R. R. *Toward Effective Counseling and Psychotherapy: Training and Practice.* Chicago: Aldine-Atherton, 1967.

Welander, G. Familjeinteraktion. Pedagogiska Institutionen, Stockholm Universitet, 1972.

Wolpe, J. *The Practice of Behavior Therapy.* Elmsford, N.Y.: Pergamon, 1969.

Yates, A. J. *Behavior Therapy.* New York: Wiley, 1970.

# 27 TRAINING NONPROFESSIONALS IN BEHAVIOR MODIFICATION

**James M. Gardner**

## Introduction

The nonprofessional revolution in the mental health and mental retardation services delivery system has been nowhere more evident than in the area of behavior modification. A cursory review of current journal articles reveals a plethora of research and demonstration programs in which nonprofessionals serve as the principal change agents within a behavior modification framework. These change agents have been institution aides, parents, and teacher's aides. Correspondingly, the major loci of intervention have been the mental health and retardation institution, the home, and the classroom. Other loci (e.g., prisons, mental health centers, universities) have been the province of more traditional change agents, namely, mental health professionals.

From a historical perspective the juxtaposition of behavior modification and nonprofessional manpower utilization was a logical outgrowth of post-World War II developments in the United States. Some of the relevant socioeconomic-political forces in operation at that time were the identified need for a tremendous expansion in the delivery of mental health services and the large surpluses of money diverted from the war effort and channeled into domestic programs within the newly created National Institute of Mental Health. Of more direct relevance to mental health and mental retardation delivery systems, the post-World War II era was characterized by an expanded definition of mental health, an extension of the primary help-giving function from psychiatry to psychology and social

469

work, the decline of classical psychoanalysis as the principal treatment approach in mental health, and the rise of alternative forms of intervention such as group, filial, child, milieu, and client-centered therapies. Behavior modification, prominent in the 1920s and 1930s in the United States, enjoyed a new popularity in the 1950s. Simultaneously, experiments with "Big Brothers" and housewife psychotherapists offered beginning evidence of the potential for nonprofessional manpower utilization.

Behavior modification as a strategy for individual and group intervention was consonant with the limit-setting boundaries defining the use of nonprofessionals. The principles of behavior modification were relatively simple and straightforward when compared to the complicated "cerebral" training of psychoanalysts. Another reason that behavior modification and the development of nonprofessionals as manpower sources were related is that behavior modification principles suggested that direct intervention in "deviant" environments was the most efficient and effective method. More often than not, the commitment to restructuring the environment required that the principal caretakers of the identified client be (re)trained. These caretakers, whether institution aides or parents, were largely nonprofessionals. Finally, it can be noted that the settings in which behavior modification was applied were highly structured, role definitions could be made clear, and client–trainer relationships could be somewhat controlled. In such settings, nonprofessionals could perform adequately without fear of counterproduction as a result of their lack of education and/or training.

The purpose of this paper is to summarize research on the training of nonprofessional change agents who employ behavior modification techniques as their principal method for facilitating adaptive behavior change. The subpopulation under consideration is the institution aide, although information relevant to other populations (e.g., parents, teacher's aides, peers) will be introduced as appropriate. The major focus of this paper will be on research conducted by the author in the areas of selection, training, and supervision of nonprofessionals.

## Selection

Mental health professionals undergo extensive training prior to assuming their positions in a delivery system. This training consists of undergraduate preparation as well as specific vocational training (e.g., nursing schools, medical academies, university graduate schools). As a result of this extended training, some minimal level of competence can be assumed;

nonetheless, mental health professionals are often subjected to extensive selection procedures prior to being retrained. The selection of nonprofessionals, on the other hand, is often a mute point. When the nonprofessionals are parents, intervention is planned through the parents; there is no selection procedure. Given the fact that most parent-training programs are limited to mothers (for whatever reason), this limits the variance even further. At the institution level, many people believe that the high degree of structure in most behavior modification programs allows for the employment of a wide variety of people, most of whom can be trained to administer the behavioral procedures required under given conditions; again, there is no selection procedure. Thus, the selection of nonprofessional behavior modifiers has resembled the sophistication and precision characteristic of hiring grocery clerks.

There are a number of reasons for the importance of developing appropriate mechanisms for the selection of nonprofessional behavior modifiers. First, there is a need to select individuals who will be competent. While it may be true that highly structured systems produce an environment in which most people can perform adequately, effective selection would allow for maximizing the progress that can be made. Moreover, appropriate selection procedures may allow for a reduction in program structure, which in turn might result in increased client progress. If highly competent individuals can be selected and trained, behavior modification programs could be more individualized for staff as well as clients. When large masses of nonprofessionals are hired without selection, the program structure inspires an average degree of progress for most, but maximizes no single person's performance.

A second reason for effective selection procedures relates to the need to reduce employee turnover, which in turn reduces the direct and indirect costs associated with employee processing, orientation, and inservice education.

Various studies by the author relate to the issue of effective selection. These studies have dealt with variables such as length of experience, personality of the aide, and socioeconomic status.

## The Experience Factor

A major problem reported in the literature has been the resistance of experienced employees to behavior modification programs (Baumeister and Klosowski, 1965; Watson, 1970; Thompson and Grabowski, 1972).

The implication of these ancedotal reports is that new employees should be selected for initiating programs. Gardner (1972a) differentiated two groups of institution aides: new (less than 1 year's employ) and experienced (1 or more years). These employees were transferred into a behavior modification program for severely and profoundly retarded residents, and it was found that experienced employees had significantly less absence and requests for transfers. To control for differences in base rates between new and experienced employees, a within-subject design was used—rates of absence or transfers were compared for 4 months preceding and following the start of the program.

This study indicates that turnover resulting from the inception of a behavior modification program was less likely among experienced employees. Of course, the possibility exists that those factors that resulted in the less frequent absences and transfers are counterproductive from a programming viewpoint. For example, individuals who are resistant to change are not likely to request a transfer; *nor* are they likely to adjust to change to a new training program.

In a related study, Gardner (1972a) examined the effects of experience on knowledge of behavior modification principles and attitude toward working in a behavior modification program. The measure of behavior modification knowledge was the *Behavior Modification Test* or *BMT* (Gardner, Brust, and Watson, 1970); a 229 item, true–false, multiple-choice, fill-in test. The attitude measure was a three-point scale that required that the aide indicate degree of willingness to work in an area where behavior modification was being used. The results indicated that there were no significant differences between newly hired, recent (1–2 years employed), and experienced (2+ years) aides. This study supports the previous study and suggests that experienced personnel may not conform to the stereotype present in the field.

## The Personality Factor

Gardner (1972a) reported the only study that relates the personality of the trainer to the progress of the client. The purpose of the study was to investigate staff characteristic correlates of client behavior change. The clients were 39 severely and profoundly retarded children, adolescents, and young adults ranging in age from 7 to 23 (mean = 15) and in social age from .18 to 8.9 (mean = 3.3). The trainers ranged in age from 21 to 41 (mean = 27). There were four married females, two married males, and one single female. All the trainers were high school graduates; two had some college training. The personality and vocational tests used were the Minnesota Multiphasic Personality Inventory, the Edwards Personal Preference Schedule, and the Strong Vocational Interest Blank. Standard subscales from these tests totaled 74 variables.

During an intensive training program in behavior modification, the trainers were placed on a unit and instructed to familiarize themselves with the residents. Following the training course, they were instructed to choose a group of residents with whom they would work. Two conditions were imposed on their choices: (1) Each group should contain both severely and profoundly retarded children and adults, and (2) groups should be of approximately equal size. The final groupings for each trainer are listed in Table 27.1.

All the residents were involved in an intensive self-care and social skills training program for 2 months. The trainers initially worked with the profoundly retarded residents on a one-to-one basis until they were able to work with them in small groups. Severely retarded residents were worked in with small groups from the start. Training for each group was scheduled for 8 hours per day, 5 days per week. Residents continued to live on their home ward and received training in small adjacent rooms.

Social age scores from the Vineland Social Maturity Scale (Doll, 1935) served as the dependent variable. The scale was administered by a psychologist before the study began, and at 2–3 month intervals thereafter. After the first 2 months, only 3 of the 74 test variables were significantly related to change in social age score. These were need for achievement ($r = .85$, $p < .05$), need for affiliation ($r = .76$, $p < .05$), and need for intraception ($r = -.77$, $p < .05$). All scores were from the Edwards Personal Preference Schedule.

It is clear that the need for achievement plays a crucial role in determining outcome; however, the relationship between outcome and the other two variables (i.e., low need for intraception, high need for affili-

**TABLE 27.1**
CHARACTERISTICS OF CLIENT GROUPS IN GARDNER (1972a)

| | Client groups | | | | | | |
|---|---|---|---|---|---|---|---|
| | A | B | C | D | E | F | G |
| N | 5 | 6 | 6 | 5 | 5 | 7 | 5 |
| Mean CA | 16.2 | 14.1 | 17.2 | 14.6 | 16.3 | 17.3 | 13.9 |
| Mean SA | 3.4 | 4.5 | 3.7 | 2.5 | 2.9 | 2.7 | 3.6 |
| Mean SQ | 24.0 | 33.0 | 26.0 | 17.0 | 18.0 | 23.0 | 30.0 |

ation) is not as clear. In fact, the finding that people with low needs to analyze their own or other people's motives make significant progress with clients is unexpected when traditional educational ideas regarding behavior modification are considered (e.g., Lindsley, 1968; Patterson, 1969).

## Socioeconomic Status

Socioeconomic status is an important variable in the selection of non-professionals, while it is not as critical in the selection of professionals. Gardner (1970a) trained two groups of institution aides: a high-unemployment, exclusively black, inner-city group (sponsored by the Office of Economic Opportunity) and regular aides. After 20 hours of training, there were no significant differences between the two groups on knowledge of behavior modification principles (*BMT* scores) or proficiency in applying behavior modification techniques (see next section). Related to this study, Staats, Minke, and Butts (1970) found no significant differences between inner-city welfare clients, middle-class housewives, and high school students in their success in correcting reading deficits among culturally deprived children.

These studies in the area of experience, personality, and socioeconomic status illustrate that research on the selection of nonprofessionals for inclusion in behavior modification programs can be used to reduce employee turnover and increase employee effectiveness. Findings such as these should be useful in initiating new programs or expanding existing ones.

## Training

While there are numerous films, manuals, and training programs in behavior modification, there has been little attention to research in this area. This is a paradox, since the majority of professional time is spent in teaching behavior modification and not in application. In 1969 Poser noted: "Despite the recent spate of publications on behavior modification there is little in the literature to guide those responsible for the training of behavior therapists [p. 37]." In 1972, Poser's lament is still true.

Five different levels of the behavior modification worker can be distinguished. At the most elementary level, there is the behavior modification *applicator* (Patterson and Reid, 1969), who is trained to apply specific techniques under highly structured conditions with supervision. Next there is the behavior modification *technician* (Risley, Reynolds, and Hart, 1972), who can apply a small number of techniques under moderately structured conditions without supervision. The next level is represented by the *specialist* (Watson, 1970), who is highly trained in one area. The behavior modification *generalist* (Schell and Adams, 1969) is not as highly trained in any one area, but he is trained to apply a wide variety of techniques to a large number of areas. Finally, there is the *consultant* (Lovitt, 1970), who develops and implements training programs for individuals at the other four levels.

The importance of theory, techniques, and personal qualities in training curricula is related to the level of skill of the trainer. In turn, the level of skill required by the behavior modification worker is related to the demands of the environment, the client characteristics and nature of the problem, the organization structure, and the available technology. Despite the fact that there are hundreds of behavior modification programs, there appears to be little communality between programs in terms of curricula content and practicum experiences. Some basic elements, however, are present in most programs: behavioral measurement and observation, discussions of reinforcement, shaping, stimulus control, and deceleration techniques.

While there is fairly high agreement that training should take place in the natural environment, this has not always been possible. Therefore, alternative methods have been developed such as role playing and critical incident modeling. In some cases, on-the-job modeling has been used. Under experimental conditions various kinds of feedback mechanisms have been used, including signaling systems, bug-in-the-ear sound systems, and audiovisual tape.

Over the past few years, I have been involved in a series of studies designed to create a more efficient and effective training program for nonprofessionals at the applicator, technician, and generalist level. The first step in this series of investigations was the development of the *Training Proficiency Scale* (Gardner, 1969; Gardner *et al.,* 1970). The Training Proficiency Scale (*TPS*) is a 30-item, five-point rating scale; items include "Gives reinforcement correctly," "Determines operant level," and so on. Interscorer, test–retest, and split-half reliabilities were all high. The validity of the test was determined in two ways. First, concurrent validity was measured by correlating scores on the *TPS* with scores on the *BMT* (see previous section): the correlation was .89. Next, total *TPS* scores for a group of aides were found to correlate highly (.90 or higher) with an independent (expert) judge's rank ordering of trainer proficiency. In a later study (Gardner, 1970a), scores on the *TPS* were found to increase significantly as a result of inservice training in behavior modification.

Having developed two measures of proficiency in behavior modification (i.e., *TPS* and *BMT*), an inservice training program was constructed based on behavior modification principles (Watson, Gardner, and Sanders, 1971). A contingent teaching format was adopted, and scores for parts of the *BMT* and the *TPS* were used as the criteria at each decision point. Behavior modification skills were broken down into two major systems: verbal and motor. The verbal system was further broken down into three major subsystems: reinforcement, stimulus control, and shaping. The motor system was also broken down into four subsystems: administering rewards, shaping responses, communicating, and miscellaneous.

The entire sequence of training both verbal and motor skills has been described in detail elsewhere and is presented in part here (Watson *et al.,* 1971):

> Teaching is accomplished through a contingent textbook-lecture-discussion series. There are nine such units. The trainee starts by receiving her first textbook assignment. In order to be admitted to the corresponding lecture, she must make a high passing grade (90% correct) on an examination that evaluates her understanding of the textbook assignment. If she passes, she can proceed to the lecture; if she fails, she must repeat the textbook assignment and take a second examination. . . .
>
> Lecture material is presented by tape recorder along with 35 mm slides that illustrate the recorded subject matter. The lecture is an extension and further illustration of the material presented in the text, designed to clarify and amplify the text. The same contingencies required for progressing from the textbook assignment to the lecture are also required for moving on to the corresponding discussion. . . . After the trainee completes the discussion, she receives her next textbook assignment. . . .
>
> After all nine textbook-lecture-discussion units are successfully completed, the trainee progresses to actual behavior shaping training. She begins by seeing a movie and a demonstration. . . . Next she attempts to apply behavior modification skills herself with a fellow trainee in a role playing situation. . . . When the trainee can pass a behavioral test that assesses how well she can actually apply behavior modification techniques (at a 90% level), she is assigned a severely or profoundly retarded child and attempts to teach him self-help skills. When she passes a second behavioral test in the one-child situation (again at a 90% level) she has completed classroom training, receives her ward assignment, and begins an internship [pp. 40–41].

The contingent textbook series outlined above was evaluated with four groups of subjects: institution aides ($N = 8$), Neighborhood Youth Corps ($N = 5$), mothers of autistic children ($N = 7$) and Foster Grandparents ($N = 6$). The first three lecture units were presented noncontingently, while the following three units were administered contingently. Finally, the last units were presented noncontingently.

The four groups differed widely on their unit test scores during the noncontingent phases. However, under contingent conditions, there were no significant differences among the four groups. The performance of the mothers remained high (90% or higher) throughout the study, while the contingent phase resulted in significant gains for the other three groups. Since the bulk of nonprofessional institution aides are drawn from these three groups, the importance of using a contingent-reinforcement teaching series was clearly demonstrated.

One critical question concerning the effects of the training program described above is whether the aides behaved differently as a result of the training. This question was explored by measuring on-ward behavior of aides who had completed the training program and aides who had not been trained in behavior modification (Gardner and Giampa, 1971). Both groups were working in the same area with the same residents. The Attendant Behavior Checklist developed by Bensberg and Barnett (1966) was adapted for the purposes of this study. The aide's behaviors were classified into nine categories: personal care, supervision, training, punishment, socialization, ward management, clothing and linen management, record keeping, and leisure time. Ratings were made by psychologists through one-way mirrors using time-sampling techniques. The psychologists were unaware of the training status of the aides. Despite the fact that the total amount of contact between residents and staff were similar for both groups of aides, the behavior modification aides spent significantly more time in training activities, whereas the untrained aides spent significantly more time in supervision (e.g., watching residents). Thus, the contingent teaching program was successful; as a result of the training, aides were spending significantly more time training residents.

The development of the two measures of behavior modification proficiency and a standardized curricula for teaching behavior modification allowed for further research. In a subsequent study (Gardner, 1972b), for example, the differential effects of role playing and lectures were examined. Twenty female aides were matched in terms of socioeconomic status, knowledge of nursing, mental retardation, and behavior modification and then randomly assigned to one of two groups. Group L attended the lecture series followed by role playing while Group R entered role playing and then the lectures. The differences between role playing and lectures were compared separately, and the effects of the different sequences (i.e., which came first) were also analyzed.

The aides were tested with the *TPS* and the *BMT* at three points: pre-course, following the first phase (role playing for Group R and lectures

for Group L), and post-course. The mean scores for both groups at all
three stages are presented in Table 27.2.

In terms of training proficiency, there were no differences between
the two groups on pre- or post-course scores; however, Group R exceeded
Group L following phase 1. Thus, training in role playing increased training proficiency, but the sequence of role playing followed by lectures did
not matter in the final analysis. An opposite pattern emerged for knowledge of behavior modification principles: No differences were found on
pre- or post-course tests, while Group L exceeded Group R following
phase 1. Thus, the lecture series contributed to knowledge of principles
but not to training proficiency, and the role playing contributed to training
proficiency but not to knowledge of principles. The sequence of experiences did not result in differential performance in terms of either proficiency or knowledge.

Research cited in the previous section on the achievement levels of
aides from different socioeconomic backgrounds (Gardner, 1970a) or with
varying lengths of employment (Gardner, 1972a) was also made possible
through the development of the standardized curricula and the measures
of behavior modification skills.

At this point, considerably more research needs to be done. For example, the relationship between *TPS* and *BMT* scores and client progress
should be assessed in the same way that staff characteristic correlates
were determined. While there is evidence that the standardized curricula
results in aides who behave differently, it remains to be demonstrated that
the altered behavior is related to client progress. Although the prescribed
teaching techniques described here result in little variation in trainer skills
(despite differences in experience, socioeconomic status, and target behavior), there may be undesirable side effects that ultimately limit the
creativity of the trainer. These are only a few of the major questions that
remain to be answered.

**TABLE 27.2**
PRE-, PERI-, AND POST-COURSE MEAN SCORES ON THE TRAINING PROFICIENCY SCALE
AND THE BEHAVIOR MODIFICATION TEST

|                    | Training proficiency scale | | | Behavior modification test | | |
|--------------------|-------|------|---------|-------|-------|--------|
|                    | R     | L    | t       | R     | L     | t      |
| Pre-course         | 45.4  | 45.6 | 0.025   | 138.7 | 139.1 | 0.625  |
| Following phase 1  | 94.8  | 52.4 | 6.235[a] | 150.1 | 163.7 | 2.193[b] |
| Post-course        | 108.3 | 96.0 | 1.618   | 168.5 | 162.9 | 0.718  |

[a] .001.
[b] .05.

## Supervision

Following appropriate selection and training procedures, individuals should be placed in a management system that provides for the continued development of the client, the staff, the organization, and the community. Various types of supervisory strategies can be adopted to attain these goals. One increasingly popular strategy is labeled "consulting supervision" (Colarelli and Siegel, 1966; Gardner, 1972c). This model is designed to foster the creativity of each member of a group, and to increase the power of individual decision making through group action. The consultant's role is faciliatory and the help giver assumes increasing responsibility at all levels of planning, decision making, and implementation.

The consulting-supervision model is also designed to foster psychological ownership, which refers to the extent to which an individual identifies with an idea or action. There are a few studies that suggest that psychological ownership may be a major factor in achieving client behavior change (Galloway and Galloway, 1970; Rose, Parson, Jarman, and Hetchenthol, 1971). Gardner (1975) conducted a behavior modification training program in which the trainer's psychological ownership was the major strategy for consultant–trainer contact. Trainers were encouraged to order their own supplies, choose their own schedules, develop their own techniques, choose their own residents, and so on. Over the course of 6 months, residents in that program made social quotient gains (as measured by the Vineland Social Maturity Scale) that averaged more than ten points: the client:trainer ratios averaged 15:1 during this period. The gains made using this method are far in excess of the gains reported in any other behavior modification study using comparable trainer and client populations.

Since behavior modification techniques were effective in changing the behavior of a wide variety of client groups, it was only a matter of time before these same procedures were incorporated into supervisory strategies for managing staff. At present there are more than a dozen published accounts of research findings on the effects of using reinforcement with staff (Gardner, 1975). In large measure, the results have been uniformly positive.

Gardner (1970b) attempted to reduce lateness and absence of institution aides. One group of aides received one-half day off for each 5 weeks of perfect attendance (i.e., no lateness, no absence); the other group were under the traditional institutional system of having their pay "docked" (i.e., response cost) for each lateness and absence. Over the course of the study, the positive reinforcement group had less absence and lateness, although the differences between the groups did not reach significance at the .05 level. Attendance has also been studied by Hirsch and Walder (1969), who reported that parents who deposited $50 (return of the money was contingent upon perfect attendance) to attend nine parent training sessions had 100% attendance records.

One of the necessary ingredients of any management system is the accumulation of accurate data. One problem in obtaining accurate data is that data collection is often viewed as an aversive stimulus—nonprofessional aides are not used to dealing with numbers and figures and are uncomfortable when doing so. Gardner (1975) reinforced aides with time off from work for data collection. On a weekly basis, one-half day off was awarded to the aide who had collected the largest number of toileting incidents for her group of residents. During baseline conditions the incidence of proper toilet incidents and soiling/wetting averaged less than 50 per day for the entire group. Under reinforcement conditions, the average daily rate for both incidents (i.e., proper use and soiling/wetting) nearly tripled. Following the removal of the contingency a marked reduction in recording soiling/wetting was noted, but recording of proper usage remained above the baseline condition. Unfortunately, independent measures of toileting frequency were not maintained, so it is not possible to determine whether the increased frequency was a result of more accurate recording or of fabulations. Nonetheless, the dramatic results of applying reinforcement as a supervisory strategy are evident.

While it has been demonstrated that the behavior of nonprofessional behavior modifiers can be modified, it remains to be seen whether a comprehensive management system utilizing behavior modification principles and techniques can be made operational. Such systems do exist on a microscopic level in complex token economies for client populations (e.g., Ayllon and Azrin, 1968). In at least one instance, the basic ingredients and requirements for a comprehensive reinforcement system for staff have been put forward (Gardner, 1975), but implementation and further development are as yet unaccomplished.

## Ethical Issues

For whatever reason, ethical issues are often ignored in discussions of the application of behavior modification principles. In the light of events in the past few years, such an approach seems at best fruitless, and at

worst, destructive. The professional behavior modification consultant oper-
ates in a world where personal, social, economic, and political forces shape
and maintain his behavior as well as the behavior of individuals to whom
he relates. Recognition and attention to the full range of issues presented
is the only approach that can ensure continued growth and development.

Ethical issues are of paramount importance in discussions of nonprofessional manpower utilization. Professionals from various fields have
established codes of ethical behavior that (hopefully) guide their behavior;
nonprofessionals do not belong to such organizations. Moreover, in none
of the behavior modification curricula familiar to this author is there inclusion of ethics as subject matter (Yen and Gardner, 1972).

One of the most serious ethical concerns when nonprofessionals are
trained in behavior modification is the spread of effect. It has been commonly observed (e.g., Fredericks, Baldwin, McDonnel, Hofman, and
Harter, 1971; Patterson, Shaw, and Ebner, 1969) that once parents are
trained to modify the behavior of one deviant child, they begin establishing behavorial programs for all family members. Such a spread of effect
raises a number of issues. First, what is the nature of the checks on the
parent? Certainly the normal checks (e.g., child abuse laws, child labor
laws) against exploitation have not been wholly adequate in the past. Although the systematic application of behavior modification by parents may
reduce the incidence of various classes of "undesirable" behavior, what is
to prevent movement in an opposite direction? For example, what is to
prevent a mother from programming her child to be "my son, the psychologist"? At present any mother will tell you: "Plenty." However, if
given the potentially powerful tools of behavior modification, such accom-
plishments are not improbable. Would not this kind of insidious and conscious programming violate the child's basic civil rights?

This problem is important, particularly when the trainer population
is considered. Parents who are trained as behavior modifiers are almost
always those parents who are experiencing extreme difficulties with their
children, indicating that the parent's responses are maladaptive (i.e., they
lead to "undesirable" responses by the children). Are these the people,
then, to whom the tools of behavior modification are to be entrusted?

Another issue in training parents is the effects of the training on the
entire family constellation. Professional workers need to anticipate the results of a "successful" intervention. How will this "success" change the
family's habitual ways of relating to each other? Although hard data is
lacking, Liberman (1969) described a case where as the child developed
more independence from his parents (the goal of the intervention), his
parents began to argue considerably.

Most parent-training programs operate with the mother as the change agent. To what extent does this modus operandi reinforce a matriarchy in the family structure? To what extent do parent-training programs further isolate the father, whose isolation may be one source of problem? Patterson and Reid (1969) have noted in this regard that in one family setting fathers dispensed and received the least reinforcement and the lowest rates of aversive consequences.

Turning from parent-training programs to institution programs increases the need for concern with ethical issues. Home-based children are protected from exploitation by various laws; institutionalized residents are almost always deprived of basic civil rights. Where else, for example, would people be allowed to give electric shocks to other human beings because they screamed (Hamilton and Standahl, 1969)? While the application of electric shock to eliminate self-destructive behaviors is not universally accepted (Buddenhagen, 1971; Gardner, 1972c), its use to decelerate other forms of behavior is questionable at best. What limits are to be placed on the use of shock? Who will use it? On whom? For what reason? What checks will be instituted to protect the institutionalized resident against the wanton use of electric shock? Once electric shock is introduced and efficient results are obtained, will expediency discourage developing alternative methods of deceleration? All these questions need to be answered. At least they need to be asked!

Another very serious ethical question concerns the extent to which effective reinforcement systems in the institution, the home, or the school will eliminate exploratory or limit-testing behavior. If a behavior modification program were successful, the client would soon adhere to the established contingencies—indeed, failure to do so would be increasingly punishing. The establishment and continual reinforcement of a passive-accepting attitude toward authority has great implications for the generation of societal change. The Viet Nam War provides an excellent example. In the mid-1960s the war was accepted by most Americans as a moral, righteous adventure. By the end of that decade the moral certitude was in doubt, and in the next decade U.S. involvement in Viet Nam had run the full circle and was viewed as morally reprehensible. Massive societal change was not accomplished through policies and dictates ushered forth from the establishment, but rather through the consistent and diligent work of a small group of men who would not accept the standards promulgated by authority. Such acts of noncompliance are possible only from individuals who have been successful in the past in deviating from societal norms and mores. To the extent that child-rearing practices and culturally based limits allow for the occasional development of individuals who are deviant, to that extent the culture as a whole provides one mechanism for renewal. What would the world be like today if Martin Luther King had been raised by parents trained in behavior modification techniques?

## References

Ayllon, T., and Azrin, N. *The Token Economy*. New York: Appleton-Century-Croft, 1968.

Baumeister, A., and Klosowski, R. An attempt to group toilet train severely retarded patients. *Mental Retardation*, 1965, **3**(6), 24–26.

Bensberg, G., and Barnett, C. *Attendant Training in Southern Residential Facilities for the Mentally Retarded*. Atlanta, Ga.: Southern Regional Education Board, 1966.

Buddenhagen, R. Until electric shocks are legal. *Mental Retardation*, 1971, **9**(6), 48–50.

Colarelli, N., and Siegel, S. *Ward H*. New York: Van Nostrand Reinhold, 1966.

Doll, E. The vineland social maturity scale. *Training School Bulletin*, 1935, **32**, 1–7.

Fredericks, H., Baldwin, V., McDonnel, J., Hofman, R., and Harter, J. Parents educate their trainable children. *Mental Retardation*, 1971, 24–26.

Galloway, C., and Galloway, K. Parent groups with a focus on precise behavior management. *IMRID Papers and Reports*, 1970, **7**, No. 1.

Gardner, J. M. *The Training Proficiency Scale: Manual*. Columbus, Ohio: St. Joseph Guild, 1969.

Gardner, J. M. Differential effects of two methods of teaching behavior modification. In J. M. Gardner (Ed.), *Mental Retardation 1970*. Columbus, Ohio: Ohio Department of Mental Hygiene, 1970, pp. 1–20.(a)

Gardner, J. M. Effects of reinforcement conditions on lateness and absence among institutional personnel. *Ohio Research Quarterly*, 1970 (9)3, 315–316.(b)

Gardner, J. M. Selection of nonprofessionals for behavior modification programs. *American Journal of Mental Deficiency*, 1972, **76**, 680–685.(a)

Gardner, J. M. Teaching behavior modification to nonprofessionals. *Journal of Applied Behavior Analysis*, 1972, **5**, 517–521.(b)

Gardner, J. M. Alternatives to the fist. Unpublished manuscript, 1972.(c)

Gardner, J. M. *Training Nonprofessionals in Behavior Modification*. Worthington, Ohio: Jones Publishing Co., 1975.

Gardner, J.M., Brust, D., and Watson, L. A scale to measure skill in applying behavior modification techniques to the mentally retarded. *American Journal of Mental Deficiency*, 1970, **74**, 633–636.

Gardner, J. M., and Giampa, F. The attendant behavior checklist: Measuring on-the-ward behavior of institutional personnel. *American Journal of Mental Deficiency*, 1971, **75**, 617–622.

Hamilton, J., and Standahl, J. Suppression of stereotyped screaming behavior in a profoundly retarded institutionalized female. Unpublished manuscript, 1969.

Hirsch, I., and Walder, L. Training mothers in groups as reinforcement therapists for their own children. *Proceedings of the 77th American Psychological Association*, 1969, pp. 561–562.

Liberman, R. Behavioral approaches to family and couple therapy. Unpublished manuscript, 1969.

Lindsley, O. Training parents and teachers to precisely manage children's behavior. Unpublished manuscript, 1968.

Lovitt, T. Behavior modification: The current scene. *Exceptional Children,* 1970, **37,** 85–91.

Patterson, G. Behavioral intervention procedures in the classroom and in the home. In A. Bergin and S. Garfield (Eds.), *Handbooks of Psychotherapy and Behavior Change.* New York: Wiley, 1969.

Patterson, G., and Reid, G. Reciprocity and coercion: Two facets of social systems. In C. Neuringer and J. Michael (Eds.), *Behavior Modification in Clinical Psychology.* New York: Appleton-Century-Crofts, 1969.

Patterson, G., Shaw, D., and Ebner, M. Teachers, peers and parents as agents of change in the classroom. In F. Benson (Ed.), *Modifying Deviant Social Behaviors in Various Classroom Settings.* Eugene, Ore. University of Oregon Press, 1969, pp. 13–48.

Poser, E. The teaching of behavior modification in an interdisciplinary setting. In R. Rubin and C. Franks (Eds.), *Advances in Behavior Therapy 1968.* New York: Academic Press, 1969.

Risley, T., Reynolds, N., and Hart, B. Behavior modification with disadvantaged children. In R. Bradfield (Ed.), *Behavior Modification: The Human Effort.* Palo Alto, Calif.: Science and Behavior Books, 1972.

Rose, S., Parson, R., Jarman, B., and Hetchenthal, C. Group training of parents as behavioral modifiers of their own mentally retarded children. Unpublished manuscript, 1971.

Schell, R., and Adams, W. Training parents of a young child with profound deficits to teacher-therapists. *Journal of Special Education,* 1969, **2,** 439–453.

Staats, A., Minke, K., and Butts, P. A token reinforcement remedial reading program administered by black therapy-technicians to problem black children. *Behavior Therapy,* 1970, **1,** 331–353.

Thompson, T., and Grabowski, J. *Behavior Modification of the Mentally Retarded.* New York: Oxford University Press, 1972.

Watson, L. Behavior modification of residents and personnel in institutions for the mentally retarded. In A. Baumeister and E. Butterfield (Eds.), *Residential Facilities for the Mentally Retarded.* Chicago: Aldine, 1970, pp. 199–245.

Watson, L., Gardner, J. M., and Sanders, C. Shaping and maintaining behavior modification skills in staff members in an MR institution. *Mental Retardation,* 1971, **9** (3), 39–42.

Yen, S., and Gardner, J. M. Ethical considerations in training parents as behavior modifiers. *Behavior Therapy,* 1972, **3,** 151–152.

# IX CONTROL AND COUNTERCONTROL: A PANEL DISCUSSION

## PATRICK BATESON

As I see it, two quite separate issues lie embedded within the problem we are discussing. The most tractable of the two, and the one most clearly involving the expertise of people working on behavior modification, concerns the kind of knowledge that would be required if we were to improve methods of government and opportunities for dissent. However, behind the glittering possibilities of a major program of research and development lies a quite different problem. On what factors does the preferred area of technical application depend? Why should particular questions about methods of government or dissent seem important to us? It will be argued that these questions can in principle be tackled at the behavior level. But even if they can, I suggest that their analyses will require a very different expertise from that involved in devising a program that will, say, encourage more people to use contraceptives or relieve the plight of oppressed groups. To take an analogy, it is not obvious that the skills involved in building a bridge are the same or even remotely similar to those involved in assessing the need for a bridge in the first place. The technology involved in choosing materials and methods of construction appropriate to the estimated loads on the bridge is very different from the body of knowledge required to anticipate the load, to calculate changes of traffic flow and to assess what will happen to the economies of nearby towns. The distinction will doubtless seem obvious, and it would be scarcely worth pursuing were it not that Skinner and many of his followers operate as though a solution to one problem is the solution to all problems. The argument appears to be that if it is possible to change human behavior by certain procedures, then those same methods can be used to analyze and control all the determinants of human behavior. Thus, when Skinner deals with the problem of human values he writes: "If a scientific analysis can tell us how to change behavior, can it tell us what changes to make? This is a question about the behavior of those who do in fact propose and make changes" (*Beyond Freedom and Dignity*, p. 103). Admittedly, Skinner attempts to justify this statement by sketching ways in which values might develop by analogy with what is thought to happen in phylogenetic evolution. Behavior that increases the chances of a culture surviving is retained, and behavior that decreases its chances of survival is eliminated. Now, even if Skinner is partly right (and I find it hard to believe he is anything more than that), nothing that I know of in operant–conditioning technology will allow him or anyone else to state with confidence what types of behavior are appropriate when present circumstances change. The survival explanation is necessarily post hoc, and Skinner is quite unable to state in advance when cultures should be highly specialized and conformist and when cultures should be diversified and heterodox. And yet some means of determining the extent of diversity appropriate to the existing social conditions is necessary if we are not merely to ask for controls and countercontrols that suit our existing ideologies. As things stand, the science of behavior has not provided us with any understanding of why some questions seem more important than others. Furthermore, by claiming that their methodology is appropriate to dealing with the problem, Skinnerians are in danger of suppressing any introspection into why they behave scientifically in the way they do. Skinner asserts that the technology he advocates is ethically neutral (*Beyond Freedom and Dignity*), and yet it is relevant to ask why he thinks that the way he selects the evidence is better than the way other scientists who study human behavior select it. There are vast areas of knowledge, ranging from ethology to social psychology and epidemiology, that Skinner ignores or chooses to disregard. Of course, it is an open question as to which theory of human behavior is going to be most productive, and Skinner's may be partly vindicated. Nevertheless, his evaluation of what is important and his assertions about the right course of action for humans depends on all sorts of preconceptions and, indeed, gaps in knowledge. For example, in company with some of the modern pop-ethologists, some Skinnerians will claim that capitalist societies are based on sounder principles of behavior than socialist societies. Is this attitude a consequence of the kinds of things they work at or is it perhaps a cause? May it not be the case that certain methods of description and analysis are chosen because they generate results that are intuitively plausible? If so, why are the results plausible? Not, I suspect, for reasons that are ethically or ideologically neutral. Indeed, I wonder whether Skinnerian methodology particularly appeals to those who have consciously or unconsciously accepted white American conventions about the value of monetary rewards and the need for material success.

Whatever the relationship between one's ideology and the results one prefers to accept, it is as well to realize that the design for a perfect society rests as always on what one happens to like, and so far no design has been produced by methods independent of anyone's initial preconceptions.

I believe, therefore, that in a discussion of methods of control and countercontrol we must be honest as well as clear headed. We should avoid phony rationalizations for what we like and dislike in terms of hypothetical behavior principles and state quite simply what sort of society we should prefer to live in. Having specified the amount of dissent that we want built into the system, and whether or not we want to consider the possibility of the system being totally overhauled from time to time, questions can then be asked about ways in which goals can be attained more quickly. At that stage the behavioral technologist may have a useful role to play. However, one would hope that techniques would be based on a broad area of knowledge and would be handled as gingerly as though they were drugs with therapeutic but potentially dangerous properties.

Just because a technique can be made to work does not necessarily mean that there are not other, better ways of doing the same job. Nor does it mean that there will be no long-term damaging side effects. For example, by using banks of magnificent equipment it may be possible to teach every 2-year-old child to read and write, and many people would doubtless argue that if it is possible it should be done. No expense should be spared in furthering the education of our children. But the costs may take a quite unexpected form. Two-year-olds are not vegetables. They actively explore and test their environments, they begin to interact socially with other children of the same age, and so on. If we were to deny them this experience by attempting to force the pace of development in one very restricted direction, we may be laying up all sorts of social and personal problems for those children later in their lives. Of course it is an open question, and all I wish to do is make a plea for caution in all areas of technical application.

In conclusion, I also wish to make a plea for collaboration between scientists from different disciplines. I admire both the skill and the sense of social responsibility of my colleagues who were trained as Skinnerians and who are now applying their expertise in areas of great human distress. But my admiration would be even greater if they were a little more eclectic in their choice of techniques and more sensitive to the biological and social determinations of behavior. Rather than selling the virtues of our various methods and concepts, and attacking or ignoring those of scientists with a different training, there is everything to be gained from combining our knowledge. But even when we do bring our different perspectives to bear on particular social problems, the question remains of why they appear to us as problems and why we place a higher priority on solving them rather than alleviating other areas of human misery.

# WILLARD F. DAY

In considering the notion of countercontrol, one confronts at once a difficulty of a sort frequently discussed by Skinner in *Beyond Freedom and Dignity*. When one thinks of issues related to countercontrol as a *problem,* one may be already deeply enmeshed in the skein of questions and concerns that easily prompt themselves as aspects of the conceptual equipment figuratively associated by Skinner with the notion of "autonomous man." The difficulty arises because it is easy to hamstring the technical behaviorist notion of "control" with irrelevant and inappropriate conceptual moves stemming from the way the term functions as a part of ordinary language.

When, following Skinner, one thinks as a behaviorist of the concept of "control," one has in mind primarily the neat adjustment of any individual's behavior to the particulars of his environmental situation. When, as a behaviorist, one speaks of the environmental control over behavior, no personification of the concept of control is involved. When the behaviorist speaks of control, what he is talking about is a *relation* between what a particular individual does, or can do, and the circumstances of his environment. The behaviorist's concept of control engages theory when it is held that the circumstances of one's environment determine whether one will have this particular behavioral repertoire rather than that, and whether on any particular occasion a specific piece of behavior is likely to occur or not. To be sure, other people can form part of the environment for behavior, and they can enter into controlling relations with behavior much as with any other aspect of the environment. However, only a very small proportion of such controlling relations involving other people are aptly describable as intentionally manipulative, and of course the patterns of behavioral control that support such manipulative behavior are themselves subject to a behavioral analysis. In sum, for a behaviorist the concept of control specifies predominantly patterns of relations, both actual and potential, in terms of which an individual's interaction with his environment can be characterized.

However, when viewed within the perspective of the interrelated concepts that define "autonomous man," the concept of control takes on an entirely different nature from the behaviorist one outlined above. When we regard ourselves as autonomous agents, we are likely to resist others whom we regard as seeking to exert control over us in some way. We often take it to be vaguely unethical to be seen too conspicuously attempting to exert "undue" influence over the behavior of others, as, for example, the model of the university professor of political science who conscientiously tries to be truly impartial in his lectures. The exercise of effective control is often associated wtih the notion of the will. People fear someone who claims to be effective in controlling behavior because they do not want to "submit" to his will, which they suspect may take a capricious turn. Self-control, of course, is widely thought to involve an exercise of will. The popular concept of control is closely interrelated to that of the exercise of power. People in power are often feared because of the opportunities they are taken to have for exercising control. Knowledge of factors involved in behavioral control, even at the purely scientific level, is regarded as dangerous because someday someone may find himself in a position of power such that he can make use of it. Perhaps most important, the popular notion of control is generally asociated with aversive practices. People fear the control exercised on them by others because they suspect it will be used to harm them.

I have taken the trouble to call attention here to some of the facets involved in our use of the concept of control simply to show that it functions hand in glove with the conceptual scheme that Skinner has characterized as "autonomous man." Of course, Skinner has argued in *Beyond Freedom and Dignity* that to interpret human actions in the light of such a conceptual scheme, and to rely on it in making important social decisions, is a major obstacle to making significant progress in solving the pressing problems of the current human situation.

The same conclusion must be said to apply to the concept of countercontrol, conspicuously at least to the extent to which the concept of countercontrol is parasitic upon that of control. However, with countercontrol the frame of reference shifts away from one in which we are conceptualizing those individuals or agencies that we regard as having the power to control us, to one in which we are conceptualizing ourselves as the objects of the (potentially malevolent) designs of someone else. The inherent focus of the concept of countercontrol is again centered on matters of damage, pain, or other aspects of personal aversion, much as it is with respect to the set of concepts within which our use of "control" is embedded. Yet the change of the frame of reference now leads us to speak of rights and responsibilities. We attempt to protect ourselves from abuse by others by making an appeal to *our* rights and *their* responsibilities. In the case of individuals "conditioned to behave for the good of others" (to use Skinner's expression), the situation may often be the other way around. There are civic-minded individuals who exhort us to keep in mind the responsibilities we must exercise with regard to others. We have similarly the charitable and the compassionate, whose behavior is powerfully reinforced by attention to the rights of others, often at the expense of their own. It is particularly clear with respect to the concept of countercontrol that relevant verbal behavior occurs predominantly within a context of concern over possibilities of aversive control. The concepts of rights and responsibilities, as with the related concepts of freedom and the self, have largely negative definitions, and they are concerned with the range of things that people do, or try to do, to protect themselves from harm.[1] However, once again, I have no purpose here other than to identify the application of the concept of countercontrol as a part of the package of conceptual equipment figuratively referred to by Skinner as "autonomous man." One can, of course, make no objection to the efforts people undertake to protect themselves from possible damage by others. The objection is to patterns of conceptualizing, and of thinking about, individual and social action that we now have reason to believe may well stand in the way both of mutual social protection and the achievement of constructive solutions of social problems that are widely acknowledged to exist.

The preceding considerations will, I hope, permit me to show now how it is that current interests in techniques for behavior modification, as representatively illustrated in the body of this volume, raise not in the slightest, in and of themselves, the threat of totalitarian political and social control. Neither is such a threat intrinsically present in the conceptual equipment employed by behaviorists in their analysis of the contingencies involved in behavioral control. The first thing to realize is that everybody, always, lives in some sort of reciprocal relation with his environment. It is the current interest of behaviorism to emphasize the overwhelming importance of environmental factors in determining what an individual's behavioral equipment and capacities will turn out to be. However, whenever one focuses attention on controlling contingencies between behavior and the social environment—that is, whenever one focuses on controlling contingencies that determine the form of behavioral interaction among people —then it is important to note than one is *always* in a position to bring into play the conceptual nexus within which the concepts of "control" and "countercontrol" characteristically function, even though such considera-

---

[1] It is also in this context that we meet application of such concepts as justice, the law, and behavior governed by rule. The intelligibility of these concepts offers no systematic problem to the behaviorist. The method Skinner outlines in the 1945 Symposium on Operationism (*Psychological Review*, 1945, **52**, 270–277, 291–294) for the clarification of the meaning of psychological ascriptions can be applied without change to such concepts as "justice," and in practice it resembles closely the "conceptual analysis" that is currently fashionable in certain philosophical circles. If one is not satisfied with the discussion of rule-following behavior in *Beyond Freedom and Dignity,* then he might pursue with profit the more detailed treatment of the issue in *Contingencies of Reinforcement* (pp. 160 ff).

tions may be intrinsically misleading and irrelevant to an accurate specification of the realities of the relations between behavior and the environment that are actually operative.

I have made the claim that any instance of social interaction, no matter how patently innocuous it would ordinarily be judged to be, provides a setting within which it is possible to respond by raising the range of issues with which one becomes involved by conceptualization in terms of "control" and "countercontrol." Actually, however, this conceptual equipment is brought to bear on only a restricted segment of social interactions that are behaviorally significant. Discussions of control and countercontrol are not likely to arise with respect to specific social interactions unless aversive factors, or the threat of such factors, are clearly present. Thus, children complain when they are picked on or teased by others, and parents rush to stand up for their own by initiating one or another form of countercontrol. The highly significant consequences of the particular form in which peer-group play happens to be successful go largely unnoticed. Issues of school busing quickly become matters of intense social concern, and an assessment of the rights and responsibilities involved, which we have seen are intrinsically associated with the concept of countercontrol, sooner or later involve the highest judiciary processes in the land. Yet the successfully regimented functioning of private parochial schools may well stimulate only contented approbation. Unfortunately, the social adjustments that are made by way of instigating countercontrol typically involve the use or threat of punishment, much as that at the heart of the control problem that was troublesome to begin with. The complex network of checks and balances involved in the administration of our own representative government provide ample illustration of the wide range of ways in which our society at present handles the countercontrol problem, namely, the problem of protecting the interests of one social entity from aversive control by some other.

It is a mistake to conceptualize the issues involved in effective social management basically in terms of possible opportunities for aversive control and protective measures that can be taken against them by way of countercontrol. The management of social problems, if it is to be effective, must inevitably deal with an appropriate adjustment of all the contingencies between social behavior and the environment that are actually operative and relevant. Thus, a more adaptive way to consider the ethical and practical issues involved in the rational planning of optimally desirable interrelationships among social agencies is to move at once to an assessment of relevant contingencies, rather than to concentrate only on those special types of problems that become conspicuous as the locus of opportunities to administer aversive control.

Once again, it is a mistake to think that one is engaging relevantly the major ethical and practical issues involved in social planning when one conceptualizes the issues as having to do largely with the design of sufficient opportunities for countercontrol essentially to protect us from aversive manipulation. The problem of social planning is misconceived if it is viewed basically as one of the protection of our "rights" by ensuring that others will live up to their "responsibilities." Intelligent discussion of practical issues associated with social organization can be expected to be effective only if it is expanded to include an analysis of *all* the relevant controlling contingencies that are operative. However, when the interest in and knowledge of relevant controlling contingencies is expanded in this way, the nature of public interest in the problem of social organization changes. The issue changes from a focal concern with guarantees of sufficient countercontrol to protect us from unwanted control, to a concern with the realities of whatever controlling contingencies are actually involved in social interaction, and with what sorts of social organizations best embody those types of contingencies that are socially desirable.

Let me illustrate the kinds of differences these concepual changes make by considering an actual example of an instance of social planning. This example avoids the problem of major differences in values, which can often complicate group efforts at social planning, by centering on a group consisting solely of Christians, persons who by identifying themselves by that name presumably commit themselves to a certain agreement in the area of values. In the illustration I shall briefly discuss, the vestry of a particular church faced the practical problem of selecting a new rector. A Search Committee had screened the applicants and made a recommendation to the vestry of what it considered to be the top four candidates. The vestry, upon whom the responsibility of making the final selection utlimately rested, had heard of something new that is being tried out by way of interviewing priests in the final stages of selection. The new plan is to bring all four of the top candidates together at the same time, where they can all be seen together, and where they can all be intensively interviewed over the same 3-day period. It was decided to try this new method for the first time at this particular church.

Now, what sort of issues arise in connection with this problem in social planning? Who is controlling whom, in the sense of who is manipulating whom? Is the ethical issue one of protecting the vestry from the competitive salesmanship of the applicants? Or do the applicants need to be protected from the competitive impulses of each other, or from the aversiveness of being interviewed under these possibly compromising circumstances by the vestry? Do the applicants have "rights" that may be threatened in this particular interview situation? Does the vestry have "responsibilities" that they may themselves happen to compromise by interviewing the applicants in this way? Who is controlling whom? Where does the countercontrol problem come in? Should the applicants concern themselves with countercontrol in order to protect themselves from the vestry, or is it the other way around? Being all members of a Christian community, should each tend to ignore his own interest in countercontrol out of a charitable interest in looking first to the countercontrol problems of the other?

What actually happened, fortunately, was that the interview situation was not conceptualized by the vestry in terms of control versus countercontrol, or of manipulation versus self-protection. The vestry did indeed attempt to make an assessment of the central controlling contingencies likely to be operating in the situation (although they are hardly ones to describe their activities along this line in these words), and they simply went ahead to plan the weekend so that the chances seemed best for getting the relevant information from the applicants, of letting the applicants see as much as possible of the idiosyncracies of this particular church and community, and of seeing to it that as pleasant a time could be had by all as possible. Particularly interesting was the fact that a Caring Committee was set up to be sure that regardless of how the fortunes of individual applicants seemed to be faring at any one moment, all of the applicants could be sure that their own special skills, talents, and capabilities were being positively seen and appreciated by those involved in the interview. It is my point to claim that in no sense would it be appropriate to conceptualize the Caring Committee as an effort at countercontrol on anyone's part. The Committee was simply a reasonable effort at social planning which followed naturally from a self-conscious attempt to be aware of controlling contingencies likely to be operative in the particular case.

But what has this to do with behavior modification, and the threat that some people see in it to our right to plan our own future for ourselves? Since behavior modification is explicitly concerned with behavioral control, do we not need to be especially concerned to protect ourselves from malevolent behavior modifiers by giving sufficient attention to prudent practices of countercontrol? In terms of the conceptual contrast I have tried to outline above, there are two ways of looking at this.

From the first perspective, behavior modifiers must be regarded as dangerous in the same way that parents, nursery school teachers, primary and secondary teachers, and university professors are dangerous. This is to say nothing of social workers, nurses, psychiatrists, judges, jurors, legislators, and people who vote, who are also dangerous in precisely the same way: They all play some active part in the complex network of mutual behavioral control that constitutes social interaction. The mistaken thing to do is to conceptualize this whole scene in such a way that individuals are regarded as entities essentially isolated from behavioral influence except when, out of weakness, they fall into some morally reprehensible condition of social susceptibility from which they need protection. If one is afraid of, or otherwise opposed to, behavior change or behavior influence, then behavior modification is indeed something to be concerned about (provided, of course, that behaviorist technology lives up in fact to the grand promises that its advocates blueprint on paper). However, it is my point to claim that if one grants the legitimacy of this fear, then there is no reason that the fear of behavior modification should not be extended to a fundamental fear of any sort of meaningful interaction with any other person under any circumstances.

The other way to look at it is to realize that behavior modification, and other behaviorist initiatives in the direction of rational social and cultural planning, are social practices, which are in fact taking place now within the fabric of society such as we know it in the West. The practice of behavior modification, and other experimental work in the management of social contingencies, is consequently subject to the same countercontrolling "safeguards" that apply to the wide range of social practices that occur in a "free" society such as ours. Surely there is no great mystery as to how it is within the constraints of representative government as we know it in this country that new forms of legislation emerge as the need for social protection becomes apparent in the faces of innovative social change. There is no more reason to associate behavior modification with the specter of totalitarian government than there is to make the same association with the wide range of institutional practices that constitute the mechanisms of public instruction in this country. (I am aware of the fact, of course, that there are indeed people in this country who have this latter fear.)

However, there are some positive things to say about protection from malevolent practices of control that follow from the proposed conceptual shift away from thinking of suggested social changes as instances of intentional efforts at personal manipulation. When one views all forms of social interaction, whether institutionalized or not, as dynamic patterns of interrelated controlling contingencies, then what might have been regarded as aspects of the problem of countercontrol become instead simply aspects of the more general problem of the analysis of controlling contingencies. When the interaction of social institutional agencies is regarded in this light, a number of constructive moves become apparent that pertain not only to the increasing public concern with innovative attempts to find new solutions to pressing social problems but also to the current widespread interest in the reform of existing governmental institutions.

1. One thing that it would be clearly worthwhile to do would be to try to identify as explicitly as possible, and to make part of the domain of public knowledge, what the characteristic patterns of social control actually are in the social and governmental institutions that exist at the present time. With an increased awareness of the realities of social controlling contingencies, the public can reasonably be expected in the future to demand information of this kind to the extent that it bears on the administration of any governmental practice. It is undoubtedly the fact that for the most part only people who function in governmental circles have accurate knowledge of the controlling contingencies actually effective in practice that are responsible for the apparently immense amount of both unethical and frankly illegal activity occurring in the administration of the kind of representative government we know in this country.

2. With increased public interest in having specific knowledge about the controlling contingencies that define the effective distribution of power in the functioning of social institutions, explicit efforts can be made to finance and support at a governmental level new techniques for identifying with increased precision the range of variables that act in behavioral control. I am thinking here of increased support for acquiring technical knowledge of how to identify the variables taken in one way or another to act in the control of behavior. Behaviorists are the first to speak with great confidence of the power of their method. Yet a more accurate assessment of the situation might suggest instead that whatever promise the behaviorist perspective may hold for the amelioration of social problems in the future will depend on the solution of both conceptual and methodological problems that deeply infect the behaviorist orientation at the present time.

3. A third move suggested by a conceptual shift away from the pattern of thinking associated with "autonomous man" would be the explicit, and much needed, education of people in the rudiments of the principles of behavioral control. Education in the realities of behavioral control, as they are manifest for example in the most common social situations such as the family and the school, should begin at a very early level, so that even children can learn to become aware of how it is that the consequences of their behavior affect the person that they are to become, and how it is that the pattern of their interaction with others has an enormous influence on the lives of those with whom they interact.

4. Finally, thought should be given to establishing agencies at the governmental level that would function specifically in the analysis of controlling contingencies involved in the administration of government. The

function of such agencies would be to keep the members of our society informed of the realities of the controlling contingencies that in fact operate to control our lives. With the knowledge of such realities, it is reasonable to expect that more enlightened practices of social control would emerge than those that currently exist.

It is undoubtedly the case that the four aforementioned possible developments will occur only gradually as the results of applied behaviorist technology, for ill or for good, become more widely known, and as effective dialogue between behaviorists and others opposed to the behaviorist outlook begins to take place. However, what I have tried to illustrate by these four suggestions is that when the conceptual model associated with "autonomous man" is replaced by one in which one attempts to look realistically at whatever controlling contingencies can be seen to exist, then the change in outlook that follows is one of a constructive, positive, and humanistic kind. Instead of regarding man as fundamentally a source of evil from which we need primarily to protect ourselves and each other, the behaviorist outlook sees humans as participating in a dynamic interaction with each other which has as its consequence what it is that people are themselves to become. Should we not make every effort to gain whatever knowledge we can of the important factors that act to determine what it is we turn out to be? Is it not possible for us to become what we would like to become?

# HERBERT McCLOSKY

In order that the nature of my critical comments not be misunderstood, let me stipulate at the outset that, like the "behaviorists," I accept the following:

1. That human behavior is "determined" (i.e., lawful).
2. That operant conditioning can be a powerful tool for behavior modification within certain narrowly defined contexts or stimulus fields.
3. That behavior can be modified by altering the "environmental contingencies."
4. That we are all continuously under some form of "control," in the (trivial, I suppose) sense that we respond to reinforcements that have been, are being, or will be, exerted upon us.
5. That positive reinforcement is generally more effective than punishment.
6. That behavior is not likely to change unless some force or influence is introduced to change it (although, unlike many behaviorists, I consider internal motivations as "forces" capable of redirecting behavior).
7. That man can and should be studied scientifically and that to do so need not (or does not in principle) dehumanize him.
8. That within the limited contexts for which it is "appropriate" (e.g., psychotherapy), it is both ethical and socially useful to employ operant principles to alter behavior, providing, of course, that there are effective countercontrols and/or that the accepted moral and professional norms of the community are not violated.

Along with other critics, however, I begin to take issue with behaviorists such as Skinner when they seek to apply their limited, rudimentary, (and still poorly understood) tools to large-scale, complex forms of social organization, including (in Skinner's case) entire societies. In their putative role as universal saviors, they are likely (from the point of view of democratic sensibility and freedom) to generate far more mischief than benefit. To state the essence of the criticism, I see little ground for believing in in either the efficacy or desirability of systematically applying operant principles to large-scale, pluralistic, complex, industrial societies. On the one side, I doubt that it is *possible* to do so effectively; on the other, I believe that the very effort to enforce such principles would require a gigantic, pervasive, control apparatus and a virtually unlimited grant of power to those who govern. The question of who will control the controllers is by now a tired one, but no less inappropriate on that account.

As to the first point, it should be obvious to any student of society that our present knowledge of even the simpler forms of social behavior is pitifully inadequate and is likely to remain so for generations to come. It is one thing to grasp the *principles* of operant conditioning, quite another to translate those principles into policies that alter environmental contingencies on a large scale in the desired direction. It is a long way from the use of reinforcement theory in the simple and protected context of the laboratory to its systematic and effective application in such matters as the reduction of political conflict, the maintenance of a stable economy, the prevention of wars, the achievement of genuine social and political equality among people of different backgrounds and capacities, the elimination of poverty and starvation, industrial advancement without attendant pollution, and many other such momentous and bewildering issues.

A modern industrial society places men and women in numerous social, political, moral, sexual, and vocational roles and interest groups. The interplay of these roles and interests, in turn, raises an endless number of issues arising out of conflicting claims for society's rewards, questions of rights and duties, variations in the degree of political awareness and involvement, changing patterns of subordination and superordination, vexing uncertainties about the meaning of such fundamental constructs as equality and freedom, persistent disagreements about the boundaries of permissible behavior—to say nothing of the overwhelming issues of control and countercontrol. Even if we had far more knowledge of these matters than we do, our ability to apply it for the purpose of manipulating large-scale environmental contingencies would remain pathetically inadequate. What we have to face, after all, is not the intermittent control of the environment for one or a few individuals, but the *simultaneous* control of a vast array of settings for tens—indeed hundreds—of millions of people! When we consider the difficulty of significantly altering the behavior of even a single individual under the most concentrated and intensive therapeutic conditions, it seems the sheerest *hubris* to suppose that one can achieve a sufficiently firm grip on the control levers of the society substantially to refashion the behavior patterns of the millions of people of every imaginable personality and social configuration who compose a complex society. When we are advised to apply behavior modification principles systematically to the entire society, we are being asked in effect to assume that we have "solved" most, if not all of the important problems to which thousands of social scientists and other observers and practitioners are now addressing themselves. I regard this suggestion as, to say the least, naive.

It is also naive to suppose that most men and women could be induced to cooperate—even if one were to employ only positive reinforcements and avoid aversive control techniques. One has to start with existing men and women who (despite Skinner's preference for other language) have beliefs, convictions, superstitions, ideologies, attitudes, conflicting interests, loyalties, standards, conventions, norms, mores, investments, personality needs, ambitions, prejudices, and various other social and mental orientations that are enormously stubborn and difficult to change, even under the most extensive environmental manipulation. I am not saying that change is impossible, or that change in a favorable direction has not occurred (indeed, I think it has). I *am* saying, however, that to manipulate large numbers of entrenched, powerful institutions in the same direction simultaneously is a task vastly beyond the power of present-day social engineering, especially in societies that are in any sense free and democratic. Indeed, one reason we choose "weak" methods of control is that we do not know enough, even about some of the simplest matters, to propose and enforce stronger controls. It is one thing to recognize that environmental changes induce changes in response, and quite another to say that one knows with confidence how to manipulate the environment on a grand scale without producing costs and damages that may be far greater than the gains. We may have discovered certain regularities or even "laws" of behavior, but it is hopelessly presumptuous to assume that we know enough about the laws or their application to introduce the "strong controls" recommended by some proponents of behavior modification.

One may also ask whether systematic behavior modification on a large scale can be approximated, let alone achieved, without the exercise of extraordinary power by the rulers (or social engineers).

The attempt to rearrange environmental contingencies within entire societies so as to alter behavior is not new. It has been tried not only in numerous small experimental societies (almost all of which have failed), but is currently being tried in what were once quaintly described as Communist "experiments." What one sees from the Soviet experience (as well as the Chinese, the Czech, the Hungarian, the Cuban, the Polish, etc.) is how difficult or impossible it is for even the most powerful, zealous, dedicated, and all-controlling regimes to achieve conformity to its norms without reliance upon the most severe aversive reinforcements.

The most serious problems for the regime arise precisely among its elite, those who are most intelligent, creative, original, and responsible. Whether they are influential by special characteristics of genetic endowment or by their social roles to resist the dread conformity of those grim prisons, one cannot say. What is clear is that large numbers of men and women in the elite roles of these relatively closed, powerfully controlled, and highly manipulated systems have given every evidence of breaking out, even at the cost of great personal sacrifice. Solzhenitzyn and Pasternak are only the most dramatic examples of a pervasive problem faced by totalitarian regimes. Although writers, poets, painters, ballet dancers, scientists, and industrial managers are among the most favored members of these societies, and although they are for the most part positively rather than aversively controlled, the regimes under which they live must sooner or later resort to the most punishing aversive controls in order to keep them in line.

The problem may to some extent be genetic, that is, the human organism is itself so complicated and comes in so many different configurations that even the most cruel and omnipotent forms of behavioral engineering cannot control the environment effectively enough to bring everyone into line. There is bound to be a good deal of slippage, no matter how determined the systems of control.

Another obstacle to full-scale behavioral engineering lies in the inevitable contradictions or conflicting goals characteristic of any large-scale society. It wants compliance but also creativity. It wants stability and conformity, but it also requires new ideas. It wants to impose uniformity of beliefs and values on all of its citizens but yet cannot function without some degree of differentiation that distinguishes elites from nonelites, and some groups within the elite from other groups. To the extent that such societies seek to grow stronger, industrialize, advance, become competitive with other societies, protect themselves militarily, promote national pride, and the like, they must perforce provide for a division of labor, a differentiation of roles and status, personal advancement and the crystallization of elites, and all of the other trappings from which they had presumably rid themselves when they seized power and began their flirtation with utopia. The difficulty is, among other things, that all such developments greatly complicate the problem of control, introduce diversity where uniformity was sought, promote conflict and dissent which, if permitted to express itself freely, would soon produce organized political opposition. Hence, the most brutal controls are often employed, and the effort to bring all members of the society under the single totalitarian canopy is unremitting.

I am not speaking of ghosts or imaginary societies. These are actual political systems that have tried social engineering on a large scale, and that originally intended to employ positive reinforcement in the main. But their very ambitions have contributed to their totalitarian and cruel form.

Their commitment to progress, their desire for scientific advancement, their cultural pride, their hope of seducing the masses into obedience through the products of art and culture, their desire to prove the superiority of their system—these and other such goals, together with an obsessive belief in the efficacy of planning and control over environmental contingencies, has led them to construct a barbaric political culture that has known few equals in the history of man.

The point, let us remind ourselves, is not that men yearn to be free by nature and will not accept controls, but that the conditions of a modern, complex, industrial society with its vastly proliferated roles, division of labor, conflicts, specializations, and the like, will not yield easily to a single, systematic, consciously directed and planned pattern of environmental controls and behavior modification, even if benign. In fact, however, we have reason to doubt that the total or near-total control required for effective, predictable behavior modification on a large scale can be achieved without totalitarian and highly authoritarian political systems that most of us would find repugnant.

Not only totalitarian communists but socialists of more benign persuasion have also championed large-scale solutions through extensive environmental manipulation. Through communal ownership of the means of production, economic and social planning, the elimination of social classes and other sources of economic, political, and social conflict, society was to evolve into a great harmonium in which happiness would reign supreme. Unfortunately for this vision, the reality (insofar as socialism has ever been attained) has been disappointing. The results can scarcely be considered a rousing success. Where socialism has not taken the form of brute totalitarianism—where, in other words, it has been benevolent—it has generally lacked vitality and has been economically and culturally torpid. It is by no means obvious—indeed economists largely deny it—that centralized planning and economic control are more advantageous for productivity and other economic benefits than is the free competitive market. Where planning has actually been introduced on a large scale, as in communist societies, it does not have a distinguished record. Great pressure has been building in those countries to return to some of the elements of economic competition and the free market. Were it not a useful adjunct to the maintenance of dictatorial power in the USSR, large-scale economic planning might well have been abandoned by now. Economic planning under more benevolent societies, such as England and Scandinavia, has not demonstrated particular superiority over more traditional economic practices.

Nor have socialist societies achieved dramatic improvements in domains other than the economic, such as military affairs, population control, pollution, optimal use of natural resources, the reduction of privilege and inequality, and the quality of life. A benign socialism, in short, appears to work no better than a benign form of mixed capitalism, and a totalitarian or aversive form is an abomination. Socialists, it turns out, do not know all the answers either.

One might argue, of course, that socialism has never been tried in a truly effective and scientific way, and that a proper scientific effort would produce different results. This, unfortunately, is a hypothesis contrary to fact, and one can take it or leave it as one chooses. One may well ask, however, why it has never been practiced more effectively. One may also ask how one gets to the point where it can be practiced effectively. One may also want to ask whether we are certain we would really want it. One might consider, for example, whether it is not likely to promote uniformity and hence discourage originality, change, diversity, and evolution; whether the price for the bureaucratic apparatus required to manage it is not exorbitant; whether one wishes to live under societies that are so heavily rule-bound; and whether the realization of absolute equality (if it could be realized) and the elimination of all elites and status differentiations among men is a realistic or desirable goal (the question of its desirability arises because of the tendency of equalitarian ideals, when pressed to an extreme, to be translated into an urge toward uniformity and identity of treatment). Every social institution and practice has its price, and the price for planned, internal harmony may very well be stagnation and the ant heap.

This is not to say that some measure of economic and social planning —some effort to rearrange the environmental contingencies—cannot or should not be attempted. It is, of course, being continually attempted in modern nations, even in the United States. What must be avoided, however, is the simplistic assumption that large-scale, complex, industrialized societies can be severely controlled to the degree recommended by some advocates of behavior modification without a cost that most of us would regard as prohibitive—if indeed it is possible at all. If all we are talking about is the more rational use of positive reinforcements to reorder some priorities and allocate rewards in a fashion that will more effectively achieve such goals as the elimination of poverty, the reduction of the birth rate, or the restoration of a more salutary physical environment, there is not much to quarrel about. But even these more modest objectives are by no means simple to achieve, and the answers for achieving them are not readily at hand.

One difficulty with all-encompassing schemes for behavior modification for the sake of social reform is that no one has yet thought of, much less introduced, a political system that simultaneously can furnish the opportunities as well as the safeguards offered by democracy. Inadequate though democratic government may be in some respects, no one has invented an appropriate alternative—a political and social order that provides for both stability and change, freedom and control, the expertise of elites together with the participation of the governed. By the values most of us hold (and since these *are* our values, they are the values by which we must and do judge), all alternative forms of political management are likely to be less desirable—less free, less progressive, less civilized, more dependent on aversive control, less salutary, less concerned with individual rights or the correction of social injustice and inequities. The difficulty from the point of view of behavior modification, however, is that democracy encourages diversity, competition, free exchange, individual self-determination and choice, and related conditions that do not easily lend themselves to behavioral controls and environmental management of the kind envisioned by universal saviors. Thus, from the point of view of universal behavior modification, democracy is a stumbling block. It cannot be manipulated easily, and it certainly cannot be manipulated in a systematic and uniform manner. One takes one's chances with it.

Behavioral engineers, eager to reorganize the environment in order to improve the reinforcement contingencies, are required (by us, at least) to come up with something as good as or better than democracy. Some very smart people have thought about this problem over the past 2000 years, but so far no one has invented a *feasible* alternative that most of us would regard as preferable. By democracy, I refer primarily to the political system, and not to all the forms of human interaction or engagement. But it is precisely the political system that is at issue in recommendations for sweeping behavior modification, since the changes that would be needed to manipulate the total environment require political action and decision. We are, after all, talking about forms of authority, control, power, laws, rules, perhaps even force—and these belong primarily to the domain of politics. Since the problem, then, is to a considerable extent political, there is no escape from the problem of having to find an appropriate alternative to democracy. It is scarcely an adequate answer to say, as Skinner does in effect, that countercontrols are implicit in all relationships between ruler and ruled. He argues, for example, that the slave "in a very real sense" controls the slave driver, the child the parent, the citizen the government, the employee the employer, and so forth. This, of course, is a bit of casuistry that a Jesuit or Talmudic scholar might envy. In a single stroke, it succeeds in eliminating the entire concept of control or domination of one individual by another. It would, I am certain, bring great comfort to a prisoner in a Soviet or Nazi concentration camp to tell him that his very existence as a prisoner represents "in a very real sense" a form of control over the camp commandant!

One would thing it obvious by this time in history that there are no effective countercontrols except the ability to remove oneself or, alternatively, to remove the superordinate or to be able, by legal means, to prevent him from exercising his power. No amount of facile argument can displace this hard fact. Nor is it adequate to say that since we are all being "controlled" anyway, we should be properly controlled so as to maximize the possibility of achieving the goals of social improvement and cultural survival. The argument has a certain superficial plausibility, but it is facile, misleading, and begs the most important questions. For example: Who will be the social engineers and how will they be chosen and controlled? (An obvious question, of course.) If they themselves are severely limited by popular controls, how will they be able to manipulate the environment as they deem necessary? If, on the other hand, they are permitted great latitude to manipulate the contingencies and reinforcement schedules so as to ensure what they regard as *desired* forms of behavior, what is to prevent them from employing their power to promote behavior the rest of us consider undesirable? A power bestowed without limit to enlarge human capacity inevitably contains the possibility of diminishing them.

Either the power to shape our destiny remains with those who are governed—in which case the ability of social engineers to manipulate environmental contingencies is narrowed to the point at which systematic control becomes impossible—or the power to plan, organize, and manipulate the social environment is bestowed upon (or seized by) the social engineers who, without the checks of democratic consent and accountability, will inevitably abuse and misuse their power in a manner that *invites,* if it does not *guarantee,* absolutism. This is a central difficulty in any proposal for behavior modification on the scale of an entire culture.

## PAUL E. MEEHL

History, whether we call it a science or not, is an empirical discipline, containing a vast body of material about human behavior. A fair-minded reading of the history of man in his political and economic life can hardly lead one to conclude that he is a gentle, sweet, loving animal, closer to the bunny rabbit than the wolverine. As Freud puts it, the verdict of history is rather clearly *homo homini lupus.* Anyone, even if he is a genius like B. F. Skinner, who tells us, in effect, "I know how to fix that up, do not worry about the power of the state, do not worry about the corruption of politicians, do not worry about the degeneration of humanitarian regimes into tyrannies, do not worry about human aggressiveness or territoriality or whatever. Because of the new science of operant behaviorism, we can assure you that this can now be fixed up," may conceivably be right—and I do not prejudge the matter—but I want to say loud and clear that such a claim carries with it a tremendous burden of proof. And I want to maintain, with Herbert McClosky, that Skinner has not sustained such a heavy burden. He has not sustained it, as I view the matter, mostly because in his writings on social and political life, whether in the fictional form we find in *Walden Two* (which I had the great pleasure of hearing read by Skinner in manuscript when I was a graduate student), or in passing remarks in the recent contingencies book, or more explicitly in *Beyond Freedom and Dignity,* has never thought it necessary to spell out details of the countercontrol mechanisms. One way of saying this is that he has never told us just how the political relay programming equipment is to be wired up. It is not sufficient merely to say, "We are not going to rely on aversive control, as mankind has done excessively in the past; we are going to be nice guys and give each other pellets, on powerful schedules." This is a very important theoretical contribution and a powerful technological point; but I repeat, it is *not* an adequate characterization of the institutional Skinner box wiring.

I shall confine myself to only one dramatic historical example, and you can all provide others for yourselves, depending on how much history you have read. Consider the Bolsheviks. We had here a group of men who were, by and large, of superior education and intelligence (Lenin, for instance, graduated first in his law class, and had he not become a revolutionary would have had a promising career as a lawyer); they were mostly intellectuals (very few of the Old Bolsheviks were drawn from the ranks of the proletariat, and almost none from the peasantry); and among

them were many who were no cultural slouches. People like Lenin, Buk-
harin, Trotsky, and Preobrazhensky, were cultivated, well-informed, intel-
lectually able persons. They were convinced that they had diagnosed the
source of the social cankers that we find on the body politic, and that they
had a radical surgery to cure it. One that went to the roots of the matter,
because it had a truly "scientific," *causal* insight into the origin of human
exploitation and strife and misery, rather than a speculative, religious,
utopian, or dilettante understanding of human affairs. Further, there can
be no serious question about the humanitarian sincerity of these men, who
proved it by spending years freezing in Siberia, by renouncing the normal
gratifications of social, economic, political, and family life, by heroically
undergoing tortures at the hands of the Tsarist police, by living in penurious
exile—I metion again the great leader Lenin himself, who we find living
in dire poverty in Zurich, scribbling articles for *Iskra* and trying to get
hectograph copies smuggled into Russia to foment the Great Revolution,
and the like. I rather doubt, with the possible exception of the founding
fathers at Philadelphia who created our own remarkable American Constitution, that you could find a collection of such bright, learned, objectively
oriented, and humanitarian zealots gathered anywhere comparable to those
of the Bolshevik Party. Well, when the Tsarist regime finally fell apart
under the impact of World War I and the coalition government headed
by Kerensky proved impotent (and persisted in carrying on the hopeless
war with the Germans), the Bolsheviks seized power in what was a remarkably easy and bloodless revolution. And what happened? In some of his
remarks I have seen on television, Skinner shows an amazing naivete about
the Russian Revolution. Somebody should explain to him that this group
of dedicated humanitarian intellectuals, having seized power rather pain-
lessly, and having defeated the actual counterrevolutionaries in the civil
far, proceeded to usher in one of the bloodiest tyrannies in human history,
in the course of which as many innocent people underwent what in the
jargon of Stalinism is known as "physical liquidation" as under Adolf Hitler.
Lenin and Stalin killed as many people as Hitler did; they just picked them
on a different basis. That one single gigantic historical paradigm, the degeneration of the humanitarian socialist ideal under the Bolsheviks, should
give anybody pause in contemplating a proposal as to how we are going
to increase total social control and bring about the social millennium,
especially when he does not tell us anything about the institutional arrangements for providing adequate countercontrols, or what Montesquieu called
"checks and balances" of the kind that McClosky, as a political scientist,
would be concerned about.

In *Contingencies of Reinforcement,* Skinner dismisses concepts such as "aggression," "territoriality," "social structure," and "communication" as being attractive but not really powerful concepts because they are not at a proper level of behavior analysis. The premise here seems to be that there can be *only one "proper"* (I take it this means useful, fruitful, conceptually powerful, scientifically respectable?) level to analyze human behavior in the social context. Who told Skinner this? So far as I am aware there is nothing in logic, epistemology, history, or philosophy of science, or analogies in the current theory and technology of the physical or biological sciences, that warrants such a dogmatic statement about the unique appropriateness of a certain level of analysis.

Further: Behavioral control systems always have a *content*—whereas Skinner, in discussing society's problems, tends to write as if they had only a *form;* that is, that it suffices to characterize what the general laws of behavior are like. One must address himself to this social content: To what are the properties of the discriminative and reinforcing stimuli, to what are the dispositions of the "social Skinner box" in which we find ourselves, to what are the actual characteristics, topographical and otherwise, of the strings of behaviors people learn in society, especially in connection with political control and countercontrol? And when you address yourself seriously to this content of stimuli and response on the social scene, such constructs as "rule," "justice," "power," "veto," "accountability," "collective choice," "communication," emerge willy-nilly *in some guise or other.*

In answer to what is probably the most common criticism of his approach since the appearance of *Walden Two,* "Who controls the controllers?" (an ancient question in political science, generally found in its Latin form, *"quis custodiet ipsos custodes?"*), it is insufficient to reply, "We rabbits (controllees) schedule the lions and foxes (controllers) just as they schedule us." If the controller has a machine gun and all I have is some spit-balls, it is rather obvious who really controls whom. (Cf. Lenin on barricades and the machine gun.)

I want to include in our discussion somewhere, if possible, the problem of the aberrant individual, on whom the souped-up, nonaversive educational regime has failed. Most of you know the classic study by Kuo on rodent slaying in the cat (1928), in which he showed that if you rear kittens with rats or mice as litter mates, and also see to it that they never get a chance to see mother cat slay any rodents, then, as adult cats— and the hunger drive appears in his data to be irrelevant in potentiating this piece of typical feline behavior—the cats do not tend to act like "normal cats" in that they do not tend to kill rodents. This is an important finding, although it has sometimes been given much too strong a construc-

tion by sociologists. The fact that you can stamp out a strong feline disposition by an artificial, aberrated, atypical nonfeline kittenhood does *not,*
of course, refute the idea that there is some innate rodent-slaying propensity
in the feline wiring diagram; it just tells you that it is possible to stamp
it out by a sufficiently aberrant upbringing. However, the point I want to
stress about Kuo's study is that he did not succeed completely in eliminating
this murderous propensity, because there were a few adult cats who,
despite their sweetness-and-light training *vis-à-vis* the rodent order, as
adults took the occasion to commit a few interspecies slayings nevertheless.
Now the appearance of an aggressive, dominant, would-be alpha baboon,
despite the sweetness-and-light society painted in *Walden Two,* raises a
statistical question in political theory. That is, not even Skinner can
presumably "fix it" so that nobody ever experiences anything aversive in
the whole course of his life history (I remind you that the distinction between positive and aversive controls has been fuzzed up for several years
now by the experimental and clinical observation of the aversive properties
of extinction following continuous reinforcement, or the aversive properties of time out, so that it is no longer as clear as it once seemed to be
when we are using punishment or avoidance learning or positive reinforcement and so on). And Skinner's lack of interest in genetics leads him not
to tell us very much about the paranoid schizotypes (like Hitler) who will
periodically arise in his utopian society. The point is, of course, that a
generic statement about the average quantitative level of society's reliance
(in home, neighborhood, Boy Scout troop, school) on positive reinforcement schedules rather than aversive, punishing systems for "stamping out"
behavior we do not like, does not solve the stomach ache of the political
scientist in his fear of Leviathan. It cannot solve it adequately, because
there is some reason to suppose that the people who get to *be* alpha
baboons are different sorts of people, genetically and otherwise, from the
rest of us bunny rabbits who do not belong to the power elite. The alpha
baboons of the human species do not tend to write books—as a matter of
fact, they have a regrettable tendency not even to read books. How many
Hitlers does it take to wreck the Weimar Republic? It is necessary, in
order to reassure those of us who have a deep, pervasive, pessimistic, and
I would say thoroughly justified fear of Leviathan, to—I repeat myself—
spell out in some concrete detail the system of interpersonal political
institutional countercontrols by means of which I am protected against
the aberrated individual who, by a combination of genes and low-prob-
ability events in the Skinnerized culture, nevertheless emerges as a dominant, aggressive, predatory specimen. I remind you in this connection of
Sorokin's statistical documentation showing that, prior to the rise of

modern constitutional democracies with their multiple constraints on the exercise of naked power, the incidence of major felonies (such as murder, rape, kidnapping, larceny, conspiracy, robbery, and the like) among heads of state in recorded Western history is something like 50 to 100 times higher than the rate of these major crimes as committed by the general population. That is the way alpha baboons are!

Finally, I hope we can say something about the problems of rules and validity in Skinner's thinking. He has always permitted himself a major philosophical blind spot on this subject, applying what his friend Feigl the philosopher calls "the behaviorist Midas touch" to everything. Everything, including concepts like truth and validity, is to be behaviorized. I have never seen the slightest shred of philosophical defense for Skinner's idea that the study of behavior is an autonomous discipline depending on nothing else (like logic or mathematics), whereas logic and mathematics are *not* autonomous but have to be reduced to the study of behavior. Skinner has never proved it, and he has never come anywhere close to proving it. I want to argue that on the distinction between *description* and *prescription,* Skinner, for unaccountable reasons (I must have spent a minimum of 100 hours debating this with him when he was at Minnesota, to no avail) persists in making a fundamental blooper that most of us got cured of in a beginning course in logic, ethics, or economics. And the sad thing about it is that while one is willing to permit a genius (whether he is Freud or Skinner or Marx or Newton) to make egregious mistakes, this particular blooper is a mistake that Skinner *does not need* for any of his purposes. It is not easy to formulate in positive terms precisely what we mean by the word "rule." But that shouldn't bother you, because everybody in this room is accustomed to using words such as "aversive" or "punishment" or "reinforcement" or "operant," despite the fact that these terms are also still what the late logician Arthur Pap calls "open concepts," and there is nothing sinful about an open concept so long as you can operate with it. It is perhaps easiest to characterize a rule negatively, by pointing out how it differs from an alleged law of nature. When an empirical generalization is confronted with an unblinkable *fact*-exception, we consider the exception to have refuted the generalization. That is what it is to be an empiricist. Whereas when a *rule* is confronted with an "exception," we do not automatically (or even necessarily in the long pull) abandon the rule—rather we *classify* the particular action as "rule-violative," as a *delict,* as somebody's failure to conform to that which is required. The distinction has been put by logicians in several ways, such as the difference between fact and norm, between empirical generalization and rule, between the descriptive and prescriptive, between ontology and axiology, between what *is* and what *ought to be,* or—if I may permit myself a bit of Hegelian lingo for once—between the actual and the ideal. This is not some deep metaphysical distinction you first come across in your second year of Ph.D. candidacy in a philosophy department. It is an undergraduate distinction, which it continues to amaze me that a man of Skinner's intellect so persistently refuses to see. (See Addendum for a post-panel elaboration of this point and related ones.)

Suppose we are studying which kind of reinforcement schedules and what types of reinforcers are most effective in teaching children how to do fractions. According to Skinner's way of talking (when he falls into his philosophical-blooper frame of mind), the right answer to a problem in fractions is *defined* as "the answer for which the child is reinforced." Whereas the reality of the situation is quite different; surely we decide, in programming the teaching machine, *which responses we shall reinforce on the basis of their being correct* according to the rules of arithmetic. So if somebody did an experiment in which it turned out that operant-behavior methods were extremely ineffective compared with hitting kids over the head with baseball bats in teaching them fractions, one of the first things any rational man—Skinner included, of course—would do would be to take a good look at the Foringer apparatus and see whether somebody had goofed it up so that the *arithmetically incorrect* responses were being reinforced instead of the *right* ones. Now of course I am well aware that Skinner might say—as I have heard him say—"But that merely refers to what we, the teachers and experimenters, call the 'right ones,' which in turn is a matter of what *we* are reinforced for believing arithmetically." That reply begs the whole philosophical question raised by John Stuart Mill in his theory of why we believe the truths of mathematics. To my knowledge, there is not one single competent logician or mathematician who holds that Mill held in this respect, including those who are very strongly "empiricist" in their general philosophical outlook.

## Addendum

Professor Skinner's "hard-line" followers have a distressing tendency to liquidate complex issues in almost any subject matter by two quick-and-easy controversial tactics, to wit, (1) they translate the other person's language into Skinnerese, seeming often unconcerned as to whether he would find the translation an acceptable rendering of his meaning; or (2) they offer to give (or more commonly simply assert that they *could* give) a causal account of how the other comes to employ the language he does. The first technique must, of course, be examined on the merits (of each proposed translation). As a sometime philosopher and clinical practitioner, I am fully prepared to discover that the reason somebody's sentence *S* cannot be translated is that it was mostly nonsense to begin with. But I do not routinely *assume* this as the outcome of careful analysis; and my Skinnerian friends are not entitled to do so either. It should not be neecssary, among educated persons, to point out the illegitimacy of the second of these two moves; but one finds it made with remarkable frequency by Skinnerians. This fallacy is called the *genetic fallacy,* and usually has overtones of the *argumentum ad hominem.* The tactic puts a non-Skinnerian at a controversial disadvantage (to naive eyes) for the simple reason that the non-Skinnerian does not permit himself to commit the *ad hominem* or genetic fallacy, and so is precluded from replying in kind. Thus, I would *never* find myself saying to one of my Skinnerian brethren, in response to some evidence, argument, or definition that he was offering me in a scientific discussion, "Well, of course, you say that because you are a committed follower of Skinner." I can discern no essential difference between such argumentative tactics and a Marxist telling me, "Well, you say that because you are not a proletarian but a petit-bourgeois intellectual," or a Freudian saying, "The reason you don't accept the concept of castration anxiety is that you are a behaviorist and have not been psychoanalyzed" (or, among Freudians themselves, the sometimes-offered polemical comment, "Well, I can see that your analysis was not complete!"); or, for that matter, a Christian saying, "You do not understand the New Testament message because you are blinded by sin."

The point is obvious and simple: It is never (read: *never*) an answer to an argument or alleged fact or objection or definition or criticism, to "explain" to the maker of it why, in the causal sense, he comes to talk the way he does. This is simply irrelevant. If I enunciate the Pythagorean theorem or a doubtful proposition in jurisprudence, it is completely irrelevant—and ought not to be permitted in discussion among cultivated minds —that I espouse a certain ideology, or that I took my B.A. at a certain institution, or that my racial or religious class origins are such and such, or that I studied with a teacher who held certain theoretical opinions, or that I have a compulsion neurosis, or that I am under 20 or over 60 or, for that matter, even that I am offering the argument or definition I am offering because in fact I am under the control of a post-hypnotic suggestion given me 2 hours previously. All of this is beside the point. Presumably if we are determinists, we can all all explain each other's verbal behavior (better, "could in principle," since I notice that people can never

really deliver the goods on this when engaged in a discussion of complicated philosophical matters). It cuts no ice for me to make that generic
statement about you when you talk Skinnerese, nor for you to make it
about me when I talk something else.

The temptation on the part of Skinner's followers to fall into this
elementary fallacy is in part fostered by Skinner's own "behaviorist Midas
touch" in matters linguistic. If we read for either "truth-condition of sen-
sentence *p*" or "confirmatory evidence *e* for sentence *p*," the like-sounding
(but utterly distinct) "condition under which utterance of *p* is [usually]
reinforced," and then equate this in turn to "discriminative stimulus $S^D$
controlling emission of '*p*'," we are closest to the idea that "explaining *p*
causally is discussing the merits of *p*." Each equivalence is a mistake, as
Skinner's critics have pointed out repeatedly, to no avail. If we start this
way, then whenever a subject matter is not congenial or an objection is
unpleasant to face, it is easier to by-pass addressing it on the merits, and
instead to "explain" why somebody says what he says.

The error in this can be best illustrated by taking any technical controversy in some formal field and asking oneself *what question is being
put*. Consider a problem in mathematics. In 1742 Goldbach sent Euler a
letter in which he conjectured that every even number can be represented
by the sum of two primes, asking Euler whether he could prove it. Euler
could not. Nor has anybody else. No exception has ever been found, and
most (not all!) mathematicians are inclined to believe that the conjecture
is true; but a proof is still lacking. For almost two centuries there was no
significant advance toward finding a valid demonstration of Goldbach's
"theorem" (as it came to be called); but beginning in the 1930s, with
proofs of weaker related theorems by Schnirelmann ("Every positive integer can be represented as the sum of not more than 800,000 primes")
and Vinogradoff ("There exists an integer *N* such that an odd integer
$n > N$ can be represented as the sum of not more than three odd primes"
—proved, however, nonconstructively, by an indirect argument *reductio,*
and hence unacceptable to intuitionist mathematicians), several powerful
developments have occurred. The reader is referred to the article, "Theory
of Numbers," in *Enyclopaedia Britannica* for a survey of this fascinating
field of formal knowledge. The point of this example, chosen from among
thousands of examples in mathematics and logic, is that we have had a
highly technical problem belonging to a rich, complex, and *autonomous*
subject matter, whose rigor and intellectual beauty far exceeds anything
we have to offer in the behavioral sciences. The Goldbach problem is, of
course, not being approached by means of the *psychologist's* facts, categories, or methods. No one in his senses would suggest doing anything so

silly. We may as psychologists hypothesize (by extrapolation) that the "mathematizing behavior" of Goldbach, Hardy, Ramanujan, Schnirelmann, Vinogradoff, and so on satisfied suitable behavioral principles—although *what* kind, and now purely "behavioral," we cannot know pending resolution of the Chomsky–Skinner controversy, which an unbiased mind must, I think, consider to be presently *sub judice.* If the so-called deep structure of a mathematician's verbal behavior requires explicit reference to the "rules" of mathematics, then Skinner's famous (1945, p. 277) boast that "logic will be embraced by our analysis" would be fulfilled only in a very odd sense: The mathematician's behavior will be determined (hence, "embraced") by psychology, but the psychologist's analysis of that behavior's "determination" will have to *include* those formal concepts that occur in the deep structure's rules (Meehl, 1970). I should think that in such a case it would be misleading to speak of either discipline as "embracing" the other. Meanwhile, no informed mind is urging that mathematicians suspend their autonomous efforts to crack the formal problem of Goldbach's conjecture, pending "empirical" developments in psychological science and, in particular, a definitive resolution of the Chomsky–Skinner issue.

The fallacy of addressing oneself to the question "Is Goldbach's conjecture valid?" by saying, "I think I could explain why Goldbach came to write this letter to Euler" or, in the case of contemporary mathematicians interested in Goldbach's problem, "We should make a careful study of the reinforcement schedules of assistant professors in the mathematics department" is so apparent as to need no discussion beyond presenting the above example.

Formal logic, as is well known, presents numerous similar examples. Thus, we know that the propositional calculus is complete, and that an effective decision procedure exists for deciding, given any well-formed formula ("wff," to logicians) whether or not it is a theorem. Whereas the lower functional calculus, also known to be complete, *cannot* have a general effective decision procedure written for it (Church's theorem, 1936). Given a wff in that calculus, is it a theorem or not? It *may* be a theorem, but even so, the sun may burn out before any logician can cook up a valid proof of it; and no "mechanical" procedure (such as the truth tables used in the propositional calculus) can, even *in principle,* be set forth that will enable us to ascertain, in a finite number of prescribed steps, whether it is a theorem or not. This is a question in *logic,* not *psychology.* Nothing we can say about discriminative stimuli or response chains or VR schedules helps us one iota in dealing with it. But in the case of logic (which, so far as I am aware, has as good a claim to subject matter autonomy as mathe-

matics), the program of a translation into behaviorese can be made to
sound plausible (not to me—but apparently to some people). And of
course when we get into such a highly controversial and murky domain as
ethics—or axiology in general—most fair-minded and informed persons
would probably opine that the possibility of translating *all* of their predicates into behaviorese *without significant conceptual residuals* may arguably
be considered still open, although somewhat unlikely. I do not myself
have a "rigorous account" of concepts such as "justice," "obligation," or
"liberty," and therefore I am not prepared to maintain that they could not
conceivably be rendered in behaviorese. I have not, however, as yet seen
any rendition that would satisfy me. I believe this is the well-nigh universal
judgment of those who have inquired into these ancient matters in scholarly
depth and breadth. I would be extremely skeptical of a one-paragraph
rendition of the concept *justice* in behaviorese, especially while I am currently struggling with Professor John Rawls' brilliant, profound, and
magisterial treatise on that difficult subject (Rawls, 1971). Consideration
of the "social engineering" potentialities now available to us from Skinner's work will demand a high-level, deep-thinking, sophisticated combination of varied skills and kinds of knowledge. Psychologists are under-
standably concerned with the need for lawyers, political theorists, moral-
ists, economists, and so on (broadly, the intellectual tradition sometimes
designated as "documentary social science") to be better informed than
most of them are about the science of operant behavior. It would be stupid
of me to quarrel with that desire to "educate the others." However, I cannot resist commenting that everyone who is somewhat knowledgeable about
*both* intellectual traditions will find considerably more naivete among
operant behaviorists than among more "traditional" thinkers. (That such
should originate from a man like Skinner, whose wide culture and imaginative intellect is obvious to those of us who have had the privilege to know
him personally, may seem strange. But one may remark that Freud, Marx,
Einstein, and Spengler suffered a similar fate. One may also comment that
the "full Skinner" of conversation somehow fails to come through in his
writings. Further, in the matter of logic as an autonomous technical discipline, Skinner himself is gravely at fault.) I am not here arguing *ad
hominem* myself—I am simply pleading for intellectual honesty, breadth
of view, and a modicum of curiosity, partly in the interest of our objective
need for better "PR" in the eyes of cultured nonpsychologists! I have personally found my students and colleagues in law, philosophy, medicine,
and political science remarkably open to learning about the facts and
concepts of operant behaviorism. I cannot honestly say that a similar open-
ness to learning the language and traditional problem formulations of
psychodynamics, diagnosis, ethics, jurisprudence, logic, epistemology, eco-

nomics, political theory, or axiology generally is typical of Skinnerians. I rarely feel the oppressive atmosphere of a rigid ideology when discussing behavior or society with representatives of these other fields; but the rigid ideological flavor is often present—and sometimes overpowering—when one engages a Skinnerian in such discussions. This doctrinal religiousity is regrettable, and will only serve to slow down our progress. I shall content myself with a single example of what I mean, not using it to prove the point but merely to put some flesh on the bones of my criticism. Traditional axiology, whether pursued by a scholar whose union card is in philosophy, theology, political science, economics, or the strange modern subject matter called "decision theory," uniformly recognizes that a fundamental problem—either to be explored in depth or "settled" for discussion purposes by an explicit statement of what will be presupposed *arguendo*—is the problem of what axiological concepts will be taken as primitive. Thus, for example, some students of ethical theory opt for the term *good* as primitive; others take the notion of *obligation* as primitive; still others hold that neither of these concepts is reducible to the other. Furthermore, whatever set of (one or several) axiological *predicates* are chosen as primitive, there then arises the question concerning primitive *propositions* capable of generating the axiology. Thus, for example, utilitarians have held that an adequate "system" for ethical and legal decision making can be erected on the single axiological premise that (roughly put) "We ought to maximize utility," a notion severely criticized by others who insist, I think rightly, that our cultural ethos *cannot* be adequately expressed by this single principle, but rather that *we aim to increase utility within constraints imposed by other axiological predicates,* such as justice or fairness, these latter *not* being fully reducible to the utilitarian predicate. And then at the other extreme we have moral philosophers such as Prichard, who repudiate the whole enterprise of "axiological reductionism" as impossible, on the ground that corresponding to each of our major obligations, whether in individual life or political affairs, is a separate, distinguishable, and irreducible *kind* of ethical relationship, so that the search for one single value to which all other value concepts can be reduced, and from which all axiological propositions can in principle be derived, is simply based on a mistake.[1]

Now it is interesting to ask what is and ought to be the impact of modern developments in behavior control on questions of this nature. Does

---

[1] During the period since this paper was read, ethical reading and reflection have nearly persuaded me that all ethico–legal–political predicates but one might, in principle, be definable in terms of psychologese (although not, perhaps, in behaviorese). The irreducible one is *obligation*. Of course, even if "obligatory" were taken as the sole primitive axiological predicate, the number of primitive axiological statements required would still remain unsettled.

our present-day knowledge of operant-behavior technology (such as the quantitative characteristics of positive reinforcement scheduling contrasted with the traditional emphasis on aversive control) help us to think better about these centuries-old axiological questions? Can the conceptual task of reducing axiological predicates to a convenient minimum number, and the further task of formulating our value beliefs in terms of a minimum number of primitive axiological propositions, be facilitated by a knowledge of operant behaviorism? I hope, and one would tend to think, that this is the case. But what *ought* to happen in this area will probably *not* happen if those psychologists who possess the basic brains and the scientific knowledge to contribute to a solution of these deep questions permit themselves cavalier dismissal of the axiological concepts and questions transmitted to us by the great intellects of the past—not to mention such brilliant contemporaries as Professor Rawls, whose book on justice I have alluded to earlier.

As for epistemology, that involves extraordinarily deep questions, beyond the scope of this paper and my competence. I merely record here my personal hunch, shared with most of the ablest living philosophers and historians of science, that epistemology is a complex interweaving of three components that I shall label "logical," "empirical," and "decisional"— the last of these having, as I think, an irreducible, uneliminable *axiological* element.

## References

Meehl, P. E. Psychological determinism and human rationality: A psychologist's reactions to Professor Karl Popper's "Of Clouds and Clocks." In M. Radner and S. Winokur (Eds.), *Minnesota Studies in the Philosophy of Science,* Vol. IV. Minneapolis, Minn : University of Minnesota Press, 1970, pp. 310–372.
Rawls, John. *A Theory of Justice.* Cambridge, Mass.: Harvard University Press, 1971.
Skinner, B. F. The operational analysis of psychological terms. *Psychological Review,* 1945, **52**, 270–277.

Not being a political scientist, I am hesitant about recommending readings in that area. However, for those psychologists who have essentially no familiarity with the literature of political science, I suggest the following books as "starters" in getting the flavor—and the historical and theoretical origins—of the fear of Leviathan expressed here:

Buchanan, James M., and Tullock, Gordon. *The Calculus of Consent: Logical Foundations of Constitutional Democracy.* Ann Arbor, Mich.: University of Michigan Press, 1962.

Burnham, James. *Machiavellians: Defenders of Freedom.* Chicago: Henry Regnery Co., 1962.

Dahl, Robert A. *Who Governs? Democracy and Power in an American City.* New Haven, Conn.: Yale University Press, 1961.

Dennis, Lawrence. *The Dynamics of War and Revolution.* The Weekly Foreign Letter, 1940. (The "American intellectual fascist," and on the edge of academic respectability, but an insightful book and useful for the purposes of this list.)

Downs, Anthony. *An Economic Theory of Democracy.* New York: Harper & Row, 1957.

Michels, Robert. *Political Parties.* Gloucester: Peter Smith, 1960.

Mosca, Gaetano. *The Ruling Class.* New York: McGraw-Hill, 1939.

Nomad, Max. *Aspects of Revolt.* New York: Twayne Publishers, 1959.

Olson, Mancur, Jr. *The Logic of Collective Action: Public Goods and the Theory of Groups,* rev. ed. New York: Schocken Books, 1971.

Schumpeter, Joseph A. *Capitalism, Socialism, and Democracy,* 3rd ed. New York: Harper & Row, 1950.

Sorokin, P. A., and Lunden, W. A. *Power and Morality.* Boston: Sargent Publisher, 1959.

Spengler, Oswald. *The Decline of the West. Volume I, Form and Actuality; Volume II, Perspectives on World-History.* New York: Knopf, 1926, 1928. (Dogmatic, mystical, intuitive, Teutonic bombast; hence regularly despised by professional historians. In my inexpert opinion, a work of genius, nevertheless, which I predict will be judged by the future as one of the towering intellectual achievements of the first half of our century, along—as I believe—with Freud, Einstein, Keynes, the quantam mechanicians, and Skinner.)

# JACK MICHAEL

As we drive along a two-way highway and pass another car going in the opposite direction we are only a few feet away from sudden death. A similar contingency is in effect when we stand on the curb near fast traffic. These severe punishment contingencies generate a good deal of behavior that usually prevents the fatal errors. Any attempt, however, to utilize deliberately a severe punishment contingency to control human behavior meets with a good deal of spontaneous and eventually organized resistance. For example, a college instructor who fails any student caught cheating on an exam is often in conflict with the college ombudsman, the dean of students, the college counseling staff, and others who describe his cheating policy as "unnecessarily rigid." The students involved readily cite extenuating circumstances, insufficient knowledge of the contingency, and the fact that the punishment is much too severe for the offence. The sudden-death traffic contingency, on the other hand, receives little attention.

Although one might attempt to distinguish between our behavior toward these two types of situations in terms of the difficulties and cost of improving or avoiding them, it seems to me that a more relevant explanation is in terms of what Skinner has called "countercontrol." Most of us have, as a part of our social repertoires, a good deal of behavior that functions to counteract the control of our behavior by others—since much control by others is for their benefit, not ours. We develop some of this counter-control repertoire as a result of our own social interactions, but much of it is transmitted culturally as part of our ethical and legal tradition. And although countercontrol may occur, by stimulus generalization, with respect to the control of our behavior by the physical environment, it is not effective in altering this control and therefore not maintained. The harsh cheating policy is exactly the kind of controlling relationship that is susceptible to countercontrol; the harsh driving-error contingency is not.

The use of reinforcement is also subject to countercontrol, as when we describe some particular reinforcement contingency as "bribery," even though it does not involve payment for unethical or socially disapproved behavior; or when any work requirement for welfare payments is resisted as a form of possible "exploitation."

As behavioral technology is extended beyond institutional settings, and particularly as we attempt to develop whole social systems based on it, will these efforts not be in direct conflict with the extensive countercontrol repertoires of our present society? Many of the public reactions to Skinner's *Walden Two,* and more recently *Beyond Freedom and Dignity,* would seem to exemplify this type of resistance. No matter how much some critics agree with any of Skinner's general goals, the fact that they are to be reached by the deliberate control of human behavior renders the whole approach "antidemocratic," "totalitarian," and so on. I shall assume that this is, at least, a part of the topic proposed for the present symposium.

As stated, however, the issue has several faults. First, it does not seem to me that the impact of an improved behavioral technology will be sudden, nor will it affect most of us by serving as a basis for a new, behaviorally designed society. The most probable effects of the behavior modification "movement" will be an improvement in the general effectiveness of existing social agents—parents, teachers, government agencies, businesses concerned with behavior, and so on. Professional behavior managers are beginning to appear under a variety of titles, and they will undoubtedly increase in number if their services continue to be useful. Also, some form of behavioral technology is increasingly being considered an essential part of many other fields—education, law, medicine, business—and the more recent graduates of such training will, themselves, be behavioral technologists within these fields.

Second, although it may for various expository purposes be convenient to group a variety of behaviors under the rubric "countercontrol," in any particular individual or subdivision of society these different behaviors are probably not a very coherent repertoire, the evocation of a part of which brings into play the whole. Proposed procedural changes may evoke various aspects of this poorly integrated repertoire, but these changes will be relevant to areas that differ from one another along many other dimensions. Because of these differences they will be reacted to, not as manifestations of "the new and dangerous behavioral technology," but rather as a new check-cashing policy, a new welfare law, a new classroom grading procedure, and so on.

Furthermore, behavioral technologists will, in general, bring their expertise to bear on any problem in such a way as to maximize their short-range *and* long-range effectiveness. Existing practices contradictory to some proposed change, because it is seen as a form of deliberate control, or for any other reason, will be taken into consideration as factors determining the particular change strategy.

In summary, although there is certainly a behavioral revolution, it does not seem likely that there will be a counterrevolution. It would appear that the "issue of countercontrol" is no issue at all; or said another way, countercontrol is simply another facet of the familiar problem of technological assimilation.

# AUTHOR INDEX

Numbers in italics refer to the pages on which the complete references are listed.

## A

Abel, L., 12, 18, *29*
Ackerman, J. M., 173, *179*
Adams, S., 83, *92*
Adams, W., 475, *484*
Agras, W. S., 13, *29, 30*, 48, 51, *62*
Aitken, R. C., 99, *103*
Alberti, R. E., 453, *465*
Alder, C., 25, *28*
Alker, H., Jr., 437, *439*
Allen, K. E., 166, 174, *179*
Alper, T., 20, *29*
Anastasi, A., 108, *134*, 170, *179*
Andersson, S. J., 387, 395, *398*
Andrews, L. M., 457, 462, *466*
Archibeque, J. D., 239, *259*
Armstrong, M., 237, *261*
Arnold, C. R., 237, *259*
Aronfreed, J., 454, *465*
Ashby, E., 238, 239, *261*
Atthowe, J. M., 18, *27*, 345, *364*
Auerbach, A. H., 83, *95*
Auerswald, E. H., 426, 429, *439*
Ault, M. H., 166, 168, 174, *179*
Ayllon, T., 14, 26, 27, 48, *61*, 109, 131, *135*, 173, *179*, 265, *284*, 291, *297*, 345, 346, 347, 353, *364*, 388, 392, 394, *398*, 413, *422*, 436, *439*, 462, *465*, 480, *483*
Azerrad, J., 52, *61*
Azrin, N. H., 14, *27*, 79, *94*, 109, *135*, 173, *179*, 265, *284*, 291, 297, 345, 346, 353, *364*, 388, 392, 394, *398*, 413, *422*, 436, *439*, 462, *465*, 480, *483*

## B

Bachrach, A. J., 51, *61*
Bachrach, H. M., 83, *95*

Baer, D. M., 61, *61*, 109, 111, 116, *135*, 162, *179*, 237, *260*, 293, *298*, 354, 362, *364*, 365, *384*
Bahm, A. K., 300, *319*
Baker, B. L., 15, *27*
Baker, J. B., 240, *259*
Baker, S. L., 415, *422*
Balance, W. D. G., 162, *179, 180*
Baldwin, L. A., 295, *297*
Baldwin, V., 481, *483*
Bancroft, J. H. J., 24, *27*, 74, *77*
Bandura, A., 7, *10*, 18, 20, *27*, 58, *62*, 287, *297*, 452, 455, 456, 458, 463, *465*
Banuazizi, A., 39, *40*
Barber, T., 455, *465*
Barcai, A., 61, *62*
Barlow, D. H., 13, *29*
Barnett, C., 477, *483*
Barrett, C. L., 3, *10*, 13, *27*
Barrish, H. H., 237, *259*
Bateman, B., 163, 164, *179*
Batstone, D., 270, *284*
Baumeister, A., 471, *483*
Beach, D. R., 299, *320*
Beavin, J. H., 81, 88, *96*
Becker, W. C., 109, *135, 136*, 139, 144, 147, *159*, 237, 238, *259, 261*, 308, *320*, 453, *465*
Behrens, W., 182, *199*
Bell, N. W., 89, *96*
Benning, J. J., 299, *320*
Bensberg, G., 477, *483*
Bercovici, A. N., 109, *135*
Bergin, A. E., 455, 463, *465*
Bergman, P., 429, *439*
Bermann, E., 299, *322*
Bernstein, A., 84, *94*
Bernstein, D. A., 12, *27*

Bersoff, D. N., 166, *179*
Bettleheim, B., 410, *422*
Bienvenu, M. J., 88, *92*
Bijou, S. W., 162, 166, 168, 169, 174, *179, 180, 320,* 365, *384*
Bird, E., 330, *344*
Birdwhistle, R. L., 435, *439*
Birky, H. J., 12, 18, *27*
Birnbrauer, J. S., 173, *179,* 238, 239, *259*
Bis, J. S., 414, *422*
Blackham, G. J., 453, *465*
Blanchard, E. B., 7, *10*
Blattner, J. E., 239, *260*
Blau, P. M., 80, *94*
Bleecker, E. R., Jr., 100, *103*
Blinder, B. J., 52, 54, *62*
Bliss, E. L., 46, *62*
Bloom, B. S., 107, *135*
Bobrove, P. H., 18, *31*
Bolstad, O. D., 307, *320*
Boren, J. J., 412, *422*
Borkovec, T. D., 13, *28*
Born, D. G., 460, *465*
Boulougouris, J., 3, 4, 6, *10,* 13, 17, *30*
Brady, J. P., 47, 58, *62*
Brady, R., 102, *103*
Branch, C. H. H., 46, *62*
Braver, J., 82, *94*
Bricker, D. E., 109, *135*
Bringmann, W. G., 162, *179, 180*
Brock, L., 13, *29*
Broden, M., 237, *259*
Broderick, C. B., 92, *94*
Brodsky, G., 303, *321*
Bronfenbrenner, U., 108, *135*
Brown, A. C., 99, *103*
Brown, B., 108, *135*
Brown, G. D., 239, *261*
Brown, P. L., 431, *439*
Browning, R. M., 288, 293, *297,* 453, *465*
Bruce, C., 237, *259*
Bruch, H., 59, *62*
Brust, D., 472, 475, *483*
Buchanan, J. M., *520*
Buchwald, A. M., 19, *28*
Buckholdt, D., 238, 239, *259*
Buckley, N. K., 301, *322*
Buddenhagen, R., 482, *483*
Budzynski, T., 25, *28*

Bugental, J. F. T., 444, *448*
Burchard, J. D., 173, *179*
Burchard, S. N., 173, *179*
Burgess, E. W., 82, *94*
Burnham, J., *520*
Burton, R. V., 162, *180*
Bushell, D., 237, *259*
Butts, P., 474, *484*
Byrne, D., 89, *94*

**C**

Caddy, G., 25, *30,* 401, 404, 405, *406*
Caditz, R., 240, *259*
Cahoon, D. D., *28*
Caldwell, B. M., 169, *180*
Calf, R. A., 13, *28*
Calhoon, B., 296, *298*
Calhoun, J. B., 410, *422*
Campbell, J. D., 162, *180*
Carkhuff, R. R., 84, *96,* 458, *467*
Carmona, A., 431, *440*
Carter, V., 237, *259*
Catania, A. C., 431, 434
Cautela, J. R., 20, *28,* 296, 297, *297,* 396, 397, *398,* 437, *440*
Chadwick, B. A., 238, 239, *259*
Chamblis, J. E., 12, 18, *27*
Chandler, C., 300, *319*
Chandler, M., 83, *95*
Check, J. F., 240, *259*
Chesser, E. S., 15, *30,* 461, *466*
Chomsky, N., 432, *440*
Christelman, W. C., 25, 26, *31*
Church, J., 111, *135*
Clark, F. W., 453, *466*
Clement, P. W., 173, *180*
Cobb, J. A., 80, 82, *95,* 301, 303, 305, 306, 308, 316, *321*
Cohen, H. L., 414, *422*
Cohen, J., 83, *95*
Cohrssen, J., 12, *31*
Colarelli, N., 479, *483*
Colby, K. M., 411, *422*
Coleman, R. A., 116, *135*
Colman, A. D., 412, 415, *422, 422, 423*
Conderman, L., 237, *260*
Cooper, A. J., 70, *77*

Cooper, B., 99, *103*
Corey, J. R., 460, *465*
Cormier, W. H., 292, *298*
Cost, J. C., 240, *261*
Cranston, S. S., 109, 111, 134, *135,* 354, 362, *364*
Cristler, C., 109, 111, 134, *135,* 354, 362, *364*
Cronbach, L. J., 170, *180*
Cross, M., 401, 404, 405, *406*
Csanyl, A., 296, *297*
Cumming, W. W., 432, 433, *441*
Curtiss, K. A., 239, *260,* 296, *298*


**D**

Dahl, R. A., *520*
Dally, P., 46, 47, 49, 50, 57, 58, *62*
Darbyshire, M., 330, *344*
Davis, A., 107, *135*
Davison, G. C., 14, 18, 25, *28, 31*
Day, R. C., 238, 239, *259*
de Kruijff, G., 297, *297*
DeLauwe, C., 410, *422*
DeLeon, G., 12, *28*
De Moor, W., 13, *28*
Dennis, L., *521*
de Ruyter, P. A., 293, *298*
de Souza e Silva, Sebastiao, 231, *235*
Deutsch, F., 49, *63*
Deutsch, M., 108, *135*
Dittman, D. T., 300, *321*
Dockens, W. S., III, 425, 437, 438, *440*
Dogan, M., *440*
Doll, E., 473, *483*
Donahoe, J., 432, *440*
Downs, A., *521*
Drewery, J., 69, *77*
Duhl, F., 426, *440*
Duhl, L. J., 428, *440*
Duncan, A. D., 197, *199*
Dunn, L. M., 170, *180*
Dworkin, S., 34, *40*
Dyrud, J. E., 422, *422*


**E**

Ebner, M., 481, *484*
Edmonds, V. H., 82, *94*

Edwards, J. A., 13, *29*
Efran, J. S., 13, *31*
Eisenberg, L., 300, *319*
Ekman, G., 432, *440*
Emmons, M. L. L., 453, *465*
Engelmann, S., 145, 147, *159*
Engelmann, T., 145, *159*
England, G., 328, 330, *343, 344*
England, K., 330, *343*
Frickson, M., 302, *322*
Eriksson, B., 453, *465*
Ernst, F. A., 11, *28*
Erwin, W. J., 51, *61*
Espich, J. E., 212, *219*
Esveldt, K. A., 238, *260*
Evans, D. R., 24, *28*
Evans, G. W., 239, *259*
Evans, M. B., 238, *261*
Evans, N. D., 240, *259*
Evans, W. I. M., 20, *31*
Eyberg, S. M., 316, *320*
Eysenck, H. J., 12, *28*


**F**

Falkowski, W., 15, *29*
Falliers, C. J., 99, *103*
Farmer, J., 433, *440, 441*
Feldhusen, J. F., 299, *320*
Feldman, M. P., 12, 14, 15, *28, 66,* 73, 77
Fensterheim, H., 455, *467*
Ferkiss, Victor, 181, *199*
Ferritor, D. E., 238, 239, *259*
Ferster, C. B., 109, *135, 196, 199,* 235, 236, *422, 422,* 433, 435, 436, *440,* 455, 463, *465, 466*
Fixen, D., 197, *199*
Fixsen, D. L., 265, *284*
Fleming, J. C., 239, *259*
Floyer, Sir John, 103, *103*
Forrester, R. H., 12, *28*
Fournier, E. P., 290, *297*
Francis, B., 79, *94*
Frank, G. H., 300, *320*
Frank, J. D., 84, *94*
Frankl, V., 38, *40*
Franks, C. M., 11, *28, 455, 465, 467*
Frederick, C. J., 458, *465*

Fredericks, H., 481, *483*
Freeman, D. M., 52, 54, *62*
Frost, J. L., 108, *135*
Fullard, J. P. P., 297, *297*

**G**

Gaind, R., 6, *10*
Gainer, P., 412, *423*
Galbraith, G. G., 15, *28*
Gale, D. S., 35, *40*
Gale, E. N., 35, *40*
Galeano, C., 37, *41*
Galloway, C., 479, *483*
Galloway, K., 479
Gallup, H. F., 460, *465*
Gannon, L., 25, *28*
Gardner, J. E., 109, *135*
Gardner, J. M., 472, 474, 475, 476, 477, 478, 479, 480, 481, 482, *483, 484*
Gardner, S. I., 327, *343*
Gardner, W. I., 453, 462, *465*
Garfield, S. L., 455, 463, *465*
Garton, K. L., 116, *136,* 239, *260*
Gaupp, L. A., 15, *28*
Gelder, M. G., 12, 17, *28*
Gelfand, D. M., 287, *297*
Geus, R. F. B., 296, 297, *297*
Giampa, F., 477, *483*
Giles, D. K., 239, *261*
Gilmore, S. K., 306, 317, *322*
Glaser, R., *440*
Glynn, E. L., 296, *297*
Goldberg, M. L., 108, *135*
Goldiamond, I., 79, *94,* 422, *422*
Goldstein, A. P., 20, *29,* 35, 38, *40,* 240, *259*
Goldstein, M. K., 79, 92, *94, 96*
Gonzalez, M., 296, *297*
Goodman, J., 295, *298*
Goodman, P., 182, *199*
Gotestam, K. G., 437, *440*
Grabowski, J., 327, *344,* 365, *384,* 419, *423,* 453, *467,* 471, *484*
Graham, P. J., 66, 67, 74, 77, *78*
Gray, W., 426, *440*
Graziano, A. M., 457, 462, *465*
Gregson, R. A. M., 429, *440*
Gripp, R. F., 12, *29*

Gruber, R. P., 25, *29*
Guess, D., 109, *135*
Gullion, M. E., 272, *284,* 303, *321,* 462, *467*
Gull, W. W., 45, *62*
Gunne, L. M., 387, 395, *398*
Guppy, T. E., 239, *260*
Gurney, B. G., Jr., 462, *466*
Guthrie, E. R., 34, *40*

**H**

Hall, E. E., 410, *423*
Hall, R. V., 109, 111, 134, *135,* 237, 238, 239, *259, 261,* 354, 362, *364*
Hallam, R. S., 15, *29*
Hallsten, E. A., Jr., 51, *62*
Hamblin, R. L., 238, 239, *259, 260*
Hamerlynck, L. A., 453, *466*
Hamilton, J., 482, *483*
Hanley, E. M., 239, *260*
Hannon, A. E., 20, *31*
Hanson, L., 87, *94*
Harbison, J. J. M., 65, 66, 67, 72, 74, 77, *78*
Hardiker, P., 25, *29,* 453, *466*
Harell, J. A., 79, *95*
Haring, N. G., 453, *466*
Harris, A., 306, 307, *320*
Harris, F. R., 166, 174, *179*
Harris, L. C., 18, *31*
Harris, M. S., 241, 243, 245, 250, 252, 253, 254, 255, 256, 258, *260*
Harris, V. W., 238, 239, 241, 243, 244, 245, 247, 248, 249, 250, 251, 252, 253, 254, 255, 256, 258, *260*
Hart, B. M., 109, 116, 117, *136,* 171, *180,* 221, *236,* 475, *484*
Hart, J., 14, *29*
Harter, J., 481, *483*
Hartmann, D. P., 287, *297*
Hassinger, J., 240, *260*
Hathaway, C., 239, *260*
Haughton, E., 48, *61*
Hawkes, G. B., 108, *135*
Hawkins, N., 303, *321*
Hawkins, R. O., 238, *261*
Hawkins, R. P., 302, *320*
Hebb, D. O., 108, *136*

Heiner, J., 296, 297, *297*
Heller, K., 20, *29*
Henderson, D. G., 241, 243, 245, 250, 252, 253, 254, 255, 256, 258, *260*
Henderson, J. D., 12, *29*
Hendin, E., 84, *94*
Hendricks, A. F. C. J., 300, 304, 306, 307, 308, *320*
Heseltine, G. F. D., 14, *31*
Hess, R., 107, *135*
Hesse, R. M., 210, *219*
Hetchenthal, C., 479, *484*
Hinde, R. A., 435, *440*
Hirsch, I., 480, *483*
Hively, W., 197, *199*
Hodgson, R. J., 13, *29*
Hoekstra, F., 297, *297*
Hofman, R., 481, *483*
Hogan, R. A., 13, 17, *29, 31*
Hollingshead, A. B., 305, *320*
Holz, W. C., 14, 26, 27
Homans, G. C., 80, *94*
Homme, L. E., 296, *297, 388, 398*
Honig, W. K., 435, *440*
Hopkins, B. L., 116, *136,* 239, *260*
Hops, H., 79, 80, 82, 85, 86, 87, *95, 96*
Horst, H. M., 240, *260*
Hubbard, M. C., 210, 211, *219*
Humphreys, L. G., 170, *180*
Hunt, E. P., 98, *103*
Hunt, G. M., 79, *94*
Hunt, J. McVicker, 108, *136*
Hunt, S., 238, 239, *261*
Hurvitz, N., 86, *94*
Hussain, M. Z., *10*
Huxley, J., 446, *448*

**I**

Illich, I., 182, *199*

**J**

Jackson, D. D., 81, 88, *96,* 237, 238, *259*
Jacobs, A., 455, *466*
Jacobson, E., 35, *40, 440*
Janczarek, K. M., 210, *219*
Jarman, B., 479, *484*
Jastak, J. F., 169, *180*

Jastak, S. R., 169, *180*
Jayaratne, S., 83, 84, *96*
Jehu, D., 25, *29,* 453, *466*
Jenkins, H. M., 431, *439*
Jensen, A. R., 108, *136*
Jensen, V., 330, *344*
Johnson, D. F., 91, *95*
Johnson, S. M., 306, 307, *320*
Johnson, V. E., 21, *30,* 69, *78,* 83, *95*
Johnston, M. S., 166, 174, *179*
Jones, M. C., 34, *40*
Jones, R. R., 309, *320*
Jourard, S., 411, *423*

**K**

Kalton, G., 99, *103*
Kaminski, G., 455, *466*
Kamiya, T., 455, *465*
Kanfer, F. H., 20, 21, 22, *29,* 294, *297,* 463, *466*
Kanouse, D. E., 87, *94*
Kaprowy, E., 328, *344*
Karlins, M., 457, 462, *466*
Katzenberg, A. C., 212, *219*
Kaufman, M. R., 48, *63*
Kehoe, B., 330, *344*
Kelleher, R. T., *440*
Keller, F. S., 460, *466*
Keller, S., 108, *136*
Kelley, H. H., 80, *96*
Kelly, G. A., 86, *94*
Kendall, J. W., 38, *40*
Kennedy, W. A., 108, *136*
Kent, R. N., 13, *29,* 306, *320*
Kerr, N., 378, *384*
Kidder, J. D., 238, 239, *259*
Kilgour, K., 328, *344*
Kimble, G. A., 38, *40*
Kimmel, H. D., 39, *40*
Kirby, F. D., 238, 239, *260*
Kirchner, J. H., 13, *29*
Klosowski, R., 471, *483*
Knapp, J., 435, *441*
Koniarski, C., 238, 239, *261*
Konorski, J., 431, 432, *440*
Kornreich, M., 83, *95*
Kraft, T., 25, *29*
Krams, M., 238, 239, *261*

Krasner, L., 18, *27,* 345, *364,* 430, *441*
Krop, H., 296, *298*
Krumboltz, J. D., 453, 462, *466*
Kugel, R., 342, *343*
Kushner, H., 435, *440*

Lund, D., 237, 238, *259*
Lunden, W. A., *521*
Luparello, T., 100, *103*
Luthe, W., *441*
Lyons, H. A., 100, *103*

**L**

Lader, M. H., 14, *29*
Lahey, B. B., 109, *136*
Laird, J. D., 299, *320*
LaMontia, M., 342, *343*
Landrum, J. W., 240, *260*
Lang, P. J., 14, *29,* 35, *40,* 50, *62*
Langdon, G., 240, *260*
Lazarus, A. A., 19, 21, *29,* 453, 455, 458,
    462, 463, *466, 467*
Lederer, W. J., 79, 86, 88, 89, 91, *95*
Ledwige, B., 14, *31*
Lee-Evans, M., 74, *78*
Leitenberg, H., 13, *29, 30,* 48, 51, *62*
Lennard, H., 84, *94*
Levinger, G., 80, 88, *94*
Levis, D. J., 4, *10,* 38, *41*
Levitt, E. E., 300, *320*
Lewinsohn, P. M., 20, *29*
Liberman, R. P., 20, 26, *29,* 79, *94,* 463,
    *466,* 481, *484*
Liebold, K. E., 412, *422*
Lilienfeld, A. M., 299, *321*
Linder, L. H., 13, *30*
Lindsley, O. R., 182, *199,* 474, *484*
Lippitt, P., 239, *260*
Lloyd, K. E., 12, 18, *29*
Lobitz, G., 306, *320*
Locke, H. J., 82, *94*
Lomont, J. F., 13, *29*
London, P., 457, *466*
LoPiccolo, J., 83, *94*
Lorr, M., 84, *94*
Lott, L., 87, *96*
Lovaas, O. I., 48, *62,* 222, *236*
Lovibond, S. H., 25, *30,* 401, 404, 405,
    *406*
Lovitt, T. C., 238, 239, *260,* 296, *298,*
    475, *484*
Lowther, G. H., 329, *343*
Lowther, R., 330, *343*
Luborsky, L., 83, *95*

**M**

Mabry, T. R., 288, 291, *298*
McAllister, H., 65, 66, 67, 72, 74, 77, *78*
McAllister, L. W., 237, *260*
McClure, D. J., 14, *31*
MacCulloch, M. J., 12, 14, 15, *28,* 66,
    73, *77*
McDonald, S., 330, *344*
McDonnel, J., 481, *483*
McFadden, E. R., 100, *103*
McGinnies, E., 436, *440,* 455, 462, *466*
McGlynn, F. D., 13, *30*
McHugh, R. B., 102, *103*
McIntire, R. W., 109, *136*
Mackenzie, J. N., 100, *103*
Maclean, G. D., 13, *28*
McMichael, J. S., 460, *465, 466*
McMurchy, M., 270, *284*
McNeal, S., 303, *321*
Macpherson, E. L. R., 25, *30*
Madsen, C. H., Jr., 109, *136,* 237, *259*
Maertens, N., 240, *261*
Magaro, P. A., 12, *29*
Mahoney, M. J., 20, *30*
Malleson, N., 38, *40*
Malott, R. W., 202, 211, *219*
Mandell, W. A., 12, *28*
Mapp, R. H., 13, *30*
Marks, I. M., 3, 4, 6, 9, *10,* 12, 13, 17,
    *28, 30, 31*
Marks, J., 12, *30*
Marset, P., 3, 4, 6, *10,* 13, 17, *30*
Marshall, K. E., 422, *423*
Martin, G. L., 328, 330, *343, 344*
Martin, M. D., 240, *260*
Martin, P. L., 345, 347, 353, *364,* 390,
    *398,* 453, 455, 461, *467*
Martin, S., 25, *29*
Masserman, J. H., 33, 34, *40,* 412, *423*
Masters, W. H., 21, *30,* 69, *78,* 83, *95*
Mathews, A. M., 14, *29*
Matijiw, S. L., 162, *179, 180*

Mayer, G. R., 453, 462, *467*
Meadows, D. H., 182, *199*
Meadows, D. L., 182, *199*
Mealiea, W. L., 3, *10, 13, 30*
Meehl, P. E., 517, *520*
Mees, H., 109, *137,* 302, *322*
Mehrabian, A., 461, *466*
Meichenbaum, D. H., 295, *298*
Melamed, B. G., 14, *29*
Melin, G. M., 437, *440*
Mellor, V., 66, 73, *77*
Meltzoff, J., 83, *95*
Merrill, M., 170, *180*
Meyer, V., 15, *30,* 461, *466*
Meyerson, L., 378, *384*
Michael, J. L., 109, *135,* 378, *384,* 436, *439,* 462, *466*
Michaelis, M. L., 237, *259*
Michels, R., *521*
Miller, D. R., 108, *136*
Miller, G. A., 131, *136*
Miller, J. G., 439, *440*
Miller, L. K., 132, *136,* 239, *261*
Miller, N. E., 39, *40,* 431, *440*
Miller, O. L., 132, *136*
Miller, S., 431, 432, *440*
Miller, S. B., 13, *30*
Mills, K. C., 25, 26, *30, 31*
Minke, K., 474, *484*
Mischel, W., 65, *78*
Mitchell, M. A., 237, *259*
Mohr, J. P., 51, *61*
Moore, N. A., 102, *103*
Moore, R. D., 13, *30*
Morris, H. H., 299, *320*
Morrison, D. C., 302, *322*
Morse, W. H., *440*
Mosca, G., *521*
Mowrer, O. H., 36, *40,* 458, *466*
Mueller, R. H., 162, *179, 180*

**N**

Nathan, P. E., 26, *30*
Nawas, M. N., 3, *10,* 13, *30*
Nelson, R., 13, *29*
Nemiah, J. C., 49, *62*
Newringer, C., 462, *466*
Nomad, M., *521*

**O**

O'Brien, J. S., 26, *30*
Öst, L. G., 453, *466*
Österling, L., 453, *465*
O'Gorman, E., 72, *78*
O'Leary, K. D., 109, *136,* 238, *261*
Oliveau, D. C., 13, *29, 30*
Olson, D. H., 82, 89, 92, *95*
Olson, M., Jr., *521*
Omichinski, M., 330, *344*
Osborn, J., 145, *159*
Oswalt, G. L., 239, *259*
Otto, H. J., 240, *261*

**P**

Packard, R. G., 237, *261*
Palm, J. M., *219*
Parrino, J. J., 13, *30*
Parson, R., 479, *484*
Pasamanick, B., 299, *321*
Patterson, G. R., 79, 80, 82, 85, 86, 87, *95, 96,* 272, *284,* 299, 301, 303, 304, 305, 306, 307, 308, 309, 316, *320, 321,* 453, 462, *467,* 472, 475, 481, 482, *484*
Paul, G. L., 12, 13, 14, 18, *27, 30, 31,* 35, *40*
Pavlov, I. P., 33, 34, 37, 38, *40*
Pear, J. J., 328, *344*
Pearson, D. T., 109, *135*
Perelman, P. F., 239, *260*
Perrott, M. C., 463, *465*
Pescor, F. T., 395, *398*
Peterson, A. F., 302, *320*
Peterson, R. F., 166, 168, 174, *179,* 302, *322*
Pettigrew, T. F., 108, *136*
Phelps, R., 303, *321*
Phillips, E. A., 265, *284*
Phillips, E. L., 195, 197, *199,* 265, *284,* 453, *466*
Phillips, J. S., 20, *29,* 294, *297,* 463, *466*
Philpott, W. M., 36, *41*
Piaget, J., 35, *40*
Pickens, R., 395, *398*
Pilek, V., 328, *344*
Pinschoff, J. M., 66, 73, *77*
Pomerleau, O. F., 18, *31*

Poppen, R., 35, *41*
Poser, E., 474, *484*
Premack, D., 59, *62,* 388, *398,* 432, 433, *441*
Prokaska, J. O., *3,* 10
Pruitt, D. G., 91, *95*
Punke, H. H., 240, *261*


**Q**

Quinn, J. T., 65, 66, 67, 72, 74, 77, *78*


**R**

Rabunsky, C., 89, *95*
Rachman, S., 13, 14, 15, 17, 25, *29, 31,* 38, *41,* 453, *467*
Rae, J. B., 69, *77*
Raines, J., 38, *41*
Randers, I., 182, *199*
Rappaport, A. F., 79, *95*
Rausch, H. L., 300, *321*
Rawls, J., 518, *520*
Ray, A., 13, *31*
Ray, R. S., 301, 303, 305, 306, 308, 316, 319, *321*
Rechs, J., 296, *297*
Reese, D. G., 212, *219*
Reichenbach, H., 435, *441*
Reid, G., 475, 482, *484*
Reid, J. B., 87, *95,* 303, 304, 306, *321*
Reid, W. J., 83, 87, *94, 95*
Reynolds, E. J., 13, *30*
Reynolds, N. J., 109, 116, *136,* 171, *180,* 221, *236,* 475, *484*
Rhamey, R., 89, *94*
Ribes-Inesta, E., 171, *180*
Rice, D. L., 299, *322*
Rice, G. E., 412, *423*
Richard, R. C., 173, *180*
Rieger, W., 47, *62*
Riessman, F., 108, *136*
Ringold, A. L., 52, 54, *62*
Risely, T. R., 61, *61,* 109, 111, 116, 117, *135, 136, 137,* 171, *180,* 221, *236,* 302, *322,* 354, 362, *364,* 475, *484*
Ritter, D., 7, *10*
Rizzo, N., 426, *440*
Roach, J. L., 299, *322*

Roberts, M. D., 109, 110, *135, 136*
Robins, L. N., 299, *322*
Rönnberg, S., 451, 453, *467*
Rogers, C. R., 196, *199,* 456, *467*
Rogers, M., 299, *322*
Roig, J. A., 37, *41*
Rokkan, S., *440*
Rollofson, R. L., 211, *219*
Rose, S., 479, *484*
Rosenthal, S. V., 99, *103*
Rossi, T. P., 239, *261*
Rubin, R. D., 455, *467*
Russell, B., 444, *448*
Russell, G. F. M., 46, 47, *62*
Rutherford, G., 109, *135*
Ryder, R. G., 82, *95*


**S**

Sachs, L. B., 455, *466*
Sailor, W., 109, *135*
Sallows, G., 301, *322*
Samels, J., 330, *344*
Sampen, S. E., 109, *137*
Sanders, C., 476, *484*
Sargant, W., 50, 57, 58, *62*
Saslow, G., 21, 22, *29*
Saudargas, R. A., 238, *261*
Saunders, M., 237, *259*
Scales, P. E., 12, *29*
Schaefer, H. H., 25, 26, *30, 31,* 345, 347, 353, *364,* 390, *398,* 453, 455, 461, *467*
Schalack, R., 12, *30*
Scheflen, A. E., 435, *441*
Schnell, R., 475, *484*
Schiffer, C. B., 98, *103*
Schiller, B., 240, *261*
Schmidt, G. W., 237, *261*
Schneider, R., 239, *261*
Schoenfeld, W. N., 432, 433, *440, 441*
Schultz, J. H., *441*
Schumpeter, J. A., *521*
Schutte, R. C., 116, *136,* 239, *260*
Schweid, E., 302, *320*
Scrignar, C. B., 52, *62*
Sechrest, L. B., 20, *29*
Segundo, J. P., 37, *41*
Senn, D. J., 88, *94*
Serber, M., 35, *40,* 102, *103*

Sergeant, H. G. S., 100, 101, 102, *103*
Shafir, M., 45, *62*
Shaw, D. A., 301, 303, 306, *321, 322,* 481, *484*
Shaw, M., 453, *466*
Shean, G. D., 12, 18, *31*
Shepherd, M., 99, *103*
Sherman, J. A., 109, *135,* 238, 239, 241, 243, 244, 245, 247, 248, 249, 250, 251, 252, 253, 254, 255, 256, 258, *260,* 293, *298*
Shields, F., 238 239, *260*
Shuey, A. M., 108, *136*
Shyne, A. W., 83, *95*
Sidman, M., 109, 134, *136,* 427, 432, *441*
Siegel, S., 393, *398,* 479, *483*
Silberman, A., 453, *465*
Siller, J., 108, *137*
Silverstone, J. T., 46, *62*
Skindrud, K. D., 306, *322*
Skinner, B. F., 109, 110, 113, *135, 137,* 161, 162, *180,* 196, *199,* 222, 231, *236,* 345, *364,* 412, *423,* 425, 431, 432, 433, 435, *440, 441,* 444, *448,* 453, 456, 457, 463, *467,* 517, *520*
Sloane, H. N., 109, *137*
Slosson, R. L., 170, *180*
Smart, R. G., 34, *41*
Smith, L., 238, 239, *259*
Snapper, A. G., 435, *441*
Sobell, I. C., 25, 26, *31*
Sobell, M. B., 25, 26, *30, 31*
Solyom, C., 14, *31*
Solyom, L., 14, *31*
Sommer, R., 410, *423, 436, 441*
Sommer-Smith, J. A., 37, *41*
Sonoda, B., 12, *30*
Sorokin, P. A., *521*
Spence, I., 197, *199*
Spengler, O., *521*
Staats, A., 474, *484*
Stachowiak, J. G., 237, *260*
Stampfl, T. G., 4, *10,* 38, *41*
Standahl, J., 482, *483*
Stanford, R. L., 52, *61*
Stein, S., 12, *28*
Stern, R. M., 15, *28*
Sternbach, R. A., 25, *28*
Stout, I. W., 240, *260*

Stover, D. O., 288, 293, *297,* 453, *465*
Stoyva, J., 25, *28*
Strang, R., 240, *261*
Straus, M. A., 82, *95*
Stuart, R. B., 79, 80, 82, 83, 84, 85, 86, 87, 88, 89, 91, *94, 95, 96,* 457, 458, *467*
Stunkard, A., 46, 47, 48, 50, 52, 54, *62, 63*
Sturmfels, G., 35, *40*
Sulzer, B., 109, *137,* 238, 239, *261,* 453, 462, *467*
Surrat, P. R., 238, *261*
Susser, M. W., 12, *28*
Svinicki, J. G., 202, *219*
Swanson, G. E., 108, *136*
Swenson, E. J., 240, *261*
Szasz, T. S., 457, *467*

**T**

Tague, C. E., 238, 239, *259*
Taylor, G. Y., 240, *261*
Taylor, R. G., 240, *261*
Taylor, T. J., 300, *321*
Teasdale, J., 14, 25, *31,* 453, *467*
Terman, L. M., 170, *180*
Terris, W., 412, *423*
Tharp, R. G., 288, 290, 293, *298,* 302, *322,* 436, *441*
Thelen, H. A., 239, *261*
Thibaut, J. M., 80, *96*
Thoma, H., 46, *63*
Thomas, D. R., 109, *136,* 147, *159,* 237, *259, 261*
Thompson, L. E., 48, 51, *62*
Thompson, T., 327, *344,* 395, *398,* 419, *423,* 453, *467,* 471, *484*
Thoresen, C. E., 453, 461, 462, *466, 467*
Throne, J. M., 436, *441*
Thurston, J. R., 299, *320*
Tilepczak, J. A., 414, *422*
Toffler, A., 108, *137*
Treffry, D., 330, *344*
Tripodi, T., 83, 84, *96*
Truax, C. B., 26, *31,* 84, *96,* 458, *467*
Tucker, B., 109, 111, 134, *135,* 354, 362, *364*

Turk, J. L., 89, *96*
Turner, A. J., 79, 83, *96*
Turner, R. K., 15, *31*
Tyler, V. O., 239, *261*

**U**

Ullman, L. P., 430, *441*
Ulrich, R. E., 237, 238, *261*

**V**

Valius, S., 13, *31*
Van de Riet, V., 108, *136*
Van Egeren, L. F., 14, *31*
Verrier, R., 296, *298*
Via, M., 250, *260*
Viek, P., 36, *40*
von Bertalanffy, L., 88, *96,* 426, 429, *441*

**W**

Wagner, B. R., 288, 291, *298*
Wahl, G., 301, *322*
Wahler, R. G., 292, *298,* 301, 302, 317, *322*
Walder, L., 480, *483*
Walker, H., 301, *322*
Wallace, K. M., 82, *94*
Waller, J. V., 48, *63*
Waller, W., 91, *96*
Wallin, P., 82, *94*
Walter, H., 306, 317, *322*
Walton, D., 100, *103*
Watson, C., 330, *344*
Watson, J. B., 6, 9, *10,* 443, *448*
Watson, L. A., 471, 472, 475, 476, *483, 484*
Watzlawick, P., 81, 88, *96*
Wechkin, S., 412, *423*
Wechsler, D., 170, *180*
Weinstein, M. S., 20, *29*
Weiss, R. L., 79, 80, 82, 85, 86, 87, *96*
Welander, G., 453, *467*
Welch, J. C., 79, 92, *96*
Werry, J. S., 12, *31*
Westman, J. C., 299, *322*
Wetzel, R. J., 288, 290, 293, *298,* 302, *322,* 436, *441*
Wheeler, A. J., 109, *137*

White, G., 307, *322*
White, J. C., Jr., 108, *136*
Wikler, A., 395, *398*
Williams, B., 212, *219*
Williams, C. W., 13, *30*
Willis, R. W., 13, *29*
Wilson, G. T., 13, 14, 20, 25, *29, 31*
Wiltz, N. A., Jr., 317, *322*
Winkle, G. H., 302, *322*
Wodarski, J., 239, *260*
Wolf, M. M., 61, *61,* 109, 111, 116, *135, 137,* 197, *199,* 237, 238, 239, *259, 261,* 265, *284,* 302, *322,* 354, 362, *364*
Wolfensberger, S., 342, *343*
Wolfensberger, W., 342, *344*
Wolff, H. H., 12, 17, *28*
Wolpe, J., 4, *10,* 12, *31,* 33, 34, 35, 36, 37, 38, *41,* 430, *442,* 455, 458, 463, *467*
Wolpin, M., 38, *41*
Woodward, R., 66, *78*
Woody, R. H., 299, *322*
Woolfenden, R. M., 212, *219*
Woy, R., 13, *31*
Wright, D. E., 13, *30*
Wright, P., 109, 131, *135*
Wrobel, P. A., 237, *259*
Wyrwicka, W., 431, *442*

**Y**

Yamaguchi, K., 365, *384*
Yarrow, M. R., 162, *180*
Yates, A. J., 453, 455, 463, *467*
Yelloly, M., 25, *29,* 453, *466*
Yen, S., 481, *484*
Yorkston, N. J., 100, 101, 102, *103*
Young, G. C., 15, *31*
Young, R. D., 19, *28*

**Z**

Zbrozyna, A., 37, *41*
Zealley, A. K., 99, *103*
Zeidberg, A., 12, 18, *31*
Zeilberger, J., 109, *137*
Zifferblatt, S. M., 109, *137*
Zimmerman, E. H., 133, *137*
Zimmerman, J., 133, *137*
Zuckerman, M., 74, *78*

# SUBJECT INDEX

## A

Absence, classroom, 207–208
Academic performance (behavior), 118, 271, 275, 329
Academic probation, 202
Academic skills
  teaching to retarded children, 383
Aggressive children, 266, 278, 299–322
Agoraphobia, 4, 22, 36
Alcoholism
  aversion therapy, 25
Amphetamine addiction
  as a problem for behavioral ecology, 437
  treatment of, 387–398
Anorexia nervosa, 45–61
  assertive training, 50–51
  chlorpromazine treatment, 50, 56, 58
  clinical description, 45–46
  etiology, 48–49
  imipramine treatment, 56
  mother daughter relationship, 47
  treatment procedures, 49–58
Antiscientific feelings
  effects in behaviorism, 446
Anxiety, 33, 34, 35, 39–40
  level of exposure, 7, 8
  relief conditioning, 37
  treatment for, 3–10, 23
Arden House Conference, 412
Arithmetic, teaching, 142
Army
  behavior modification and the, 416
Assessment, 164, 165
Assistant, teaching, 217–219
Asthma, desensitization, 100–103
Attendance of trainees, 132, *see also* absence, classroom

Attendant behavior checklist, 477
Audience control, 223, 231
Authoritarian, 195
Autism, 328
  retarded child, 380–383, 411, 413
Autonomous man, 491–493, 498–499
Aversion–relief model, 15
Aversion therapy, 14–15, 24–25
Aversive control, 132
Aversive stimulus, 300–302, 307
Axiology, 518, 519

## B

Backup reinforcers, 173
Baseline measures, 268–269, 305–306, 311–316, 332, 336, 338–340, 354, 355–356, 362
Behavior, topographical, 118
Behavioral ecology
  applications of, 437–438
  and evolution, 436
Behavioral technology, 523–524
Behavior inventories, 171
Behavior modification
  applicator, 475
  consultant, 475
  generalist, 475
  specialist, 475
  technician, 475
Behavior Modification Test, 472
Behavior therapists, training of classes, 452–455
  comprehensiveness, 455–456
  future programs, 459–464
  issues, 456
  levels, 458–460
Body awareness, 111, 113, 120
Bolsheviks, 509

Brethalyzer, 400, 401
Bronchial asthma, 97–103
  behavioral approach, 40
  treatment, 98–103

**C**

Caldwell Preschool Test, 169
CASE project, 414
Cerebral–organic disturbance, 266, 267,
  286
Cerebral palsy, 369
Changing clothes
  retarded child, 370–374
Character disorders, 415
Child
  participation in treatment choice/plan,
    290–293
Children's Reinforcement Survey, 173
Civil Rights
  of the child, 481
  of institutionalized patients, 483
Classical conditioning, 14–15
Closure
  of behavior modification programs,
    418–419
Coding systems, 307–309
Cognitive desensitization, 15
Cognitive factors in anxiety, 9, *see also*
  Anxiety
Community involvement, 266, 281, 283,
  329, 342
Comparative studies
  behavior modification techniques
    versus nontreated controls, 317,
    318–319
    versus placebos, 317
  of self control, 295
Compulsive patients, 17
Conceptualization
  teaching of, 212–213
Concurrent operants, 434–435
Conditioned inhibition, 34–37
Conduct disorders, 300
Consultant, 288, 289, 342
  function of large treatment facilities,
    342–343
Contingency manager, 296
Contract, contingency or behavioral, 293,
  296
Control, 488, 491–496, 504, 511

Convulsions, 378, 380
"Cookbook," 107, 119
Cost efficiency, 302, 341
Counterconditioning, 33, 34, 35
Countercontrol, 488, 491–496, 506–508,
  523–524
Count sheets, 186
Course objectives, 203
Course syllabi, 203
Coverant, 296
Covert conditioning, 396–398, 437
Covert extinction, 396–397
Criterion teaching, 146
Cross–cultural comparisons, 435
Culture, design of, 487–489, 501–508,
  *see also* Society

**D**

Descriptive psychiatry, 26
Desensitization, 12–13, 15–17, 23–24, 26,
  430
  compared with implosion, 3–10
Detoxification
  of amphetamine addicts, 388, 391
Diagnosis, current assumptions, 163, 164
Diazepam
  use in anxiety, 8
Discriminated aversive conditioning, 402
Discrimination learning, 296
Disruptive behavior
  effects on study behavior, 237–238
DISTAR™, 142
"DO IT" signals, 145
Down's Syndrome, 370
DRO probes, 226, 231

**E**

Eating problems, 48
Ecology
  and a general systems approach,
    427–439
  and learning, 428
  and mental health, 428
Edwards Personal Preference Schedule,
  69, 473
Elimination of inappropriate behavior,
  33, 269–275, 279–281
  aggression, 300–319
  lying in bed, 346, 348–352

Emotionally disturbed children, 286, 292, 295, 296
Encounter group, 422
Enuresis
  treatment of, 366–370
Environmental control, 491
Environmental design
  defined, 410
  and operant conditioning, 409–423
Epilepsy, 366, 375
Epistemology, 520
Ethical issues, 518
  in social planning, 494–495
  in training nonprofessionals, 480–483
Etiology in diagnosis, 161
Evolution
  and environmental design, 412
Exposure hypothesis, 6, 7
Expressive language, 110, 113, 121
Extinction, experimental, 38, 39
Extinction scheduling, 133

**F**

Facilitative conditioning, 458
Fading, 414, 376–377
Family intervention, 286, *see also* Parents
  as treatment modality, 302–322
Father–absent families, 304–305
Fixed interval schedule, 434
Flash sampling, 223
Food, as reinforcer, 47, 48
Foster grandparents, 476
Frigidity, 72

**G**

General systems theory
  defined, 426
  operant conditioning and, 424–442
Generalization, 107, 133, 287, 288, 289
  internal, 291–292, 295
Genetic fallacy, 515
Genetics, 504
Goldbach's theorem, 516–517
Government, 497–499
Grading scale, 206
Graph construction
  teaching of, 213

**H**

Higher education
  behavior technology and, 200–219
  purpose of, 202
  remediation in, 205
  systems analysis in, 202–219
History, personal, 162
Homework, effects of, 250–259
Homosexuality, 66–69, 73, 74
  aversion therapy in, 24, 25
Humanism
  and applied behaviorism, 443–450
Humanistic goals
  and behaviorism, 446–447
Hyperactive children, 266, 267, 275, 304–305

**I**

Illness model, 162
Implosion, 12–13, 38
  compared with desensitization, 3–10
Independent study
  compared with tutoring, 243, 246 247
Individual differences
  in treatment procedures, 17, 18
Inhibition
  direct, 37
  external, 36
  protective, 37–38
  supramaximal, 37–38
  transmarginal, 37–38
Inner behavior, 189
Institutional aides, 470–484
Institutional professionalization, 182
Instructions, effects of, 335, 341, 353–364
Interpersonal Perception Technique, 69–71
Interview, 21–23, 294
Intraresponse reciprocal
  inhibition, 35
Intraverbals, 222

**J**

Jacobsonian relaxation, 51

**K**

Kinesics, 435
Kin Kare, 325–344

# L

Learning systems, 200, 201, 209

# M

Mands, 113, 222
Marital communication, 88, 89
Marital interaction
    assessment of, 82
    and sexual problems, 69–70
Marital treatment
    behavioral approaches, 79, 80
    goals of, 81, 82
    operant–interpersonal approach, 80–92
    structure, 83–85
Mathematics
    as a descriptive language, 429
Mediators, 288, 290, 291
Meningitis, 375
Mental retardation, 304
    mental defective with psychotic re-
        actions, 346
    mild and moderate retardates, 326–327
    severe and profound retardates, 325–
        344
Methodone patients, treatment of, 438
Minnesota Multiphasic Personality In-
    ventory, 473
Modeling, 271, 303
    imitation training, 335
Monitoring system, 147
Monitoring techniques, 173, 174
Morphine, 388
Multiple baseline design, 107, 111, 116,
    354

# N

Need for achievement
    relationship to performance, aides,
        473–474
Neighborhood Youth Corps, 476
Nonprofessionals
    personality variables, 473–474
    resistance to retraining, 471–472
    selection of, 471
    socioeconomic status, 474
    training, 474–483
    training in behavior modification, 469–
        484

# O

Observation, direct, 165
Observers, 269, 272–273, 303, 305–307,
    310–311
On–task behavior, 166
Operant principles
    application to society, 501
Open ward
    token economy in, 388
Operational space, 431–433
Ordering systems, 426
"Other" management, 183
Oversimplification
    in applied behaviorism, 447

# P

Pacing, 146
Paraprofessionals, 109, 117, 131
Parental training program, 272, 280, 283,
    287, 288–289, 289–290, 299–322
Parents as teachers, 140
Pavlovian conditioning, 431
Peer tutoring, 238–250, 257–259
    math, 244–246
    spelling, 241–243
Personal uniqueness, 447
Personalized Instruction System, 460
Phobias, treatment, 3–10, 17
Play therapy, 286
Point systems, 269–271, 273–275, 414–
    415, *see also* Token economies
Political factors
    in treatment programs, 418–420
Positive reinforcer
    versus positive consequence, 301
Potency disorders, 72
Premack Principle, 388, 437
Prepositional language, 111, 114, 121
    125
Probe, behavioral, 112
Procedural space, 431–433
Programmed lessons, 141
Prompt sessions, 224, 226
Psychological mechanism, 6
    in desensitization, *see* Exposure
        hypothesis
    in flooding, *see* Exposure hypothesis
Psychological ownership

effects on nonprofessional aide, 479–480

Punishment, 26, 523

**Q**

Quizzes, daily, 204–212

**R**

Reading, teaching, 143
Receptive language, 110, 113, 121, 125
Reciprocal inhibition, 34
Reciprocity count, 188
Reinforcer survey, 172
Relapse, in drug abuse, 395
Relaxation
  compared with desensitization, 102–103
  in desensitization, 14
Reliability checks, 227, 233
Remediation, 206–208, 211
Repeated presentation, 111
Residential treatment settings, 265–284, 285–298, 300, 328–343
  as temporary treatment, 285–298, *see also* Kin Kare
Response cost
  for lying in bed, 346, 349–352
Responsibilities, 492–493
Retarded children
  treatment of, 366–384
Reversal design, 271, 354
Rights, 492–493
Road accidents, alcohol-related
  legislation, effects on, 400
  medical approach to, 400–401
  modification of, 399–406
  recommendations for treatment, 404
Rule of relevance, 388, 394

**S**

Schizophrenics
  institutionalized psychotics, 265, 304, 346
Self-care skills
  development of, 328–329, 330–337, 341, 346–348, 353–364
Self-control

in behavior modification programs, 287, 292–297, 492
Self-knowledge, 457
Self-mutilating behavior, 413
Self-recording, 296, 307–308
Sexual evaluation
  defined, 65
Sexual Interest Measure, 72–73
Sexual orientation
  defined, 65
Sexual Orientation Method, 66–69, 73–76
Skinner box
  as a designed environment, 413
  relation to human ecology, 429
Slosson Intelligence Test, 150
Social engineering (planning), 495–499, 504–507, 518
Social environment and behavior, 493
Social interactions
  development 337, 338
  recording 268
Socialism, 505–506, 510
Social problems, 494
Social reform, 506–507
Social reinforcers, 223, 272, 293, 301, 338
Social space, 410
Social workers, 438
Society, applications of behavior modification, 496–497, 501–508
Soldiers, delinquent
  behavioral requirements, 415
  measurement system, 416
  social and institutional reinforcement, 416
  treatment goals, 415
  treatment of, 415
Specialists, 141
Species–specific anxiety stimuli, 430
Specification, of material to be learned, 203, 204
Staff
  feedback, 276–277, 330
  training, 271–272, 288–290, 319, 328, 330, 337–338, 341, 346, 395–397
Stimulus generalization, 523
Structural analysis, 429
Student-Centered Education Project, 213–216

Stuart Marital Precounseling Inventory, 82
Stuttering, 413
Successful behavior modification programs
characteristics of, 418
Supervision, of nonprofessional aides, 479–480
Synonyms, acquisition of, 229–230
Systems analysis, 214

**T**

Tacts, 222
Target, subject, 288, 289, 306
Target behavior, 24, 25, 289, 290, 291, 293, 309, 311, 316, 317
Task components, 144
Technical eclecticism, 20, 21
Television watching
reinforcing, 352–353
Temporary substitution treatment, 292
Tests, standardized, 169, 170
Therapeutic instructions, 13, 14, 23
Therapist–patient relationship, 13
Threats
by amphetamine abusers, 387
Time-out, 269, 270, 272, 274, 277, 334, 337, 339
Toilet training
retarded child, 375–378
Token economies, 12, 17, 265, 269, 277, 291, 293, 296, 297, 330, 334–337, 338, 341, 346, 353–364, 368–369, 413–14, 436

T-system, 433
Training Proficiency scale, 475
Treatment
choice of, 291, 294–297
family intervention as treatment modality, 302–322
goal, 290
of mentally retarded, history, 325–328
packages, 319
Treatment setting, 23
Tricycling
retarded child, 374–376
Turnover, institutional aides, 471–472

**V**

Value, in Premack's formulation, 434
Values, 487
in behaviorism, 445–446
Verbal development
in preschool children, 221–236
Verbal prompts, 223
Viet Nam War, 482
Vineland Social Maturity Scale, 473
Vocational Interest Blank, 473

**W**

Warmth, 188
Working behavior, 338–339, 340, 346, 348, 352, 377–381
Wide Range Achievement Test (WRAT), 150, 169

A 5
B 6
C 7
D 8
E 9
F 0
G 1
H 2
I 3
J 4